CHRISTIANITY
IN CELTIC LANDS

CHRISTIANITY IN CELTIC LANDS

A History of the Churches of the Celts,
their origin, their development, influence,
and mutual relations

By Dom LOUIS GOUGAUD

Benedictine Monk of St. Michael's Abbey, Farnborough

Translated from the Author's MS
by Maud Joynt

With an Introduction (1992)
by Jean-Michel Picard

FOUR COURTS PRESS

FIRST PUBLISHED BY SHEED & WARD, LONDON, 1932
REISSUED WITH AN INTRODUCTION BY J.-M. PICARD, 1992
BY FOUR COURTS PRESS LTD,
KILL LANE, BLACKROCK, CO. DUBLIN

© FOUR COURTS PRESS LTD 1992

A CATALOGUE RECORD FOR THIS TITLE
IS AVAILABLE FROM THE BRITISH LIBRARY

ISBN 1-85182-097-3
ISBN 1-85182-113-9 pbk

PRINTED IN IRELAND BY
COLOUR BOOKS LTD, DUBLIN

INTRODUCTION BY JEAN-MICHEL PICARD

IN the decade preceding World War II three books were published in short succession which soon became essential reading for every student of early Irish history for generations to come. These were James F. Kenney's *The sources for the early history of Ireland* (Columbia 1929), John Ryan's *Irish monasticism* (Dublin 1931) and Louis Gougaud's *Christianity in Celtic lands* (London 1932). Even though their data is sometimes incomplete by modern standards and their analyses old-fashioned, these books are still mines of information for the modern scholar. We had reprints of Kenney's *Sources* in 1966 and 1979 and of Ryan's *Irish monasticism* in 1972 and 1986 but a reprint of Gougaud's *Christianity* has long been overdue.

The author of this once famous book was a native of Britanny, born in 1877 in the small town of Malestroit, some twenty miles from the medieval monastery of Redon. Although showing a keen personal interest in literature and local history, he went to the University of Rennes to study law. This early legal training would later help him when dealing with the complexities of early Irish Church organisation. He did not become a lawyer but joined the Benedictine order in 1904 and was allowed to engage in research concerning the Church. He was not a scholar of the Celtic languages but his Breton background drew him to the history of the Church in the Celtic-speaking countries. The material he explored was mostly in Latin and he had at his disposal the pioneer work of eminent celticists such as Kuno Meyer, Whitley Stokes, Ernst Windisch or Heinrich Zimmer. He was also fortunate to be the contemporary of Osborn Bergin, R.I. Best, Charles Plummer, Rudolf Thurneysen, Joseph Vendryes and he made good use of current scholarship in Celtic studies.

In 1910 he joined the community of St Michael's Abbey, at Farnborough (Hampshire), which brought him nearer to the treasures of the British Library. The publication of his first major book, *Les chrétientés celtiques,* in 1911 established his reputation as a world expert on the Celtic Church. The book showed not only a detailed knowledge of a wide range of original sources—lives of saints, annals and chronicles, biblical and patristic commentaries, liturgical texts, laws tracts, glosses and glossaries, inscriptions—but a sharp sense of analysis, of clarity, and of balance in controversial subject matters. This book was to form the basis of *Christianity in Celtic lands,* published twenty-one years later. Meanwhile he had been asked to write articles on Celtic subjects in Cabrol and Leclerq's *Dictionnaire d'archéologie chrétienne et de liturgie,* where his notice "Celtiques (Liturgies)"—DACL, Tome II, 2, Cols 2969-3032—is still a reliable guide on the difficult subject of liturgical practices in Celtic countries.

His work at Farnborough was interrupted by World War I when he was mobilised into the French army. Between 1914 and 1918, he was interned in prison camps in Germany. There he devoted his free time to perfecting his knowledge of modern Celtic languages. He returned to England after the war and resumed his work: between 1920 and 1940, he published six books[1] and more than 200 articles in scholarly journals in the field of Celtic hagiography, history, liturgy and folklore. While his scholarly work called him from time to time outside the cloister, he remained at Farnborough Abbey until his death on 24 March 1941.

Louis Gougaud had close associations with Ireland. His first publication in an Irish periodical was in 1909 when his "Notes on Latin writers of Medieval Ireland" appeared in *Irish Theological Quarterly*.[2] In subsequent years he became a regular contributor to *Irish Ecclesiastical Record, Studies* and *Ériu.* Before the first world war he visited the Irish countryside and saw at first hand the early Christian sites. In 1911 he had published a small pamphlet in Paris about early Christian art, and the following year he visited Cashel

---

1 *Gaelic pioneers of Christianity* (Dublin 1923), Irish translation: *Cinnirí gaedhealacha na críostaidheachta* (Dublin 1939); *Dévotions et pratiques ascétiques du moyen-âge* (Paris 1925), English translation: *Devotional and ascetic practices in the middle ages* (London 1927); *Ermites et reclus. Études sur d'anciennes formes de vie religieuse* (Ligugé 1928); *Anciennes coutumes claustrales* (Ligugé 1930); *Christianity in Celtic lands* (London 1932); *Les saints irlandais hors d'Irlande, étude dans le culte et la dévotion traditionnelle* (Louvain and Oxford 1936).

2 L. Gougaud, "Notes on Latin writers of Medieval Ireland" *Irish Theological Quarterly* 4 (1909) 57-66.

and Clonmacnois in the company of his friend and colleague Victor Collins. He was invited several times to give lectures at University College Dublin. One of his books, *Gaelic pioneers of Christianity*, was published in Dublin by M. H. Gill & Son in 1923. In this work he dealt with the work of the Irish missionaries on the continent in the Middle Ages and the place of Irish saints in the folklore of continental Europe. This book was later translated into Irish and published in 1939 by the Dublin Stationery Office under the title *Cinnirí Gaedhealacha na Críostaidheachta*.

His scholarly achievements and his important contribution to the history of the early Irish Church were officially recognised in Ireland when the NUI conferred on him a honorary D Litt. Celt. in October 1925, in the same year as Joseph Loth, Charles Plummer, Julius Pokorny, Rudolf Thurneysen and Joseph Vendryes, all eminent Celtic scholars. The lectures he gave at UCD in April 1929 were very successful and were published by Hodges Figgis as a pamphlet entitled *Modern research, with special reference to early Irish ecclesiastical history* (Dublin 1929). This work is a gem of good sense and sound advice to the scholar of early Irish history. The methodological principles expressed in this pamphlet—close study of original sources, precise textual criticism, acquaintance with the Irish language, patience, absence of bias, attention to detail, self-criticism— are those which are found at work in *Christianity in Celtic lands*.

During his travels in Ireland and in Great Britain as a scholar and a lecturer, Gougaud was repeatedly asked whether he would allow his now famous *Les chrétientés celtiques* to be translated into English. When he finally consented, nearly twenty years had elapsed since the publication of the French work and the author's views had changed in the light of more recent research, not least his own. Rather than produce a translation of *Les chrétientés celtiques*, Gougaud decided to write a new book, keeping the framework of the original work but substantially changing the content. Like most of his work, the new draft was written in French and had to be translated into English. Father Paul Grosjean, the Celtic studies specialist among the Bollandists, introduced him to the London publishing house of Sheed & Ward. An Irish scholar, Maud Joynt, was chosen as the translator, not only because of her interest and expertise in the field of early Irish studies, but also because of her excellent knowledge of French. Maud Joynt is best known for her work as a lexicographer for the Royal Irish Academy's *Dictionary of the Irish language*,[3] but she also was a scholar of Irish hagiography and monastic history. The introduction to her English translation of Walahfrid Strabo's *Vita sancti Galli* published by the SPCK in 1927 remains an excellent treatment of the Irish involvement in the ecclesiastical and literary life of Carolingian Europe. She had studied on the continent and was fluent in French, German and Italian. She is responsible for the clear and elegant style of *Christianity in Celtic lands* and also for the correction of minor imperfections which she was able to bring to the author's attention. The book came out in 1932, the same year as the Fasciculus E of the *Dictionary of the Irish language* edited by Maud Joynt, and was an instant success. Scholars such as Mario Esposito, James F. Kenney and Felim Ó Briain who reviewed the book were unanimous in praising its excellence and recommending it as an indispensable guide for the student of the early Irish Church.[4]

Nowadays, sixty years after its original publication, the book can no longer be described as an "indispensable guide" but it remains an interesting and useful interpretation of early Irish sources. One of its main advantages is that, as a general survey of the period between the fifth and the twelfth century, it offers a collection of references to primary documents conveniently arranged in a single volume. However, statements and conclusions based on secondary material should be treated with caution and with the same critical mind advocated by Gougaud himself in *Modern research*. There is now a good deal of primary and secondary material in print which was not available when *Christianity in Celtic lands* was first published and relevant recent publications are listed in the annex of this introduction.

3   For an assessment of the scholarly career of Maud Joynt see, E. Knott, "Maud Joynt (†July 24, 1940)", *Éigse* 2 (1940) 226–9.

4   Reviews of Christianity in Celtic lands were published in the following journals: M. Esposito, *Archivio Storico Italiano* 90 (1932) 110–2; P. Le Roux, *Annales de Bretagne* 40 (1933) 571–3; J. A. Geary, *American Historical Review* 37 (1933) 308–10; H. Watt, *Journal of Theological Studies* 34 (1933) 87–9; D. A. Robeyns, *Recherches de Théologie Ancienne et Médiévale* 5 (1933) 335–6; F. Ó Briain, *Revue d'Histoire Ecclésiastique* 29 (1933) 126–8; J. F. Kenney, *Speculum* 8 (1933) 89–92; F.A. Walsh, *Catholic Historical Review* 19 (1933–34) 73–6.

Throughout the book Gougaud offers challenging views, taking care to derive statements from a logical presentation of his sources and avoiding imposing his point of view on the reader. In general he takes a balanced approach and is ready to take account of evidence which goes against the main trend of his argument. For example, when dealing with monasticism, he points out that despite the importance of the monastic element in the Irish Church, there was room for a secular clergy and an independent episcopal jurisdiction. An exception to the balanced approach is the first chapter, which deals with the Insular Celts. In an effort to rectify the romantic view portrayed by Ernest Renan at the end of the nineteenth century, Gougaud gives an excessively negative view of the pagan Celts which is at variance with the findings of modern scholarship. However, we should remember that modern archaeology was at its beginning and he was obliged to rely on the works of ancient and medieval writers who had little knowledge or understanding of Celtic civilisation. In matters of Church organisation, he is both more accurate and more original. He knew and admired Father John Ryan's recently published *Irish monasticism*, but did not use the findings of the Irish scholar and was able to present a different and independent voice which can still interest the modern reader. Some of his views now appear old-fashioned but he offers such a wealth of information that even the seasoned scholar of medieval studies will find details or useful references which have been overlooked in more recent publications. *Christianity in Celtic lands* is now a collector's item of interest to antiquarians, but as a well written and proven tool it will find a distinguished place in the library of any person interested in early Irish history.

ANNEX

To complete the bibliography compiled by Gougaud in his introduction, recent bibliographical material concerning primary sources will be found in M. Lapidge and R. Sharpe, *A bibliography of Celtic Latin literature 400–1200* (Dublin 1985) and R. Baumgarten, *Bibliography of Irish linguistics and literature* (Dublin 1986). Most of the journals listed are still in progress (*Revue Celtique* is now continued as *Études Celtiques*) but one should add to his list two new publications which are relevant to the subject matter of *Christianity in Celtic lands*: *Cambridge Medieual Celtic Studies*, published by James Hall, Cambridge, since 1981 and *Peritia*, published by the Medieval Academy of Ireland, Cork, since 1982.

The following references, which are by no means exhaustive, are intended for the reader who wishes to supplement Gougaud's bibliography with works of more recent scholarship.

CHAPTER I: THE HEATHEN CELTS IN THE BRITISH ISLES

J. Raftery, *The Celts* (Cork 1964); A. and B. Rees, *Celtic heritage* (London 1973); A. Ross, *Pagan Celtic Britain* (London 1974); J. Filip, *Celtic civilisation and its heritage* (Prague 1977); B. Cunliffe, *The Celtic world* (London 1979); P. Mac Cana, *Celtic mythology* (Feltham 1983); B. Raftery, *Celtic art* (Paris 1990); S. Moscati (ed.), *The Celts* (London 1991).

CHAPTER II: THE RISE OF CHRISTIANITY IN THE INSULAR COUNTRIES

The most challenging contribution to the debate concerning the mission of St Patrick is probably D. A. Binchy, "Patrick and his biographers, ancient and modern", *Studia Hibernica* 2 (1962) 7–173. A bibliography of the literature concerning the Patrician controversy up to 1963, compiled by Father F. X. Martin, is to be found in the reprint of E. Mac Neill, *Saint Patrick* (Dublin and London 1964). Further studies are: L. Bieler, *St Patrick and the coming of Christianity* (Dublin 1967); R. P. C. Hanson, *St Patrick: his origins and career* (Oxford 1968); J. Carney, *The problem of St Patrick* (Dublin 1973); E. A. Thompson, *Who was St Patrick?* (Woodbridge 1985) and for the readers of Italian, E. Malaspina, *Patrizio e l'acculturaziona latina dell'Irlanda* (Rome 1984). On the posthumous fame of St Patrick, which is the subject of the last section in this chapter, see now C. Doherty, "The cult of St Patrick and the politics of Armagh in the seventh century" in J.-M. Picard (ed.), *Ireland and Northern France, AD 600–850* (Dublin 1991) 53–94.

CHAPTER III: THE EXPANSION OF CHRISTIANITY—MONASTICISM

L. Bieler, *Ireland, harbinger of the Middle Ages* (London 1966); K. W. Hughes, *The Church in early Irish society* (London 1966); M. W. Barley and R. P. C. Hanson, *Christianity in Britain 300–700* (Leicester 1968); K. W. Hughes, *Early Christian Ireland* (London 1972); P. J. Corish (ed.) *A history of Irish Catholicism*, vol 1 (Dublin 1972); G. Mac Niocaill, *Ireland before the Vikings* (Dublin 1972); L. & M. De Paor, *Early Christian Ireland* (London 1978); C. Thomas, *Christianity in Roman Britain to AD 500* (Berkeley 1981).

CHAPTER IV: THE BRITONS IN ARMORICA

N. K. Chadwick, *Early Britanny* (Cardiff 1969); E. G. Bowen, *Saints, seaways and settlements in the Celtic lands* (Cardiff 1969); J. Delumeau, *Histoire de Bretagne* (Toulouse 1969); L. Fleuriot, *Les origines de la Bretagne* (Paris 1980); A. Chédeville and H. Guillotel, *La Bretagne des saints et des rois* (Rennes 1984); *Landévennec et le monachisme breton dans le haut moyen-âge* (Bannalec 1986).

CHAPTER V: THE IRISH ABROAD

B. Bischoff, "Il monachesimo irlandese nei suoi rapporti col continente" *Settimane di Studio* 4 (Spoleto 1957) 121–38; T. Ó Fiaich, "Irish peregrini on the continent", *Irish Ecclesiastical Record* 103 (1965) 233–400; A. Angenendt, *Monachi Peregrini* (Munich 1972); J. J. Contreni, *The Cathedral school of Laon from 850 to 930* (Munich 1978); P. A. Breatnach, "The origins of the Irish monastic tradition at Ratisbon (Regensburg)", *Celtica* 13 (1980) 58–77; H. B. Clarke and M. Brennan (eds), *Columbanus and Merovingian monasticism* (Oxford 1981); H. Löwe, *Die Iren und Europa im früheren Mittelalter* (Stuttgart 1982); P. Ní Chatháin and M. Richter (eds.), *Ireland and Europe: the early Church* (Stuttgart 1984); H. Dopsch and R. Juffinger, *Virgil von Salzburg, missionar und Gelehter* (Salzburg 1985); J.M. Picard (ed.), *Ireland and Northern France, AD 600–850* (Dublin 1991).

CHAPTER VI: CONTROVERSIES IN MATTERS OF DISCIPLINE

J. Ryan, "The early Irish Church and the Holy See", *Studies* 49 (1960) 1–16; E. James, "Bede and the tonsure question", *Peritia* 3

(1984) 85–98; M. Walsh and D. Ó Cróinín, *Cummian's letter "De controversia paschali"* (Toronto 1988).

CHAPTER VII: THE CLERGY AND ECCLESIASTICAL INSTITUTIONS

K. W. Hughes, *The Church in early Irish society* (London 1966); L. De Paor, "The agrandisement of Armagh", *Historical Studies* 8 (1971) 95–110; D. Ó Corráin, "The early Irish churches: some aspects of organisation", in D. Ó Corráin (ed.), *Irish antiquity. Essays and studies presented to Professor M.J. O'Kelly* (Cork 1981) pp. 327–41; T. Charles-Edwards, "The Church and settlement", in P. Ní Chatháin and M. Richter (eds), *Ireland and Europe: the early Church* (Stuttgart 1984) 167–75; R. Sharpe, "Some problems concerning the organization of the Church in early Medieval Ireland", *Peritia* 3 (1984) 230–70.

CHAPTER VIII: INTELLECTUAL CULTURE AND THEOLOGICAL DOCTRINES

J. W. Smit, *Studies on the language and style of Columba the younger* (Amsterdam 1971); L. Bieler and J. J. O' Meara (eds.), *The mind of Eriugena* (Dublin 1973); M. McNamara, *The Apocrypha in the Irish Church* (Dublin 1975); B. Bischoff, "Turning points in the history of Latin exegesis in the early Middle Ages" in M. McNamara (ed.), *Biblical Studies. The medieval Irish contribution* (Dublin 1976) 74–160; J. J. O'Meara and B. Naumann, *Latin script and letters AD 400–900* (Leiden 1976); L. Holtz, *Donat et la tradition de l'enseignement grammatical* (Paris 1981); M. Herren, *Insular Latin studies* (Toronto 1981); D. Ó Corráin, L. Breatnach, A. Breen, "The laws of the Irish", *Peritia* 3 (1984) 382–438; F. Kerlouégan, *Le De Excidio Britanniae de Gildas* (Paris 1987); M. Herren, *The sacred nectar of the Greeks: The study of Greek in the West in the early Middle Ages* (London 1988); J. J. O' Meara, *Eriugena* (Oxford 1988).

CHAPTER IX: LITURGY AND PRIVATE DEVOTION

J. Hennig, "Studies in the liturgy of the early Irish Church", *Irish Ecclesiastical Record* 75 (1951) 318–32; J. Ryan, "The mass in the early Irish Church", *Studies* 50 (1961) 371–84; "The sacraments in the early Irish Church", *Studies* 51(1962) 508–20; P. Ní Chatháin,

"The liturgical background of the Derrynavlan altar service" *Journal of the Royal Society of Antiquaries of Ireland* 110 (1980) 127–148; W. Godel, "Irish prayer in the early Middle Ages", *Milltown Studies* 4–8 (1979–1981); P. O'Dwyer, *The Celi Dé: spiritual reform in Ireland, 750–900* (Dublin 1981); M. Curran, *The Antiphonary of Bangor* (Dublin 1984).

CHAPTER X: CHRISTIAN ART

F. Henry, *Irish art in the early Christian period to AD 800* (London 1965); A. T. Lucas, *Treasures of Ireland: Irish pagan and early Christian art* (Dublin 1973); J. Alexander, *Insular illuminated manuscripts, 6th to the 9th century* (London 1978); M. Werner, *Insular art: an annotated bibliography* (Boston 1981); T. O'Neill, *The Irish hand* (Dublin 1984); M. Ryan, *Ireland and insular art, AD 500–1200* (Dublin 1987); S. McNab, "Styles used in twelfth century Irish figure sculpture", *Peritia* 6–7 (1987–88) 265–297; S. Young, *The work of angels: Masterpieces of Celtic metalwork, 6th to 9th centuries* (London 1989)

CHAPTER XI: THE GRADUAL DECLINE OF CELTIC PARTICULARISM

A. Gwynn, *The twelfth century reform* (Dublin 1968); D. Bethell, "English monks and Irish reform in the eleventh and twelfth centuries", *Historical Studies* 8 (1971) 11–35; D. Ó Corráin, *Ireland before the Normans* (Dublin 1972); J. Watt, *The Church in medieval Ireland* (Dublin 1972); B. Ó Cuiv, *The impact of the Scandinavian invasions on the Celtic-speaking peoples, 800–1000* (Dublin 1975); A. P. Smyth, *Scandinavian York and Dublin,* 2 vols (Dublin 1975 and 1979; reissued in one volume, Dublin 1987).

FOREWORD

THE present work is based on a book of mine entitled *Les chrétientés celtiques* which was published in Paris in 1911. It now appears under the title *Christianity in Celtic Lands*, revised, corrected and considerably enlarged, with such improvements as the incessant researches and ripening process of the intervening twenty years have suggested.

The title has been changed because the English language contains no word corresponding exactly to the French " chrétienté ", used in the sense of a Church in process of formation and as yet imperfectly organized, such as were those Christian communities of the Celtic world in the early Middle Ages whose history is sketched in this book. A good many writers speak unhesitatingly of a " Celtic Church " ; but that such a thing never existed has been, I trust, demonstrated in the following pages. The expression " Celtic Churches," used by some good writers,[1] might perhaps serve our purpose and has indeed been adopted as an equivalent in the explanatory sub-title of the book.

However, there is no reason to regret the issue of the work under a new title, since its contents differ largely from those of the French book of 1911. It is by no means a mere translation of *Les chrétientés celtiques*. I shall presently point out the respects in which the two works differ ; but first I may be allowed to dwell on two other words which occur in the new title. It is needless to say that by " Celtic lands " is meant " lands of Celtic speech." In this connection we may here reproduce the opening lines of the foreword of *Les chrétientés celtiques* (pp. i and ii) : " The expressions ' Celtic Church ' and ' chrétientés celtiques,' commonly used at the present day, are not of ancient date. Neither Irish, Welsh nor Bretons in

---

[1] For instance, J. E. Lloyd, who entitles one section of his *History of Wales* " The Celtic Churches and Rome " (London, 1912, I, p. 171).

vii

the Middle Ages called themselves by the name Celts. That name, now employed as a common denomination for the old Scottish, Irish, Welsh, Cornish and Breton peoples, is based on the resemblance of the languages spoken by those peoples in early times, as well as on a [certain] racial relationship.[1] For our present purpose, the development, nearly parallel in respect of time, of Christian institutions in the different sections of the Celtic world, both in the islands of the West and in Brittany, the resemblance between these institutions (at least in their general outlines), the similarity of the spirit and even in some respects of the religious temperament from which they derived their characteristic colouring, finally, the reciprocal influence exercised by these various Churches on one another—cut off as they were geographically and politically from the rest of Western Christianity—all these reasons seem to furnish sufficient justification for including in a single survey the origin and progress of Christianity in these countries down to the time when at last they lost their peculiar religious physiognomy, that is to say, down to the eleventh and twelfth centuries."

The walls and framework of a house are generally more solid and enduring than the rest of the structure. In like manner, the framework of the book of 1911 has been found to be still solid and has been retained almost intact. It has, however, been necessary to reconstruct some sections of the original fabric and to add new ones. The following is a summary of the principal changes and additions made.

To the bibliographical introduction, which has been revised throughout, a section has been added containing publications which have appeared between the years 1911 and 1931.

The plan and in consequence the contents of the first

[1] In 1911 I had written " vague " instead of " certain." A text of the eleventh century, quoted below in ch. xi, § 2, asserts the tie of kinship between British and Bretons. On the revived use of the classical word " Celtic " see Eoin MacNeill, who writes : " There must have been a time when the Celts of Ireland, Britain and Gaul were fully aware that they were nearer akin to each other than to the Germans and Italians, but this knowledge perished altogether from the popular memory and the popular consciousness. It was re-discovered and re-established by a Scottish Gael, George Buchanan, in the sixteenth century " (*Phases of Irish History*, Dublin, 1919, pp. 4–5). Cf. Robin Flower, *Ireland and Medieval Europe* (London, 1929), p. 5.

chapter, *The Heathen Celts in the British Isles,* have been radically altered, only a very small portion of the original text being left unchanged.

In Chapter II, *The Rise of Christianity in the Insular Countries,* a tenth section devoted to the posthumous glory of St Patrick has been added, and numerous changes have been made in other sections.

Chapter III, *The Expansion of Christianity,* has also been enlarged by the addition of a new section dealing with anchorites and recluses.

In Chapter IV, the long fourth section dealing with the ecclesiastical organization of Brittany has been entirely recast.

Chapter V, *The Irish Abroad,* now contains twelve sections instead of eight.

The plan of Chapters VI and VII remains unaltered.

Chapter VIII, *Intellectual Culture and Theological Doctrines,* retains its six divisions, but all have been considerably augmented.

Chapter IX, *Liturgy and Private Devotion,* has likewise undergone a good many alterations in detail, rendered necessary by the large number of publications, both sources and works by writers of to-day, which have appeared since it was originally written.

Chapter X, *Christian Arts,* has been subjected to revision in all its parts, and a fifth division has been added on music, as well as a conclusion summarizing what can be divined of the influence exercised overseas by Irish art in some of its branches.

Chapter XI, *The Gradual Decline of Celtic Particularism,* contains an additional section on the ecclesiastical reforms in Cornwall between the ninth and eleventh centuries.

Independently of the author's own researches, carried on during the twenty years which have elapsed since the publication of the French work,[1] it has been necessary to take into account many new publications (sources, fresh editions of texts and numerous historical studies) which have appeared

---

[1] Save for the period between August 3rd, 1914, and March 3rd, 1919, which was spent far from the cloister and devoted to occupations of a wholly different nature.

in the interim. Only the chief of these have been mentioned in the new section (1911-1931) of the bibliography ; but all that have come within the author's way have received his attention, as will be seen by the references in the footnotes.

There is no need to dwell further on the new features introduced in the general plan or the details of the present work. Those who desire to form an idea of the extent of the changes made need only glance at the list of abbreviations which follows the introduction. There they will see how many works published between 1911 and 1931 the author has had to pass under review ; in some cases adopting, in others rejecting the conclusions reached by their writers ; sometimes being led by the discovery of fresh material or of new points of view to correct, complete or modify his own text.

In conclusion, it gives me pleasure to express my gratitude to the many persons without whose aid this book would have been even more imperfect ; in the first place, to the translator, who has executed the English version of the revised text with much care and with a sympathy arising from interest in the subject-matter, and who has, moreover, supplied some useful information on points of philology ; to my friend Mario Esposito, who was kind enough to draw up, at my request, a detailed list of the misprints or other mistakes which his practised eye had discovered in the bibliography and footnotes of *Les chrétientés celtiques ;* to the R.P. Paul Grosjean, S.J., who placed me in communication with the publisher of the present volume ; to Mr. C. P. Curran for various wise suggestions ; to all those with whom for years past I have carried on an exchange of publications, by means of which I have been able to form a collection of off-prints (some from journals otherwise difficult of access) which has proved of great service ; finally to Miss Daisy Dunn of the National Library, Dublin, to Mlle. Françoise Henry of the Musée of Saint-Germain-en-Laye, to Canon Gilbert H. Doble, to the RR. PP. Hieronymus Frank, O.S.B., and Emmanuel de Severus, O.S.B., of the Abbey of Maria Laach, as well as to other friends and colleagues, for verifying references in libraries or supplying other valuable information.

Several suggestions on points calling for expert knowledge,

both in text and notes, have been made by Maud Joynt, P. Paul Grosjean, and Mario Esposito, through whose hands the proofs of the book have passed. To them I desire to express my gratitude, and also to Mlle. Françoise Henry, who was so kind as to read Chapter X and place at my disposal some of her special knowledge of the subject with which it deals. In the task of final revision I have had the aid of my *confrère*, Dom Adrien Eudine, O.S.B.

CONTENTS

xii

CHAPTER III

THE EXPANSION OF CHRISTIANITY— MONASTICISM

CHAPTER IV

THE BRITONS IN ARMORICA

CHAPTER V

THE IRISH ABROAD

CHAPTER VI

CONTROVERSIES IN MATTERS OF DISCIPLINE

CHAPTER VII

THE CLERGY AND ECCLESIASTICAL INSTITUTIONS

CHAPTER VIII

INTELLECTUAL CULTURE AND THEOLOGICAL DOCTRINES

CHAPTER IX

LITURGY AND PRIVATE DEVOTION

CHAPTER X

CHRISTIAN ARTS

CHAPTER XI

THE GRADUAL DECLINE OF CELTIC PARTICULARISM

INTRODUCTION

SOURCES AND AIDS TO RESEARCH

I PROPOSE here to indicate the original sources, the later works, the journals and academy publications, an acquaintance with which is necessary or useful to anyone who wishes to study the Celtic Churches as a whole or at some particular phase of their history. Lest this introduction should attain a length altogether out of proportion to the rest of the volume, I have omitted from my lists all periodical literature except publications which consist of original texts or which deal directly with bibliography or criticism of sources. As for books, I have mentioned only those which are really of value. If I name any works which are faulty or quite uncritical, it is only in order to point out their defects and put the reader on his guard against the undeserved popularity they enjoy in certain quarters.

I have thought it best to arrange this table of the sources and aids to research in the chronological order of their publication, thus enabling the reader to obtain a summary view of the gradual progress of studies, while at the same time observing the logical order in each section.

The first division contains publications of the sixteenth and seventeenth centuries, the second of the eighteenth century, the third those which appeared between 1800 and 1853 (in the latter year was published the first edition of the *Grammatica Celtica* of Johann Kaspar Zeuss, an event of great importance in the history of Celtic philology), the fourth those which appeared between 1853 and 1911, and the fifth those which appeared between 1911 and 1931 (inclusive).

I.—SIXTEENTH AND SEVENTEENTH CENTURIES.

I.—SOURCES

GENERAL

Bollandus (Ioannes) and successors, *Acta Sanctorum quotquot toto orbe coluntur* . . . f° original ed. Antverpiae, Tongerlaae, Bruxellis, 1643 sq.; 3rd ed. Parisiis et Bruxellis, from T. I of January to T. IV of November (1863–1925).

Mabillon (Iohannes) et D'Achery (Lucas), *Acta Sanctorum ordinis Sancti Benedicti* (Parisiis, 1668–1701), 9 vols. f°.

SPECIAL

(*a*) Great Britain

Bale (John), *Index Britanniae scriptorum*, ed. R. L. Poole and Mary Bateson (Anecdota Oxoniensia.—Mediaeval and Modern Series, IX, Oxford, 1902, 4°).

Capgravius, *Nova legenda Anglie*, impressa Londonias, 1516, 4°; latest ed. C. Horstman (Oxford, 1901), 2 vols. 8°.

Wharton (Henry), *Anglia sacra, sive Collectio historiarum partim antiquitus, partim recenter scriptarum de archiepiscopis et episcopis Angliae a prima fidei Christianae susceptione ad annum* MDXL (Londini, 1691), 2 vols. f°.

(*b*) Ireland

Messingham (Thomas), *Florilegium insulae Sanctorum* (Parisiis, 1624) f° [contains, by way of introduction, a dissertation by David Roth on the ancient names of Ireland].

Usserius [Ussher], *Veterum epistolarum Hibernicarum sylloge quae partim ab Hibernis, partim ad Hibernos, partim de Hibernis vel rebus Hibernicis sunt conscriptae* (Dubl., 1632) 4° [Ussher's complete works were collected and edited by Elrington and Todd and published in 13 vols. in Dublin between 1847 and 1864. The 40 letters contained in the *Sylloge* occupy pp. 383–572 of the fourth volume].

The Irish Franciscans were the first to get into direct contact with the early sources of the ecclesiastical history of their country. Between 1632 and 1636 in the convent of

Donegal the lay brother Michael O'Clery, assisted by three principal collaborators, compiled the *Annals of Donegal* (generally known as the *Annals of the Four Masters*, a title given to them by Colgan) from old Irish chronicles, some of which are now lost. These annals extend from the year of the world 2242 to A.D. 1616. The chronology of the Middle Ages is often at fault. They were published, with a Latin translation, by Charles O'Conor, *Rerum Hibernicarum scriptores veteres* (Buckinghamiae, 1824, 4°, T. III), and, with an English translation, by John O'Donovan (Dublin, 1848-51, 6 vols. 4°).

Michael O'Clery also compiled various Genealogies and a Martyrology of Irish saints drawn from earlier martyrological writings. This compilation is known as the *Martyrology of Donegal;* it was edited, with an English translation by J. O'Donovan, by James Henthorn Todd and William Reeves (Dublin.—Irish Archaeol. and Celtic Soc., 1864. 8°).

Finally, O'Clery drew up a glossary of the difficult and obscure Old and Middle Irish words which he had met in the course of his reading ; this work was published at Louvain in 1643. A new edition by Arthur W. K. Miller appeared in the *Revue celtique* (IV, 1880, pp. 349-428 ; V, 1881, pp. 1-69).

The Franciscan John Colgan made use of the Latin and Irish materials supplied to him by Bollandus, by his fellow workers O'Clery and Hugh Ward and by Brendan O'Connor and Stephen White, in the publication of his two famous hagiographical collections : (1) *Acta Sanctorum veteris et maioris Scotiae seu Hiberniae, Sanctorum insulae* (1 vol. f°, Lovanii, 1645) ; (2) *Triadis Thaumaturgae seu divorum Patricii, Columbae et Brigidae . . . acta* (1 vol. f°, Lovanii, 1647).— Colgan left, besides, three folio volumes of unedited writings.

Another Franciscan, Patrick Fleming, published *Collectanea sacra seu S. Columbani Hiberni abbatis . . . necnon aliorum . . . Sanctorum acta et opuscula* (Lovanii, 1667, f°).

For the works and various undertakings of the Irish Franciscans in the seventeenth century, the reader may consult : (1) Ch. P. Meehan, *The rise and fall of the Irish Franciscan monasteries* (1st ed., Dublin and London, 1869, 2nd ed., Dublin,

1877, 8°) ; (2) Victor De Buck, *L'archéologie irlandaise au couvent de Saint Antoine de Padoue à Louvain* (*Études publiées par les Pères de la Société de Jésus*, XXIII, 1869, pp. 409–37, 586–603) ; (3) Denis Murphy, *The College of the Irish Franciscans in Louvain* (*JRSAI*, 5th ser., III, 1893, pp. 237–50) ; (4) Brendan Jennings, *The return of the Irish Franciscans to Louvain* (*Studies*, XIV, 1925, pp. 451–58).

II.—HISTORICAL RESEARCH

GENERAL

Camden (William), *Britannia sive florentissimorum regnorum Angliae, Scotiae, Hiberniae et insularum adiacentium ex intima antiquitate chronographica descriptio* (Londini, 1586) [many editions].

Usserius [Ussher], *Gravissimae quaestiones de Christianarum Ecclesiarum in Occidentis praesertim partibus ab Apostolicis temporibus ad nostrum usque aetatem* (Londini, 1613) [*Works*, ed. Elrington and Todd, vol. II]. *S.a.*, *A Discourse on the Religion anciently professed by the Irish and British* (Dubl., 1613) [*Works*, vol. IV].—*S.a.*, *Britannicarum Ecclesiarum antiquitates*, etc. (Dubl., 1639) [*Works*, vol. V and VI].—For the age he lived in, Ussher shows considerable knowledge of Irish antiquities ; but his critical judgment is often at fault, especially when he is endeavouring to discover Protestant tendencies in ancient Celtic Christianity.

Tillemont (Le Nain de), *Mémoires pour servir à l'histoire ecclésiastique des six premiers siècles* (Paris, 1691–1738, 2nd ed. 1701–1712). [I have used this second edition.—Before the end of the nineteenth century no insular writer brought so much critical acumen to the investigation of the sources with which we are concerned as the French scholar Tillemont. Unfortunately he had to do with only a few of the personalities connected with the history of Christianity in Celtic lands, Prosper of Aquitaine, Germanus of Auxerre, Lupus of Troyes, Faustus of Riez and St Patrick].

SPECIAL
(a) Scotland

Dempster (Thomas), *Apparatus ad historiam Scoticam. Accesserunt Martyrologium Scoticum Sanctorum et scriptorum Scotorum nomenclatura* (Bononiae, 1622, 4°).—*S.a.*, *Historia ecclesiastica gentis Scotorum, sive de scriptoribus Scotis* (Bononiae, 1627, 2nd ed. Edinburgh, Bannatyne Club, 1829, 2 vols., 4°) [Perhaps no writer has ever handled historical questions so recklessly and with such utter absence of impartiality and restraint as Dempster].

(b) Brittany

Albert Le Grand, *Les Vies des saints de la Bretagne armorique* (1636 or 1637 ; 2nd ed., 1659 ; 3rd ed., 1680 ; ed. de Kerdanet, 1837 ; ed. Thomas and J.-M. Abgrall, Quimper and Paris, 1901) [In this work, the worthy Friar Preacher had no aim beyond the moral edification of his readers].

Pierre Le Baud, *Histoire de Bretagne avec les chroniques des maisons de Vitré et de Laval* (Paris, 1638, f°) [This compilation was written between 1498 and 1505].

(c) Ireland

Ware (Sir James), *De Hibernia et antiquitatibus ejus disquisitiones*, etc. ¦(Londini, 1654, 4°).—*S.a., Commentarium de praesulibus Hiberniae a prima gentis Hiberniae ad fidem Christianam conversione ad nostra usque tempora* (Dubl., 1665, f°). An English version of these works has been published in *The whole works of Sir James Ware concerning Ireland*, by Walter Harris (Dublin, 1739–64) [At the present day these writings possess but slight value owing to the mass of mistaken opinions they contain].

Lynch (John), *Cambrensis eversus seu potius historica fides in rebus Hibernicis Giraldo Cambrensi abrogata* (Saint-Malo,? 1662, f°). New ed. with Engl. transl. by Matthew Kelly (Dublin, Celtic Soc., 1848–52, 3 vols.)

O'Flaherty (Roderick), *Ogygia seu rerum Hibernicarum chronologia* (Londini, 1685, 4°). Engl. transl. by J. Hely, 2 vols. 8°, Dublin, 1793 [a rather fictitious history of Ireland from the remotest times down to the seventeenth century].

II.—EIGHTEENTH CENTURY
I.—SOURCES
GENERAL

Bouquet (Martin), *Rerum Gallicarum et Francicarum scriptores : Recueil des historiens des Gaules* (Paris, 1738–1876, 23 vols. f°; ed. L. Delisle, Paris, 1869–79, 17 vols. f°).

Mansi (J. D.), *Sacrorum conciliorum nova et amplissima collectio* (Florentiae, 1759–1798. New impression, Paris, 1901–1913, 48 vols., f°) [I have used this new impression].

SPECIAL
(a) Great Britain

Wotton (William), *Cyfreithjeu Hywel Dda ac Eraill, seu Leges Wallicae ecclesiasticae et civiles Hoeli Boni et aliorum Walliae principum* . . . (Londini, 1730, f°) [The first edition of Welsh laws].

(b) Scotland

Pinkerton (John), *Vitae antiquae Sanctorum qui habitaverunt in ea parte Britanniae nunc vocata Scotia vel in ejus insulis* (Londini, 1789, 8°) [contains nine Lives of Scottish Saints, re-edited by Metcalfe (Paisley, 1889, 2 vols.)].

(c) Brittany

[See below, Hyacinthe Morice under the heading " Historical Research."]

II.—HISTORICAL RESEARCH
(a) Cornwall

Borlase (William), *Historical and monumental Antiquities of the County of Cornwall* (Oxford, 1753, 2nd ed. 1769).

(b) Ireland

Between 1628 and 1640 Geoffrey Keating composed in Irish a History of Ireland, *Foras Feasa ar Éirinn*, extending from the Flood to the seventeenth year of the reign of Henry II. This work was translated into English by Dermot O'Connor (Dublin, 1723, f°, re-edited in 1726, 1817, 1854), and by John O'Mahony (New York, 1866, 8°). The Irish text was edited for the first time, with translation, by William Haliday (Vol. I., Dublin, 1811, 8°. Only Vol. I. appeared). The Gaelic text (Book I., Part I.) was edited again, with literal translation, by P. W. Joyce (Dublin, 1900). David Comyn and Patrick S. Dinneen have published a complete and better edition, with Engl. transl. (London, Irish Texts Society, 1902–14, 4 vols. 8°). For other editions and translations see Best,

Bibl., pp. 254–55. As a compiler Keating was devoid of critical judgment, but he made use of manuscripts which are now lost, and on this account his testimony is sometimes valuable.

Ledwich (Edward), *Antiquities of Ireland* (Dublin, 1790, 2nd ed. 1794–96, 2 vols. 4°) [Thoroughly sceptical in his tendencies, an Irish counterpart of Launoi, this historian went so far as to assert that St Patrick's *Confessio*, the authenticity of which, nowadays, is hardly called in question, was the fabrication of a monk of the eleventh or twelfth century].

Astle (Thomas), *The origin and progress of writing . . . illustrated by engravings . . .* (London, 1784, 4°, 2nd ed. 1803) [In this work Irish script and illumination are dealt with for the first time and at considerable length. Some of the plates still deserve attention].

Archdall (Mervyn), *Monasticon Hibernicum, or an History of the Abbies, Priories and other religious Houses in Ireland* (Dublin, 1786, 4°) [a work with many defects, re-edited by Patrick F. Moran (Dublin, 1873–76, 2 vols. 4°). See L. G., *Modern research* (Dublin, 1929), p. 53].

(c) Brittany

Just as in the preceding century, the Irish Franciscans (emulated by some Jesuits) had laid the foundation of the religious history of their country, in the eighteenth a group of French Benedictines, some of them natives of Brittany, devoted themselves to the study of Celtic antiquities, both continental and British. Unfortunately Dom Paul Pezron, author of *L'antiquité de la nation et de la langue des Celtes autrement appelés Gaulois* (Paris, 1703, 8°), was one of the first, along with Simon Pelloutier, to fall a victim to Celtomania.—*La religion des Gaulois tirée des plus pures sources de l'antiquité* by Dom Jacques Martin (Paris, 1727, 2 vols.) may still be consulted for its plates, on which are figured some objects now lost.—In 1752, Dom Louis Le Pelletier published a *Dictionnaire de la langue bretonne*.

It is chiefly the historical works of the Breton Maurists which are still of value : (1) *L'histoire de Bretagne composée sur les actes et auteurs originaux* (Paris and Rennes, 1707, 2 vols. f°) by

Dom Gui-Alexis Lobineau ; (2) his *Histoire des saints de la province de Bretagne et des personnes qui s'y sont distinguées par une éminente piété* (Paris and Rennes, 1723, 2 vols. f° ; revised edit. by Tresvaux, 1836–39, in 6 vols. 8°).—At the beginning of the second volume of Lobineau's *Histoire de Bretagne* are three " éclaircissements " or dissertations by Dom Antoine-Paul Le Gallois, the first dealing with the date of the second journey of St Germanus of Auxerre to Britain, the second with the establishment of the Christian religion in that country and the earliest saints, the third with the date of the Council of Vannes in 468.

Of the writings of Dom Hyacinthe Morice de Beaubois the two following deserve special mention : (1) *Mémoires pour servir de preuves à l'histoire ecclésiastique et civile de Bretagne* (Paris, 1742–46, 3 vols., f°) [a veritable storehouse of texts ; the first volume contains documents of the early Middle Ages] ; (2) *Histoire ecclésiastique de Bretagne* (Paris, 1750–56, 2 vols. f°) [a very unsatisfactory edition of these two works together appeared at Guingamp in 1836–37, 20 vols. 8°].

Cf. Maurice Lecomte, *Les Bénédictins et l'histoire des provinces aux* XVII° *et* XVIII° *siècles* (Liguge, 1928), Ch. II, *Histoire de Bretagne*, pp. 13–18).

III.—ACADEMY PUBLICATION

Royal Irish Academy.—*Transactions : Polite Literature and Antiquities* (Dublin, 1786–1907).

III.—FROM 1800 TO 1853
I.—SOURCES
GENERAL

Monumenta Germaniae historica [For the details of the various series see below, List of Abbreviations.]

Migne (J.-P.), *Patrologiae cursus completus :* (*a*) Series Latina (221 vols., Parisiis, 1844–64) ; (*b*) series Graeca (161 vols., Parisiis, 1857–66.)

Wasserschleben (F. W. B.), *Die Bussordnungen der abendländischen Kirche* (Halle, 1851, 8°).

SPECIAL

(a) Great Britain

Myvyrian Archaiology of Wales collected out of ancient Manuscripts (3 vols., London, 1801–1808) [the product of the labour of Owen Jones, Edward Williams and William Owen [Pughe], containing poetic, historical, moral, legal and didactic materials in Welsh, without translation : 2nd ed., 1 vol., 1860].

Probert (William), *The ancient Laws of Cambria . . . to which are added the historical Triads of Britain translated from the Welsh* (London, 1823–28).

Owen (Aneurin), *Ancient Laws and Institutes of Wales* (London, 1841, f°) [Text with translation. Best edition of Welsh Laws].

Iolo Manuscripts, a selection of ancient Welsh MSS. in prose and verse from the collection made by the late Edward Williams, Iolo Morganwg, for the purpose of forming a continuation to the Myvyrian Archaiology . . . with English translation and notes by his son, the late Taliesin Williams [Ab Iolo] (Llandovery, 1848) [contains genealogies, historical pieces, stories, etc.].

Petrie (H.) and Sharpe (J.), *Monumenta historica Britannica* (London, 1848, f°) [contains inscriptions, Gildas, Nennius, Bede's *Hist. Eccl.*, the *A-S. Chronicle*, Asser, *Annales Cambriae* to A.D. 1066, *Brut y Tywysogion* to the same date, etc.]

(b) Ireland

Letronne (Jean-Antoine), *Recherches géographiques et critiques sur le livre ' De Mensura orbis terrae,' composé en Irlande au commencement du ixe siècle par Dicuil, suvies du texte restitue* (Paris, 1814).—The *Liber de mensura orbis terrae* has been re-edited by Gustav Parthey (Berolini, 1870) [I use the latter edition].

O'Conor (Charles), *Rerum Hibernicarum scriptores veteres* (Buckinghamiae, 1814–28, 4 vols. 4°) [contains the Irish text, with a Latin translation, of the Annals of Tigernach, of a portion of the Annals of Innisfallen (A.D. 428–1196), of the Annals of Boyle (A.D. 420–1245), of the Annals of the Four Masters and of the Annals of Ulster].

Villanueva (J. L.), *Sancti Patricii, Ibernorum apostoli synodi, canones, opuscula et scriptorum quae supersunt fragmenta scholiis illustrata* (Dubl., 1835).

Jubinal (Achille), *La Légende latine de S. Brandaines* (Paris, 1836).

Retting (H. C. M.), *Antiquissimus quatuor Evangeliorum Codex Sangallensis Graeco-Latinus* (Zürich, 1836) [St. Gall, Cod. 48].

Ormonde (Marquis of), *Life of St Cainnech* (1848, published for private distribution) [From Cod. Salmanticensis with variants from MS. Z. 3. I, 5 of Marsh's Library, Dublin].

Todd (J. H.), *Irish Version of the Historia Britonum of Nennius* (Irish and English) (Dublin, 1848) [A Latin translation of this Irish version by H. Zimmer is given side by side with the original text of Nennius in Mommsen's edition published in the *Monumenta Germaniae historica* (*Auct. Antiq.*, XIII, *Chron. min.* III, 1894)].

II.—HISTORICAL RESEARCH

(a) Wales

Rees (Rice), *An Essay on the Welsh Saints* (London, 1836, 8°).

Williams (John), *The ecclesiastical antiquities of the Cymry or the ancient British Church* (London, 1844).

(b) Ireland

Betham (Sir William), *Irish antiquarian researches* (Dublin, 1827, 2 vols. 8°) [swarms with errors].

Wakeman (W. F.), *Handbook of Irish Antiquities, Pagan and Christian* (Dublin, 1848) [re-edited by John Cooke in 1903].

Lanigan (John), *An ecclesiastical History of Ireland from the first introduction of Christianity . . . to the beginning of the thirteenth century* (1st ed., 1822, 4 vols. ; 2nd ed., Dublin, 1829, 4 vols.) [a work of merit, far surpassing all its predecessors, displaying vast learning, written with judgment and vigorous style ; directed chiefly against the errors of Ussher and Ledwich, the latter in particular being Lanigan's *bête noire*].

Wright (Thomas), *The Purgatory of St Patrick* (London, 1844).

Petrie (George), *The ecclesiastical architecture of Ireland anterior to the Anglo-Norman invasion, comprising an Essay on the origin and uses of the Round Towers of Ireland,* a work accompanied with

256 engravings which was printed in vol. XX. of the *Trans. of the Roy. Irish Academy*, and in reprint (Dublin, 1845, 4°).

III.—PERIODICAL AND ACADEMY PUBLICATIONS

The Celto-Briton (3 vols., 1820–22) [contains translations of several texts printed in the *Myvyrian Archaiology of Wales* (See above)].

Proceedings of the Royal Irish Academy : I. Ser., *Science, Polite Literature and Antiquities* (10 vols., 1836–69) ; II. Ser., *Pol. Lit. and Antiq.* (2 vols., 1870–88) ; III. Ser., *Science, Pol. Lit. and Antiq.* (1888, in progress) [Since 1902 each vol. is divided into three sections, sect. C including archaeology, linguistics and literature].

Archaeological Journal (London, 1845, in progress), published by the Royal Archaeological Institute of Great Britain.

Archaeologia Cambrensis (London, 1846, in prog.), organ of the Cambrian Archaeological Association.

Journal of the Royal Society of Antiquaries of Ireland (Dublin, 1849, in prog.) [Continuation of the *Journal of the Royal Historical and Archaeological Association of Ireland*, originally founded as the Kilkenny Archaeological Society in the year 1849].

Proceedings of the Society of Antiquaries of Scotland (Edinburgh, 1852, in prog.).

IV.—FROM 1853 TO 1911

I.—SOURCES

GENERAL

Potthast (August), *Bibliotheca historica medii aevi : Wegweiser durch die Geschichtswerke des Europäischen Mittelalters bis* 1500 (2nd ed., 2 vols., Berlin, 1896).

Rerum Britannicarum medii aevi scriptores, or Chronicles and Memorials of Great Britain and Ireland during the Middle Ages, published . . . under the direction of the Master of the Rolls, (London, 1858–96, 8°) [several volumes of this important series will be specially mentioned further on, according to their contents ; but in the present section may be placed the following work of Thomas Duffus Hardy, *Descriptive catalogue of materials relating to the History of Great Britain and Ireland to the end of the Reign of Henry VII* (4 vols., London, 1862–71), a repertory of the historiographical sources for the history of England, Scotland, Wales and Ireland. The lists of MSS. given are of necessity very incomplete].

Haddan (A. W.) and Stubbs (W.), *Councils and ecclesiastical documents relating to Great Britain and Ireland* (Oxford, 1869–78, 3 vols. 8°).

Venerabilis Bedae Historia ecclesiastica gentis Anglorum, ed. Charles Plummer (Oxford, 1896, 2 vols. 8°).

Bibliotheca hagiographica latina antiquae et mediae aetatis, ediderunt Socii Bollandiani (Bruxellis, 1898–1901, 2 vols. 8° and a supplement vol., 1911).

Brash (R. B.), *The Ogam inscribed monuments of the Gaedhil in the British Islands* (London, 1879, 4°).

Cooper (Charles Purton), *Appendix A to Rymer's Foedera and Supplement to Appendix A* (*s.l.* 8°, 1869) [An ill-digested compilation giving accounts of the English and Irish MSS. preserved in the British Isles or on the Continent. The pressmarks of the MSS. are not given. Except for the facsimiles it contains the work is of no value].

Omont (Henri), *Catalogue des manuscrits celtiques et basques de la Bibliothèque nationale* (*Revue celtique*, XI, 1890, pp. 389–433) [29 Irish and 73 Breton MSS.].

Stokes (Whitley), *The Breton Glosses at Orleans : The Irish passages in the Stowe Missal* (Berlin, 1882).

Loth (Joseph), *Vocabulaire vieux-breton avec commentaire contenant toutes les gloses en vieux-breton, gallois, cornique, armoricain* (Bibliothèque de l'École des Hautes Études.—Paris, 1884, 8°).

Schmitz (H. J.), *Die Bussbücher und die Bussdisciplin der Kirche* (Mainz, 1883, 8°).—*S.a.*, *Die Bussbücher und das kanonische Bussverfahren* (Düsseldorf, 1898, 8°). [See important reviews of both works in *Bulletin critique*, of the first by L. Duchesne (IV, 1883, p. 365–71), of the second by Paul Fournier (*ib.*, 2nd Ser., VII, 1901, p. 601–607].

Jenkinson (F. J. H.), *The Hisperica Famina* (Cambridge, 1908, 8°).

Dottin (Georges), *La littérature gaélique de l'Écosse. La litté-*

rature cornique. La littérature bretonne armoricaine (Revue de synthèse historique, t. VIII, 1904).

Maclean (Magnus), *The literature of the Celts* (London, 1902).

Hinneberg (Paul), *Die Kultur der Gegenwart, ihre Entwickelung und ihre Ziele.* Teil I, Abteilung XI, 1 : I. *Die keltischen Literaturen.*—(1) H. Zimmer, *Sprache und Literatur der Kelten im Allgemeinen.*—(2) *Die einzelnen keltischen Literaturen :* (a) Kuno Meyer, *Die irisch-gälische Literatur ;* (b) L. C. Stern, *Die schottische gälische und die Manx Literatur ;* (c) L. C. Stern, *Die kymrische (walische) Literatur ;* (d) L. C. Stern, *Die kornische und die bretonische Literatur* (Berlin and Leipzig, 1909).

SPECIAL

(a) Ireland

(1) *Bibliography of Sources*

O'Curry (Eugene), *Lectures on the Manuscript Materials of ancient Irish History* (Dublin, 1861, 8°, 2nd ed. 1878) [Still useful, though now out of date. At an early age O'C. was attracted by the old national literature, and he passed his life among the Irish MSS. preserved in Dublin, studying them and transcribing a great number. With those of the Continent he had far less acquaintance].

Arbois de Jubainville (Henri d'), *Essai d'un catalogue de la littérature épique de l'Irlande* (Paris, 1883, 8°) [mentions other texts besides the tales and sagas. See *Addenda et corrigenda* by Zimmer (*Göttingische gelehrte Anzeigen*, 1887, 169–75, 184–93), by Kuno Meyer (*R. Cel.*, VI, 1884, pp. 187–88), by Whitley Stokes (*Academy*, May 10, 1890), by G. Dottin, *Supplément à l'Essai d'un catalogue* (*R. Cel.*, 1912, XXXIII, pp. 1–40)].

Abbott (T. K.), *Catalogue of the manuscripts of Trinity College, Dublin* (Dublin and London, 1900, 8°), new ed. of the Catalogue of Irish MSS. only, by T. K. Abbott and E. J. Gwynn (1921).

Dottin (Georges), *Notes bibliographiques sur l'ancienne littérature chrétienne de l'Irlande* (*Revue d'histoire et de littérature religieuses*, V, 1900, pp. 162–67) ; *s.a.*, *La littérature gaélique de l'Irlande* (*Revue de synthèse historique*, III, 1901, pp. 60–97) [brought up to date in 1906 by J. Dunn, *The Gaelic literature of Ireland* (Washington : *privately printed*)].

Extremely useful bibliographies of the Latin writers of medieval Ireland have been published by Mario Esposito in *Hermathena*, (XV, 1909, pp. 353–64, XVI, 1910, pp. 58–72), *Irish Theological Quarterly* (IV, 1909, pp. 181–85) [See also below, Sect. V. of this Introduction].

L. G., *Notes on the Latin writers of Mediaeval Ireland* (*Irish Theological Quarterly*, IV, 1909, pp. 57–65).

(2) *Epigraphy*

Petrie (George), *Christian Inscriptions in the Irish language from the earliest known to the end of the twelfth century.* Edited with introduction by Margaret Stokes (Dublin, 1872–78, 2 vols. 4°)

Gaidoz (Henri), *Notice sur les inscriptions latines de l'Irlande* (*Mélanges publiés par la Section historique et philologique de l'École des Hautes Études*, Paris, 1878, pp. 121–35).

Macalister (R. A. Stewart), *Studies in Irish Epigraphy, a Collection of revised readings of the ancient Inscriptions of Ireland* (London, 3 parts, 1897–1907).

(3) *Annals and Chronicles*

Three Fragments of Irish Annals, edited by John O'Donovan (Dublin, 1860).

Cogadh Gaedhel re Gallaibh. The War of the Gaedhil with the Gaill or the Invasions of Ireland by the Danes and other Norsemen, edited with transl. by J. H. Todd (London, *RS.*, 1867, 8°).

Chronicon Scotorum from the earliest times to 1135 *with a Supplement*, 1141–50, *by Duald MacFirbis*, edited with transl. by William M. Hennessy (London, *RS.*, 1866, 8°).

Annals of Ulster, edited with transl. by W. M. Hennessy and B. MacCarthy (Dublin, 1887–1901, 4 vols., 8°) [*AU* are the most reliable of all Irish Annals printed to this date. Vol. IV contains a valuable introduction by B. MacC. For various criticisms of the edition and lists of corrigenda see Best, *Bibl.*, p. 252, and, on the language, Thomas O'Maille, *On the language of the Annals of Ulster* (Manchester, 1910)].

The Annals of Loch Cé (1014–1590), edited with transl. by W. M. Hennessy (London, *RS.*, 1871, 8°).

The Annals of Tigernach, edited with transl. by Whitley Stokes (*R. Cel.*, XVI–XVIII, 1895–97) [See Eoin MacNeill, *The authorship and structure of the 'Annals of Tigernach'* (*Ériu*, VII, 1913, pp. 30–113)].

(4) *Hagiography*

Reeves (William), *The Life of St Columba written by Adamnan* (Dublin, 1857, 8°.—Irish Archaeological and Celtic Society) [An edition of Adamnan's text with notes which have not lost their value with time ; Whitley Stokes, in the *Academy* of Oct. 2, 1886, has corrected some errors.—It has been re-edited by J. T. Fowler with notes abridged from those of Reeves, *Adamnani Vita S Columbae* (Oxford, 1894 ; new ed., Oxford, 1920.—See sect. V of this Introduction].

Caulfield (Richard), *Life of St Fin Barre* (London, 1864) [From MS. Z, 3. I, 5 of Marsh's Library, Dublin].

Schröder (Carl), *Sanct Brandan. Ein lateinischer und drei deutsche Texte* (Erlangen, 1871).

Moran (Patrick, later Cardinal), *Acta Sancti Brendani* (Dublin, 1872).

Whitley Stokes, *Three Middle Irish Homilies, or the Lives of Saints Patrick, Brigit and Columba* (Calcutta, 1877, 8°).— S.a., *The Tripartite Life of Saint Patrick with other Documents relating to that Saint* (London, *RS.*, 1887, 2 vols.) [Contains the works of St Patrick and all documents affording evidence of any value on the saint, together with translations of the Irish texts, a long introduction, and excellent notes and glossaries of marked excellence. For criticism see B. MacCarthy, *The Tripartite Life of St Patrick : new textual studies* (*Trans. of the R. Irish Academy*, XXIX, 1889, pp. 183–206) and Best, *Bibl.*, p. 240. Cf. Sect. V of this Introduction].

White (Newport J. D.), *Libri Sancti Patricii, The Latin writings of St Patrick* (*PRIA*, XXV, Sect. C, 1905) [contains a new edition of St Patrick's *Confessio* and *Epistola.* See Sect. V of this Introduction].

The Passions and Homilies from the Leabhar Breac, edited with transl. and glossary by Robert Atkinson (Todd Lecture Series, II, Dublin, 1887, 8°) [contains 15 Passions and 21 Homilies. For criticism see Best, *Bibl.*, p. 231].

Conchubrani Vita S. Monennae, edited by Mario Esposito (*PRIA*, XXVIII, Sect. C, 1910, pp. 202–51).

The Irish Nennius from the Leabhar na Huidre and Homilies and Legends from the Leabhar Breac, edited by Edmund Hogan (Todd Lecture Series, VI, Dublin, 1895).

De Smedt (Charles) and De Backer (Joseph), *Acta Sanctorum Hiberniae ex codice Salmanticensi* (Edinburgi et Brugis, 1888) [Detailed reviews and criticisms in *Göttingische gelehrte Anzeigen*, March, 1891, by Zimmer, and *AB*, XI, 1892, p. 479].

Documenta de St. Patricio . . . ex Libro Armachano, ed. by Edmund Hogan (*AB*, I–II, 1882–83) and separately.

Whitley Stokes, *Lives of Saints from the Book of Lismore* (Anecdota Oxoniensia : Mediaeval and Modern Series, V, Oxford, 1890, 4°) [Extremely valuable. For criticism by Standish H. O'Grady and B. MacCarthy, and replies to them, see Best, *Bibl.*, p. 234].

Standish H. O'Grady, *Silva Gadelica. A Collection of tales in Irish . . . edited from MSS. and translated* (London, 1892, 8°) [vol. I, Irish text ; vol. II, Translation and notes and some texts at end. Contains several Lives of Saints. Review with corrigenda by K. Meyer in *R. Cel.*, XIV, 1893, pp. 321–37 ; XV, 1894, pp. 108–22, 371–82].

Plummer (Charles), *Vitae Sanctorum Hiberniae partim hactenus ineditae* (Oxonii, 1910, 2 vols. 8°) [Excellent edition of 34 Lives of saints, 13 of which are edited for the first time ; very valuable introduction, notes and glossary].

The series *Scriptores rerum Merovingicarum* (7 vols., 1885–1920) of the *Monumenta Germaniae historica* includes several Lives of Irish saints.

(5) *Biblical texts*

Abbott (T. K.), *Evangeliorum versio antehieronymiana ex codice Usseriano* (Dublin, 1884, 8°).

Lawlor (H. J.), *Chapters on the Book of Mulling* (Edinburgh, 1897, 8°).

(6) *Liturgical texts*

Kelly (Matthew), *Calendar of Irish saints, the Martyrology of Tallagh* (Dublin, 1857, 8°) [superseded by the new edition of the Martyrology of Tallaght by R. I. Best and H. J. Lawlor, see sect. V of this Introd.].

Todd (James H.), *Leabhar Imuinn. The Book of Hymns of the ancient Church of Ireland* (Irish Archaeological and Celtic Soc., Dublin, 1855–69, 4°) [publication not completed and superseded by *The Irish Liber Hymnorum*, edited with translations, notes and glossary by John H. Bernard and Robert Atkinson (London, *HBS*, 1898, 2 vols. [Vol. I. Text and Introduction ; Vol. II, Translation and Notes)].

Whitley Stokes, *The Calendar of Oengus* (Dublin, Trans. of the Roy. Irish Acad.—Irish MSS. Series, 1880, 4°). Superseded by a subsequent edition by the same editor : *Félire Oengusso Céli Dé. The Martyrology of Oengus the Culdee* (London, *HBS*, 1905) [List of *addenda et corrigenda* in *ZCP*, VI, 1907, pp. 235–42 and *R. Cel.*, XXIII, 1902, pp. 83–87. On the composition and date of the *Félire* see R. Thurneysen, *Die Abfassung des Félire von Oengus* (*ZCP*, VI, 1907, pp. 6–8)].

The *Stowe Missal* has been published three times : (1) by F. E. Warren in *The Liturgy and Ritual of the Celtic Church*, (Oxford, 1881) ; (2) by B. MacCarthy in *TRIA* (XXVII, *Lit. and Antiq.* VII, 1886) ; (3) by Sir G. F. Warner (London, *HBS*, 1906–1915, 2 vols.) [Vol. I, Facsim.].

The *Antiphonary of Bangor* has been edited by F. E. Warren (London, *HBS*, 1892–95, 2 vols. 4to) [Vol. I, Facsim.].

Olden (Thomas), *Early Irish Service of the Consecration of a Church* (*Trans. of the St. Paul's Ecclesiological Soc.*, IV, 1897, pp. 98–104, 177–80) [Text from the Leabhar Breac, pp. 277–78, with transl. and introd., re-edited, with transl. and glossary, by Whitley Stokes. *The L.B. tractate on the consecration of a church* (*Miscellanea linguistica in onore di Graziadio Ascoli*, Torino, 1901, pp. 363–87). See G. Mercati, *Il trattato irlandese circa la consecrazione della chiesa* (*Studi e testi*, VII, Roma, 1902, pp. 28–32)].

Kuypers (A. B.), *The Prayer Book of Aedeluald the Bishop, commonly called the Book of Cerne* (Cambridge, 1902, 4°) [with valuable notes by Edmund Bishop].

Meyer (Wilhelm), *Das turiner Bruchstück der ältesten irischen Liturgie* (*Nachrichten von der k. Gesellschaft der Wissenschaften zu Göttingen.*—Philol.-hist. Kl., 1903, pp. 163–214).

Bannister (H. Mariott), *Some recently discovered Fragments of Irish Sacramentaries* (*JTS*, V., 1904).—*S.a.*, *Liturgical Fragments*, (*Ib.*, IX, 1908).

(7) *Civil and Canon Law*

Ancient Laws of Ireland (Dublin, 1865–1901, 6 vols., 8°) [several editors and translators; very imperfect. For criticisms see Best, *Bibl.*, pp. 258–60].

Wasserschleben (Hermann), *Die irische Kanonensammlung* (2nd ed., Leipzig, 1885, 8°).

Kuno Meyer, *An Old Irish Treatise de Arreis* (*R. Cel.*, XV, 1894, pp. 485–98. Cf. XVII, p. 320).

(8) *Glosses and Glossaries*

Stokes (Whitley), *Three Irish Glossaries* (London, 1862, 8°) [contains text, without translation, of Cormac's Glossary (Leabhar Breac recension), of O'Davoren's (B.M., Egerton 88), and of the glossary to the Félire of Oengus (T.C.D., H. 3 18)].

O'Donovan (John), *Sanas Chormaic. Cormac's Glossary, translated and annotated by the late John O'D.*, edited, with notes and indices, by Whitley Stokes (Calcutta, 1868, 4°) [The text is the one printed in *Three Irish Glossaries*, with additional articles from the Yellow Book of Lecan].

For Old-Irish glosses published by Whitley Stokes, H. Zimmer, Ascoli, Nigra and others, see Best, *Bibl.*, pp. 68–74. The fundamental publication is *Thesaurus Palaeohibernicus. A collection of Old-Irish Glosses, Scholia, Prose and Verse*, edited by Whitley Stokes and John Strachan (Cambridge, 1901–1903, 2 vols. 8°, with a Supplement by Stokes alone, Halle a. S., 1910).

(9) *Monastica*

L.G., *Inventaire des Règles monastiques irlandaises* (*RB*, XXV, 1908, pp. 167–84, 321–33 ; XXVIII, 1911, pp. 86–89).

(10) *Miscellaneous*

Irische Texte mit Wörterbuch, edited by Ernst Windisch and Whitley Stokes (Leipzig, 1880–1909).

Saltair na Rann, edited by Whitley Stokes (Anecdota Oxoniensia. Mediaeval and Modern Series, Oxford, 1883, 4°) [A collection of early Middle Irish Biblical poems from MS. Rawl. B. 502 in the Bodleian Libr.].

Very imperfect facsimiles of the most important Dublin MSS. have been published : *Leabhar na hUidhri* (1870), *Leabhar Breac* (1872–1876), *Book of Leinster* (1880), *Yellow Book of Lecan* (1896).

Nigra (C.), *Reliquie celtiche*. I. *Il manoscritto irlandese di S. Gallo* (Torino, 1872, 4°) [No more published].

Besides numerous Irish *anecdota* printed in reviews and Academy publications, Kuno Meyer has published : *Hibernica minora* (Anecdota Oxoniensia, Mediaeval and Modern Series, Oxford, 1894) [a fragment of an O.I. treatise on the Psalter, with translation, notes and glossary, from MS. Rawlinson B. 512 in the Bodleian Libr.] ; *Liadain and Curithir* (London, 1902) ; *King and Hermit* (London, 1901) ; *Cáin Adamnain, Lex Adamnani* (Anecdota Oxoniensia, Mediaeval and Modern Ser., Oxford, 1904) ; *The Triads of Ireland* (Todd Lecture Series, XIII, Dublin, 1906) ; *Rawlinson B. 502. A Collection of pieces in prose and verse in the Irish language* (Oxford, 1909, f°) [Facsimile].

In Traube's *Quellen und Untersuchungen zur lateinischen Philologie*, Latin texts of Sedulius Scottus along with a study of that writer have been published by Siegmund Hellmann : *Sedulius Scottus* (München, 1906, 8°), and in the same series, *Der Kommentar des Iohannes Scottus zu den Opuscula sacra des Boethius* by E. K. Rand (München, 1906).

In *Texte und Untersuchungen* of Harnack and Schmidt, S. Hellmann has published a new edition of *Pseudo-Cyprianus De duodecim abusivis saeculi* (Vol. XXXIV, 1, 1909).

(b) Wales

Dottin (Georges), *La littérature bretonne du Pays de Galles* (*Revue de synthèse historique*, VI, 1903).

Hübner's *Inscriptiones Britanniae Latinae* (Berlin, 1876) form the 7th vol. of the *Corpus inscriptionum Latinarum*.

Westwood (John Obadiah) *Lapidarium Walliae* (Oxford, 1876–79) [contains Ogham inscriptions of Wales].

W. H. Skene's *The four ancient Books of Wales* (Edinburgh,

1868, 2 vols.) includes the Books of Carmarthen, Aneurin, Taliessin and Hergest.

The *Book of Llan Dâv* has been edited twice : (1) by W. J. Rees, with Engl. transl. (Llandovery, 1840) ; (2) by J. Gwenogvryn Evans (Oxford, 1893).

The same Rees has published for the Welsh Manuscripts Society the *Lives of Cambro-British Saints, with English transl. and explanatory notes* (Llandovery, 1853, 8°) [This collection of Latin and Welsh Lives has been very badly edited. Some of the numerous errors have been rectified in Kuno Meyer's collation of the MSS. printed in *Y Cymmrodor* (XIII, 1900, pp. 76–96)].

The *Annales Cambriae*, compiled in the tenth century, have been edited twice : first by J. Williams [Ab Ithel] (London, RS, 1860) ; secondly by Egerton Phillimore in *Y Cymmrodor* (IX, 1888, pp. 141–84), the latter a far better edition [For the best MS. of *AC* see Phillimore, *ib.*, pp. 141–51, and Lloyd, *HW*, I, pp. 159–60].

Giraldus Cambrensis, *Opera*, ed. Dimock, Brewer and Warner (London, RS, 1861–91, 8 vols.).

Wade-Evans (A. W.), *Welsh Mediaeval Law* (Oxford, 1909) [Text, with Engl. transl., of the Laws of Hywel Dda from MS. B.M. Harl. 4353].

(c) Scotland

Chronicles of the Picts, Chronicles of the Scots, and other early memorials of Scottish History, edited by William Forbes Skene (Edinburgh, 1867) ['The literal accuracy of Skene's transcriptions is not certain ' (Anderson, *Early Sources*, I, p. LXXXVIII). On these chronicles see *ib.*, pp. XLV–XLVIII].

Book of Deer, edited by John Stuart (Aberdeen, 1869).

Sir Archibald Campbell Lawrie, *Early Scottish Charters prior to A.D. 1153* (Glasgow, 1905) ; *s.a.*, *Annals of the reigns of Malcolm and William, kings of Scotland, 1153–1214* (Glasgow, 1910).

Lives of St Ninian and St Kentigern edited from the best MSS. by A. P. Forbes (Historians of Scotland.—Edinburgh, 1874).

Robertson (Joseph), *Statuta Ecclesiae Scoticanae* (Bannatyne Club.—Edinburgh, 1866, 2 vols.).

(d) Brittany

Courson (Aurélien de), *Le cartulaire de l'abbaye de Redon en Bretagne* (Collection de documents inédits sur l'histoire de France.—Paris, 1863) [Map of Brittany in front of prolegomena. For chronology of the Chartulary see A. de La Borderie, in *An. Br.*, V, 1886].

Le Men and Ernault, *Cartulaire de Landévennec* in *Mélanges historiques* edited in *Collection des documents inédits*, V, Paris, 1886, pp. 533–600.

La Borderie (A. de), *Cartulaire de l'abbaye de Landévennec* (*Société archéologique du Finistère*, Rennes, 1888).

Maître (Léon) and Berthou (Paul de), *Le cartulaire de l'abbaye de Sainte-Croix de Quimperlé* (Paris, 1896, 2nd revised ed., Rennes, 1904) [Cf. Whitley Stokes, *A Collation of the Cartulary of Quimperlé* in *Archiv für celtische Lexicographie*, I, 1898, pp. 143–50].

Vie de S. Paul de Léon [by Wrmonoc], edited by Ch. Cuissard (*R. Cel.*, V, 1881–83).

La chronique de Nantes, edited by René Merlet (Collection de textes pour servir à l'étude et à l'enseignement de l'histoire.—Paris, 1896).

Duine (François), *Bréviaires et missels des églises et abbayes bretonnes de France antérieurs au xvii⁴ siécle* (Rennes, 1906, 8°).

II.—MODERN WORKS
GENERAL

Arbois de Jubainville (Henri d'), *Introduction à l'étude de la littérature celtique* (*Cours de littérature celtique*, I, Paris, 1883, 8°).

Tourneur (Victor), *Esquisse d'une histoire des études celtiques* (Bibliothique de la Faculté de Philosophie de l'Université de Liége, XV.—Liége, 1908, 8°).

Dottin (Georges), *Manuel pour servir à l'étude de l'antiquite celtique* (Paris, 1906 ; revised and enlarged edition, 1915).

Holder (Alfred), *Alt-celtischer Sprachschatz* (Leipzig, 1896–1913, 3 vols.).

Rhys (Sir John), *Lectures on the origin and growth of religion as illustrated by Celtic heathendom* (*The Hibbert Lectures for* 1886) (London, 1888) [Adventurous].—*S.a., Celtic Folklore, Welsh and Manx* (London, 1901, 2 vols.).

Varin, *Mémoire* [see List of Abbreviations].

Arbois de Jubainville (Henri d'), *Études sur le droit celtique ; le Senchus Mór (Cours de littérature celtique,* VII–VIII. Paris, 1895, 2 vols.).

Allen (J. Romilly), *Celtic art in Pagan and Christian times* (London, 1904, 8°).

Brown (G. Baldwin), *The Arts in early England* [*V. infra.,* pp. 83, 339, 347].

Warren (F. E.), *The liturgy and ritual of the Celtic Church* (Oxford, 1881, 8°) [See L. Duchesne's review in *Bulletin critique,* II, 1881, p. 263–66].

Arbois de Jubainville (Henri d'), *Les premiers habitants de l'Europe* (Paris, 1894, 8°).

Montalembert, *Les moines d'occident* (1st ed., Paris, 1860–67, 5th ed., Paris, 1878, 7 vols., 8°).

Baring Gould and Fisher, *Lives of the British Saints* (Cymmro-dorion Society, 4 vols., 1907–13) [The critical sense of the writers is not sufficiently on the alert. Vol. I, p. 35, contains a map of the monastic foundations of Wales].

C. Schoell is the author of *De Ecclesiae Brittonum Scotorumque historiae fontibus* (Berolini, 1851) and of the article *Keltische Kirche in Britannien und Ireland* in the *Realencyclopaedie für protestantische Theologie und Kirche* edited by Herzog and Plitt (Leipzig, 1881, Vol. VIII, pp. 334–55), both works too often tainted by denominational prejudice.—In the third edition of the *Realencyclopaedie,* Schoell's article has been replaced (Vol. X, 1901, pp. 204–243) by one written by Heinrich Zimmer, which is also not without faults. This latter work has been translated into English by Antonie Meyer, *The Celtic Church in Great Britain and Ireland* (London, 1902), and to her translation, as more accessible and convenient, I shall refer in quoting Zimmer.

Loofs (Friedrich), *Antiquae Britonum Scotorumque Ecclesiae quales fuerint mores, quae ratio credendi et vivendi, quae controversiae cum Romana Ecclesia, causa atque vis* (Lipsiae, 1882).

Schmid (Joseph), *Die Osterfestberechnung auf den britischen Inseln vom Anfang des 4. bis zum Ende des 8. Jahrhunderts* (Regensburg, 1904, 8°).

Bruun (J. A.), *An inquiry into the art of the illuminated manu-*

scripts of the Middle Ages. Part I. *Celtic illuminated* MSS. (Stockholm, 1897, 4°).

Roger (M.), *L'enseignement des lettres classiques d'Ausone à Alcuin* (Paris, 1905) [a very fine piece of criticism ; embodies much important information on the history of education in the Western isles and on the Irish teachers of the early Middle Ages].

SPECIAL

(a) Ireland

(1) *Palaeography*

Westwood (J. O.), *Palaeographia sacra pictoria. . . .*(London, 1845, 4°).—*S.a., Facsimiles of Miniatures and Ornaments in Anglo-Saxon and Irish Manuscripts* (London, 1868, f°).

A dissertation by J. H. Todd entitled *Remarks on illuminations in some Irish Biblical* MSS. (with plates) is to be found in *Vetusta monumenta* (Vol. VI, 1869), published by the Society of Antiquaries of London.

Gilbert (J. T.), *Facsimiles of national manuscripts of Ireland* (London, 1874–84, 5 vols. f°).—*S.a., Account of Facsimiles of national manuscripts of Ireland* (London, 1884, 8°).

Celtic Ornaments from the Book of Kells (Dublin and London, 1892–95, f°) [with a preface by T. K. Abbott].

Robinson (Stanford F. N.), *Celtic illuminative art in the Gospel Books of Durrow, Lindisfarne and Kells* (Dublin, 1908, f°).

Lindsay (W. M.), *Early Irish minuscule script* (St. Andrews University Publications, VI.—Oxford, 1910).

(2) *Hagiography and Liturgiology*

O'Hanlon (John), *The Lives of the Irish Saints* (Dublin, 1875–1903, 9 vols.) [The best popular collection of Lives of Irish Saints. Incomplete, reaches October].

The principal works on St Patrick are : Robert (B.), *Étude critique sur la vie et l'œuvre de Saint Patrick* (Paris, 1883, 8°) [a thesis for the Faculty of Protestant theology of Paris] ; Todd (J. H.), *Saint Patrick, apostle of Ireland* (Dublin, 1864) ; Bury (J. B.), *The life of Saint Patrick and his place in History* (London, 1905, 8°) [an epoch-making work].

Martin (Eugène), *Saint Colomban* (Paris, 1905).

Schirmer (Gustav), *Zur Brendanus-Legende* (Leipzig, 1888).

Geyer (Paul), *Adamnanus, Abt von Iona* (*Programm zu dem Jahresberichte des Gymnasiums St Anna in Augsburg.*—Augsburg, 1895 ; vol. II, Erlangen, 1897).

Blume (Clemens), *Hymnodia Hiberno-Celtica saec.* v–ix (in Dreves, *Analecta Hymnica*, LI, pp. 257–372 (Leipzig, 1908).

(3) *Monographs on early Irish Christianity*

Moran (Patrick), *Essays on the origin, doctrines and discipline of the early Irish Church* (Dublin, 1864, 8°).

Greith (Carl J.), *Geschichte der altirischen Kirche* (Freiburg i. Br., 1867, 8°).

Ebrard (F. H. A.), *Die iroschottische Missionskirche* (Gütersloh, 1873) [a book full of erroneous opinions].

Killen (W. D.), *The ecclesiastical History of Ireland* (London, 1875, 2 vols., 8°).

Bellesheim (Alfons), *Geschichte der katholischen Kirche in Ireland von der Einführung des Christenthums bis auf die Gegenwart* (Mainz, 1890–91, 2 vols., 8°).

Olden (Thomas), *Church of Ireland* (London, 1895).

Salmon (John), *The ancient Irish Church as a witness to Catholic doctrine* (Dublin, 1897) [This booklet of 225 pages gives more information than many a folio. The author has gone direct to the sources and quotes them copiously and to the point].

Stokes (G. T.), *Ireland and the Celtic Church* (Dublin, 1888, revised by H. J. Lawlor in 1907 and again in 1928).

(4) *Christian art in Ireland*

O'Neill (Henry), *The most interesting of the ancient crosses of ancient Ireland* (London, 1853–57, f°) [large plates in colours].

Lord Dunraven, *Notes on Irish Architecture*, edited by Margaret Stokes (London, 1875, 2 vols. with photographic plates).

Stokes (Margaret), *Early Christian art in Ireland* (London, 1887).—Revised by G. N. Count Plunkett (Dublin, 1911).— New impression of the first edition (Dublin, 1928) [with new pagination, but same number and numbering of illustrations].

Wilde (Sir W. R.), *Descriptive catalogue of the antiquities in the Museum of the Royal Irish Academy* (Dublin, 1857–62).—Coffey

(George), *Guide to the Celtic antiquities of the Christian period preserved in the National Museum, Dublin* (Dublin and London, 1909, 2nd ed., 1910).

(5) *Mythology and Folklore*

Arbois de Jubainville (Henri d'), *Le cycle mythologique irlandais et la mythologie celtique* (*Cours de littérature celtique*, II.—Paris, 1884, 8°).

Wood-Martin (W. G.), *Traces of the elder Faiths of Ireland, a folk-lore sketch* (London, 1902, 2 vols., 8°).

Krapp (George Philip), *The Legend of St Patrick's Purgatory, its later literary History* (Baltimore, 1900, 8°).

Félice (Philippe de), *L'autre monde, mythes et légendes : le Purgatoire de S. Patrice* (Paris, 1906, 8°) [thesis].

(6) *Miscellaneous*

King (Robert), *A Memoir introductory to the early History of the Primacy of Armagh* (Armagh, 2nd ed., 1854, 4°).

Reeves (William), *The Culdees of the British Islands* (*TRIA*, 1860, reprinted, Dublin, 1864, 4°).

O'Curry (Eugene), *On the Manners and Customs of the ancient Irish* (London, 1873, 3 vols. 8°).

Zimmer (Heinrich), *Ueber die Bedeutung des irischen Elements für die mittelalterliche Cultur* (Preussische Jahrbücher, LIX, 1887) [essay translated into English by J. L. Edmands, *The Irish element in mediaeval culture*, New York, 1891].

Stokes (Margaret), *Six months in the Apennines in search of vestiges of the Irish saints in Italy* (London, 1892, 8°).—*S.a., Three months in the forests of France : a pilgrimage in search of vestiges of Irish saints* (London, 1895, 8°).

Traube (Ludwig), *O Roma nobilis. Philologische Untersuchungen aus dem Mittelalter* (Abhandlungen der k. bayer. Akademie der Wissenschaften, I. Cl., XIX, II).—*S.a., Perrona Scottorum* (*Sitzungsberichte* of the same Academy, 1900, pp. 469–538), reprinted in *Vorlesungen und Abhandlungen* (München, 1920, vol. III, pp. 95–119).

Malnory (A.), *Quid Luxovienses monachi, discipuli Sancti Columbani, ad regulam monasteriorum atque ad communem Ecclesiae profectum contulerint* (Parisiis, 1894, 8°) [thesis].

Healy (John), *Insula Sanctorum et doctorum. Ireland's ancient schools and scholars* (Dublin, 1890, 4th ed. 1902) ['a quite untrustworthy combination of romance and pseudo-criticism' (Kenney, *Sources*, I, p. 288)].

Zimmer (Heinrich), *Pelagius in Irland* (Berlin, 1901, 8°) [brilliant, but at times adventurous].

Joyce (P. W.), *A social History of ancient Ireland* (London and Dublin, 1903, 8°, 2nd ed. 1913).

(b) Great Britain

Walter (Ferdinand), *Das alte Wales, ein Beitrag zur Völker-, Rechts-, u. Kirchengeschichte* (Bonn, 1859, 8°) [valuable].

Bright (William), *Chapters of early English Church History* (Oxford, 1878, 8°, 3rd ed. 1897).

Pryce (John), *The ancient British Church* (London, 1878).

Rhys (John), *Celtic Britain* (London, 1884, 4th ed. 1908).

La Borderie (Arthur de), *L' 'Historia Britonum' attribuée à Nennius et l' ' Historia Britannica' avant Geoffroy de Monmouth* (Paris, 1883, 8°).

Zimmer (H.), *Nennius Vindicatus* (Berlin, 1893, 8°).

Seebohm (F.), *The tribal system in Wales* (London, 1895, 8°) [misleading].

Newell (F. J.), *History of the Welsh Church to the dissolution of the Monasteries* (London, 1895, 8°).

Bund (J. W. Willis), *The Celtic Church of Wales* (London, 1897, 8°) [a work composed without method and with a decided bias].

Rhys (Sir John) and Brynmore-Jones (D.), *The Welsh People* (London, 1900, 8°, 6th impr. 1923).

(c) Scotland

Anderson (Joseph), *Scotland in Pagan times* (Edinburgh, 1883–86, 2 vols., 8°) ; *s.a.*, *Scotland in early Christian times* (2 Ser., Edinburgh, 1881, 8°).

Stuart (John), *The sculptured stones of Scotland* (Spalding Club. —London, 2 vols., 1856–67).

Allen (Romilly), *The early Christian monuments of Scotland* (Edinburgh, 1903) [Part I, Introduction (pp. iii–cxxii) by Joseph Anderson ; an authoritative survey].

Skene (William Forbes), *Celtic Scotland. A History of ancient Alban* (Edinburgh, 1876, 3 vols., 8° ; 2nd ed. 1886–90). Vol. II, *Church and culture* (1887) [' It has become the custom to condemn Skene for uncritical work. It is true that his theories must not be accepted without examination of their bases ; and that later writers have frequently been misled by his errors. But it is also true that some of Skene's theories will stand examination, and that in spite of errors he did much useful pioneer work in Scottish history. All those that condemn him use his books. He had to rely upon untrustworthy editions of the Irish annals ; and in his own editions he suffered from lack of the most necessary aids to Celtic study ' (Anderson, *Early Sources*, I, p. lxxx)].

Bellesheim (Alfons), *Geschichte der katholischen Kirche in Schottland* (Mainz, 1883, 2 vols., 8°) [translated into English by Sir David O. Hunter-Blair, Edinburgh, 1887–90, 4 vols.].

Mackinnon (James), *Ninian und sein Einfluss auf die Ausbreitung des Christenthums in Nord-Britannien* (Heidelberg, 1891, 8°).

Dowden (John), *The Celtic Church in Scotland* (London, 1894).

Edmonds (Columba), *The History of the early Scottish Church* (Edinburgh, 1906) [uncritical].

Forbes (A. P.), *Kalendars of the Scottish Saints* (Edinburgh, 1872).

Walcott (M. E. C.), *Scoti-Monasticon. The ancient Church of Scotland, a History of the cathedrals, conventual foundations, collegiate churches and hospitals of Scotland* (London, 1874, 4°).

(d) Cornwall

Blight (J. T.), *Ancient crosses and other antiquities in East and West Cornwall* (London, 1872, 4°).

Langdon (A. G.), *Old Cornish crosses* (Truro, 1896, 4°) ; s.a., *Early Christian monuments* [of Cornwall] in the *Victoria History of the County of Cornwall* edited by William Page (London, 1906, pp. 407–49).

(e) Brittany

Mottay (J. Gaultier du), *Essai d'iconographie et d'hagiographie bretonne* (*Mémoires de la Société archéologique des Côtes-du-Nord*, 1st Ser., III., 1857–69, pp. 112–44, 205–66).

Loth (J.), *L'émigration bretonne en Armorique* (Paris, 1883, 8°) [fundamental].

La Borderie (Arthur Le Moyne de), *Histoire de Bretagne*, t. I–III (Rennes, 1896–99, 4°) [a work deserving attention, although open to criticism in some places].

Lot (Ferdinand), *Mélanges d'histoire bretonne* (Paris, 1907, 8°) [a work of first-rate importance, the fruit of vast learning and penetrating criticism].

III.—PERIODICAL AND ACADEMY PUBLICATIONS

The Ulster Journal of Archaeology (Belfast, 1853, in progress).

The Irish Ecclesiastical Record (Dublin, 1864, in progress).

The Academy (London, 1869—1909).

Revue celtique (Paris, 1870, in progress).

Hermathena (Dublin, 1874, in progress).

Y Cymmrodor, the Magazine of the Hon. Society of Cymmrodorion (London, 1877, in progress).

Mélusine, recueil de mythologie, littérature populaire, traditions, mœurs et usages, published by H. Gaidoz and Eugène Rolland (Paris, 1878–1912).

Annales de Bretagne (Rennes, 1886, in progress).

Transactions of the Hon. Society of Cymmrodorion (London, 1822–43).

Zeitschrift für celtische Philologie (Halle a. S., 1897, in progress).

Archiv für celtische Lexicographie (Halle a. S., 1898–1907).

The Celtic Review (Edinburgh, 1904–1916).

Ériu, the Journal of the School of Irish Learning (Dublin, 1904, in progress).

Anecdota from Irish Manuscripts, edited by O. J. Bergin, R. I. Best, Kuno Meyer, J. G. O'Keeffe (Halle a. S., 1907–1913).

V.—FROM 1911 TO 1931
I.—SOURCES
GENERAL

Manitius (Max), *Geschichte der lateinischen Literatur des Mittelalters* (Iwan E. P. Müller's Handbuch der Altertumswissenschaft. (München, 1911–31, 3 vols., 8°) [standard work].

Mackinnon (Donald), *A descriptive catalogue of Gaelic manuscripts in the Advocates' Library, Edinburgh, and elsewhere in Scotland* (Edinburgh, 1912) [pp. 72–105, religious and ecclesiastical texts].

Dottin (Georges), *Les littératures celtiques* (Paris, 1924).

Hamel (A. G. van), *De oudste keltische en angelsaksische geschiedbronnen* (Middelburg, 1911).

SPECIAL

(a) Ireland

(1) *Bibliography of sources*

[Best (Richard Irvine)], *Bibliography of Irish philology and of printed Irish literature* (Dublin, 1913) [a monument of patient erudition, indispensable to the student].

Catalogue of the Irish manuscripts in the Library of T.C., Dublin [See above, IV, 1, 1°].

Catalogue of the Irish manuscripts in the British Museum (London, 1926, 2 vols., 8°) [Vol. I, by Standish Hayes O'Grady, nearly the whole of which was printed between the years 1889 and 1892 ; Vol. II, by Robin Flower, a truly descriptive and comparative catalogue].

Catalogue of Irish manuscripts in the Royal Irish Academy, [Dublin]. In progress, 6 fasciculi issued, Dublin, 1926–31, by T. F. O'Rahilly, Kathleen Mulchrone, Mary E. Byrne, James H. Delargy.

Die Handschriften der Grossherzoglich Badischen Hof- und Landesbibliothek in Karlsruhe.—Vol. V, VI. Die Reichenauer Handschriften beschrieben und erläutert von Alfred Holder (Leipzig, 1906–14) [The Reichenau mss. include several Irish codices].

Lebor na Huidre, Book of the Dun Cow, edited by R. I. Best and Osborn Bergin (Dublin, 1929).

Kenney (James F.), *The Sources for the early History of Ireland. An introduction and guide.*—I. *Ecclesiastical* (New York, Columbia University Press, 1929) [a masterly survey of the medieval Irish ecclesiastical literature and historical sources descending to the minutest details. Indispensable].

Continuing his labours in the description and critical examination of the Latin writings of medieval Ireland, Mario Esposito has added to his previous publications [see above IV, 1, Ireland, (1)] the following : *Hiberno-Latin* MSS. *in the Libraries of Switzerland* (*PRIA*, Sect. C, XXVIII, 1910, pp. 62–95, XXX, 1912, pp. 1–14) ; *A Bibliography of the Latin writers of mediaeval Ireland* (*Studies*, II, 1913, pp. 495–521) ; *Some further notes on mediaeval Latin and Hiberno-French literature* (*Hermathena*, XVI, 1911, pp. 325–33) ; *Miscellaneous notes on mediaeval Latin literature* (*ib.*, XVII, 1912, pp. 104–14) ; *Notes on Latin learning and literature in mediaeval Ireland* (*ib.*, XX, 1930, pp. 225–60).

(2) *Hagiography*

Plummer (Charles), *A tentative catalogue of Irish hagiography* (*Subsidia Hagiographica*, XV : *Miscellanea Hagiographica Hibernica*, Bruxelles, 1925, pp. 171–288) [extremely useful].

Editions of Latin or Irish hagiographical texts and English translations :

Bethada Náem nÉrenn : Lives of Irish saints, ed. C. Plummer (Oxford, 1922, 2 vols., 8°).

St Patrick's *Confessio* and *Epistola*, edited by Newport J. D. White in 1905, have been re-issued in a revised edition with the same title (London, S.P.C.K., Texts for students, No. 4, 1918) [handy and cheap : Patrick's *Opera omnia* for 6*d*.]. English translation of the same and, in addition, of Muirchu's Life of the saint by the same writer, *St Patrick, his writings and Life* (London, S.P.C.K., 1920).

All texts of the Book of Armagh relating to St Patrick have been re-edited by John Gwynn, *Liber Ardmachanus* [see below (9)].

C. Plummer has edited, with Engl. transl., three Irish Lives (Mac Creiche, Naile, Cranat) in the first part of *Subsidia Hagiographica*, XV (Bruxelles, 1925), pp. 1–169, and *Vie et miracles de S. Laurent, archevêque de Dublin* (*AB*, XXXIII, 1914, pp. 121–86).

In addition to the Lives included in Boll., *AS*, Nov. IV (1925), Paul Grosjean has edited the following texts : *De S. Flannano ; Vita S. Flannani* (*AB*, XLVI, 1928, pp. 122–45) ;

Vita S. Brendani Clonfertensis e cod. Dubl. (*ib.*, XLVIII, 1930, pp. 99–123) ; *The Life of St Columba from the Edinburgh* MS. (*SGS*, II, 1928, pp. 111–71. Cf. *ib.*, III, 1929, pp. 84–85).

Joynt (Maud), *The Life of St Gall* (London, 1927).

Macalister (R. A. Stewart), *The Latin and Irish Life of Ciaran* (London, 1927).

Power (P.), *Life of St Declan and Life of St Mochuda* (Irish texts Society.—London, 1914).

Lawlor (H. J.), *St Bernard of Clairvaux's Life of St Malachy of Armagh* (London, 1920).

Betha Coluim Chille, written by Manus O'Donnell, in 1532, edited by A. O. Kelleher and Gertrude Schoepperle (Irish Foundation series of America, I.—Chicago, 1918).

Discussions of hagiographical texts :

Mulchrone (Kathleen), *Die Abfassungszeit und Ueberlieferung der Vita Tripartita* (*ZCP*, XVI, 1926, pp. 1–94).

MacNeill (Eoin), *Dates of texts in the Book of Armagh relating to St Patrick* (*JRSAI*, LVIII, 1928, pp. 85–101) ; *s.a., The origin of the Tripartite Life of St Patrick* (*ib.*, LIX, 1929, pp. 1–15) ; *s.a., The Vita Tripartita of St Patrick* (*Ériu*, XI, 1930, pp. 1–41).

Grosjean (Paul), *Recent research on the Life of St Patrick* (*Thought*, V., 1930, pp. 22–41).

Brüning (Gertrud), *Adamnans Vita Columbae und ihre Ableitungen* (*ZCP*, XI, 1917, pp. 213–304) ; Kenney (J. F.), *The earliest Life of St Columcille* (*Catholic Historical Review*, N.S., V, 1926, pp. 636–44).

Lawlor (H. J.), *Notes on St Bernard's Life of St Malachy* (*PRIA*, XXXV, sect. C., 1919, pp. 230–64).

(3) *Annals*

On the Irish Annals see Anderson, *Early Sources*, I, pp. LXVII–LXIX.

(4) *Biblical texts*

Lawlor (H. J.), *The Cathach of St Columba* (*PRIA*, XXXIII, sect. C, 1916, pp. 241–443).

The Biblical texts in the Book of Armagh have been edited by John Gwynn (see below, 9).

(5) *Liturgical texts*

The Martyrology of Tallaght, edited by R. I. Best and H. J. Lawlor (*HBS*, London, 1931, 8°).

The Lebar Brecc tractate on the Canonical Hours, edited by R. I. Best (*Miscellany presented to Kuno Meyer*, Halle a. S., 1912, pp. 142–66).

Irish Litanies, edited by Charles Plummer (*HBS*, London, 1925, 8°).

T. F. O'Rahilly, *The history of the Stowe Missal* (*Ériu*, X, 1926, pp. 95–109).

L.G., *Étude sur les 'loricae' celtiques et sur les prières qui s'en rapprochent* (*BALAC*, I, 1911, pp. 265–81, II, 1912, pp. 33–41, 101–27).

(6) *Monastica*

Gwynn (E. J.) and Purton (W. J.), *The Monastery of Tallaght* (*PRIA*, XXIX, 1911, pp. 115–79).

Gwynn (E. J.), *The Rule of Tallaght* (*Hermathena*, No. XLIV. Second supplemental vol., Dublin, 1927).

(7) *Canon Law*

An Irish Penitential, edited by E. J. Gwynn (*Ériu*, VII, 1914, pp. 121–95).

(8) *Cormac's Glossary*

Sanas Cormaic, an Old-Irish Glossary compiled by Cormac úa Cuilennáin, edited by Kuno Meyer (*Anecdota from Irish Manuscripts*, IV, 1912).

R. Thurneysen, *Zu Cormacs Glossar* (*Festschrift Ernst Windisch*, Leipzig, 1914, pp. 8–37).

(9) *Miscellaneous*

Liber Ardmachanus, edited by John Gwynn (Dublin, 1913) [this diplomatic edition of the famous MS. is an achievement of scholarship and criticism].

Seymour (St John D.), *Irish Visions of the Other World : a contribution to the study of medieval visions* (London, 1930).

Selections from ancient Irish poetry, translated by Kuno Meyer (London, 1911).

Irish Texts, edited by J. Fraser, P. Grosjean, and J. G. O'Keeffe (London, 1931, three fasciculi published) [Transcripts of texts which have not been previously published].

(b) Wales

Macalister (R. A. S.), *The ancient inscriptions of Wales* (*A. Camb.*, VII Ser., VIII, 1928, pp. 285–315).

The text of Ricemarch's *Life of St David* has been edited by A. W. Wade-Evans in *Y Cymmrodor* (XXIV, 1913, pp. 1–73) and translated by him into English : *Life of St David* (London, 1923).

The text of Ricemarch's *Martyrology and Psalter* has' been edited by H. J. Lawlor for the *HBS* (London, 1914, 2 vols., 8°). The *Martyrology* has also been edited by P. H. Delehaye (*AB*, XXI, 1913, pp. 369–407).

Lewis (Timothy), *Bibliography of the Laws of Howel Dda* (*Aberystwyth Studies*, X, 1928, pp. 151–82) ; *s.a.*, *A Glossary of mediaeval Welsh Law* (Manchester, 1913).

Griscom (Acton), *The Historia Regum Britanniae of Geoffrey of Monmouth* (London, 1929).

Lloyd (John Edward), *The Welsh chronicles* (The Sir John Rhys Memorial Lecture. British Academy, 1928.—*PBA*, vol. XIV).

Liebermann (F.), *Nennius the author of the Historia Brittonum* (*Essays in medieval History presented to T. F. Tout*, Manchester, 1925, pp. 25–44).

(c) Scotland

Anderson (Alan Orr), *Early Sources of Scottish History*, A.D. *500–1286*, collected and translated (Edinburgh, 1922, 2 vols., 8°) [very useful ; excellent bibliographical notes and comments].

Strecker (K.), *Zu den Quellen für das Leben des hl. Ninian* (*NA*, XLIII, 1920, pp. 1–26).

(d) Brittany

Duine (François), *Memento des sources hagiographiques de l'histoire de Bretagne, V^e–Xe siècles* (Rennes, 1918) ; *s.a.*, *Catalogue des sources hagiographiques pour l'histoire de Bretagne jusqu'à la fin du XIIe siècle* (Paris, 1922) ; *s.a.*, *Inventaire liturgique de l'hagiographie bretonne* (Paris, 1922) [These three books are a treasure-store of information on Breton hagiographical literature].

Fawtier (Robert), *La Vie de saint Samson, essai de critique hagiographique* (Bibliothèque de l'École des Hautes Études, cxcvii.—Paris, 1912) [contains an excellent edition of the earliest *Vita Samsonis*].—An English translation of which by Thomas Taylor was published by S.P.C.K. (London, 1925).

Burkitt (F. C.), *St Samson of Dol* (*J.T.S.*, XXVII, 1926, pp. 42–57).

Latouche (Robert), *Mélanges d'histoire de Cornouaille, VIe–XIe siècles* (Bibliothèque de l'École des Hautes Études, cxcii.—Paris, 1911) [discusses texts relating to Cornouaille. Cf. André Oheix in *BSAF*, XXXIX, 1912].

Oheix (André), *Vie inédite de S. Cunival* (*R. Cel.*, XXXII, 1911, pp. 154–83) ; *s.a.*, *Notes sur la Vie de S. Gildas* (Nantes, 1913).

Oheix (André) and Fawtier-Jones (Ethel C.), *La ' Vita' ancienne de S. Corentin* (*MSHAB*, VI, 1925, pp. 3–56).

Morey (C. R.), Rand (E. K.), Kraeling (C. H.), *The Gospel-Book of Landevennec* (*Art Studies*, VIII, Part II, 1931) [Edition of a New York Public Library MS., with 40 plates].

II.—MODERN WORKS

GENERAL

Loth (Joseph), *Les études celtiques, leur état présent, leur avenir* (*Revue internationale de l'enseignement*, LXII, 1911, pp. 201–29).

MacNaught (John Campbell), *The Celtic Church and the See of Peter* (Oxford, 1927) [valuable].

O'Rahilly (Cecile), *Ireland and Wales, their historical and literary relations* (London, 1924).

Slover (Clark Harris), *Early literary channels between Britain and Ireland* (University of Texas.—Studies in English, No. 6, 1926, pp. 5–52 ; No. 7, 1927, pp. 5–111).

MacNeill (John Thomas), *The Celtic Penitentials and their influence on continental Christianity* (Paris, 1923), reprinted from *R. Cel.*, XXXIX, pp. 257–300, XL, pp. 51–103, 320–41.

Workman (Herbert B.), *The evolution of the monastic ideal from the earliest times down to the coming of the Friars* (London, 1913) [Ch. IV, The ideals of monasticism in the Celtic Church].

SPECIAL

(*a*) **Ireland**

(1) *Palaeography*

Zimmermann (E. Heinrich), *Vorkarolingische Miniaturen* (Berlin, 1916) [a volume of text and 4 portfolios containing 332 plates, many of them reproductions of Irish MSS.].

The Book of Kells described by Sir Edward Sullivan (London, 1914, 2nd ed. 1920).

Schiaparelli (Luigi), *Note paleografiche intorno all'origine e ad alcuni caratteri della scrittura e del sistema abbreviativo irlandese* (*Archivio storico italiano*, LXIV, 1916, pp. 116–239) ; *s.a.*, *Avviamento allo studio delle abbreviature latine nel medioevo* (Firenze, 1926) ; *s.a.*, *Influenze straniere nella scrittura italiana dei secoli* VIII *e* IX (*Studi e testi*, XLVII, Roma, 1927) [pp. 15–23, insular influence].

L. G., *Répertoire des fac-similés des manuscrits irlandais :* I, *R. Cel.*, XXXIV, 1913, pp. 14–37 [Dublin MSS.], II, *ib.*, XXXV, 1914, pp. 403–30 [Cambridge, Durham, Litchfield, London, Oxford MSS.] ; III, *ib.*, XXXVIII, 1920, pp. 1–14 [MSS. preserved in continental libraries].

Plummer (Charles), *On the colophons and marginalia of Irish scribes* (*PBA*, 1926, 34 p.).

(2) *Christian archaeology and art*

Power (P.), *Early Christian Ireland. A manual of Irish Christian archaeology* (Dublin, 1925).

Macalister (R. A. S.), *The archaeology of Ireland* (London, 1928) [extremely useful].

A sketch of the history of Irish archaeology will be found in Macalister's *Ireland in Pre-Celtic Times* (Dublin, 1921), Ch. I, pp. 1–18.—See also an address delivered by the same scholar at a meeting of the Royal Society of Antiquaries of Ireland, Jan. 27, 1925, on *The present and future of archaeology in Ireland* (Dublin, 1925).

Crawford (Henry S.), *Handbook of carved ornament from Irish monuments of the Christian period* (Dublin, 1926) [essential].

Henry (Françoise), *Les origines de l'iconographie irlandaise* (*RA*, 5th Ser., XXXII, 1930, pp. 89–109) [sane and sagacious criticism].—Through Mlle. Henry's kindness, I have been privileged to read in proof her forthcoming book, *La sculpture irlandaise pendant les douze premiers siècles de l'ère chrétienne*, a work of primary importance.

Hemphill (S.), *The Gospels of MacRegol of Birr. A study in Celtic illumination* (London, 1911).

Porter (A. Kingsley), *The crosses and culture of Ireland* (New Haven, 1931).

(3) *Hagiography*

Hitchcock (F. R. Montgomery), *St Patrick and his Gallic friends* (London, 1916).

Czarnowski (S.), *Le culte des héros et ses conditions sociales. Saint Patrick, héros national de l'Irlande* (Paris, 1920) [brilliant but venturesome].

Concannon (Helena), *The life of St Columban* (Dublin, 1915) ; *s.a.*, *Saint Patrick, his life and mission* (Dublin, 1931).

(4) *Monastica*

Ryan (John), *Irish monasticism. Origins and early development* (Dublin, 1931) [a very fine piece of criticism and reasoning].

(5) *Liturgiology*

Edmund Bishop's *Liturgica historica* (Oxford, 1918) is a work of scholarly insight which offers many a judicious suggestion to the student of Celtic Christianity.

(6) *Miscellaneous*

MacNeill (Eoin), *Phases of Irish History* (Dublin, 1919) [very important].

Meyer (Kuno), *Learning in Ireland in the fifth century and the transmission of letters* (Dublin, 1913).

Esposito (Mario), *The knowledge of Greek in Ireland during the Middle Ages* (*Studies*, I, 1912, pp. 665–83) [searching criticism].

Clark (J. M.), *The Abbey of St. Gall as a centre of literature and art* (Cambridge, 1926).

L. G., *Modern research with special reference to early Irish ecclesiastical History* (Dublin, 1929).

(b) Wales

An Inventory of the ancient Monuments in Wales and Monmouth-shire (London.—Royal Commission on the ancient and historical Monuments and Constructions in Wales and Monmouthshire, 1911, in progress) [I, Montgomery; II, Flint; III, Radnor; IV, Denbigh; V, Carmarthen; VI, Merioneth; VII, Pembroke].

Lindsay (W. M.), *Early Welsh script* (Oxford, 1912).

Lloyd (John Edward), *A History of Wales from the earliest times to the Edwardian conquest* (London, 1911, 2 vols. 8°; 2nd ed., 1912) [a fine piece of work]; s.a., *A History of Wales* (Benn's sixpenny Library, London, 1930) [popular account].

Grosjean (Paul), *Cyngar Sant* (*AB*, XLII, 1924, pp. 100–20).

Williams (Hugh), *Christianity in early Britain* (Oxford, 1912) [valuable].

Chevalier (Jacques) *L'Église celtique en Grande-Bretagne du IIIe au VIIe siècle* [art. printed under the word 'Angleterre' in A. Baudrillart's *Dictionnaire d'histoire et de géographie ecclésiastiques*, Paris, 1914, col. 145–56]; s.a., *Essai sur la formation de la nationalité et des réveils religieux du Pays de Galles des origines à la fin du vi^e siècle* (Annales de l'Université de Lyon, N.S., II. Droit, Lettres: XXXIV, Lyon and Paris, 1923) [authoritative survey; judicious reasoning].

Hirsch-Davies (J. E. de), *Catholicism in mediaeval Wales* (London, 1916).

Jones (G. Hartwell), *Celtic Britain and the Pilgrim movement* (London, 1912) [uncritical theories].

(c) Scotland

Royal Commission on ancient and historical Monuments and Constructions in Scotland.—*Ninth Report with inventory of Monuments and Constructions in the Outer Hebrides, Skye and the small Isles* (Edinburgh, 1928).

Watson (W. J.), *History of Celtic place-names of Scotland* (London, 1926).

Hay (M. V.), *A chain of error in Scottish History* (London, 1927).

Simpson (W. Douglas), *The historical Saint Columba* (Aberdeen, 1927) [a ventursome account of the career of the saint].

(d) Cornwall

Up to the end of 1931 Canon Gilbert H. Doble has published 29 monographs of Cornish saints.

The Cornish Church guide (Truro, 1928) contains a valuable *Parochial History of Cornwall* (pp. 51–223) by Charles Henderson, ' a brief summary of his forthcoming *History of Cornwall*, where authority for all the statements will be found.'

Taylor (Thomas), *The Celtic Christianity of Cornwall. Diverse sketches and studies* (London, 1916).

(e) Brittany

Lindsay (W. M.), *Breton scriptoria, their Latin abbreviation-symbols* (*Zentralblatt für Bibliothekswesen*, XXIX, 1912, pp. 264–72) [Orleans MSS., 255 (302) and 193 (221)].

Largillière (René), *Les saints et l'organisation chrétienne primitive dans l'Armorique bretonne* (Rennes, 1925) [very important. See, on this book, J. Loth, in *MSHAB*, VII, 1926, pp. 1–24].

Duine (François), *Le schisme breton* (Rennes, 1915) ; *s.a.*, *La métropole de Bretagne* (Paris, 1916) [two valuable contributions to the ecclesiastical history of Brittany].

III.—PERIODICAL AND ACADEMY PUBLICATIONS

Aberystwyth Studies (Aberystwyth, 1912, in progress).

Bulletin de la Société d'histoire et d'archéologie de Bretagne and *Mémoires* of the same Society (Rennes, 1920, in progress).

Scottish Gaelic Studies (Aberdeen, 1926, in progress).

IV.—BIBLIOGRAPHIES OF DECEASED SCHOLARS

Whitley Stokes (†1909), by R. I. Best in *ZCP*, VIII, 1911, pp. 351–406.

Henri d'Arbois de Jubainville (†1910), by P. d'Arbois de Jubainville in *R. Cel.*, XXXII, 1911, pp. 456–74.

Heinrich Zimmer (†1910), by T[imothy] L[ewis] (Aberystwyth, 1911) ; *Addenda* by R. I. Best in *ZCP*, VIII, 1912, pp. 593–94.

François Duine (†1924), by Georges Collas in *An. Br.*, XXXVIII, 1928, pp. 96–126.

Georges Dottin (†1928), by himself, 1896–April, 1910 (Rennes, April, 1910) ; by P. Le Roux in *An. Br.*, XXXVIII, 1929, pp. 505–25.

Charles Plummer (†1927), appended to his obituary by P. S. A[llen], F. M. S[tenton] and R. I. B[est] in the *Proceedings of the British Academy* (XV, 1931), pp. 14–17 of the reprint.

LIST OF ABBREVIATIONS

a.a. = *ad annum.*

AB = *Analecta Bollandiana* (1882, in progress).

AC = *Annales Cambriae,* ed. Egerton Phillimore (*Y Cymmrodor,* IX, 1888, pp. 141–84).

A. Cam. = *Archaeologia Cambrensis* (1846, in progress).

Adam., *Vita Col.* = Adamnán, *Vita Columbae,* ed. J. T. Fowler (Oxford, 1894), new ed., 1920 (same pagination).

AJ = *Archaeological Journal* (1845, in progress).

Allen, *CA* = J. Romilly Allen, *Celtic Art in Pagan and Christian times* (London, 1904).

Allen, *ECMS* = J. Romilly Allen, *The Early Christian Monuments of Scotland* (Edinburgh, 1903) [Introduction, pp. III–CXXII, by Joseph Anderson].

An. Ban. = *Antiphonary of Bangor,* ed. F. E. Warren, 2 vols. (Henry Bradshaw Soc., IV, X) (London, 1893, 1895).

An. Br. = *Annales de Bretagne* (1886, in progress).

Anderson, *Early Sources* = Alan Orr Anderson, *Early Sources of Scottish History,* A.D. 500–1286, 2 vols. (Edinburgh, 1922).

AT = *Annals of Tigernach,* ed. Whitley Stokes (*Revue celtique,* XVI–XVIII, 1895–97).

AU = *Annals of Ulster,* ed. William M. Hennessy and B. MacCarthy, 4 vols. (London, 1887–1901).

BALAC = *Bulletin d'ancienne littérature et d'archéologie chrétiennes* (1911–14).

BC = *The Prayer Book of Aedeluald the Bishop commonly called the Book of Cerne,* ed. Dom A. B. Kuypers, with notes by Edmund Bishop (Cambridge, 1902).

Bede, *HE* = Bede, *Historia Ecclesiastica gentis Anglorum,* ed. Charles Plummer, 2 vols. (Oxonii, 1896).

Bernard, *Vita Mal.* = S. Bernard, *Vita Malachiae,* ed. Migne, *PL,* CLXXXII.

Best, *Bibl.* = *Bibliography of Irish philology and of printed Irish literature* [by Richard Irvine Best] (Dublin, 1913).

Bishop, *LH* = Edmund Bishop, *Liturgica historica* (Oxford, 1918).

BNE = *Bethada Náem nÉrenn : Lives of Irish Saints,* ed. Charles Plummer, 2 vols. (Oxford, 1922).

Boll, *AS* = Bollandists, *Acta Sanctorum,* many vols., in progress.

BSAF = *Bulletin de la Société archéologique du Finistère* (1873, in progress).

Bury, *Pat.* = J. B. Bury, *The Life of St Patrick and his Place in History* (London, 1905).

Buss. = *Die Bussordnungen der abendländischen Kirche,* ed. F. W. H. Wasserschleben (Halle, 1851).

Catalogus = *Catalogus sanctorum Hiberniae secundum diversa tempora,* ed. A. W. Haddan and W. Stubbs, *Councils and Ecclesiastical Documents,* II, II (Oxford, 1878), pp. 292–94.

CBS = *Lives of Cambro-British Saints,* ed. W. J. Rees (Llandovery, 1853).

CED = *Councils and ecclesiastical documents relating to Great Britain and Ireland,* ed. A. W. Haddan and W. Stubbs, 3 vols. (Oxford, 1869–78).

Chevalier, *Essai* = Jacques Chevalier, *Essai sur la formation de la nationalité et les réveils religieux au Pays de Galles des origines à la fin du sixième siècle* (Annales de l'Université de Lyon, Nouv. série, XXXIV, Lyon and Paris, 1923).

Chr. Nam. = *La chronique de Nantes*, ed. René Merlet (Collection de textes pour servir à l'étude et à l'enseignement de l'histoire, Paris, 1896).

CMH = *Cambridge Medieval History* (1911, in progress).

Coffey, *Guide* = George Coffey, *Guide to the Celtic Antiquities of the Christian period preserved in the National Museum, Dublin* (Dublin, 1909).

Cogadh Gaedhel = *Cogadh Gaedhel re Gallaibh : The War of the Gaedhil with the Gaill*, ed. J. H. Todd (*RS*) (London, 1867).

Cogitosus, *Vita Brig.* = Cogitosus, *Vita Brigidae* (Boll, *AS*, Feb., I, 135–41).

Colgan, *ASH* = J. Colgan, *Acta sanctorum Hiberniae*, Lovanii, 1645.

Columban, *RM* = S. Columban, *Regula monachorum*, ed. Otto Seebass (*ZK*, XV, 1895, pp. 366–86).

Conchubran, *Vita Mon.* = Conchubranus, *Vita S. Monennae*, ed. Mario Esposito (*PRIA*, XXVIII, Sec. C., 1910, pp. 202–51).

Corp. SEL = *Corpus scriptorum ecclesiasticorum latinorum.* In progress.

Crawford, *Handbook* = Henry S. Crawford, *Handbook of carved ornament from Irish monuments of the Christian period* (Dublin, 1926).

Cummian, *DCP* = Cummian, *De controversia paschali*, ed. Migne, *PL*, LXXXVII.

Cursus = *Ratio de cursus qui fuerunt ex auctores* (*sic*), ed. J. Wickham Legg (*Miscellanea Ceriani*, Milano, 1910, pp. 156–67).

DACL = *Dictionnaire d'archéologie chrétienne et de liturgie*, edited by F. Cabrol and H. Leclercq (1907, in progress).

De arreis = *An Old Irish treatise de Arreis*, ed. Kuno Meyer (*R. Cel.*, XV, 1894, pp. 485–98).

Dottin, *Manuel* = Georges Dottin, *Manuel pour servir à l'étude de l'antiquité celtique* (Paris, 1915).

Duchesne, *Fastes* = Louis Duchesne, *Fastes épiscopaux de l'ancienne Gaule*, 3 vols. (Paris, 1907–15).

Duine, *Inventaire* = F. Duine, *Inventaire liturgique de l'hagiographie bretonne* (Paris, 1922).

Duine, *Memento* = *Memento des sources hagiographiques de l'histoire de Bretagne*, V*ᵉ*–X*ᵉ siècle* (Rennes, 1918).

Duine, *Métropole* = *La métropole de Bretagne* (Paris, 1916).

Duine, *Schisme* = *Le schisme breton* (*An. Br.*, XXX 1915, pp. 424–68) [Anonymous].

EHR = *English Historical Review* (1886, in progress).

ERE = *Encyclopaedia of Religion and Ethics*, edited by James Hastings, 13 vols. (Edinburgh, 1908–26).

Esposito, *Bibliography* = Mario Esposito, *A bibliography of the Latin writers of Mediaeval Ireland* (*Studies*, II, 1913, pp. 495–521).

Esposito, *Latin Learning*, I = *Notes on Latin Learning and Literature in Mediaeval Ireland.*—(I *Hermathena*, XX, 1930, pp. 225–60).

Esposito, *PADM* = *On the Pseudo-Augustinian treatise "De Mirabilibus Sanctae Scripturae"* (*PRIA*, XXXV, Sec. C., 1919, pp. 189–207).

Fél. Oeng. = *Félire Oengusso Céli Dé : The Martyrology of Oengus the Culdee*, ed. Whitley Stokes (*HBS*, XXIX) (London, 1905).

Fuhrmann, *IMM* = Joseph Fuhrmann, *Irish Medieval Monasteries on the Continent* (Washington, 1927).

Gesta Caroli Mag. = *Die Gesta Caroli Magni der Regensburger Schottenlegende*, ed. by A. Dürrwächter (Bonn, 1897).

Gilbert, *SE* = Gilbert, *De statu Ecclesiae*, ed. Migne (*PL*, CLIX).

Gildas, *De exc.* = Gildas, *De excidio et conquestu Britanniae*, ed. Th. Mommsen (*MG. Auct. ant.*, XIII, pp. 1–85).
Giraldus, *DK* = Giraldus Cambrensis, *Descriptio Kambriae* (*RS*), ed. J. F. Dimock (*Opera*, Vol. VI).
Giraldus, *EH* = *Expugnatio Hibernica*, ed. J. F. Dimock (Vol. V).
Giraldus, *IK* = *Itinerarium Kambriae*, ed. J. F. Dimock (Vol. VI).
Giraldus, *TH* = *Topographia Hibernica*, ed. J. F. Dimock (Vol. V).
GSR = *Gesta Sanctorum Rotonensium*, ed. J. Mabillon (*Acta Sanctorum Ordinis S. Benedicti*, IV, Part II, Venetiis, 1738).
HBS = Henry Bradshaw Society.
Henry, *Origines* = Françoise Henry, *Les origines de l'iconographie irlandaise* (*RA*, 5th ser., XXXII, 1930, pp. 89–109).
Henry, *SI* = Françoise Henry, *La sculpture irlandaise pendant les douze premiers siècles de l'ère chrétienne* (forthcoming book).
Hibernensis = *Die irische Kanonensammlung*, ed. H. Wasserschleben (Leipzig, 1885).
Ir. Lit. = *Irish Litanies*, ed. C. Plummer (*HBS*, LXII) (London, 1925).
Ir. Pen. = *An Irish Penitential*, ed. E. J. Gwynn (*Ériu*, VII, 1914, pp. 121–95).
James, *Learning* = Montague Rhodes James, *Learning and Literature till the death of Bede* (*CMH*, III, 1922, ch. XIX, pp. 485–513).
Jonas, *Vita Col.* = Jonas, *Vita Columbani*, ed. Bruno Krusch (*MG. Scr. RM*, IV, pp. 1–152).
JRSAI = *Journal of the Royal Society of Antiquaries of Ireland* (1852, in progress).
JTS = *Journal of Theological Studies* (1900, in progress).
Kenney, *Sources*, I = James F. Kenney, *The Sources for the early History of Ireland.—I. Ecclesiastical* (New York, Columbia University Press, 1929).
Krusch, *Studien* = Bruno Krusch, *Studien zur christlichmittelalterlichen Chronologie. Der 84 jährige Ostercyclus und seine Quellen* (Leipzig, 1880).
LA = *Liber Ardmachanus. The Book of Armagh*, ed. by John Gwynn (Dublin, 1913).
La Borderie, *HB* = Arthur Le Moyne de La Borderie, *Histoire de Bretagne*, I–III (Rennes, 1896–99).
Largillière, *Les saints* = René Largillière, *Les saints et l'organisation chrétienne primitive dans l'Armorique bretonne* (Rennes, 1925).
Lawlor, *BLM* = H. J. Lawlor, *St Bernard of Clairvaux's Life of St Malachy of Armagh* (London, 1920).
Lawlor, *Cathach* = *The Cathach of St Columba* (*PRIA*, XXXIII, Sec. C, 1916, pp. 241–443).
Levison, *Die Iren* = Wilhelm Levison, *Die Iren und die Fränkische Kirche* (*Historische Zeitschrift*, CIX, 1912, pp. 1–22).
L.G. in front of a title denotes a work by the author of the present book.
LH = *The Irish Liber Hymnorum*, ed. by J. H. Bernard and R. Atkinson (*HBS*, XIII, XIV), 2 vols. (London, 1898).
Lismore = *Lives of saints from the Book of Lismore*, ed. Whitley Stokes (*Anecdota Oxoniensia.—Mediaeval and Modern Series*, V) (Oxford, 1890).
Lloyd, *HW* = John Edward Lloyd, *A history of Wales from the earliest times to the Edwardian Conquest*, 2 vols. (London, 1912).
Lot, *Mélanges* = Ferdinand Lot, *Mélanges d'histoire bretonne (VIe–XIe siècle)* (Paris, 1907).
Loth, *Émigration* = Joseph Loth, *L'émigration bretonne en Armorique* (Paris, 1883).
Macalister, *AI* = R. A. S. Macalister, *The Archaeology of Ireland* (London, 1928).

Macalister, *Inis Cealtra* = *The history and antiquities of Inis Cealtra* (*PRIA*, XXXIII, Sec. C, 1916, pp. 93–174).

Macalister, *Mem. slabs* = *The memorial slabs of Clonmacnois* (Dublin, 1909).

MacNeill, *Phases* = Eoin MacNeill, *Phases of Irish history* (Dublin, 1919).

Malnory, *Quid Luxov.* = A. Malnory, *Quid Luxovienses monachi, discipuli Sancti Columbani, ad regulas monasteriorum atque ad communem Ecclesiae profectum contulerint* (Parisiis, 1894).

Manitius, *Geschichte* = Max Manitius, *Geschichte der lateinischen Literatur des Mittelalters*, 3 vols. (München, 1911, 1923, 1931).

Mansi, *Concilia* = Mansi, *Sacrorum conciliorum nova et amplissima collectio* (many vols.).

Martène and Durand, *Thesaurus* = E. Martène and U. Durand, *Thesaurus novus anecdotorum*, 5 vols. (Lutetiae Parisiorum, 1717).

Mem. SHAB = *Mémoires de la Société d'histoire et d'archéologie de Bretagne* (1920, in progress).

MG. Auct. ant. = *Monumenta Germaniae historica.—Auctores antiquissimi.*

MG. Dipl. imp. = *Diplomata imperii.*

MG. Dipl. Kar. = *Diplomata Karolinorum.*

MG. Dipl. reg. = *Diplomata regum et imperatorum Germaniae.*

MG. Epist. = *Epistolae.*

MG. Leges : Sect. II. Cap. = *Leges : Sect. II. Capitularia regum Francorum.*

MG. Leges : Sect. III. Conc. = *Leges : Sect. III. Concilia.*

MG. Necrol. = *Necrologia.*

MG. Poet. Lat. = *Poetae Latini aevi Carolini.*

MG. Scr. = *Scriptores.*

MG. Scr. RM = *Scriptores rerum Merovingicarum.*

MHMA = *Mélanges d'histoire du moyen âge offerts à Ferdinand Lot* (Paris, 1925).

MIOG = *Mitteilungen des Instituts für oesterreichische Geschichtsforschung* (1880, in progress).

Morice, *Preuves* = Hyacinthe Morice de Beaubois, *Mémoires pour servir de preuves à l'histoire ecclésiastique et civile de Bretagne*, 3 vols. (Paris, 1742–46).

Muirchu = Muirchu [Documents concerning St Patrick], ed. Whitley Stokes, *The Tripartite Life of Patrick*, II, pp. 269–300 (*RS*) (London, 1887).

NA = *Neues Archiv der Gesellschaft für ältere deutsche Geschichtskunde* (1876, in progress).

Nennius, *HB* = Nennius, *Historia Brittonum*, ed. Th. Mommsen (*MG. Auct. ant.*, XIII, pp. 112–222).

Pat., *Confessio* = S. Patricius, *Confessio*, ed. Newport J. D. White, *Libri S. Patricii* (London, 1918), pp. 1–26.

Pat., *Epistola* = S. Patricius, *Epistola*, ed. N. J. D. White, *ib.*, pp. 26–32.

PBA = *Proceedings of the British Academy* (1903, in progress).

PG = Migne, *Patrologia Graeca* (many vols.).

PL = Migne, *Patrologia Latina* (many vols.).

PRIA = *Proceedings of the Royal Irish Academy* (1841, in progress).

PSAS = *Proceedings of the Society of Antiquaries of Scotland* (1852, in progress).

RA = *Revue archéologique* (1870, in progress).

RB = *Revue bénédictine* (1884, in progress).

R. Bib. = *Revue biblique* (1892, in progress).

R. Cel. = *Revue celtique* (1870, in progress).

RH = *Revue historique* (1876, in progress).

RHE = *Revue d'histoire ecclésiastique* (1900, in progress).

Ricemarch, *PM* = *The Psalter and Martyrology of Ricemarch*, ed. H. J. Lawlor, 2 vols. (*HBS*, XLVII, XLVIII).

Roger, *Enseignement* = M. Roger, *L'enseignement des lettres classiques d'Ausone à Alcuin* (Paris, 1905).

RS = Rolls Series.

Ryan, *Monast.* = John Ryan, *Irish Monasticism : Origins and early Development* (Dublin and Cork, 1931).

s.a. = by the same author.

Sal. ASH = *Acta sanctorum Hiberniae ex codice Salmanticensi*, ed. De Smedt and De Backer (Edinburgi and Brugis, 1888).

Schiaparelli, *Note* = L. Schiaparelli, *Note paleografiche intorno all'origine e ad alcuni caratteri della scrittura e del sistema abbreviativo irlandese* (*Archivio storico Italiano*, LXXIV, 1916, pp. 116–239).

SGS = *Scottish Gaelic Studies* (1926, in progress).

Skene, *CS* = William F. Skene, *Celtic Scotland, a History of ancient Alban*, 3 vols. (Edinburgh, 1876).

Slover, *Channels* = Clark Harris Slover, *Early literary Channels between Britain and Ireland* (University of Texas—*Studies in English*, No. 6, 1926, pp. 5–52 ; No. 7, 1927, pp. 5–111).

Stephen, *Vita Wilfridi* = Stephanus Eddius, *Vita Wilfridi*, ed. W. Levison (*MG. Scr. RM*, VI, pp. 193–263).

Stokes, *ECAI* = Margaret Stokes, *Early Christian Art in Ireland* (London, 1887).

Stokes, *Ireland* = G. T. Stokes, *Ireland and the Celtic Church*, edit. revised by H. J. Lawlor (London, 1928).

Stokes and Strachan, *TP* = Whitley Stokes and John Strachan, *Thesaurus palaeohibernicus*, 2 vols. (Cambridge, 1901–1903 ; Supplement, Halle, 1910).

Stowe = *The Stowe Missal*, ed. G. F. Warner, 2 vols. (*HBS*, XXXI, XXXII) (London, 1906, 1915).

Tallaght (1911) = *The Monastery of Tallaght*, by E. J. Gwynn and W. J. Purton (*PRIA*, XXIX, Sec. C, 1911, pp. 115–179).

Tallaght (1927) = *The Rule of Tallaght*, by Edward Gwynn (*Hermathena*, No. XLIV, Second Supplemental Volume, Dublin and London, 1927).

Theodore, *Canones* = *Die Canones Theodori Cantuariensis und ihre Ueberlieferungsformen*, ed. Paul Willem Finsterwalder (Weimar, 1929).

Tirechán = Tirechán [Documents concerning St Patrick] (*LA*, pp. 17–31).

Traube, *Vorlesungen* = L. Traube, *Vorlesungen und Abhandlungen*, 3 vols. (München, 1909–20).

TRIA = *Transactions of the Royal Irish Academy* (1787–1907).

TSC = *Transactions of the Honourable Society of Cymmrodorion* (1892, in progress).

Turner, *Irish teachers* = William Turner, *Irish teachers in the Carolingian revival of letters* (reprinted from *The Catholic University Bulletin*, XIII, Washington, 1907).

UJA = *Ulster Journal of Archaeology* (1853, in progress).

Van der Essen, *Étude* = L. Van der Essen, *Étude critique et littéraire sur les Vitae des saints mérovingiens de l'ancienne Belgique* (Louvain and Paris, 1907).

Varin, *Mémoire* = Varin, *Mémoire sur les causes de dissidence entre l'Église bretonne et l'Église romaine relativement à la célébration de la fête de Pâques* (*Mémoires présentés par divers savants à l'Académie des Inscriptions et Belles-lettres*, I. Ser., V, Part II, 1858).

Vita Gildae = *Vita Gildae* auct. Monacho Ruiensi, ed. Th. Mommsen (*MG. Auct. ant.*, XIII, pp. 90–106).

Vita Sam. = *Vita Samsonis*, ed. Robert Fawtier, *La Vie de Saint Samson* (*Bibliothèque de l'École des Hautes Études*—Sciences historiques et philologiques, CXCVII, Paris, 1912, pp. 91–172).

Vita Trip. = *Vita Tripartita S. Patricii*, ed. Whitley Stokes, *The Tripartite Life of Patrick* (*RS*), London, 1887, Vol. I.

VSH = *Vitae sanctorum Hiberniae*, ed. C. Plummer, 2 vols. (Oxonii, 1910).

Wade-Evans, *David* = A. W. Wade-Evans, *Life of St David* (London, 1923).

Walahfrid, *Vita Galli* = Walahfrid Strabo, *Vita Galli*, ed. Bruno Krusch (*MG. Scr. RM*, IV, pp. 280–337).

Warren, *Lit.* = F. E. Warren, *The Liturgy and Ritual of the Celtic Church* (Oxford, 1881).

Westwood, *MO* = J. O. Westwood, *Facsimiles of miniatures and ornaments in Anglo-Saxon and Irish Manuscripts* (London, 1868).

Westwood, *PSP* = *Palaeographia sacra pictoria* (London, 1845).

White, *Patrick* = Newport J. D. White, *St Patrick, his Writings and Life* (London, 1920).

Williams, *Christianity* = Hugh Williams, *Christianity in early Britain* (Oxford, 1912).

YC = *Y Cymmrodor* (1880, in progress).

ZCP = *Zeitschrift für celtische Philologie* (1897, in progress).

Zimmer, *CC* = H. Zimmer, *The Celtic Church*, transl. from the German by A. Meyer (London, 1902).

Zimmermann, *VM* = E. Heinrich Zimmermann, *Vorkarolingische Miniaturen* (Berlin, 1916).

ZK = *Zeitschrift für Kirchengeschichte* (1876, in progress).

CHRISTIANITY IN CELTIC LANDS

CHAPTER I

THE HEATHEN CELTS IN THE BRITISH ISLES

§ 1.—Divisions of the Celtic Insular World.—Result of the Roman Influence.—Geographical Distribution

Leaving aside the question of the European *Urheimat* of the Celts and the history of their successive migrations through Western Europe and crossings to the British Isles—a history the chronology of which is still a matter of debate—let us give the names of the various peoples who were settled in the islands at the time when the first tidings of Christianity reached them.

The ancients were accustomed to speak, not of races, but of peoples or tribes, and languages. In the first chapter of his *Historia Ecclesiastica gentis Anglorum,* one of the most valuable among all the early works on which we shall have to draw, the Venerable Bede says that in his time five languages were spoken in Britain, to wit, those of the Angles, Britons, Scots and Picts, and finally Latin, " which the study of the Scriptures," he adds, " has rendered familiar above all others " [1]— to churchmen, be it understood. Taking them in the order of priority of arrival in the island of Britain, we should have to arrange the peoples who spoke these several tongues as follows : Picts, Britons, Romans, Scots hailing from Ireland, and Anglo-Saxons.

The two leading Celtic peoples of the islands were, on the one hand, the Goid ls or Gaels, called also in Latin *Scotti,* and on the other, the Britons (*Brittani, Britanni*). The two corre-

---

[1] Bede, *HE,* i, 1.

sponding linguistic branches of the Indo-European stock are Gaelic, a language which is still spoken in Ireland and the Highlands of Scotland, and to which the Manx tongue, formerly spoken in the Isle of Man but now almost wholly fallen into disuse, is closely akin ; and Brythonic, comprising Welsh, Cornish (now extinct) and Breton.

The Picts, who inhabited the north and centre of the Scotland of to-day, have been looked upon by some scholars as an aboriginal pre-Celtic population not of Aryan origin [1] ; but at present ethnologists and linguists regard them as Celts, and believe that their language may be referred to the Brythonic branch. [2] Professor J. Fraser is of opinion that they did not form " a racially homogeneous population." [3] The name Picts appears for the first time in A.D. 297 in the Latin form *Picti*. [4] But at an earlier period, before the Christian era, they occupied far vaster territories in Britain and in Ireland (where even in Christian times there were *Cruithni* or *Cruithin* in Ulster), insomuch that Pytheas, a citizen of Massilia (fourth century B.C.) and other geographers give to the two large islands the name of πρετανικαὶ νῆσοι, the Pretanic islands or isles of the Picts, identical with the Welsh *Ynys Prydyn*. [5]

From the middle of the ninth century of our era the Picts were absorbed by the Scots of Dál Riada and their language became gradually extinct ; only traces of it remain in place-names in Scotland. [6]

Several different names were used to denote Ireland : 'Ιέρνη, *Iuverna* (**Iverio*). To the last form may be traced *Éire*

[1] Sir John Rhys, *The Inscriptions and Language of the Northern Picts* (*PSAS*, XXVI, 1892, pp. 263–351) ; *Addenda et corrigenda* (*ib.*, XXVII, pp. 411–12) ; *s.a.*, *A revised Account of the Inscriptions of the Northern Picts* (*ib.*, XXXII, 1897–98, pp. 324–98).

[2] Whitley Stokes in A. Bezzenberger's *Beiträge zur Kunde der indogermanischen Sprachen* (XVIII, 1892, pp. 84–115) ; J. Loth, *Les Pictes d'après les travaux les plus récents* (*An. Br.*, VI, 1890–91, pp. 111–16).

[3] J. Fraser, *The Question of the Picts* (*SGS*, II, 1928, p. 176).

[4] VI (VII) *incerti panegyricus Constantino Aug. dictus*, 7 ; VIII (V) *inc. pan. Constantio Caesari dictus*, 11, ed. Guilielmus Baehrens (Lipsiae, 1911), pp. 205, 240.

[5] Ed. C. Müller, *Geographi Graeci minores*, I (Paris, 1855), p. 561 ff. Cf. Kenney, *Sources*, I, p. 124 ff. ; T. Rice Holmes, *Ancient Britain and the Invasions of Julius Caesar* (Oxford, 1907), pp. 411, 459–61.

[6] Cf. W. C. Mackenzie, *Scottish Place-Names* (London, 1931), p. 287.

(anciently *Ériu*), the Gaelic name of the country, and the Welsh *Iwerddon*.[1] St Patrick calls Ireland *Hiberio*.[2]

By a process of popular etymology, the term *Iverni*, which originally designated one of the tribes of the island and later the entire group of its inhabitants, was changed by the Romans into *Hiberni*, " the wintry people." [3] The name *Hibernia* appears for the first time in the writings of Julius Caesar.[4] But about the year 600 St Columban still calls his fellow-countrymen *Iberi*,[5] and a Breton hagiographer of the eleventh century, writing in Latin, has preserved the Irish equivalent in the slightly altered form *Iren*.[6]

Throughout all the earlier Middle Ages writers who used Latin called Ireland *Scottia* and its inhabitants *Scotti*. The earliest instance of the latter word occurs in a passage of Ammianus Marcellinus relating to events of the year A.D. 360 approximately.[7] *Scottus*, signifying a raider or reaver, is conjectured to be of Gaelic origin.[8]

The oldest name given to the other large island by Greek writers was *Albion*.[9] The Pseudo-Aristotle who wrote a treatise *Concerning the World* in the first or second century of our era, still calls the two islands by the names of *Albion* and *Ierne*.[10] Caesar is the earliest known writer to use the words *Britannia* and *Britanni*.[11]

Driven westwards by the Anglo-Saxons to the territory

---

[1] 'Ιέρνη (Strabo) ; Iuverna (Pomponius Mela ; Juvenal). Cf. MacNeill, *Phases*, pp. 67, 133.

[2] Pat., *Confessio*, 1, 16, 23, 28, 41 ; *Epistola*, 1, 5, 10, 12.

[3] MacNeill, *Phases*, p. 65.

[4] Julius Caesar, *Commentarii de bello Gallico*, V, xiii.

[5] Columban, *Epp.* 2, 5, ed. W. Gundlach (*MG. Epist.*, III, pp. 164, 171).

[6] " Valedicens pio magistro venerandisque condiscipulis, [Gildas] Iren perrexit " (*Vita Gildae*, p. 93).

[7] Ammianus Marcellinus, *Historia Romana*, XX, 1, 1.

[8] MacNeill, *Phases*, p. 145 ; R. A. S. Macalister, *Tara* (London, 1931), p. 92.

[9] Periplus of Himilco (quoting Festus Avienus, *Ora maritima*, 108-12) ; Pliny, IV, 30, 1.

[10] Didot's ed. of Aristotle, III, 630. Cf. L.G., *Les noms anciens des Iles Britanniques* (*Revue des questions historiques*, LXXXII, 1907, pp. 537-47) ; E. Windisch, *Das keltische Britannien bis zu Kaiser Arthur* (*Abhandlungen der philol.-hist. Kl. d. kön. Sächsischen Gesellschaft der Wissenschaften*, XXIX, 1913, pp. 3-9).

[11] J. Caesar, *Com. de bello Gallico*, V, II, VI, etc. Cf. MacNeill, *Phases*, p. 58.

which subsequently formed Wales (*Wallia*), the Britons, during the struggles which they maintained against the invaders, took the name of *Cymry* (singular *Cymro*, meaning " fellow-countryman "), which reappears in *Cambria*, the Latinised form of *Cymru*, " country of the Cymry," and in *Cumbria* (*Cumberland*), a district which long continued to be occupied by the Britons.[1]

In the early centuries of the Christian era, the *Scotti* of Ireland founded colonies in various parts of the island of Britain, in Cornwall and in Demetia [2] ; especially, from the fourth century on, they ensconced themselves firmly to the south of the Picts in Dál Riada (a name which they brought with them from Ireland), a district corresponding to the present county of Argyll in Scotland (*Airer nGaidhel* = coast or district of the Gaels), and in the neighbouring islands.[3] The Venerable Bede denotes this region by the term *Provincia Scottorum* or *septentrionalis Scottorum provincia*, i.e., the province of the Irish settled in Britain.[4] He never calls it simply *Scottia*. It was only in the period following on the absorption of the Picts by the immigrant *Scotti* (ninth century) that Scottic nationality really gained firm hold in the north of Britain and that the name *Scottia* began to be used to denote that territory.[5]

The Britons on their side also made settlements in Ireland.[6]

The two invasions of Britain by Julius Caesar (55 and 54 B.C.) did not result in the conquest of the island. It was not till a century later, in the year 43 of our era, that Claudius subdued the southern part of the country. In 83 and 84

---

[1] Lloyd, *HW*, I, pp. 164, 191–92. Cf. J. Loth, *Persistance des institutions et de la langue des Brittons du nord* (*R. Cel.*, XLVII, 1930, pp. 387–88) ; Chevalier, *Essai*, pp. 254–56.

[2] Sir John Rhys, *The Goidels in Wales* (*A. Cam.*, 5th Ser., XII, 1895, pp. 18–39) ; Kuno Meyer, *The Expulsion of the Déssi* (*YC*, XIV, 1901, pp. 104–35) ; *Ériu*, III, 1907, pp. 135–42 ; *Anecdota from Irish Manuscripts*, I, 1907, pp. 15–24 ; MacNeill, *Phases*, pp. 46, 155–56. Cf. Kenney, *Sources*, I, pp. 148–49. Henry Jenner, *The Irish Immigrations into Cornwall in the Late Fifth and Early Sixth Centuries* (*Roy. Cornwall Polytechnic Society*, 1917).

[3] Cf. L.G., *Les noms anciens*, pp. 541–42 ; MacNeill, *Phases*, pp. 194–97.

[4] See C. Plummer's note in Bede, *HE*, Vol. II, pp. 11–12.

[5] L.G., *op. cit.*

[6] MacNeill, *Phases*, p. 203.

Agricola carried the Roman arms to the foot of the Grampian Mountains ; but Rome never succeeded in reducing the tribes of the north of the island to subjection. Ireland likewise remained independent ; not till the ninth century did she feel for the first time the weight of a foreign yoke, that of the Scandinavians.

To secure themselves against the incessant incursions of the northern tribes, the Romans raised gigantic fortifications, the wall of Hadrian in 122 and that of Antoninus in 142, the latter strengthened by Septimius Severus (208). The most formidable of these northern peoples who harried Britons, Romans and Anglo-Saxons in turn, were the Picts. Either in concert with the Picts or acting independently, the *Scotti* (those of Ireland or those already settled in Britain) and the *Atacotti* or *Atecotti* also organized frequent expeditions against the inhabitants of Britain. Roman documents attest the presence of contingents drawn from the *Atecotti* in the imperial armies stationed in Gaul.[1]

Opinions are divided as to the importance of the influence exercised by Roman civilization on the Celtic population of Britain. Some writers are convinced that it left only a slight varnish on British institutions, which rapidly disappeared after the withdrawal of the legions.[2] Others, on the contrary, are of opinion that the Romanizing process was carried very far, especially in the southern and eastern parts of the island, where, they would have us believe, mere handicraftsmen were already speaking Latin before the country was converted to Christianity.[3]

That the Latin language and culture may have gained a foothold in the towns where the representatives of the imperial power resided and in military centres, we will not deny. But

---

[1] Ammianus Marcellinus, *Historia Romana*, XXVI, 4 ; XXVII, 8 ; *Notitia dignitatum*, ed. Böcking (Bonn, 1839–53) ; Jerome, *Adv. Iovin.*, II, 7 (*PL*, XXIII, 335). Cf. Kenney, *Sources*, I, pp. 136–38.

[2] J. Loth, *Les noms latins dans les langues brittoniques* (Paris, 1892), pp. 9–60 ; *s.a.*, *R. Cel.*, XXII, 1901, pp. 91–92.

[3] F. J. Haverfield, *The Romanization of Roman Britain*, 4th ed. revised by George Macdonald (Oxford, 1923) ; R. E. Zachrisson, *Romans, Kelts and Saxons in Ancient Britain, an Investigation into the Two Dark Centuries* (400–600) *of English History* (Skrifter utgivna av K. Humanistika Vetenskaps-Samfundet i Uppsala, XXIV, Upsala, 1927), pp. 23–26.

if the Latin language had been so widely spoken by the
Britons, it would in the natural course of evolution have given
birth to a Romance language, as happened in Gaul. Now
there is not the least trace of such an evolution of Latin into
Romance on British soil.[1] The Roman conquest was
belated, slow, difficult and never brought to completion.
Up to the Anglo-Saxon domination it seems that the British
tongue was spoken throughout the length and breadth of the
country.

During the first decade of the fifth century the Roman
troops withdrew to the Continent. But the prestige of Rome,
heightened by the growing ascendancy of the Christian faith,
kept its hold on the minds of the people for some time longer.
We can discern its influence in St Patrick, who was the son
of a *decurio* or town councillor,[2] and in Gildas, who has
nothing but contempt for Celtic names and speaks of Latin as
" *lingua nostra.*" [3]

The first Saxon invasions of Britain began about the year
428.[4] For long after that date numerous reinforcements
from the mother-country continued to join the conquerors.
During the fifth and sixth centuries the Britons offered them a
vigorous resistance ; but they were little by little split asunder
by the invaders and driven to the west. The Britons of
Strathclyde, intrenched to the south of the Picts and the west
of the Angles of Bernicia, maintained their independence
against these formidable neighbours up to the end of the ninth
century. Other British tribes held their ground in the
territories of the ancient Cumbria, to the south of those of
Strathclyde. The Brythonic language was still spoken in the
fourteenth century in some districts in the north of England.[5]

[1] Roger, *Enseignement,* p. 210 ; F. Sagot, *La Bretagne romaine* (Paris,
1911), pp. 274, 276.

[2] Pat., *Epistola,* 1, 2, 10.

[3] Gildas, *De exc.,* 23, p. 38. Cf. Lloyd, *HW,* I., p. 140 ; Jacques
Chevalier, art. *Angleterre.* I. *L'Église celtique en Grande-Bretagne* in Baudrillart's *Dictionnaire d'histoire et de géographie ecclésiastiques* (1914), col. 148.

[4] R. Thurneysen *Wann sind die Germanen nach England gekommen?* (Köl-
bing's *Englische Studien,* XXII, 1896, pp. 163–79) ; J. Loth in *R. Cel.,*
XXII, 1901, p. 94. Cf. Chevalier, *Essai,* p. 223–24.

[5] Sir John Rhys, *Celtic Britain* (London, 1904), p. 149. Cf. Eilert
Ekwall, *Scandinavians and Celts in the North-West of England* (Lunds Universitets
Årsskrift, N.F. Avd. 1, Bd. 14, No. 27, Lund and Leipzig, 1918), p. 117.

But it was in Wales, Cornwall and Brittany that the British beliefs, traditions and language found their surest refuge and persisted longest.

In the regions adjoining these chief strongholds of the insular Celts, the Celtic and Saxon elements were inter-mingled in varying proportions. The progress of linguistic research has brought to light the existence of a mixed popula-tion, which might be termed Anglo-Celtic, in the territories forming the present counties of Somerset, Gloucester and Cumberland.[1]

Such was the distribution of the several sections of the Celtic world in the period bordering on their conversion to Christianity. Before we describe the pagan beliefs of these various racial groups, it may be well to sketch the chief features of their political and social organization.

§ 2.—POLITICAL AND SOCIAL ORGANIZATION OF THE ANCIENT GAELS

In the days of pagan Ireland the country was divided into five large states called " the five fifths of Ireland." At the beginning of the Christian era, this pentarchy was replaced by a heptarchy, the seven divisions of which were as follows : Ailech, Airgialla and Ulaid, these three in the north together covering an area slightly less than that of modern Ulster ; Connacht ; Mide (Meath) and Laigin, these two comprising approximately the territory of modern Leinster ; and finally Mumu, corresponding to the present Munster.[2]

Each of these seven great divisions was ruled over by a king. They were subdivided into a large number of petty kingdoms (tuatha), the territory of a tuath corresponding in

---

[1] Cf. J. Loth in R. Cel., XX, 1899, pp. 340-42 ; XXIX, 1907, pp. 281-82 ; XXX, 1908, p. 287 ; s.a., Contributions à l'étude des romans de la Table Ronde (R. Cel., XXXII, 1911, p. 419). Cf. Zachrisson, Romans, Kelts and Saxons, p. 64 and passim.

[2] MacNeill, Phases, pp. 112–13 ; Alice Stopford Green, History of the Irish State to 1014 (London, 1925), pp. 16–19. See map showing the "Five fifths of Ireland " (Cúig cúigi na h-Éireann) in A. S. Green, op. cit., p. 17, and in John Ryan, Ireland from the Earliest Times to A.D. 800 (Dublin, n.d., p. 181), and also map of Ireland divided into the seven main provinces in A. S. Green, op. cit., p. 57, and in J. Ryan, op. cit., p. 183.

most cases to a barony of the present day.[1] Between the petty kings who ruled each over a single *tuath* and the five great kings, there were others of intermediate rank, each of whom had under him several kings (three at least). Finally, above all the kingdoms of Ireland was the high-king (*ardrí*).[2] Loegaire, son of Niall of the Nine Hostages, was high-king in the time of St Patrick. Ireland, we see, was truly a land of kings :

> " High Éire, island of the kings,
> Illustrious scene of mighty deeds." [3]

The *Book of Rights*, compiled about the year 900 and revised a century later, enumerates from 90 to 100 petty kings.[4]

Within his state the king was territorial lord, president of the assembly, judge, and over and above all, commander in chief. It was absolutely essential that he should be able to lead his people to battle, for feuds between different states were exceedingly frequent.[5]

To be eligible for the throne, the individual had to belong to the same *derbfine* (family group comprising four generations) as some king who had already reigned. Among the members of a royal family the succession was determined by election.[6]

Secular learning was represented in the state by two classes who occupied the highest rank in the social hierarchy, the *filid* and the brehons (*brithemain, breithemain*). The *filid* were professors of profane learning, soothsayers, poets and judges. The brehons were not judges, but it was their charge to safeguard, develop and interpret the laws.[7] Their legal maxims were laid down in the *Brehon laws*. The body of Irish law was revised after the conversion of the country to Christianity ; the code thus revised received the title of *Senchus Mór* or great collection of antiquities.

[1] Eoin MacNeill, *Celtic Ireland* (Dublin, 1921), p. 4.
[2] E. MacNeill, *Celtic Ireland*, p. 104.
[3] Metrical list of Irish monarchs ascribed to Gilla Coemáin (†1072), ed. B. MacCarthy, *Codex Palatino-Vaticanus* (Todd Lecture Ser., 1892), p. 142.
[4] E. MacNeill, *Celtic Ireland*, pp. 122–23.
[5] E. MacNeill, *ib.*
[6] E. MacNeill, *op. cit.*, p. 114.
[7] E. MacNeill, *Celtic Ireland*, p. 25 ; Kenney, *Sources*, I, pp. 3–4 ; A. S. Green, *History*, ch. XII.

§ 3.—POLITICAL AND SOCIAL ORGANIZATION OF THE CELTS OF BRITAIN

We have not many documents which throw light on the political and social organization of the ancient Britons. Gildas is lacking in precision. The two best sources of information for the study of the political life and of the social and territorial conditions in Wales are the Welsh laws, codified by King Hywell Dda (†949 or 950), and the writings of Giraldus Cambrensis. These sources, it is true, are somewhat late, but, as J. Loth says, " the life of the Welsh people between the tenth and twelfth centuries offers nearly the same features as that of the Britons at the time when they entered into relations with the Romans " [1] ; and A. W. Wade-Evans observes : " Throughout the fifth century we discern Wales dividing or already divided into a number of small kingdoms, which remain very much the same till Norman and post-Norman times." [2]

The Britons, like the Irish, had no towns. They led the life of herdsmen and warriors. Their dwellings, even those of the nobles, were mere huts constructed of timber and wattle, and situated, so Giraldus observes, in the heart of forests like those of hermits. [3] In the middle of the house the fire blazed on an open hearth ; at night the firebrands were covered with cinders and the fire was stirred up to new life next morning. [4]

Welsh society was divided into three classes of freemen and three classes of the non-free. The three former classes were composed respectively of the members of royal families, of the nobles (*nobiliores, optimates* ; *uchelwyr, breyryeit, gwyrda*), and of simple freemen (*boneddigyon, kynhwynawl*). Among the non-free were classed villeins (*talogyon, eilltyon* ; *nativi, villani*), menial and domestic slaves (*caethyon*), and foreigners residing temporarily in Cymric territory (*alltudyon*). [5] The path to liberty was opened to these latter classes by three callings,

---

[1] Loth, *Émigration*, p. 104.
[2] A. W. Wade-Evans, *Welsh Mediaeval Law* (Oxford, 1909), p. xxxviii.
[3] " Non urbe, non vico, non castris cohabitant, sed quasi solitarii silvis inhaerent " (Giraldus, *DK*, I, 17, p. 200).
[4] Giraldus, *DK*, I, 10, p. 184. Cf. Lloyd, *HW*, I, pp. 298–304.
[5] T. Gwynn Jones, *Social Life as reflected in the Laws of Hywel Dda* (*Aberystwyth Studies*, X, 1928, pp. 103–104).

those of scholar, smith and bard ; for, according to a triad, the race had three jewels : book, sword and harp.[1]

Much has been said about the clan system among the Celts, both Gaels and Welsh ; but the latest historians of these peoples reject what has been written on the subject as an invention of theorists.[2] In speaking of the Welsh they use the terms " household " (*teulu*), " kindred " (*cenedl*) and *gwlad* (*patria*), but not " clan." The *pencenedl* (head of the *cenedl*), the guardian of the *gens*, the champion bound to protect it from oppression, the censor of those belonging to it, men and women, was chosen for life.[3]

The members of the same *cenedl* were bound to assist one another and to avenge the murder of any of their number or else obtain compensation, estimated according to the three juridical considerations, namely, the condition of the person killed (*gwerth*), the amends payable for the insult (*sarhaed*), and the blood-fine, amount of retribution for murder, assessable upon the criminal and his kindred (*galanas*).[4]

A passage written by the Venerable Bede, which has been wrongly interpreted, has been the source of much debate. It relates to a peculiar feature of the law of succession to the kingship among the Picts. Bede says that in a case of contested succession (*ubi res veniret in dubium*), probably when more confidence was placed in the son of the deceased king's sister than in the king's own son, his nephew was chosen as his successor.[5] This statement has been taken as a proof that matriarchy prevailed among the Picts, and consequently that they were not of Indo-European origin : a conclusion which is justified neither by Bede's words nor by the lists of kings preserved in the *Pictish Chronicle*, which the supporters of the matriarchal theory have tried to interpret according to their views.[6]

---

[1] *Myvyrian Archaiology of Wales* (Denbigh, 1870), p. 922 (No. 54).
[2] A. W. Wade-Evans, *Welsh Med. Law*, p. LV ; MacNeill, *Phases*, pp. 289–95 ; *s.a., Celtic Ireland*, pp. 144, 152.
[3] Lloyd, *HW*, I, p. 285.
[4] Giraldus, *DK*, I, 17, pp. 200-201. Cf. T. Gwynn Jones, *op. cit.*, p. 108.
[5] Bede, *HE*, I, 1.
[6] The legend of Pictish matriarchy has been accepted as a historical fact by Heinrich Zimmer. See *Das Mutterrecht der Picten und seine Bedeutung für die arische Alterthumswissenschaft (Zeitschrift der Savigny-Stiftung für Rechts-*

§ 4.—Moral Temperament of the Insular Celts

Among the Celts of the two insular branches the marriage tie was far less binding than among the Continental Gauls.[1] It consisted in the sale of the bride by her parents to her future husband. There were marriages which lasted only for a year. Ancient writers accuse the Britons, as well as the Caledonians and the Irish, of practising polygamy and community of wives, and even of not shrinking from incest[2]; and in fact, in the epic literature of Ireland, we come across more than one incestuous king.[3] Most of the kings are represented as given to gluttony, theft, quarrelling and debauchery. It seems to have been an accepted custom that kings in their " circuits " should even go so far as to enjoy the wives of their hosts.[4] To this dark picture of morals some early writers added the charge of cannibalism, which, however, according to some modern critics is inadmissible.[5]

The early Scots and Britons were of extremely bellicose disposition. For a tribute withheld or not paid in full, for cattle stolen, for some point of honour on which they conceived themselves affronted, a tribe went to war against a neighbouring tribe, a province against another province; so that warfare was a well-nigh permanent condition among them. Even the women took part in hostilities[6]; it was not till near the end of the seventh century that Adamnán, abbot of Iona, is

geschichte, XV, 1894.—Romanist. Abteil., pp. 209–40). Zimmer's views have been criticised by the following writers : J. Loth, Les études celtiques, leur état présent, leur avenir (Revue internationale de l'enseignement, LXII, 1911, p. 220) ; J. Fraser, The alleged Matriarchy of the Picts (Medieval Studies in Memory of Gertrude Schoepperle-Loomis, Paris and New York, 1927, pp. 407–12) ; s.a., The Question of the Picts (SGS, II, 1928, pp. 172–201).

[1] See Camille Jullian, Histoire de la Gaule (Paris, 1914), II, pp. 407–409.

[2] J. Caesar, V, xiv, 4 ; Dion Cassius, LXXVI (LXXVII), 12, 2 ; Strabo, IV, v, 4 ; Jerome, Adv. Iov., ii, 7 (PL, XXIII, 309). Cf. Eusebius, Praep. Evangel. vi, 10 (PG, XXI, 472).

[3] Dottin, Manuel, p. 181.

[4] H. d'Arbois de Jubainville, Le droit du roi dans l'épopée irlandaise (RA, XLII, 1881, p. 331). Cf. Whitley Stokes in R. Cel., XIII, 1892, pp. 54, 58 ; Ériu, IV, 1910, pp. 20, 25.

[5] Besides the texts of Strabo and St Jerome referred to above, see Diodorus Siculus, v, 32 ; Pliny, Hist. nat., xxx, 13. Cf. C. S. Greaves in AJ, XXXVI, 1879, pp. 38–55 ; J. O'Donovan in UJA, VIII, p. 239.

[6] Tacitus, Annales, xiv, 35–36 ; The oldest version of the Tochmare Emire, ed. Kuno Meyer (R. Cel, XI, 1890, p. 451).

said to have procured exemption from military service for Irishwomen.[1]

In assemblies and banquets etiquette had to be scrupulously observed. In Wales, as in Ireland, the question of precedence roused keen susceptibilities. At a feast the right of carving was reserved to the most valiant, in other words, to him who had cut off the largest number of human heads ; accordingly each guest began by enumerating his bloody exploits, and there ensued heated disputes which generally ended in fresh bloodshed.[2]

Side by side with these barbarous customs, the most striking traits of the temperament and character of the pagan insular Celts are love of music, poetry, feasting and gaily coloured raiment, a predilection for fables and symbols, riddles, allegories and triads, and the practice of a naturalistic religion along with belief in a fancifully conceived other world. We shall now proceed to examine their religious ideas.

§ 5.—Religious Beliefs

(a) Gods.—Tacitus tells us that the cults and superstitions of Gaul were easily to be recognized among the Britons.[3] Traces of the worship of Lugus and Ogmios have been found in the islands as well as on the Continent. On the other hand, other divinities appear to have been known only to the island dwellers, for instance, Nodons, Briganti, Dagda and Mider. But as our knowledge of these is almost exclusively drawn from epic tales, we cannot tell whether they were really the objects of popular worship. However, in Britain four dedications have been discovered to the goddess Briganti, who became in Latin *Brigantia* and in Irish *Brigit*, " the mother of the Gods." [4]

As the Romans never penetrated to Ireland, it is not surprising that no trace of their gods has been found in that

---

[1] *Cain Adamnáin, An Old Irish Treatise on the Law of Adamnán* (Anecdota Oxoniensia : Med. and Mod. Ser., xii, Oxford, 1905). Cf. *Lismore*, p. 361.

[2] *Scél Mucci Maic Dáthó*, ed. E. Windisch (*Irische Texte*, I, 1880, p. 96 ff.) ; *Fled Bricrend*, ed. E. Windisch (*Irische Texte*, I, p. 254 ff.). Cf. Dottin, *Manuel*, pp. 164–65.

[3] Tacitus, *Agricola*, 11.

[4] H. d'Arbois de Jubainville, *Les Celtes depuis les temps les plus anciens jusqu'à l'an 100 avant notre ère* (Paris, 1904), pp. 33–37.

country. It is otherwise with Britain. Not only the Roman cults, but those of the East were introduced by Roman legionaries and by colonists. According to Artemidorus, in an island lying off Britain rites used to be celebrated which recalled in all respects those practised in honour of Demeter and Kore in the isle of Samothrace.[1] From inscriptions we learn that Jupiter, Serapis, Hercules, Sul, Diana and Mithras had worshippers in various places in British territory.[2] If we are to believe Donald A. Mackenzie, Buddhism had also its adepts in pre-Christian Britain[3]; but this writer's arguments are far from convincing.

In Armorica, which before the arrival of the Britons was a Gallo-Roman territory, Gaulish and Roman divinities appear side by side on the menhir of Kernuz.[4] A Mars, but of Gaulish rather than Roman type, was honoured among the *Namnetes*. Venus had her statues on the banks of the Blavet and the Vilaine and in several other places, as had also the mother-goddesses.[5]

(b) *Naturalistic Cults.*—In the time of St Patrick we find the Irish paying divine honours and making offerings to fountains.[6] The worship of fountains likewise appears among the Picts[7] and the Britons; the latter extended it to the stream which issued from the fountain and the mountain in which it rose.[8]

Trees—yew, ash and oak—and stones were also venerated. In the Brehon Laws the stones which served as boundary marks to territories are called by the name *lia adartha*, " *stone of worship.*"[9] A Life of St Samson, drawn up probably in

---

[1] Strabo, *Geogr.*, IV, 4, 6.

[2] Hübner, *Inscriptiones Britanniae Latinae* in *Corpus inscr. Lat.*, VII, Nos. 316, 95, 240, 39, 236, 924, etc. ; F. Cumont, *Textes et monuments figurés relatifs aux mystères de Mithra* (Bruxelles, 1899) (See map in Vol. I) ; W. J. Williams, *The Cult of Mithra in Britain and the Rhineland in the First Century A.D. (AJ*, LXXXII, 1925, pp. 1–24). Cf. Chevalier, *Essai*, pp. 190–91.

[3] D. A. Mackenzie, *Buddhism in Pre-Christian Britain* (London, 1928).

[4] See G. Guénin in *An. Br.*, 1910, pp. 453–54 ; Paul du Chatellier, *Les époques préhistoriques et gauloises dans le Finistère* (Rennes, 1907), Pl. XXIX.

[5] La Borderie, *HB*, I, pp. 172–87.

[6] Tirechán, p. 26 ; *Vita Trip.*, pp. 122–23.

[7] Adam., *Vita Col.*, II, 11 (p. 81).

[8] Gildas, *De exc.*, 4, p. 29.

[9] *Ancient Laws of Ireland*, IV, p. 142.

the seventh century, shows us the peasants of the Pagus Tricurius in Britain, in the sixth century, dancing round a standing stone on which the saint carved a cross.[1]

An oriented stone bearing an Ogham inscription, which was found at Drumlusk near Kenmare (Kerry) has incised on it a circle which has been conjectured to be a trace of a sun-cult.[2] As a matter of fact, Cormac's Glossary (ninth–tenth century) tells us that the Irish heathens were wont to portray on their altars the forms of the creatures they adored, and especially the figure of the sun[3]; and St Patrick alludes to sun-worship in his *Confessio*.[4] The primitive inhabitants of Albion used also to celebrate the recurring motions of the day-star with religious ecstasies.[5] On May 1st the Gaels used to hold the solar festival of Beltane by kindling great fires and dancing round them.[6]

(c) *Druids and Magic*.—According to a common belief mentioned by Caesar, the doctrine of the druids was supposed to have had its birth in Great Britain and the druids of Gaul used to cross the sea to study it more thoroughly.[7] But was Britain really the cradle of druidism, or did it first arise in Ireland? Or had the institution its origin among the predecessors both of Gaels and Britons? These are questions to which only vague conjectures can be offered in answer.[8] So much is certain—druidic discipline was in a highly flourishing condition in Britain about the year 53 before our

---

[1] *Vita Sam.*, I, 48 (pp. 143–144).

[2] R. A. S. Macalister, *Studies in Irish Epigraphy* (London, 1902), II, p. 117.

[3] *Sanas Cormaic*, 752, ed. Kuno Meyer (*Anecdota from Irish Manuscripts*, IV, Halle, 1912, p. 63) ; ed. Whitley Stokes and J. O'Donovan (Calcutta, 1868), p. 94.

[4] Pat., *Confessio*, 60 (p. 25).

[5] Diodorus Siculus, *Bibl.*, II, 47, 2 (quoting Hecataeus of Abdera).

[6] H. d'Arbois de Jubainville, *Les Celtes*, p. 54. See *R. Cel.*, XXV, 1904, pp. 86–87.

[7] " Disciplina in Britannia reperta atque inde in Galliam translata esse existimatur, et nunc qui diligentius eam rem cognoscere uolunt plerumque illo discendi causa proficiscuntur " (Caesar, *De bello Gal.*, VI, XIII).

[8] According to Julius Pokorny, Druidism is to be traced among the non-Celtic folks whom the Celts subjugated in Ireland. See *Der Ursprung des Druidentums* (*Mitteilungen der anthropologischen Gesellschaft in Wien*, XXXVIII, 1908, pp. 34–45). This memoir has been translated into English : *The origin of Druidism* (*Annual Report of the Smithsonian Institution for 1910*, Washington City, 1911, pp. 583–97).

era, the period to which Caesar's testimony refers us. Pliny the Elder states that in his time, that is to say, about the year 77 of the Christian era, it still maintained its repute there.[1] We find druids in the isle of Mona (Anglesey) in 61 A.D.,[2] and an Ogham inscription attests their presence in the Isle of Man.[3] Vortigern, the somewhat legendary king of the Britons in the fifth century, had relations with druids if we may believe Nennius.[4] After Vortigern there is no further trace of druidism in the south and west of the island. But in the following century St Columba, the abbot of Iona, on making his way to the Picts, found it still amongst them.[5]

In Armorica the last druids seem to have disappeared before the arrival of the Britons. In Welsh and in Breton the words for " druid " are of comparatively recent formation. The title of druid does not appear in the Welsh laws.[6]

It was in Ireland that they held their ground longest. There is frequent mention of them in texts. Patrick waged an unceasing combat with them. " He warred against hard-hearted druids ; he crushed the proud with the help of our Lord of fair heaven. He purified Ireland's meadow-lands," so we read in an ancient hymn.[7]

But the Irish druid, as he is presented to us in epic or hagiographic narratives, little resembles the Gaulish druid of Caesar's time. Such texts as are available for information about Ireland never represent him as exercising priestly functions. He took no part in sacrifices, though he may perhaps have presided at the funeral obsequies of heroes. The druids of the Continent were priests and in addition judges, professors, diviners and, towards the end, more cattle-doctors and sorcerers than anything else. In Ireland they were not competent to act as judges ; that was the

---

[1] Pliny, *Hist. nat.*, xxx, 13.
[2] Tacitus, *Annales*, xiv, 30.
[3] P. M. C. Kermode in *PSAS*, XLV, 1911, p. 437 ; T. D. Kendrick, *The Druids : a Study in Keltic Prehistory* (London, 1927), p. 100.
[4] Nennius, *HB*, 40 (p. 181).
[5] Adam., *Vita Col.* I, 1, 37 ; II, 33, 34.
[6] H. d'Arbois de Jubainville, *Les druides et les dieux à formes d'animaux* (Paris, 1906), p. 81.
[7] Ninine's Prayer (Stokes and Strachan, *TP*, II, p. 322 ; *LH*, I, p. 105 ; II, p. 36).

province of the *filid* or poets. We find two druids entrusted with the education of the daughters of Loegaire, king of Ireland and contemporary of St Patrick ; but we do not know whether teaching formed a regular part of the druidic functions. The Irish druid resembles rather the Gaulish druid of the decadent period. He was before all else a prophet and a magician ; even Christians believed in the prophetic powers of the druids.

In the time of Pliny magic was in high repute in Britain.[1] That writer calls the druids *magi*, a title always given them in Latin texts written in Ireland, *magus* being the equivalent of the Irish *druí*. It is generally as magicians that they figure in the early literature of the country. They were supposed to have the power of calling up dense fogs, causing showers of fire or blood, making snow fall in midsummer, raising tempests on land or sea, and driving men out of their senses. Adamnán, the biographer of Columba, shows us the saint engaged in a contest of miracles with the druids and triumphing over them.[2]

The power of magic continued to be the most lasting source of Irish superstitions in the Christian period. A penitential of the eighth century deems it advisable to ordain a severe penance against the sin of " druidism " (*druidecht*), by which we are evidently to understand the practice of magic arts.[3]

(*d*) *Idols and Human Sacrifices.*—We have seen that St Samson in the sixth century put an end to a stone-worshipping cult in Britain. The Irish too had their idols, as St Patrick in his *Confessio* and his biographer Muirchu avouch.[4] The most famous was a standing stone called *Cenn Cruaich* covered with gold and silver, which stood on the plain of Magh Slecht, popularly interpreted as Magh Slécht, " the plain of genuflexions." It was surrounded by twelve other idols of stone which were adorned with copper.[5] The *Dindsenchas*, a work dealing with the local legends of the country, the oldest parts

---

[1] Pliny, *Hist. nat.*, xxx, 4, 13.
[2] Adam., *Vita Col.*, *l. cit.*
[3] *De arreis*, pp. 488, 497. Cf. L.G., *Les chrétientés celtiques* (Paris, 1911), p. 24, note 2.
[4] Pat., *Confessio*, 41 (p. 19) ; Muirchu, p. 275.
[5] *Vita Trip.*, pp. 90–92.

of which go back to the eleventh century, still speaks in the article devoted to Magh Slecht of this idol, " the chief idol of Ireland," calling it *Cromm Cruaich*, and says that up to the arrival of St Patrick it was worshipped by all the peoples dwelling in Ireland. Even children used to be sacrificed to this stone to secure milk and corn.[1] Another stone idol, likewise decorated with gold and silver, and called *Cermand Cestach*, is spoken of in the notes to the Martyrology of Oengus.[2]

The passage in the *Dindsenchas* just referred to is the most explicit mention of human sacrifices in Ireland, a late text, it is true, but one which may be the echo of an ancient tradition. Other Irish texts appear to allude to the custom of human sacrifice either to make a piece of land fertile or to secure a firm foundation for a house in process of building.[3] In Nennius we read of the sacrifice of a child for this latter object.[4]

The ancient writers also represent the Britons as cruel sacrificers of human beings. According to Dion Cassius, the followers of Boudicca used to put their female captives to death with refinements of torture in honour of the goddess Adraste[5] ; and Tacitus tells of the baneful superstition of the inhabitants of Mona (Anglesey), who held it a religious act to pour on their altars the blood of human victims and to interpret the will of the gods from their entrails.[6] It seems that in the year 77 of our era the custom of human sacrifices still persisted in certain districts of Britain.[7]

Vestiges of these heathen cults survived for long among the Celts both of the Continent and the insular countries. Many traces of pre-Christian religious practices may be observed even in our own day. Did the practice of bloody

---

[1] Ed. Whitley Stokes in *R. Cel.*, XVI, 1895, pp. 35–36, 163. Cf. F. N. Robinson, *Human Sacrifice among the Irish Celts* (*Anniversary Papers by Colleagues and Pupils of George Lyman Kittredge*, Boston, 1913), p. 189.

[2] *Fél. Oeng.*, pp. 186, 187, 378.

[3] See Kuno Meyer, *Human Sacrifice among the Ancient Irish* (*Ériu*, II, 1905, p. 86) ; F. N. Robinson, *art. cit.*

[4] Nennius, *HB*, 40–41.

[5] Dion Cassius, *Hist. Rom.*, LXII, 7.

[6] Tacitus, *Annales*, XIV, 30.

[7] Pliny, *Hist. nat.*, XXX, 4, 13.

sacrifices continue among the Celts after they had become Christians ? From certain medieval texts we might infer that such was the case in Ireland and Scotland. The sacrifice was sometimes commuted by drawing blood from the first animal met by troops on their way to battle,[1] or again by sprinkling the foundations of a building with the blood of a human being or an animal.[2]

Divination by means of the song of birds (raven, wren) was still practised in the Christian period.[3] The bonfires of the festival of May 1st (Beltane) continued to be kindled in Ireland and Scotland up to the eighteenth century and even later.[4]

(e) *Immortality of the Soul ; the Other World.*—Tirechán, who wrote a narrative of the apostolate of St Patrick, has left a story about Loegaire, the high-king of Ireland, from which we may infer that the Irish pagans believed in the survival of the soul after death. Tirechán tells us that the king desired to be buried standing and in arms, for, he adds, the heathens are accustomed to await fully armed in their tombs the day called *erdathe* by the druids, that is, the day of judgment of the Lord.[5]

It must, however, be observed that " far from being the outcome of the meditations of the philosophers of Great Britain, the belief in the survival of souls is Indo-European ; it is found already in the Vedas, and Herodotus has recorded it among the Egyptians and the Getae. It is not therefore a religious belief peculiar to the Celts." [6]

As for inquiring into the fate in store beyond the grave for heroes and for ordinary men, or describing the Celtic Elysium and explaining how it may be reconciled with the belief in metempsychosis, which has also been discovered among the early Irish pagans, we deem it better to leave these questions

[1] Martin, *Description of the Western Islands of Scotland* (1716) in Pinkerton's *Voyages* (III, p. 607).
[2] F. N. Robinson, *art. cit.*, pp. 186, 196.
[3] R. I. Best, *Prognostication from the Raven and the Wren* (Ériu, 1916, pp. 120–26). Cf. L.G., *Les chrétientés celtiques*, p. 22.
[4] P. W. Joyce, *A Social History of Ancient Ireland* (London, 1913), I, p. 291 ; Kendrick, *The Druids*, pp. 129–30.
[5] Tirechán, p. 19.
[6] Dottin, *Manuel*, p. 356.

to be dealt with by specialists in the imaginative literature of Ireland and Wales ; for that literature alone can furnish us with some notions (very vague at best) on these problems, which from the very nature of our sources of information belong to the domain of legend and folklore rather than of the history of Celtic religion.[1]

Conclusion

It was the idealistic tendencies of the Celts which impressed Renan and inspired those pages he has written on the genius of the Celtic peoples—pages full of exquisite literary skill, but to some extent fallacious.[2] In glowing terms he describes a race, small in numbers, timid, self-centred, chaste, melancholy, far removed from all thought of aggression or conquest, thirsting for the ideal and the infinite, in short " naturally Christian." We must not allow ourselves to be deceived by the magic art of the great master. The pagan Celt, from the glimpses we catch of him in his literature, does not stand revealed in such a poetic light. His manners and morals are violent and barbarous ; his nobles are under the sway of gross appetites ; the conscience and destiny of the subject are entirely within the power of the chief. Every-where we meet with beliefs marked by a crude naturalism and utterly devoid of moral character, with minds held captive and enslaved under the tyrannic rule of sorcery. There is nothing in all this to denote a race peculiarly pre-adapted to Christianity.

It is true that these peoples, once converted, were to remain, for the greater part, long and deeply attached to their faith. But, as we shall see, the work of converting them was not accomplished without great toil and long-continued effort on the part of the missionaries and often active resistance on that of the peoples.

[1] See L.G., *Les chrétientés celtiques*, pp. 24–25, and the following art. in *ERE : Blest (Abode of the)*, by A. MacCulloch ; *Transmigration (Celtic)*, by G. Dottin.

[2] E. Renan, *De la poésie des races celtiques* in *Essais de morale et de critique* (4th edit., Paris, 1890), pp. 375–456. Cf. Anatole Le Braz, *Le théâtre celtique* (Paris, *n.d.*), ch. i.

CHAPTER II

THE RISE OF CHRISTIANITY IN THE INSULAR COUNTRIES

§ 1.—The Earliest Evidence Relative to the Conversion of the Britons

The Christian faith was first propagated in the insular Celtic countries from Roman Britain as a base. At what time and by what missionaries was it spread? Our sources of information are far too vague and brief to allow of an answer to these questions. The most ancient do not go back as far as the year 200.[1] The earliest fact of which we can be sure is the presence of three British bishops at the Council of Arles in 314.[2] The first Christians of Great Britain were Romans who had come in the train of the Roman legions.[3] However, one of the bishops present at Arles, Eborius (or more correctly Eburius), bears a name derived from a Celtic theme.[4] We find several British bishops at the Council of Rimini in 359.[5] In the preceding year, St Hilary of Poitiers, then an exile in Phrygia, dedicated his treatise *De Synodis* to the bishops of the British provinces as well as those of the Continent.[6] We may infer that in the fourth century the British Church was already well known.[7]

---

[1] *CED*, I, p. 3 ff.

[2] *CED*, I, p. 7. Cf. S. N. Miller, *The British Bishops at the Council of Arles, 314* (*EHR*, XLII, 1927, pp. 79–80).

[3] Williams, *Christianity*, ch. III.

[4] H. d'Arbois in *R. Cel.*, XXV, 1904, p. 100. Haddan and Stubbs (*CED*, I, p. 7, note *b*) mention several Welsh bishops bearing the names *Ebur, Ibarus, Ywor*.

[5] Sulpicius Severus, *Historia sacra*, II, 41 (*PL*, XX, 152).

[6] *CED*, I, pp. 9, 10 ; *PL*, X, 479.

[7] On his arrival at Canterbury (A.D. 597), Augustine found a church dedicated to St Martin, ' *antiquitus facta, dum Romani Brittaniam incolerent* ' (Bede, *HE*, I, 26). On that church see C. R. Peers, *The Earliest Christian*

According to Gildas, the natives of Great Britain accepted Christianity for the most part without enthusiasm (*tepide*) [1] ; and this is all he tells us about the conversion of the country. Elsewhere, however, he records that British Christianity was watered with the blood of several martyrs ; he mentions the names of St Alban of Verulam, and of St Aaron and St Julius, both of Caerleon. [2]

The Christian inscriptions of Britain do not go back beyond the middle of the fourth century.

St Germanus of Auxerre, whose missions had so great an influence on the Celtic Churches, arrived in Britain for the first time in 429. At that date the Romans had abandoned the country ; the first Saxon invaders had barely landed and had as yet ventured only on a few raids through the regions which were the area of the Gaulish bishop's activity. [3] Christianity seems to have been fairly widespread at the time. The biographer of Germanus represents him as preaching not only in the churches, but at cross-roads and in the open country, so large were the crowds eager to hear his words. [4] Ferdinand Walter has even conjectured that there were no pagans left in the island when the Roman dominion came to an end. [5]

Gildas draws a tragic picture of the havoc wrought by the Saxons among the British Christians : priests put to death, churches sacked and burnt, altars profaned. The inhabitants were driven to hide in the mountains or the recesses of the sea-coast, or even compelled to seek refuge beyond seas. [6] Eddius, the biographer of St Wilfrid, records also that the

---

Churches in England (*Antiquity*, III, 1929, pp. 67–68). The remains of two basilicas of the Roman period have been found in Great Britain, one at Silchester (Hampshire), excavated in 1892, another (possibly not a Christian church) at Caerwent (Monmouthshire), excavated in 1923 (cf. R. E. M. Wheeler, *Prehistoric and Roman Wales* (Oxford, 1925), p. 248 ; A. W. Clapham, *English Romanesque Architecture before the Conquest* (Oxford, 1930), pp. 13–14 ; R. G. Collingwood, *The Archaeology of Roman Britain* (London, 1930), p. 145.

[1] Gildas, *De exc.*, 8.
[2] Gildas, *De exc.*, 10.
[3] Cf. J. Loth in *R. Cel.*, XXX, 1900, p. 398.
[4] Constantius, *Vita Germani*, 14, ed. W. Levison (*MG. Scr. R. M.*, VII, pp. 260–61).
[5] F. Walter, *Das alte Wales* (Bonn, 1859), p. 217.
[6] Gildas, *De exc.*, 23–25.

British clergy were attacked by the forces of the enemy and forced to desert the " holy places." [1]

The orthodoxy of the infant Church of Great Britain on the article of the Trinity has been called in question. It is true that the insular bishops who were present at Rimini signed the obnoxious homoiousian formula dictated by the Emperor, just as did their continental brethren. But they were taken by surprise at the moment ; and they were not slow in returning to the doctrine of Nicaea, on their faithful profession of which St Hilary of Poitiers, only a year before the Council, had congratulated them, because they had kept themselves " pure from all contagion of the detestable [Arian] heresy." [2] St Athanasius, too, in 363, places Britain among the nations which had remained true to the Catholic doctrine.[3] Gildas and the Venerable Bede, who accepted his statements, have therefore greatly exaggerated the influence of Arianism in their country.[4]

Again, it has been asserted that the baptism of the Britons was irregular and invalid, being administered without the invocation of the three Divine Persons.[5] This statement cannot be accepted ; it rests, as will be shown later, on texts which do not apply to the Britons.

At the end of the fourth century there arose grave dissensions among the bishops of Britain, to such a degree that St Victricius, bishop of Rouen, was obliged to cross the sea to restore peace among them. Whether their disagreement rose out of theological disputes is not known.[6]

The most real danger to the integrity of the faith was the spread of the heresy of Pelagius among the British Churches in the first half of the fifth century.

---

[1] Stephen, *Vita Wilfridi*, 27 (p. 212). Cf. *The Life of Bishop Wilfrid* by Eddius Stephanus. Text, transl. and notes by Bertram Colgrave (Cambridge, 1927), p. 164, note.

[2] Hilary, *De synodis*, Prol. and ch. II (*CED*, I, p. 9 ; *PL*, X, 481).

[3] Athanasius, *Ad Iovinianum imp.*, 2 (*CED*, I, pp. 7, 8 ; *PG*, XXVI, 815-17).

[4] Gildas, *De exc.*, 12 ; Bede, *HE*, I, 8.

[5] F. C. Conybeare, *The character of the heresy of the early British Church* (*TSC*, 1897–98, pp. 84–117). Cf. Zimmer, *CC*, pp. 4–6.

[6] Victricius, *De laude Sanctorum*, I, 2 (*PL*, XX, 443). Cf. E. Vacandard, *Saint Victrice évêque de Rouen* (Paris, 1909), pp. 126–27.

§ 2.—PELAGIANISM AND THE MISSIONS OF ST GERMANUS

Pelagius was by birth a Briton or an Irishman. St Augustine, Orosius, Marius Mercator and Prosper of Aquitaine—all contemporaries—give him as a native of Britain.[1] On the other hand, St Jerome, in his *Commentary on Jeremiah*, speaks of an ignorant slanderer who had criticised one of his works and whom he qualifies as a " most stupid fellow, heavy with Irish porridge (*Scottorum pultibus praegravatus*)." [2] But it is not absolutely certain that the person so referred to was the heresiarch Pelagius. In another passage of the same commentary Jerome assails some individual (or rather two) in the following terms : " Although silent himself, he does his barking through an Alpine dog, huge and corpulent, who can rave more with his claws than with his teeth, for he has his lineage of the Irish race, from the neighbourhood of the Britons (*habet enim progeniem Scoticae gentis de Britannorum vicinia*)." [3] This was evidently written *ab irato*. We do not know whether the last lines refer to Pelagius or to his principal disciple Caelestius. From the fiery pen of the solitary of Bethlehem we may be prepared to meet with an occasional exaggeration. St Jerome, as L. Duchesne remarks, " calls [Pelagius] a Scot (Irishman), so as to be able to fasten on him the legends current at the time about the Scots, their barbarism, their cannibalism and so forth." [4] There are, however, some writers on whom Jerome's testimony has made a deeper impression than that of the other contemporaries of Pelagius and who make his words a foundation for the assertion that Pelagius was born in Ireland.[5] The terms *Brito*, *Britannus*, used by other authors were, they aver, employed in a wide sense to denote any native of the lands called by the Greek geographers αἱ πρετανικαὶ νῆσοι, hence also of Ireland.[6]

[1] Augustine, *Ep.* CLXXXVI, 1 (*Corp. SEL*, LVII, 45 ; *PL*, XXXIII, 816). Orosius, *Liber apologeticus*, XII, 3 (*Corp. SEL*, V, 620). Marius Mercator, *Liber subnot. in verba Iuliani*, Praef. 2 (*PL*, XLVIII, 111).—Prosper, *Epitoma chron.*, A.D. 413, ed. Th. Mommsen (*MG. Auct. ant.* IX : *Chron. min.* I, p. 467) ; *Carmen de ingrat.*, I (*PL*, LI, 94).
[2] Jerome, *In Hieremiam proph.*, Prol. Lib. I (*Corp. SEL*, LIX, 4).
[3] Prol. Lib. III, p. 151.
[4] Louis Duchesne, *Histoire ancienne de l'Église* (Paris, 1910), III, p. 207.
[5] Mario Esposito, *Latin Learning*, I, p. 227-28.
[6] Different opinions have been advanced on the matter. See A. Souter,

Others try to reconcile conflicting testimonies in a different way, alleging that Pelagius was born in Britain, but of parents belonging to a Gaelic colony settled in that island.[1]

We find Pelagius at Rome during the pontificate of Anastasius (399–401).[2] It was not till he had reached the Eternal City that he began openly to avow those erroneous views on Divine Grace with the germ of which he had been inoculated by the Syrian Rufinus.[3]

He was a monk [4] and a man of culture, and had learnt enough Greek to be able to dispense with an interpreter at the Assemblies of Jerusalem (July, 415) and Diospolis (December 20th–26th, 415), where he was summoned to give an account of his doctrine. His adversary Orosius, on the contrary, had to have recourse to an interpreter, who, so he tells us, acquitted himself very badly of his office.[5]

St Augustine credits the heresiarch with an active, subtle, and penetrating intellect, an ardent soul, and even a certain reputation for holiness.[6]

After 429 we hear no more of him. Probably he never returned to his native land. Before going to Africa, he made a stay in Sicily. One of his compatriots, Bishop Fastidius, who was likewise a wanderer in Sicily and at Rome between 413 and 418, was seduced by his opinions.[7] It is not, how-

Pelagius's Expositions of Thirteen Epistles of St Paul. I. *Introd.* (*Texts and Studies*, IX. Cambridge, 1922), pp. 2–3 ; Kenney, *Sources*, I, pp. 161–62.

[1] Bury, *Pat.*, pp. 15, 43.

[2] Marius Mercator, *l. cit.*

[3] Marius Merc., *l. cit.*

[4] Marius Merc., *l. cit.* ; Augustine, *De gestis Pelagii*, xiv, 36 (*Corp. SEL*, XXXXII, 92).

[5] Orosius, *Liber apol.*, vi, 1, p. 610. Cf. L. Duchesne, *Op. cit.*, p. 207. Orosius was present at the Council of Jerusalem, but he did not attend the synod of Diospolis. Cf. F. Cavallera, *Saint Jérôme, sa vie et son œuvre* (Louvain and Paris, 1922), I, p. 327. " He (Pelagius) had certainly not learned Greek in his early life, as has sometimes been stated, for it has been recently shown [Burkitt, *JTS*, XXVIII, 1927, p. 99] that when he wrote his Commentary on St Paul he was ignorant of that language, and had not consulted Greek MSS," notes M. Esposito (*Latin Learning*, I, p. 228). " Dom Chapman has justly cast suspicion on Pelagius' knowledge of Greek at the time he wrote his exposition " (A. Souter, *The Earliest Latin Commentaries of the Epistles of St Paul*, Oxford, 1927, p. 225).

[6] Augustine, *De peccat. mer.*, iii, 1, 5 (*Corp. SEL*, LX, 129 ; *PL*, XLIV, 185–86) ; *Retractat.*, ii, 33 (*PL*, XXXII, 644).

[7] On Fastidius, his life and works, see Germain Morin, Le " *De vita christiana* " de l'évêque breton Fastidius et le livre de Pélage " ad viduam " (*RB*,

ever, Fastidius who is said to have introduced the leaven of
the heresy into Britain, but one Agricola, the son of another
Pelagian bishop, Severianus.[1] Among the Britons it made
such rapid progress that the orthodox party, feeling themselves
no longer strong enough to fight it unaided, besought help
from the Church of Gaul. Germanus, bishop of Auxerre, was
appointed by a synod as the best fitted to bring back the
British Pelagians to orthodox belief; and it seems that Pope
Celestine himself, at the request of the deacon Palladius,
exerted himself to confirm the chosen bishop in his mission.[2]
With him was associated St Lupus of Troyes.[3] The two
bishops acquitted themselves of their task with remarkable
zeal and led back into the right path many who had gone
astray.

This first mission lasted from 429 to 431. But after the
departure of the Gaulish bishops the heresy raised its head
once more; and fifteen years later St Germanus was obliged
to cross the Channel a second time (446–447). On this occasion he was accompanied by a bishop of the name of Severus,
whose diocese is not mentioned by Constantius, the saint's
biographer, but who is given by Bede as bishop of Trèves.[4]
Pelagianism did not survive this new campaign. Gildas, who
wrote in the following century, does not make the least
allusion to it, though it was in a way the national heresy of
the Britons.[5]

XV, 1898, pp. 481–93); *s.a.*, *Études, textes, documents* (Maredsous and
Paris, 1913, pp. 25–27); *s.a.*, *Un manuscrit inconnu et complet de trois des
opuscules de l'évêque breton Fastidius* (*A travers les manuscrits de Bâle* in *Basler
Zeitschrift für Geschichte und Altertumskunde*, XXVI, 1927, pp. 234–41);
R. S. T. Haslehurst, *The Works of Fastidius* (London, 1927).

[1] Prosper, *Epitoma chron.* (*MG. Auct. ant.*, IX : *Chron. min.*, I, p. 472).

[2] " . . . sed ad insinuationem Palladii diaconi papa Caelestinus
Germanum Autissiodorensem episcopum vice sua mittit" (Prosper, *Epit.
chron., l. cit.*).

[3] *Vita Lupi ep. Trecensis*, 4, ed. Br. Krusch (*MG. Scr. RM*, III, 121);
Constantius, *Vita Germani*, 12, ed. W. Levison (*MG. Scr. RM*, VII, 259).

[4] Constantius, *Vita Germani*, 25–27 (pp. 269–71); Bede, *HE*, I, 21.
Cf. W. Levison, *Bischof Germanus von Auxerre und die Quellen zu seiner Geschichte*
(*NA*, XXIX, 1903, pp. 128–129).

[5] The semi-Pelagian Faustus, abbot of Lérins and afterwards bishop of
Riez (462), was a Briton, as was also Riocatus (Riochatus), " *antistes ac
monachus*," whose visit to Sidonius Apollinaris at Clermont gave the latter
an opportunity of reading some books of Faustus's which Riocatus was
carrying to Britain (Cf. Sidonius, *Epist. Fausto*, ed. Luetjohann (*MG.*

Germanus appears to have made a considerable impression on the Christians of the British Isles, who instituted a lasting cult in his memory and found a place for him in their legends.[1]

§ 3.—St Ninian among the Southern Picts

At a date unknown, but previous to the time when Germanus was carrying out his first mission, a Briton who had been instructed in the faith and the holy scriptures at Rome, traversed Gaul and south Britain in order to carry the light of the Gospel to the peoples of the north, especially the Picts of Galloway. His name was Ninian.[2] The holy bishop took up his abode in the peninsula of Galloway in a spot which received the name of *Candida Casa*, because of the light colour of the stone he used to build his church.[3] Among the Celts a church of stone was a rarity ; for long they were contented with rustic oratories constructed of planks, stakes or wattle. Is it a fact that St Ninian on his way home from Italy visited St Martin of Tours and got from him masons to build his church ? We have no means of deciding ; and, in any case, on account of the late appearance of the story, it must be received with caution. However, we have the authority of the Venerable Bede for believing that the holy bishop placed his church under the patronage of the great Confessor of Gaul.[4]

The southern Picts converted by Ninian did not persevere in the Faith. In a letter written about the middle of the fifth century St Patrick speaks of them already as apostates.[5] It was the lot of St Columba and his disciples and successors, the

Auct. ant., VIII, p. 157). See Williams, *Christianity*, pp. 242–43. Faustus of Riez is mentioned by Nennius (48, p. 192). Cf. F. Liebermann, *Nennius the Author of the Historia Brittonum (Essays in Med. Hist. presented to T. F. Tout*, Manchester, 1925), pp. 35–37.

[1] Williams, *Christianity*, pp. 229–33 ; W. Levison, *Bischof Germanus*, pp. 172–74 ; Duine, *Inventaire*, pp. 39–41, 42 ; Louis Prunel, *Saint Germain d'Auxerre* (Paris, 1929), pp. 93–102.

[2] For the discussion of the time of Ninian's apostolate see Varin, *Mémoire*, pp. 117–20, and C. Plummer's notes on Bede, *HE*, III, 4 (Vol. II, p. 128).

[3] Ailred of Rievaulx (†1167), *Vita Niniani*, 2, ed. A. P. Forbes, *Historians of Scotland* (Edinburgh, 1874), V, p. 143.

[4] Bede, *HE*, III, 4.

[5] Pat., *Epistola*, 2.

monks of Iona and Lindisfarne, to take up the work begun by
Ninian among these uncivilized tribes and to extend the
dominion of the Gospel further north.

§ 4.—The Beginnings of Christianity in Ireland before St Patrick

We now come to Ireland. As Christianity had already
about the year 400 penetrated to the Solway Firth and the
banks of the Clyde, it would be strange if Ireland, so close to
Britain, had remained untouched by any Christian influence
up to 430. The commercial relations of the Irish Scots with
the Britons and with the peoples of the Continent, their hostile
raids outside their own country, the foundation of Gaelic
colonies in Great Britain, the slave trade, actively carried on
at that time, and war, which brought captives of whom many
were Christians to the shores of Ireland—all these opportunities of contact were likely to disseminate the Christian
religion from individual to individual and from nation to
nation.[1] But, in any case, we have texts which afford explicit
proof that it was so propagated.

From at least one passage of the *Confession* of St Patrick, a
work which is nowadays allowed by almost all critics to be
genuine,[2] it appears that missionaries had preceded the saint
in certain districts of Ireland, since he speaks expressly of
certain other districts in which none had arrived before him
to baptize, to ordain clergy or to confirm.[3] The earliest
biographers of the saint, Tirechán and Muirchu maccu
Machteni, tell us also that in Connacht Patrick was surprised
to find a cross erected over a grave.[4] If it were true, moreover, that king Loegaire, when pressed to believe in Christ,
answered that his father Niall of the Nine Hostages had for-

---

[1] Pat., *Confessio*, 1. Cf. Kuno Meyer, *Early Relations between Gael and
Brython* (*TSC*, 1895–96, pp. 55–86) ; Cecile O'Rahilly, *Ireland and
Wales : their historical and literary Relations* (London, 1924) ; Slover
Channels, No. 6 (1926), pp. 5–35, 42–45.

[2] Mario Esposito, *Notes on the Latin Writings of St Patrick* (*JTS*, XIX,
1918, pp. 342–44) ; Kenney, *Sources*, I, pp. 166–67.

[3] Pat., *Confessio*, 51. On the alleged pre-Patrician Irish saints (Ailbhe,
Declán, Ciarán of Saighir, etc.) see MacNeill, *Phases*, p. 161, and Kenney,
Sources, I, pp. 309–19.

[4] Tirechán, p. 34 ; Muirchu, p. 325.

bidden him that belief,[1] we should have to conclude that the doctrines of Christ had already in some form or other come within the knowledge of Niall, who reigned over Ireland from 379 to 405. But no testimony is more positive than that of Prosper of Aquitaine, according to whom Pope St Celestine in 431 sent to the Scots " who believed in Christ " (*ad Scottos in Christum credentes*) as their first bishop Palladius, whom he had ordained.[2] The sending of a bishop from Rome to Ireland leads us to suppose that in the latter country there existed Christian communities of some importance.

It would, however, be a grave mistake to assert with Zimmer that in the year 431 the conversion of the island was already well advanced.[3] For in another work Prosper says in eulogy of St Celestine that that Pope sought, on the one hand, to keep the Roman island Catholic (an allusion to the anti-Pelagian mission of St Germanus in Great Britain), and, on the other, to convert to Christianity the " barbarian " island, *i.e.*, Ireland (*dum Romanam insulam studet servare catholicam, fecit etiam barbaram christianam*).[4] The necessity of converting the " barbarian " island of the Scots is sufficient proof that it had so far made but slight progress in the Faith.

This, too, is the impression left by the writings of St Patrick. He depicts Paganism as still holding the mastery in the Ireland of his day, that is to say, in the second half of the fifth century, during which he wrote.[5] He dwells, he says, among *gentiles*, in the midst of pagan barbarians, worshippers of idols and of unclean things.[6] It is, then, certain that before the arrival of Patrick and Palladius there were Christians in Hibernia. But it is equally certain that Christianity was so

---

[1] Tirechán, p. 19.

[2] Prosper, *Epitoma chron.* (*MG. Auct. ant.*, IX ; *Chron. min.*, 1, p. 473).

[3] One of Zimmer's arguments is that several Old-Irish words of Christian religious significance derived from Latin, but through the medium of British speech, can only be explained by the fact that they were learned by the Irish people from British missionaries labouring in Ireland before the coming of Patrick. But was not Patrick himself a Briton ? Besides, other interpretations of the linguistic evidence have been offered. See Dr. James MacCaffrey in *Irish Theological Quarterly*, I, 1906, pp. 58–62 ; Bury, *Pat.*, p. 351, Kenney *Sources*, I, p. 160 ; Ryan, *Monast.*, p. 380.

[4] Prosper, *Liber contra Collatorem*, XXI, 2 (*PL*, LI, 271).

[5] He was in advanced age when he wrote his two *opuscula*.

[6] Pat., *Confessio*, 34, 37, 38, 41, 48, 50, 51 ; *Epistola*, 1.

little spread that the country, in the judgment of the chronicler of Aquitaine, did not merit the title of a Christian land.

Who was this Palladius, first bishop of the Scots, and what work did he accomplish ?

§ 5.—THE MISSION OF PALLADIUS

His nationality is unknown to us. We have seen that he enjoyed the confidence of Pope Celestine, who at his request determined or confirmed the mission of Germanus of Auxerre to Britain in 429.[1] Two years later he himself was consecrated bishop by the Pope and placed in charge of the nascent Church of the Scots. Of what nature were the relations between Palladius and St Germanus ? We cannot tell, nor do we even know whether Germanus himself had any share in the mission of Palladius. It has been conjectured that the latter accompanied the bishop of Auxerre to Britain and thence passed to Ireland, but that, finding it needful to strengthen himself with some additional authority, or perhaps in compliance with the wishes of the Scots who wanted him for their bishop, he returned to Rome to be consecrated.[2] But all this is pure hypothesis.

In any case, the apostolic labours of Palladius were of very short duration. Perhaps he failed in his mission ; perhaps it was his death which brought his career to a speedy end after the lapse of a few months. Be that as it may, the short-lived attempt of the " phantom missionary " [3] was soon thrown completely into the shade by the fruitful apostolate of his glorious successor.

§ 6.—THE ASSUMED IDENTITY OF PALLADIUS AND ST PATRICK

The coincidence to within about a year of the arrival of Palladius in Ireland with that of St Patrick, the relations kept

[1] On the deaconship of Palladius see Alfred Anscombe, *Professor Zimmer and the Deaconship of Palladius* (*Ériu*, IV, 1910, pp. 233–34).

[2] Cf. Pope Celestine, *Ep.* IV : " Nullus invitis detur episcopus " (*PL* L, 434).

[3] Roger's expression (*Enseignement*, p. 218). Tirechán writes that he was martyred in the land of the Scotti " *ut tradunt sancti antiqui* " (p. 31), and Nennius, that, after his return to Britain, he died " *in terra Pictorum* " (*HB*, 50, p. 195)

up by both with St Germanus of Auxerre, the successive changes of name of St Patrick, who is said to have been called in turns Sucat, Palladius, Patricius and Cothraige, while on the testimony of Tirechán, bishop Palladius himself bore the name of Patricius : these facts have led some writers, notably Heinrich Zimmer, to suggest that Palladius and Patrick were one and the same individual.[1]

It must be admitted that on the first glance the suggestion is plausible enough. But when we come to examine details we are soon led to reject it and to hold by the traditional opinion which regards them as two distinct persons.[2]

In the first place, the relations of both missionaries with St Germanus are neither well ascertained nor identical ; in the case of Palladius they are less firmly established. As for the variations in Patrick's name, they have not the weight which Zimmer assigns to them as proofs. That at the beginning of the fifth century *Cothraige* was the Irish pronunciation of the Latin *Patricius*, may be admitted. But Zimmer goes on to say that *Palladius*, derived from the name of Pallas, a goddess of war, is the Latin translation of *Sucat* " good warrior," Patrick's British name, and that consequently Patrick is identical with Palladius : this seems a far-fetched and, to say the least, a questionable assumption.[3]

The name of *Patricius*, given by Tirechán to Palladius, may be accounted for by the wish to assign a historic rôle, by equating him with Palladius, to a legendary personage, *Sen-Pátraic*, " old Patrick," who, if he ever existed, played only a shadowy part in the conversion of Ireland before the genuine St Patrick.

[1] Zimmer, *CC*, pp. 35–41. The identification theory had been advocated by several writers before Zimmer : Schoell, *De Ecclesia Brittonum Scotorumque historiae fontibus* (Berolini, 1851), p. 77 ; Loofs, *Antiquae Britonum Scotorumque Ecclesiae quales fuerint mores* (Lipsiae, 1882), p. 51 ; B. W. Wells in *EHR*, V, 1890, pp. 475–85 ; E. O'Brien and W. J. D. Croke in *Irish Ecclesiastical Record* (Aug. 1887, pp. 723–31 ; Nov., 1902, pp. 442–450).
[2] According to Muirchu, after his failure in Ireland, Palladius " returned to him that sent him. Returning then hence, he crossed the first sea (Irish sea) ; and, continuing his journey by land, he died in the country of the Britons " (p. 272).
[3] Sound critics like Bury (*Pat.*, pp. 343–44), W. Levison (*Bischof Germanus*, p. 166 ff.), Roger (*Enseignement*, p. 218) reject the identification theory.

Zimmer brings forward two other arguments. Palladius and St Patrick were, according to him, of the same nationality, both being born in Great Britain. He further adduces the fact that neither Prosper of Aquitaine nor the Venerable Bede make any mention of Patrick, both apparently being acquainted with only one apostle of Ireland, namely, Palladius.

We have seen that the native country of Palladius is absolutely unknown. It is a purely gratuitous hypothesis to make him out a Briton. In the next place, it is not in the least surprising that Prosper should have been ignorant of the doings and achievements of Patrick, who in all likelihood never quitted the distant scene of his apostolate and whose renown cannot have crossed the seas till a much later date. As for Bede, in his *Historia Ecclesiastica gentis Anglorum*, he refers to the evangelization of Ireland only incidentally, and confines himself to quoting Prosper's narrative on the subject almost word for word.[1]

For our part, then, we shall still continue to hold Palladius and Patrick for two distinct persons. We have seen how ephemeral was the apostolic career of the former. It remains to set forth the life and wonderful labours of his successor, who so well deserved the title which remains attached to his name of Apostle of the Irish.

§ 7.—LIFE OF ST PATRICK TO HIS PASSAGE TO THE CONTINENT

Patrick was born in Great Britain in the last quarter of the fourth century. He was grandson of the priest Potitus and son of the deacon Calpurnius, who was also a decurion. Calpurnius lived in the *vicus* of Banavem Taberniae, in the neighbourhood of which he worked a small farm.[2] Where are we to locate Banavem Taberniae? Certainly not far from the

---

[1] Cf. James MacCaffrey, *Rome and Ireland : Pre-Patrician Christianity* (*Irish Theological Quarterly*, I, 1906, p. 63) ; H. d'Arbois, *R. Cel.*, XXII, 1901, pp. 335–36 ; H. Williams, *ŽCP*, IV, 1903, pp. 546–47 ; Bury, *Pat.*, pp. 343–44. On the theory of the three Patricks launched by J. H. Shearman (*Loca Patriciana*, Dublin, 1879, p. 395 ff.) see B. Robert, *Étude critique sur la vie et l'œuvre de saint Patrick* (Paris, 1883), and H. d'Arbois, *Saint Patrice et Sen Patrice* (*R. Cel.*, IX, 1898, pp. 111–17).

[2] Pat., *Confessio*, 1.

sea, for it was at the little farm that young Patrick was seized by pirates. In the seventh century the name had already passed out of use. But Muirchu identifies it unhesitatingly (*indubitanter*) with a locality called *Ventre* or *Nemtrie*,[1] which is without doubt the *Nemthur* of Fiacc's hymn. According to the glossator of that hymn (eleventh century), it corresponded to the place called Ail Clúade (the cliff of the Clyde) near Dumbarton.[2] " Banavem " or " Banaven " is a name which occurs more than once in Celtic local nomenclature ; it signifies a river-mouth,[3] which very well suits a spot situated at the mouth of the Clyde. Besides, Dumbarton means " fortress of the Britons." [4] The fortress was intended to protect an important strategic point at the end of the wall of Antoninus. The military station may have given rise to a Roman-Briton municipality governed by decurions.[5] This, in my opinion, is the most likely theory that can be advanced as to the birthplace of St Patrick.

Several other places have been suggested, even outside Great Britain, in spite of the express testimony of Patrick himself, who tells us that his family inhabited Britain.[6] Bury was

---

[1] Muirchu, p. 494. Cf. F. Lot in *An. Br.*, XV, 1900, p. 514, note 4.

[2] " Nemthur, *i.e.*, a city which is among Britons of the North, viz., Ail Clúade " (*LH*, I, p. 97, II, p. 176).

[3] " I cannot help thinking that Lanigan was right in supposing that Banavem (or Banaven, as he spells it) might represent a Celtic place-name, *river's mouth* (Todd, *St Patrick*, p. 357) ; and that *taberniae* is connected with *taberna*, a tavern. It is not a fatal objection to this theory that it is inconceivable that a Celtic town should have only one *taberna* in it " (White *Patrick*, p. 111).

[4] * Duno-n Britonon. Cf. H. Maxwell, *Scottish Land-Names, their Origin and Meaning* (Edinburgh and London, 1894), p. 35 ; H. d'Arbois de Jubainville, *R. Cel.*, XV, 1894, p. 234 ; W. J. Watson, *History of the Celtic Place-names of Scotland* (London, 1926), p. 15.

[5] A view taken by T. W. Rolleston (*Hibbert Journal*, IV, 1906, pp. 450–51).

[6] " Et iterum post paucos annos in Britanniis eram cum parentibus meis " (*Confessio*, 23). " Et ita pergens in Britanniis—et libentissime paratus eram—quasi ad patriam et parentes " (*Confessio*, 43). " Patricius . . . , Brito natione, in Britannis natus " (Muirchu, p. 494). It would be an arduous task to compile a complete catalogue of the various opinions advanced as to the birthplace of St Patrick. An attempt has been made by Stephen de Leigh, *St Patrick in Britain* (*Tablet*, March 14th, 1925, pp. 340–41). Boulogne-sur-Mer, Pont-Aven (Finistère), Nanterre (Seine), Daventry (Northamptonshire), even Ireland, have found supporters. According to Michael T. McSweeney, Patrick was born at Terracina (Anxur) in Latium, a town situated at the point where the Via Appia reaches the sea (*The Birthplace of St Patrick* in *Irish Eccles. Record.* 5 Ser.,

inclined to place the saint's native spot in the shire of Glamorgan in the region of the lower Severn, where three places of the name of Banwen are found.[1] On various grounds, both philological and historical, Eoin MacNeill has likewise reached the conviction that St Patrick's birthplace is to be sought not far from the sea in the south of Wales.[2]

At the age of about sixteen Patrick was seized by pirates, who carried him off captive to Ireland with many of his compatriots.[3] We do not know to what part of the island he was taken. Perhaps it is true that he was sold to a magician or druid of the name of Miliucc, whose flocks he herded.[4]

In his *Confession* he reproaches himself bitterly with having lived up to the period of his captivity in forgetfulness of the Lord and neglect of his duties as a Christian.[5] But in the hardships of exile and servitude his heart turned towards God ; he learnt to know His mercies and to respond to His grace, and his piety was heightened. " Day by day," he says, " I used to pasture the flock and I used to pray constantly in the daytime. More and more the love of God came to me, and the fear of Him ; my faith was increased and the Spirit wrought within me ; insomuch that in a single day I would offer as many as a hundred prayers and nearly as many by night, while I abode in the fields and on the mountains. Before sunrise I used to wake to pray, in spite of snow or frost or rain, and I felt no ill, nor was there any slothfulness in me, as I now see, because the Spirit was then fervent within me." [6]

XI, 1918, pp. 265–85). According to the Rev. John E. Sexton, DD, he was born just outside Rome (*The Birthplace of St Patrick, an Essay in textual Criticism*, a paper read at the annual meeting of the American Catholic Historical Association held on December 28th to 31st, 1930, at Boston). An amusing anecdote concerning a Dublin P.P. and Dr. Lanigan in connection with this prolific source of speculation, dispute and blunders among historians and preachers alike is recorded in W. J. Fitzpatrick's *Irish Wits and Worthies, including Dr. Lanigan, his Life and Times* (Dublin, 1873), pp. 186–87.
[1] Bury, *Pat.*, p. x, 17, 322–25.
[2] Eoin MacNeill, *The Native Place of St Patrick* (PRIA, XXXVII, 1926, pp. 118–40).
[3] "Annorum eram tunc fere sedecim . . . in captiuitate abductus sum cum tot milia hominum . . ." (*Confessio*, 1).
[4] Tirechán, p. 17 ; Muirchu, p. 275.
[5] *Confessio*, 1, 2.
[6] *Confessio*, 16.

During his captivity he acquired that knowledge of the Irish language which was destined to prove so necessary to him in the future. This first captivity lasted six long years. At the end of that time he managed to escape. He reached a port two hundred miles distant where he had never yet been. There he found a vessel about to start. At first they made difficulties about taking him on board, but at last he was allowed to embark. After three days' sailing the passengers reached a desert land which it took them twenty-eight days to traverse, their provisions running short on the way.[1] Was this desert situate in Great Britain or on the Continent? We have no means of finding out, but Gaul suits the narrative of Patrick in his *Confession* better than Britain.[2] At any rate, after a considerable lapse of time Patrick was again reduced to slavery, but on this occasion for two months only.[3]

At last he returned to Great Britain and had the happiness of seeing his family once more, who welcomed him with affection and earnestly begged him, having undergone so many hardships, never to leave them again.[4] It was just then that in a vision he received his first call to evangelize Ireland—a vision which reminds us strongly of the one which St Paul had at Troas, when a man from Macedonia appeared to him and said, "Pass over into Macedonia and help us."[5] Let us leave it to Patrick himself to relate this mysterious episode of his life :

" In a vision of the night I beheld a man of the name of Victoricus coming as it were from Ireland with countless letters. And he gave me one of them, and I read the beginning of the letter with the words ' The Voice of the Irish ' ; and while reading the beginning of the letter aloud methought

---

[1] *Confessio*, 18–20, 22. The cargo of the ship may have been of dogs. Celtic hounds were highly valued in the south of Europe (Bury, *Pat.*, pp. 340–41). " Et canes eorum repleti sunt, quia multi ex illis defecerunt et secus uiam semiuiui relicti sunt " (*Confessio*, 19).

[2] Bury, *Pat.*, pp. 338–42.

[3] *Confessio*, 21. This passage is not clear (cf. White, *Patrick*, p. 114). F. R. Montgomery Hitchcock suggests that it should be regarded as a parenthesis in the narrative, and that it simply means that Patrick's treatment by the sailors was like a second captivity, not that he was taken prisoner a second time (*St Patrick and his Gallic Friends*, London, 1916, p. 52).

[4] *Confessio*, 23.

[5] *Acts*, xvi, 9.

that in the same moment I heard the voice of those who were beside the forest of Foclut which is near the western sea,[1] and they cried out as with one mouth, 'We beseech thee, holy youth, to come and walk again amongst us.' And I was deeply moved in heart and could read no further, and so I awoke. Thanks be unto God that after many years the Lord granted unto them according to their cry." [2]

This passage suggests that in the time of his captivity he had made a first attempt to evangelize the rude people around him. This was not the only vision he had. He heard voices urging him to concern himself with the salvation of others— he who for long had not even thought of his own.[3] He recalled to mind his days of trial, which, as often happens, were also days of penitence and fervour. He had sought God and had found Him.[4] He remembered the poor island in which Providence had cast him among uncivilized and barbarous people on whom the kindly light of the Gospel had not yet shone. The affection of his family was powerless to hold him back. Filled with zeal and compassion for these unhappy idolaters, he resolved to search out God's intentions concerning him, to make sure of his vocation, and also to get instruction and gain that knowledge of the Divine law and the sacred writings which he lacked—in what measure, none knew better than himself—in order that afterwards, if God still called him, he might carry out his arduous mission.[5]

§ 8.—PATRICK ON THE CONTINENT

In that age it was necessary to undertake long journeys in order to gain knowledge and become acquainted with the traditional Christian teachings. Patrick went to Gaul and travelled on to the isles of Lérins. Of these journeys there can be little doubt. In a *dictum* attributed to him, as it seems, on

---

[1] The " Silua Focluti quae est prope mare occidentale " (*Confessio*, 23) has been identified by E. MacNeill with *Silua Uluti*, the "Wood of the Ulaid," now Killultagh, east of Loch Neagh (*Silva Focluti* in *PRIA*, XXXVI, Sec. C, 1923, pp. 249-55). "Mare occidentale" must be understood from the standpoint of the writer, a Briton by birth.
[2] *Confessio*, 23.
[3] *Confessio*, 28.
[4] *Confessio*, 33.
[5] *Confessio*, 35–62.

good grounds, the saint has given us some hint as to his wanderings : " I have had," he says, " the fear of God as the guide of my journey through the Gauls and Italy, and also in the isles which are in the Tyrrhenian Sea." [1]   Elsewhere he speaks of the desire he felt towards the end of his life to return to Gaul " to visit my brethren and to behold the faces of the saints of my Lord." [2]

In the fifth century the Gulf of Genoa and even that part of the Mediterranean which washes the coast of Provence were regarded as forming part of the Tyrrhenian Sea, which geographers at the present day apparently confine between Sardinia, Corsica, the western coast of Italy, and Sicily. So that according to the geography of the time the isles of Lérins were actually in that sea. [3]   There is therefore nothing unusual in St Patrick's statement.

The monastery of Lérins had been founded in 410 by St Honoratus, and already possessed a strong attraction for religious souls. [4]   Lupus, the future companion of St Germanus in Britain, was a monk of Lérins about the time that Patrick stayed there. [5]   The Briton Faustus, future bishop of Riez, was to be elected abbot of Lérins some years later (433).

Besides Lérins the young traveller perhaps also visited several of those other solitary islets of the Tyrrhenian Sea, retreats of cenobites or anchorites, which St Ambrose gracefully compares to a necklace of pearls cast upon the waves [6]— Capraria, Gorgona, Palmaria and Gallinaria. St Martin had come between 356 and 360 to seek edification among the hermits of the last-mentioned island. [7]

Patrick says further that he went to Italy. At that period Rome and the south of the peninsula did not form part of

---

[1] *LA*, p. 17. For a critical examination of the *Dicta Patricii* see Bury, *Pat.*, pp. 228–33. The first two must be regarded as genuine.

[2] Pat., *Confessio*, 43.

[3] Cf. L.G., *Bulletin critique*, 2nd Ser., XI, 1905, pp. 694–95. The "una ex insolis quae dicitur Aralanensis" mentioned by Tirechán (p. 17) is to be identified with Lérins. Cf. Bury, *Pat.*, p. 294.

[4] " Etenim quae adhuc terra, quae natio in monasterio illius (Honorati) cives suos non habet ? " (Hilary, *Sermo de vita Honorati*, 17 : *PL*, L, 1258).

[5] Lupus left Lérins in A.D. 426 or 427 (Duchesne, *Fastes*, II, p. 453).

[6] Ambrose, *Hexameron*, III, 5 (*PL*, XIV, 165).

[7] Cf. Bury, *Pat.*, pp. 294–95.

Italy properly so called.[1] It does not seem likely that on this occasion he went as far as the Eternal City. In Muirchu' account the journey to Rome is mentioned only as an unrealized project.[2]

It was at Auxerre that Patrick seems to have stayed longest. There he was trained most likely under the direction of two bishops of eminent piety—Amator, who died about 418, and Germanus.[3] He applied himself not so much to the study of letters as to exercises of devotion and to doctrinal instruction. The Latin of his works is barbarous to a degree, but from the way he quotes the holy scriptures and draws inspiration from them it can be seen that he had made a searching study of the Bible and assimilated it thoroughly. His theological tenets are of the most orthodox type. He has left a summary of them in the *Credo* inserted in his *Confession*. Although the word *consubstantial* does not find place in it, Jesus Christ is declared " to have existed always with the Father before the beginning of time, spiritually in the bosom of the Father, ineffably engendered before all beginnings." [4]

It is possible that deacon's orders were conferred on Patrick by Amator in his last days. As far as can be judged, the young Briton spent more than fifteen years at Auxerre.[5] During these long years he was able to prepare at leisure for his future mission. On the return of St Germanus from Great Britain in 431, he would have been sure to inquire eagerly about the religious condition of his native country and, above all, about the spiritual needs of the neighbouring isle, the object of his constant thought.

[1] See H. d'Arbois, *R. Cel.*, XII, 1891, p. 292 ; XVII, 1897, p. 251.
[2] Muirchu, p. 270.
[3] In several Irish texts Germanus is called Patrick's master or tutor. See *Fél. Oeng.*, p. 126, 220–21 ; *Vita Ciarani de Saigir*, 4 (*VSH*, I, p. 219). Cf. J. Vendryes, *R. Cel.*, XXXVIII, 1920–21, p. 73.
[4] *Confessio*, 4. On the borrowing of the wording of this creed from Victorinus of Pettau in Upper Pannonia, who lived at the close of the third century see Mario Esposito, *Notes on the Latin Writings of St Patrick* (*JTS*, XIX, 1918, pp. 342–43). Some less striking parallels between Patrick's creed and that of St Irenaeus have been pointed out by Dr. F. R. Montgomery Hitchcock (*Hermathena*, XIV, 1906, pp. 168–82). Cf. White, *Patrick*, p. 112.
[5] See a tentative chronology of the life of St Patrick from 411–12 (escape from his ship-companions) to 432 (consecration by Germanus) in Bury, *Pat.*, p. 338.

It was in that same year (431), as we know, that Palladius had just been sent to the Scots by the pope himself. We do not know whether Patrick was fully informed of this mission at the start. But, in any case, at the end of a few months grave tidings reached him : Palladius had hardly begun his work in Ireland when death carried him off. It was from two disciples of the deceased missionary that he learnt the event.[1]

The field of action was now open. The Scots had lost their first bishop. Ripe for the work of an apostle, long trained by the counsels and examples which he found among the ascetic monks of the southern isles and the holy bishops of Gaul, Patrick received consecration as a bishop probably from the hands of Germanus himself,[2] and then without delay set out with some companions towards the distant island whither God was calling him.[3]

§ 9.—THE SAINT'S APOSTOLIC WORK

It was in the year 432 that Patrick set sail for Ireland.[4] It is supposed that he landed in Leinster at the mouth of the Vartry (anciently the Dee), not far from the present town of Wicklow. But he soon embarked again to coast along the eastern shore, touching at Inishpatrick and at the mouth of the Boyne, and finally reaching Ulster by way of Loch Cúan (Strangford Lough). There he converted a powerful chief named Dichu and founded the church of Sabal Pátraic, later called Saul.[5]

The conversion of a king, the head of a *tuath* or several *tuatha*, was an event of particularly happy omen. The masses often adopted Christianity in the train of their chiefs, drawn by their example. Moreover, since kings and nobles were the sole possessors of the soil, they alone could provide the mis-

---

[1] *Ebmoria*, the place where, according to Muirchu (p. 272), they met Patrick, has not yet been identified with certainty.

[2] On Muirchu's confusions of Patrick's various ordinations, and for the historical evidence concerning the events previous to his coming to Ireland, see Bury, *Pat.*, pp. 347-49, and E. J. Newell, *St Patrick, his Life and Teaching* (London, 1907), pp. 43-44.

[3] *Confessio*, 43.

[4] *AU*, *a.a.* 432 ; *Chronicon Scottorum*, ed. Hennessy (*RS*), pp. 20-23.

[5] Muirchu, p. 275.

sionary with a site whereon to build a church.[1] Thus we find Patrick everywhere setting himself first of all to convert the great.

We do not propose to follow the apostle in his manifold wanderings through the island ; to do so would indeed be impossible on account of the insufficient data we possess of his various journeys. The seventh century biographers, especially Tirechán, have collected precious local traditions as to the districts he evangelized and the churches founded in them.[2] It is not hard to believe that an ecclesiastical community should have faithfully preserved for the space of two centuries the memory not only of its foundation by the great St Patrick, but even of the more important circumstances which attended the foundation. But it is not so easy to accept the itinerary allotted to the saint by the hagiographer. Such an itinerary could be known only by means of a journal of its successive stages kept either by Patrick himself or one of his companions.[3] No such document any longer exists, and it is questionable whether any such ever existed. It has therefore been said with perfect justice that " if we attempted to follow the saint's missionary journeys on a map we should constantly encounter insuperable difficulties."[4]

It seems certain that Patrick traversed the five provinces of Ireland ; but he carried on his apostolate chiefly in those of Leinster, Ulster, Meath and Connacht. Thanks to Tirechán, we are particularly well informed of his doings in the last province. We know further that he made frequent tours in districts already evangelized.[5]

[1] Cf. Bury, *Pat.*, pp. 71–74, 176, 311.
[2] On Bishop Tirechán's homeland, sources of information, topographical sequence of his narrative and leading motive of his writings see Bury, *Tirechán's Memoir of St Patrick* (*EHR*, XVII, 1902, pp. 235–67) and *Pat.*, pp. 248–51 ; John Gwynn, *LA*, pp. xliii–lxiii ; Kenney, *Sources*, I, pp. 329–31 ; Paul Grosjean, *Recent Research on the Life of St Patrick* (*Thought*, V, 1930, pp. 22–41). On Muirchu's priority and Tirechán's authorship of the *Vita tripartita* in its original form see Eoin MacNeill's following essays : *Dates of Texts in the Book of Armagh relating to St Patrick* (*JRSAI*, LVIII, 1928, pp. 85–101), *The Origin of the Tripartite Life of St Patrick* (*JRSAI*, LIX, 1929, pp. 1–15), *The Vita Tripartita of St Patrick* (*Ériu*, XI, 1930, pp. 1–41).
[3] Bury, *EHR*, XVII, p. 266.
[4] B. Robert, *Op. cit.*, p. 77.
[5] *Pat., Confessio*, 53.

The methods employed by the missionary in his work of evangelization are of much more interest than his itineraries. The chief influence he had to contend with was that of the druids, who in Ireland were practically magicians. It was his wont, it appears, to challenge them to thaumaturgic contests, so to speak, in which each party tried to outdo the other in working wonders before the eyes of the dumbfounded crowd, the druids relying on the aid of the powers of darkness, Patrick on the grace of the Most High. This was the course he followed at Tara, at the well of Findmag, and among the sons of Amolngid.[1]

When he had succeeded in converting a certain number of pagans, he set about obtaining a site on which to build a church. He ordained on the spot one of his disciples as deacon, priest or bishop and committed to him the charge of the infant mission. Sometimes he left the care of his neophytes to monks.[2] Before taking his departure he often placed in the hands of the new converts or of their pastors a little book which Tirechán calls sometimes *elementa* (*elimenta*), sometimes *abgitorium* (abecedary), and which was most likely a compendium of Christian doctrine and the Canons.[3] Nennius records that Patrick wrote with his own hand at least three hundred and sixty-five of these *abgitoria*.[4]

It happened occasionally that the saint in one place or another gave the veil to Christian women of marked piety,[5] who thenceforth, it may be, retired to places of seclusion, or else, like the earliest Christian virgins, led a life of continence in their families.

Among the chief persons who received baptism from the hands of Patrick must be mentioned Dubthach, supreme head of the *filid*,[6] and Conall son of Niall and brother of king Loegaire, who bestowed the site on which was built Patrick's

---

[1] Tirechán, pp. 26–28 ; Muirchu, pp. 281–85.
[2] Tirechán, pp. 24, 27, 29.
[3] Tirechán, pp. 25, 26, 28, 29.
[4] Nennius, *HB*, 54 (p. 196). On *abgitoria* or *elementa* see Bury, *Pat.* p. 311.
[5] ". . . et accepit pallium de manu Patricii " (Tirechán, p. 25 (twice), 28). A " *monacha* " is mentioned by Tirechán, p. 22. Cf. *Confessio*, 42 ; *Epistola*, 12.
[6] Muirchu, p. 283 ; Additions to Tirechán's Memoir (*LA*, p. 35).

large church or Domnach Mór.[1] As for Loegaire, the high-king of Ireland, he refused to be converted. He even thought at one time of compassing Patrick's death,[2] but filled with amazement at sight of the wonders wrought by the saint at Tara to confound the druid Lucat Moel, he did not thence-forward dare to hinder him from preaching.

Loegaire desired to be buried according to the rites of his pagan ancestors. His two daughters, on the contrary, died in the Christian faith. The story of their conversion is so curious and throws so much light on Patrick's missionary methods that we cannot refrain from repeating it here.

One day at sunrise, when he was beside a spring close to Cruachan, the daughters of Loegaire, Ethne the Fair and Fedelm the Red, came to wash themselves, as was the custom of women. Seeing the clerics assembled in white vestments, they were surprised, believing them to be phantoms, and they said to Patrick, " Where is your home and whence do you come ? " And Patrick answered, " It were better to believe in God than to ask us about our race." Then the elder of the girls asked, "Who is God? Where is he? Whose God is he ? Where is his abode ? Has your God sons and daughters, gold or silver ? Does he live for ever ? Is he always beauti-ful ? Had he many fosterers for his son ? Are his daughters fair and dear to the men of the world ? Is he in heaven or on earth, in the sea or the rivers or the mountains ? How is he loved ? How is he found ? Is he young or is he old ? " And Patrick, filled with the Holy Spirit, replied, " Our God is the God of all men, the God of heaven and earth, of sea and rivers, of the sun and the moon and all the stars, the God of high mountains and low valleys. God has His dwelling-place above heaven, in heaven and below heaven, in earth and sea and all that in them is. He inspires all, He gives life to all, He is above all, He sustains all. He kindles the light of the sun

[1] Tirechán, p. 19.

[2] Muirchu, p. 285. According to Muirchu, Loegaire became a Christian, but Tirechán affirms the contrary (p. 19). The latter is right as shown by Bury (*Pat.*, p. 353). The story from Lebor na Huidre (p. 117b20), *Comthoth Lóegairi*, edited by C. Plummer (*The Conversion of Loegaire and his Death* : R. Cel., VI, 1884, pp. 162–172), is a tale destitute of historical basis. Cf. R. I. Best and Osborn Bergin, *Lebor na Huidre* (Dublin, 1929) p. xxxv.

and the light of night ; He makes springs in the thirsty land and dry islands in the sea, and He has set the stars to serve the greater lights. He has a Son coeternal with Him and like unto Him, and the Son is not younger than the Father, neither is the Father older than the Son. And the Holy Spirit breathes in them, and Father, Son and Spirit are not divided. And I desire to join you to the heavenly King, for ye are children of an earthly king." And the girls spoke as if they had but one voice and one heart, " Teach us how to believe in the heavenly King, that we may see Him face to face, and as thou sayest we will do." " Do you believe," said Patrick, " that through baptism the sin of your father and your mother is taken away ? " " We believe," they answered. " Do you believe in repentance after sin ? " " We do." " Do you believe in the life after death and the resurrection on the day of judgment ? " " We believe." " Do you believe in the unity of the Church ? " " We do." And they were baptised and a white veil was laid on their heads. But they asked that they might see God face to face. Then the saint said to them, " You cannot see the face of Christ unless you taste of death and receive the Communion." They answered, " Then give us the Communion that we may see the Son, our Bridegroom." And they received the Eucharist of God and fell asleep in death ; and they were laid on a couch under the one covering. Their friends bewailed them with loud cries, and the druids who had brought them up came to weep over them ; and Patrick preached to them and they believed in God. When the days of mourning were ended, the king's daughters were buried near the fount in a round pit such as the pagans used to make." [1]

Patrick had from his youth been fashioned in the hard school of adversity. Like all great servants of God, he had all his life to endure many discomfitures and all kinds of vio-

---

[1] Tirechán, pp. 23-24. According to Whitley Stokes, the account of the meeting with King Loegaire's daughters and of their baptism " bears internal evidence of antiquity and genuineness." He adds : " I refer in particular to the five baptismal interrogations put by the Saint ; to the mention of the chrisom-cloth, and the naïveté of the questions asked by the girls about God and His sons and daughters—questions which no mere legendmonger ever had the imagination to invent " (Vita Trip., pp. CXLII–CXLIII).

lence.[1] When he was preparing to evangelize a new district, the druids used to gather together to plot his ruin. He was exposed to outrage and persecution from unbelievers, who more than once sought to lay hold of him and put him to death.[2] To die for Christ would have been for him the height of happiness and glory. " If I have ever imitated aught of good for the sake of my God whom I love, I ask Him to allow me to shed my blood for His name along with those converts and captives, even though I should go without burial or have this miserable corpse torn limb from limb as a portion for dogs or wild beasts or devoured by the birds of heaven." [3] It did not enter into the counsels of God that the soil of Ireland at this early beginning should be watered with the blood of martyrs. Trials of another kind were reserved for Patrick ; and they were all the more painful to him because they came from his fellow-believers and even, it would seem, from priests, his fellow-workers.

There were persons whom he calls his elders, *seniores mei*, who took advantage of some fault which he had committed at the age of fifteen and confessed before being made deacon, in order to cast discredit on his laborious episcopate and to trample him under foot.[4] Even his best friend was not afraid to dishonour him openly.[5] It was to justify himself in the eyes of these accusers that in his old age he wrote his admirable *Confession*. In it he thanks God who has delivered him out of all his distress and deigned to make use of him to accomplish great things, to preach the Gospel even in the land beyond which no man lives.

His other work, the *Epistola*, is addressed to the soldiers of Coroticus, the British prince of Strathclyde,[6] a Christian by

[1] *Epistola*, 12 ; *Confessio*, 35–37.
[2] *Confessio*, 52 ; Muirchu, p. 285 ; Tirechán, p. 28.
[3] *Confessio*, 59. Cf. 37.
[4] *Confessio*, 26.
[5] *Confessio*, 27, 29.
[6] " Coroticus " (*Epistola*, 2, 6, etc.) is called " Coirthech regem Aloo " by Muirchu (p. 271). Rex Aloo = " King of the Rock," *i.e.*, of Ail Clúade (in British *Alclut*), " the Rock of the Clyde." Cf. Watson, *History of the Celtic Place-names of Scotland*, p. 33. " *Ceretic gueletic* appears in the pedigree of the princes of Strathclyde at a point consistent with the floruit here suggested, viz., A.D. 450 " (Lloyd, *HW*, I, p. 126). See J. Loth, *R. Cel.*, XLVI, 1929, p. 2 ; XLVII, 1930, pp. 181–82. About the words

baptism but a heathen in conduct, who in a raid on the Irish coast had massacred believers and taken captive a number of converts anointed only the day before with the holy chrism. With accents of the liveliest grief the apostle protests against these hateful acts of violence ; he weeps and laments for his sons and daughters carried off to distant lands where iniquity abounds, among the Picts, worthless and evil backsliders ; and he implores that they may be restored to him.

With the help of these two works, we can discern the prominent traits of the great apostle's religious temperament. He recognizes the success which has crowned his efforts and declares it marvellous ; he has caught a multitude of souls in his nets. But he is careful not to ascribe these amazing results to his own weakness ; he gives all the credit to the grace of God, the source for him of light and strength. His humility, his simplicity, the candour of his soul are revealed in almost every line of his writings. He constantly speaks of himself as a sinner, rustic and ignorant. " I was like a stone which lies in deep mire. He that is mighty came and in His mercy took me and of a truth lifted me up and placed me on the top of the wall." [1] He is filled with distrust of self and the fear of God, consumed to the uttermost with apostolic zeal. Certainly it was no worldly motives which made him come to Ireland ; rather was it the Gospel and its promises which drew him to that idolatrous land, from which in times gone by he had had such difficulty in escaping. It was his robust faith and his unshaken trust in God that sustained him among the countless trials of his hard career.

It is easy to understand the charm which such a nature, ardent, strong and tender, steeped in a faith which in danger stood him in lieu of armour, must have exercised over spirits fierce and withal childlike. Most certainly he did not succeed in converting all the heathens of the island [2] ; but he won so

---

of Patrick speaking of the soldiers of Coroticus " non dico ciuibus meis atque ciuibus sanctorum Romanorum, etc.," [see White, *Patrick* (p. 119), and E. MacNeill, *The Native Place of St Patrick* (*PRIA*, XXXVII, Sec. C. 1926, p. 134).

[1] *Confessio*, 12.

[2] Note in Stowe Missal (first decade of the ninth century) the words : " adque omnem populum ab idulorum cultura eripias et ad té deum uerum patrem omnipotentem conuertas " (*Stowe*, p. 12), written by one of

many of them for Christ, he founded so many churches, ordained so many clerics, kindled such a zeal in men's hearts, that it seems right to believe that to him was directly due the wonderful out-blossoming of Christianity which distinguished Ireland in the following ages.

He had helpers of different nationalities. Tirechán speaks of Gauls and Franks.[1] An eighth century text, the *Catalogue of the Saints of Ireland*, mentions in addition Romans, Britons and Scots.[2]

Of one of Patrick's British disciples we hear from Adamnán, the *quidam proselytus Brito homo sanctus*, Mochta, whom Patrick settled at Ardpatrick in the east of Louth.[3] The nationality of Auxilius is unknown ; another disciple, Iserninus, was an Irishman.[4] Both, it is said, accompanied Patrick on the Continent in the period of his clerical training, but did not join him in Ireland till the year 439.[5] " Auxilius and Iserminus," says James F. Kenney, " were contemporaries of Patricius who have escaped in some degree the activities of the myth-makers. They are noticed in the annals ; they were sent into Ireland as bishops to assist Patricius in 439, and died in 459 and 468 respectively. The name of Auxilius is commemorated in the church of Cell-Usailli or Auxili, now Killossy or Killashee, near Naas. To Iserninus, whose Irish name is given as Fith, are ascribed the foundations of Cell-Chuilind (Kilcullen) in Kildare and Ath-Fithot (Ahade) in Carlow." [6]

Among the other natives of Ireland whom Patrick joined with him in his work must be named Benén (Benignus), his

the earliest hands. " The conventional picture of an Ireland transformed instantaneously by St Patrick from a Salvage Island to an Island of Saints is only fit for the nursery " (E. J. Gwynn, *Some Saints of Ireland* in *Church Quarterly Review*, LXXIV, 1912, pp. 74–75).

[1] Tirechán, pp. 17, 18.
[2] *Catalogus*, pp. 292–93.
[3] Adam., *Vita Col.* Praef, II, p. 4 ; *Vita Trip.*, pp. 226–28. According to *AU* (*a.a.* 534, 536), Mauchteus died in A.D. 535 or 537. A work by Mochtae was quoted in the *Liber Cuanach* (*AU*, *a.a.* 471), and the opening words of a letter (now lost) of his are given *a.a.* 534.
[4] His native name was Fith (Additions to Tirechan's Memoir : *LA*, p. 35).
[5] *AU*, *a.a.* 439 ; Additions to Tirechán's Memoir, *l. cit.* Cf. Bury, *Pat.*, p. 348.
[6] Kenney, *Sources*, I, pp. 169–70.

successor in the see of Armagh,[1] and Fiacc, bishop of Slébte (Sletty, Co. Leix).[2]

It is possible that popular tradition has attached to Patrick's outstanding personality many of the doings of his companions and disciples. Only to the rich do men lend. However, the writings of the saint are fortunately at hand to bear witness to his own activity. The *Catalogue of Saints* above mentioned divides the most illustrious saints of Ireland into three classes. The first comprises the companions and immediate successors of Patrick. "They," it says, "were very holy and filled with the Holy Spirit. They had only one head, Christ, and only one chief, Patrick." [3]

A good many historians have sought to represent Christianity as making easy way among the Celts, thanks to the accommodating temper of their apostles.[4] The latter, they aver, were not unduly disturbed by the remnants of paganism which remained mingled with Christian beliefs. " No race," Renan declares, " took over Christianity with so much originality. . . . The Church did not feel herself bound to be hard on the caprices of religious imagination, but gave fair scope to the instincts of the people, and from this liberty there resulted a cult perhaps the most mythological and the most analogous to the mysteries of antiquity to be found in the annals of Christianity."[5]

Without denying that the Celtic peoples remained strongly attached to many superstitious practices, we find it hard to accept Renan's estimate of the attitude adopted by the apostles of the British Isles towards paganism. St Patrick, as we have seen, exerted himself to the utmost of his power to

---

[1] Tirechán, p. 18. Some poems agree in ascribing to him the original codification of the *Book of Rights*, and tradition associates him also with the compilation of the *Senchus Mór* (Eoin MacNeill, *Celtic Ireland*, pp. 84–85. Cf. Paul Grosjean, *De S. Benigno commentarius praevius :* Boll., *AS*, Nov. IV, pp. 166, 180).

[2] Muirchu, p. 283. Cf. Kenney, *Sources*, I, p. 340.

[3] *Catalogus*, p. 292.

[4] John Rhys, *Lectures on the Origin and Growth of Religion as Illustrated by Celtic Heathendom* (The Hibbert Lectures for 1886), London, 1888, p. 224 ; A. Nutt, *The Celtic Doctrine of Re-birth*, in *The Voyage of Bran* (London, 1897), II p. 101.—Views expressed by Bury, *Pat.* (pp. 76–78), Joyce, *Social hist.*, I, p. 173 note, and Newell, *St Patrick* (p. 200) are sounder.

[5] E. Renan, *Essais de morale et de critique* (Paris, 1890), pp. 437–38, 442.

fight the druids and root out idolatrous customs. As long as the claims of religion were not in question, he made it his care to conform with the customs of the country and to show a conciliatory spirit.[1] But to believe him capable of any compromise with paganism on the ground of doctrine is to misunderstand the whole character of his work. Besides, we have texts which bear explicitly on the subject. The *Senchus Mór* tells us that when he made alliance with the *filid* he required of them that they should renounce any practice that could not be carried out without sacrificing to false gods. " He did not leave them any rite of which an offering to the Devil formed part." [2] And, according to *Cormac's Glossary*, he said that " whosoever continued to observe these old rites would have neither heaven nor earth, for that to practise them was to renounce baptism." [3]

In 444, so it is believed, Patrick founded the see of Armagh, which was destined one day to become the primatial see of Ireland.[4] Some years previously he is said to have visited Rome, but this journey is very doubtful.[5] His death is believed to have taken place in the year 461.[6]

Armagh, Downpatrick and Saul (not to mention Glastonbury) have claimed to possess Patrick's remains.[7] With more discretion the Book of Armagh, in the passage in which a parallel is drawn between Moses and the apostle of Ireland, says : " *Ubi sunt ossa eius nemo novit.*" [8]

§ 10.—POSTHUMOUS FAME : THE OLDEST TESTIMONIES

The cult devoted by the Irish to Patrick's memory is well known. For having annexed the isle of the Scots to the king-

---

[1] Pat., *Confessio*, 13.
[2] *Ancient Laws and Institutes of Ireland*, I, p. 44.
[3] Cormac's Glossary, 136, ed. K. Meyer, *Anecdota from Irish Manuscripts*, IV, p. 64. Cf. H. d'Arbois, *Introduction à l'étude de la littérature celtique* (Paris, 1883), pp. 158–59.
[4] Cf. Bury, *Pat.*, p. 308.
[5] Cf. Mario Esposito, *Notes* (*JTS*, XIX, 1918, p. 344) ; Warren (*EHR*, XXI, 1906, p. 348) ; F. R. Montgomery Hitchcock, *JTS*, VIII, 1906, pp. 91–95). According to Bury (*Pat.*, pp. 367–69), the journey to Rome took place in A.D. 441.
[6] Cf. Bury, *Pat.*, pp. 382–84 ; E. MacNeill, *Phases*, p. 222.
[7] See H. J. Lawlor, *Rosslyn Missal* (*HBS*), pp. xiv–xix.
[8] Fol. 15ᵛ (*LA*, p. 30). " . . . sepulchrum illius nemo scit, sed in occulto humatus est nemine sciente " (Nennius., *HB*, p. 198).

dom of God, in the midst of many hardships and tribulations, with a Christian heroism which has never been equalled, his people have honoured and blessed him throughout the ages as no other national saint has ever been honoured and blessed.[1]

Testimonies are not wanting to prove the antiquity of the cult bestowed on his memory both in Ireland and in foreign centres where Irish influence has been felt. The oldest text exalting Patrick is the Latin hymn attributed to Secundinus (Sechnall), one of his followers ; it was composed perhaps as early as the fifth century, probably in the sixth (in any case, certainly before the end of the seventh).[2] In his letter to Segéne, abbot of Iona, and Beccán, a recluse, written in 632 or 633, Cummian speaks of " Sanctus Patricius, noster papa." [3] The saint's name has a place of honour in the law-treatise *Córus Béscna*, one of the books of the *Senchus Mór*, written most likely in the second half of the seventh century.[4]

Later such testimonies are multiplied. We have a passage in the Life of St Gertrude of Nivelles, the oldest text which mentions Patrick's *natale* on March 17 (the saint died in A.D. 659, and her Life was written about 670) [5] ; we have the hagiographical works of Muirchu and Tirechán (last quarter of the seventh century), which, it will be hereafter seen, are based on specified traditions and biographical documents ; further, the so-called hymn of Fiacc, composed in the seventh or eighth century.[6] The saint's name appears once in the writings of Adamnán, abbot of Iona (†704),[7] in

---

[1] See a not altogether satisfactory book by S. Czarnowski, *Le culte des héros et ses conditions sociales : Saint Patrick, héros national de l'Irlande* (Travaux de l'année sociologique publiés sous la direction de M. E. Durkheim, Paris, 1920).

[2] *An. Ban.*, II, pp. 14–16. Cf. Kenney, *Sources*, I, pp. 258–60.

[3] Cummian, *DCP*, 975.

[4] *Anc. Laws and Institutes of Ireland* (Dublin, 1873), III, pp. 28, 30. Cf. E. MacNeill, *The Fifteenth Centenary of St Patrick* (*Studies*, XIII, 1924, p. 179).

[5] *Vita Gertrudis*, 7, ed. B. Krusch (*MG., Scr. RM.*, II, p. 463). For the date of the *Vita* see p. 448.

[6] *LH*, I, pp. 96–103, II, pp. 31–35. E. MacNeill regards that hymn as the work of Aed (†700), the successor of Fiacc in the see of Slébte : *The Earliest Lives of St Patrick* (*JRSAI*, LVIII, 1928, pp. 1–21).

[7] Adam., *Vita Col.*, Praef. II, p. 4.

verses by Cellanus, abbot of Péronne (†706),[1] in the treatise entitled *Ratio de cursus* (sic) *qui fuerunt ex auctores* (sic), also probably composed in the eighth century,[2] as well as the *Catalogus Sanctorum Hiberniae*, in which, as has been seen, Patrick—*superno oraculo edoctus*—is given as the chief of the first order of Catholic saints.[3]

To these panegyrics of the saint in hagiography, law and literature we must not forget to add liturgical honours of even greater significance. Patrick's *natale*, fixed on March 17,[4] is given under that date in the Calendar of St Willibrord (beginning of the eighth century),[5] in a fragmentary calendar of ·Luxeuil (eighth century),[6] and, as might be expected, in the earliest Irish martyrologies, that of Tallaght [7] and the Félire of Oengus, both composed at Tallaght, the latter between the years 797 and 808, the former a little earlier.[8] The Félire, which is a metrical martyrology, has a quatrain for each day in the year. The following quatrain is found at March 17: "The flame of a splendid sun, the apostle of virginal Erin, may Patrick, with many thousands, be the shelter of our wretchedness." And again in the Epilogue are invoked "the troop of the noble saints of Erin, with Patrick who is highest" (Stan. 277).[9]

Between 680 and 691, the compiler of the Antiphonary of Bangor inserted in that book Sechnall's hymn, in the title of which Patrick is called *Magister Scottorum*.[10]

---

[1] Ed. L. Traube, *Vorlesgunen*, III, p. 107 ; ed. Kuno Meyer, *Ériu*, V, 1911, p. 110.

[2] *Cursus*, p. 163.

[3] *Catalogus*, p. 292. Cf. 293-94.

[4] "Septima decima martii die translatus est Patricius ad caelos" (Note written by the scribe Ferdomnach in A.D. 807 in the Book of Armagh, fol. 24ᵛ [*LA*, p. 48]).

[5] "Sancti patrici episcopi in scotia" (ed. H. A. Wilson [*HBS*], p. 5).

[6] Ed. Martène and Durand, *Thesaurus*, III, 1592 ; ed. Br. Krusch (*NA*, X, 1885, p. 92). See also some eighth-century *codices pleniores* of the Hieronymian Martyrology and some posterior recensions (*Martyrologium Hieronymianum*, ed. De Rossi and L. Duchesne : Boll., *AS*, Nov. II, 1, [p. 33]).

[7] Ed. R. I. Best and H. J. Lawlor (*HBS*), p. 24.

[8] R. Thurneysen, *Die Abfassung des Félire von Óengus* (*ZCP*, VI, 1907, pp. 6-8).

[9] Ed. Whitley Stokes (*HBS*), pp. 82, 277.

[10] Ed. Warren (*HBS*), II, pp. 14-16. The title in *LH* is *Incipit ymnu sancti patricii episcopi scotorum* (I, p. 7).

Tirechán speaks of the receipt of a *Missa Patricii* by the church of Achadfobuir (Aghagower) in Connacht.[1] Are we to understand by this a Mass composed by Patrick or one composed in his honour on the celebration of his festival ? The most likely interpretation of the words appears to us to be the celebration of the Mass according to Patrick's use, not the saint's festival on March 17 or a proper Mass in his honour, since the receipt of the *Missa Patricii* seems to have taken place at Achadfobuir in Patrick's lifetime. But in the eleventh century the chronicler Marianus Scottus, who uses the term " Missa sancti Michaelis " in the sense of " Michaelmas " in English, also employs the words " Missa sancti Patricii " to denote the festival of March 17.[2]

St Patrick is invoked in a very old colophon in the Book of Durrow,[3] in a liturgical text of Irish origin of the eighth or ninth centuries (MS. Harl. 7653, f. 7ᵛ).[4] The saint's name figures no less than four times in the ordinary of the Mass in the Stowe Missal (first decade of the ninth century), the fourth occurrence being in the embolism of the Pater (*Libera nos, Domine*),[5] as is also the case in a liturgical fragment in the Library of St. Gall (Stiftsbibl. 1394, iv. 97, ninth century ?).[6]

No other Celtic saint has been so much venerated in Ireland, nor from so remote a period. And in speaking of the oldest testimonies, it must not be forgotten that we are dealing with

---

[1] " . . . et missam Patricii acceperunt " (Tirechán, p. 26).—Note the following lines in the Book of Armagh (fol. 16ʳ) : " Patricius sanctus episcopus honorem quaternum omnibus monasteriis et aeclessiis per totam Hiberniam debet habere, id est, 1. Solempnitate dormitationis eius honorari in medio ueris per tres dies et tres noctes omni bono cibo praeter carnem . . . 11. Offertorium eius proprium in eodem die immolari, etc." (*LA*, p. 31).

[2] " Missa S. Patricii " (*Chronicon, a.a.* 1079 [MLVII], *PL*, CXLVII, 786) ; " Missa S. Michaelis " (*Ib., a.a.* 1094 [MLXXII], col. 789). Cf. L.G., *The Liturgical Year in English Garb* (*Month*, CLV, 1930, pp. 320–22, 327).

[3] MS. T. C. Dublin, 57 [A. 4, 5], fol. 12ᵛ. See W. M. Lindsay, *The Colophon of the Durrow Book*, a note appended to Lawlor, *Cathach*, pp. 403–407. Cf. L.G., *Les scribes monastiques d'Irlande au travail* (*RHE*, XXVII, 1931, p. 296) ; Kenney, *Sources*, I, pp. 324, 631.

[4] *An. Ban.*, II, p. 86.

[5] (*a*) In the litany (*Stowe*, p. 14 ; see note 2) ; (*b*) after *Memento etiam, Domine* (p. 15 ; see note 6) ; (*c*) in the prayer *Nobis quoque* (p. 16) ; (*d*) in the prayer *Libera nos* (p. 17).

[6] Ed. Warren, *Lit.*, p. 177.

the oldest texts known, those which have escaped the numerous agents of destruction in the course of centuries. How many others have perished ! " It is a well known error," a judicious critic has written on the subject of the hagiographical works of Muirchu and Tirechán, " to regard the date of the first attestation of any fact to be the date of the fact itself ; so in the present case we have intimations that the records called by Zimmer the ' earliest ' seem to be such simply because they are the earliest that have survived to us." And again, " It is difficult, on such grounds, not to conclude that these two ' earliest ' records were preceded by a mass of more or less imperfect writings, as well as a volume of tradition going back to the time, or nearly so, of St Patrick himself." [1]

[1] H. Williams, *Heinrich Zimmer on the History of the Celtic Church* (*ZCP*, IV, 1903, pp. 557, 559).

CHAPTER III

THE EXPANSION OF CHRISTIANITY— MONASTICISM

§ 1.—Lives of the Celtic Saints : their Worth and their Character

THE Lives of Irish, British and Breton saints form our most abundant source for the history of the Celtic Churches after they had reached full development, that is to say, from the sixth to the end of the eighth century. A copious literature sprang up dealing with the saints whose activity was specially remarkable during that period. Unfortunately, the greater number of these Lives were written some three, four or five centuries later than the persons whose doings they profess to record [1]; moreover, they too often startle us by their glaring improbabilities, their puerilities and anachronisms. Another cause of confusion is the fact that many Irish saints bore the same name ; there are ever so many St Fintans, St Molaisses and St Colmáns on record.[2] When, therefore, we come across a casual reference to a saint possessed of several homonyms in the Life of some other saint, it will be readily understood that it is difficult to identify him with any certainty.

Everywhere in the Middle Ages men's imaginations were avid of the marvellous. But there was perhaps no people whose taste for the extraordinary and the fantastic was so

---

[1] It is notably the case for the Latin Lives of Welsh Saints edited by W. J. Rees in *CBS* ; for the Latin Lives of Irish Saints edited by De Smedt and De Backer in *Sal. ASH* (cf. H. Zimmer, *Göttingische gelehrte Anzeigen,* 1891, pp. 153–200), by C. Plummer in *VSH* ; for the Irish Lives of Irish Saints edited by Whitley Stokes in *Lismore* and by C. Plummer in *BNE.* —C. Plummer has compiled a most useful *Tentative Catalogue of Irish Hagiography* (*Subsidia hagiographica,* XV : *Miscellanea hagiographica Hibernica,* Bruxelles, Soc. des Bollandistes, 1925, pp. 171–285).

[2] See lists of homonymous saints in the Book of Leinster (pp. 366 *e* 30–369 *c* 23).

keen as that of the Celts.[1] All their literature, religious as well as secular, bears witness to this pronounced trait of their national genius. The author of a saint's Life was naturally led to embroider the bare background of his narrative with patterns borrowed from legend in order to gratify the propensities of his readers.

And, after all, why should we reproach the hagiographers for their shortcomings as witnesses ? Their aim in writing was by no means to fulfil the office of the historian. The methods on which the modern historian prides himself were altogether foreign to their purpose, as well as to the demands of the public for whom they wrote. Their sole object was to provide edification by means of narratives abounding in marvellous incidents or striking traits of virtue, calculated to impress the mind of the reader and stir up his feelings to reverence and emulation. It would be doing them great injustice to judge their naïve productions by the severe canons of modern criticism.

In many Irish hagiographical narratives the Christian miracle takes the place of the traditions, mythological or tribal, of the secular legends [2] ; and numerous are the points of resemblance between the methods of the miracle-working saint and those of the magician of pre-Christian times.[3]

The Life of an Irish saint is a series of episodes, nearly always miraculous in nature, interspersed with prophecies, benedictions and maledictions all intended to glorify the subject of the biography and demonstrate his power.[4] If we set aside the miracles, information of a strictly biographical order is very scanty.

It is usually the further aim of the hagiographer to set forth prominently the tributes, privileges and rights of all kinds

[1] For the view of the Irish Jesuit Stephen White on the matter see De Buck, *L'archéologie irlandaise au couvent de Saint-Antoine de Padoue à Louvain* (*Études publiées par la compagnie de Jésus*, XXII, 1869, p. 597), and Adrien Baillet, *Les vies des saints* (Paris, 1704, I, pp. 62–63).

[2] E. J. Gwynn, *Some Saints of Ireland* (*Church Quarterly Review*, LXXIV, 1912, pp. 64–66).

[3] E. J. Gwynn, *art. cit.*, pp. 77 ff ; Kenney, *Sources*, I, pp. 202 ff.

[4] On the maledictory powers of Irish saints see C. Plummer, *VSH*, I, pp. CLXXIII–CLXXIV (*introd.*) ; P. Power, *Early Christian Ireland* (Dublin, 1925), pp. 100–101 ; of Welsh saints, Giraldus, *IK*, I, 2 ; II, 7 (pp. 27, 130).

which the successor (*comarba*) of the saint who founded a monastery claims as his due throughout the entire extent of the *paruchia* [1] ; as well as the ties of confraternity, or of subordination, existing between the different monasteries of the *paruchia*.[2]

However, we should be deprived of much useful information, often unique in its kind, were we summarily to reject all the literature of this class. We possess some comparatively ancient Lives of Breton saints ; one—that of St Samson—of the seventh century ; several of the ninth, including two Lives of St Malo, one of St Turianus (Turiau), one of St Winwalloc (Winwaloeus, Guénolé) by Wrdisten, one of St Paul Aurelian by Wrmonoc. A Life of St Maglorius and one of St Tutwal (Tugdual) belong perhaps also to the ninth or the following century. The Life of St Conwoïon was written in the tenth century.[3] It is true that in order to disentangle the historical element—generally minute—in these Lives, we have to peruse many pages filled with what a writer of the eleventh century called the *Britannica garrulitas* [4] ; but, after all, is garrulity a defect wholly monopolized by the hagiographers of the Armorican peninsula ? [5]

The majority of the Lives of Irish saints were drawn up after the Viking epoch, most of them indeed in the age which followed the Anglo-Norman invasion. However, some are fairly early. We possess several belonging to the seventh century : the *Vita Columbani* of Jonas of Bobbio, written on the Continent, Adamnán's *Vita Columbae*, the *Vita Brigidae* of Cogitosus, another Life of the same saint perhaps even of anterior date,[6] and, finally, the Patrician records of Muirchu and Tirechán preserved in the Book of Armagh.[7] Generally speaking, the Lives of Irish saints composed in Latin represent

[1] *VSH*, p. xcii (*introd.*) ; Kenney, *Sources*, I, pp. 299–301 ; Paul Grosjean, *Recent Research on the Life of St Patrick* (*Thought*, V, 1930, p. 35).

[2] *VSH*, p. xci (*introd.*).

[3] On the Breton hagiographical literature see Duine, *Memento* (1918), *Inventaire* (1922).

[4] Vitalis, *Vita Pauli Aureliani*, Praef. 1 (Boll., *AS*, Mart., II, p. 111).

[5] Duine, *Memento*, p. 61.

[6] The *Vita prima anonyma* of the Bollandists (Colgan's *Tertia Vita*), as suggested by M. Esposito, *Latin Learning*, I, pp. 256–57.

[7] See Eoin MacNeill, *Dates of Texts in the Book of Armagh relating to St Patrick* (*JRSAI*, LVIII, 1928, pp. 85–101).

an earlier tradition than those in Irish.[1] However, among the latter there is one the study of which must not be neglected, the *Tripartite Life* of Patrick, which has reached us in a recension of the end of the ninth century.[2]

Apart from the *Vita Columbae* of Adamnán, the only hagiographical literature available for Scotland is of late origin and inconsiderable value.

Of late provenance also and of doubtfully genuine character are the Latin Lives of Welsh saints which have come down to us. We may mention two : that of David of Menevia by Rhygyfarch (written about 1079)[3] and that of Cadoc of Llancarvan, the work of a certain Lifris, who also flourished in the second half of the eleventh century.[4] All the Welsh Lives published by W. J. Rees in 1853 are largely fabulous in content and have been deplorably edited.[5]

Such a Life as that of Columba of Iona by Adamnán gives information of very definite value on certain aspects of monasticism ; and even from Lives strongly tinged with legend it is not impossible, we believe, to disengage some historical facts. When it is a question of the foundation of a monastery or a celebrated school by some great British or Irish monk, or of journeys made by an Irishman to Wales or a Welshman to Ireland—journeys which are often of great use in determining the line of descent of ascetic doctrines or accounting for the propagation of knowledge—there is no reason for entrenching ourselves in absolute scepticism. In a matter of that sort a

[1] Kenney, *Sources*, I, pp. 294-95.
[2] Kathleen Mulchrone, *Die Abfassungszeit und Ueberlieferung der Vita Tripartita* (*ZCP*, XVI, 1926, pp. 1-94). Cf. E. MacNeill, *The Origin of the Tripartite Life of St Patrick* (*JRSAI*, LIX, 1909, pp. 1-15), s.a. *The Vita Tripartita of St Patrick* (*Ériu*, XI, 1930, pp. 1-41).
[3] Ed. Rees, *CBS* (pp. 117-44) together with an English translation (418-38) ; ed. A. W. Wade-Evans in *YC*, XXIV, 1913, pp. 4-28 ; English translation by the same author, *Life of St David* (London, 1923).
[4] Ed. Rees, *CBS* (pp. 22-96). Lifris (Lifricus) was probably the son of Bishop Herwald of Llandaff († 1104). Cf. Chevalier, *Essai*, p. 263.
[5] Kuno Meyer has published a collation of *CBS* in *YC* (XIII, 1900, pp. 76-96). On Rees' " most unsatisfactory performance, teeming with blunders " see Egerton Phillimore (*YC*, XI, 1892, pp. 127-29) ; J. Loth (*R. Cel.*, XX, 1899, p. 207 ; XXIII, 1906, p. 150) ; E. J. Newell, *A History of the Welsh Church* (London, 1895), pp. 39-47 ; Lot, *Mélanges*, p. 274 ; Wade-Evans, *David*, p. xi.—On the Welsh hagiographical literature see Williams, *Christianity*, pp. 300-303 ; Chevalier, *Essai*, pp. 262-65.

pure invention on the narrator's part would have clashed with the local traditions, which, it may be supposed, were still alive and flourishing even after a considerable lapse of time and substantially true on such points of major importance, and would have called forth protest and denial. Finally, as regards journeys undertaken from one island to the other for the purpose of acquiring ascetic or scientific training, it is fortunately possible in several cases to check the statements of the hagiographers of one country by those of another or, what is still more satisfactory, to corroborate the basis of fact in the Lives by the aid of the Annals or other non-hagiographical writings.[1]

Again, these Lives supply us with useful information concerning the remnants of paganism, the superstitious practices, the folklore and the social conditions of the period to which they refer or else of the writer's own times.[2]

Let us finally draw attention to another feature of Celtic hagiography, to wit, the large space allotted in it to scenes of nature, familiar or picturesque, and to animals, which are represented at the saint's beck and call. On this subject Jacques Chevalier has said : " Celtic Christianity, sombre and forbidding in aspect, often violent and of mixed nature, reveals itself, on closer acquaintance, as animated throughout by the love of nature and of native country, by a winning familiarity with our ' unknown brothers,' animals or angels, and by ardent passion for spirituality." [3] From materials furnished by these Lives it would be easy to compile a delightful collection of anecdotes and legends, a forerunner of the *Fioretti*.[4]

---

[1] " The Lives must be tested by the annals, not vice versa " (Plummer, *VSH*, I, p. xcv).

[2] *VSH*, I, p. xciii. Cf. L. G., *Modern Research* (Dublin, 1929), pp. 14–18.

[3] Chevalier, *Essai*, p. 276.

[4] On the feeling for nature in the Lives of saints and the friendly intercourse between Celtic saints and animals, the reader may be referred to C. Plummer, *VSH*, I, pp. cxliii–cxlvii ; F. Duine, *Memento*, pp. 46–47 ; Irène Snieders, *L'influence de l'hagiographie irlandaise sur les Vitae des saints irlandais de Belgique* (*RHE*, XXIV, 1928, pp. 624–25) ; Gerard Murphy, *The Origin of Irish Nature Poetry* (*Studies*, XX, 1931, pp. 87–102). Cf. L. G. in *RHE*, XXVII, 1931, p. 700.—Miss Maud Joynt's book, *The Golden Legends of the Gael* (Dublin, *n. d.*), contains but three Christian legends. What a charming continuation of this book could be compiled from Irish hagiographical sources !

§ 2.—Origin and Development of the Monastic Life in Great Britain

There can be no doubt, as we have seen, that Pelagius was a monk. The difficulty is to find out in what monastery he lived, if indeed at that period every monk was necessarily attached to a monastery in the modern sense of the word.[1] We do not know of any monastery in the British Isles whose existence goes back to such early times. It is, however, possible that Pelagius did not embrace the religious life till he had left Britain.

We know that St Athanasius, who was thoroughly conversant with the monastic customs of the East, was exiled for the first time to Trèves in 336–337. He had not yet written his *Life of St Antony*, which he probably did not compose till during his third exile in Upper Egypt between 356 and 362.[2] This work was written at the request of the monks of the West and dedicated to them. It exercised an extraordinary influence over its readers and contributed powerfully to the development of monastic life in our part of the world.[3] Was its influence felt as far as Britain ?

St Athanasius, as we have seen, had information touching the doctrinal condition of the British Church. Rouen at the end of the fourth century possessed a monastery of men and a *chorus virginum*. St Victricius, the bishop of Rouen, according to the statement of his biographer, may have borrowed the Rule of his monks from Trèves.[4] Perhaps Victricius himself carried to Great Britain some seeds of the monasticism which had sprung from the teachings of St Athanasius.

The Britons were not afraid of long journeys. In St Jerome's time they willingly set out on pilgrimage to the Holy Places.[5] A pilgrimage of this kind generally involved a

---

[1] Μοναστήριον, originally means a place where one lives alone, which is exactly the opposite of the evolved meaning of the term.

[2] See *RB*, VIII, 1891, p. 56. On the authorship of St Athanasius see Ryan, *Monast.*, p. 16.

[3] Augustine, *Confessiones*, VIII, 6.—The *Vita Antonii* had been translated into Latin, *c.* A.D. 380 (Cuthbert Butler, *The Lausiac History of Palladius* in *Texts and Studies*, VI, I, p. 249).

[4] E. Vacandard, *Saint Victrice*, pp. 50–54.

[5] Paula and Eustochium, *Ep. ad Marcellam* among Jerome's *Epistolae* 46, § 10, ed. Hilberg (*Corp. SEL*, LIV, 340), ed. Migne (*PL*, XXII, 489). Jerome

digression, either going or coming, to the hermits of Egypt, whose angelic life aroused the wonder of the West ; moreover, Palestine itself was rich in monasteries.[1] Among the foreigners whom St Simeon Stylites, " miracle of the universe," as he is called by Cyril of Scythopolis,[2] drew to the foot of his pillar, were many Britons ; a fact we learn from Theodoret of Cyrrhus, who wrote during the lifetime of the Stylite.[3]

All this meant frequent opportunities of contact between the people of the West and the East, not to speak of the journeys which have left no trace in history.

The missions of St Germanus of Auxerre had not, as their sole result, to lead the British Church back to orthodoxy ; they also contributed to the development of monasticism in Britain. A document of the eighth century attributes to him as well as to St Lupus of Troyes the introduction of the *cursus* of Lérins into these islands.[4] Unlike his companion, Germanus had not himself been a monk ; but, owing to the influence of Trèves, Lérins and Tours, monasticism had made such remarkable progress in the Gaul of his day that it seems likely he endeavoured to assure its development on the far side of the Channel. As a matter of fact, the biographer of St Samson speaks of a British monastery which was supposed to have been founded by Germanus.[5] The same writer relates that the Gaulish bishop ordained as priest, no doubt on the occasion of his second visit (447), Illtud, *egregius magister Britannorum,*[6] " the first great abbot of the British Church," [7] who had for his disciples St Samson, St Paulus

says that the Britons were acquainted with the *xenodochium* founded by Fabiola at Ostia (*Ep.* 77, § 10, ed. Hilberg, LV, 47, ed. Migne, *PL,* XXII, 697).

[1] L. Duchesne, *Histoire ancienne de l'Église,* II (Paris, 1907), pp. 512–18.

[2] *Vita Euthymii magni,* xiv, 84 (Boll., *AS,* Jan., II, p. 679). Cf. R. Génier, *Vie de Saint Euthyme le Grand* (Paris, 1909), pp. 6–52.

[3] Theodoret of Cyrus, *Religiosa historia,* 26 (*PG,* LXXXII, 1471–72).

[4] *Cursus,* pp. 160–63.—Malnory has well shown the part taken by St Lupus in the propagation of the monastic institution from Lérins (*Saint Césaire, évêque d'Arles,* Paris, 1894, p. 251).

[5] " in monasterio quod, ut aiunt, a sancto Germano fuerat constructum " (*Vita Sam.,* II, 42, p. 138).

[6] *Vita Sam.,* I, 7, p. 105.

[7] Ryan, *Monast.,* p. 110.

Aurelian and perhaps Gildas, all of them—at any rate, the two former—subsequently destined to go to Armorica ; perhaps also St David.[1]

David's active influence seems to have been very powerful. He remains the great national saint of Wales. Many churches of that country are still dedicated to Dewi Sant.[2] He founded the see of Mynyw (Old Welsh *Moniu*, Latin *Menevia*) on a rugged promontory overlooking the Irish sea, in a wild and picturesque situation, better adapted to the contemplative life of monks than to the needs of an episcopal see. This monastic centre, of special importance in the religious annals of the Cymry, was also called by them Ty Ddewi (the house of David), and received the further name of Vallis Rosina. The Irish called it Cill Muine.

St Cadoc was another great British monk of the sixth century. Trained by a Scottic master, he crossed over to Ireland, where he recruited a large number of followers, among them Finnian of Clonard. On his return to his own country he founded the monastery of Llancarvan (or Nant-carvan).[3]

Monasticism was, therefore, flourishing in Great Britain in the sixth century. It has even been held that the clergy of that period was exclusively monastic. This, however, is an extreme view. There existed also a secular clergy, whose

[1] *Vita Iltuti* (*CBS*, p. 167) ; Wrmonoc, *Vita Pauli Aurel.*, 3 (*R. Cel.*, V, 1881–83, p. 421) ; *Vita Gildae*, 3–5 (pp. 92–93). The latter text mentions only Samson, Paul and Gildas among Illtud's pupils. According to Wade-Evans (*David*, p. 73), little credence can be attached to the statement that David belonged to the group. The objection is valid if the date of David's death given by *AC* (A.D. 601) is correct, but not if we accept the obit given by the *Chronicon Scottorum*, A.D. 588. Lloyd (*HW*, I, pp. 158–63) proposes A.D. 589.—Llanilltud, Illtud's monastery, was situated on an island (" quae insula usque in hodiernum diem Lanna Hilduti vocitatur " : (*Vita Gildae, l. cit.*). This island described by Wrmonoc as " insula Pyrus nomine, Demetarum patriae in finibus sita " (*Vita Pauli*, 2, p. 419) has been identified with Caldey Island (called Ynys Pyr by the Welsh), a small island near Dyfedd. But Illtud may have had another monastery at Llanilltyd Fawr (Llantwit Major), S. W. Cowbridge, on the mainland. Cf. Williams, *Christianity* (pp. 322–25) ; Robert Fawtier, *La Vie de S. Samson* (1912, pp. 41–44) ; Chevalier, *Essai* (pp. 317–18) ; Lloyd, *HW*, I, p. 144.
[2] Fifty-three churches in Wales were dedicated to St David (Rice Rees, *An Essay on the Welsh Saints*, London, 1836, p. 45).
[3] *Vita Cadoci*, 40 (*CBS*, p. 79).—Llancarfan (Llancarvan) is a corruption which arose under the Norman occupation. Compare " in Carbana valle," " Nancarbanensis," " Carbanam vallem," as quoted by Lloyd, *HW*, p. 7.

disorders are vehemently denounced by St Gildas, the Jeremiah of Britain.[1] We must beware of looking for an exact picture of the British Church of the time in his diatribes, for Gildas exaggerates after the fashion of austere and indignant pulpit orators. It has been observed that in this part of the *De excidio Britanniae*, where he depicts the evils of the British Church in such gloomy hues, he says nothing about monks ; whence it has been inferred that it was only after the composition of the work (about 540), that is, in the second half of the sixth century, that British monasticism attained its full expansion.[2] To this we reply that Gildas, himself a monk, had doubtless no reproach to bring against the monastic institution, and for that reason passed it over in silence. He alludes, however, to monastic life incidentally in a passage of his book dealing with Maelgwn (Maglocunus), king of Gwynedd.[3]

In these British cloisters the monks prayed, led a life of rigorous asceticism and cultivated letters classical and sacred. Manual toil also formed a large part of their occupations.

At the beginning of the seventh century the monastery of Bangor-is-Coed on the Dee, not far from Chester, passed for the most celebrated one on British soil.[4] It had for abbot Dinoot, who took part in the negotiations between the adherents of Celtic customs, of whom he himself was one, and St Augustine of Canterbury, the spokesman of Rome and the apostle of the Anglo-Saxons. The Venerable Bede tells us that the population of Bangor comprised seven cloistral divisions, each containing at least three hundred monks, having provosts placed over them ; all lived by the labour of their hands.

These monks took an interest in the fortunes of their country. On learning that Ethelfrid, king of Northumbria, was bearing on Chester with a large army, they began a three

---

[1] " Si vero sine monachi voto presbiter aut diaconus peccaverit, sicut monachus sine gradu sic peniteat " (*Praefatio Gildae de poenitentia*, 3 : *CED*, I, p. 114, ed. Th. Mommsen, p. 89).
[2] See a note by Hugh Williams in his edition of the *De excidio* (*Cymrodorion Record*, No. 3, p. 151).
[3] Gildas, *De exc.*, 33 (p. 45).
[4] " Nobilissimum eorum monasterium " (Bede, *HE*, II, 2).

days' fast ; then, when the hour of combat had arrived, they repaired to a spot not far distant from the battle-field and engaged in prayer to secure the success of their fellow-countrymen. The latter were commanded by a leader called Brocmail. In the course of the engagement Brocmail and his soldiers took to flight, and Ethelfrid avenged himself by hurling his Saxons on the band of praying monks. They perished to the number of twelve hundred ; only fifty succeeded in escaping (c. 615).[1]

Bede represents this massacre as a chastisement inflicted by Heaven on the Celtic monks for not having consented to renounce their erroneous religious customs and co-operated with Augustine in the task of converting the Saxons. The Irish annalist, Tigernach, on the contrary, speaks of the mournful event as " the combat in which the saints were slaughtered ".[2]

§ 3.—THEORIES AS TO THE ORIGIN OF IRISH MONASTICISM

To a greater extent even than Britain, Ireland, converted in the fifth century, experienced in the sixth a prodigious development of monastic institutions. Whence was this principle of the religious life, so fruitful in its workings, derived ? On this question various opinions have been advanced, which we shall proceed to examine.

The most original one is assuredly that of Alexandre Bertrand.[3] In the judgment of this scholar, Irish monasticism was indigenous. It proceeded directly from the native druidism, the monasteries being only Christianized fraternities of druids. The druids had received the glad tidings of the Gospel with favour and had been converted in a body. Their colleges, retreats of learning and asylums of religious and moral culture, similar to the lamaseries of Tartary or Tibet, had become, under the influence of Christianity, highly flourishing centres of proselytism and study. Not otherwise

---

[1] *Ib.*—For the date of the battle of Chester see C. Plummer (Bede, *HE*, vol. II, p. 77) ; A. W. Wade-Evans, *Welsh Mediaeval Law*, p. xliii ; Lloyd, *HW.*, I, p. 179.

[2] *AT*, p. 171.

[3] A. Bertrand, *Nos origines. La religion des Gaulois* (Paris, 1897), pp. 297–312, 417–24.

can Alexandre Bertrand account for the rapid progress of Christianity in Ireland, the immediate foundation of so many great monasteries, the monastic character of the Celtic Church, its particularism, and finally the amazing intellectual activity which it displayed in an age of prevailing ignorance and barbarism.[1]

Unfortunately this ingenious hypothesis lacks proof. It is not true, as we have seen, that the druids received Christianity with favour. St Patrick's mission encountered no more formidable and irreconcilable opponents. D'Arbois de Jubainville believed in the existence of a sort of vast national druidic congregations. The druids had not indeed (to use his own expression) a General like the Jesuits, but like them, they were subordinated to Provincials, one in Gaul, one in Ireland, and one in Great Britain.[2] The " Provincial " of Gaul may be conceded, since a text of Julius Caesar seems to indicate his existence.[3] But there is nothing to prove that the Rechrad, *primus magum*, of whom Tirechán speaks[4] and whom d'Arbois de Jubainville invokes in aid of his theory, was the head of all the druids of Ireland. In any case, the existence of a national association of Irish druids, even were it proved, would lend no support to Bertrand's thesis. To make the latter plausible, he would have to establish the existence of local druidic communities, and this he has failed to do. Consequently his hypothesis, despite its attractive originality, has not succeeded in gaining ground.[5]

Some British writers, anxious at all costs to safeguard the early Celtic Church from Roman influence, have conceived the idea of deriving insular monasticism directly from the East.[6] This is just a particular instance of that Oriental

----

[1] An analogous theory on the origin of British monasticism, in which not only Druidism but Bardism also played a large part, was advanced by John Williams, *Ecclesiastical Antiquities of the Cymry* (London, 1844), pp. 167 ff., 229.

[2] H. d'Arbois, *Les druides et les dieux à formes d'animaux* (Paris, 1906), pp. 6–7.

[3] *De bello gallico*, vi, 13.

[4] Tirechán, p. 28.

[5] See H. Hubert, *Revue critique*, 1898, p. 120 ; G. Dottin, *Manuel*, p. 386 ; H. d'Arbois, *Les druides*, p. 109 ff.

[6] See notably Th. Olden, *The Church of Ireland :* ch. viii, *Its Eastern*

" mirage " so frequently met with in all branches of historical research. It cannot indeed be disputed that the teachings of the Egyptian monks reached Ireland and played an important part in the ascetic development of the country.[1] But whereas we have been able to point out some relations between Britons and Orientals which allow us to believe, if need be, in a direct take over of the monastic doctrines of the East, such is not the case with the Irish. Later converts to Christianity, they received the traditions of Eastern askesis, already propagated in the West, from St Patrick and other British or Gaulish intermediaries ; they had not therefore to go and draw for themselves from the original sources. That propaganda the monks of Lérins and Cassian took on themselves, and it is certain that their influence was felt as far as Ireland.[2]

William Forbes Skene admits intermediaries between East and West. In his opinion the first principles of Celtic monasticism proceeded from St Martin of Tours and reached Ireland by two channels, on the one hand through Candida Casa in Galloway, on the other through Brittany and Wales.[3]

It is certain that Irish monks used to visit Candida Casa, but they did so at a time when monasticism was no longer in its initial stages among them. As for St Martin's influence in Brittany, and notably at Landouart and Landévennec, the monasteries which Skene has specially in view,[4] it is not easy to prove, any more than the influence of Brittany on Wales. With regard to the latter country, it is an established fact that Brittany, at the period with which we are dealing, received incomparably more than she gave.

Origin (London, 1895) ; G. T. Stokes, *Ireland and the Celtic Church :* Lect. IX, *Ireland and the East.*

[1] See H. Williams, *Some Aspects of the Christian Church in Wales during the Fifth and Sixth Centuries* (*TSC*, 1893–94, p. 78).—Haeften is quite wrong when he writes : " Hiberniae monachi nihil cum Aegyptiis commune habuerunt " (*Disquisitionum monasticarum libri* XII, Antverpiae, 1644, p. 58).

[2] Cf. *Cursus*, pp. 160–63. Cf. Warren in *An. Ban.*, II, p. XXVI (*introd.*) ; *LH*, I, p. 85, II, pp. 67, 170, 171.

[3] W. F. Skene, *CS*, II, pp. 45–51.—" Of direct intercourse between Ireland and the lesser Britain or Brittany we do not hear very much," writes judiciously C. Plummer (*VSH*, I, p. CXXVI, *introd.*).

[4] Skene, *CS*, II, p. 49.

§ 4.—THE PROBABLE ORIGIN OF IRISH MONASTICISM AND ITS DEVELOPMENT

Monasticism had perhaps found its way into Ireland before St Patrick in those parts of the country already Christianized by his predecessors. In any case, it is certain that the great apostle, not content with winning over crowds of heathens to the Christian religion, initiated a large number of chosen converts of both sexes into the perfect life. " The sons of the Scots and the daughters of chieftains who have become monks and virgins of Christ I cannot count," he says [1] ; and he relates the following significant incident : " There was a blessed lady, a Scot by birth, of noble rank, very beautiful and of adult age, whom I baptized ; a few days afterwards she came to us for some reason and made known to us that she had received an answer through the will of God and that He had warned her to be a virgin of Christ and draw nigh unto God. Thanks to God, six days after she laid hold full well and eagerly on that which all virgins of God do ; not with the consent of their fathers, for they suffer persecution and unmerited reproaches from their parents ; nevertheless their number increases and we know not the number of those of our race who are born here, besides widows and continent persons. But it is the women kept in slavery who suffer most. They constantly endure even terrors and threats ; but the Lord has given grace to many of His handmaidens, for though forbidden they follow with courage the example set them." [2]

There is also mention of monks and consecrated virgins in the canons ascribed to Patrick, Auxilius and Iserninus, the authenticity of which Bury has proved.[3] We have seen too that more than once Patrick left monks as pastors of the tribes he had evangelized.[4] These " monks of Patrick," as Tirechán calls them,[5] had to lead the life of missionaries for a fairly long time, for the work of the holy apostle was not completed and consolidated without persevering effort. The first

[1] Pat., *Epistola*, 12. Cf. *Confessio*, 41.
[2] Pat., *Confessio*, 42.
[3] *CED*, II, 328. Cf. Bury, *Pat.*, pp. 233–45 ; Kenney, *Sources*, I, pp. 169–70.
[4] Tirechán, pp. 24, 27, 29.
[5] Tirechán, pp. 22, 27.

monasteries were doubtless missionary stations, similar to those which were to be founded later in the eighth century by St Boniface and his companions in heathen Germany. After some time they became in addition influential centres of cenobitic and intellectual life.

There are in our opinion two causes which account for the extraordinary development of the Irish monasteries. First, the burning zeal of the apostles of the country, themselves very often monks, who, from the outset, set their hearts on promoting monastic institutions, as may be seen from the writings of Patrick. Their aim was wonderfully furthered by the ardent temperament of the newly won converts. We have seen how unreservedly the daughters of Loegaire gave themselves to Christ. A large number of the baptized had scarcely felt the regenerating touch of the sacramental waters, when they were drawn to follow the evangelic counsels ; once become Christians, they were impelled by holy zeal to vow themselves forthwith to the Christian religion in its entire extent. A strong outburst of asceticism manifested itself among the converts. " The first ardour of faith," Frédéric Ozanam has justly said, "which everywhere else led Christians to martyrdom, impelled the Irish converts to the monastery." [1]

Moreover, the political and social condition of the country helps to explain the rapid development of monastic life. Irish society was divided into a multitude of petty states. When it came to pass that a chieftain was converted, he would grant the missionary a site not only for a church, but also for a monastic settlement, maintained from the very beginning by the people of his tribe. [2] The incident related in a Life of St Maedóc of Ferns may be taken as typical. A chieftain of Leinster, having been baptized by that saint, made him a gift of land whereon to establish a religious settlement, saying : " I offer myself to God and to thee, and with myself I offer all my race ; be thou the master of all." [3]

[1] F. Ozanam, *La civilisation chez les Francs* (Paris, 1849), p. 97. Cf. Ryan, *Monast.*, p. 186.
[2] Additions to Tirechán's Memoir (*LA*, p. 33). Cf. E. MacNeill, *Celtic Ireland*, p. 148.
[3] *Vita Aidani* [i.e., Maedoci] (*Sal. ASH.*, 473). Cf. *ib.*, cols. 214–15, 521–24.

There were no towns in Ireland. The need of union and close cohesion made itself felt in the midst of a people as yet little civilized, still heathen in many ways, and distracted by slavery, dissension and wars. The monastery became the sure and peaceful refuge of elect souls as well as a centre of intellectual culture.

In the period of the great expansion of religious life, it is ascertained that there existed great monastic federations presided over by powerful abbots who exercised jurisdiction throughout the whole extent of the *paruchia*.[1] A goodly number of these abbots were also bishops.[2] There is no trace of episcopal dioceses at this time. Bishops who were not abbots were certainly treated with all due respect, but were relegated to the background. It is, however, possible that, as has been observed, " a kind of *fainéant* episcopal jurisdiction survived over some churches or districts that the monastic system had not absorbed." [3]

A striking proof among many of the remarkable ascendancy enjoyed by the heads of these great monastic " cities," as they were called,[4] is furnished by the curious inflections of meaning which the Irish words for " abbot " and " abbotship " (*abb*, *abdaine*) acquired from this time forth. They were used to denote any eminent authority, whether temporal or spiritual. In a poem ascribed to Gilla Coemáin (†1072) Astyages, king of the Medes, is called an " abbot." [5] Pope Sylvester is called " abbot of Rome " in the work of the tenth or eleventh century known as the *Vision of Adamnán*,[6] and in the glosses to the *Félire* of Oengus St Gregory the Great is styled " abbot of Rome and of the whole of Latium." [7] Still more, Christ

---

[1] C. Plummer, *VSH*, I, pp. cxi f. (*introd.*) ; *BNE*, II, p. 324.

[2] About the period referred to Fr. Ryan even says : " Comparing the list of monastic rulers who were bishops with the list of monastic rulers who were priests, we find that there is no great difference in numbers between the two " (*Monast.*, p. 176).

[3] Kenney, *Sources*, I, p. 292.

[4] Ir. *cathair*.—" In the Patrician documents the word is used of Armagh, Slane and Sléibte, and is in general connected with bishops and with the National Apostle " (Ryan, *Monast.*, p. 88). In *AU* " civitas " always denotes a monastery. Cf. *VSH*, II, p. 382 (Latin glossary).

[5] Chronological Poem, ed. Whitley Stokes (*Vita Trip.*, pp. 534–35).

[6] Ed. C. S. Boswell, *An Irish Precursor of Dante* (London, 1908), p. 45.

[7] *Fél. Oeng.*, pp. 96–97.

himself is called " the great Abbot " [1] and to him is assigned " the abbotship and sovranty of the heavenly city." [2] God is called " *ar n-abb* " (our Abbot) in the *Saltair na Rann*.[3] What is still more startling, according to another text, " the devil is the Abbot of Hell." [4]

The monastery of Killeany (Cell Enda), situate in the largest of the Aran Islands in Galway Bay, is considered to have been the oldest of those famous centres which from the first half of the sixth century onwards were the glory of Ireland. Its founder was St Enda († *c.* 530), chieftain of a powerful tribe. On his baptism Enda, it is said, repaired to Candida Casa ; then, having obtained Aranmore from the king of Cashel, he opened a monastery there which was soon filled with chosen disciples. Among them was St Ciarán of Clonmacnois.[5]

St Finnian († 549) crossed the sea to visit David, Cadoc and Gildas, and he came back to Ireland accompanied by British disciples.[6] His chief foundation was Clonard in Meath, which, like all these great religious centres, was at once a monastery and a school of renown.[7]

The Abbey of Moville (Magh Bile), which stood north of Loch Cúan (Strangford Lough) in Ulster, was founded about 540 by the other Finnian († 589). Like Enda, he was of royal descent and like him is said to have spent some time at Candida Casa.[8]

St Columban tells of a neat reply given by Gildas to a certain Vennianus who had consulted him on the subject of anchoritism.[9] A penitential attributed to a certain Vinniaus has

---

[1] In a poem ascribed to Columcille, edited by J. O'Donovan (*The Miscellany of the Irish Archaeological Society*, Dublin, 1846, pp. 12–13) and by Kuno Meyer (*Mitteilungen aus irischen Handschriften* : *ZCP*, VII, 1910, pp. 302–303).

[2] Leabhar Breac. Facs., pp. 135 *b*, 43.

[3] *Saltair na Rann*, l. 831, ed. Whitley Stokes (*Anecdota Oxoniensia, Mediaeval and Modern Ser.*, I, III, Oxford, 1883).

[4] See refer. in *VSH*, I, p. CXI, and in *BNE*, II, p. 338.

[5] *Vita Endei*, 25 (*VSH*, II, pp. 71–72).

[6] *Acta Finniani de Cluain Eraird*, 4–11 (*Sal. ASH*, cols. 191–95).

[7] *Ib.*, 19 (cols. 199–200).

[8] Cf. Ryan, *Monast.*, p. 106.

[9] *Ep.* 1, ed. Gundlach (*MG, Epist.*, III, p. 159). Cf. Esposito, *Latin Learning*, I, p. 238.

also come down to us [1] ; and the question has been raised to which Finnian its authorship is to be ascribed, to him of Moville or him of Clonard, or someone else. [2] Mario Esposito is of opinion that it is the work of Finnian of Moville. [3]

Trained at Clonard and Aranmore, St Ciarán mac in tsaír (son of the carpenter) (†549) founded several monasteries, the most celebrated being Clonmacnois on the left bank of the Shannon (544 or 548). He did not long survive its foundation, [4] but his monastery continued to flourish for several centuries. At the end of the eighth century we find a certain Colcu (†796) there, whom it has been attempted to identify, but without sufficient proof, with a correspondent of Alcuin who bore the same name. [5]

We cannot enter into the origin of all the great monasteries. Mention must, however, be made of Derry and Durrow, founded by St Columba before his departure for the isle of Iona, of Glendalough, founded by St Coemgen (Kevin) (†618 or 622), [6] of Clonfert, founded by St Brendan the Navigator (†577 or 583), [7] and finally of Bangor, erected by Comgall (†602) to the north of Moville on the southern shore of Belfast Lough. [8] Here it was that St Columban and St Gall acquired the virtues, learning and traditions which they passed on later to continental Europe with such happy results.

From the foregoing it will be seen that monastic Ireland kept up constant relations with Britain. The two countries

---

[1] *Poenitentiale Vinniai* (*Buss.*, pp. 108–19).

[2] Cf. Otto Seebass, *Ueber Columbas von Luxeuil Klosterregel* (Dresden, 1883), p. 58 ; Wasserschleben, *Buss.*, pp. 10–11 ; H. J. Schmitz, *Die Bussbücher und die Bussdisciplin der Kirche* (Mainz, 1883), p. 499.

[3] Esposito, *Latin Learning*, I, pp. 236–40.

[4] " Uno tantum anno vixit in ciuitate Cluain " (*Vita Ciarani de Cluain*, 32 : *VSH*, I, p. 215) ; " emisit spiritum trigesimo tercio etatis sue anno " (*Ib.*).

[5] *MG. Epist.*, IV, pp. 437 f. Cf. Charles MacNeill (*Studies*, XIV, 1925, p. 504).

[6] *Vita Coemgeni*, 6 (*VSH*, I, p p. 237 ff.).

[7] *Vita* Iᵃ *Brendani*, 91, 92 (*VSH*, I, p. 145).

[8] *Vita Comgalli*, 13 (*VSH*, II, p. 7).—Cf. Félim O'Briain, art. *Bangor* in the *Dictionnaire d'histoire et de géographie ecclésiastiques* edited by Baudrillart, De Meyer and Van Cauwenbergh (1931). On the etymology of Bangor see K. Meyer, *Zur keltischen Wortkunde*, IV (*Sitzungsberichte der königl. Preuss. Akad. der Wissenschaften.* Philos.-hist. Cl., 1913, XLIX, pp. 952–53).

aided one another in their progress in the religious life.[1] St Cadoc of Llancarvan, it will be remembered, had an Irish master. He passed several years in Ireland as well (in particular he stayed three years at Lismore), "until he acquired the perfection of the learning in the West." [2] St Finnian of Clonard is said to have been connected with St Cadoc. He returned from Llancarvan accompanied by two Britons, Bite and Genoc.[3] The latter appears in a list of Finnian's pupils.[4] Afterwards close relations of friendship existed between Llancarvan and Clonard.[5] Cybi, another British saint, is credited in Cymric traditions with a visit to Aranmore, where he is said to have lived four years.[6] St Samson, who came to Ireland with some highly educated Scots who were returning from Rome, did not remain so long in that country.[7] Maedóc of Ferns was a disciple of St David.[8] Brendan of Clonfert is reported to have visited Gildas in Britain.[9]

St David of Menevia seems to have been much sought out as a teacher by Irish monks.[10] The *Catalogue of the Saints* says that those of the second order (from 544 to 598) received a new liturgy of the Mass from three British saints, Bishop David, Gilla and Docus.[11] The two former are easily identified with David of Menevia and Gildas.[12] As for

---

[1] See Roger, *Enseignement*, pp. 232–35 ; C. Plummer, *VSH*, pp. cxxiv–cxxv (*introd.*) ; Slover, *Channels* (1927), pp. 19–26, 30–32, etc. ; Ryan, *Monast.*, pp. 105–16.

[2] *Vita Cadoci*, 7 (*CBS*, pp. 35–36).

[3] *Vita Cadoci* (*CBS*, pp. 36, 39, 44, 85, 88) ; *Acta Finniani*, 11 (*Sal. ASH*, cols. 191–95). Cf. Slover, *Channels* (1927), pp. 20 ff. ; Ryan, *Monast.*, p. 115 ; Chevalier, *Essai*, p. 350.

[4] *Acta Finniani*, 19 (Kayneacus) (*Sal. ASH*, col. 200).

[5] *Vita Cadoci* (*CBS*, p. 79).

[6] *Vita Kebii* (*CBS*, pp. 184–85). Cf. Slover, *Channels* (1927), pp. 30 ff.

[7] *Vita Sam.*, 37–38 (pp. 133–35).

[8] *Vita Aidui sive Maedoc*, 11 (*VSH*, II, p. 297). Ricemarch, *Vita Davidis*, 42. Cf. Slover, *Channels* (1927), p. 13.

[9] *Vita Iᵃ Brendani*, 83–85 (*VSH*, I, pp. 141–43) ; *Vita Brendani e cod. Dubl.*, 15–16, ed. P. Grosjean (*AB*, XLVIII, 1930, pp. 111–13).

[10] Slover, *Channels* (1927), pp. 7–19 ; Chevalier, *Essai*, pp. 349 ff.

[11] " A Davide Episcopo et Gilla et a Doco Britonibus missam acceperunt " (*Catalogus*, p. 293).

[12] *Gillas* = Gildas. Cf. Kuno Meyer, *Ein mittelirisches Gedicht auf Brendan der Meerfahrer* (*Sitzungsberichte d. königl. Preuss. Akad. der Wissenschaften*, 1912, XXV, p. 440). Cf. R. Thurneysen, *Handbuc hdes Alt-Irischen*

" Docus," he is generally identified with Cadoc of Llancarvan. Is this a mistake ? [1] There certainly was a British abbot-bishop of the name of Doccus, but he is known to us only by an entry in the Annals of Ulster, which give his death under A.D. 473 : *Quies Docci episcopi sancti Britonum abbatis,*[2] a date much too early for the saint to have been associated with David and Gildas. On the other hand, we find the same triad of saints mentioned in another text in connection with a circum-stance which brought them together at Menevia. This other text is a Life of Finnian of Clonard in which we read : " *Ibi sanctus Finnianus tres viros sanctos videlicet sanctum David et sanctum Cathmaelum et sanctum Gildam invenit.*" [3] Now Cath-mael is another name for Cadoc ; that no one disputes.[4] Therefore, it seems, if not certain at least probable, that the names which appear in the passage of the Catalogue referred to are those of the three contemporaries, David, Gildas and Cadoc.

Unlike the two others, David does not seem to have come to Ireland. On the contrary, the journey of Gildas to Ireland is attested by his biographer as well as by the *Annales Cambriae ;* it took place in the reign of the Irish king Ainmire (565–568).[5]

§ 5.—THE ALLEGED PAGAN REACTION IN IRELAND IN THE SIXTH OR SEVENTH CENTURY

A most improbable theory has been built up on the state-ment of the *Catalogue* to which allusion has just been made : *A Davide episcopo et Gilla et a Doco Britonibus missam acceperunt.*

(Heidelberg, 1909), I, p. 91.   Cf. J. Loth, *Le nom de Gildas dans l'île de Bretagne, en Irlande et en Armorique* (*R. Cel,* XLVI, 1929, p. 13).
    [1] J. Loth believes *Doccus* and *Cadocus* to be two distinct men. See *Le nom de Gildas* (pp. 12–13) and *Saint Doccus et l'hagio-onomastique* (*Mem. SHAB,* X, 1929, pp. 1–12). Cf. J. Vendryes (*R. Cel.,* XLVII, 1930, pp. 259–60). For the opposite view see E. Phillimore (*YC,* 1890–92, p. 92, note 6) and Slover, *Channels* (1927), pp. 6–7.
    [2] W. M. Hennessy, who, in *AU,* identifies Doccus with Cadoc the Wise, abbot of Llancarvan, notes that the entry in *AU* must be out of its place (pp. 24–25).
    [3] *Acta Finniani,* 4 : *Sal. ASH.,* col. 193). Also in *Betha Fhindein (Lismore,* pp. 75, 222).
    [4] Cathmael is the Irish form of Cadvael, *i.e.,* Cadoc (Cadog).
    [5] *Vita Gildae,* 11, 12 (pp. 94–95) ; *AC, a.a.* 565.

It has been assumed that the faith underwent an eclipse in Ireland at some period of the sixth century. Some have even gone so far as to believe in an almost general apostasy.[1] Just as their distant kinsfolk, the Galatians, after receiving St Paul as an angel of God, had renounced his Gospel, even so the Gaels had at that time completely forgotten the teachings of Patrick ; and the sole object of the mission of the British saints was to inculcate these anew.

Such a supposition is wholly irreconcilable with the highly prosperous condition of the Irish Churches which has just been described. The author of the *Catalogue*, it is true, in order to keep up his arrangement in grades, compares the holiness of the saints of the second order to the lustre of the moon, while that of Patrick and his disciples is likened to the radiance of the sun. But to ground on metaphors like these a theory involving an eclipse of the faith during the second age seems to me a very hasty inference. Besides, the work of the British saints is stated to have been purely liturgical, and from this passage alone we should not be justified even in concluding that any one of them ever came to Ireland in person.

Accordingly further support has been sought in two hagiographical texts which depict the state of the Irish Church in the most sombre hues. The first is taken from the Life of St Gildas by the monk of Ruis. According to this writer, Gildas was invited by king Ainmire to come and restore the ecclesiastical doctrine in his dominions. " All, from the least to the greatest, had utterly abandoned the Catholic faith. Then St Gildas, armed with the shield of faith and wearing the helmet of salvation, traversed all the regions of Hibernia, raising up the churches, instructing the entire clergy in the Catholic faith, restoring the dogma of the Holy Trinity, healing the peoples who were badly hurt by the bites of the heretics, and, in short, scattering afar the deceptions of heresy and those who abetted them. Then in the bosom of the mother Church there sprang up a rich harvest of believers,

---

[1] This view has been held by Whitley Stokes (*On the linguistic Value of Irish Annals : Transact. of the Philol. Soc.*, 1888–90, p. 389) ; Haddan and Stubbs (*CED*, I, pp. 115–16) ; Th. Olden (*Church of Ireland*, pp. 49–52) ; J. Fonsagrives (*Saint Gildas de Ruis et la société bretonne au VIe siècle*, Paris, 1908, pp. 142 ff.), etc.

and the soil, long barren, being at last cleared of the briars
of heresy and learning its supernatural vocation, brought forth
under the fertilizing dew of the divine grace fruits of better
flavour. The Catholic faith made progress and the country
hailed such a patron with joy." [1]

If we are to believe this writer, all the clergy of Ireland had
lost faith ; Irish Christianity had long remained barren,
having been profoundly laid waste by heresy. All this is pure
invention. The monk of Ruis, who wrote this page in the
eleventh century, was simply drawing on his own imagination.
As a general rule, he does not scruple to embellish his narrative
or even to indulge in sheer invention. As for the passage in
question, " we have here an absolutely falsified picture of the
religious situation in Ireland in the sixth century," so Ferdinand
Lot, who has made a close study of the methods of our author,
does not hesitate to affirm. [2]

The other text adduced is taken from the Life of St Disibod
by St Hildegard. The holy bishop Disibod by his fruitless
efforts to lead back a people no longer possessing faith or
morals to the right way brought about his own expulsion from
Ireland. Thereupon he undertook long wanderings over the
Continent and finally settled in the diocese of Mainz, where
he founded the monastery of Disibodenberg. Hildegard gives
the following description of the state of Ireland at the moment
when Disibod had to leave the country : " At that time, while
the saint was guiding the people in the faith both by word and
example, the whole district was stirred up by a spirit of
derision and a great schism. Some rejected the Old and New
Testaments, renounced Christ and embraced the errors of
heretics ; others joined themselves to the sect of the Jews ;
others reverted to paganism ; others in the depravity of their
instincts began to live not like men but after the disorderly
fashion of brutes. Some still preserved some human decency,
but without applying themselves to aught of good." [3]

St Hildegard's Life of the founder of her first monastery
dates from the twelfth century, and apart from it we do not

---

[1] *Vita Gildae, l. cit.*
[2] Lot, *Mélanges*, p. 261. Cf. *ib.*, pp. 247-48 ; 252-56.
[3] *Vita Disibodi*, I, 11 (*PL*, CXCVII, 1099-1100).

possess the least biographical information about the obscure Disibod.[1] It is difficult even to fix the main points of his chronology. In reliance on the chronicler Marianus Scottus (†1082 or 1083) some place his death in the year 674. If this date is correct, the assumed apostasy of Ireland would have arisen in the seventh century, not the sixth. But neither the testimony of the monk of Ruis nor that of the great German abbess can be received in this matter ; both exhibit a tendency to verbosity which excites suspicion and they are moreover very late. Both come to us from distant parts, do not agree with each other and are directly contrary to the indigenous sources, which tell only of progress in faith and holiness during the period. Giraldus Cambrensis says expressly that from the time of St Patrick to the reign of the Irish king Feidhlimidh, who lived in the second quarter of the eighth century, the Christian faith remained intact and unadulterated in Ireland.[2]

The belief, therefore, in the breakdown of Christianity in the island, either in the sixth or the seventh century, cannot be held. On the contrary, we have shown that it was highly flourishing ; and we do not doubt that what we have still to say on the subject will serve only to strengthen that conviction in the reader.

§ 6.—THE LARGE POPULATION OF THE MONASTERIES.—WAS THE EARLY IRISH CHURCH EXCLUSIVELY MONASTIC ?

We have hitherto borrowed no information from Jocelin of Furness, a writer by no means trustworthy, who composed his *Vita Patricii* about 1183 ; nor do we feel at all inclined to begin laying him under contribution by repeating his statement that Patrick exacted for the benefit of the Church a tithe of the people of Ireland as well as of its territory, thus engaging a tenth of the population in the religious life.[3] None the less, it is beyond doubt that the Celtic monasteries were extraordinarily populous.

[1] A. Poncelet, *Treverensia* (*AB*, XXII, 1903, p. 455) ; Kenney, *Sources*, I, pp. 513–14.
[2] Giraldus, *TH*, III, 36, p. 182.
[3] Jocelin, *Vita Patricii*, 152 (Boll., *AS*, II Mart., p. 572).

St Comgall of Bangor and St Brendan of Clonfert are said to have had each 3,000 disciples [1] ; St Laisrén, abbot of Leighlin (Co. Carlow), 1,500.[2] Finnian, we are told, was surrounded by " 3,000 saints " at Clonard.[3] Other texts speak with less precision of a " *magna multitudo monachorum*," [4] or describe certain abbots as " *multarum millium animarum duces.*" [5]

Let us confront these figures with those furnished by other texts relating to monastic establishments in other parts of the Celtic world or on the Continent. We have already spoken on Bede's authority of the monastery of Bangor on the Dee in Wales with its seven groups of 300 monks apiece.[6] According to a source much less deserving of confidence, St Kentigern reckoned 965 monks under his governance at St. Asaph ; of these 300, who were unlettered, were engaged in agricultural labour, 300 worked inside the monastery, and the remaining 365 devoted themselves to the service of the *laus perennis*.[7]

None of these numbers, taken separately, seems altogether excessive if we remember the 5,000 monks of Tabennisi, the thousands of disciples who gathered round Serapion or St Martin of Tours,[8] or, at less remote periods, the monks, close on 600, whom Ceolfrid counted in his monastery at Wearmouth and Jarrow at the time of his death (716),[9] and the large populations of the monasteries of Lérins, Agaune, Corbie, Fontenelle and Jumièges when at the height of their prosperity.[10]

---

[1] *Cursus*, p. 163 ; *Vita Comgalli*, 13 (*VSH*, II, p. 7) ; *Vita Mochoemog*, 9 (*VSH*, II, p. 168) ; *Vita I[a] Brendani*, 71 (*VSH*, I, p. 136).
[2] *Vita Munnu*, 26 (*VSH*, II, p. 236).
[3] *Betha Fhindein* (*Lismore*, pp. 79, 226).
[4] *Vita Moluae*, 28 (*VSH*, II, p. 216).
[5] See a list of monasteries with the largest population in Reeves' edit. of Adamnán's *Vita Col.* (p. 336).
[6] Bede, *HE*, II, 2 (p. 84).
[7] *Vita Kentigerni*, 25, ed. Forbes, *Historians of Scotland* (Edinburgh, 1874), V, pp. 78–79.
[8] Cassian, *Instit.*, IV, 1 ; Jerome, *Ep.* 22, § 33, ed. Hilberg (*Corp. SEL*, LIV, pp. 195–96), ed. Migne (PL, XXII, 418) ; Sozomenus, *HE*, VI, 28 (*PG*, LXVII, 1371–72) ; Sulpicius Severus, *Ep.* 3 *ad Bassulam* (PL, XX, 183 ; *Corp. SEL*, I, p. 150).
[9] Bede, *Historia quinque abbatum Benedicti, Ceolfridi, etc.*, 17, ed. C. Plummer (*HE*, Vol. I, p. 382).
[10] For Gaulish monasteries see A. Marignan, *Études sur la civilisation française* (Paris, 1899), II, pp. 225–26

Here some explanatory remarks are called for. In the first place, beside these multitudes of cenobites recorded in Ireland, the religious life was represented, especially from the seventh century on, by a very large number of hermits.[1] Next let us bear in mind with Charles Plummer that " when we hear of the enormous number of monks under a single abbot we must remember that they were not necessarily all in the same monastery." [2] We read in the *Vita Comgalli* : " *Et in diuersis cellis et monasteriis tria millia monachorum sub cura sancti patris Comgalli fuerunt,*" [3] and many other texts use similar language.[4] " The larger monasteries," Plummer adds, " were continually throwing off new swarms, an ecclesiastical ' ver sacrum,' which settled at a greater or less distance from the parent hive." [5]

However, important as the monastic element in the Church may have been, there was room for a secular priesthood beside it. This indeed is not the common opinion ; many historians represent the Church of Ireland as a purely monastic one. " There is no fact," says George T. Stokes, " more patent on the face of history than this—the early Irish Church was thoroughly monastic. Monasticism pervaded every department of the Church, and was the secret of its rapid success." [6] We feel it our duty to be less positive and to content ourselves with saying that the Irish Church was almost exclusively monastic. Tirechán, as we have seen, takes care to make special mention of the monks among St Patrick's helpers [7] ; if they had all been monks, why should he have drawn attention to the fact in some cases only ?

---

[1] On the anchorites of the third Order of Irish Saints—" *ordo sanctus* " (A.D. 598–664)—" who dwelt in desert places and lived on herbs and water and by alms, for the idea of possessing anything of their own was repugnant to them," see *Catalogus* (p. 293). Cf. Ryan, *Monast.*, pp. 220 ff.

[2] C. Plummer, *VSH*, I, pp. cxi–cxii (*introd.*).

[3] *Vita Comgalli, l. cit.*

[4] ". . . et multa monasteria et cellas per diversas regiones Hybernie fundavit, in quibus tria milia monachorum, ut perhibetur a senioribus, sub eo erant " (*Vita Brendani*, 12, ed. P. Grosjean : *AB*, XLVIII, 1930, p. 109). See other texts in Plummer, *Op. et l. cit.*

[5] C. Plummer, *Op. et l. cit.*

[6] G. T. Stokes, *Ireland and the Celtic Church* (London, 1907), pp. 166–67. Cf. Kenney, *Sources*, I, p. 291.

[7] *V. sup.* § 4.

Among the canons wrongly attributed to St Patrick, which were however known in Ireland at the time with which we are dealing, there are some which appear to make a distinction between secular priests and monks. Treating of the Gospel parable of the Sower, it is said that those who bring forth a hundredfold are bishops and doctors, monks and virgins; those who yield sixtyfold are clerics and chaste widows.[1] Again St Columban, writing to the bishops of Gaul, observes that the functions and ideals of the secular clergy are different from those of monks [2]; which leads us to believe that the distinction was not unknown in the ecclesiastical discipline of his native country. Finally, on the testimony of the Venerable Bede, the missionaries of St. Aidan of Lindisfarne were monks for the most part, but not all : *monachi erant maxime qui ad praedicandum venerant.*[3]

§ 7.—THE CULDEES

Many erroneous opinions have been expressed concerning the *Céli Dé*, " those pathetic relics of a lost Celticity," as they have been called.[4] The title has sometimes been improperly bestowed on Irish and Scottish monks in general. But it was really used to denote only a special class of monks gathered into communities here and there, as to whose manner of life we have scanty information.[5]

" The word *céle* (plur. *céli*)," says Dr. J. F. Kenney, " had the general significance of ' companion,' and more particularly the companion of lower *status* who was attached by a sense of love and duty." [6] *Céle Dé* (anglicised " Culdee ") means,

---

[1] II. Ser. Can. 18 : *De tribus seminibus Evangeliorum (CED*, II, p. 336). On these canons see Bury, *Pat.*, pp. 235 ff. On episcopal jurisdiction exercised independently of monasteries see Ryan, *Monast.*, pp. 168–70.

[2] Columban, *Ep.* 2 (*MG., Epist.*, III, p. 163).

[3] Bede, *HE*, III, 3.

[4] W. C. Mackenzie, *Scottish Place-Names* (London, 1931), p. 237.—The most misleading treatise on the matter is Ebrard's disquisition, *Die kuldeische Kirche der 7. 8. u. 9. Jahrhunderte (Zeitschrift für die historische Theologie*, 1862–63). Untrustworthy also is A. Paumier, art. *Culdées* in *Encyclopédie des sciences religieuses* edited by F. Lichtenberger (Paris, 1878).

[5] See Kenney, *Sources*, I, pp. 468–71 ; L. G., art. *Culdées (DACL*, 1914) ; T. Jones Parry, art. *Culdees (ERE*, 1911) ; A. W. H[addan], art. *Colidei* in Smith and Cheetham, *Dictionary of Christian Antiquities* (1875).

[6] Kenney, *Sources*, I, p. 470.

then, something like " servus Dei." Mediaeval writers Latinized the term *Céle Dé* as *colideus, colledeus, keledeus.*

In patristic Latin literature the expression *servus Dei* is often applied to monks and ascetics.[1] It occurs also in the writings of the hagiographer Tirechán (end of the seventh century).[2] But the earliest Irish texts which mention the *Céli Dé* belong to the eighth and ninth centuries.[3]

Zimmer's hypothesis that the *Regula canonicorum* of St Chrodegang of Metz († 766) gave rise to the institution of the Culdees of Ireland or aided in its development is without foundation.[4]

In the twelfth century Giraldus Cambrensis still speaks of Culdees, settled on an island in a lake in Munster (Loch Cré) : " *Minor vero [insula] capellam [habet], cui pauci coelibes, quos Coelicolas vel Colideos vocant, devote deserviunt.*" [5]

From Ireland the institution of the Culdees passed to Wales [6] and Scotland.[7] There were Culdees at Armagh down to the sixteenth century.[8]

The only community of *Céli Dé* about which we have satisfactory information is that of Tallaght (Co. Dublin), governed by Máel Rúain († 792). Tallaght seems to have been a religious centre of some importance in the eighth and ninth centuries.[9] Two texts make known to us the manner of life observed there by Máel Rúain and his monks : (1) a Rule placed under his own name,[10] and (2) a collection of his teachings and of *memorabilia* relating to the community of

---

[1] L.G., *art. cit.*
[2] Tirechán, p. 22.
[3] L.G., *art. cit.*
[4] Zimmer, *CC*, pp. 99–100.
[5] Giraldus, *TH*, II, 4 (p. 80).
[6] On the Bardsey Culdees see Giraldus, *IK*, II, 6 (p. 124). Certain Welsh communities of celibates were called " meudwyaid," *i.e.,* " servi Dei " (Lloyd, *HW*, I, pp. 203, 217).
[7] William Reeves, *On the Céli Dé commonly called Culdees* (*TRIA*, XXIV, 1864, pp. 216–63). In his *Disquisitio in Culdeos eorumque institutum et fata,* the Bollandist Joseph Van Hecke (Boll., *AS.*, Oct. VIII, 1870, pp. 165–68) is mainly concerned with Scottish Culdees, on whom also *v. inf,* ch. XI, § 5.
[8] W. Reeves, *op. cit.*
[9] The Martyrology of Tallaght, the Félire of Oengus and the Stowe Missal come from that monastery.
[10] Ed. W. Reeves, *op. cit.*, pp. 202–15 ; ed. Ed. Gwynn, *Tallaght* (1927), pp. 64–87. Cf. No. 36 (p. 73).

Tallaght, of which two recensions have come down to us [1] ;
it was compiled apparently in the first half of the ninth
century (between 831 and 840) from the recollections of a
certain Maeldithruib, a disciple of Máel Rúain.   In reading
these texts we are chiefly struck by the austere life of the
Culdees on the one hand, and, on the other, by the singularity
of some of their liturgical practices.

Finally, we have a section (the seventh) of a metrical Rule
attributed variously to Mochuta (or Carthach) of Rahen and
Lismore, or to Fothad na canóine ; this may belong to the
beginning of the ninth century and is entitled *Of the Culdee or
cleric of the enclosure.*[2]

§ 8.—Monastic Rules

It may be presumed that every monastery of importance
had its own Rule, which however, it is likely, preserved many
of the regulations in use in the monastery where its founder
had himself been initiated into the religious life.

The *Catalogue of the Saints* tells us that there were varieties
of discipline in different ages [3] ; and the Irish canonical
collection ascribes to Gildas a regulation in which mention is
made of an abbot whose Rule was stricter than that of
another.[4]

The Lives of saints and the Annals occasionally attribute
to individual churchmen " laws " or " rules," which have
been erroneously taken for monastic rules.   The " laws " or
" rules " in question are either the measures produced by some
great ecclesiastical or social reform (*Lex Patricii, Ríagail
Pátraic, Cáin Adamnáin*) [5] or else acknowledgments of tributes
levied by monasteries in districts where the memory of the
sainted founder or his relics were venerated (*Law of Ciarán,
Law of Commán*, etc.) [6]   Often too the word " rule " is used

---

[1] Ed. Purton and Gwynn, *Tallaght* (1911) ; ed. Gwynn, *Tallaght* (1927)
pp. 2–63.

[2] Ed. MacEclaise (*Irish Ecclesiastical Record*, 4th Ser., XXVII, 1910,
pp. 508–11). Cf. Kenney, *Sources*, I, pp. 473–74

[3] *Catalogus*, pp. 292–93.

[4] *Hibernensis*, xxxix, 9 (p. 151).

[5] Cf. Kenney, *Sources*, I, p. 237.

[6] Cf. W. Reeves, *Primate Colton's Visitation of the Diocese of Derry* (Dublin,
1850), pp. iii ff. Cf. Kenney, *Sources*, I, p. 377.

in the Lives of saints in a sense other than that of a systematic routine of religious life drawn up and written down ; it signifies merely the ascetic teaching of a saint communicated by word of mouth or by example, or else the traditional, but not codified, observance of a monastery.[1]

Many compositions have come down to us in Old or Middle Irish, both prose and verse, brief collections of aphorisms and pious exhortations, which hardly correspond to the modern idea of a monastic rule. The Rule ascribed to St Mochuta ór Carthach of Rahen [2] († 637) is of more systematic nature than other writings of the kind. The metrical form was no doubt adopted to make it easier for disciples to commit its maxims to memory. Among these metrical rules we may mention further those attributed to St Ailbe of Emly († c. 540),[3] St Ciarán of Clonmacnois († 548?),[4] St Comgall of Bangor († c. 602) [5] and Cormac mac Cuilennáin († 908) [6] ; finally, the Rule of the Grey Monks (*Ríagul na manach líath*),[7] and that of Echtgus úa Cúanáin of the community of Roscré.[8] As for the authorships assigned to these various rules, they must be received with caution, for in Irish literature it very often happens that the person to whom a composition is assigned was not the actual author.[9]

There has come down to us also a very short Rule in Irish prose placed under the name of St Columcille and intended for an anchorite.[10] We have already mentioned the Rule of the Culdees attributed to Máel Rúain of Tallaght, which is likewise in prose but much more detailed.

[1] L.G., *Inventaire des règles monastiques irlandaises* (*RB*, XXV, 1908, pp. 167–84, 321–33). Detailed bibliography in Best, *Bibl.*, pp. 228–30 ; Kenney, *Sources*, I, pp. 474–75.
[2] Ed. Kuno Meyer, *Archiv für celtische Lexicographie*, III, 1907, pp. 312–20 ; ed. MacEclaise, *op. cit.*, pp. 495–517.
[3] Ed. Joseph O'Neill, *Ériu*, III, 1907, pp. 92–115.
[4] Ed. J. Strachan, *Ériu*, II, 1905, pp. 227–28.
[5] Ed. J. Strachan, *Ériu*, I, 1904, pp. 191–208.
[6] Ed. J. Strachan, *Ériu*, II, 1905, pp. 62–68.
[7] Ed. J. Strachan, *Ériu*, II, 1905, p. 229.
[8] Ed. A. G. Van Hamel, *R. Cel.*, XXXVII, 1919, pp. 345–49.
[9] L.G., *art. cit.* Cf. J. Strachan, *R. Cel.*, XVII, 1896, p. 41.
[10] Ed. W. Reeves, *Primate Colton's Visitation*, pp. 109-12 ; Adam., *Vita Col.* (Reeves' ed.), p. 337 ; *CED*, II, p. 119 ; Skene, *CS*, II, p. 508 ; E. V[enables] art. *Monastery* (Smith and Cheetham, p. 1238) ; Kuno Meyer, *Mitteilungen aus irischen Handschriften* (*ZCP*, III, 1899, pp. 28-30).

The monks of Bangor celebrated the rule of their monastery in their Antiphonary in the following words :

> Benchuir bona regula
> Recta atque divina,
> Stricta, sancta, sedula,
> Summa, iusta ac mira . . . [1]

It cannot be said whether the " *Benchuir bona regula* " is the same as the metrical Rule of St Comgall, the founder of Bangor, spoken of above.

In Latin we possess the Rule of St Columban, Comgall's disciple. This rule, it is true, was composed for continental monks, but contains many regulations which throw light on insular monastic life. It is distinguished by its austere and drastic character. It is divided into two parts, often separated in manuscripts, the *Regula monachorum* and the *Regula coenobialis*. The former consists of ten chapters : I. *De obedientia.*—II. *De silentio.*—III. *De cibo et potu.*—IV. *De paupertate.*—V. *De vanitate calcanda.*—VI. *De castitate.*—VII. *De cursu psalmorum.*—VIII. *De discretione.*—IX. *De mortificatione.*—X. *De perfectione monachi.* The last chapter, borrowed from St Jerome, is not found in all manuscripts of the Rule.[2]

The *Regula coenobialis*, sometimes also entitled *Regula fratrum* (or *patrum*) *Hiberniensium* in manuscripts, is a list, in fifteen sections, of punishments to be undergone by the monks for various sins and offences. There are two recensions, a shorter and a longer.[3] In one text of St Benedict of Aniane the *Regula coenobialis* appears as Chapter X of the *Regula monachorum*, and it is so given in Migne's edition, which reproduces that of Holstenius-Brockie.[4]

No Rule has reached us which was followed by monks living in other parts of the Celtic world, Britain, Brittany or Scotland ; for it has, we think, been proved that the so-called *Ordo monasticus de Kilros*, given as the Rule observed in a com-

---

[1] *An. Ban.*, II, p. 28.
[2] Ed. Otto Seebass ' (*ZK*, XV, 1895, pp. 366–86) ; ed. Migne (*PL*, LXXX, 209–16). Cf. O. Seebass, *Ein Beitrag zur Rekonstruktion der Regel Columbas des Jüngeren* (*ZK*, XL, 1922, pp. 132–37) ; Br. Krusch, *Zur Mönchsregel Columbans* (*NA*, XLVI, 1925, pp. 148–57).
[3] Ed. O. Seebass (*ZK*, XVII, 1897, pp. 215–34).
[4] *PL*, LXXX, 216–24.

munity of Scotch Culdees, is only an extract from Rhygyfarch's Life of St David of Menevia, not *vice versâ*.[1]

§ 9.—Religious Vows

Obedience, poverty and chastity, which lie at the basis of
the monastic idea, formed the foundation of the ascetic life of
Celtic monks also.[2] The Irish canonical collection contains
a regulation of native origin pertaining to the burial of a monk,
which is couched in the following terms : " The monk enjoys
no liberty outside the command of his abbot during his lifetime, much less after his death." [3] So much for obedience.
Poverty is no less plainly prescribed. The same collection
includes a chapter entitled : *De eo quod non oportet monachum
habere proprium*, taken from Gildas ; and other dispositions
declare that he has no power to dispose of anything at his
death save at the command of his superior.[4] St Columban
places the highest perfection of the monk in utter abnegation
and contempt of riches. The first chapter of his Rule is
devoted to obedience, the fourth to poverty.[5] Speaking of
St Colmán of Lindisfarne and of the Scots who preceded him,
the Venerable Bede tells us that they possessed no wealth
beyond their cattle. If they received any money from the
wealthy, they were not slow in distributing it among the
poor.[6]

As for chastity, in spite of Ebrard's assertions,[7] there is no
lack of texts also to prove that it was strictly required from
Celtic monks and nuns. " If a virgin who has vowed herself

---

[1] L.G., *Étude sur l'Ordo monasticus de Culross* (*RHE*, XXIII, 1927,
pp. 764–78).

[2] See Ryan, *Monast.*, pp. 240–54.

[3] *Hibernensis*, xli, 8 (p. 160).

[4] *Hibernensis*, xxxix, 5 (p. 150) ; xviii, 3, 6 (pp. 56–57). This collection
has been compiled from various sources, both continental and insular,
but all referred to above are headed " *Sinodus Hibernensis*."

[5] Ed. Seebass (*ZK*, XV, 1895, pp. 374–75 ; 376–77) ; ed. Migne (*PL*,
LXXX, 209–11).

[6] Bede, *HE*, iii, 26.—On cattle kept for their personal use by monks or
ecclesiastics, see *Hibernensis*, xviii, 6, p. 57 ; Giraldus, *EH*, i, 35, p. 283.

[7] A. Ebrard, *Die iroschottische Missionskirche* (Gütersloh, 1873), pp.
206–22. Refuted by F. Loofs, *Antiquae Britonum Scotorumque Ecclesiae
quales fuerint mores* (Lipsiae, 1882), pp. 5–8, 14–15, and by F. X. Funk,
Kirchengeschichtliche Abhandlungen und Untersuchungen (Paderborn, 1897), I,
p. 442).

to God, after having remained chaste marries a husband according to the flesh, let her be excommunicate until she amend her ways," so runs a canon of St Patrick.[1] Another text from the same source forbids a monk and a virgin to stay at the same hostel, to travel from one place to another in the same vehicle, and, finally, to keep up a conversation of any length with one another.[2] The penitentials inflict severe punishments on violations of chastity committed either against persons consecrated to God or by them.[3]

It has further been denied by Ebrard that these three obligations of the religious calling formed the subject of vows in early Celtic monasticism ; we have not the shadow of a doubt, however, that such was the case.   In one of the canons just quoted reference is made to a virgin who has made her vows to God, *virgo quae voverit Deo*.   The expressions " *votum perfectionis*," " *votum monachicum*," " *votum monachi*," occur very frequently.[4]   From the time of Gildas on, there were monks who bound themselves by solemn oath and in perpetuity.   Addressing Maelgwn, king of Gwynedd, who after becoming a monk had belied the promises of his pro- fession, Gildas reminds him of the perpetual vows which he had publicly pronounced *coram omnipotente Deo, angelicis vultibus humanisque*.[5]   To such explicit texts there is nothing to oppose.

§ 10.—THE CELTIC MONASTERY

There are few literary data concerning the early monastic architecture of the Celtic countries.   To compensate for this there are fairly numerous archaeological remains still existing in different districts which help us to form some notion of the construction of monastic establishments.[6]

---

[1] Can. 17 (*CED*, II, p. 329).

[2] Can. 9 (*CED*, II, p. 328).

[3] *Excerpta quaedam de Libro Davidis*, 5 (*CED*, I, p. 119) ; *Praefatio Gildae de poenitentia*, 1 (*CED*, I, p. 113) ; *Ir. Pen.*, II, 8–10 (pp. 142–43) ; *Peniten- tiale Vinniai*, 37 (*Buss.*, p. 116), ed. Schmitz, *Die Bussbücher* (Mainz, 1883), p. 507 ; *Penit. Cummeani*, II, 22–23 (*Buss.*, 470–71).

[4] *Altera synodus Luci Victoriae*, 9 (*CED*, I, p. 118) ; *Praefatio Gildae*, 1, *l. cit.* ; Columban, *Ep.* 1, 4, ed. Gundlach (*MG.*, *Epist.*, III, p. 159) ; Adam., *Vita Col.*, II, 40 (p. 112).

[5] Gildas, *De exc.*, 34 (p. 45).

[6] See G. Petrie, *The Ecclesiastical architecture of Ireland anterior to the*

It would be a very false conception to imagine them built in the style of the medieval European monasteries, with lofty and spacious buildings symmetrically arranged round a central cloister. The architecture of the Celts of that age was far different in its primitive simplicity. Their cenobitic establishments resembled rather the settlements of pioneers in territories newly opened to exploitation. They comprised a large number of separate cells, each forming the abode of one or more cenobites, and constructed sometimes of wood, sometimes of stone.[1] Those of the latter class, round, oval or rectangular in shape, were built without mortar, the roof being formed by the gradual convergence of the walls corbelwise.[2] At Iona the abbot inhabited a small lodge (*tuguriolum*) situated on a hillock.[3] Besides the cells of the monks, the monastic city included one or more oratories, likewise very modest in construction and dimensions, and, in addition, a kitchen, a refectory, a guest-house [4] and workshops.[5]

Independently of the monks' cells or taking their place, it has been ascertained that in certain Celtic monasteries of Great Britain and the Continent there existed a dormitory (*dormitorium*).[6]

At Devenish, in Molaisse's time, a modest structure termed *secretum monasteriolum*, adjoining the main monastery, served the purposes of a monastic school.[7]

A monastery of this pattern was quickly built. In Ireland the founders often chose the site of an ancient fort of pagan times, in other countries that of a fortified enclosure dating back to the Roman occupation.[8] The rampart of the fort

Norman Conquest (Dublin, 1845), pp. 124–25 ; G. Baldwin Brown, *The Arts in Early England*, new and revised edit., I (London, 1926), II (1925) ; Ryan, *Monast.*, pp. 285–94. *V. inf.*, ch. x, § 1.

[1] *Betha Brenainn Clúana Ferta*, 30 (*BNE*, I, p. 49, II, p. 49). Cf. Plummer, *VSH*, I, p. cxiii (*introd.*) ; Ryan, *Monast.*, pp. 287, 290.

[2] G. Baldwin Brown, *Op. cit.*, II, pp. 41–49.

[3] Adam., *Vita Col.*, iii, 2 (p. 152).

[4] Adam., *Vita Col.*, ii, 29 (p. 108). Cf. Plummer, *VSH*, I, p. cxiii ; Ryan, *Monast.*, pp. 202, 274, 289, 318.

[5] Ryan, *Monast.*, pp. 289, 291–92.

[6] Adam., *Vita Col.*, ii, 13. Cf. Ryan, *Monast.*, p. 289 ; Duine, *Memento*, p. 117.

[7] *Acta Dagaei*, 1 (*Sal. ASH*, 891).

[8] In East Anglia, St Fursa " curauit locum monasterii . . . uelocissime construere . . . Erat autem monasterium siluarum et maris uicinitate amoenum, constructum in castro quodam . . ." (Bede, *HE*, iii, 19)

or the *castrum* served as the enclosure of the new establish-ment.[1] The three vast concentric cashels, or dry-built stone walls, surrounding the monastery of Nendrum on Mahee Island in Strangford Lough (Co. Down) call for special notice.[2]

The earliest monastic colonies of the East and of Gaul were similarly constituted of separate cells enclosed within a *vallum*.[3]

As for the dress of monks, very little information can be gathered from ancient texts,[4] but the pointed hood appears in figures carved on sculptured stones in Scotland and Ireland.[5]

§ 11.—MONASTICISM AND WOMEN

We have seen that St Patrick consecrated a large number of virgins.[6] Did these virgins from the beginning join together in the life of community ? We cannot say. Tirechán calls some of them *monachae*,[7] a term that never occurs in Patrick's own writings. The oldest monasteries of women recorded in Ireland are those of Brigid at Kildare, of Moninne (Darerca, Monenna) at Killeevy,[8] of Ita at Killeedy.[9] We

---

[1] Many Irish monasteries or churches have taken their names from the nature of their enclosure : (*a*) from *less* or *rath* " earthen rampart " (*e.g.*, Lismore, Rathan) ; (*b*) from *caisel* " stone rampart " (*e.g.*, Cashel).—In Wales, Cornwall and Brittany, *llan* or *lan*, meaning " enclosure " is very frequent as first term in names of monasteries. Cf. Williams, *Christianity*, pp. 266–68.—For Irish monastic place-names beginning with *Lann*, " all within easy reach of the Irish sea," see Ryan, *Monast.*, pp. 129–30. In Latin *vallum monasterii* occurs in Adam., *Vita Col.* (I, 3, II, 19) ; Columban, *Reg. coenobialis* (*ZK*, XVII, 1897, p. 225 ; *PL*, LXXX, 219) ; Columban, *Poenitentiale* (*ZK*, XIV, 1894, p. 446 ; *PL*, LXXX, 229). Cf. Ryan, *Monast.*, pp. 285–86. On the enclosure built by St Cuthbert in Farne see Bede, *Vita Cuthberti*, 17 (*PL*, XCIV, 757).
[2] H. C. Lawlor, *The Monastery of Saint Mochaoi of Nendrum* (Belfast, 1925), Ch. VII and plates.
[3] Ryan, *Monast.*, p. 293 ; E. V[enables], art. *Monastery* in Smith and Cheetham, *Dictionary of Christian Antiquities* (pp. 1238–43).
[4] Ryan, *Monast.*, pp. 384–85.
[5] Allen, *ECMS*, Figs. 4, 4A, 5, 6, 255B, 235B, 278, 305B, 378 ; A. W. Brøgger, *Ancient Emigrants : a History of the Norse Settlements of Scotland* (Oxford, 1929), Fig. opposite pp. 52, 56 ; Crawford, *Handbook*, No. 148.
[6] *V. sup.*, Ch. II., § 9.
[7] Tirechán, pp. 22, 24. Cf. *LA*, p. 454.
[8] Barony of Upper Orior, Armagh.
[9] Barony of Glenquin, Limerick.

are told by Adamnán of the existence of *monasteria puellarum* in the time of St Columba (597).[1]

In the following century we find the Scot Aidan, the first abbot of Lindisfarne, acting as director of the abbess Hilda and giving the veil to Heiu, the first Northumbrian nun.[2]

There certainly existed cloisters of women in Brittany prior to the eleventh century, although I do not know whether any mention of such establishments can be found older than one in the *Vita Gildae*, which belongs to that century.[3]

The most celebrated Irish virgin whose name history has handed down to us is St Brigid of Kildare. Unfortunately, the inexact and incoherent character of the biographies of the saint make it hard to find out anything definite about her life. She lived, it seems, in the second half of the fifth century and the first quarter of the sixth. After receiving the veil (from the hands of bishop Mac Caille?)[4] she founded a convent of nuns at Kildare in Leinster, which soon became an ardent centre of religious life. She is even said to have induced a bishop named Conlaed to leave his solitude and come to share with her in directing the community and those attached to it, by consecrating churches, ordaining priests and officiating in the church she had built at Kildare, one exceptionally large and well endowed.[5]

Cogitosus, who wrote in the seventh century,[6] even gives us to understand that Brigid, not content with ruling nuns, presided over a double community, members of both sexes

[1] Adam., *Vita Col.*, II, 41 (p. 115).—" Monialium monsaterium " in *Vita Boecii*, 10 (*VSH*, I, p. 90) ; " Sanctarum virginum locum " in *Vita Aidi I*[a], 15 (p. 509), *II*[a], 11 (p. 519), *III*[a], 11 (p. 527), ed. P. Grosjean (Boll., AS, Nov., IV). The word " *caillech*," nun (from " *caille* " borrowed from Lat. *pallium* " veil "), occurs in *Fél. Oeng.* (p. 58), in *Tallaght* (1911), §§ 7, 62. A " caillech " from Caill Uaitne is mentioned, § 32 (p. 140).

[2] Bede, *HE*, IV, 23.

[3] *Vita Gildae*, 32 (p. 101). Cf. A. Oheix, *Vie inédite de Saint Cunwall* (*R. Cel.*, XXXII, 1911, p. 169).

[4] *Vita I*[a] *Brigidae*, III, 16 (Boll., AS, Febr. I, p. 121); Cogitosus, *Vita Brig.*, II, 5 (p. 136). " In campo Teloch in qua sancta Brigita pallium cepit sub manibus filii Caille " (Tirechán, p. 21). Cf. *Vita Brigitae*, ed. C. Plummer, J. Fraser and P. Grosjean, 19–21 (*Irish Texts*, London, 1931, I, pp. 6–7).

[5] Cogitosus, *Vita Brig.*, I, 8 (pp. 135, 141).

[6] M. Esposito, *On the earliest Latin Life of St Brigid of Kildare* (*PRIA*, XXX, Sect. C, 1912, pp. 319–24), corrected by a further paper of the same writer (*Latin Learning*, I, pp. 256–57). Cf. Kenney, *Sources*, I, pp. 359–60.

having flocked from all sides to place themselves under her
direction.   However, as he is the only biographer of the holy
abbess to record this important fact, it has been questioned
if the double monastery of Kildare, which seems really to have
existed in his time, actually went back to the days of Brigid.[1]
Be that as it may, no other example of a monastery of the
kind can be adduced in Ireland or in any other Celtic
Church.[2] If in the sixth and seventh centuries the great
abbesses who were at the head of houses of this type in England and Gaul, St Hilda, St Salaberga, Itta and Gertrude,
the foundresses of Nivelles, and St. Burgundofara, were more
or less directly influenced by Scottic monks, that is no reason
for supposing that the latter were the first to introduce into
those countries an institution almost unknown in their own.
The best explanation that has been offered of the phenomenon
is that such an organization had no chance of surviving save
in an extremely pure spiritual atmosphere, and this the
influence of the Scottic monks of that age was certainly likely
to produce.[3]

That the association of the sexes in monasticism was contrary to the discipline of Irish saints of the second order
(second half of the sixth century) is clearly attested by the
passage of the *Catalogue* already referred to, which is couched
as follows : *Abnegabant mulierum administrationem separantes eas a
monasteriis.*[4] On the contrary, the saints of the primitive
period, according to the same author, " neither refused to
govern women nor to live with them, for, being firmly founded
on Christ as on a rock, they feared not the wind of temptation."   But does this imply that at the outset double monasteries existed as an institution in Ireland ?   I do not think so.
The passage seems rather to allude to a kind of life analogous
to that of the *agapetae* or the *subintroductae* of the first Christian
centuries ;   and in that sense it has been interpreted by

[1] Stephanus Hilpisch, *Die Doppelklöster. Entstehung und Organisation*
(*Beiträge zur Geschichte des alten Mönchtums und des Benediktinerordens*, XV,
Münster i, W., 1928), pp. 30–31.
[2] For a discussion of some doubtful statements see Ryan, *Monast.*, p. 143.
[3] Cf. Mary Bateson, *Origin and early History of Double Monasteries*
(*Transactions of the Royal Historical Society*, XIII, 1899, p. 197). Cf. S.
Hilpisch, *op. cit.*
[4] *Catalogus*, p. 292.

Thomas Olden, Hans Achelis and P. Stephanus Hilpisch.[1] In any case, a ready explanation is to be found in the circumstances of the times. Speaking of that Scottic lady of noble rank who vowed herself to Christ, St Patrick observes that Irish virgins had to endure the reproaches and persecution of their kinsfolk, some being threatened with slavery, others subjected to constant molestation.[2] In the possible absence of convents for women, such virgins were naturally led to have recourse to the churchmen who had initiated them into the life of faith and continence ; these were their only protectors in the midst of a society still partly heathen and given over to violence of all kinds.

The institution of *conhospitae* existed in Brittany at the beginning of the sixth century. It gave rise to abuses which were attacked by three bishops of the province of Tours in a curious letter addressed by them, between 515 and 520, to two Breton priests, Lovocat and Catihern. The following passage calls for notice : " You cease not from bearing to your fellow-countrymen from cot to cot certain tables on which you celebrate the divine sacrifice of the Mass with the assistance of women to whom you give the name of *conhospitae*. While you distribute the Eucharist, they take the chalice and administer the blood of Christ to the people. This is a new thing, a superstition hitherto unheard of. We have been deeply grieved to see an abominable heresy, never before introduced into Gaul, reappearing in our time. The Eastern fathers call it ' Pepundian' from the name of Pepundius, the author of the schism, who presumed to join women unto him in the ministry of the altar. Renounce these abuses . . ." [3]

It is possible that the practice of having spiritual sisters (or, as it is now sometimes called, syneisactism),[4] some traces

---

[1] Th. Olden, *On the " Consortia " of the First Order of Irish Saints (PRIA*, 3rd Ser., III, 1893–96, pp. 415–20) ; H. Achelis, art. *Subintroductae* in *Realenzyclopaedie f. prot. Theologie* (Leipzig, 1907), p. 124 ; *s.a.* art. *Agapetae (ERE*, 1908, p. 178) ; S. Hilpisch, *op. cit.*

[2] Pat., *Confessio*, 42.

[3] Ed. L. Duchesne, *Lovocat [et Catihern (Revue de Bretagne et de Vendée*, LVII, 1885, pp. 6–7) ; P. de Labriolle, *La crise montaniste* (Paris, 1913), pp. 499–501 ; *s.a. Les sources de l'histoire du montanisme (Collectanea Friburgensia*, N. Ser., XV, Fribourg and Paris, 1913), pp. 226–30. Cf. L.G., *Les chrétientés celtiques*, pp. 95–96.

[4] On " syneisactism " see Hans Achelis, above-mentioned art. ; *s.a.*

of which have been noted in Ireland, led some ascetics of that country to engage in strange and extremely risky experiments in order to test their sexual ἀπάθεια ; of such there is record in a few writings. Certain ascetics of the East had already conceived such experiments,[1] and, if we may believe the biographer of St Aldhelm of Sherborne († 709), that Anglo-Saxon monk too was addicted to practices of the same nature.[2] These strange self-tests, if they really occurred at all, seem to have been extremely rare in Ireland.[3] As for syneisactism itself, which led to such excesses, it is manifestly a great exaggeration to assert, as Achelis has done, that " the early Church of Ireland made this form of asceticism the basic column of its organization," [4] for the recklessness of the over-daring was always held in balance by the vigilance of the prudent.[5]

Women were strictly excluded from the confines of monasteries and hermitages.[6] To build a convent for women, Buite mac Brónaigh, the founder of Monasterboice (sixth century), chose a spot sufficiently distant from the monastery to ensure the reputation of the monks from being exposed to any danger.[7] It is told that St Ciarán, the future abbot of Clonmacnois, when studying the Psalter and the Scriptures at the school of St Finnian of Clonard, had as his fellow-pupil the daughter of a king. Taking as the rule of his conduct the

---

Virgines subintroductae, ein Beitrag zu I. Cor. 7 (Leipzig, 1902) ; Ad. Jülicher, *Die geistlichen Ehen in der alten Kirche* (*Archiv für Religionsgeschichte*, VII, 1904, pp. 373–86) ; P. de Labriolle, *Le " mariage spirituel " dans l'antiquité chrétienne* (*RH*, CXXXVII, 1921, pp. 204–25).

[1] Cassian, *Conlationes,* xv, 10 (*PL*, XLIX, 1009–1011) ; Evagrius Scholasticus, *Historia eccles.*, I, 21 (*PG*, LXXXVI, II, 2480–81) ; Nicephorus Callistus, *Eccles. hist.*, XIV, 50 (*PG*, CXLVI, 1236–37).

[2] William of Malmesbury, *De gestis pontificum Angliae*, ed. Hamilton (*RS*), pp. 357–58 ; ed. Migne (*PL*, CLXXIX, 1633–34) ; Capgrave, *Nova Legenda Angliae*, ed. Carl Horstman (Oxford, 1901), I, p. 39 ; ed. Migne (*PL*, LXXXIX, 85).

[3] See L.G., *Mulierum consortia* (*Ériu*, IX, 1923, pp. 147–56).

[4] H. Achelis, art. *Subintroductae* (p. 124), art. *Agapetae* (p. 178).

[5] L.G., *Mulierum consortia*, pp. 154–55.

[6] *Ib.* Cf. Ryan, *Monast.*, p. 227.

[7] *Vita Boecii*, 10 (*VSH*, I, p. 90). So did Daig of Inis Cain Dega in Louth, who, having first accepted to govern some virgins who had come to live under his rule, soon after sent them to various monasteries of their own (*Acta Dagaei*, 16 : *Sal. ASH*, col. 898). Cf. Ryan, *Monast.*, pp. 143–44.

words of the Book of Job : " I made a covenant with mine
eyes ; how then should I look upon a maid ? " (xxxi, 1), he
never allowed himself to gaze on the young princess, whom
he would have been unable to distinguish from other girls, for,
as he said, " he saw naught of the body of the maiden, so long
as they were together, save her feet only." [1] Maignenn,
abbot of Kilmainham, would never look on a woman, lest
he should see her " guardian devil." [2] It is related also of
St Enda of Aran that when his sister came from a great
distance to visit him, he would only consent to converse with
her through a veil stretched between them. [3] An Irish
hagiographer places the following *dictum* in the mouth of a
saint : " *In hoc loco non ero, ubi enim ovis, ibi mulier, ubi mulier,
ibi peccatum.*" [4] And it would be easy to multiply instances
showing the same extreme caution in associating with the other
sex. [5]

§ 12.—Ascetic Life

The primary mortification for the monk as for every
Christian is work. The threefold division of the day between
prayer, study and manual labour is frequently indicated in
the Rules. [6] In certain monasteries of Britain, as well as at
Rahen in the beginning of St Carthach's abbotship, agricultural labour was carried on without the aid of animals,
everyone being his own ox and his own horse. [7] To feed
flocks, to gather in the harvest, to thresh the corn and grind

[1] *Vita Ciarani*, 16 (*VSH*, I, 205–206) ; *Betha Ciarain Clúana meic Nois*
(*Lismore*, ll. 4128 ff., pp. 123, 268) ; R. A. Stewart Macalister, *The Latin
and Irish Lives of Ciaran* (London, 1921), pp. 25, 77.
[2] *Betha Mhaignenn*, ed. Standish H. O'Grady, *Silva Gadelica* (London,
1892), I, p. 37, transl. II, p. 35.
[3] *Vita Endei*, II, 9 (Boll., *AS*, Mart. III, p. 269).
[4] *Vita Coemgeni*, 32 (*Sal. ASH*, 273) ; *Vita Coemgeni*, 31 (*VSH*, I, p. 250.
Cf. Plummer, *VSH*, I, p. cxxi (*introd.*).
[5] Conchubran, *Vita Mon.*, II, 16 (p. 226) ; *Tallaght* (1911), 62, p. 151.
Cf. L.G., *Mulierum consortia*, pp. 153–55.
[6] *Rule of the Céli Dé*, 55, ed. E. Gwynn, *Tallaght* (1927), p. 79 (cf. note,
p. 101) ; *Rule of Colum Cille*, 16, ed. K. Meyer (*ZCP*, III, 1901, p. 29) ;
Regula Columbani, 3 (*PL*, LXXX, 211) ; *Rule of Fothad na canóine*, ed. W.
Reeves, *Culdees* (p. 83) ; *Vita Moluae*, 51 (*VSH*, II, p. 222) ; Wrdisten, *Vita
Winwaloei*, I, 20, ed. C. De Smedt (*AB*, VII, 1888, p. 208).
[7] *Vita Carthagi*, 20, 25, 46 (*VSH*, I, pp. 178, 179, 188) ; *Vita Fintani*, 4
(*VSH*, II, p. 98) ; Ricemarch, *Vita Davidis*, 22, ed. A. W. Wade-Evans
(*YC*, 1913, p. 13) ; *Vita Kentigerni*, 20, ed. Pinkerton, p. 237.

it in a hand-quern, these were the commonest manual industries. The monasteries had also their craftsmen, gold-smiths, scribes and illuminators.[1]   Columcille was re-nowned as a scribe.[2]   We shall see later what prodigious patience and skill were displayed by Irish calligraphers and painters on vellum.

We will also speak elsewhere of the liturgical prayers of the Celtic monks, in which the psalms formed the largest element. In private devotion also it was to the Psalter they most readily had recourse, " the three fifties " (na trí cóecait), as it was currently termed.[3]   The daily recitation of the " three fifties " is prescribed by several monastic Rules and is found as a voluntary devotional practice.[4]   The psalm Beati immaculati, the Hymnum dicat (wrongly ascribed to St Hilary of Poitiers),[5] certain forms of confession of sin, and those curious prayers named after the saints supposed to be their authors, the lorica of Patrick, the lorica of Gildas, etc., such were the vocal prayers in commonest use.[6]

Prayer was often accompanied by gestures of adoration, demonstrations of penitence, prostrations, genuflexions and the attitude of the arms outstretched to form a cross.[7]   In the Teaching of Máel Rúain we read : " ' I have heard,' said

[1] Ryan, Monast., pp. 362–64.

[2] Adam., Vita Col., III, 23 (p. 157).

[3] Fél. Oeng., 177 (p. 272) ; Teaching of Máel Rúain, 36, 37, 65 (Tallaght, 1927, pp. 22–23, 38–39) ; Rule of Céli Dé, 32 (Tallaght, 1927, pp. 72–73). "Ter quinquagenos decantat in ordine psalmos " (Versiculi Ricemarch, ed. H. J. Lawlor : Ricemarch, PM, I, p. 29).—Irish psalters are divided into three parts, each containing fifty psalms. The tripartite division, however, was not peculiar to the Irish ; see Lawlor (Ricemarch, PM, p. 118). Cf. R. L. Ramsay, Theodore of Mopsuestia in England and Ireland (ZCP, VIII, 1912, p. 487).

[4] Rule of the Céli Dé, 30, 58 (Tallaght, 1927, pp. 72–73, 80–81) ; Rule of Comgall, 13 (Ériu, I, 1904, p. 196) ; Rule of Ailbe, 17 (Ériu, III, 1907, p. 100) ; Wrdisten, Vita Winwaloei, II, 10, ed. C. De Smedt (AB, VII, 1888, p. 225). Cf. Gildae Translatio, 45 (St Goustan), ed. F. Lot, Mélanges (p. 472).

[5] Hymnum dicat in LH, I, pp. 35–42 ; ed. A. Feder, S. Hilarii Opera, IV (Corp. SEL, LXV, pp. 217–23). Cf. Esposito, Latin Learning, I, p. 231.

[6] On these prayers v. inf., ch. IX, § 6.

[7] On these practices see H. Zimmer, On Prostration in the early Irish Church (Irish Eccles. Record, 3rd Ser., V, 1884, pp. 242–46) ; L.G., Some liturgical and ascetic Traditions of the Celtic Church : I, Genuflexion (JTS, IX, 1908, pp. 556–61) ; s.a. La prière les bras en croix (Rassegna gregoriana, VII, 1908, cols. 343–54) ; s.a. Devotional and ascetic Practices in the Middle Ages (London, 1927, pp. 3–17).

Mael Dithruib, ' that Dublitir's customary form of vigil is to say the hundred and fifty psalms standing, with a genuflexion at the end of each psalm.' ' Such is not my command,' said Mael Ruain, ' but to chant every other fifty (or, every other psalm—the old book says, ' each division,') sitting and standing alternately. If any one,' said he, ' were to remain seated longer than this, he would fall asleep : and if he remained standing longer, he would be tired out.' "

The same text continues : " The vigil which Muirchertach mac Olcobhair, erenagh [1] of Clonfert, used to keep was to say the *Beati* twelve times in place of the hundred and fifty psalms, because he knew that there were more of the monks or penitents who knew the *Beati* by heart than knew the Psalms ; and he used to say the *Magnificat* after each repetition of the *Beati* . . ." [2]

Prostration was, as we know, much practised by the early monks of the East, just as it is by their successors at the present day. [3] The early Irish ascetics likewise employed it frequently. However, it is often hard to say whether the Gaelic verb *slechtaim* (from the Latin *flecto*) denotes the act of prostrating oneself at full length or merely putting one or both knees to earth. [4] St Iarlaithe of Tuam (fl. *c.* 540) is said to have been in the habit of making three hundred genuflexions or prostrations by night and three hundred by day, [5] and Oengus the Culdee to have made the same number by day. [6] According to Tirechán, St Patrick had already set the example of the practice. On one occasion the saint engaged in a fast of three days and three nights accompanied by a hundred prayers and by constant genuflexion or prostration (*cum centenis oraculis flectenisque assiduis*). [7]

James the Less, of whom it was related that, owing to his

---

[1] *Airchennech* (*anglice*, erenagh) = head, leader, superior. On this word see Kenney, *Sources*, I, p. 12, n. 17 ; Ryan, *Monast.*, p. 264, n. 5.

[2] *Teaching of Máel Rúain*, 36, 37, ed. Gwynn, *Tallaght* (1927), pp. 22–23.

[3] On the metanœas (μετάνοιαι) of the Greeks see H. Thurston, *Genuflexions and Aves* (*Month*, CXXVII, 1916, pp. 196, 442–46) ; Placide de Meester, *Voyage de deux Bénédictins au Mont Athos* (Paris, 1908), p. 214.

[4] See H. Zimmer's above-mentioned paper on Prostration.

[5] Cuimin's Poem on the Saints of Ireland, ed. Wh. Stokes (*ZCP*, I, 1897, pp. 66–67).

[6] *Fél. Oeng.*, p. xlviii.

[7] Tirechán, p. 22.

constant prayers, his knees had become like those of a camel, had come to be a favourite among the Irish ascetics, who called him " Iacob glúnech " (*i.e.*, James of the knees).[1]   It was told that " he used to make two hundred genuflexions in the day and two hundred in the night on the bare flags of marble in the great Temple at Jerusalem, so that his knees were as large as a camel's knees : wherefore he was called ' James the kneed.' "[2]

In practices of this kind as well as others, veritable contests of emulation seem to have arisen, one ascetic trying to outdo the performance of another, the result being often manifest excesses.   We hear of an anchorite of Clonard who made it his rule " to make two hundred genuflexions at lauds, a hundred at each of the canonical hours, and a hundred at matins.   Seven hundred genuflexions in all did he make in the twenty-four hours.   This was told to Máel Rúain.   " ' My word for it,' said he, ' there will be some space of time before his death when he will not be able to make a single genuflexion.'   And this came true, for his legs became crippled, so that for a long while before his death he was unable to make a single genuflexion, by reason of the excessive number he had formerly made." [3]

Among the Scottic monks who went to the Continent there were evidently some who distinguished themselves by faithful adherence to this ascetic tradition of their country, for several Continentals were struck by, and noted, the peculiarity. Walahfrid Strabo, abbot of Reichenau, wrote in 841 on the subject : " While the whole Church maintains this practice of kneeling, more especially do men of Irish nationality (*Scotorum natio*) lay stress upon this observance, many of whom —some with more, some with less, but in any case with genuflexions during the day or night, which are fixed and counted—are found to be constant in this exercise of bending the knees, not only to bewail their past sins, but also for the discharge of their daily devotions." [4]

[1] Cf. C. Plummer, *Ir. Lit.*, pp. 33, 112.
[2] Gloss in Lebar Brecc (p. 151ᵃ) transl. by Wh. Stokes, *The Irish Verses, Notes and Glosses in Harl.* 1802 (*R. Cel.*, VIII, 1887, p. 365).
[3] *Tallaght* (1911), 34, p. 141 ; *Tallaght* (1927), 103, p. 61.
[4] Walahfrid Strabo, *De exordiis et incrementis quarundam in observationibus*

The custom of praying with the arms extended like a cross was particularly well known to the early Irish, both as an ordinary private devotion and imposed as a penance. The expression " to crucify oneself," which is found in the writings of some Irish hagiographers, must be taken as an allusion to this penitential practice.[1] There is even a special word in Old Irish to denote it, *crossfigell*, which means " the vigil of the cross " (*crucis vigilia*) or prayer of the cross.[2] In the *crossfigell* the ascetic was sometimes lying down, but more often standing. In a penitential written in Irish in the eighth century, in which the different ways of commuting the canonical punishments (*De arreis*) are discussed, it can be seen that the horizontal position, with the face to the earth, for carrying out the *crossfigell*, was in certain cases left to the choice of the penitent.[3] It is related in the Life of St Féchín of Fore that when the parents of the young Féchín lay down to sleep, they used to place the child between them in bed, but often when they awoke they found him stretched on the floor with his arms in the form of a cross.[4]

However, as we have said, the *crossfigell* was generally practised in an upright position. An Irish penitential pre-scribes *manus sopinate ad orationem*.[5] This position, if kept up for long, was far more painful than lying on the ground with the arms forming a cross. The treatise *De arreis*, already quoted, orders a *crossfigell* at the end of every hundred psalms, and it is further directed that it should only last till fatigue began to be felt. For more serious faults the same position was to be kept up for a longer time—in one instance, during the double recitation of the psalm *Beati immaculati*, " without

---

ecclesiasticis rerum, ed. A. Knöpfler (München, 1899), pp. 74–75. Cf. *Miracula Columbani*, ed. Mabillon, *Acta Sanct. O.S.B.* (Paris, 1669), II, p. 42 ; *Codex Bernensis* 363 *phototypice editus*, ed. H. Hagen (Lugduni Batavorum, 1897), p. 208.

[1] *Vita Abbani*, 22 ; *Vita Albei*, 47 (*VSH*, I, pp. 17, 63).

[2] J. Vendryes, *De Hibernicis vocabulis quae a Latina lingua originem duxerunt* (Lutetiae Parisiorum, 1902), pp. 30, 133 ; S. Malone, *The vicissitudes of* " *Vigil* " (*Dublin Review*, 3rd Ser., XII, 1884, p. 354) ; L.G., *La prière les bras en croix*, cols. 348–49.

[3] *De arreis*, p. 494.

[4] *Life of St Fechin of Fore*, ed. Wh. Stokes (*R. Cel.*, XII, 1891, p. 323).

[5] *Canones Hibernenses*, II, *De arreis*, 2 (*Buss.*, p. 139).—" Coram altari in modum crucis stans " (*Vita Findani*, 10 ; *MG, Scr.* XV, I, p. 505).

lowering the arms " ; in another, during the recital of fifty
psalms or, at choice, of four *Beati*, during which, says the text,
" the penitent should not allow his arms to touch his sides or
procure any support." [1]

In the minds of the Irish ascetics, the remembrance of
Moses praying on the mountain with outstretched arms during
the fight between the children of Israel and Amalek was
associated with the crucifixion of our Lord.   Proof of this may
be found in the second Vision of Adamnán, where the term
crossfigell is used to describe the attitude of Moses during the
battle. [2]

The practice of this species of mortification, as well as that
of repeated genuflexions, was suspended between the two
Christmases (*i.e.*, Christmas Day and Epiphany [*notlaic
stéill*]) and also between the two Easters (Easter Day and
Low Sunday). [3]

The ascetic writers and hagiographers of Celtic countries
have preserved numerous striking examples of the extension
of the arms during prayer.   The author of a Life of Gildas
represents his hero as mortifying his body with fasts and
vigils and spending the nights in prayer standing without
any support (*stans sine aliquo sustentaculi adminiculo*). [4]   Legend
took firm hold of a practice so dear to the ascetic spirit of the
Celts.   Once St Finnian of Clonard " sent his pupil, even
bishop Senach, to find out what the folk of his school were
doing.   Different, in sooth, was that at which each of them
was found, yet all were good.   Colomb, son of Crimthann,
was found with his hands stretched forth and his mind contemplative of God, and birds resting on his hands and on his
head.   When that was told to Finnian : ' The hands of that
man,' saith he, ' shall give me communion and sacrifice at the
ending days.' " [5]   A gloss of the *Liber Hymnorum* tells us how
Kevin remained seven years standing in Glendalough, " with
a board under him merely and he without sleeping during

---

[1] *De arreis, l. cit.*—For some minor infractions the penance lasted during
twelve or even only three Our Father's (*Ir. Pen.*, pp. 142–45).
[2] *Hibernensis*, p. 41.   Cf. L.G., *La prière les bras en croix*, col. 351.
[3] *Tallaght* (1911), 30 (p. 138) ;   *Tallaght* (1927), 95 (pp. 54–55).
[4] *Vita Gildae*, 6 (p. 93).
[5] *Betha Fhindein Chiana hEraird* (*Lismore*, ll. 2646 ff.).

that time, *ut ferunt*, in ' crosfigill,' so that the birds made their nests in his hands, *ut ferunt*." [1] Apart from their poetic beauty, such stories should be taken into account, since in their own way they show the extraordinary vogue of this old Christian custom in the medieval Celtic world. A noteworthy example of psalm-singing combined with both *crossfigell* and repeated genuflexions is offered by a Life of the Breton saint Winwalloc (Guénolé). [2]

Another strange form of mortification consisted in plunging into a stream or pond and remaining there petrified with cold for a greater or less time, meanwhile reciting psalms or other prayers. According to the Gaelic hymn ascribed to Fiacc, " cold of weather did not keep [Patrick] from sleeping at night in pools." [3] These words are echoed in a homily of the eleventh century on the saint, [4] as well as in his biography by Jocelin of Furness (A.D. 1185–86). [5] Four biographers of Patrick, in particular Muirchu (seventh century), allude to the same practice. [6]

A considerable number of Irish, Scotch, Welsh and Breton saints, male and female, are recorded as having regularly practised ascetic immersion with accompanying prayers, generally during the night ; likewise a certain number of Anglo-Saxon ascetics of the seventh and eighth centuries (Cuthbert of Lindisfarne, Drithelm of Melrose, Wilfrid, Aldhelm), and it is likely that these latter borrowed their favourite exercise of mortification from the *Scotti*. [7] The

---

[1] *LH*, I, p. 114 ; II, p. 193. Cf. *Lismore*, p. 344.
[2] " Quinquagenos namque ter cotidie particulatim psalmos consuebat psallere, nunc in crucis modo, nunc immobilis fixus statura, nunc fixis provolutis genibus " (Wrdisten, *Vita Winwaloei*, II, 9, ed. C. De Smedt (*AB*, VII, 1888, p. 225). *Ib.*, II, 14, p. 227.
[3] *LH*, II, p. 33.
[4] Edited by Whitley Stokes in *Trip. Life*, p. 485. On the date see *R. Cel.*, XXXII, 1911, p. 351.
[5] Jocelin, *Vita Patricii*, 160 (Boll., *AS*, Mart. II, p. 574).
[6] Muirchu, 27, ed. E. Hogan (*AB*, I, 1882, p. 577) ; *Vita tertia*, 86, ed. J. Colgan, *Triadis Thaumaturgae, seu divorum Patricii, Columbae et Brigidae . . . Acta* (Lovanii, 1645), p. 28, col. 2 ; *Vita tripartita*, III, 96, ed. Colgan, pp. 166–67 [this passage is wanting in the text of *Vita Trip.* edited by Wh. Stokes] ; *Vita quinta*, II, 2, ed. Colgan, p. 52. On this point see Paul Grosjean, *Patriciana* (*AB*, XLIII, 1925, pp. 250 ff. and XLVI, 1928, p. 206).
[7] See L.G., *Ascetic Immersions* in *Devotional and ascetic Practices in the Middle Ages*, pp. 159–78.

nightly immersions, accompanied by the recital of psalms, which were practised by the Frankish monk Wandrille († 667) according to the account of a well-informed contemporary, seem to have been also a legacy of the same ascetic tradition.[1]

During the Middle Ages proper and down to a time far less remote from our own, this method of mortifying the body was often practised outside the Celtic world, but nearly always with the view of taming the outbreaks of the flesh, an object not habitually mentioned in the case of Celtic ascetics.[2] However, Giraldus Cambrensis relates that an old Welsh saint named Dogmael was in the habit of plunging into the river which flowed close by his hermitage *ad domandam libidinem*.[3] And centuries later we hear of a Breton penitent, Pierre de Keriolet († 1660), who threw himself into a ditch full of water one winter day to overcome a sinful desire and then walked several miles in his frozen clothing.[4]

Similar immersions were sometimes imposed as a penance for grave misdeeds.[5]

One of the rites which every pilgrim to the Purgatory of St Patrick (Loch Derg) was obliged to observe as late as the seventeenth century consisted in plunging naked, even in winter, into the waters of the lake which surrounds the island of the Purgatory.[6] At the present day this performance no longer forms part of the exercises, though these are still severe enough.[7]

The monastic diet was exceedingly austere. As a rule monks abstained from flesh-foods. Vegetables seasoned with

---

[1] *Vita Wandregisili*, I, 12, ed. Br. Krusch (*MG. Scr. RM*, V, 267). The author of this Life died before A.D. 672.

[2] L.G., *op. cit.*

[3] Giraldus, *Gemma Ecclesiae*, II, 10 (*RS*), pp. 214–15.

[4] H. Le Gouvello, *Pierre de Keriolet* (Paris, 1910), pp. 220–21.

[5] *De arreis*, pp. 493, 495. Cf. L.G., *op. cit.*, p. 163.

[6] " Deducuntur [peregrini] ad marginem stagni, ibique se nudos immergunt aquis lacustribus, et hac lustrali expiatione veluti novi milites e balneo poenitentiae renati purgatique progrediuntur ad ecclesiam " (T. Messingham, *Tractatus de Purgatorio S. Patricii*, 30, 31, in *Florilegium Insulae Sanctorum* (Parisiis, 1624, p. 96), reprinted in *PL*, CLXXX, cols. 985–86).

[7] Cf. Daniel O'Connor, *St Patrick's Purgatory, Lough Derg* (Dublin, 1895), pp. 210–11.

salt, eggs, occasionally fish, and bread twice baked (*paximatium*), already a classic item of fare among the Eastern monks (παξαμάδιον, παξαμάτιον), formed the basis of their solid food [1]; they drank milk, whey-water or simply water.[2] St David of Menevia was surnamed "the Aquatic" (*Aquaticus*), in Welsh *Dewi Ddyvrwr* (Dewi the Waterman),[3] and the Book of Llandaff mentions other *aquatici viri*.[4] "Not a drop of beer was drunk in Tallaght in Maelruain's lifetime. . . . Not a morsel of meat was eaten in Tallaght in his lifetime [unless] it were a deer or a wild swine. What meat there was [at Tallaght used to be consumed by] the guests." [5]

As for the practice of fasting, it was carried to great lengths. "Just as one ought to pray each day," St Columban writes in his monastic Rule, "so ought one to fast each day." [6] Ratramnus, a monk of Corbie, remarks in a treatise *Contra Graecorum opposita* that, "among the *Scotti* who live in the island of Hibernia, there is a custom in the monasteries of monks, canons, and other religious, of fasting on every day except Sundays and feast days, in such a manner that no bodily nourishment is taken before none in summer or before vespers in winter." [7]

The Wednesday and Friday fasts were observed in Ireland even outside the monasteries. In other parts of Christendom these two days were likewise distinguished by fasting. But it is to be believed that the custom flourished particularly in Ireland, for from a very remote period the name given to Wednesday in the language of the country was *cétaín*, which means "first fast," and Friday was called *oín diden*, the "last fast," or *dia oíne didine*, "day of the last fast." [8]   This

---

[1] Ricemarch, *Vita Davidis*, 24 (cf. Wade-Evans, *David*, pp. 96–97) ; Wrdisten, *Vita Winwaloei*, II, 11 (*AB*, VII, 1888, p. 226) ; *Tallaght* (1927), 2, 3 (pp. 1–5). Cf. Ryan, *Monast.*, pp. 386–88.—On "*paxamatium*" see Ryan, *Monast.*, p. 389, n. 13 ; L.G., *Étude sur l'Ordo monasticus de Culross* (*RHE*, XXIII, 1927, p. 775).

[2] *Tallaght* (1927), 55 (pp. 34–35). Cf. Ryan, *Monast.*, pp. 388–89.

[3] Ricemarch, *Vita Davidis*, 2 ; Wade-Evans, *David*, pp. VIII, 62–63.

[4] Cf. Du'ne, *Memento*, p. 123 ; Ryan, *Monast.*, p. 163.

[5] *Tallaght* (1911), 6 (p. 129).

[6] *Regula*, 3 (*PL*, LXXX, 211).

[7] *Contra Graec. opposita*, IV, 3 (*PL*, CXXI, 315–16).

[8] L.G., *Fasting in Ireland*, in *Devotional and ascetic Practices in the Middle Ages*, p. 148 ; H. d'Arbois de Jubainville, *Le jeûne du mercredi et du vendredi chez les Irlandais du moyen âge* (*R. Cel.*, IX, 1888, pp. 269–71).

latter name is met with in an Irish gloss of the eighth century.[1]

The introduction of this custom into Ireland has been attributed to St Patrick himself.[2] Although this opinion is not based on any formal proof, there are many facts which render it probable.[3] The Scot Aidan († 651), first abbot of Lindisfarne and the apostle of Northumbria, inculcated the practice among the pious Christians whom he had evangelized.[4]

" *Superpositio* " was the term used in the vocabulary of asceticism to denote the particular mortification which consisted in abstaining from all food for two or three or even four days.[5] These prolonged and consecutive fasts were called respectively *biduanum* (sc. *ieiunium*), *triduanum*, *quatriduanum*. Instances of *biduana* and of *triduana* are not rare in Irish hagiographic literature.[6] The latter word passed into Gaelic in the form *trédenus*.[7]

Individual cases of great austerity are on record. St Paul Aurelian was accustomed to remain for two or three days at a time without eating.[8] Adamnán of Coldingham is said to have abstained from food and drink except on Sundays and Thursdays.[9] For men living in a harsh northern climate such privations call for amazing heroism.

This is not the place to speak of certain curious purposes for which fasting was sometimes employed and which do not come under the head of asceticism but belong to the history of law and to folklore.[10]

---

[1] Stokes and Strachan, *TP*, I, pp. 4, 383 ; II, p. 32.
[2] Ussher, *Works* (Dublin, 1847–64), Vol. VI, p. 444.
[3] L.G., *Devotional and ascetic Pract.*, pp. 148–49.
[4] Bede, *HE*, III, 5.
[5] See Du Cange, *Glossarium mediae et infimae latinitatis*, s.v. " *Superpositio*," and *Glossarium mediae et infimae graecitatis*, s.v. ὑπερθέσις. Cf. Duguet, *Jeûnes de superposition et du samedi*, in his *Conférences ecclésiastiques* (Cologne, 1742), I, p. 411.
[6] *Vita Abbani*, 22 (*VSH*, I, 17) ; *Vita Albei*, 29 (p. 57) ; *Vita Barri*, 12 (p. 70) ; *Vita Comgalli*, 14 (II, p. 7) ; *Vita Itae*, 5, 10 (pp. 117, 119).
[7] *Betha Máedóc Ferna*, I, 150 (*BNE*, I, 190, 233) ; *Life of St Fechin of Fore*, ed. Wh. Stokes (*R. Cel.*, XII, 1891, pp. 326–27). See a note of C. Plummer in Bede, *HE*, Vol. II, p. 78.
[8] Wrmonoc, *Vita Pauli Aurel.*, 7 (*R. Cel.*, V, 1881–83, p. 431).
[9] Bede, *HE*, IV, 25.
[10] R. Thurneysen, *Aus dem irischen Recht.*, III. *Das Fasten beim Pfändungs-*

§ 13.—Hermits and Recluses

At every period of the Middle Ages the life of the solitary had numerous adepts in all the Celtic countries. Both types of solitary are to be found in them, the hermit living far apart from the world of men in the midst of nature, and the recluse enclosed in his *carcair* (Lat. *carcer*) in proximity to a church or monastery. The *Liber Angeli* inserted in the Book of Armagh mentions the anchorites attached to the church of Armagh.[1]

The cells shaped like beehives on the Skellig Rock, an islet very difficult of access situated in a wild sea about seven miles and a half from the coast of Kerry, were the abodes of hermits. Others lived in the depths of the woods, in pleasant spots, on familiar terms with the animals around them[2] ; such a one was Marbán, brother of king Guaire mac Colmain, who has left us a charming picture of his retreat.[3] " These anchorites were not necessarily morose or unsociable. They had no objection to being visited and consulted by their fellow-men. We hear of one Cronan of Glen Essa, who was a notable hand at the pipes and anxious to prove his skill."[4] Bede and Alcuin tell us of some Anglo-Saxons who left their country in order to follow the hermit life in Ireland.[5] As a rule monks set out for the desert after long years of cenobitical life.[6]

verfahren (*ZCP*, XV, 1924, pp. 260–76) ; L.G., *op. cit.*, pp. 151–54.—For further ascetical practices such as silence, curtailment of sleep and other monastic austerities see Ryan, *Monast.*, pp. 397–401.

[1] " In australi vero bassilica aepiscopi et presbiteri et anchoritae ecclessiae et caeteri religiossi laudes sapidas offerunt " (*LA*, fol. 21r). " Christi miles Finanus nomine, qui vitam multis anachoreticam annis iuxta Roboreti monasterium campi [Durrow] irreprehensibiliter ducebat " (Adam., *Vita Col.*, I, 49, p. 62). Note the Welsh " gwr ystafellog " (chambered man = recluse). Cf. Lloyd, *HW*, I, p. 218 ; *Fél. Oeng.*, pp. 45, 320 ; *Cuimín's Poem*, ll. 21, 33, 105 (*ZCP*, I, 1897 and index, p. 71) ; *De arreis*, pp. 495–96.—On discussions which arose in Ireland in the sixth century concerning the life of solitude see Columban, *Ep.* 3 *ad Gregor. Papam* (*MG. Epist.*, III, p. 159). Cf. Ryan, *Monast.*, pp. 260–61.

[2] Cf. Gerard Murphy, *The Origin of Irish Nature Poetry* (*Studies*, xx, 1931, pp. 87–102).

[3] *The Hermit's Song ; King and Hermit*, transl. by K. Meyer, *Selections from Ancient Irish Poetry* (London, 1911), pp. 30–31, 47–50.

[4] E. J. Gwynn, *Some Saints of Ireland* (*Church Quarterly Review*, LXXIV, 1912, p. 71).

[5] Haemgils (Bede, *HE*, v, 12) ; Wigbert (Bede, *HE*, V, 9) ; Alcuin, *Versus de sanctis Eubor. Eccl.*, V, 1024 (*MG. Poet. Lat.*, I, 192).

[6] " Qui videlicet Virgnous, post multos in subiectione inter fratres

Even without finally renouncing the advantages of the life in community, it occasionally happened that monks felt the need of giving themselves up for a season to more intense contemplation and severer mortifications in solitude ; and an island was sometimes chosen for the purpose.[1] But some islands were difficult of access and moreover exposed to the danger of visits from pirates [2] ; those who cared not to face the risk of crossing the waves to find solitude, could retire to lonely spots on the mainland, often not far distant from their monastery. In Ireland the *disert*, in Brittany the *penity* met the needs of these lovers of retreat. The Irish *disert*, the Welsh and Cornish *diserth*, the Breton *penity* have left their traces in the local nomenclature of those several countries.[3]

The *Catalogus Sanctorum* tells us that many Irish saints of the third order (598–665) attained to sanctity in solitude.[4]

Hermits were the objects of singular regard and veneration. A hermit was chosen by Brigid to be the bishop of her monastery at Kildare.[5] In the course of their famous discussions with Augustine of Canterbury, the British bishops would come to no decision without first seeking advice from a wise and holy anchorite.[6] Cummian's important letter on the Paschal question is addressed jointly to abbot Segéne and Beccán the solitary.[7] In the twelfth century the hermit life was still in vogue and held in respect in Wales. "Nowhere," says Giraldus Cambrensis, " are hermits and anchorites to be

---

irreprehensibiliter expletos annos, alios duodecim in loco anachoretarum in Muirbulcmar, vitam ducens anachoreticam, Christi victor miles, explevit " (Adam., *Vita Col.*, III, 23, pp. 160–61).

[1] Adam., *Vita Col.*, I, 20, II, 42 ; *Vita Sam.*, I, 20, 21 (pp. 119–21). Cf. Lloyd, *HW*, I, p. 213.

[2] " [insulae] nunc causa latronum Nortmannorum vacuae anachoritis " (Dicuil, *Liber de mensura orbis terrae*, VII, 15, ed. G. Parthey, Berolini, 1870, p. 44). See the story of Donnán of Eig and his disciples in *Fél. Oeng.*, pp. 114–17.

[3] See E. Hogan, *Onomasticon Gadelicum* (Dublin, 1910) ; *VSH* and *BNE*, index of places ; *Fél. Oeng.* Glossarial index, *s.v. disertán.* Cf. Lloyd, *HW*, I, p. 213, note 103. R. Largillière, *Pénity* (*BSAF*, LVII, 1930, pp. 18–30) ; E. Ernault, *Glossaire moyen-breton* (Paris, 1896), II, pp. 472–73.

[4] *Catalogus*, p. 293.

[5] Cogitosus, *Vita Brig.* Prol. 2 (p. 135).

[6] Bede, *HE*, II, 2.

[7] Cummian, *DCP*, col. 969.

found who practise greater abstinence and lead a more spiritual life." [1]

CONCLUSION

Such—hastily and imperfectly sketched—was the kind of life led by these heroic servants of God who by their virtues and their imposing number gained for Ireland the distinguishing title of the Isle of Saints.[2] Such a continuous outflowering of sanctity, prolonged throughout three or four centuries, is a spectacle which does honour to our human nature and shows all that can be produced from it by Christianity. From the age of the Fathers of the desert the annals of the Church had never recorded equal ascetic fervour.

It has been justly said : " The extraordinary severity of the ascetic practices which prevailed in early Irish Christianity, and of the penances which it imposed, is often a matter of wonder in these latter and, it is to be feared, degenerate days. But it must be remembered that in a primitive and hardier age, with a far different standard of physical comfort, such mortifications were not felt to be exactly what they appear to us ; moreover, that they were designed for a people in whom the sap of life was yet young, whose passions were more easily kindled and more violent in explosion than ours. However, that the character of the Irish saints and ascetics stood high is beyond dispute. . . ." [3]

To some, indeed, the spectacle has seemed too extraordinary and they have tried to make us believe that it is only a mirage, a deception having its source in legend. If we accept their views, the notion which the early Celts had of sanctity was quite different from ours. In the first place, sanctity had for them an altogether local character. " A saint in Wales was not necessarily a saint in Ireland, and the Latin Church would decline to recognise the claims of either Welshman or Irishman." In the next place, the Celt did not invoke the protection of his saints, because he did not believe that they had

---

[1] Giraldus, *DK*, 1, 18 (p. 204) ; *s.a. De jure et statu Menevensis Ecclesiae* Prol. (*RS. Opera*, III, p. 115).
[2] Cf. L.G., *The Isle of Saints* (*Studies*, XIII, 1924, pp. 363–80).
[3] Maud Joynt, *Aspects of Celtic Christianity* (*The Irish Review*, July, 1911, p. 258).

attained celestial bliss ; so far from invoking them or regarding them as intercessors, he prayed for them. Moreover, the title of saint by no means implied individual merit, personal holiness acquired by effort. It was a title of honour in which the members of a certain tribe, a certain family or a certain monastery shared without further reason.[1]

Without denying that the word " saint " was sometimes used by Celtic writers of the Middle Ages (especially those of Cymric race) in a special sense to denote merely either " monk " or " ascetic " or even a member of some particularly famous family,[2] it is none the less true that the notion of " sanctity " as we understand it at the present day existed also in that age among the Celtic Churches. A few concrete facts will suffice to show the weak points in these abstract arguments.

Not only was the sanctity of the Irish ascetics recognized by the Welsh and reciprocally, as is proved by the intimate relations between the saints of both countries, but even an Anglo-Saxon like the Venerable Bede, who, himself a saint, had a claim to judge of sanctity, and who moreover, as we know, was by no means prepossessed in favour of the Celts, delights in dwelling on the special characteristics of sanctity, in the modern sense of the word, among the Scots who lived in the age preceding his own, Aidan, Tuda, Fursa and others.

Neither is it difficult to show that the Celts were given to invoke their saints, to venerate them and to place themselves under their protection. An Irish scribe of the ninth century writes on the margin of a manuscript invocations such as the following : " *Sancta Brigita intercedat pro me.*" " *Sancta Brigita adiuva scriptorem istius artis.*" " *Patricie adiuva,*" etc.[3] In the seventh century St Columba was invoked and his festival celebrated at Iona.[4] In a hymn dating at latest from the

[1] J. W. Willis Bund, *The Celtic Church of Wales* (London, 1897), p. 411 ; s.a. *Welsh Saints* (*TSC*, 1893–94, pp. 21–54).

[2] A. W. Wade-Evans, *Brychan Brycheiniog* (*Transactions of the Brecknock Society*, 1928–29) ; G. H. Doble, *The Children of Brychan in Cornwall* (*Downside Review*, XLVIII, 1930, pp. 217–36, XLIX, 1931, pp. 149–72). Cf. Paul Grosjean, *AB*, XLVIII, 1930, pp. 395–96 ; Chevalier, *Essai*, pp. 270, 288.

[3] Stokes and Strachan, *TP*, II, p. xx.

[4] Adam., *Vita Col.*, II, 45.—St Comgall was invoked at Bangor (*An. Ban.*, II, pp. 16, 19, 33). On the cult of saints and the veneration of relics, see Ryan, *Monast.*, pp. 357–59.

eighth century, St Aed mac Bricc († c. 589) is invoked for the cure of headaches.[1] Finally, the study of Breton local nomenclature leads to the conclusion that some Armorican parishes were from an early date dedicated to national saints, immigrants or natives, whose names they still bear.[2] In the Book of Armagh, written in 807, in the Life of Findan of Rheinau, also composed in the ninth century, we have proof of the celebration of the *natale* of St Patrick and that of St Columba and of the festivals of St Aidan and St Brigid,[3] and it has been already seen that we possess attestations of still earlier date of a cult bestowed on St Patrick.[4]

In the ranks of these saints various types of sanctity were represented. Nevertheless, if it be true that in the course of the Church's history " we meet, as it were, with two races of saints, embodying, on the one hand, the influence of love and tenderness, on the other, vigorous action and the spirit of ardent propaganda," [5] it is rather to the second class that most of our Celtic saints belong through their ardent temperament and their tendency to plunge overdeep into austerities. Not having been called to the glories of the martyrdom of blood, the " red martyrdom " as they called it, they sought to make up for it by devoting themselves to the sternest sacrifices and labouring to spread religion far and wide, whilst crucifying the flesh in the protracted martyrdom of penitence.[6]

---

[1] Prayer " *O rex, o rector regminis* " in an eighth-cent. MS. Ed. Mone, *Lateinische Hymnen des Mittelalters* (Freiburg, 1885), III, 181–82 ; *Lismore*, p. 324 ; P. Grosjean (Boll., *AS*, Nov. IV, p. 503) ; Blume, *Analecta hymnica*, LI (1908), pp. 315–16. Cf. *Vita Aedi*, 13 (17) (*VSH*, I, pp. 38–39 ; Boll., *AS*, Nov. IV, p. 150).

[2] J. Loth, *Les noms des saints bretons* (Paris, 1910).—At the beginning of the seventh century the " magnifica illa ac sancta annualis solemnitas " of St Samson was kept at Dol (*Vita Sam.*, II, 2, p. 157).

[3] *LA*, p. 31 ; *Vita Findani*, 4, 8, 9, 11, ed. Holder-Egger (MG., *Scr.*, XV, I, pp. 505–506).

[4] *V. sup.*, ch. II, § 10.

[5] Henri Joly, *Psychologie des saints* (Paris, 1900), p. 54. Cf. Sainte-Beuve, *Port-Royal* (Paris, 1901), I, pp. 216–17. " [The early Irish Saints], men of sterner stuff than we of to-day, who blessed with the right hand and cursed with the left " (A. Kingsley Porter, *Crosses and Culture*, p. 37).

[6] On the idea of the three kinds of martyrdom as adumbrated in the Cambrai homily in Irish (eighth century) and other ancient texts see L.G., *Devotional and ascetic Practices* (London, 1927), pp. 205–23.

CHAPTER IV

THE BRITONS IN ARMORICA

§ 1.—Causes and Date of the Emigration

SEVERAL opinions have been formed as to the causes of the emigration of the insular Britons to Armorica. For long it was believed that, led by the tyrant Maximus and Conan Meriadec, they had conquered the peninsula by the end of the fourth century, exterminating the native inhabitants and settling in their places. No one at the present day dreams of maintaining such a theory, founded as it is solely on legend.[1]

Still more surprising is the view propounded by Thomas Wright. According to him, no emigration of Britons to Armorica took place ; it was, on the contrary, the Celts of Armorica who peopled Wales in a period when the rest of the island was held by the Anglo-Saxons.[2]

A writer who places the emigration at the end of the fourth century has asserted that it was immediately due to the invasion of west Britain by the Scots from Ireland. Harassed and ousted from their homes, the Britons were obliged to forsake their country.[3] It is certain that Irish settlements were made in that part of Britain, but they did not by any means entail the consequences ascribed to them by this writer, and no historical text records the presence of Britons in Brittany before the second half of the fifth century.

Not by the Scots were the Britons compelled to cross the sea, but by the Anglo-Saxons. The earliest descents of these

---

[1] Gallet and Dom Hyacinthe Morice, in the eighteenth century, drew that fable from Geoffrey of Monmouth. A refutation of this theory may be found in Arthur de la Borderie, *HB*, II, pp. 441–56. Dom François Plaine elaborated another theory in which Maximus and the legend of St Ursula played a conspicuous part. See his treatise, *La colonisation de l'Armorique par les Bretons insulaires* (Paris, 1899).

[2] Thomas Wright, *On the Origin of the Welsh* (*A. Cam.*, 3rd Ser., IV, 1858, pp. 289–305).

[3] F. Lot in *Bibliothèque de l'École des Chartes* (LXI, 1900, pp. 547–49).

invaders date, as we have seen, from the year 428. Their number increased rapidly in the course of the following years. They began straightway to roam through the country in various directions, scattering terror and leaving ruins on every side. At the outset, and for a considerable time, the Britons held out against them ; but large bodies of them, dispossessed of their goods and driven from their territories, fled for refuge to the farthest bounds of the west ; there, brought to bay by the sea, they had soon no resource left but to seek a foreign country.[1]

Some of them went as far as Galicia and settled there. The councils of Lugo, Braga and Toledo mention British bishoprics and bishops in that country in the sixth and seventh centuries. The see of Britonia in Galicia survived at least as late as the year 900.[2] The earliest bishop of that see whose name is known was called Mailoc ; he was present at the second Council of Braga in 572.[3]

The majority of the emigrants landed on the coasts of Brittany. In the second half of the fifth century they had already settled in large numbers in that region. We find a certain Mansuetus, who is styled " bishop of the Britons " without any mention of his see, present at the Council of Tours in 461.[4] About 470 twelve thousand Britons coming by sea reached the country lying north of the Loire and afterwards stationed themselves on the territory of the Bituriges to lend their aid to the emperor Anthemius in his struggle with Euric king of the Visigoths.[5] The general in command of the army was called Riothimus, a British name which was later borne by a king of Armorican Dumnonia.[6]

Throughout the whole sixth century the insular Cornavii

---

[1] Loth, Émigration, ch. IV, § 1.

[2] CED, II, 99–101.—F. Fita, Concilio Ovetense del año 900 ? Texto inedito (Boletin de la Real Academia de la Historia, Madrid, 1901, XXXVIII, pp. 113–33).

[3] CED, II, 99.

[4] Mansi, Concilia, VII, col. 947.

[5] Jornandes, Getica, 45 (MG. Auct. ant., V, pp. 118–19) ; Sidonius Apollinaris, Ep. I, 7, ed. Luetjohann (MG. Auct. ant., VIII, p. 11).

[6] Loth, Émigration, p. 154.—On possible vestiges of these Bretons in the toponymy of the territory of the Bituriges see Auguste Longnon, Les noms de lieu de France, leur origine, leur signification (Paris, 1920–29), p. 136.

and Dumnonii sent forth large bands of recruits to the emigration.

§ 2.—SETTLEMENT OF THE EMIGRANT TRIBES ON THE SOIL OF BRITTANY

At the time when the first batches of emigrants landed on the peninsular seaboard of the *tractus Armoricanus*, that country, like all the rest of Gaul, was under Roman rule.[1] Administratively it formed part of the *Provincia Lugdunensis Tertia*. Its territory was shared between five Gallo-Roman cities, belonging respectively to the *Namnetes* (district of Nantes), the *Redones* (district of Rennes), the *Veneti* (district of Vannes), the *Curiosolites* (more correctly *Coriosopites*), and the *Osismi*.[2]

Like the rest of Gaul, the peninsula had been Romanized. The old Celtic or Gaulish tongue does not seem to have held its ground there any more than elsewhere. When the Britons arrived, the vulgar Latin, already in process of transformation into the *lingua Romana*, was spoken by the inhabitants.[3] For this Romance language the Britons substituted their own, the Armorican British or Breton, still spoken at the present day in Finistère and in part of Morbihan and Côtes-du-Nord.[4] The settlement of the islanders led to the change of the name of the country. This change was an established fact in the sixth century : Marius of Avenches († 593 or 594), Gregory of Tours († 595) and Venantius Fortunatus († 600) call the region *Brittania* (*Britannia*) and its inhabitants *Brittani* (*Britanni*) or *Brittones*.[5]

[1] J. Loth, *De vocis Aremoricae ad quintum post Christum natum saeculum forma atque significatione* (Redonibus, 1883).

[2] *Notitia Galliarum* (*MG. Auct. ant.*, IX, pp. 586–87). Cf. Duchesne, *Fastes*, II, pp. 242–45 ; H. Waquet, *De Corisopitum à Conflans-Saint-Corentin* (*Mélanges bretons et celtiques offerts à Joseph Loth*, Rennes and Paris, 1927, pp. 12–17).

[3] J. Loth, *Les langues romane et bretonne en Armorique* (*R. Cel.*, XXVIII, 1907, pp. 374–403).

[4] Albert Dauzat, *Le breton et le français* (*La Nature*, No. 2717, May 1, 1926, pp. 273–78, with three maps). Cf. J. Loth, *Les langues bretonne et française en Bretagne d'après un travail récent* (*R. Cel.*, XLIII, 1926, pp. 419–27). A. Dauzat, *La pénétration du français en Bretagne du XVIIIe siècle à nos jours* (*Revue de philologie française*, XLIII, 1929, pp. 1–55, with 3 graphs and 1 map). Cf. J. Vendryes, *R. Cel.*, XLVII, 1930, pp. 249–50.

[5] Marius Aventicensis, *Chronica*, a.a. 560 (*MG. Auct. ant.*, XI, p. 237) ; Gregory of Tours, *Hist. Franc.*, IV, 4, 20 ; v, 16, 27, etc., ed. B. Krusch

The Britons crossed the sea in numerous fleets of small vessels, a band at a time, all hailing from the same district. Those of the north, of Cumbria and Strathclyde, do not appear to have emigrated in large bodies ; at the most they sent a few individuals to Brittany, perhaps among others that St Ivy who gave his name to Pontivy and several place-names called Loguivy.[1]

The chief centre of emigration was probably the ancient Dumnonia (the modern counties of Cornwall and Devon). The name of Dumnonia, in any case, crossed the Channel with the emigrants from that region. In the ninth century this name stood for the whole north of Brittany from the mouth of the Elorn to the Couesnon.[2] This vast tract did not, however, represent an unmixed unity of race ; its western end, the district of Léon, was probably occupied by Welsh immigrants from Caerleon on the Usk.[3] The great monks who founded the chief episcopal or monastic establishments of Armorican Dumnonia, Samson, Paul Aurelian, Lunaire (Leonorius), Maglorius, Méen (Mevennus) and Malo, were of Welsh origin. Tutwal, the first bishop of Tréguier, was, on the other hand, a native of insular Dumnonia.

Ptolemy mentions the Cornavii ($Ko\rho\nu\alpha o\acute{\upsilon}\iota o\iota$) as belonging altogether to the north of the isle of Britain.[4] At the period of the Saxon invasion we find the Cornavii settled in the east of the present Wales. Their principal towns were Chester (Deva) and Wroxeter (Viroconium).[5] Under the stress of the Teutonic invasion, the tribe gradually moved further south and settled in the angle of Dumnonia, to which it gave its name, Cornovia or Cornubia [6] (A.S. Corn-wealas = Corn-

---

(*MG. Scr. RM.*, I, pp. 143, 157, etc.) ; Venantius Fortunatus, *Carmina*, III, 8, ed. Leo (*MG. Auct. ant.*, IV, p. 59), *s.a. Vita Paterni*, 10 (*Ib.*, p. 36) ; *s.a. Vita B. Maurilii*, 16 (*Ib.*, p. 93) ; Council of Tours, A.D. 567, Can. 9 (*MG. Leges* ; III. *Concilia*, I, p. 124). Cf. L.G., *Un point obscur de l'itinéraire de S. Colomban venant en Gaule* (*An. Br.*, XXXI, 1907, p. 329).

[1] Largillière, *Les saints*, pp. 26, 76, 151.

[2] J. Loth, *L'étendue de la Domnonée armoricaine* (*R. Cel.*, VIII, 1887, pp. 156–57).

[3] Loth, *Émigration*, p. 191.

[4] Ptolemy, *Geographia*, II, 3, 11. Cf. Alfred Holder, *Alt-Celtischer Sprachschatz* (Leipzig, 1896–1913), I, col. 1131, III, col. 379.

[5] H. d'Arbois de Jubainville, *Les Celtes depuis les temps les plus anciens jusqu'à l'an 100 avant notre ère* (Paris, 1904), pp. 28–29.

[6] " *Cornubia* " occurs for the first time in a poem of St Aldhelm, *Carmina*

wall). In the fifth or sixth century a large section of this tribe separated from the main body to found the Armorican Cornouaille between the Elorn and the Ellé. The Cornavii played an important part in the emigration ; so much so that a host of names of parishes in Cornwall are to be met with in Brittany,[1] and, according to celtologists, Cornish and Breton are very closely connected dialects. " The main point to be emphasized," says J. Loth, " is that Breton and Cornish together form an intimate group as opposed to Welsh." [2]

It is not so easy to find out the exact region from which came the Britons who settled south-east of the Ellé. This district was called Broerec (O. Bret., *Bro-Weroc*), " the country of Weroc," the name of the famous British chief who directed the expeditions against the Franks. It would not do to conclude that because of its greater distance this tract was the last to be colonized. Einhard declares that the earliest emigrants settled on the territory of the *Veneti* and the *Curiosolites*.[3] The city of Vannes did not pass into the power of the British settlers till the ninth century, but all the coast south of that town as far as the Loire, as well as the adjacent islands, was no doubt in their hands at an early period.[4] Towards the middle of the sixth century one of their number, Macliau, being pursued by his brother the Count Chanao, took refuge in Vannes, received the tonsure and actually became a bishop. On the death of Chanao he forsook his bishopric, reassumed the garb of a layman, took back his wife and installed himself again in his brother's " kingdom," for which proceedings he was excommunicated by the bishops.[5]

It was probably Welsh tribes that took possession of the

---

rhythmica, I, ed. R. Ehwald (*MG. Auct. ant.*, XV, p. 524). Cf. J. Loth, *R. Cel.*, XXII, 1901, p. 96.

[1] See G. H. Doble, *Les relations durant les âges entre la Bretagne et le Cornwall* (*Bulletin diocésain d'histoire et d'archéologie de Quimper et de Léon*, 1924) ; J. Loth, *R. Cel.*, XXI, 1901, pp. 98–100 ; A. Oheix and Ethel C. Fawtier-Jones, La " *Vita* " ancienne de Saint Corentin (*MSHAB*, VI, 1925, p. 26).

[2] J. Loth, *R. Cel.*, XXII, 1901, p. 99 ; XVIII, p. 402 ; XXX, p. 397.

[3] *Annales*, a.a. 786 (*MG. Scr*, I, p. 169).

[4] Loth, *Émigration*, p. 185.

[5] Gregory of Tours, *Hist. Franc.*, IV, 4, ed. B. Krusch (*MG. Scr. RM.*, I, pp. 143–44).

Vannetais [1] ; the eastern part of the Vannetais remained Gallo-Roman, only slightly affected by British influences. [2]

The central part of the peninsula from the Monts d'Arrée to the Rance and the Vilaine was far less populous and was occupied by the vast forest, interspersed with moors, of Brécilien (Brocéliande), a forest which figured largely in the Romance literature of the country in the Middle Ages.

From Ermold the Black we gather that the Armorican Gallo-Romans received the Britons out of pity, because they were Christians. [3] The Britons did not show much gratitude. They displayed towards their hosts and benefactors the same violence as the Saxons had offered them. The Britons of Broerec, who were especially truculent, in the sixth century laid waste the territories of Rennes and Nantes unceasingly and fought desperately against the Franks. [4] " Oppressed by the Britons, we are under the yoke of a hard slavery," complains Regalis, bishop of Vannes, about 590. [5] The Christian profession of their enemies did not check the warlike ardour of the Britons. In 849 Nominoé was not afraid to set fire to the monastery of Saint-Florent-le-Vieil and to drive Actard, bishop of Nantes, from his see. [6]

J. Loth considers that the fusion of the Gallo-Roman and British elements was hardly completed until the tenth century. [7]

§ 3.—The Religious Condition of Armorica on the Arrival of the Britons

The martyrdom of the young brothers Donatianus and Rogatianus of Nantes about 288 is the earliest evidence of Christianity in the Armorican region. [8] Nothing is known

---

[1] Loth, *Émigration*, pp. 186–87.

[2] Loth, *Émigration*, pp. 185, 195–99 ; *s.a. Les noms latins dans les langues brittoniques* (Paris, 1892), pp. 25 ff. Cf. *R. Cel.*, XXII, pp. 104 ff. ; XXVIII, 1907, pp. 374 ff.

[3] Ermold, *Carmina*, III (*MG. Poet. Lat.*, II, p. 490).

[4] La Borderie, *HB*, I, pp. 442–58.

[5] Gregory of Tours, *Hist. Franc.*, x, 9, ed. B. Krusch, p. 417.

[6] *Versus de eversione monasterii Glonnensis*, ed. Dümmler (*MG. Poet. Lat.*, II, pp. 146–49). Cf. Lot, *Mélanges*, p. 41.—*Chr. Nam.*, 9, 10 (pp. 25–28). Cf. Lot, *Mélanges*, p. 474.

[7] *R. Cel.*, XXII, p. 106.

[8] *Passio SS. Rogatiani et Donatiani*, ed. Ruinart, *Acta martyrum sincera*

of St Clarus, whom the Church of Nantes hails as its first bishop. The pontiff Similianus, called by Gregory of Tours " *Similinus magnus confessor*," seems to have lived in the second half of the fourth century.[1] Eumelius, bishop of Nantes, is perhaps the same as the Eumerius who appears in 374 at the Council of Valence on the Rhône. Eusebius, another bishop of the same see, attended the Council of Tours in 461.[2]

Besides the city of the *Namnetes*, two other cities, those of the *Redones* (Rennes) and the *Veneti* (Vannes), were certainly provided with episcopal sees at the time when the Britons arrived. St Paternus was consecrated bishop of Vannes at the Council which met in that town under the presidency of Perpetuus, metropolitan of Tours, about 465.[3] Paternus was a Gallo-Roman, not a Breton. His relations with the mythical Breton chief Caradoc Breichbras are pure fiction.[4] Paternus was not the first bishop of Vannes.[5]

Some historians believe that the two other *civitates* mentioned in the *Notitia Galliarum*, those of the *Coriosopites* and the *Osismi*, were similarly each equipped with an episcopal see before the close of the Roman period.[6] But where were these sees fixed ? No one can tell. In the Breton period four bishoprics were established in the territories of these two *civitates*, Quimper, Léon, Tréguier and Saint-Brieuc.[7]

Many biographers of the emigrant British saints give as their motive for crossing the Channel the desire of evangelizing the people of Armorica, of whom a great part were still heathens. We find Paul Aurelian, Brieuc, Lunaire, Malo, Samson and Maglorius devoting themselves to spread the

---

(Parisiis, 1689), pp. 295–98 ; Boll., *AS*, Maii, V, pp. 282–84. Cf. Gregory of Tours, *De gloria martyrum*, 59, ed. B. Krusch, p. 528.

[1] *De gloria martyrum*, 59 (p. 529).

[2] Mansi, *Concilia*, III, 493 ; VII, 947. Cf. Duchesne, *Fastes*, II, p. 365.

[3] Mansi, *Concilia*, VII, 951–55.

[4] F. Lot, *Caradoc et Saint Patern (Romania*, XXVIII, 1899, pp. 568–78).

[5] L. Duchesne, *Saint Patern (R. Cel.*, XIV, 1893, pp. 238–40) ; *s.a. Fastes*, II, pp. 247, 377 ; J. de La Martinière, *Vannes dans l'ancien temps (Bulletin de la Société polymathique du Morbihan*, 1913, pp. 44–48).

[6] Lot, *Mélanges*, pp. 200–206 ; Duchesne, *Fastes*, II, pp. 244–50.

[7] Julius Caesar, who mentions the Namnetes, the Redones, the Veneti, the Osismi, says nothing of Alet, but the *Notitia dignitatum* has a *Praefectus militum Martensium Aleto*. However, it seems that the *pagus Aletensis* was included in the *civitas Redonum*. So believes F. Duine, *Inventaire*, p. 190.

Gospel among the unbelievers.[1]   Even at the end of the fifth
or beginning of the sixth century, the *Veneti*, if we may credit
the interpolator of the Life of St Melanius, were still " almost
all heathens." [2]   However, it would not do to place implicit
faith in such informants ; the sole thought of the authors of
these Lives of saints was to exalt their heroes by depicting
them as grappling with a firmly rooted paganism.   It cannot
be denied that Christianity was not very flourishing and that
in the sixth century there were still heathens remaining in
Brittany.[3]   But it was not so much the wish to convert the
Gallo-Romans that drew the British clergy into the stream
of emigration as the necessity of providing for the spiritual
needs of their own countrymen, immigrants or descendants of
immigrants.   They are seldom found in contact with the
natives, who in the west and north were probably swamped
by the tide of the British occupation.   The native tongue was
moreover a foreign one to them, and the missionary zeal
which led so many Scots to cross the seas does not seem to
have animated the early British monks in the same degree.
In any case, their own countrymen, the settlers, though
nominally Christian, had great need of being catechized, confirmed in the faith and recalled to the practice of morality and
the Christian virtues which their impetuous temperament so
often led them to forget.   It may readily be conceived that the
British clergy had their hands full merely in organizing their
monasteries, their places of worship and their bishoprics and
dispensing day by day the light and succour of religion to the
Christians of their own race in the midst of the perils and
disorders of emigration.

From Wales came the most famous founders of Breton
Christianity.   The largest number of emigrants may indeed
have been supplied by Cornwall ; but, if we may judge from
the documents that have come down to us, that country does
not seem to have ever possessed an influential religious organization.   " There everything seems, so to speak, a fresh impor-

---

[1] Texts collected by La Borderie, *HB*, I, pp. 264–66. Cf. Lot, *Mélanges*,
p. 174, note 1.

[2] *Vita Melanii*, 23 [interpolated] (Boll., *AS*, Jan. I, 331).

[3] G. Guénin, *Le paganisme en Bretagne au sixième siècle* (*An. Br.*, XVII,
1902, pp. 216–34).

tation."[1] Cornwall received much from Christian Ireland.[2] Some Irish saints—Fingar, Briac, Maudez, Vougay—also landed in Brittany, some of them after having first passed through Wales or Cornwall. Zimmer has, moreover, drawn attention to certain linguistic peculiarities of the Gaels found in use among the monks of Landévennec.[3] But, on the whole, Irish saints played a very subordinate part in organizing the Christian life of the peninsula.[4]

§ 4.—Ecclesiastical Organization of Brittany

At a time previous to the ecclesiastical reforms of Nominoé, six new bishoprics were founded in Brittany.

The origin of the see of Quimper is obscure. Concerning St Corentin, generally regarded as its first bishop, our sole information, apart from mere mentions of the name of the saint in some earlier litanies,[5] depends on Lives of a very late period containing manifest errors.[6]

Paul Aurelian, a native of South Wales, set up his first monastery on the island of Ushant, where he landed, then another on the mainland at Lampaul in Ploudalmézeau (*Lanna Pauli in plebe Telmedoviae*), and finally a third on the island of Batz. The tiern Withur, by a ruse, procured his consecration as bishop at Paris, to some extent against his own

---

[1] J. Loth, *R. Cel.*, XXII, p. 90.

[2] W. Bright, *Chapters of early English Church History* (Oxford, 1897), p. 30.

[3] H. Zimmer, *Nennius vindicatus* (Berlin, 1893), pp. 258–59, *s.a. CC*, pp. 67–69. Cf. J. Loth, *Landevennec et Saint Guénolé* (*An. Br.*, VIII, 1893, pp. 488–91).

[4] See Largillière, *Les saints*, pp. 128–30, 141 ; Vendryes, *R. Cel.*, XXXVIII, 1920–21, p. 360 ; F. Lot, *R. Cel.*, XLIII, 1926, p. 456.—It is great exaggeration to call Brittany " a spiritual colony of Ireland," as did Samuel Berger (*Histoire de la Vulgate pendant les premiers siècles du moyen âge*, Paris, 1893, p. 49). For specific Irish influence at Landévennec *v. inf.* ch. VIII, § 4.

[5] A. Oheix and Ethel C. Fawtier-Jones, *La " Vita " ancienne de Saint Corentin* (*MSHAB*, VI, 1925, p. 30) ; L.G., *Notes sur le culte des saints bretons en Angleterre* (*An. Br.*, XXXV, 1923, p. 603). A still earlier mention of " *Courentinus* " is to be found in the *Vita Winwaloei* by Wrdisten written between 857 and 884 (II, 19, ed. De Smedt, *AB*, VII, p. 231). Cf. J. Loth, *Les noms des saints bretons*, p. 29 [*Couran*].

[6] *Vita Corentini* (thirteenth century), ed. F. Plaine (*BSAF*, XIII, 1886, pp. 119–72). Cf. Duine, *Memento*, pp. 79–80 ; *Vita Corentini*, ed. A. Oheix (*MSHAB*, VI, 1925, pp. 38–56). Cf. *ib.*, pp. 33–37 ; R. Largillière, *Saint Corentin et ses Vies latines à propos d'une publication récente* (*BSAF*, LII, 1925).

will.[1] Paul was the first bishop of Léon.   The foundation
of the see of Castel-Pol, which became subsequently the little
town of Saint-Pol-de-Léon, is placed about 530.

The *Vita prima Samsonis*, written about sixty years after the
saint's death, which took place about 565,[2] tells us that St
Samson was already a bishop (though not a diocesan)[3] and an
abbot before crossing the Channel.   In Brittany he founded
the monastery of Dol (*fundavit monasterium quod usque hodie
proprio vocabulo Dolum nuncupatur*).[4]   " The earliest title given
to Dol," observes F. Duine, " is that of monastery ; and the
designation *monasterium Sancti Samsonis* persisted for about two
centuries after the archbishopric [of Dol] was instituted." [5]

To the abbey of Dol were attached monasteries and
parishes scattered throughout the whole of Armorican
Dumnonia and enclosed in the neighbouring territories.   All
these dependencies, together with the *pagus Dolensis*, formed
the *paruchia* of St Samson, the territory over which the founder
and his successors exercised personal influence and jurisdiction.[6]   One of Samson's foundations, the monastery of
Pental, was even situated in Neustria in the archbishopric of
Rouen.[7]   Even so, in Great Britain Cedd († 664), the bishop
of the East Saxons, an alumnus of Lindisfarne, ruled as abbot
the monastery of Lastingham in Yorkshire, founded *juxta ritus
Lindisfarnensium*, which was situated outside his diocese.[8]

[1] Wrmonoc, *Vita Pauli Aurel.* (*R. Cel.*, V, 1881–83, pp. 437–38,
450–52).   On the foundations of Paul Aurelian and the evangelization of
Finistère, see G. Guénin, *L'évangélisation du Finistère* (*Bulletin de la Société
académique de Brest*, 2nd Ser., XXXII, 1906–1907, pp. 29–82).

[2] Duine, *Memento*, p. 31.—According to Charles de Calan, the Frankish
king mentioned in the *Vita Samsonis* is not Childebert I (511–558), but
Childebert II (575–596) (*Études de chronologie bretonne : S. Samson et le roi
Childebert, Gradlon, Conomor* (*MSHAB*, XI, 1930, pp. 1–4).

[3] F. C. Burkitt suggests that Samson may have been consecrated to
the then vacant see of Evoracum (York) : *St Samson of Dol* (*JTS*, XXVII,
1926, p. 52).

[4] *Vita Sam.*, I, 52.—" *Dolo monasterio* sancti Samson *abb.* " (Hieronymian Martyrology [in 5 *codices pleniores*].   Cf. Fawtier, *Vita Sam.*, p. 53 ;
Duine, *La Vie de S. Samson à propos d'un ouvrage récent* (*An. Br.*, XXVIII, 1913,
p. 347).

[5] F. Duine, *Histoire civile et politique de Dol jusqu'en 1789* (Paris, 1911),
p. 7.

[6] See map in Duine, *Métropole*.

[7] *Vita Sam.*, I, 38 (p. 135).   Cf. F. Duine, *Saint Samson*, Rennes [1909],
p. 13.

[8] Bede, *HE*, III, 23.

The oldest Life of St Samson gives the names of Leucher and Tigerinomal, who were Samson's successors and, like him, bishops and abbots of the monks of Dol, where they resided.[1]

The first to occupy the adjoining see, that of Alet on the banks of the Rance, is said to have been St Maclovius (Malo, also called Machutes, Machutus). At Alet, in its immediate vicinity and in the islands round, St Malo founded monasteries " *ubi non modice monachorum congregationes Deo servire videbantur.*" [2] When did St Malo live ? We cannot tell whether it was in the sixth or the seventh century.[3] According to his earliest Life (second half of the ninth century), he had been raised to the episcopacy before coming to the *pagus Aletensis*,[4] while according to his biographer Bili, who wrote nearly at the same time, he was consecrated bishop only after his arrival in Brittany.[5] His career cannot be compared to that of St Samson ; his influence was far more restricted. Nor does it appear that the monastery of Alet ever played the part of a mother-abbey, the head and centre of the diocesan *paruchia*. The great monastery of that *paruchia* is not to be sought on the banks of the Rance. Its chief abbey in the ninth century was that of St. Méen in Poutrocoët.[6] Now Helogar, who was alive in 811 and of whom we have further record in 816, is styled *episcopus Alethensis et abbas sancti Mevenni*.[7] Does this not imply that he was an abbot-bishop ? Certainly ; but an abbot-bishop of a type by no means unusual. Many diocesan bishops of the eighth and ninth centuries can be mentioned who were at the same time abbots of a monastery in their

---

[1] *Vita Sam.*, I, I (p. 95), II, 15 (p. 171). Cf. Duine, *La Vie de S. Samson* (*An. Br.*, XXVIII, 1913, pp. 351–52) ; J. Loth, *La plus ancienne Vie de S. Samson* (*R. Cel.*, XXXV, 1914, pp. 279, 286).

[2] Bili, *Vita Machutis*, 31, ed. F. Lot, *Mélanges*, p. 373.—Little credence can be accorded to Bili (see Lot, *Mélanges*, pp. 142 ff. ; F. Duine, *Memento*, p. 51–54). On Alet see Duine's art. in the *Dictionnaire d'histoire et de géographie ecclésiastiques*, edited by Baudrillart, Vogt and Rouziès.

[3] Duine, *Memento*, pp. 54–55.

[4] Ch. 8, ed. Lot, *Mélanges*, pp. 304–305.

[5] Bili, 37, ed. Lot, *Mélanges*, p. 377.

[6] " *Pou-tro-coet*," *i.e.*, " region beyond the forest," in opposition to the coastal region of the diocese of Alet. The archdeaconry of Porhoët (a name derived from Poutrocoët) corresponds to that wooded territory (cf. Lot, *Mélanges*, p. 29). On the central forest, see P. Vidal de la Blache, *Tableau de la géographie del a France* in *Histoire de France*, edited by E. Lavisse (Paris, 1905), I, pp. 332–33.

[7] Morice, *Preuves*, I, p. 225.

diocese ; for instance, Erkambodus († *c.* 742), who was bishop of Thérouanne and at the same time abbot of Sithiu (St. Bertin),[1] and Salomon III (890–919), who was bishop of Constance while continuing to be abbot of St. Gall.[2] Helogar, who was simultaneously bishop of Alet and abbot of St. Méen, cannot on that ground alone be regarded as the head of a monastery-bishopric.

The *Chronicle of Nantes*, composed between 1050 and 1059, also gives to Dol the designation of *monasterium Doli* and calls St. Brieuc *monasterium Brioci* and Tréguier *monasterium Sancti Tutualis Pabut.*[3] St Brieuc is said to have founded on the Gouet at a place called *Campus Roboris* a monastery which was the nucleus of the city which now bears his name.[4] Was this monastery originally the see of the bishopric ? No Life of St Brieuc assigns the rank of bishop to the founder of *Campus Roboris.* An inscription on his tomb at Angers, whither his bones are supposed to have been transferred in the reign of king Erispoé (851–857), styles him *episcopus Britanniae.*[5] This inscription is much later than Erispoé's time ; it existed, however, in the eleventh century.[6] It may further be observed that in the fifteenth century Pierre Le Baud saw a *Vita Brioci* which placed the ordination of the saint as bishop in Britain.[7] " Whatever may be the truth regarding the episcopal rank of its founder," such is the conclusion of Louis Duchesne, " it is certain that the monastery of St. Brieuc remained a simple monastery up to the time of Nominoé. It must also be noted that no legend ever arose about the saint's successors in the rule of his foundation." [8]

The earliest biography of Tutwal, believed to have been composed in the ninth century, informs us that that bishop, a native of Britain, founded in the *pagus Treher* the monastery

[1] Duchesne, *Fastes*, III, pp. 134–35 ; Duine, *Schisme*, p. 431, n. 1.
[2] *Formulae*, ed. K. Zeumer (*MG. Leges*, sect. V, pp. 395–96, 435). See, however, reservations made by E. de Rozière, *Recueil géneral des formules* (Paris, 1859), I, p. 192.
[3] *Chr. Nam.*, p. 39.
[4] *Vita Brioci*, 45, etc., ed. F. Plaine (*AB*, II, 1883, pp. 182 ff.).
[5] Lobineau, *Histoire de Bretagne* (Paris, 1717), II, cols. 55–56.
[6] Duchesne, *Fastes*, II, pp. 390–91.
[7] Cf. Duine, *Memento*, p. 85.
[8] Duchesne, *l. cit.*

which in the *Chronicle of Nantes* is called *monasterium sancti Tutualis Pabut* (monastery of St Tutwal the monk), now the town of Tréguier.[1]   J. Loth observes that " in Breton Tréguier is known only by the name of Lan-Dreger (*monasterium Tricorium*), the *pagus*, subsequently a diocese, being called Treger." [2]   According to the earliest Life of Tutwal, the monastery of Tréguier, like that of Dol, had in its dependence churches scattered throughout the whole of Dumnonia, which might likewise have constituted a *paruchia* of the monastery-bishopric type.[3]   Finally, the Life of St Cunwal (eleventh century) mentions a *monasterium Cunuali episcopi*, a monastery which must have been that of Tréguier, as Cunwal passed for a successor of Tutwal.[4]   This is all the evidence we have in support of the monastery-bishopric of Tréguier ; and, taking into consideration the small historical value of the hagiographical writings to which alone we can appeal, we cannot draw any definite conclusion.[5]

Two other celebrated monasteries, neither of which was ever the seat of a bishopric, arose at opposite ends of the country, one at the mouth of the Aulne, the other on the bank of the Vilaine : Landévennec and Redon.

All that is known of St Winwalloc (Guénolé), the founder of Landévennec, is derived from the learned abbot Wrdisten, who composed a *Vita Winwaloei* partly in prose and partly in verse about 880, that is to say, nearly four centuries after the founder's death.[6]   Guénolé was born in Brittany of an immigrant family.   He was educated by St Budoc in the island of Lavré.[7]   Towards the end of the fifth century he went with some disciples to settle in the peninsula of Crozon

---

[1] *Vita I^a Tuduali*, 1, ed. A. de La Borderie, *Mémoires de la Société archéologique des Côtes-du-Nord*, 2nd Ser., II, p. 84. On the episcopal character of Tutwal, *ib.*, 4 (p. 85).

[2] J. Loth, *La plus ancienne Vie de S. Samson*, p. 280.

[3] *Vita I^a*, pp. 84 ff.

[4] *Vita Cunuali*, 11, 13, ed. André Oheix (*R. Cel.*, XXXII, 1911, p. 165).

[5] Cf. Duine, *Memento*, p. 62.

[6] Duine, *Memento*, pp. 40-48.—On the MSS and various editions of Wrdisten's *Vita Winwaloei* see Robert Latouche, *Mélanges d'histoire de Cornouaille* (*Bibl. de l'École des Hautes Études*, CXCII, 1911), pp. 6-7 ; Duine, *Schisme*, p. 24 ; René Largillière, *Mélanges d'hagiographie bretonne* (Brest, 1925), pp. 5, 15.

[7] Wrdisten, *Vita Winwaloei*, 1, 2-4 (*AB*, VII, 1888, pp. 176-79).

to the north of the *pagus* Porzoed and founded there a *lann* which was called after him *Lan-Towennoc* from the hypocoristic name *To-Winn-oc* bestowed on him in Irish fashion. Before long monks and hermits issued in swarms from this monastery to all corners of Cornouaille. There are various indications which lead to the belief that Irish influence was felt at Landévennec more than in any other Breton monastery.[1] The monastic observance and the tonsure of the monks were Scottic, and remained in force till 818, in which year Louis the Pious, having become master of Brittany by his triumph over Morvan, enjoined on the abbot Matmonoch to substitute the Rule of St Benedict for the insular monastic customs and the Roman *corona* for the Celtic tonsure.[2]

Landévennec seems to have kept up close relations with Cornwall.[3]

Conwoïon, born at Camblessac, was archdeacon of Vannes at the time when he settled with five other priests on the land of Roton in the *plou* of Bain, given to him by the machtiern Ratwili (832).[4] It was not long until the Rule of St Benedict was introduced at Redon, if indeed it was not followed from the beginning.[5] Conwoïon supported the designs of Nominoé, and that prince bestowed his protection on the abbey. The *Gesta sanctorum Rotonensium*, a work composed some ten years after Conwoïn's death (January 5, 868),[6] in which his acts and the story of the early times of his monastery are related, by its partiality attests the friendly relations between the prince and the abbey.

---

[1] St Patrick was venerated there (*Vita Winwaloei*, I, 19, II, 9, pp. 205–206, 225). The feast-day of St Brigid of Kildare occurs in the *comes* joined to the *Gospel-book of Landevennec* (latter part of the ninth century). See C. R. Morey, E. K. Rand, C. H. Kraeling, *The Gospel-book of Landevennec* (*Art Studies*, VIII, Part II, 1930, p. 264. Cf. pp. 273–74). St Guénolé is alluded to in Jocelin's *Vita Patricii*, 159 (Boll., *AS*, Mart. I, p. 574). Cf. F. Duine, *Bréviaires et missels des églises et abbayes bretonnes de France antérieurs au XVIIe siècle* (Rennes, 1906), p. 149 ; Duine, *Memento*, p. 43. *V. sup.* ch. IV, § 2.

[2] Wrdisten (*Vita Winwaloei*, II, 13, p. 227) quotes verbatim the document of Louis the Pious, whose genuineness cannot be doubted : *CED*, II, p. 79. Cf. R. Latouche, *op. cit.*, p. 37 ; A. Oheix, *L'histoire de Cornouaille d'après un livre récent* (*BSAF*, XXXIX, 1912, reprint p. 9).

[3] J. Loth, *Les noms des saints bretons*, pp. 53–54 (Guénolé).

[4] On the " machtiern " see Largillière, *Les saints*, p. 202.

[5] *GSR*, p. 194.

[6] Lot, *Mélanges*, pp. 1–13.

As for St Gildas, the author of the *De Excidio*, said to have
been the founder of the abbey of Rhuys (Ruis), did he ever
come to Brittany ? The texts at our disposal do not allow of a
decisive answer. The monk (Vitalis ?) who wrote a *Vita
Gildae* in the eleventh century, has—whether intentionally or
otherwise—probably confounded a local saint of the name of
Gueltas with the great St Gildas, who was celebrated not
only in Britain but also in Ireland, and whom it was an
honour to claim as founder.[1] We know nothing of the abbey
of Ruis previously to its restoration in the year 1008.[2] At first
glance, the topography of the cult of St Gildas, especially in
the Vannetais, is calculated to impress us ; but the extension
of that cult was due simply to the rapid rise of the abbey of
Ruis, which after its restoration in 1008 became speedily
celebrated, thanks to the gifts of the Breton princes and
nobles.[3]

In Brittany, as in Britain and Ireland, the monastic element
predominated. It would be puzzling to determine what part
the secular clergy played before the ninth century. However,
we must not imagine the Breton monks as wholly given up
to the contemplative life. It was their task to provide the
nascent Church with an ecclesiastical organization and to
set the pastoral ministry among the immigrants on a sure
basis. Worship, preaching and the administration of the
sacraments formed their chief business, for in the regions
newly occupied by immigrants everything had to be started
and organized afresh.

Besides the large abbeys, the country was dotted with
monasteries of minor importance (*lann*) and hermitages

[1] " [Gildas] venit ad quandan insulam, quae in Reuvisii pagi prospectu
sita est, ibique aliquamdiu solitariam duxit vitam [Houat] . . . Veniens
itaque ad quoddam castrum in monte Reuvisii in prospectu maris situm ibi
potioris fabricae construxit monasterium atque in eo claustra coenobitali
ritu perfecit " (*Vita Gildae*, 16, p. 96).

[2] We only learn from *Vita Gildae* (32, 33, p. 102) and from a charter of
A.D. 1134 (see Lot, *Mélanges*, p. 244, note) that a little party of monks of
Ruis, together with a certain Daioc, their leader, took refuge in Berry
(c. A.D. 920), first at Déols and afterwards at Issoudun.

[3] On the Armorican career of Gildas see Duine, *Memento*, pp. 27–31 ;
Lot, *Mélanges*, p. 257 (cf. *RHE*, XXV, 1929, pp. 395–96) ; R. Largillière,
La topographie du culte de Saint Gildas (*MSHAB*, V, 1924, pp. 3–25) ; J. Loth,
Le nom de Saint Gildas (*R. Cel.*, XLVI, 1929, pp. 1–15) ; E. Faral, *La légende
arthurienne* (*Bibl. de l'École des Hautes Études*, CCLV, 1929), I, pp. 3–8.

having a small oratory or chapel (*loc*). The word *lann* would seem to have had in divers Celtic lands the primary sense of " enclosure." In Brittany and Wales (Welsh *llan*) it often bore the further sense of church or chapel.[1]

There are no place-names formed with *loc* (from Lat. *locus*) either in Wales or Cornwall. In Brittany names so formed are posterior to the tenth century and are found only in Lower (*i.e.*, Breton-speaking) Brittany. The term *loc* is always followed by the name of a saint, there being only one exception, Locminé (*Locmenech = locus monachorum*). But the eponyms of the place-names containing *loc-* are not those saints whose cult is of ancient date in Brittany, and these names are not of any use in clearing up the history of the rise of Christianity in the peninsula.[2]

On the contrary, the term *plou* (Lat. *plebem*) is of the utmost importance in the study of Breton religious place-names, as has been shown by the thorough-going researches of René Largillière.[3] This writer has proved that the term *plou* always denotes the territory of a parish, and of a primitive one going back to the initial organization of religious life in the country. In Wales the word *plwyf* has to the present day the sense of " parish." [4]

The term *plou* may be followed by a common noun (Plougastel, Pléchâtel = *plebs castelli* ; Plescop = *plebs episcopi*) or by an adjective (Plémeur, " big parish " ; Plounévez, Pléneuf, " new parish "), but is far oftener associated with the name of a saint. For instance, Plestin has for its eponym St Gestin ; Pleucadeuc, St Cadoc ; Ploërmel, St Armel. The proper name is very often that of some little-known saint, some humble missionary whose memory has been preserved in no written record. This lowly labourer in the Lord's vineyard

---

[1] " quae insula usque in hodiernum diem Lanna Hilduti vocitatur " (*Vita Gildae*, 5, p. 93) ; " Coetlann, quod sonat interpretatum monasterium nemoris " (*Ib.*, 27, p. 100) ; " Lanna Pauli id est monasterium Pauli " (*Vita Pauli, R. Cel.*, V, p. 440), etc. Cf. Lloyd, *HW*, I, p. 149 ; Largillière, *Les saints*, pp. 212, 227 ; J. Loth, *Les saints et l'organisation chrétienne primitive dans l'Armorique bretonne d'après un livre récent* (*MSHAB*, VII, 1926, pp. 5–6).
[2] Largillière, *Les saints*, pp. 18–19 ; J. Loth, *Les saints*, p. 4.
[3] Largillière, *Les saints*, pp. 169 ff.
[4] J. Loth, *Les saints*, p. 7. Cf. Williams, *Christianity*, pp. 289–91.

must nevertheless be regarded as the original organizer of the parish which still bears his name at the present day.[1]

Place-names compounded with *plou-* are found in all parts of Brittany and are even preserved within the French zone from which the Breton tongue has long since retreated.

The word *tré* denotes a village. When a village possessed a chapel, it was frequently one erected as a chapel of ease, and thus the village and the adjoining district constituted a *trêve* in the ecclesiastical sense of the word.[2]

These parochial and *trévial* churches, these chapels called *lann* and *loc*, which have perpetuated the memory of their primitive pastors throughout the ages, have remained dear to the piety of the Breton people ; and on the feast-day of the local saint the faithful flock to them to get the indulgence or " pardon."

In the ninth century we find not only chapels but even some parochial churches in Brittany which had become the private property of laymen, though indeed in far less number than in other parts of Gaul.[3]

Such is the outline which can be traced of the ecclesiastical organization of Brittany during the early Middle Ages, either with the aid of such documents as have been preserved or by using the data furnished by the study of its toponymy. Let us conclude with the words of René Largillière : " The priests who came from the isle of Britain found in Armorica a virgin soil and a population wholly unsettled which had scarce taken up its abode and had as yet no social organization. They were not subjected to any previously existing local authority, and they acted in complete independence, founding parishes wherever it seemed needful

[1] Largillière, *l. cit.* ; F. Lot, *R. Cel.*, XLIII, 1926, pp. 456–58.

[2] Largillière, *Les saints*, p. 182 ; Émile Ernault, *Glossaire moyen-breton* (Paris, 1896), *s.v. Trev.*

[3] Charter of A.D. 843 (ed. Paul Marchegay, *Archives de l'Anjou : Cartulaire de Saint Maur-sur-Loire*, Angers, 1843, pp. 363–64 ; Planiol, *La donation d'Anouuarth : An. Br.*, IX, 1894, p. 235).—Charter of A.D. 847 (*Cartulaire de l'abbaye de Redon*, edited by Aurélien de Courson, Paris, 1863, pp. 26–27).— Charter No. xxiv in *Cartulaire de Landévennec*, ed. L. Maître and Paul de Berthou (Paris, 1886). Cf. R. Latouche, *Mélanges d'histoire de Cornouaille*, pp. 65–68 ; Largillière, *Les saints*, pp. 241–42 ; Planiol, *La donation*, p. 232 ; Imbart de la Tour, *Les origines religieuses de la France. Les paroisses rurales du IVᵉ au XIᵉ siècle* (Paris, 1900), pp. 198–215.

to do so, without waiting for the bishop to establish a rural church in the place and appoint them to officiate in it.   The situation was therefore altogether different from that in Gaul, where the rural churches were subservient to the primary baptismal church established in the chief centre of the *civitas*.   In Armorica there were no rural churches affiliated to the urban church ; all the churches were rural, independent and contemporary." [1]

§ 5.—The Emancipation of the Church of Brittany

In the fifth century Brittany was under the jurisdiction of the ecclesiastical province of Tours.   The metropolitan Perpetuus presided over the Council assembled at Vannes about 465.   The metropolitan Licinius it was who, about 515, conjointly with his suffragans of Rennes and Angers, addressed to the two Breton priests Lovocat and Catihern those remonstrances spoken of in the preceding chapter.   But if the authority of the metropolis was recognized at first by the Breton Church, it waned more and more in the course of the following centuries.   It happened occasionally that Breton bishops took part in councils outside the ecclesiastical province. For instance, St Samson, bishop of Dol, subscribed in 557 (?) to the third Council of Paris ; Garurbius, bishop of Tréguier or St. Brieuc, attended the synod of Quierzy at which Gottschalk was condemned (March–April, 849) [2] ; whereas bishops of Breton race never took part in the councils of the province of Tours.   A formal charge is brought against them on that score in the letter addressed by the Fathers of the Council of Soissons to Pope Nicholas I (866).[3]

Nor were they more concerned to obtain the sanction of the metropolitan for episcopal consecrations.   The ninth canon of the Council of Tours in 567 calls them to order on that head : " Let no pontiff presume to give episcopal consecration in Armorica either to a Briton or a Roman without the sanc-

---

[1] Largillière, *Les saints*, p. 208.
[2] Mansi, *Concilia*, IX, col. 747 ; *MG. Leges*, III, *Concilia*, I, p. 146.
—Hincmar, *De praedestinatione*, 2 (*PL*, CXXV, 85). Cf. Lot, *Mélanges*, pp. 85–86.
[3] Mansi, *Concilia*, XV, 732.

tion of the metropolitan or the bishops of the province ; otherwise he shall hold himself excommunicate." [1] The " Romans " referred to are the bishops of Rennes, Nantes and Vannes. As a fact, Felix of Nantes and Victorius of Rennes were present at this council, and it was no doubt they who drew the attention of the Fathers to the proceedings of their neighbours. It is hardly likely that the Bretons subsequently obeyed the injunction.

In spite of the efforts of Charlemagne and Louis the Pious, the cleavage between the Church of Brittany and the see of Tours, or rather the entire Frankish Church, grew more and more decided. The Bretons had not grown accustomed to the institution of metropolitan sees ; they had known nothing of the sort in the country whence they came. Even the notion of a diocese was probably foreign to them. On the other hand, their episcopal organization, their abbot-bishops, their monastic clergy, their tonsure and their Easter were in the eyes of the Franks reprehensible irregularities calling for urgent and radical reform.

Add to this the fact that on political grounds there were constant and implacable outbursts of hostility between Bretons and Franks, under the Merovingians as well as the Carolingians, and it will be conceived that the relations between the prelates of the two countries were further embittered. In Great Britain it had been impossible to establish any mutual understanding between the British clergy and Augustine of Canterbury, the apostle of their enemies the Saxons. It must moreover be borne in mind that the Frankish episcopate, though entirely within its rights in protesting against the insubordination of the Bretons in ecclesiastical matters, more than once with its canonical reprimands mingled allusions to political questions which were bound to irritate the Bretons. [2]

If finally we take into consideration that obstinate adherence to their religious customs which was characteristic of the Celts, and of which St Columban gave a striking example in Gaul itself in his altercations with the Burgundian prelates

[1] Mansi, IX, 794 ; ed. Maassen (*MG. Leges*, III, *Concilia*, I, p. 124).
[2] Mansi, XV, 533, 733.

at the end of the sixth century,[1] we have a full explanation of the separatist movement which was brought to a head by the exorbitant claims of king Nominoé.

The refusal of the Bretons to pay the tributes imposed by the Carolingians was the cause of the campaigns undertaken against Brittany by Pippin the Short and afterwards by Charlemagne. The Frankish annals record the result of the expedition of 799 as follows : " The whole province of Brittany was conquered by the Franks, a thing never witnessed before." [2] Nevertheless, the imperial armies were obliged to take the field on three subsequent occasions under Louis the Pious to put down the revolts of Morvan (818) and of Wiomarc'h (822–825). In 826 Louis committed the government of Brittany to the Breton Nominoé with the title of duke. There was hardly any disturbance of the peace under Nominoé's administration as long as the king lived ; but on his death (840) Nominoé held himself no longer bound towards Louis' successors and boldly raised the standard of independence. In 843 he threw himself on the territory of Rennes ; in the following year he crossed the Loire and penetrated into Poitou. Charles the Bald marched against Brittany with a large army. Nominoé awaited him between the Oust and the Vilaine, and on November 22, 845, gained a brilliant victory over him at Ballon.[3] The war of independence being now over, the Breton became a conqueror. He assumed the title of king of Brittany, took possession of Rennes, Nantes and Angers, flung himself on Le Mans " with unspeakable fury," [4] and carried his daring excursions as far as the plain of Beauce.

Arrived at the zenith of his political fortunes, the victor was unhappily so misguided as to conceive the project of reforming the Church of Brittany in his own fashion. The sees of Vannes, Quimper, Alet and Léon were held by bishops devoted to the Frankish princes. Anxious to get rid of these,

---

[1] E. Martin, *Saint Colomban* (Paris, 1905), p. 76. *V. inf.* ch. VI, § 1.

[2] *Annales regni Francorum*, A.D. 799, ed. Pertz and Kurze, *Script. rer. German. in usum scholarum*, Hannoverae, 1895, p. 108.

[3] Cf. René Merlet, *Les guerres d'indépendance de la Bretagne sous Nominoé et Érispoé* (*Revue de Bretagne*, 1891, pp. 6 ff.)

[4] *Chron. Fontanellense* (*MG. Scr.*, II, 301–304).

Nominoé eagerly listened to the charges of simony brought against them by Conwoïon, abbot of Redon, and sent the abbot as his deputy to Rome to procure their condemnation and deposition by the Holy See.[1] Two of the accused prelates, Susannus of Vannes and Felix of Quimper, repaired on their own account to the Pope to justify themselves. The decision of Leo IV was not such as Nominoé expected. The Pope wrote to him personally a letter which has not come down to us.[2] He also wrote to the bishops of Brittany ; and in this letter, which has been preserved, he expressed himself to the following effect : Those who are convicted of simony are to be deposed, but only in council and by twelve bishops, or on the testimony of seventy-two witnesses ; should the accused bishop claim to be heard at Rome, he is to be sent there. The Pope then specifies the canonical texts according to which the trial is to be conducted.[3]

Such methods of procedure were too complicated for the Breton prince. At Coëtleu, between Redon and Ploërmel,[4] he convened a large assembly of priests and laymen to judge the accused bishops. These latter, having been threatened with death unless they confessed to the charge of simony, made the desired confession, laid down their insignia and departed to seek refuge among the Franks (849).[5] Nominoé replaced the unfortunate prelates by creatures of his own.

Had the four bishops been really guilty of the crime of simony ? The uncanonical procedure at Coëtleu, the kindly welcome bestowed on the accused by the Frankish bishops, the testimony of the *Indiculus de episcoporum Britonum depositione* and of the *Chronicle of Nantes*,[6] and a passage in a letter from Pope Nicholas I to the Breton king Salomon (862), leave room for doubt on the point. " It is said," so ran the last document, " that these bishops confessed their crime ; but it may be

[1] *GSR*, ii, 10 (p. 211).
[2] Document analysed in *Chron. Nam.*, pp. 34, 35, 59.
[3] Leo IV, *Ep.* 8 (*MG. Epist.*, V, 593).
[4] Com. Saint-Congar ; Cant. Rochefort-en-Terre ; arr. Vannes (Morbihan). Cf. La Borderie, *HB*, II, p. 55, n. 5 ; Rosenzweig, *Dictionnaire topographique du département du Morbihan* (Paris, 1860), p. 48.
[5] For the date see Lot, *Mélanges*, p. 87, and F. Lot and L. Halphen, *Le règne de Charles le Chauve* (Paris, 1909), I, p. 217.
[6] *Indiculus* (Bouquet, VII, p. 288) ; *Chron. Nam.*, pp. 33 ff.

believed that under the constraint of violence and fear they avowed things which they had not done, because they beheld laymen and seculars united with the king against them." [1]

In any case, the choice made by Nominoé of men to take their place does not seem to have been a happy one. A synodal letter of the Frankish bishops (850 or 851), drawn up by the pen of Lupus, abbot of Ferrières, describes the new bishops as "*mercenarii*." [2] Shortly after, Nominoé, having ejected bishop Actard of Nantes, replaced him by a certain Gislard whom Leo IV stigmatized as "robber" and "thief." [3] The new prelates were called "pseudo-bishops" by the Fathers of the Council of Soissons (866). [4] Nevertheless, Nicholas I, writing to king Salomon in 865, considers Festinian of Dol, the second successor of Salocon who had been deposed by Nominoé, as a genuine bishop, for he speaks of him in the following terms : "*Fratri et coepiscopo nostro Festiniano qui ecclesiae Sancti Samsonis praeesse dinoscitur.*" [5]

It is generally agreed that another reform carried out by Nominoé, this time in perfect accordance with Frankish and Roman ideas, was to transform the monastery-bishoprics of Celtic type into dioceses with strictly defined areas. [6]

Was the establishment of a metropolitan see at Dol an immediate consequence of the spurious Council of Coëtleu, and was Nominoé directly responsible for the blow thus dealt to the jurisdiction of Tours ? It has been hitherto believed that such was the case. [7] However, Ferdinand Lot seems to me to be right in assigning the creation of the archbishopric of Dol to a later date. In the letters of remonstrance addressed either by the Pope or the Frankish bishops to the Breton bishops or princes, there is no mention before the year 862 of this grave infraction of the prerogatives of Tours. Before the Council of Soissons in 866 Dol is not even named. In

---

[1] Nicholas I, *Ep.* 107, ed. E. Perels (*MG. Epist.*, VI, p. 621).

[2] Lupus, *Ep.* 84 (*MG. Epist.*, VI, p. 76 ; *PL*, CXIX, 554). For the date see Lot and Halphen, *op. cit.*, p. 200, and Duine, *Schisme*, p. 440.

[3] Leo IV, *Ep.* 20 (*MG. Epist.*, V, p. 598).

[4] "Duobus in ipsa sede nuncupative subrogatis" (Mansì, *Concilia*, XV, 733).

[5] *Ep.* 122 (p. 640).—In *Ep.* 126, the Pope calls Festinian "venerabilis, Dolensis antistes" (p. 647).

[6] Largillière, *Les saints*, p. 223.

[7] La Borderie, *HB*, II, p. 57.

documents anterior to 862 there is indeed some mention of the violation of the rights of the Church of St Martin,[1] but this may be understood to refer to the old determination of the Bretons not to take part in the synods of the province and the custom no less old of proceeding to episcopal consecration without the sanction of the metropolitan. Evidently that sanction had not been asked for in the consecration of the four bishops appointed by Nominoé.[2] " It appears," as Ferdinand Lot justly observes, " that this idea [of the metropolis of Dol] took shape in the minds of the Breton prince [Salomon (857–874)] and his bishops as a direct consequence of the vehement reproaches of the synods. Subjected to threats, they grew restive, and their resistance, hitherto passive, became active." [3]

Festinian took possession of the see of Dol in 859.[4] Four or five years later he took it into his head to ask the Pope for the pallium. This request shows that he considered himself thenceforth really a metropolitan or at least that he was determined to pass for one.[5]

The reigning Pope at the time was Nicholas I (858–867). Writing to Salomon, king of the Bretons, in 862, he touches on the matter of the bishops whom Nominoé had dismissed without complying with canonical rules, and he declares that all the Breton bishops are suffragans of the metropolitan see of Tours and that there is no witness to the existence of a metropolitan Church in Brittany. But, he adds, since the Bretons feel so deeply on this question, let them come to Rome to discuss it.[6]

As for the bestowal of the pallium solicited by the king for Festinian " who presides over the Church of St Samson," the Pope, in another letter addressed on May 26, 865, to Salomon and his wife, requires that the pontifical documents which had

---

[1] Mansi, *Concilia*, XV, col. 533.

[2] *Epist. altera conc. Suessionensis ad Nicolaum* (Mansi, *Concilia*, XV, col. 733) ; John VIII, *Ep.* 92 (*MG. Epist.*, VII, pp. 87–88).

[3] Lot, *Mélanges*, p. 25.

[4] Lot, *Mélanges*, p. 14 ; Duine, *Schisme*, pp. 446–59.

[5] The pallium was generally attached to metropolitan sees ; there were very few exceptions. See E. Lesne, *La hiérarchie épiscopale en Gaule et en Germanie* (Lille and Paris, 1905), pp. 94 ff.

[6] Nicholas I, *Ep.* 107 (*MG. Epist.*, VI, pp. 610–22).

accompanied its bestowal on Festinian's predecessors should be submitted to him and further, that Festinian should send him a profession of the Catholic faith and of submission to the Chair of Peter by an envoy chosen from among his clergy and qualified to take an oath in the name of his bishop.[1]

In the same or the following year a new letter came from Nicholas to Salomon, in which the Pope repeats what he has already said touching the bestowal of the pallium on Festinian, " the venerable bishop of Dol," and the metropolitan authority of Tours, against which no conclusive document has hitherto been produced. " If you have really solid reasons in support of a Breton metropolis," adds the Pope, " let them be brought forward." [2]

Driven thus to the necessity of adducing precedents in support of the privileges claimed by Dol, Festinian urged the Pope to consult the *gesta* of the Roman Church (*i.e.*, the *Liber Pontificalis*), in which he would find that in times past Pope Severinus had consecrated Restoald, one of his predecessors, as archbishop.[3]

In the *Liber Pontificalis* there does indeed occur the following sentence in the notice of Sergius (not of Severinus) : " *Hic ordinavit Bertoaldum Britanniae archiepiscopum* " [4] ; this, as Louis Duchesne has shown, is the passage which led Festinian into temptation or error.[5] For the name Bertoaldus he probably read (or someone read for him) Restoaldus. Unfortunately, the *archiepiscopus Britanniae* referred to occupied a see not of Brittany but Britain, to wit, that of Canterbury (692–730). The Pope was not to be convinced by this alleged precedent, nor yet by the further statement of Festinian that a certain Iuthmaël had also received the pallium from Pope Adrian [6]—a statement the source of which has not been discovered.

[1] *Ep.* 122 (p. 640).—On the collation of the pallium in the ninth century and the accompanying formalities, see Duine, *Schisme* (p. 450) and H. Thurston, *The pallium and the pallium oath* (*Month*, CLIV, 1929, pp. 152–58).
[2] *Ep.* 126 (pp. 646–47).
[3] *Ep.* 127 (pp. 648–49).
[4] *Liber Pontificalis*, ed. L. Duchesne (Paris, 1886), I, p. 376.
[5] *R. Cel.*, XXII, 1901, p. 244.
[6] The letter of Hadrian II conferring that dignity on Festinian is a forgery. See Lot, *Mélanges*, p. 31, n. 2.

After due investigation, the sovereign Pontiff declared that he found nothing in ecclesiastical tradition which would authorize the Bretons to have a metropolis of their own. Nicholas I died in 867. On June 25, 874, king Salomon, the ardent supporter of the primacy of Dol, was assassinated. In Brittany he was regarded as a holy martyr.[1]

The popes did not cease to protest against the ecclesiastical revolution which had been carried out in Dol.[2] The conflict lasted over three centuries. We will relate hereafter how it was brought to an end by a bull of Innocent III dated June 7, 1199, requiring the bishop of Dol to renounce his chimerical rights and submit to the jurisdiction of the see of Tours.[3]

The ecclesiastical affairs of Brittany called forth lively emotions in France, as has been sufficiently seen from the councils which dealt with them and from the measures they provoked. Now, as Paul Fournier has with keen insight observed, the two main reproaches formulated against the Bretons, namely, the assaults made on the episcopacy by seculars and the illegal dismemberment of an ecclesiastical province, are the very evils which the author of the False Decretals sought above all to remedy. Many other points of resemblance have been established between the situation of the Breton clergy in the middle of the ninth century and that which Pseudo-Isidore exerted himself to amend. "No region could furnish an original more closely resembling the picture which Isidore tried to paint."[4] P. Fournier has therefore been led by consideration of these facts to locate the "pseudo-Isidorian workshop" in the province of Tours and the neighbourhood of Brittany, probably at Le Mans.

[1] F. Le Lay, *La mort de Salomon, roi de Bretagne* (*MSHAB*, V, 1924, pp. 3–22).

[2] John VIII, *Ep.* 159 *ad episcopos Britanniae* (*PL*, CXXVI, 801–802).

[3] *V. inf.* ch. XI, § 8.

[4] Paul Fournier, *Étude sur les Fausses Décrétales* (*RHE*, VII, 1906, pp. 761–84), *s.a.* art. *Décrétales* (*Fausses*) in *Dictionnaire apologétique de la foi catholique*, edited by A. d'Alès, I, cols. 907–908. P. Fournier and G. Le Bras, *Histoire des collections canoniques en Occident* (Paris, 1931), I, pp. 196–201. On the Pseudo-Isidorian Decretals see Langen, *Nochmals : Wer ist Pseudoisidor ?* (*Historische Zeitschrift*, XLVIII, 1882, pp. 473-94) ; W. Levison in Gebhardt's *Handbuch der Deutschen Geschichte* (Stuttgart, 1926), I, p. 262 ; L. J. Paetow, *A Guide to the Study of Medieval History* (New York, 1931), p. 205.

CHAPTER V

THE IRISH ABROAD

ONCE converted, Ireland, as we have seen, made rapid progress in the faith. Churches and monasteries were multiplied on her soil; and piety blossomed and bore fruit. From an early time, strong impulses towards expansion were at work among the religious. Anchorites sought a fuller solitude beyond the seas, monks were inflamed with the desire of carrying their ascetic practices to foreign lands. We need not seek any other motives to account for the movement of emigration which set in from the sixth century among the Irish.[1]

Later, under the Carolingians, we shall see scholars, artists and pilgrims from the islands arriving in numbers on the Continent ; but the emigrants who landed in England and spread thence to the neighbouring continental countries from the sixth century on were actuated almost exclusively by ascetic and missionary impulses.[2]   Monks for the most part, voluntary expatriation appeared to them in the light of a

---

[1] See on the subject : A. W. Haddan, *Scots on the Continent* (*Remains*, edited by A. P. Forbes, Oxford and London, 1876, pp. 258–94) ; J. von Pflugk-Harttung, *The old Irish on the Continent* (*Transactions of the Royal Historical Society*, New Ser., V, 1891, pp. 75–102) ; Margaret Stokes, *Six Months in the Apennines in Search of the Vestiges of Irish Saints* (London, 1892) ; s.a. *Three Months in the Forests of France : a Pilgrimage in Search of Vestiges of Irish Saints* (London, 1895) ; J. J. Dunn, *Irish Monks on the Continent* (*Catholic University Bulletin*, Washington, X, 1904, pp. 307–28) ; L.G., *L'oeuvre des " Scotti " dans l'Europe continentale* (*RHE*, IX, 1908, pp. 21–37, 255–77) ; s.a. *Gaelic Pioneers of Christianity* (Dublin, 1923) ; W. Levison, *Die Iren und die Fränkische Kirche* (*Historische Zeitschrift*, CIX, 1912, pp. 1–22) ; Anton Mayer, *Die Iren auf dem Kontinent im Mittelalter* (*Hochland*, XIII, 1915–16, pp. 605–14) ; Boissonnade, *Les relations entre l'Aquitaine, le Poitou et l'Irlande du Ve au IXe siecle* (*Bulletin de la Société des Antiquaires de l'Ouest*, 2nd Ser., IV, 1917, pp. 181–202) ; J. P. Fuhrmann, *Irish Medieval Monasteries on the Continent* (Washington, 1927) ; Kenney, *Sources*, I, ch. VI, pp. 486–621.

[2] Adam., *Vita Col.*, Praef. II (pp. 5–6) ; Jonas, *Vita Col.*, I, 3, 4, 5 (pp. 68, 71) ; Columban, *Ep.* 4 (*MG. Epist.*, III, p. 167 : " Mei voti fuit, gentes visitare, et evangelium eis a nobis praedicari "). Cf. C. Plummer's Note on " Peregrinam ducere vitam " in Bede, *HE*, Vol. II (pp. 170-71) ; Ryan, *Monast.*, pp. 262–63.

supreme self-sacrifice, the fittest crown to the task of renunciation in which they had engaged.[1]   To leave their country
" for the love of God," " for the name of the Lord," " for the
love of the name of Christ," " for the healing of the soul,"
" in order to win the heavenly fatherland," such are the
phrases which the biographers of these holy travellers choose
to describe the motive of their wanderings.[2]   They called
themselves *peregrini*, a word which as a general rule we must
beware of translating by " pilgrims."   The real pilgrim is one
who repairs to some shrine which is the object of his special
devotion and, his pious journey ended, returns to his own
land and resumes his usual life.   Such pilgrims there were
undoubtedly among the Irish, and even more among the
Anglo-Saxons, who swarmed over the highways of Europe,
especially from the eighth century [3] ; but the earlier *peregrini*
were not, properly speaking, pilgrims.   In a far fuller sense
they were voluntary exiles who had pledged themselves not
to return to their native land for a considerable period or
indeed, in most cases, for the rest of their life, whether or
not they undertook the duties of the missionary as well.[4]
Hence by the writers of their Lives they are often compared
to Abraham ; and it might indeed be imagined that they had
all heard the voice which bade the Patriarch : " *Egredere de
terra tua et de cognatione tua.*" [5]

[1] Ryan, *Monast.*, pp. 261–62 ; H. von Campenhausen, *Die asketische
Heimatlosigkeit im altkirchlichen und frühmittelalterlichen Mönchtum* (Sammlung
Gemeinverständlicher Vorträge und Schriften aus dem Gebiet der Theologie
und Religionsgeschichte, CXLIX, Tübingen, 1930).
[2] PEREGRINATIO PRO DEI AMORE : *Vita Walarici*, 4 (*MG. Scr. RM.*, IV,
162) ; Walahfrid Strabo, *Vita Galli*, I, 30 (*MG. Scr. RM.*, IV, 308).—PEREGRI-
NATIO PROPTER NOMEN DOMINI : *Vita Cadroe*, II, 19 (Boll., *AS.*, Mart., I,
p. 476).—OB AMOREM ;   PRO AMORE ;   PRO NOMINE CHRISTI : Alcuin,
Inscriptiones in monast. S. Petri Salisburgensi, 24 (*MG. Poet. Lat.*, I, p. 340) ;
s.a. Ep. 287 (*MG. Epist.*, IV, 446) ;   *Vita Vodoali*, ed. Mabillon, *Acta Sanct.
O.S.B.* (Parisiis, 1668–1701), IV, II, 545).—PRO CHRISTO : Adam., *Vita
Col.*, Praef. 2 (pp. 5–6).—PRO REMEDIO ANIMAE : *Chron. abbat. S. Martini
Colon.* (*MG. Scr.*, II, 215).—PRO ADIPISCENDA IN CAELIS PATRIA : Bede,
HE, V, 9.—PRO AETERNA PATRIA : Bede, *HE*, III, 13, V, 9 ; *Vita Mariani
Scotti*, I (Boll., *AS*, Febr., II, 365).
[3] *V. inf.* § 8.
[4] " . . . et peregrinationem suscipiens, ad patriam nequaquam sum
reversurus " (*Vita Findani*, 5, 6 : *MG. Scr.*, XV, I, p. 504).
[5] Jonas, *Vita Col.*, I, 4 (p. 10) ; *Betha Phátraic* (*Lismore*, pp. 17, 165) ;
Betha Fhindein Clúana hEraird (*Lismore*, pp. 82, 229) ; *Betha Ciarain Clúana
meic Nois* (*Lismore*, pp. 133, 279) ; *Vita Donati*, I, 7 (Boll., *AS*, Oct. IX,

Many of these voluntary exiles were led by circumstances to devote themselves to apostolic work. However, as it has been said, " speaking generally, the primary idea of the word *peregrinatio* is not evangelistic labour, but exile from the mother country and its temptations, for the purpose of leading a life of austerity." [1]

It should be added that, beside the sacrifices inspired by asceticism and missionary zeal, *Wanderlust*, the love of adventure—a characteristic to be noticed among the Celts in all times and one which continental observers in the Middle Ages did not fail to remark—had not a little to do with the motives which drove the sons of Erin from their country in the period with which we deal.[2]

§ 1.—Irish Monks in the Northern Islands

At an early date Irish monks visited the northern seas. Some, eager for complete solitude, were in search of a place of retreat inaccessible to man [3]; such a one was that Cormac úa Liatháin, for whom St Columba of Iona obtained from Brude, king of the Picts, the protection of his suzerain, the prince of the Orkney Islands. Cormac landed in those islands, but found them inhabited by people to whom he was no doubt the first to preach the Gospel.[4]

According to the Irish geographer Dicuil, who wrote his treatise *De mensura orbis terrae* in 825, the Faroe Islands, lying beyond the *ultima Thule* of the ancients, nearly half-way between the Orkneys and Iceland, had been tenanted for a

p. 656) ; *Vita Altonis*, 2 (*MG. Scr.*, XV, II, 843) ; *Vita Cadroe*, II, 15 (Boll., AS, Mart., I, p. 476) ; *Vita Ronani*, 2 (*Catal. codic. hagiogr. Lat. Bibl. Nat. Parisiensis*, Bruxellis, 1889, I, p. 439).

[1] Lawlor, *Cathach*, pp. 303–304.

[2] " Iter direxerunt versus Romam in peregrinacione more Scottorum " (*Gesta Caroli Mag.*, p. 173). Cf. P. S. Allen, *The Romanesque Lyric. Studies in its Background and Development* (Chapell Hill, N.C., 1908), p. 159.

[3] " Eremum in oceano quaerere " (Adam., *Vita Col.*, I, 6 (p. 22), II, 42 (pp. 115–16). Cf. J. M. Mackinlay, *In Oceano desertum : Celtic Anchorites and their Island Retreats* (*PSAS*, XXXIII, 1889, pp. 129–33).

[4] Adam., *Vita Col.*, I, 6 (p. 22), II, 42 (pp. 115–18). On the doubtful existence of any extensive Celtic Christianity in the Shetlands and Orkneys before the advent of the Norsemen see A. W. Brøgger, *Ancient Emigrants, A History of the Norse Settlements of Scotland* (Oxford, 1929), pp. 55–57 ; A. B. Scott, *The Celtic Church in Orkney* (*Proceedings of the Orkney Antiquarian Society*, IV, 1925–26, pp. 45–56) [Full of hypotheses].

K 2

hundred years by Irish hermits.[1]   The geographer states
that they discovered Iceland about 795, sixty-five or seventy
years before the time generally fixed for its discovery by the
Scandinavians.[2] His testimony is confirmed by the Icelandic
tradition recorded in the *Islendígabók* [3] and the *Landnámabók*.[4]
Ari Frodi (*c.* 1067–1148), who compiled the latter book, gives
in particular the following information : " Before Iceland
was settled by Northmen there were there those people whom
the Northmen called Papas.[5] They were Christian men, and
people think that they must have been from the West of the
Sea [*i.e.*, the British Isles] because there were found after
them Irish books and bells and crooks and yet more things
by which it might be perceived that they were West-men.
These things were found in East Papey and in Papyli. And
it is also spoken of in English books that at that time men
went between the lands." [6]

It is possible that St Brendan and his companions, impelled
by the spirit of adventure, did really accomplish voyages to
distant seas.[7] At any rate, they gave birth to legendary
Odysseys which had a fascination for the people of the Middle
Ages and of which almost every literature in Europe in the
past possessed translations or imitations.[8] Other voyages of

[1] On the identification of the Thule of the Ancients with Mainland, the
principal island of the Shetland group see Mario Esposito, *An Irish Teacher
at the Carolingian Court : Dicuil* (*Studies*, III, 1914, p. 670).

[2] Dicuil, *Liber de Mensura orbis terrae*, VII, 10–13, ed. G. Parthey (Berolini,
1870, pp. 42–44). Cf. M. Esposito, *art. cit.*, pp. 670–71 ; W. A. Craigie,
The Gaels in Iceland (*PSAS*, XXXI, 1897, pp. 247 ff.) ; Eiríkr Magnússon,
The Conversion of Iceland to Christianity (*Saga-Book of the Viking Club*, II,
1897–1900, pp. 348–76).

[3] Ed. Vigfússon and Powell, *Origines Islandicae* (Oxford, 1905), I, pp. 3,
288.

[4] Ed. Vigfússon and Powell, *op. cit.*, p. 13.

[5] *I.e.*, monks or priests (L.G., *Les chrétientés celtiques*, p. 137 ; M. Esposito,
art. cit., p. 671 ; Knut Gjerst, *History of Iceland* London, 1924, pp. 21–22).

[6] *L. cit.*

[7] " It is reasonably certain that Brendan himself made a voyage to the
Scottish isles, and perhaps to Strathclyde, Cumbria or Wales. His Lives
speak of such a voyage, and, more important, Adamnan, in his Life of
Columba (III, 17), testifies that Brendan, with Comgall of Bangor, Cainnech
of Achad-bó and Cormac úa Liatháin, visited Columba in the island of
Hinba " (Kenney, *Sources*, I, p. 409). Cf. W. H. Babcock, *St Brendan's
Explorations and Islands* (*Geographical Review*, III, 1919, pp. 37–46), *s.a.
Legendary Islands of the Atlantic* (*American Geographical Society Research Series*,
No. 8, New York, 1922).

[8] See Kenney, *Sources*, I, pp. 408–12.

the same nature, undertaken by laymen or clerics from motives of piety or penance, sometimes even by way of ordeal, contributed if not to create, at least to enrich and render popular an important branch of Irish literature, the *Immrama* or sea-voyages.[1] The *immram* was one of the classes of tale from which the old *filid* could take subject-matter for an epic.[2]

It has even been asserted that the venturesome barks of the Celts, drawn by currents or driven by favouring winds to the extreme west, touched the shores of the American continent eight or nine centuries before Christopher Columbus ; but the enthusiasts who have advanced this theory have not so far succeeded in winning acceptance for it from any critics in the least inclined to be exacting.[3]

" God did not make the sea for navigation, but on account of the beauty of the element." [4] If this quaint reflection of St Ambrose ever met the eyes of our Irish wanderers, it cannot have had much weight with them. Assuredly they were susceptible to the beauty of the marine element ; but, first and foremost, they thought of using the sea for navigation : the only means which these island-dwellers had of enlarging the scope of their experience and activity.

They penetrated by degrees the regions of the north and north-west. One of the earliest stages was the settlement of St Columba on the little isle of Iona. From Iona Christianity spread to the Picts ; from Iona, too, went forth the Scottic monks who founded Lindisfarne and devoted themselves with such noble ardour to evangelizing Northumbria.

§ 2.—IONA, LINDISFARNE, AND THE EVANGELIZATION OF NORTHUMBRIA

Columba was born in 521 (?) of a noble Irish family belonging to the sept of the O'Donnells, which counted among its ancestors Niall of the Nine Hostages, high-king of Ireland from 379 to 405 (?). His original name was Crimthann, a

---

[1] Best, *Bibl.*, pp. 115–16. Cf. W. F. Thrall, *Clerical Sea Pilgrimages and the " Imrama "* (*The Manly Anniversary Studies*, Chicago, 1923, pp. 276–83).

[2] H. d'Arbois de Jubainville, *Introduction à l'étude de la littérature celtique* (Paris, 1883), p. 350.

[3] Kenney, *Sources*, I, p. 408 ; L.G., *Les chrétientés celtiques*, p. 138.

[4] Ambrose, *De Helia et ieiunio*, 19 (*PL*, XIV, 757).

fairly common Irish name, signifying " fox." [1] Later he was given the name Columcille, which means " dove of the church (or monastery)." [2] In Latin he is always called Columba.

He received his literary education and religious training at Moville and later at Clonard, and became in his turn a founder of monasteries. Derry (now Londonderry) and Durrow were the most important of his Irish foundations.

In 563 (?) Columba left Ireland. What was his reason for doing so? According to well-established tradition, it was remorse or the condemnation of his fellow-countrymen drawn on him by bloody tribal disputes of which he was deemed the author.[3] But neither Adamnán, the saint's best accredited biographer, nor the Venerable Bede give this reason for his departure. Adamnán tells us that it was the wish to become an exile for Christ (*pro Christo peregrinari volens*) which made him decide to leave the soil of Erin [4] ; Bede represents him as possessed by missionary zeal (*praedicaturus verbum Dei*).[5]

From the fifth century the Irish Scots had gained a foothold in Albion, south of the Picts, in Dál Riada, a region corresponding to the present county of Argyll (*Airer nGaidhel* = territory of the Gaels). The Scots of Dál Riada were Christians, at least in name. The southern Picts, cut off from their kinsmen to the south of Dál Riada, had been evangelized, it will be remembered, in the fifth century by St Ninian, but since then had lost the faith. As for the northern Picts, who inhabited the most northerly and inaccessible part of the island, beyond the Grampians, they were still pagans. Of them and of the Scottic colonists of Dál Riada Columba was thinking when he left Ireland.

He fixed himself within reach of both these tribes on a small island about three miles in length from north-east to south-west and varying in breadth from one mile to a mile and a half. The island belonged to one of the tribes but seems to have been under the suzerain power of the other.[6]

[1] Notes on Fiacc's Hymn (*Fél. Oeng.*, pp. 144–46 ; Stokes and Strachan, *TP*, II, p. 306).

[2] *Fél. Oeng., l. cit.*

[3] *LH*, II, pp. 75, 140.

[4] Adam., *Vita Col.*, Praef. 2 (pp. 5–6).

[5] Bede, *HE*, III, 4.

[6] Bede says (*HE*, III, 3) that the island was granted to Columba by the

Both proprietor and suzerain, however, renounced their rights in favour of Columcille, who settled there in full security. The little island, about seventy miles distant from Ireland, is separated from the Ross of Mull, the neighbouring island, by a sound or strait about a mile in width. It was called Í or Hii, whence the adjective *Iova*, which by a scribal error was changed into *Iona*, the name which has clung to it since.[1]

There the " island soldier " (*insulanus miles*), as Adamnán calls him, lived for thirty-four years. His biographer, who was also a successor in the abbotship, has drawn the following portrait of him : " He had the face of an angel ; he was of an excellent nature, polished in speech, holy in deed, great in counsel. He never let a single hour pass without engaging in prayer or reading or writing or some other occupation. He endured the hardships of fasting and vigils without intermission by day and night ; the burden of a single one of his labours would seem beyond the powers of man. And, in the midst of all his toils, he appeared loving unto all, serene and holy, rejoicing in the joy of the Holy Spirit in his inmost heart." [2]

When leaving Ireland St Columba was accompanied only by twelve monks, but before long disciples flocked in large numbers to Iona. Soon other monasteries or hermitages had to be organized in the neighbouring islands, at Ethica (Tiree), Elena, Hinba and Scia (Skye). These settlements, together with those of Scotland and Ireland, which their holy founder had not ceased to direct, formed a vast monastic confederation which is termed in texts *muinter Coluimchille, familia Columbae*.[3] In these solitary retreats and monastic establishments were trained the valiant apostles of the Picts and Anglo-Saxons.

In order more easily to overcome the paganism of the Picts, Columba did not hesitate to go in the first place to their king Brude. Like Loegaire in Ireland, Brude was surrounded by

Picts. According to *AU, AT* and *LH*, it was granted to him by Conall mac Comgaill, king of Dál Riada.
[1] G. T. Stokes, *Ireland and the Celtic Church*, pp. 361–62. On the island see C. Trenholme, *The Story of Iona* (Edinburgh, 1909).
[2] Adam., *Vita Col.*, Praef. 2 (p. 6).
[3] Skene, *CS*, II, p. 61.

druids deeply hostile to the proceedings of the Christian missionaries. But like St Patrick, Columba, by his personal influence and his miracles, triumphed over their thaumaturgic feats.[1] He succeeded in converting Brude and, that once accomplished, it was easier to spread Christianity among the uncivilized tribes. We have little information about the labours of Columba and his helpers among the Picts, but we may take for granted that the greater part of the thirty-four years over which the saint's *peregrinatio* extended was devoted to apostolic enterprises.[2]

In 574 Conall, king of the Scots of Dál Riada, died and was succeeded by his cousin Aedhán mac Gabhráin, who received his sacring in Iona at the hands of St Columba.[3]

Unlike a number of Irish abbots of the period, the abbot of Iona was not a bishop. Nevertheless he exercised over the churches and monasteries of neighbouring districts a jurisdiction which may be likened to that of a metropolitan. This anomalous state of affairs still persisted in favour of his successor in the time of the Venerable Bede. "The island," says that writer, "is ruled by a presbyter-abbot, to whose jurisdiction, by an unusual arrangement (*ordine inusitato*), the entire province, including even the bishops, is subject; in accordance with the example of the first teacher of the island, who was not a bishop but a priest and monk." [4]

According to Adamnán, the name of St Columba was venerated as far as Spain, in Gaul and beyond the Appenines in Rome, "the capital of all cities." [5] But England owes him special gratitude; for it was the sons of Columba who came to settle at Lindisfarne and spread thence among the Angles of the north to preach Christianity, the progress of

[1] Adam., *Vita Col.*, I, 1 (p. 10), I, 38 (p. 50).
[2] W. Douglas Simpson has contended that Columba's apostolic achievement among the Picts have been greatly exaggerated and that Adamnán nowhere states that Columba converted Brude. See *The Origins of Christianity in Aberdeenshire* (Aberdeen, 1925), *On Certain Saints and Prof. Watson* (Aberdeen, 1928) and, principally, *The Historical St Columba* (Aberdeen, 1927). These views have been criticized by Paul Grosjean (*AB*, XLVI, 1928, pp. 197–99) and by L.G. in *SGS*, II, 1927, pp. 106–108. See the texts referred to in both these reviews.
[3] Adam., *Vita Col.*, III, 5 (p. 134).
[4] Bede, *HE*, III, 5.
[5] Adam., *Vita Col.*, III, 23 (pp. 164–65).

which had been rudely interrupted by the victory of the heathen Penda over Edwin, king of Northumbria, at Hatfield (October 12, 633).

In consequence of that event, Paulinus, the representative of the Roman mission, who had reached York in 625 and restored the ancient episcopal see there, was obliged to flee to Kent.[1] But in the reign of Oswald (634–642), the country was opened once more to missionary enterprise. Oswald had spent his youth in exile among the Scots, either in Ireland or, more probably, in Dál Riada or Iona, and had been baptized by them.[2] From his accession he made it his aim to restore the faith in his dominions, and to Iona he applied for a bishop. He was sent a monk, a man of very austere disposition, who did not make way among the Angles.[3] Another monk, Aidan, was consecrated bishop and sent to England to replace him.

Aidan established himself on a small island in the North Sea, accessible from the mainland at low water and lying not far from the royal residence of Bamborough. This islet was called Lindisfarne ; it is now known as Holy Island. After the Celtic fashion, it became at the same time the seat of a monastery and a bishopric. For thirty years, down to the Synod of Whitby (664), it was the most powerful centre of religious influence in England.[4]

Aided by the pious king Oswald, who acted as his interpreter when necessary, Aidan displayed such missionary activity that Lightfoot has not hesitated to declare that " it was not Augustine, but Aidan, who was the true apostle of England." [5] His great love for the poor, his simplicity and straightforwardness, the austerity of his life, and his gift of reaching men's hearts are revealed in many incidents of his career. He ransomed captives and trained them for the priesthood. He trained monks and laymen in the Holy

---

[1] Bede, *HE*, ii, 20.
[2] Bede, *HE*, iii, 3. Cf. Plummer's Notes (Vol. II, p. 124) ; John Dowden, *The Celtic Church in Scotland* (London, 1894, p. 157) ; J. M. Mackinlay, *Celtic Relations of St Oswald of Northumbria* (*Celtic Review*, V, 1909, pp. 304–305).
[3] Bede, *HE*, iii, 5.
[4] Bede, *HE*, iii, 3 (Plummer's Notes, Vol. II, pp. 125–26).
[5] J. B. Lightfoot, *Leaders of the Northern Church* (London, 1890), p. 9.

Scriptures and in devotion to the Psalter.   He was the spiritual director of the abbess Hilda and gave the veil to Heiu, the first Northumbrian nun.   Bede bestows the highest encomium on the labours and virtues of this holy man ; he has only one reproach to bring against him—the observance of the heterodox Pasch.   But this nonconformity on a point of discipline did not prevent other saints who were his contemporaries, Honorius, bishop of Canterbury, Felix, bishop of East Anglia, both of them observers of the Roman Easter and the Roman tonsure, from professing the utmost veneration for the Apostle of Northumbria.[1]

Aidan died in 651 and was succeeded by another Scot, Finan.   Finan wished to build at Lindisfarne a church worthier of an episcopal see.   He did not, however, use stone, but wood, *more Scottorum*, for the edifice, and had it thatched with reeds.[2]   Finan helped in spreading Christianity beyond the frontiers of Northumbria.   He baptized two heathen kings, Peada, son of Penda, king of the Middle Angles, and Sigbert, king of the East Saxons.   He sent four priests to the Middle Angles, among them the Anglo-Saxon Cedd and the Scot Diuma.   Both of these were later raised to the episcopate, Cedd becoming bishop in Sigbert's dominions, while Diuma remained among the Middle Angles.   His episcopate was of short duration, and on his death another Scot, Cellach, succeeded him.[3]

Finan's successor in the see of Lindisfarne was also a Scot, Colmán.   It was during his episcopate that the controversy of the Celtic Easter and tonsure reached its critical stage in England [4] ;   in the following chapter we shall see how Colmán, when his party was worsted at the Synod of Whitby, chose to retire to Ireland, bearing with him the bones of St Aidan, rather than forsake the customs of his country.

The activity of the bishops of Lindisfarne and their monks was powerfully seconded by the support of the kings of Northumbria.   Oswy, the brother and successor of Oswald,

---

[1] Bede, *HE*, III, 5, 14, 23, 25.
[2] Bede, *HE*, III, 25.
[3] Bede, *HE*, III, 21, 22.
[4] Bede, *HE*, III, 25.

who reigned from 642 to 671, like him knew Irish, having been
instructed by the Scots.[1] Finally, Oswy's son, Aldfrid, who
reigned from 686 to 705, long after the Synod of Whitby,
was also a disciple of the Scots and kept up friendly relations
with Adamnán, abbot of Iona.[2] The Irish called him Flann
Fina mac Ossu, Fina being his mother's name according to
the authorities of their country. Some Gaelic verses which
have come down to us are attributed to him.[3] Bede, Eddius
and Alcuin have extolled the learning and wisdom of this
king.[4]

In the south of England we find only two monasteries which
owed their foundation to Irishmen, the little monastery of
Bosham in modern Sussex, founded by a certain Dicuil,[5] and
Malmesbury in Wiltshire, founded by another Irishman
named Maelduth or Maeldúin, from whom St Aldhelm
received his early education.[6]

At the celebrated abbey of Glastonbury (Somerset), several
Irish saints were venerated, a circumstance which drew
pilgrims from Ireland to the place. The youthful Dunstan
is said to have received, about the year 940, lessons from some
of the *peregrini* who had come from beyond the sea and settled
there.[7] In the ninth century the abbey was known in Ireland
by the name of *Glastimber na nGoídel* (Glastonbury of the
Gaels).[8] All that can be culled from the luxuriant growth
of traditions, historical and legendary, belonging to Glastonbury with regard to the ties between the monastery and
Ireland, has been summed up by Dr. James F. Kenney as
follows : " As so often happens, the associations produced the
legend and then the legend maintained the associations. The

---

[1] Bede, *HE*, III, 1, 25.
[2] Bede, *Vita Cuthberti*, 24 (*PL*, XCIV, 764, 765) ; *Vita anon. Cuthberti*,
III, 6 (Boll., *AS*, Mart., III, p. 121) ; Adam., *Vita Col.*, II, 46 (p. 126). Cf.
Kenney, *Sources*, I, pp. 284, 286.
[3] Best, *Bibl.*, pp. 142, 263.
[4] Bede, *HE*, IV, 24, V, 12 ; Stephen, *Vita Wilfridi*, 44 (p. 238) [see edit.
B. Colgrave (Cambridge, 1926), note p. 183] ; Alcuin, *Versus de sanctis
Euboricensis Ecclesiae*, V, 843 ff. (*MG. Poet. Lat.*, I, p. 188).
[5] Bede, *HE*, IV, 13.
[6] Bede, *HE*, V, 18.
[7] *Vita anon. Dunstani*, 5 ; Osbern, *Vita Dunstani*, 6 ; William of Malmesbury, *Vita Dunstani*, 4 (ed. W. Stubbs, *Memorials of St Dunstan* [*RS*]), pp. 10,
24, 256–57).
[8] Cormac's Glossary, *s.v.*, *Mug-éme* : *Fél. Oeng.*, pp. 188–89.

saints Patrick, Benignus, Brigit and, perhaps with more truth, Indract, were made to visit Glastonbury. One of the two Patricks into whom hagiography split the apostle of Ireland was buried there, but the records differ as to whether it was the elder or the younger Patrick. To visit his tomb and a church having for them so many other interests, pilgrims came from Ireland, and occasionally passed on to settle in other parts of England. At Glastonbury many Lives of Irish saints were collected or written, and from these, doubtless, were derived the majority of the texts which were used by John of Tynemouth.'' [1]

The myth of the foundation of the monastery of Abingdon (Berkshire) by an Irishman named Abban [2] may be due to the influence exercised by Glastonbury on that abbey from the tenth to the twelfth century. [3]

Let us now investigate the results of the religious activity of the Scots on the Continent of Europe.

§ 3.—St Columban and St Gall

To St Columban above all was due the initiation of these monastic and missionary migrations to the Continent. [4] Like Columba, he left Ireland with twelve companions, without any definite goal, his one idea being to go far from his native soil, spreading the Gospel among foreign peoples on his way. [5] Sailing first of all to Great Britain, he traversed that island, crossed the Channel and landed on the coast of Gaul. [6] He reached Burgundy in 590 or 591. [7] There he founded in

---

[1] Kenney, *Sources*, I, p. 607.—On the alleged connection of St Joseph of Arimathea with Glastonbury see H. Thurston, *The English Legend of St Joseph of Arimathea (Month*, CLVIII, 1931, pp. 43–54).

[2] *Chronicon monasterii de Abingdon*, 5, ed. J. Stevenson, I, p. 3 (*RS*).

[3] C. H. Slover, *William of Malmesbury and the Irish (Speculum*, II, 1927, p. 274).

[4] On St Columban, his work and religious influence, see principally Eugène Martin, *Saint Colomban* (Paris, 1905, 3rd edit. 1921) ; Geo. Metlake [J. J. Laux], *The Life and Writings of St Columban* (Philadelphia, 1914) ; J. J. Laux, *Der hl. Kolumban, sein Leben und seine Schriften* (Freiburg i. Br., 1919) ; P. Lugano, *San Colombano monaco e scrittore (Rivista storica Benedettina*, XI, 1916, pp. 5–46); Dr. Kenney's bibliography in *Sources*, I, pp. 186-87.

[5] Jonas, *Vita Col.*, I, 4, 5 (p. 71).

[6] L.G., *Un point obscur de l' itinéraire de S. Colomban venant en Gaule (An. Br.*, XXII, 1907, pp. 327–43).

[7] Cf. Kenney, *Sources*, I, p. 191.

succession the monasteries of Annegray, Luxeuil and Fontaine. Before long Luxeuil began to exercise a powerful attraction on the inhabitants of the country through the novelty of its rule and the burning zeal and personal ascendancy of its founder. The Rule of Columban soon became the object of such veneration that towards the middle of the seventh century many Gaulish cloisters adopted it conjointly with that of St Benedict.[1] In the annals of monasticism we do not think that any other example can be found of an amalgamation of rules differing so widely in spirit.[2]

Driven from Burgundy by Brunhildis in 610, Columban resumed his wanderings. Accompanied by some of his monks, he was first conducted by a strong escort to Besançon. From that place the exiles reached Nevers by way of Autun, Avallon and Auxerre. At Nevers they entered a boat to descend the course of the Loire as far as Nantes, halting at Orleans and Tours. At Nantes they found a vessel on the point of setting sail for Ireland ; Columban and his companions were taken on board, but scarcely had they weighed anchor when the ship was driven back on the shore by a violent spate of the river.[3] At the end of three days the little band, providentially rescued from danger, resumed their journey on foot, directing their course to the east of Gaul. Columban received a warm welcome at the court of Chlothair II, king of Neustria. Setting out from Paris and making always for the east, the saint crossed the district of Brie. These long wanderings were not without their fruit. By his example, his exhortations, more than once merely by the blessing which he bestowed on the child of some great feudatory who had given him shelter,

---

[1] *Vita Sadalbergae*, 3, ed. B. Krusch (*MG. Scr. RM*, V, p. 54). Cf. A. Hauck, *Kirchengeschichte Deutschlands* (Leipzig, 1904), I, p. 297 (eds. 1914, 1922, p. 296).—In addition to these two, a third Rule, that of St Caesarius of Arles, was sometimes followed in monasteries of women (Levison, *Die Iren*, pp. 7–8).

[2] Another unusual combination of rules was that obtaining at St. Yrieix (*monasterium Atanense*), in Limousin, where " non modo Cassiani verum etiam Basilii et reliquorum abbatum, qui monasterialem vitam instituerunt, celebrantur regulae " (Gregory of Tours, *Historia Francorum*, x, 29, ed. Arndt, *MG. Scr. RM*, I, p. 441). Cf. *Vitae Patrum Iurensium*, 23, ed. B. Krusch (*MG. Scr. RM*, III, p. 165).

[3] Jonas, *Vita Col.*, I, 22, 23. Cf. Columban, *Ep.* 4 (*MG. Epist.*, III, p. 169).

many a religious vocation was determined, destined in time
to be the source of fresh monastic expansion.[1] Indeed, it
may well be said that to form a clear idea of the progress of
monasticism in Gaul in the seventh century it is only needful
to follow the wanderings of the saint. The monasteries of the
Brie district, Faremoutiers (627), Jouarre (630) and Rebais
(*c.* 636), owed their foundation to his followers or friends.[2]
In later days the Irish did not forget the fact. From the *Vita
Agili* we learn that it was their wont to visit Rebais on their
way, in order to rest there and leave behind such of their
number as were exhausted by the hardships of the journey.[3]

Faro († *c.* 672), the brother of St Fara or Burgundofara,
foundress of Faremoutiers, whom St Columban had blessed
when she was but a child, was also an entertainer of Irish
travellers when he became bishop of Meaux. At his suggestion two of them settled for good in Gaul, St Kilian (Chillien)
at Aubigny near Arras, and St Fiacre in the hermitage of
Broilum near the town of Meaux.[4]

Having reached the Rhine, Columban journeyed along its
valley from the neighbourhood of Mainz to its junction with
the Aar. He followed the course of the latter river and then
of the Limmat as far as the Lake of Zurich and thence made his
way to the shores of the Lake of Constance. After halting
for a time at Bregenz at the eastern extremity of that lake, he
resumed his journey to Italy. But one of his companions,
Gall, who had mastered the dialects of the neighbouring
country and rescued several of its inhabitants from idolatry,
was seized by a sharp attack of fever, and, being unable to
continue the journey, asked to be allowed to settle in the
place (612). Columban, however, " thinking that Gall was
held back by love of a spot endeared to him by many labours
and was shirking the fatigue of a long journey, said to him :
' I know, brother, that now it seems to thee a heavy burden

[1] Cf. G. Bonet-Maury, *Saint Colomban et la fondation des monastères
irlandais de la Brie au VIIe siècle* (*RH*, LXXXIII, 1903, p. 285).
[2] Cf. L.G., *Gaelic Pioneers of Christianity*, p. 10.
[3] *Vita Agili*, 7 (Boll., *AS*, Aug., VI, p. 586).
[4] *Vita Fiacrii*, 1 (Boll., *AS*, Aug., VI, p. 605) ; *Vita Faronis*, 98–99, ed.
B. Krusch (*MG. Scr. RM*, V, p. 194) ; *Vita Killiani Albiniacensis*, ed. A.
Poncelet (*AB*, XX, 1901, pp. 432–44).

to endure toil and weariness for my sake. Nevertheless, this I enjoin on thee ere I depart, that so long as I am alive in the body, thou shalt never take upon thee to celebrate Mass.' " [1]

Gall built himself a cell in a desert spot in the valley of the Steinach, a stream flowing into the Lake of Constance, where he spent his last years. He died at Arbon, a place on the shore of the lake, but his body was buried in the spot he had chosen for his retreat.[2] "After his death the church and settlement appear to have been kept up. The earliest record extant of them is a deed drawn up about 700 for Gottfried, duke of Alemannia, granting land at Biberburg in Würtemberg for the upkeep of the church, the pastor of which, Magulfus, had appealed to him for support." [3] It was not till nearly a century after the saint's death that a regular monastery was established there, the first abbot of which was Othmar, an Alemannic priest in the service of Victor, Count of Rhaetia (720). Such was the origin of the famous abbey which gave its name to the modern town and the Swiss Canton of St. Gallen.

Meanwhile Columban, with the rest of his band, had descended from the Alps, crossed the plain of Lombardy and found a final resting-place at Bobbio, in a valley of the Ligurian Appenines. It was not long ere he entered into the supreme rest ; on November 23, 615, the dauntless monk died.

In the following centuries the abbeys of St. Gall and Bobbio were sought out with pious intent by the Scots. In the ninth century we find the Irish bishop Mark on his way back from Rome bequeathing his books to the library of St. Gall ; his

---

[1] Wettinus, *Vita Galli*, 9, ed. B. Krusch (*MG. Scr. RM*, IV, pp. 261–62) ; Walahfrid Strabo, *Vita Galli*, 1, 9 (p. 291), transl. into English by Maud Joynt, *The Life of St Gall* (London, 1927), p. 75. Cf. *Vita Galli vetustissima*, 1 (pp. 251–52).—On Columban's death Gall dispatched a deacon to Bobbio to inquire into the circumstances of his master's decease. The deacon brought back the staff of Columban " which is vulgarly called the *cambota*, saying that the holy abbot before his decease had given orders that Gall should receive his absolution by means of this familiar token " (Walahfrid, *Vita Galli*, 26 (pp. 304–305) ; M. Joynt's transl., p. 101). Cf. *Vita vetustissima, l. cit.* ; Wettinus, 26 (p. 271).

[2] Walahfrid, *Vita Galli*, 29. Cf. M. Joynt, *op. cit.*, p. 8.

[3] M. Joynt, *op. cit.*, p. 11. Cf. Hermann Wartmann, *Urkundenbuch der Abtei St Gallen* (Zürich, 1863), No. 1 (p. 1) ; B. Krusch in *MG. Scr. RM*, IV, pp. 229–30.

nephew, Moengal or Marcellus, remained in the monastery,[1] and an Irishman named Eusebius settled on the Viktorsberg beyond the Rhine, where he lived as a recluse for thirty years.[2]

With the aid of the *Necrologium* of St. Gall and other documents pertaining to the abbey, J. M. Clark has been able to draw up a list of twenty names of Irish monks who are known to have been in some way associated with the abbey from the ninth to the twelfth century.[3]

At Bobbio we find a Cummian in the eighth century, a Dungal in the ninth, and other monks bearing Irish names.[4]

At Luxeuil there were at least six Irish monks at the time of the death of Eustasius, Columban's successor († April 2, 629).[5]

The personal influence exercised by St Columban in Gaul was great. After his death his views on the exemption of monasteries,[6] penitence and confession,[7] and, above all, his monastic Rule, continued to make their way, thanks to the zeal of his numerous immediate followers or their disciples. Many influential persons of the period, notably those noblemen who in such numbers forsook the court for the cloister or the episcopate, Dado, Faro, Eligius (Éloi), Wandregiselus (Wandrille) and Philibert, seem to have highly prized the ascetic discipline of Luxeuil and laboured to spread it farther.

Wandrille, after resigning his rank as count, gave himself up in solitude to prayer and ascetic practices (such as the recitation of the entire Psalter, genuflexions and immersion in ice-cold water), which remind us strongly of the mortifications of the Irish monks. " It is likely," it has been said, " that Wandrille's thoughts were haunted by the memory of

---

[1] Ekkehard iv, *Casus S. Galli* (*MG. Scr.*, II, pp. 78 ff.).

[2] Ratpert, *Casus S. Galli* (*ib.*, p. 73).

[3] J. M. Clark, *The Abbey of St. Gall as a Centre of Literature and Art* (Cambridge, 1926), p. 31.

[4] *Epitaph. Cumiani* (*MG. Poet. Lat.*, I, p. 107) ; Kenney, *Sources*, I, p. 516. Cf. Mario Esposito, *The Ancient Bobbio Catalogue* (*JTS*, XXXII, 1931, p. 342) ; *s.a. JTS*, XXXIII, 1932, pp. 119–31.

[5] Wettinus, *Vita Galli*, 28 (pp. 271–72). Cf. *Vita vetustissima*, 3 (p. 252).

[6] *V. inf.* Ch. VII, § 2.

[7] Malnory, *Quid Luxov.*, pp. 62–80. Cf. E. Vacandard, *Le pouvoir des clefs et la confession* (*Revue du clergé français*, 1899, pp. 147 ff.).

Columban." [1] As a fact, he stayed some time near the tomb of St Ursinus, a disciple of Columban ; he visited Bobbio and even formed the plan of going to Ireland. [2]

The future abbot of Jumièges, St Philibert, seems to have been inspired by the same influence. He began by following Columban's Rule at Rebais, then visited Luxeuil and Bobbio and dedicated one of his altars at Jumièges to St Columban. [3]

St Eligius while yet a layman built the monastery of Solignac in the diocese of Limoges, and following Scottic precedents procured its exemption from the jurisdiction of the bishop in order to place it under that of the abbot of Luxeuil. The foundation charter, according to the custom of the day, established the joint Rule of St Benedict and St Columban as the norm of the religious life. [4]

When the body of St Quentin was discovered at Noyon, St Eligius, who had been made bishop of the city, built a handsome basilica to receive the holy relics, and this was entrusted to the care of Irish monks ; their abbot in the year 633 was named Ebertram. [5]

Two whilom officers of the court of Chlothair II and Dagobert I were in immediate touch with the *Scotti* : St Cyran, afterwards abbot of Longrey in Berry, who owed his conversion partly to his meeting with the Irish bishop Flavius, [6] and Desiderius of Cahors, whose friendship with a Scot named Arnanus has called for notice by his biographer. [7]

Mommelin (Mummolinus), first abbot of the monastery of Sithiu (later St. Bertin) and successor of St Eligius in the see of Noyon, was an alumnus of Luxeuil ; as were also Valéry (Walaricus), who had known Columban and who founded at the mouth of the Somme a monastery which was called after him, Omer (Audomarus), bishop of Thérouanne, who had

---

[1] E. Vacandard, *Vie de Saint Ouen, évêque de Rouen* (Paris, 1902), p. 164.

[2] *Vita Wandregiseli*, 8, 9 (*MG. Scr. RM*, V, pp. 16–18).

[3] *Vita Filiberti*, 2–5, 8 (*MG. Scr. RM*, V, pp. 585–89).

[4] Foundation charter of Solignac, edited by B. Krusch (*MG. Scr. RM*, IV, pp. 746–49). Cf. Hans von Schubert, *Geschichte der christlichen Kirche im Frühmittelalter* (Tübingen, 1921), p. 609.

[5] *Vita Eligii*, II, 6 (*MG. Scr. RM*, IV, pp. 698–99) [Cf. B. Krusch, *ib.*, pp. 424, 640] ; *MG. Dipl. imp.*, I, p. 36 ; *Scr.*, XIII, p. 608. Cf. Van der Essen, *Étude*, p. 328.

[6] *Vita Sigriamni*, 9, 10, ed. B. Krusch (*MG. Scr. RM*, IV, p. 611).

[7] *Vita Desiderii*, 32, 33, ed. B. Krusch (*MG. Scr. RM*, IV, pp. 589–90).

been the disciple of Eustasius, Bertin, second abbot of Sithiu, and others.[1] Through the medium of these missionary-monks the Irish monastic traditions took root in the north of Gaul. To Luxeuil also Bathildis, wife of Chlodwig II (639–657), applied for the first abbot of the abbey of Corbie which she had built, and from the double monastery of Jouarre she sought the first abbess of the monastery of Chelles (also a double one), which she had restored.[2]

Luxeuil had still a great name in France in the tenth century, as is testified by the following lines written in that age by Adso of Montier-en-Der : " And now what place, what city does not rejoice in having for its ruler a bishop or an abbot trained in the discipline of that cloister ? For it is certain that by the virtue of its authority almost the whole of the land of the Franks has been for the first time properly furnished with regular institutions." [3]

§ 4.—ST FURSA AND THE " PEREGRINI MINORES" OF HIS KIN.

Bede tells us that in the seventh century many English-women entered the monasteries of Gaul, especially at Chelles, where Queen Bathildis, herself of English birth, took the veil and passed the last years of her life.[4]

Was it Bathildis also who drew over to Gaul the Irish monk Fursa [5] who, after engaging in various religious enterprises and apostolic labours in his own country, emigrated to England and founded (sometime after 630) a monastery at Cnoberesburgh in East Anglia ? [6] We cannot tell. All we know of Fursa's career is that at some date after 641, when he was already raised to the episcopate, he went to Gaul, where he was cordially received by Erchinoald, Mayor of the

---

[1] Vita I*a* Mummolini, ed. J. Ghesquière, Acta Sanct. Belgii, 1787, IV, 393–413 ;   Vitae Audomari, Bertini, Winnoci, ed. W. Levison (MG. Scr. RM, V, pp. 753–75 ; see editor's introd., pp. 729–42) ; Vita Walarici, 5, ed. B. Krusch (MG. Scr. RM, IV, p. 162).
[2] Vita Balthildis, 7, 8 (MG. Scr. RM, II, pp. 490, 492).
[3] Adso, Vita Bercharii, 1, 8 (Boll., AS, Oct., VII, p. 1012).
[4] Bede, HE, III, 8 ; Vita Balthildis, 10, 11 (pp. 495–96).
[5] Called Fursy in France.
[6] Now Burgh Castle (Suffolk).

Palace—the same man who had rescued Bathildis from slavery and even wished to marry her—and that thanks to Erchinoald's patronage he was able to build a monastery in the Brie district at Lagny (*Latiniacum*), not far from Chelles.[1]

The dates of Fursa's career are far from certain. We only know that before the year 652 (perhaps in 649) he died at Mézerolles [2] while making a journey in the north of Gaul and that by Erchinoald's orders his body was taken to Péronne.[3]

Although his activity cannot be compared to that of St Columban, Fursa's name deserves special mention in the history of the Irish migrations on account of those remarkable visions of the unseen world which Bede has recorded [4] and which may have been the starting-point of an important branch of Irish religious literature [5]; on account also of the monastery which was built in the place of his burial. This monastery attracted many Scottic monks, and for more than a century its abbots were Irishmen; in consequence whereof it received the name of *Perrona Scottorum*.[6]

Fursa had two brothers, Foillan and Ultan, who had accompanied him to England [7] and followed in his wake to the Continent.[8] At first they were drawn to Péronne; but about this time another centre of attraction had just arisen in Brabant, the monastery of Itta and Gertrude at Nivelles, where the scriptural knowledge of the monks beyond the seas was highly prized.[9]

Nivelles had been founded by Itta, the wife of Pippin the Elder of Landen, and on her husband's death (640), following

---

[1] *Vita Fursei*, 9, ed. B. Krusch (*MG. Scr. RM*, IV, pp. 438–39).—Lagny, arr. Meaux (Dept. Seine-et-Marne).

[2] On the Authie, cant. Bernaville, arr. Doullens (Dept. Somme).

[3] *Vita Fursei*, 10 (pp. 439–40).

[4] Bede, *HE*, III, 19.

[5] Cf. Kenney, *Sources*, I, p. 502.

[6] On Péronne, see L. Traube, *Perrona Scottorum* (*Vorlesungen*, III, pp. 95–119).

[7] *Vita Fursei*, 9 (*MG. Scr. RM*, IV, p. 438) ; *Virtutes Fursei*, 4, ed. Krusch, *ib.*, p. 441.—These two saints are called Feuillen and Ultain in Belgium and France.

[8] *Additamentum Nivialense de Fuilano*, ed. Krusch., *ib.*, pp. 449–50.

[9] " . . . et de transmarinis regionibus gignaros viros ad docendum divini legis carmina " (*Vita Gertrudis*, A, 2, ed. B. Krusch, *MG. Scr. RM*, II, p. 457).

the advice of St Amand, she had retired there with her daughter Gertrude.

Itta († 652) gave Foillan the domain of Fosses in the diocese of Liége,[1] and there he founded a monastery which was still called " *monasterium Scottorum* " by Einhard († 840).[2] Foillan was put to death with three of his companions in the course of a journey about 655.[3] Ultan was at Fosses (as abbot?) at the time of Gertrude's death in 659. He had predicted that the holy abbess would die on the anniversary of St Patrick's death (March 17).[4] It is possible that he subsequently became abbot of Péronne.[5]

Among the abbots of the latter monastery may further be named the Irishman Cellanus († 706),[6] from whom we have a letter addressed to St Aldhelm of Malmesbury,[7] and later a certain Moinan mac Cormaic († 779).[8] The monastery was destroyed by the Northmen in 880.

§ 5.—OTHER MONASTIC FOUNDATIONS

We have seen how active was the influence of the monks of Luxeuil in disseminating monastic institutions in Gaul. The number of cloisters whose foundation was directly or indirectly due to their activity has been estimated at about fifty.[9]

The influence of Luxeuil was also felt further east. Columban's first successor, the Burgundian Eustasius († 629), and his disciples evangelized Bavaria.[10] Under the abbotship of the Frank Waldebert (629–670), who succeeded Eustasius, the number of monks at Luxeuil became so large as to call for new foundations. Detachments thrown off by Luxeuil peopled

[1] *Additamentum, l. cit.* Cf. Ursmer Berlière, *Le monasticon belge* (Maredsous, 1890), I, pp. 57–58 ; Joseph Crépin, *Le monastère des Scots de Fosses* (*La Terre Wallonne*, VIII, 1923, pp. 357–85 ; IX, 1923, pp. 16–26).

[2] Einhard, *Translatio Sanct. Marcellini et Petri*, ix, 86 (Boll., *AS*, Jun., I, p. 198).

[3] *Additamentum*, pp. 450–51.

[4] *Vita Gertrudis*, A, 7, pp. 462–63. Cf. B. Krusch, p. 428

[5] Cf. Traube, *Vorlesungen*, III, pp. 103–104 ; Kenney, *Sources*, I, p. 505.

[6] Traube, *Vorlesungen*, III, pp. 100–109.

[7] Traube, *Vorlesungen*, III, pp. 101–102 ; *Aldhelmi Opera*, ed. R. Ehwald (*MG. Auct. ant.*, XV., p. 494).

[8] *AU, a.a.* 778.

[9] Levison, *Die Iren*, p. 6.

[10] Jonas, *Vita Col.*, ii, 8 (p. 122).

Moutiers-Grandval (*monasterium Granvallense*) or Granfelden, not far from Basel, and the neighbouring *cellae* of St. Ursanne (St. Ursitz) on the Doubs, and of Vermes (Pfermund) near Delémont. One of the few surviving monks of St Columban, the priest Fridoald (*de paucis monachis domni Columbani abbatis quondam*), was a member of the party sent to Granfelden.[1]

To the second half of the seventh century belong St Disibod, whose name was preserved at Disibodenberg, a monastery situated on the Glan not far from Kreuznach, but about whom we have only uncertain information,[2] and also the much better known St Kilian, the apostle of Franconia, who was put to death along with two companions, Colman and Totman (Totnan), at Würzburg about 689.[3]

We know that the Celtic monks always showed a strong partiality for islands. Some *peregrini* discovered a little island in the Rhine, about five miles below Strasbourg, an island whose shores were in the course of following ages undermined by the current of the river, until it was at last completely submerged.[4] On this island, which was called Honau (*Honaugia*), a monastery was founded and dedicated to St Michael in the opening years of the eighth century by a certain bishop Benedictus. In several charters this abbey is styled *monasterium Scottorum* [5] or *ecclesia Scottorum*.[6] It enjoyed the favour of the great and could count on the royal protection. Pippin the Short, Carloman and Charlemagne granted it immunity and exemption from tolls and taxes.

When the Scottic monks of Honau were dispossessed of some of their property, King Charles obliged the depredators to disgorge their plunder in its entirety. The decree of Charles (772–774) calls for quotation *in extenso* : " The illustrious Charles, by the grace of God king of the Franks, gives orders

---

[1] *Vita Germani Grandivallensis*, 8, ed. B. Krusch (*MG. Scr. RM*, V, p. 36).

[2] Hildegard, *Vita Disibodi* (*PL*, CXCVII, 1095–1116).

[3] *Passio Kiliani*, ed. W. Levison *MG. Scr. RM*, V, pp. 711–28. Cf. W. Levison, *ib.*, pp. 713–17 ; Franz Emmerich, *Der hl. Kilian, Regionarbischof und Märtyrer historisch-kritisch dargestellt* (Würzburg, 1896) ; S. Riezler, *Die Vita Kiliani* (*NA*, XXVIII, 1903, pp. 232–34).

[4] Fuhrmann, *IMM*, p. 40 ; W. Reeves, *The Irish Abbey of Honau on the Rhine* (*PRIA*, VI, 1853–57, pp. 452–61).

[5] *MG. Dipl. Kar.*, I, p. 143.

[6] *MG. Dipl. Kar.*, I, p. 111.—" Pauperes et peregrinos gentis Scottorum " (Mabillon, *Annales O.S.B.*, ed. 1704, II, p. 700).

to all who have taken anything from the church of the Irish which is in the island of Honau (*de ecclesia Scotorum quae est in insula Honaugia*) that each restore again everything that he has received or carried off without the authorization of the abbot Beatus. And if anyone retains even a little, he orders all the magistrates of that region to search for all the goods of the church as per schedule, in accordance with the law of the Franks, for the goods of the pilgrims are the property of the king (*quia res peregrinorum propriae sunt regis*). Therefore let all those things we have spoken of be restored to the church of the Irish without any let or hindrance—whether land or vine or stock or vassals or silver or gold. But if any one will not do this, let him know that he is disobeying a royal command, for the kings of the Franks have given freedom to all Irish pilgrims, to the end that no one shall carry off anything of their property, and that no race except their race shall occupy their churches. So act henceforth as you wish to experience our favour." [1]

From divers charters concerning the monastery of Honau which have been preserved we learn the names of several of its abbots. Besides the founder Benedictus, Tuban, Dubanus, Stephanus and Beatus are mentioned in succession in these documents. In charters ranging from the year 748 to the year 758, Dubanus is twice called *Dubanus episcopus*, once *Dubanus abbas* and once *Dubanus episcopus vel abbas*.[2] Beatus was still alive in 778 ; it was probably in that year that he drew up at Mainz a deed of gift in favour of Honau. Among the signatures of those who countersigned this deed are those of seven bishops bearing Irish names : Coniganus, Echoch, Suathar, Maucumgib, Canicomrihc, Doilgussus and Erdomnach.[3]

---

[1] *MG. Dipl. Kar.*, I, pp. 110–11.

[2] Dubanus episcopus : Mabillon, *Annales*, II, p. 696 ; *MG. Dipl. Kar.*, I, p. 15.—Dubanus abbas : Mabillon, p. 697.—Dubanus episcopus et abbas : *MG. Dipl. Kar.*, I, p. 16.

[3] " Haec charta in Moguntia civitate scripta xi kl. iulias, anno x. regni domini nostri Caroli regis et imperatoris." The last words point to a redaction later than A.D. 800, even later than A.D. 810. W. Levison, however dates this charter rather from 778 than 810 (*Die Iren*, p. 16). The churches situated in Hesse at Lich, Lanheim, Wisseck, Sternbach, Bauernheim, Rodheim, Horloff and Schotten given by Beatus to Honau have been identified by H. G. Voigt in his article, *Von der iroschottischen Mission*

After the death of bishop John, whom St Boniface, the great organizer of ecclesiastical Germany, had placed over the see of Salzburg, we find the Irishman Ferghil (Virgilius) installed in that city and ruling the diocese as abbot of the monastery of St Peter founded by St Rupert. Abbot of Aghaboe in Ireland, Virgilius had crossed to the Continent " *Christi propter amorem* " [1] about A.D. 743. Pippin the Short kept him in his own circle for almost two years at Quierzy-sur-Oise, in the neighbourhood of Noyon, and then recommended him to Odilo, Duke of Bavaria, who placed him over the Abbey of St Peter and the diocese of Salzburg.[2] Virgil was only a priest ; to exercise the episcopal functions he availed himself of the services of a fellow-countryman, Dubdáchrích (Dobdagrecus, Tuti), who had been consecrated bishop in Ireland.[3]

On divers points of doctrine and ecclesiastical discipline, and also on account of certain cosmographical theories (to which we shall have to come back later), the Scot Virgilius was at variance with the Anglo-Saxon Boniface.[4] Moreover, the government of a diocese by an abbot—a state of affairs which recalled the system in vogue at Iona,[5] in which the authority of the abbot was supreme—was ill in keeping with the ecclesiastical organization framed by St Boniface. It was not till after the death of Boniface, possibly in A.D. 755 (according to other historians not until A.D. 767), that Virgilius received episcopal consecration.[6] He laboured zealously in disseminating the Gospel not only among the Bavarians but

---

in Hessen und Thüringen und Bonifatius' Verhältnis zu ihr (*Theologische Studien und Kritiken*, CIII, 1931, pp. 256–57, 266–69, 283–84).

[1] Alcuin, *Carmina*, CIX, 24 (*MG. Poet. Lat.*, I, p. 340).

[2] *Libellus de conversione Bagoariorum et Carantanorum*, 2 (*MG. Scr.*, XI, p. 6). Cf. H. Krabbo, *Bischof Virgil von Salzburg und seine kosmologischen Ideen* (*MIOG*, XXIV, 1903, p. 10).

[3] *Libellus de conversione, l. cit.* ; *Gesta archiepiscoporum Salisburgensium* (*MG. Scr.*, XI, p. 86). Cf. Kenney, *Sources*, I, p. 523 ; Theodor Gottlob, *Der abendländische Chorepiskopat* (*Kanonistische Studien und Texte*, hrsg. v. A. M. Königer, Bonn, 1928, I, pp. 82–83).

[4] Boniface, *Epp.* 60, 68 (*MG. Epist.*, III, pp. 336, 360). Cf. Krabbo, *op. cit.*

[5] Cf. Bede, *HE*, III, 4.

[6] *Libellus de conversione, l. cit.*—For the date A.D. 755 see B. Krusch (*MG. Scr. RM*, VI, p. 519) ; for the date A.D. 767, Levison, *Die Iren*, p. 16 ; Gottlob, *Der abendl. Chorepiskopat, l. cit.*

also the Slavonic inhabitants of the mountains of Carinthia.[1]
He died in 784, having held the see of Salzburg for nearly
forty years,[2] and left behind him a great reputation for
learning and holiness.[3]

Dubdáchrích became abbot of the monastery dedicated to
the Saviour in Chiemsee in Upper Bavaria.[4]

Scottic monks spread in considerable numbers from the
sixth to the ninth century in all the territories subject to the
rule of the Frankish monarchs. All grades of monks and
clerics were represented amongst them ; there were simple
abbots, bishops without a diocese (*episcopi vagantes*), abbot-
bishops who either governed an abbey and a diocese simultaneously or exercised their episcopal functions only within
their own monastery. Finally, several of these *peregrini* were
appointed to the rule of dioceses ; one of them even occupied
one of the most important metropolitan sees of continental
Europe.

We have already mentioned several *episcopi vagantes*. To
this category belonged Dubdáchrích and the seven bishops
whose names figure among the signatories of the deed of gift
of abbot Beatus in favour of Honau.

In the category of abbot-bishops (or bishop-abbots) are
probably to be placed Fursa, Dubanus of Honau, Virgil of
Salzburg (from A.D. 755 or 767) and a host of others.
To an Irish bishop and the companions of his wanderings
Ansoald, bishop of Poitiers, gave the derelict *cellula* of
Mazerolles. Ansoald's will, drawn up in 696, contains the
following statement on the subject : " I found the *cellula* of
Mazerolles on the Vienne deserted, without occupants and
without divine worship. I restored it completely and set over
it a holy man of Irish race who was journeying abroad for the

---

[1] *Libellus de conversione*, 5 (p. 7).

[2] *Epitaphium Virgilii*, ed. Dümmler (*MG. Poet. Lat.*, II, p. 639) ; *Epist. variorum*, 3, 4 (*MG. Epist.*, IV, pp. 497–98).

[3] *Epitaphium Virgilii*, *l. cit.* Critics believe that the *Liber confraternitatum Ecclesiae S. Petri Salisburgensis* (*MG. Necrol.*, II, i, pp. 3–64) was begun by, or under the direction of, Virgil. Cf. Kenney, *Sources*, I, p. 525.

[4] *MG. Dipl. Kar.*, I, p. 219 (No. 162). The " monasterium [virorum] constructum in Chiemse stagno " had been dedicated by Bishop Virgil, A.D. 782 (*Auctarium Mellicense* : *MG. Scr.*, IX, 536); *Auctarium Gartense* (*ib.*, p. 564). Cf. J. Doll, *Frauenwörth im Chiemsee* (München and Frieb. i. Br., 1912), p. 12.

sake of God, bishop Romanus. I placed him and his *peregrini* in possession of the spot in order that they might there persevere [in the religious life] (*in qua [cellula] sanctum Dei peregrinum ex genere Scotorum nomen Romanum, episcopum, cum suis peregrinis constitui rectorem et institueram ut ipsi peregrini inibidem perseverarent*)." [1] But after the death of Romanus, as no suitable successor could be found among its inmates, the small community was placed under a certain Chroscelmus, who seems to have been abbot of Nouaillé. [2]

Among the signatures appended to two charters emanating from Ansoald in 677 and 678 we find the name of Romanus, " *indignus tamen episcopus*," and that of Thomeneus, " *episcoporum minimus*." [3] This latter, whose name appears under the form " Tomiànus " among the signatures to the acts of a Council of Bordeaux (663/675), was bishop of Angoulême and is supposed to have been an Irishman. [4]

It is worth remarking that when the boy Dagobert II was tonsured and condemned to exile by Grimoald in 656, it was Ansoald's predecessor, bishop Dido († 673), who was commissioned to conduct the young prince to Ireland, where he remained in exile for twenty years. [5] No doubt this fact accounts for the presence of these Irishmen in Aquitaine at a later time.

Two centuries later Elias, another *Scottigena*, became bishop of Angoulême (862–875). [6]

Still more, a Scottic monk named Abel held the metropolitan see of Reims for the space of some years (probably from 744 to 748). He was placed over this see by the Council of Soissons of March, 744, and—a fact which calls for special notice—at the suggestion of St Boniface, to whom Pope Zachary wrote a letter on the 22nd of the following June confirming the nomination of Abel and sending him the pallium.

---

[1] Ed. J.-M. Pardessus, *Diplomata* (Lutetiae Parisiorum, 1849), II, 239.
[2] Cf. J. Tardif, *Les chartes mérovingiennes de Noirmoutier* (*Nouvelle revue d'histoire de droit français et étranger*, XXII, 1898, pp. 763–90) ; L. Levillain, *Les origines du monastère de Nouaillé* (*Bibliothèque de l'École des chartes*, LXXI, 1910, p. 281).
[3] J. Tardif, *art. cit.*, pp. 783–86. Cf. Kenney, *Sources*, I, p. 499.
[4] Ed. F. Maassen, *MG. Leges* : Sect. III. *Conc.*, I, 215–16.
[5] *Liber Histcriae Francorum*, A (*MG. Scr. RM*, II, p. 316).
[6] Cf. Kenney, *Sources*, I, pp. 592–93.

Being turned out of his see by the usurper Milo, Abel returned to the abbey of Lobbes whence he had come, to seek forgetfulness of his sufferings, and there he was buried.[1]

Be it noted in passing that in the same abbey of Lobbes, situated on the Sambre in Hainault and much sought out by Irishmen, we find in the eighth century down to the year 776 the superiors entitled *episcopi et abbates* or simply *episcopus*, and that other bishops besides resided in the monastery.[2]

In the preceding century Remaclus, a monk of Solignac in Aquitaine, had ruled as bishop-abbot the abbey of Stavelot-Malmédy founded by Sigebert III, king of the Franks, in the forest of Ardenne about A.D. 650.[3]

To complete this sketch of the authentic monastic foundations of the *Scotti* on the Continent, we have still to mention the monasteries founded in the tenth and eleventh centuries in the north of France, in the valleys of the Meuse and the Moselle and on the banks of the Rhine ; we shall reserve for a final section the *Schottenklöster* of Ratisbon and South Germany.

About 940 we find the Irishman Maccalan installed at St. Michel-en-Thiérache, a monastery situate in the diocese of Laon.[4]

The monastery of Waulsort on the Meuse was in Irish hands in 946. A charter of Otto I, king of the Germans (September 19 of that year), declares that the establishment was reserved for the use of *peregrini* coming from Ireland and that the abbot should be chosen from among the Irish as long as there were any dwelling in the community. Further, the monastery was

---

[1] J. Warichez, *L'abbaye de Lobbes depuis ses origines jusqu'en* 1200 (Louvain, 1909), pp. 20–24 ; M. Prou, art. *Abel* in the *Dictionnaire de biographie française*, edited by J. Balteau, A. Rastoul and M. Prevost (Paris, 1929).

[2] Folcuinus, *Gesta abbatum Lobbiensium*, 5 (*MG. Scr.*, IV, p. 58). Cf. W. Levison, *Die Iren*, p. 18, and also the prolegomena by the same author to his edit. of the *Vitae Ursmari et Erminonis episcoporum et abbatum Lobbiensium* (*MG. Scr. RM*, VI, pp. 445–47).

[3] Remaclus hailed from Solignac in Aquitaine. He had been called from Luxeuil by Eligius to be the first abbot of Solignac : *Vita Remacli ep. et abb.*, 1, ed. B. Krusch (*MG. Scr. RM*, V, p. 104). Cf. editor's prolegomena, pp. 88–92 ; J. Halkin and C.-G. Roland, *Recueil des chartes de l'abbaye de Stavelot-Malmédy* (Académie royale de Belgique, Commission d'histoire, Bruxelles, 1909, I, pp. 5–8) ; F. Baix, *L'abbaye et la principauté de Stavelot-Malmédy* (Paris, 1924), I, pp. 13–44.

[4] See Kenney, *Sources*, I, pp. 608–609 ; Fuhrmann, *IMM*, pp. 74–75.

to devote itself especially to the care of foreign pilgrims, and for that reason it received the title of *monasterium peregrinorum*.[1]

Towards the middle of the tenth century Waulsort had for its abbot Cadroe, a native of Scotland but trained in the schools of Armagh.[2] When about 953 Cadroe was called to reform the abbey of St. Felix (later St. Clement) at Metz, restored by Adalbero I, bishop of that city (929–962), he was replaced at Waulsort by the Irishman Forannán, who negotiated with Thierry, Adalbero's successor, the annexation of the neighbouring abbey of Hastières to his own monastery.[3]

Adalbero II (984–1005) showed himself no less willing than his predecessor to entrust the monastic establishments of his diocese to the care of the islanders. " *Scotti et reliqui sancti peregrini semper sibi dulcissimi habebantur,*" observes his biographer, Constantine of St. Symphorian.[4] At that time the abbey of St. Clement had at its head the Irishman Fingen. Adalbero begged him to take over in addition the government of St. Symphorian, a monastery which had been destroyed long previously, probably by the Northmen. Fingen restored the monastery and won it for the Scottic influence. A charter of Otto III, Holy Roman Emperor, dated January 25, 992, confirmed the grants made to the abbey of St. Symphorian, rebuilt outside the walls of the city of Metz, and declared that the first abbot, an Irishman named Fingenius, and his successors, shall receive Irish monks, as long as possible. Should monks from Ireland fail there, the number of inmates is always to be maintained by recruits of other nationalities.[5]

Fingen closed his career as a reformer at St. Vanne in Verdun, whither he had gone with a detachment of seven of

---

[1] *MG. Dipl. reg.*, I, ed. Th. Sickel, pp. 160–61.—Maccalan, abbot of St. Michael's, started the settlement at Waulsort and, for a short time, ruled the monastery and then returned to St. Michael's. Cf. Kenney, *Sources*, I, p. 609 ; L. Lahaye, *Étude sur l'abbaye de Waulsort* (Liége, 1890), p. 11; Fuhrmann, *IMM*, pp. 75–78 ; U. Berlière, *Monasticon belge*, I, p. 40.

[2] *Vita Cadroe* (Boll., *AS*, Mart., I, pp. 468–81). Cf. A. O. Anderson, *Early Sources*, I, p. 431 ; Faral, *La légende arthurienne*, I, p. 175.

[3] *Vita Forannani* (Boll., *AS*, April, III, 816–23).

[4] *Vita Adalberonis* II (*MG. Scr.*, IV, p. 668).

[5] Ed. T. Sickel (*MG. Dipl. reg.*, II, ii, p. 493).

his countrymen. He died in 1005 and was buried in the church of St. Felix, outside the walls of the city of Metz.[1]

Strasbourg is said to have possessed a *monasterium Scottorum* founded in honour of St Thomas under the episcopacy of St Florentius (second half of the sixth century).[2]

Mainz possessed several establishments of the same kind. This city was regularly visited by the Irish. St Columban had passed through the district. Beatus, abbot of Honau, had caused a church to be built there before the year 778. A grant was made about 817 to the monastery of Fulda of an *ecclesia Scottorum* situated in Mainz.[3] Down to the year 1749 the city possessed two *Schottenkirchen*, one of which was dedicated to St Paul.[4] We shall see later that the chronicler Marianus Scottus, who died in 1082 or 1083, spent the last thirteen or fourteen years of his life in an incluse's cell attached to the monastery of St. Martin at Mainz.

The city of Cologne—*sacrosancta Colonia*—attracted many Irishmen in the tenth and eleventh centuries. St Bruno, who was archbishop of Cologne from 953 to 965, had among his masters an Irish bishop named Israel, whose learning is extolled by the saint's biographer.[5]

The monastery of St. Martin (Gross St. Martin) was assigned to the Scots *in sempiternum* in A.D. 975, according to Marianus Scottus, who dwelt in that monastery from 1056 to 1058.[6] The chronicle left by Marianus is of all the more value to us because the documents relating to the Scottic period of St. Martin are believed to be forgeries of the eighteenth century executed by Oliver Legipont, a monk of that house.[7] Marianus gives the names of the abbots of

---

[1] *Annales S. Vitoni Virdunensis* (*MG. Scr.*, X, 526) ; *Carmen Mettense*, ed. E. Dümmler, *NA*, V, 1880, p. 437. Cf. Kenney, *Sources*, I, pp. 612, 613.

[2] Cf. Fuhrmann, *IMM*, p. 32.

[3] F. Falk, *Die irischen Mönchen in Mainz* (*Katholik*, N.S., XX, 1868, pp. 311–16) ; Fuhrmann, *IMM*, p. 37.

[4] F. J. Bodmann, *Rheingauische Alterthümer*, II, p. 593 ; Heber, *Die neun vormaligen Schottenkirchen in Mainz und Oberhessen* (*Archiv für hessische Geschichte*, IX, pp. 193–348).

[5] *Vita Brunonis*, I, 12 (Boll., *AS*, Oct., V, p. 768).

[6] Marianus Scottus, *Chronicon, a.a.* 975 (*PL*, CXLVII, 780).

[7] Oppermann, *Kritische Studien zur älteren Kölner Geschichte* (*Westdeutsche Zeitschrift für Geschichte und Kunst*, XIX, 1900, pp. 271–344). Cf. U. Berlière in *Archives belges*, 1901, pp. 89–91 ; *s.a. RB*, XVIII, ·1901, pp. 424–27 ; W. Levison, *Die Iren*, p. 21.

St. Martin from the year 975 to 1061 ; they are all Irishmen.[1] The *Chronicon* or *Catalogus abbatum Sancti Martini
Coloniensis* states further that during the abbotship of Kilian
(986–1003), Eberger, archbishop of Cologne, with the consent of the Emperor Otto III, gave various goods to that
monastery *in usu monachorum peregrinorum* [2] ; but this detail
may be an invention, as the *Catalogus* is one of the very works
which are suspected of being forgeries. In the days of the
abbot Elias, another monastery of Cologne, that of St. Pantaleon, passed in its turn into the hands of the Scots (1042).[3]

The Irish lost control of St. Pantaleon's monastery rather
early, and abbot Alcadus, who died about the year 1101, was
the last of his nation to rule the community of Gross St.
Martin.[4]

Numerous indeed, we see, were the monastic foundations
which the initiative and energy of the Irish impelled them to
make outside their own country. There is, however, a tendency on the part of some writers to exaggerate the number
of strictly Irish foundations. What establishments may
properly be classed among the *monasteria Scottorum* ? The title,
it seems, ought to be restricted solely to those cloisters which,
in the years following their foundation or their restoration or
the introduction of measures of reform, were governed by
Irishmen and which, moreover, had a majority of Irish monks
among their inmates. As we have seen, some monasteries
were intended by their founders to receive only monks of Irish
birth. When in official documents, such as authentic charters
of foundation, or in other old texts whose authenticity can be
guaranteed, we meet the expressions *monasterium Scottorum*,
monasterium peregrinorum, or something equivalent, there can
be no doubt as to the nature of the establishment. Thus it is
perfectly certain that the abbeys of Iona and Lindisfarne, the
cella of Mazerolles, the abbeys of Fosses, Péronne and Honau,
as well as the two monasteries of Metz and the two of Cologne
mentioned above, are to be classed among the *monasteria Scottorum*. On the contrary, neither Luxeuil nor Bobbio nor St.

---

[1] *Chronicon*, col. 780–87.
[2] *MG. Scr.*, II, p. 215.
[3] Marianus, *Chronicon*, *a.a.* 1064 (col. 784).
[4] Fuhrmann, *IMM*, p. 82.

Gall nor Reichenau can be placed in that category. The communities of the first two abbeys never contained more than a minority of Irish monks. The abbey of St. Gall was not founded at the beginning of the seventh century by Gall, the companion of St Columban, as is too often repeated ; its first abbot was the Alemannic priest Othmar, who governed it from the year 720. It is a still greater mistake to call Reichenau " an old Irish monastery," for its founder Pirmin was not a Scot,[1] nor can we tell whether the abbey ever counted a single Scot among its monks.

§ 6.—DOUBTFUL IRISHMEN AND PSEUDO-IRISHMEN

In order to avoid loading the remaining sections of the present chapter with a mass of legendary matter, it seems well to group together here, as far as possible in topographical and chronological order, all those persons, whether their existence be authenticated or legendary, to whom the chroniclers and hagiographers of the Middle Ages or their modern interpreters have felt themselves bound, for reasons more or less valid, to assign an Irish origin. Perhaps historical criticism will some day succeed in throwing light on the nationality of some of these monks, solitaries, missionaries or prelates ; but for the greater number we may give up all hope of gaining any certain knowledge of their native land, owing to the scarcity or the late age of the documents relating to them.[2]

Some of these doubtful cases are given as anterior to St Columban ; for instance, St Fridian (Frediano), bishop of Lucca in Tuscany (c. 560–588), who is represented as the son of a king of Ulster.[3] Tradition likewise makes a Scot of

[1] For discussion of Pirmin's native land see Kenney, *Sources*, I, pp. 518–19, 783–84.
[2] Besides modern works already referred to (*v. sup.* § 1) or to be mentioned further down, see on this category of *peregrini* : (*a*) on those labouring in Frankish lands : P. W. Finsterwalder, *Wege und Ziele der irischen und angelsächsischen Mission im fränkischen Reich* (*ZK*, XLVII, 1928, pp. 203–26) ; (*b*) in Belgium : Nicolaus Vernulaeus, *De propagatione fidei christianae in Belgio per sanctos ex Hibernia viros* (Lovanii, 1639) ; *Un poème latin du XVIIᵉ siècle sur les saints irlandais honorés en Belgique*, edited by Paul Grosjean (*AB*, XLIII, 1925, pp. 115–21) ; (*c*) in Alsace : Luzian Pfleger, *Beiträge zur Geschichte der Predigt und des religiösen Volksunterrichts im Elsass während des Mittelalters* (*Historisches Jahrbuch*, XXXVIII, 1917, pp. 661–83).
[3] Kenney, *Sources*, I, pp. 184–85.

St Cataldus, bishop of Tarentum in Apulia, who is said to have lived in the sixth or the seventh century, or even earlier.[1]

Also anterior to Columban is Gibrian (Gibrianus), who belongs to the beginning of the sixth century and is one of a party of seven brothers and three sisters who came to settle on the banks of the Marne in the time of St Remi (Remigius) of Reims.[2] In the sixth century, too, St Fridolin, founder of the abbey of Säckingen on the Rhine (east of Basel), is said to have lived.[3]

St Desle (Deicolus) and St Rouin (Rodingus) are represented as companions of St Columban, although Jonas, the biographer of the abbot of Luxeuil, does not mention either of them. Desle is associated with Lure in modern Franche-Comté, and Rouin with Beaulieu in Argonne.[4]

Likewise Sigebert, believed to be the founder of the monastery of Disentis situated some miles distant from one of the sources of the Rhine (Vorderrhein), is presented to us as a companion of St Columban and an Irishman in the *Passio Placidi*. Now this text, the oldest we possess relating to that foundation, was not written before the tenth century,[5] and the name Sigebert is certainly not Irish.

In the *Chronicon Centulense*, Hariulf († 1143) names as Irishmen the three foreigners Caidoc, Fricor and Mauguille (Madelgisilus) of the seventh century, who are associated with Ponthieu.[6] The first name of this group is Breton not Irish.

The *Vita Ettonis* gives the names of seven holy brethren of Irish birth, Foillan, Ultan, Fursa, Eloquius, Algisus, Etto and Adelgisus (*septem fratres uno spiritu et fide in Christo concordes, licet de omnibus non simus certi utrum fuerint carnali nativitate germani*).[7] The first three are known to us ; we have

---

[1] *Ib.*, p. 185.
[2] *Ib.*, pp. 183–84.
[3] Balther, *Vita Fridolini*, ed. B. Krusch (*MG. Scr. RM*, III, pp. 350–69).
[4] *Vita Deicoli* (Boll., *AS*, Jan., II, pp. 564–74); Richard of St. Vanne, *Vita Rodingi* (Boll., *AS*, Sept., V, pp. 513–17).
[5] Paul E. Martin, *Les sources hagiographiques relatives aux saints Placide et Sigebert et aux origines du monastère de Disentis* (*MHMA*, pp. 515–41).
[6] *Chronicon Centulense*, ed. Ferdinand Lot, I, 5, 6 ; II, 11 ; III, 29 ; IV, 3 (pp. 14, 15, 75–76, 169, 176, 266).
[7] *Vita Ettonis*, 1 (Boll., *AS*, Jul., III, p. 58). Cf. Van der Essen, *Étude*, pp. 282–84.

historical information about their careers. The fourth, Eloquius, is said to have succeeded St Fursa at Lagny. Adelgisus and Algisus represent the doubling of one and the same person,[1] who is localized in the Thiérache, between the Oise and the Sambre. Etto (also called Zé) lived in an unfrequented corner of Hainault not far from that district.

To St Fursa's sphere of influence belong further Mumbolus, abbot of Lagny in the seventh century,[2] and also Goban, who has given his name to the town of Saint-Gobain (Aisne), and Dicuil, both mentioned by Bede himself as companions of Fursa in East Anglia.[3] Their names are certainly Irish. Three others who pass for Scots, Corbican, Rodalgus and Caribert, are localized at Saint-Algise in the forest of Thiérache.[4]

The following are also held by some writers to have been of Irish extraction : Hidulf (Hidulfus), bishop of Trèves and founder of Moyenmoutier in the Vosges († 707 ?)[5] ; Patto († 788 ?) and Tanco († 808 ?), both at first abbots of the " monasterium Amarbaricense "[6] and then called to occupy successively the see of Verden (ancient West Saxony ; at the present day Hanover), of which they were the first bishops.[7] Furthermore, other Irishmen are said to have been in possession of the same see. Neither onomastic nor historical sources support these assertions. On the other hand, critics of no small weight are led by various clues to infer that the famous abbot of St. Mihiel, Smaragdus († c. 830), was an Irishman.[8]

Two bishops of Strasbourg in the second half of the sixth

----

[1] Cf. De Buck, Boll., *AS*, Oct., XIII, p. 380.

[2] *Vita Momboli* (Mabillon, *Acta sanct. O.S.B.*, Venetiis, 1733–40, II, 624–25). Cf. Fuhrmann, *IMM*, p. 24.

[3] Bede, *HE*, III, 19.

[4] Fuhrmann, *IMM*, p. 75.

[5] On the hypothetical character of Hidulf's episcopate, see L. Duchesne, *Fastes*, III, p. 40.

[6] Almost nothing is known of this monastery, which was situated not far from Verden. It has sometimes been confounded with Amorbach in Lower Franconia.

[7] D. Papebroch in Boll., *AS*, Apr., III, 813 ; Mabillon, *Annales O.S.B.* (1704), II, 324 ; Gams, *Series episcoporum*, p. 320. Cf. Kenney, *Sources*, I, p. 785.

[8] Manitius, *Geschichte*, I, p. 462 ; *s.a. Geschichtliches aus mittelalterlichen Bibliothekskatalogen* (*NA*, XXXII, 1906, pp. 670–71) ; Kenney, *Sources*, I, pp. 542–43.

century, Arbogast and Florentius, are likewise, according to late documents, reputed to be Irishmen.[1]

As for Pirmin († c. 753), that "shadowy and ubiquitous missionary saint," founder of the famous monastery of Reichenau in the Lake of Constance (724), of Pfäffers (?) in Rhaetia (diocese of Coire), of Murbach and Münster (Upper Alsace), of Maursmünster north-west of Strasbourg, of Hornbach (Rhenish Palatinate), and of other abbeys as well, his native country has always been a matter of dispute, but the tendency of critics at present seems to be less and less in favour of his Scottic origin.[2]

Several diplomas of immunity drawn up in favour of Murbach and dating from the eighth century contain the words " de monasterio Vivario peregrinorum." [3] It is possible that the peregrini referred to were Scots, at least some of them. We read indeed in the Annals of Murbach that devout men came from Scotia and settled in a desert place " scilicet super Vivarium," [4] but these annals are of very late date and cannot be trusted.[5]

We may further note the name of a Scot called Monon, a hermit in the forest of Ardenne in the seventh century.[6] In the seventh and eighth centuries the brothers Lugle and Luglien, sons of a king of Ireland and localized at Thérouanne on the Lys, were honoured as martyrs.[7] Oda, who died at

---

[1] Fuhrmann, *IMM*, p. 32 ; Kenney, *Sources*, I, p. 783. For the chronology of Arbogast and Florentius see Paul Wentzcke, *Die Regesten der Bischöfe von Strassburg* (Innsbruck, 1908), I, ii, Nos. 10, 14, pp. 215-18, and L. Pfleger, *Nikolaus Paulus* (Gebweiler, 1931), p. 156.

[2] See following papers by Dom Germain Morin, *D'où est venu Saint Pirmin ?* (*Revue Charlemagne*, I, pp. 1-8) ; *Le " Meltis castellum " des chorévêques Pirmin et Landri, Meltburch en Brabant* (*RB*, XXIX, 1912, pp. 262-73) [cf. *RB*, XXXI, 1914-20, pp. 178-84] ; *Études, textes, découvertes* (Maredsous and Paris, 1913), pp. 54-55, and besides : M. Coens, *AB*, XLV, 1927, p. 177 ; XLVI, 1928, pp. 417-18 ; Kenney, *Sources*, I, pp. 518-19, 783-84.

[3] Ed. E. Mühlbacher (*MG. Dipl. Kar.*, I, Nos. 17, 64, 95).

[4] *Murbacher Annalen*, ed. Theodor v. Liebenau (*Anzeiger für Schweizerische Geschichte*, XII [NS, IV], pp. 167-68).

[5] They were compiled by Sigismund Meisterlin in the fifteenth century.

[6] Van der Essen, *Étude*, pp. 144-49 ; Irène Snieders, *L'influence de l'hagiographie irlandaise sur les Vitae des saints irlandais de Belgique* (*RHE*, XXIV, 1928, pp. 848-49) ; Kenney, *Sources*, I, p. 508.

[7] Van der Essen, *Étude*, pp. 418-20 ; I. Snieders, *art. cit.*, pp. 857-58 ; Kenney, *Sources*, I, p. 510 ; Duine, *Catalogue des sources hagiographiques pour l'histoire de Bretagne jusqu'au XIIe siècle* (*An. Br.*, XXXVIII, 1928, pp. 456-57);

St. Oedenrode (North Brabant) in the Netherlands, she likewise daughter of a king of Ireland, has only the title of
virgin.[1] On the other hand, Dympna (Dimphna), the
saint of Gheel near Antwerp, also a king's daughter, is classed
among martyrs [2] ; as are St Rombaud or Rumold (Romol-
dus), honoured as the apostle of Malines (eighth century),[3]
and St. Liévin, or Livin (Livinus), the patron saint of Ghent
(c. 660).[4]

Further may be mentioned as passing for a Scot Hymelin
(Himelinus), a kinsman of St Rombaud, who lived in Brabant
in the eighth century.[5] All these names, however, will
be sought for in vain in the Irish Martyrologies of Tallaght
and Oengus, compiled at the end of the eighth or in the
beginning of the ninth century.

The saints Wiro and Plechelm are said to have founded the
monastery of St. Odiliënberg near Roermond (Limburg,
Holland) on a piece of land given them by Pippin of Heristal
(† 714).[6]

According to the fabulous *Gesta Caroli Magni*, composed in
the thirteenth century by a Gael of Ratisbon, seven brothers
of Irish extraction in the time of Charlemagne obtained from
their abbot permission to lead a more secluded life at Burt-
scheid near Aix-la-Chapelle.[7]

Wandalinus or Wendelinus, the patron saint of the town of
St. Wendel (Rhine Province), mentioned in a late Life as
" *exortus Scotorum regione*," has been variously represented as a

J. Vendryes, *Saints Lugle et Luglien, patrons de Montdidier* (*R. Cel.*, XLIV,
1927, pp. 101–108).
    [1] Van der Essen, *Étude*, pp. 192–97 ; I. Snieders, *art. cit.*, pp. 850–51 ;
Kenney, *Sources*, I, p. 510. This saint should not be confounded with St
Oda of Amay, a widow. Cf. Van der Essen, *Étude*, pp. 189–91.
    [2] Van der Essen, *Étude*, pp. 313–20 ; I. Snieders, *art. cit.*, pp. 851–52 ;
Kenney, *Sources*, I, p. 510.
    [3] I. Snieders, *art. cit.*, pp. 858–60.
    [4] Van der Essen, *Étude*, pp. 368–75 ; I. Snieders, *art. cit.*, pp. 853–56 ;
Kenney, *Sources*, I, p. 509.—Celestinus, abbot of St. Peter of Mount Blandin,
in Ghent, was of Irish origin (*Fundatio monasterii Blandiniensis : MG. Scr.*,
XV, II, p. 623).
    [5] I. Snieders, *art. cit.* .p. 853.
    [6] Van der Essen, *Étude*, pp. 105–109 ; I. Snieders, *art. cit.*, pp. 849–50 ;
Kenney, *Sources*, I., p. 509.
    [7] *Gesta Caroli Mag.*, pp. 176, 188. Cf. A. Bellesheim, *Ueber einige
Beziehungen Irlands zu Reichsstadt Aachen und Diözese Lüttich* (*Zeitschrift des
Aachener Geschichtsvereins*, XIV, 1892, pp. 38–53).

hermit, a monk or an abbot of the neighbouring abbey of Tholey.[1]

Besides Virgil of Salzburg and other authentic Scots, a good many missionaries of Bavaria are put forward by certain writers as of Irish origin : Marinus and Annianus (earlier part of the seventh century ?), who are by tradition connected with Upper Bavaria, and who were specially venerated in the monastery of Rott in the Inn valley [2] ; Alto, founder of Altomünster in the diocese of Freising (eighth century) ; Corbinian, bishop of the last-named city († c. 725) ; Rupert, bishop-abbot of Salzburg († 718 ?) ; Ehrhard and Emmeram, both bishops of Ratisbon.[3]

Finally, it may be added that the chronicler Marianus Scottus believed St Boniface himself, the apostle of Germany, to be a Scot on his father's and his mother's side, an opinion followed by Trithemius.[4]

This list of pseudo-Irishmen and persons whose Gaelic extraction is open to question, full as it is, might be still further lengthened. For it is a fact which has been often proved that, when a mediaeval hagiographer had to recount the doings of a *peregrinus* of whose native country he was ignorant, he did not hesitate to make him one of those *Scotti* " with whom the custom of travelling into foreign lands has now become almost second nature," to use the oft-quoted words of Walahfrid Strabo.[5]

---

[1] Kenney, I, p. 511. Cf. De Buck in, Boll., *AS*, Oct., IX, pp. 344 ff., 350.

[2] Kenney, I, p. 511–12.

[3] Widemann, *Die Herkunft des hl. Korbinian* (*Altbayerische Monatschrift*, XIII, 1915–16, pp. 16 ff.) ; B. Krusch, *NA*, XLI, 1917, pp. 322–23 ; R. Bauerreiss, *Irische Frühmissionäre in Südbayern* (*Wissenschaftliche Festgabe zum zwölfhundertjährigen Jubiläum des hl. Korbinian*, München, 1924, pp. 43–60) ; Michael Huber, *Der hl. Alto und seine Klosterstiftung Altomünster* (*Ib.*, pp. 209–44). Cf. Kenney, *Sources*, I, pp. 514–15, 783.

[4] Marianus, *Chronicon*, s.a. 737 [DCCXV] (*PL*, CXLVII, 756) ; J. Trithemius, *De scriptoribus ecclesiasticis*, ed. Fabricius, *Bibliotheca ecclesiastica* (Hamburgi, 1718), p. 67. Not so the author of the *Vita Burchardi episcopi Herbipol.*, who wrote the following passage at the beginning of the twelfth century : " . . . dum Scotia, quondam bruta, nunc in Christo prudentissima, nobis lumen nostrum primitivum destinavit Kylianum, Burgundis Columbanum, Alemannis Gallum, *Anglia vero universae Germaniae magnum Bonifacium* " (*Prol. ad cap.* 1 : Boll., *AS*, Oct., VI. p. 576).

[5] Walahfrid, *Vita Galli*, II, 46 (p. 336)—" Notet lector Scottos, sive Hibernos jam olim (ut et hodie) peregrinationibus deditos esse," wrote the Belgian historian, Aubert Lemire (Miraeus) († 1640), *Rerum Belgicarum*

M 2

§ 7.—Wastrels of the Emigration

Besides those *peregrini* whom the esteem of the continental clergy raised to the episcopate, there was a goodly number of their compatriots who felt ill at ease in the confines of the ecclesiastical discipline established on the Continent and whose conduct was at variance with the canons accepted in the Churches of Gaul and Germany, and these were a source of constant scandal among foreign churchmen.

The freaks of the *episcopi vagantes* gave special offence. They had already been invested with the episcopal dignity before leaving their own country; but at no time had they been attached to any diocese, and they roamed ceaselessly from place to place, exercising the powers they held in virtue of their consecration without any authorization from the Ordinary.[1] Among these men whose *Wandertrieb* suffered them not to rest, there were some who unsettled the minds of their hearers, as yet ill-grounded in the faith, by inopportune and sometimes downright heretical discourse on doctrinal points. In the course of his missions St Boniface encountered more than one adventurer of this kind and did not hesitate to procure their condemnation from the councils and the Holy See. Such a one was the bishop Clement, *genere Scottus*, who rejected ecclesiastical celibacy, the treatises of the holy fathers Jerome, Augustine and Gregory, and the decrees of the councils, enjoined Jewish customs on the inhabitants of Austrasia, and taught that when Christ descended to Hell he had delivered all confined there, good and bad.[2]

St Boniface had also to contend with a Scottic priest of the

---

chronicon (Antverpiae, 1636), quoted by J. Ghesquière, *Acta Sanct. Belgii,* VI, p. 607. See also Anton Meyer, *Die Iren auf dem Kontinent im Mittelalter* (*Hochland*, XIII, 1915–16, p. 607) ; Duine, *Memento*, p. 81 ; Fuhrmann, *IMM*, pp. 48–49 ; W. Levison, *Zur Geschichte des Klosters Tholey* (*Historische Aufsätze Aloys Schulte zum 70. Geburtstage gewidmet*, Düsseldorf, 1927, p. 67) ; P. E. Martin, *op. cit.*, p. 525 ; Kenney, I, p. 784.

[1] See B. Krusch, *Zur Eptatius-und Eparchius Legende* (*NA*, XXV, 1900, pp. 131–73) and various prolegomena by the same scholar in *MG. Scr. RM,* IV, pp. 648–49, 696 ff.

[2] Zachary to Boniface (*Ep.* 57, 60) ; *Acta Synodi Romanae* (A.D. 745), 59, ed. Dümmler (*MG. Epist.*, III, pp. 314, 324–25. Cf. G. Kurth, *Saint Boniface* (Paris, 1902), pp. 88 ff.

name of Samson, who taught that baptism was of no avail for salvation.[1]

Even before these errors had been brought to the knowledge of the Holy See, a marked tendency may be discerned in the Roman Curia to look with suspicion on all who hailed from the islands. When told that Pirmin was a bishop coming *de occidentali parte*, Pope Gregory II is reported to have said : "*De talibus nos praecavere oportet.*" [2] And a letter of Gregory III written about 737 to the bishops of Bavaria and Alemannia bids them be on their guard against the doctrine of the Britons (*doctrinam venientium Brittonum*).[3]

In order to keep these disturbers in check, the first Germanic general Council, held at the instance of St Boniface in April, 742, in what town is not known, began its work by ruling that unknown bishops or priests should not be allowed to exercise sacred ministry till they had been examined in council.[4] The Council of Soissons (744) required that the said wandering bishops and priests should obtain the approval of the diocesan bishop.[5] The Councils of Verneuil (755), of Mainz (813) and of Tours (813) passed other measures against them.[6] The twenty-second canon of Mainz bestows on these vagrants the epithets "acephalous" and "hippocentaurs" and threatens them with excommunication and imprisonment. Although Irishmen are not explicitly mentioned in these texts, there is no doubt that they were the persons chiefly aimed at.[7] In any case, the forty-third canon of the second Council of Chalon-sur-Saône (810) expressly names them. "There are in certain places "—so it runs—" Scots who pass themselves off for bishops and confer holy orders ; such ordinations are null and void, all the more so as they are often tainted with

---

[1] Boniface, *Ep.* 80 (p. 359).

[2] *Vita II^a Pirmini*, 4 (Boll., *AS*, Nov., II., p. 36).

[3] Gregory III to the Bishops of Bavaria and Alemannia (*MG. Epist.*, III, p. 292).

[4] Ed. A. Werminghoff, *MG. Leges : Sect. III Conc.*, II, p. 3 ; *Capitulare Karlmanni*, 4, ed. A. Boretius (*MG. Leges : Sect. II Cap.*, I, p. 25).

[5] Council of Soissons, c. 5 (*MG. Conc.*, II, p. 35) ; *Capitulare Suessionense*, c. 5 (*MG. Cap.*, I, p. 29). Cf. Levison, *Die Iren*, pp. 17–18.

[6] Council of Verneuil, 13 (Mansi, *Concilia*, XII, 583) ; Council of Mainz, 22 (Mansi, *Concilia*, XIV, 71 ; *MG. Conc.*, I, 1, p. 267) ; Council of Tours, 13 (Mansi, XIV, 85 ; *MG. Conc.*, ib., p. 288).

[7] Cf. Ed. Bishop, *JTS*, VIII, 1907, p. 285 ; *s.a. LH*, p. 172.

simony."[1] A capitulary dated September, 813, which
recapitulates all the enactments made in preceding councils,
enjoins on every bishop to look and see whether he has any
of these foreign clerics in his diocese and, if so, to send them
back to their own country.[2]

Charles the Great himself had been obliged, about 795,
to expel a Scottic priest who had caused scandal in the diocese
of Cologne by eating meat in Lent. However, as it was not
possible to try the culprit on the spot for want of sufficient
evidence, the king of the Franks decided to send him to Offa,
king of Mercia, who was charged to dispatch him to his native
Ireland in order to be tried by his own bishop there.[3]

But if Charles showed himself severe towards those of the
foreigners whose conduct deserved censure, he was no less
active in protecting those who travelled or settled in his states
from praiseworthy motives. We have seen all that he did to
restore the Scottic monks of the isle of Honau to the possession
of their property.[4] The sixth canon of the Council of Tours
in 813, which obliged bishops to receive at their table strangers
and the poor, was certainly due to the Emperor's influence.[5]
He loved the *peregrini*, so his biographer Einhard tells us,
and received them with such kindness that soon their con-
course became a nuisance to the palace and even a burden to the
State.[6] Consequently, we come across remarks from the
pen of some of those associated with the Palace School,
Theodulf, bishop of Orleans, and others, Alcuin perhaps among
them, which betray resentment and may have been inspired
by jealousy.[7] The most virulent of these was Theodulf,
who in a poem addressed to the monarch pours out his

---

[1] Council of Chalon-sur-Saône, 43 (Mansi, *Concilia*, XIV, 102). The
decision to restrain the action of the *Scotti* is still more sharply formulated
by the synod of Celchyth in England (c. 5) [July 27, 816] (*CED*, III,
581).
[2] *Karoli Magni capitula e canonibus excerpta* (A.D. 813), can. 23, ed.
Werminghoff, *MG. Conc.*, I, 1, p. 297 ; ed. Migne, *PL*, XCVII, p. 364).
[3] *Ep.* 12 (*MG. Epist.*, IV, 131).
[4] *V. sup.* § 5.
[5] Mansi, *Concilia*, XIV, 84.
[6] Einhard, *Vita Karoli Mag.*, 21 (*MG. Scr.*, II, p. 455).
[7] Einhard, *l. cit.* ; *Vita Alcuini*, 18 (*MG. Scr.*, XV, I, p. 793) ; Alcuin,
Ep. 145, ed. Dümmler, *MG. Epist.*, IV, pp. 231–35. Cf. Kenney, *Sources*,
I, p. 535 ; Turner, *Irish Teachers*, pp. 34–36.

bile on a certain " *Scotellus* " whose name he does not give.[1]

The want of discipline and the irregularities which brought discredit on many of the *peregrini* of the early Middle Ages are also referred to in some texts of following times. In England, at the end of the twelfth century, there were still *pseudo-episcopi Hibernenses*, against whom Richard,[2] archbishop of Canterbury (1174–84), warns his suffragans. The intemperance of some, the aggressive disposition of others, above all the incorrigible *vagatio* of the greater number, cast here and there a few ugly shadows among the swelling and motley throngs of the religious emigration.[3]

§ 8.—PILGRIMS AND SHAM PILGRIMS

As a result of the close relations between the Carolingians and the Holy See, the pilgrimage to Rome became both more popular and easier to undertake. Although the insular *peregrini*, as has been already said, were far from being all pilgrims in the strict sense of the word, there were among them many whose steps were directed towards some particular sanctuary either from the start or owing to some incident of the route. St. Gall, Bobbio and Péronne, we know, drew many Irish ; some paid only a passing visit, others settled in these monasteries.

In the tenth century Cadroe began his wanderings by a visit to the tomb of St Fursa, and Marianus Scottus was ordained a priest in the basilica of St Kilian at Würzburg.[4] But naturally the greatest attraction for the devout imagination of the islanders was the *limina Apostolorum*.[5] It is told

---

[1] Theodulf, *Carmen* 25 *ad Carolum regem* (*MG. Poet. Lat.*, I, pp. 483–89) ; *Carmen* 27 (p. 492). Cf. Kenney, *Sources*, I, p. 536.

[2] *PL*, CCVII, 160.

[3] Caesarius of Heisterbach, *Dial.*, VI, 5, ed. Strange, I, p. 353 ; Ferdinand Janner, *Geschichte der Bischöfe von Regensburg* (Regensburg, 1883), II, 268, 430 ; H. Omont, *Satire de Garnier de Rouen contre le poète Moriuht* (*Annuaire-bulletin de la Société de l'Histoire de France*, XXXI, 1894, p. 198).

[4] *Vita Cadroe*, 19 (Boll., *AS*, Mart., I, p. 476) ; Marianus Scottus, *Chronicon, a.a.* 1081 [MLIX] (*PL*, CXLVII, 786).

[5] *Vita Sam.*, I, 37 (p. 133) ; *Vita Agili*, 7 (Boll., *AS*, Aug., VI, 586) ; *Vita Fintani*, 6 (*MG. Scr.*, XV, I, 504) ; *Vita Mariani*, II, 9 (p. 357) ; *Gesta Caroli Mag.*, p. 173. Cf. A. P. Forbes in *Hist. of Scotland*, 1874, V, pp. 261–66.

that St Molua († *c.* 609), desirous of making a pilgrimage to the tomb of the apostles, went to his master St Maedóc to ask permission ; when Maedóc made some objections, the saint expressed the warmth of his desire in the concise words : " *Nisi videro Romam, cito moriar.*" [1]

Rome, therefore, was often visited by Irish pilgrims. In the twelfth century there was even a small monastic establishment in the Eternal City dedicated to the Trinity and intended for the use of Scots.[2] But during the early Middle Ages the Anglo-Saxons showed more eagerness than their neighbours to undertake the pilgrimage to Rome. It is surprising to see the enthusiasm and the readiness with which kings, priests, monks and nuns carried out this long journey.[3] The repeated expeditions of Benedict Biscop, abbot of Wearmouth and Jarrow, are well known. He made the journey to Rome six times, and always to the advantage of his monasteries in Northumbria.[4] " *Toties mare transiit,*" the Venerable Bede says of him, " *nunquam, ut est consuetudinis quibusdam, vacuus et inutilis rediit.*" [5]

The correspondence of St Boniface and also that of Charlemagne supply us with instructive details concerning the habits of the pilgrims and sham pilgrims of the age. Sometimes traders joined the pious bands on false pretences, in order to benefit by the exemption from tolls accorded to them.[6] This, however, was by no means the worst offence committed. The Apostle of Germany, writing to the archbishop of Canterbury, begs him to check the passion for pilgrimages among

---

[1] *Sal. ASH*, col. 480.

[2] Cf. A. Wilmart, *La Trinité des Scots à Rome et les notes du Vat. Lat.* 378 (*RB*, XLI, 1929, pp. 218–30).

[3] Thomas Allison, *English religious Life in the Eighth Century as illustrated by contemporary Letters* (London, 1929), pp. 13, 32–35, 133, 137.

[4] Cf. T. Allison, *op. cit.*, p. 32.

[5] Bede, *Homilia* 17 *in natale S. Benedicti* (*PL*, XCIV, 228).

[6] Charlemagne, *Ep.* 7 *ad Offam regem* (*PL*, XCVIII, 907) ; *Council of Mainz* (753), c. 6 (Mansi, *Concilia*, XII, 572).—For the relations between Charlemagne and Offa see T. Allison, *op. cit.*, pp. 14–15. On those between Charlemagne and the kings of Ireland see Einhard, *Vita Karoli Imp.*, 16 (*PL*, XCVII, 25–26). The statement made therein is, however, open to question (see L. Halphen's edition of the *Vita* (1923), pp. 46–47).—Referring to Charles the Bald, Prudentius of Troyes, in the *Annales Bertiniani*, says (*a.a.* 848) : " Unde et rex Scottorum ad Karolum pacis et amicitiae gratia legatos cum muneribus mittit, viam sibi petendi Romam concedi deposcens " (ed. G. Waitz, Hannoverae, 1883, p. 36). Cf. *ib.*, *a.a.* 839 (p. 18).

his flock, especially among nuns. He points out the resulting disadvantages and even mentions grave irregularities of which female so-called pilgrims were reported to have been guilty in several towns of France and Italy. " In a great measure they [the female pilgrims] are lost, few retaining their chastity. There are very few cities in Lombardy, in Francia and in Gaul, in which there is not an adulteress or a prostitute of English race. This thing is a disgrace and a shame to the whole of our Church." [1]

It does not appear that the flood of Irish emigration drew many women into its current. However, if we may believe a Life of St Odilia († c. 720), the *peregrinae feminae* who had left their country, whether Ireland or Britain, were warmly welcomed at the monastery of Hohenburg. [2]

A council of the year 813 disapproves of pilgrimages to Tours and Rome undertaken by clergy or laymen from superstitious or worldly motives. [3] Doubtless it was experience of the physical and moral dangers incurred on pilgrimages which inspired those somewhat melancholy verses written by an Irish hand on a page of a ninth-century manuscript :

" To go to Rome, much labour, little profit ; the King whom thou seekest here, unless thou bring him with thee, thou findest him not. Much folly, much frenzy, much loss of sense, much madness [is it], since going to death is certain, to be under the displeasure of Mary's Son." [4]

To judge from the extraordinary number of emigrant clerics, bishops and monks, we might suppose that the disciplinary regulations dealing with clerical and monastic stability were less firmly established in Ireland than on the Continent. Such, however, was not the case. There as elsewhere canons and religious Rules agree in condemning the rolling stone. A synod attributed to the time of St

[1] Boniface, *Ep.* 78 (*MG. Epist.*, III, pp. 354-55).
[2] *Vita Odiliae*, 16, ed. W. Levison (*MG. Scr. RM*, VI, pp. 45-46).
[3] Council of Chalon-sur-Saône (813), c. 45 (Mansi, *Concilia*, XIV., 102-103).
[4] Stokes and Strachan, *TP*, II, p. 296. " But that there is a real connection in the MS. (*Codex Boernerianus*) between the second stanza and the first in the verses quoted above, is not proved " (remark kindly made to me by P. Paul Grosjean). Compare the verses against Rome " *Nobilibus quondam*," etc., sometimes ascribed to John the Scot, edited by L. Traube (*MG. Poet. Lat.*, III, pp. 555-56).

Patrick declares : " His own country a man must first teach, after the example of the Saviour ; not unless it refuse to learn may he lawfully forsake it, after the example of the Apostles." [1] In what way did the behaviour of the Irish people furnish an excuse for adopting the latter alternative ? That is a question we will examine later. The collection of canons known by the name of *Hibernensis* contains an enactment, also purporting to be of Patrician origin, which runs as follows *: " Patricius ait : Monachus inconsulto abbate vagus ambulans in plebe debet excommunicari."* [2] Further, the Rule ascribed to St Ailbe of Emly and that of St Columban († 615) are explicit on the necessity of monastic stability. [3] St Máel Rúain of Tallaght († 792) and the wise men of Ireland, when consulted as to the emigratory movement which was drawing such numbers of religious out of the country, expressed their disapproval. [4] Nevertheless, the great number of monks in Ireland, examples like those of Columban, Fursa and Kilian, a genuine missionary vocation, a call to a higher level of the ascetic life, the conversion of the heathens of Gaul and Germany and the instruction of the ignorant, were not these reasons sufficient to justify the distant expeditions made by these indefatigable voluntary exiles with results which, despite the losses inevitable in all collective and prolonged undertakings, remain a lasting glory to their country and their faith ?

§ 9.—RECLUSES

Many were the *peregrini* who stopped short their journey in some spot which appealed to their love of solitude. Renouncing the society of men and confined in a narrow cell, they gave

---

[1] *CED*, II, p. 335.

[2] *Hibernensis*, xxxix, 11 (p. 151).

[3] *Rule of St Ailbe*, 33, 48, 52, ed. J. O'Neill (*Ériu*, III, 1907, pp. 105, 109).—" Mortificationis igitur triplex est ratio . . . [tertio] non ire quoquam absolute " (*Regula Columbani*, 9, ed. Seebass, p. 385 ; ed. Migne, *PL*, LXXX, 216).

[4] *Tallaght* (1911), 17 (p. 133) ; *Rule of the Céli Dé*, 44, ed. Gwynn, *Tallaght* (1927), pp. 75–77. In the same train of thought : " Nullam enim avem sua ova in volatu fovere audisti " in *Vita Coemgeni*, 29, 30 (*VSH*, I, pp. 249–50) ; *Vita Samthannae*, 24 (*VSH*, II, p. 260). Cf. E. J. Gwynn, *Some Saints of Ireland* (*Church Quarterly Review*, LXXIV, 1912, pp. 70–71).

themselves up to the contemplation of eternal truth for years, generally indeed to the end of their life. On the death of such a solitary, his body was buried beneath the floor of his cell.[1]

We have already come across more than one of these recluses who had crossed the seas : in the Merovingian period, Arnanus, *ex genere Scottorum*, a friend of St Desiderius of Cahors, in whose monastery he was first a monk [2] ; and later the solitary Eusebius, whose cell was on the Viktorsberg in Rhaetia, not far from the abbey of St. Gall.[3]

At the beginning of the ninth century we find a learned man of the name of Dungal an *inclusus* at the abbey of Saint-Denis in France,[4] and in the second half of the century a bishop named Marcus, a recluse at the monastery of Saint-Médard of Soissons. The latter, a native of Great Britain, was full of reminiscences of the missions of St Germanus of Auxerre, " the most holy apostle of his nation " ; these he imparted to Heiric of Auxerre, who made use of them in his *Miracula Germani*.[5]

Born in Ireland, Fintan († 878) was captured and carried off by the Vikings. He escaped from them in the Orkneys, trusted himself to the ocean, landed among the Picts, and, in fulfilment of a vow, went on pilgrimage to Rome. On his journey back he stopped with some anchorites dwelling on the island of Rheinau in the Rhine near Schaffhausen, where he spent the remainder of his life, the last twenty-two years in strict seclusion.[6]

In the eleventh century insular recluses become more numerous. There is first the celebrated chronicler Marianus Scottus, whose Irish name was Moel Brigte, a former monk of the monastery of Moville, which he entered in 1052 at the age of twenty-four. In 1056 for some trifling offence the abbot Tigernach sentenced him to banishment from Ireland.

[1] Cf. L. G., *Ermites et reclus* (Liguge, 1928), p. 74.
[2] *V. sup.* § 3.
[3] *V. sup.* § 3.
[4] Kenney, *Sources*, I, pp. 538–42.
[5] Heiric of Auxerre, *Miracula Germani*, 1, 8 (*PL*, CXXIV, 1245). Cf. Mommsen's edition of Nennius (*MG. Auct. ant.*, XIII, p. 113).
[6] *Vita Fintani* (*MG. Scr.*, XV, 1, 502–506).

After spending two years in the monastery of St. Martin at
Cologne, he went to Fulda in 1058 and was ordained priest
the following year in the Church of St Kilian the Irish martyr
at Würzburg.[1] Marianus was not the first Scot to visit the
abbey of Fulda ; monks of his nationality received at the time
a fraternal welcome in that monastery. A certain Anmchad,
formerly a monk of Inis Cealtra, who had likewise been
condemned to banishment for a slight infraction of cloistral
discipline, had occupied a recluse's *clausola* there, in which he
died in 1053.[2] In this cell Marianus had himself inclosed
when after his ordination he resolved to embrace the same
kind of life. For ten years he celebrated Mass over the body
of Anmchad, who was buried beneath the floor of the cell.
In 1059, by order of the bishop of Mainz and with the
consent of the abbot of Fulda, he was transferred to another
cell at the monastery of St. Martin at Mainz, where he died
in 1082 or 1083.

Marianus records in his chronicle the tragic fate of Paternus,
another Irish recluse of the monastery of Paderborn. When
that monastery caught fire, Paternus refused to leave the place
of his retreat and was burnt alive. "*Ambiens martyrium*,"
writes Marianus, "*pro nullo foris exivit, sed, in sua clausola
combustus, per ignem pertransivit in refrigerium*" (1058).[3]

In 1067 another Marianus, a contemporary of the foregoing, who bore the Irish name of Muiredach mac Robartaig,
set out on a pilgrimage to Rome with two companions, John
and Candidus. They spent a year in the monastery of
Michelsberg at Bamberg.[4] On reaching Ratisbon, they
were induced to stay by a fellow-countryman, a recluse
named Muirchertach, and continued their journey no further.
Marianus († 1088), a skilled and industrious scribe, was the
soul of a colony of Irish solitaries installed in *clausolae* attached
to the priory of Weih-Sankt-Peter near Ratisbon and another
monastery of that city. Each of these solitaries occupied a
separate cell.[5] One of them named John parted from the

[1] Marianus, *Chronicon* (*PL*, CXLVII, 784–86).
[2] *Chronicon* (col. 785). Cf. Macalister, *Inis Cealtra*, pp. 104–105.
[3] *Chronicon* (col. 786).
[4] *Vita Mariani*, II, 7–8 (p. 367).
[5] *Vita Mariani*, II, III (pp. 367–68).

group at Ratisbon in order to be further distant from his native island, and went to end his days at Göttweig in Austria.[1]

This John must not be confounded with another Irishman of the same name, a bishop, who suffered as a martyr in Mecklenburg in 1066, after baptizing thousands of pagans.[2]

§ 10.—TRAVELLING METHODS OF THE ISLANDERS

In his memoir entitled *Die Congregation der Schottenklöster in Deutschland* [3] Wattenbach has quoted a curious passage of the Chronicle of Jocelin of Brakelond which, he believes, presents a living picture of the habits of the Irish pilgrim in the later Middle Ages.[4] We must, however, abstain from making use of this document for two reasons. In the first place, Jocelin's Chronicle, which was written at the end of the twelfth century and records events belonging to the years 1159–62 in the passage in question, would be a late source for us, dealing as we are only with Irish peregrinations previous to the close of the eleventh century. In the second place, it is hard to decide whether in this passage the author is alluding to Irish or Scotch pilgrims. Used by an English writer of the twelfth century, the word *Scotti* would, we think, be more likely to mean Scotchmen [5]; if so, the passage of the Chronicle would have for us the value merely of an analogy. Therefore we prefer to turn to the contemporary documents of the period under study and glean from them here and there such traits as are best fitted to give a clear idea of the conditions under which the Irish of the early Middle Ages travelled and were received on the Continent.

[1] *Vita Mariani*, III (p. 368) ; *Vita Altmanni*, 5 (*MG. Scr.*, XII, 241 ; Boll., *AS*, Aug., II, p. 387).

[2] Adam of Bremen, *Gesta Hammaburgensis Ecclesiae pontificum*, III, 20, 50, 70, IV, 10 (*MG. Scr.*, VII, 343, 355, 367, 372). Cf. J. Fischer, *Kann Bischof Johannes aus Irland mit Recht als erster Märtyrer Amerikas bezeichnet werden ?* (*Zeitschrift für katholische Theologie*, XXIV, 1900, pp. 756–58). Cf. H. Delehaye, in *AS*, Nov., IV, pp. 564–66.

[3] *Zeitschrift für christliche Archaeologie und Kunst*, 1856, pp. 21–30, 49–58. English translation in *UJA*, VII, 1859, pp. 227–46, 295, 313.

[4] Jocelin of Brakelond, *Chronica*, 35, ed. Th. Arnold, *Memorials of St. Edmund's Abbey* (*RS*), London, 1890, I, pp. 252–53.

[5] Cf. Giraldus, *TH*, III, 7 (p. 147) ; Henry of Huntingdon, *Historiae Anglorum*, I, 11, ed. Th. Arnold (*RS*), pp. 15–16.

They generally set out in bands, a single band often consisting of twelve persons and their leader.[1] It would indeed have been imprudent to undertake a long journey through foreign parts alone in those turbulent and violent ages.[2] If they did not feel themselves sufficient in number or strength, monks and clerics gladly joined caravans of traders ; as did Clement, the vendor of wisdom, and his companion—of whom more anon.[3] It has been asserted that the emigrants generally reached Gaul by way of Brittany and the Loire.[4] This is stated in none of our texts [5] ; on the contrary, a large number explicitly attest that the Irish first set sail to Great Britain, crossed that island and then re-embarked on its southern coast, doubtless in some port of Kent, to cross the strait at its narrowest point.[6] This, we believe, was in its main lines the route followed by St Columban [7] ; it was also that of Clement the Scot,[8] of St Kilian and of many others.[9] Agilbert, the future bishop of Paris, when returning from Ireland followed the same course.[10] Moreover, Thierry of Saint-Trond tells us that from the days of St Rombaud (eighth century) it was the customary route.[11] No doubt it is the

---

[1] Reeves's note in Adam., *Vita Col.* (1874, pp. LXXI ff.) ; W. Levison's notes and comments in *MG. Scr. RM*, V, pp. 688, 714.

[2] Lupus of Ferrières, *Ep.* 104 (*MG. Epist.*, IV, p. 91) ; Einhard, *Ep.* 14 (*MG. Epist.*, V, p. 132).

[3] *V. inf.* ch. VIII, § 6.

[4] Pflugk-Harttung, *The old Irish on the Continent* (*Transactions of the Royal Historical Society*, N.S., V, 1891, p. 77).

[5] St Ronan (Renan) is said to have sailed from Ireland to the coast of Léon (N. Brittany) : *Vita Ronani*, 2 (Boll., *Catal. Cod. lat. hagiogr. Bibl. Nat. Paris.*, I, p. 439).

[6] Vulganius (*Vita*, II, 15 ; Boll., *AS*, Nov., I, p. 572), and Cadroe (Boll., *AS*, Mart., I, p. 476) sailed from the Kentish coast. Richborough, near Sandwich, in Kent, was one of the chief ports of embarkation in Roman times (Bede, *HE*, I, 4. Cf. Plummer's notes, vol. II, p. 5).

[7] L.G., *Un point obscur de l'itinéraire de Saint Colomban venant en Gaule* (*An. Br.*, XXI, 1907, pp. 327–43).

[8] Monachus Sangall., *Gesta Karoli*, I, I (*MG. Scr.*, II, p. 731).

[9] *Passio Kiliani II*ᵃ, c. 4 (Boll., *AS*, Jul., II, p. 615).

[10] Bede, *HE*, III, 7.

[11] Theodoricus, *Vita Rumoldi*, I, 3 (Boll., *AS*, Jul., I, 215). " Britain was for passengers the usual way to the Continent " (C. Plummer, *VSH*, I, pp. C–CI, introd.). See marginal note in MS. Pal. Vatic. 830 of Marianus Scottus' *Chronicle* reproduced in *MG. Scr.*, V, p. 481, and *PL*, CXLVII, 602–603. Note the name of the Irish sea, " *primum mare* " in Muirchu (p. 272), *i.e.*, in that text, " the first sea," a traveller from Ireland to the Continent having to cross two seas, *viz.*, that between Ireland and Britain and that between Britain and the Continent (cf. White, *Patrick*, p. 123).

belief in some vague affinity between the races, together with the fact that the two Britains, island and peninsula, bore the same name, that has led some modern writers to surmise that there was frequent intercourse between Ireland and Armorica. In reality, direct communication between those two countries was rather rare.[1]

Once landed on the coast of Picardy or Flanders,[2] the *peregrini* set out in widely different directions, either according to a premeditated plan or guided by impulse or the circumstances of the moment. From certain monastic traditions which were accepted among the Celts on the subject of journeying, we are led to believe that those who had entered on their wanderings from purely ascetic motives journeyed for the most part on foot. This form of mortification was, as a matter of fact, largely practised and for certain monks was even compulsory.[3] In the *Regula cuiusdam patris ad monachos*, which is Celtic in origin or at least inspiration, the abbot who allows himself the use of a horse or vehicle in his journey is held to be unmortified. According to the same Rule, a monk in good health who did not travel on foot would have incurred excommunication.[4] We know, moreover, as a fact that St Aidan, St Ceadda, St Kentigern and St Malachy made their missionary tours on foot.[5] St Wilfrid, going to Rome at the

---

[1] *V. sup.*, ch. IV, § 3, *in fine.*—In proof of a direct trade route between Brittany and Ireland there is but a single text, viz., Jonas, *Vita Col.*, I, 22. This forms the basis of all the inferences deduced by Zimmer in his paper *Auf welchem Wege kamen die Goidelen vom Kontinent nach Irland?* (*Abhandlungen der k. Preuss. Akad. der Wissenschaften*, 1912) and his followers. See reservations made by J. Vendryes, *R. Cel.*, XXXIII, 1912, p. 387.

[2] (a) On the coast of Ponthieu : Chaidoc and Fricor (*Chron. Centulense*, 6, ed. F. Lot, pp. 15–16).—(b) At Quentavic (or Quentovic), " vicus ad Quantiam," *i.e.*, on the Canche, situated near Étaples and not far from Saint-Josse-sur-Mer (Cant. Montreuil, Dept. Pas-de-Calais) [see Plummer's note, Bede, *HE*, vol. II, p. 203 ; *MG. Epist.*, IV, pp. 66, 291]. From Quentavic sailed Theodore of Canterbury (Bede, *HE*, IV, 1) ; there landed St Boniface (Willibald, *Vita Bonif.*, 5, ed. W. Levison, *Scr. rer. Germanic.*, 1905, p. 20).—(c) At Boulogne (*Vita Cadroae*, II, 19 : Boll., *AS*, Mart., I, p. 476).—(d) At Wissant (Cant. Marquise, Dept. Pas-de-Calais, between Boulogne and Calais) : *Vita Vulganii*, II, 15 : Boll., *AS*, Nov., I, p. 572). In the Middle Ages Wissant was a much frequented port of embarkation for Dover (see *PL*, CLVI, 975–76).—(e) In Flanders : *Gesta Caroli Mag.*, pp. 173, 176.

[3] Cf. L.G., *Anciennes traditions ascétiques* : 1. *L'usage de voyager à pied* (*Revue d'ascétique et de mystique*, III, 1922, pp. 56–59).

[4] Cap. 20, 21 (*PL*, LXVI, 991).

[5] Cf. L.G., *art. cit.* ; Bernard, *Vita Mal.*, 3 (col. 1084).

age of seventy, accomplished the entire land journey on foot (704).[1] It was considered an apostolic tradition to abstain from using a vehicle or a mount.[2] It is likely that Irish ascetics and missionaries had to conform to this custom on the Continent. This is not indeed explicitly stated in texts [3]; but the exhaustion of which many of our travellers complain, the poverty of most of them, the destitution to which they were sometimes reduced from want of baggage, all this leads us to suppose that as a rule walking was their sole means of locomotion.[4]

Great indeed were the privations endured by most of those who crossed to the Continent. Men like Clement, Dungal, and Sedulius Scottus are constantly reduced to entreat the benevolence of some prince, prelate or nobleman for themselves or their fellow-countrymen in need. They are conscious of being a burden to the society which receives them : "*Nos ergo pauperes et peregrini oneri forsitan et fastidio vobis videamur esse propter nostram multitudinem et importunitatem et clamositatem.*" [5] But the hunger, thirst, fatigue and stress of weather which try them so severely wring groans from them.[6] To touch the hearts of those they address, the scholars among them pour forth their plaints in Latin verses.

---

[1] Stephen, *Vita Wilfridi*, 50.
[2] L.G., *art. cit.*
[3] Cf. *Epistolae Scottorum Leodienses* (*MG. Epist.*, VI, pp. 195 ff.) ; *Vita Agili*, 24, ed. Mabillon, p. 324 ; *Vita Rumoldi*, 1 (Boll., *AS*, Jul., I, p. 215).
[4] Cf. Sedulius, *Carmina*, II, 3 (*MG. Poet. Lat.*, III, p. 168) ; *Epist. Scottorum Leod.* (*MG. Epist.*, VI, pp. 195–97). See how Duntacus, *terrae Scottorum indigena*, went on a pilgrimage to the tomb of St Heribert of Cologne and how, being cured there, " qui primus male tripes nunc bene bipes coepit discurrere " (*Vita Heriberti*, 20 : *MG. Scr.*, XV, II, pp. 1254–55). Columban, however, travelled by boat on the Loire, Dungal on horseback (*Ep.* 4 : *MG. Epist.*, IV, pp. 579–80), and St Samson made use of a chariot in Ireland (*Vita Sam.*, I, 47, p. 143).—Scanty as the baggage of those *peregrini* often was, a leather bottle was no superfluity in their travelling equipment, as can be gathered from the following gloss on the Latin word *ascopa* (see Du Cange, *s.v. ascopa, ascopera*) : " flasco, similis utri de coriis facta, sicut solent Scottones habere," quoted by J. M. Clark, *The Abbey of St. Gall as a Centre of Literature and Art* (Cambridge, 1926), p. 27.
[5] Dungal, *Ep.* 4 (*MG. Epist.*, IV, p. 580).
[6] *Epistolae variorum* XXXI, 1 (*MG. Epist.*, VI, p. 195).—" Miser," an epithet frequently used by the *Scotti* speaking of themselves. Cf. W. Wattenbach, *Un autographe de Marianus Scottus* (*R. Cel.*, I, 1870–72, p. 263) ; J. A. Endres, *Das St Jakobsportal in Regensburg und Honorius Augustodunensis* (Kempten, 1903), pp. 15, 20, 22,

A Scot threatened with punishment escapes from Bobbio and takes refuge at St. Zeno's in Verona ; there in poverty and loneliness he begins to regret the cloister of St Columban and indites the following distichs :

" *Nocte dieque gemo, quia sum peregrinus et egens ;*
    Attritus febribus nocte dieque gemo ;
Plangite me, iuvenes, animo qui me colebatis ;
    Rideat hinc quisquis ; plangite me, iuvenes.
Magne Columba, roga Dominum ne spernar ab ipso ;
    Quo reddar tibimet, magne Columba, roga . . ." [1]

Another at Soissons, benumbed with cold, envies the good fire at which Carloman, the son of Charles the Bald, is warming himself in the same town :

" *Karlomanne, tuis arridet partibus ignis ;*
    Nos vero gelidos urit iniqua hiems." [2]

One on his way to Rome is attacked and killed by brigands on the banks of the Aisne.[3] Another returning from the Eternal City is despoiled of part of his clothing by robbers. He enumerates his losses in detail in a letter to Franco the bishop of Liége, in hopes, as he says, that the prelate may of his bounty make good the damage : " *Vincat vestra pietas raptorum impietatem !* " [4]

§ 11.—" HOSPITALIA SCOTTORUM "

Many persons of rank and several kings of the Merovingian period gave a hearty welcome to our *peregrini*. In the Carolingian period the number of their protectors was still larger. The Pippins, Charlemagne and Charles the Bald lavished marks of favour on them. They found powerful support in the episcopate also ; we may recall the names of Faro of Meaux, Didier (Desiderius) of Cahors and Ansoald of Poitiers. Under the Carolingians the bishops Hartgar and Franco of Liége,[5] Hildoard of Cambrai,[6] Adalbero I and Adal-

---

[1] *Lamentum R<efugae> cuiusdam* (*MG. Poet. Lat.*, III, p. 688).
[2] *MG. Poet. Lat.*, III, p. 690.
[3] Flodoard, *Historia Ecclesiae Remensis*, IV, 48 (*MG. Scr.*, XIII, p. 597).
[4] *MG. Epist.*, VI, p. 197.
[5] *Epistolae Leod.* (*MG. Epist.*, VI, pp. 195–97). Cf. Kenney, *Sources*, I, p. 601.
[6] Cf. Bishop, *LH*, p. 65.

bero II of Metz gave them help and favoured their undertakings. St Gerard, bishop of Toul (963–994), and St
Arnold, archbishop of Mainz (1153–60), also entertained
the friendliest feelings towards the Irish.[1] Widric, the
biographer of Gerard, has preserved various traits which
prove the fact. In particular, he says : " He collected no
small number of Greeks and Irish, and fed this mingled crowd,
speaking divers tongues at his own expense." And further—
an interesting detail—" It was their custom to assemble daily
at the different altars in the chapel, where they offered the
services of supplication and praise to God after the manner
of their own countries (*more patrio*)." [2]

At the courts of princes, in many episcopal cities and in the
monasteries they came to on their way, these wayfarers
received the help they needed and found a shelter. All such
havens were known to them ; no doubt they passed on to one
another lists of the best halting places and of generous
benefactors. They had also their special monasteries, those
monasteria Scottorum of which we have spoken, marked out by
the very title as places of refuge, the hostels in which were no
doubt well frequented.[3] Moreover, *xenodochia* or hospices
intended for travellers and pilgrims were multiplied from the
seventh century on.[4] St Bertin employed four men who
came from Britain to build a refuge for the poor and for
travellers.[5] About 725 a *xenodochium* was built at Moutiers-
en-Puisaie, south-west of Auxerre, for Britons bound on
pilgrimage to Rome.[6] The former of these establishments
was destined, like other similar institutions, for the poor and
strangers in general, the second for Britons only. Besides the
hostels of their own monasteries, the *Scotti* had other religious

---

[1] *Vita Arnoldi*, ed. Ph. Jaffé, *Bibl. rerum Germanic.*, III, p. 674 (Berolini,
1866).
[2] Widric, *Vita Gerardi*, III, 25 (Boll., *AS*, Apr., III, p. 213). Cf. IV, 31,
p. 214.
[3] *E.g.*, Waulsort (*v. sup.* § 5).
[4] Hans von Schubert, *Geschichte der christlichen Kirche im Frühmittelalter*
(Tübingen, 1921), p. 698.
[5] Folcuin, *Gesta abbatum S. Bertini* (MG. *Scr.*, XIII, p. 610) ; *Vitae
Audomari, Bertini et Winnoci*, 22 (MG. *Scr. RM*, V, p. 770).
[6] *Gesta episc. Autissiodorensium* (MG. *Scr.*, XIII, p. 395). Cf. Lupus of
Ferrières, *Ep.* 11 (MG. *Epist.*, IV, p. 21).

establishments intended for travellers of their own race and called *hospitalia Scottorum.*

Under Charlemagne and his successors the number of these charitable institutions had been multiplied ; but by the middle of the ninth century their very existence was in danger. The Irish were dispossessed of their foundations, and those who usurped the direction or administration not only refused to admit travellers who came to seek a lodging, but even drove out the monks who had been living in them for years and reduced them to beggary.

These facts are made known to us by the Council of Meaux in 845. " Moreover," we read in the fortieth canon, " the hospices of the Irish, which holy men of that race built in this kingdom and endowed with property bestowed on them because of their sanctity, have been entirely alienated from that service of hospitality ; and not only are newcomers not received in those hospices, but even the very men who from infancy have in the same places been serving the Lord in religion are sent forth and compelled to beg from door to door." [1] The council demanded that the hospices of the Scots should be reorganized and restored to their lawful owners and administrators. At this council were present Wenilo, metropolitan of Sens, Hincmar of Reims and their suffragans, Rudolph of Bourges and some other bishops. The members of the council besought the intervention of the king. The king at the time was Charles the Bald, who next to Charlemagne was the best friend the Scots had ; he did not fail to respond to the appeal, and he confirmed the measures taken at Meaux towards re-establishing the *hospitalia Scottorum.*[2]

The same beneficent episcopal intervention appears in a letter addressed by the bishops of the provinces of Reims and Rouen to Louis the German, drawn up by Hincmar of Reims in A.D. 858.[3] The bishops once more demanded that the establishments of the Scots should revert to the uses for which they were originally intended, and further, that the monarch should see to it that the administrators of these

[1] Council of Meaux (845), c. 40 (Mansi, *Concilia,* XIV, 227–28).
[2] Ed. A. Boretius and V. Krause, *MG. Leges : Sect. II. Cap.,* II, p. 408.
[3] *Epistola synodi Carisiacensis ad Hludovicum regem Germaniae directa,* 10 (*Ib.,* p. 434).

houses should submit, as was required by canons and capitularies, to the jurisdiction of the bishops, who, they added, would in return make them the objects of their most benevolent solicitude.

From the middle of the ninth century onwards, Irish monasteries and hospices were multiplied, especially outside the west Frankish kingdom. The Irishman Donatus, bishop of Fiesole (829–876), on August 20, 850, bestowed on the monastery of Bobbio the church of St. Brigid in the city of Piacenza, to which a hospice was attached where two or three pilgrims could be received.[1]

In 883 Charles the Fat erected a *monasterium Scottorum* on the Viktorsberg in Rhaetia, the very spot whither the Irish hermit Eusebius had retired twenty-nine years before. Two years later the same prince handed over the revenues of one of his villas to this monastery for the upkeep of a hospice intended to receive twelve pilgrims on their way to Rome.[2]

We know how eagerly the Scots were received at Nivelles in Brabant by the abbess Gertrude, at Hohenburg in Alsace by the abbess Odilia, at Ratisbon before their own establishments were set up in that city, and in other cloisters. They were esteemed holy men, and their knowledge, as well as the feats of penmanship which they executed with consummate skill for their hosts, made their presence welcome. At Fulda, especially during the abbotship of Richard († 1039), they were received with the utmost kindness ; a *calefactorium*, or heated room, and a dormitory were set apart for their special use, and during their stay the abbot treated them with paternal care.[3]

§ 12.—THE IRISH BENEDICTINE CONGREGATION IN GERMANY

The foundation of the abbey of St. James at Ratisbon at the end of the eleventh century opens a new era in the history of the Scottic monastic establishments on the Continent. In the

---

[1] Carlo Cipolla, *Codice diplomatico del monastero di San Colombano di Bobbio* (Roma.—Fonti per la Storia d'Italia, 1918), I, pp. 165–69.
[2] Ratpert, *Casus S. Galli* (MG. Scr., II, p. 73 ; PL, CXXVI, 1077).
[3] Marianus, *Chronicon*, col. 784.

twelfth and thirteenth centuries these monasteries displayed a vigorous activity, but they declined rapidly in the course of the two following centuries.

We know that John, one of the companions of Marianus (Muiredach mac Robartaig), did not stay at Ratisbon but went farther down the Danube valley and ended his days as a recluse at Göttweig. On his way through Melk he was able to offer prayer at the tomb which the piety of the sainted emperor Henry II had erected in honour of another Irishman, St Coloman, who was assassinated at Stockerau in 1012.[1] In our own days Coloman still has an important place in the religious folklore of the peoples of Austria and south Germany.[2] The other companion of Marianus, Candidus (or else a third companion named Clemens), pursued his journey as far as Jerusalem, where he died.

Marianus lived at first in a cell placed at his disposal by the abbess of Obermünster. Both this abbess and the abbess of Niedermünster gave a cordial welcome to the strangers ; so did the inhabitants of Ratisbon, a city which the biographer of Marianus calls " *urbs inclyta, pia mater peregrinorum praecipueque Scottorum*." [3]

The first monastery occupied by the little Irish colony was the priory of Weih-Sankt-Peter, situated outside the city walls, which was given them by the abbess of Obermünster, but soon the number of monks grew so large that it was necessary to build another.[4]

---

[1] *Vita Mariani*, III, 15 (p. 368) ; *Passio Cholomanni* (*MG. Scr.*, IV, p. 675).

[2] L.G., *Gaelic Pioneers*, pp. 143–45 ; Hoffmann-Krayer and H. Bächtold-Stäubli, *Handwörterbuch des Deutschen Aberglaubens* (Berlin and Leipzig, 1927, in progress), art. *Coloman* (*Colman*) ; *Colomanibüchlein u.-segen*.

[3] *Vita Mariani*, I, 1 (p. 365). Cf. Hugo von Walderdoff, *St. Mercherdach und St. Marian und die Anfänge der Schottenklöster zu Regensburg* (*Verhandlungen des historischen Vereins von Oberpfalz und Regensburg*, XXXIX, 1878, pp. 189–232).

[4] *Vita Mariani*, III, IV (pp. 368–69) ; Th. Ried, *Codex chronologico-diplomaticus episcopatus Ratisbonensis* (Ratisbonae, 1816), I, p. 166 (No. 178).—*Weich* (Lat. *Vicus*) wrongly interpreted " *consecratus* " (*weih*) by the *Scotti* (see above-mentioned sources and the so-called *Libellus de fundatione Consecrati Sancti Petri*, partly edited by A. Dürrwächter, *Gesta Caroli Mag.*) [Cf. D. Binchy, *The Irish Benedictine Congregation in Medieval Germany* (*Studies*, XVIII, 1929, pp. 198–99)]. Cf. Aventin, *Herkommen der Stadt Regensburg* (*Sämmtliche Werke*, ed. K. von Halm, München, 1880), I, p. 294 ; J. A. Endres, *op. cit.*, p. 12.

Marianus died in 1088. Two years later the benefactions of the Landgrave Otto, the nobles of the district and the wealthy burgesses of the town made it possible to begin the building of an abbey, which was dedicated jointly to St James the Greater and St Gertrude, and which was destined to become the most important of the Irish foundations abroad.[1]

A letter written by the infant community of St. James to Wratislaw, duke of Bohemia, has come down to us. The monks ask the prince for an escort for the messenger whom they are on the point of sending to Poland.[2] This mission was carried out. The biographer of Marianus tells us that a monk named Mauricius went to Kiev, that the king and the nobles of the country offered him valuable furs with which he loaded several carts, and that he came back safe and sound to his abbey under the protection of the traders of Ratisbon. The writer adds that the cloister and roof of the monastery were constructed with the price of these furs.[3]

The abbots of St. James also on sundry occasions sent missions to Ireland, where the abbey possessed more than one priory (among them that of Our Lady in Ros Ailithir, the modern Rosscarbery, Co. Cork). As they recruited their numbers solely from Irishmen, they had to procure novices in their own country, from which they also drew important material aid.[4]

The new abbey was consecrated by the bishop of Ratisbon in 1111.[5] Even at the present day the celebrated northern portal of the *Schottenkirche*, which has often been described,

[1] Ried, *Codex*, I, p. 171 (No. 184) ; *Vita Mariani*, IV, 16 (p. 369).
[2] B. Pez, *Thesaurus anecdotarum novissimus* (Augustae Vindel., 1729), VI, I, p. 291.
[3] *Vita Mariani*, IV, 17 (p. 369). Cf. Hogan, *The Irish Monasteries of Ratisbon* (*Irish Eccles. Record*, 1894, pp. 1015–29) ; L. Abraham, *Mnisi irlandzcy w Kijowie* (*Bulletin international de l'Académie des sciences de Cracovie. Cl. de philol., d'hist. et de philosophie*, 1901, pp. 137 ff.) ; A. Parczewski, *Poczatki chrystjanismu w Polsce i Misya Irlandska* (*Annuaire de la Société des sciences de Posen*, 1902). Cf. Louis Leger, *R. Cel.*, XXVI, 1905, p. 389) ; B. Leib, *Rome, Kiev et Byzance* (Paris, 1924), p. 90 ; M. E. Schaitan (1925), see *NA*, XLVII, 1928, pp. 288–89.
[4] *Vita Mariani*, IV, 19 (p. 369) ; W. Wattenbach, *Die Kongregation der Schottenklöster*, Engl. translat, *UJA*, VII, pp. 244–45 ; Clark, *St. Gall*, pp. 48, 50 ; Binchy, *The Irish Benedictine Congregation*, pp. 195, 200, 203.
[5] G. A. Renz, *Beiträge zur Geschichte der Schottenabtei St Jakob und des Priorates Weih St Peter in Regensburg* (*Studien und Mittheilungen aus dem Bene-dictiner-und dem Cistercienser-Orden*, XVI, 1895, pp. 64 ff).

seems to bear in its iconographic and ornamental details the stamp of mediaeval Irish art.[1]

In the twelfth century St. James of Ratisbon made several new foundations in Alemannia, Bavaria and Austria, to wit, the abbey of St. James at Würzburg (1135) ; the abbey of St. James at Erfurt (1136), founded by the count of Glisberg ; St. Giles (Aegidius) at Nuremberg (1140), founded by the emperor Conrad III ; the *Schottenkloster* of Vienna (between 1158 and 1161), founded by Henry of Babenberg, duke of Austria, and dedicated to the Holy Virgin ; and, finally, the priories of St. Nicholas at Memmingen, Holy Cross at Eichstätt and St. John at Kelheim, this last founded in 1232.[2] All these establishments collectively formed what was called the Benedictine Congregation of the *Schottenklöster*, placed under the headship of the abbot of St. James of Ratisbon,[3] who in several documents is styled " *abbas matricularius, visitator et corrector omnium monasteriorum et fratrum Scoticae* (or *Ybernicae*) *nationis in Alemania constitutorum*." [4]

In the fourteenth and fifteenth centuries the congregation declined rapidly. The fount of Irish vocations dried up by degrees ; the finances were at a low ebb ; the condition of the buildings as well as the falling off in religious observances

[1] J. Sighart, *Geschichte der bildenden Künste im Königreich Bayern* (München, 1862), I, pp. 164–66 ; Ferd. Janner, *Die Schotten in Regensburg, die Kirche zu St Jakob und deren Nordportal* (Regensburg, 1885) ; A. Michel, *Histoire de l'art* (Paris, 1906), I, II, fig. 246 ; Endres, *op. cit.;* Richard Wiebel, *Das Schottentor* (Augsburg, n.d.) ; M. Leonia Lorenz, *Das Schottenportal zu Regensburg* (Walsassen, 1929).

[2] *Vita Mariani*, v, VI (pp. 370–72). Cf. M. Wieland, *Das Schottenkloster zu St Jakob in Würzburg* (*Archiv des histor. Vereins von Unterfranken und Aschaffenburg*, XVI, 1863, pp. 1–182) ; P. J. Barry, *Die Zustände im Wiener Schottenkloster vor der Reform des Jahres* 1418 (Aichach, 1927) ; Fuhrmann, *IMM*, pp. 94–111 ; Binchy, *art. cit.*, p. 202 ; E. Hauswirth, *Abriss einer Geschichte der Benedictinerabtei U.L.F. zu den Schotten in Wien* (Wien, 1858) ; *Urkunden der Benedictinerabtei U.L.F. zu den Schotten in Wien*, 1158–1418, edited by E. Hauswirth (*Fontes rerum Austriacarum*, 2. Abteil., XVIII, Wien, 1859) ; Albert Hübl, *Die Wiener Schotten und ihr Mutterkloster St Jakob in Regensburg* (*Jahresbericht des k.k. Obergymnasiums zu den Schotten in Wien*, 1909).—On the foundation charter of the Schottenkloster in Vienna of 1158 see P. J. Barry, *A Medieval Forgery* (*The Placidian*, Washington, VII, 1930, pp. 35–48).

[3] W. Wattenbach, *Die Congregation der Schottenklöster ;* Johann Meier, *Das ehemalige Schottenkloster St Jakob in Regensburg und dessen Grundherrschaft* (Regensburg, 1910) ; Binchy, *art. cit.*, p. 203 ; Max Heimbucher, *Die Orden und Kongregationen* (Paderborn, 1907), I, pp. 258–61.

[4] Binchy, *art. cit.*, p. 203 ; Barry, *Die Zustände*, p. 20.

betokened approaching ruin.   Grave disorders arose in the monasteries.[1]   However, to judge fairly of the decadence of the *Schottenklöster* we must take into account the miseries of the age, as Dr. Binchy has done with much judgment in the following words : " No doubt there were abuses ; but whether they were more serious in the Irish than in most of the German monasteries of the time may well be doubted.   The miseries of the Great Schism, the political dissensions within the Holy Roman Empire, the ravages of famine and plague, all had contributed to a general loosening of monastic discipline, abundantly testified to by the various reform movements and ' visitations ' within the Benedictine Order right through the fifteenth century." [2]

The abbeys of Nuremberg and Vienna were the first to give up being exclusively Irish ; they passed to the German Benedictines in 1418.[3]   In 1419 the abbey of St. James at Würzburg no longer possessed a single monk.   It was taken over by German monks and joined in 1506 to the Congregation of Bursfeld.[4]

The parent house of the Congregation at Ratisbon prolonged its existence until 1515, in which year the Irish were replaced by Scotchmen.   These latter took advantage of the equivocal term *Scotti* to claim that St. James, as well as the other *Schottenklöster*, had been originally founded not by the Irish but by the Scotch.[5]   In the reign of Mary Stuart they made vain efforts to get possession of the monastery *Unserer Lieben Frau zu den Schotten* in Vienna.[6]   This abbey, still bearing the same name, is now tenanted by Austrian Benedictines. As for the abbey of St. James of Ratisbon, it continued to be a Scotch monastery till 1863, when it became the diocesan seminary.

---

[1] Binchy, *art. cit.*, pp. 205–206.   Cf. Fuhrmann, *IMM*, pp. 108–109.

[2] Binchy, *art. cit.*, p. 209.   See Trithemius, quoted by Barry, *Die Zustände*, p. 6.

[3] Barry, *Die Zustände*, p. 11 ; Hauswirth, *Abriss*, pp. 560–62, 568, 569. Cf. Hauswirth, *Urkunden* ; Hübl, *Die Wiener Schotten*.

[4] Wieland, *art. cit.*, p. 124.

[5] Wattenbach, *art. cit.* (Engl. transl. *UJA*, VII, p. 310).   See documents quoted by Bernhard Sepp, *Maria Stuart und die Deutschen Schottenklöster* (*Beitrag zur Geschichte der Renaissance und Reformation*, Festgabe Joseph Schlecht, München, 1917), pp. 312, 318.

[6] B. Sepp, *op. cit.*, pp. 311–23.

CHAPTER VI

CONTROVERSIES IN MATTERS OF DISCIPLINE

§ 1.—The Paschal Question

THE most important controversy was that concerning the date of the Easter festival. This festival is the pivot of the liturgical year, and on it depends the entire cycle of movable feasts ; so that any difference in the date of its celebration is not only to be deplored on its own account, but, moreover, throws the rest of the ecclesiastical year into confusion. Consequently, from the second century on we find the Holy See busy seeking to suppress the different views which prevailed on this question in Christendom. At the Council of Arles in 314 (at which, it will be remembered, some British bishops were present) it was decreed that Easter should be celebrated *uno die et uno tempore per omnem orbem*[1] ; this decree, however, remained a dead letter. The Council of Nicaea (325) took in hand anew the task of establishing uniformity. It declared that Easter should be celebrated throughout the world on the same Sunday, but never on the same day as the Jewish Passover. It ordained further that the festival should not be celebrated till after the vernal equinox, a practice already long adopted by the Church of Alexandria. But it left the date of the equinox indeterminate and did not lay down any method for settling the lunar and solar terms between which the date of the Paschal celebration might fluctuate.[2]

Through the necessity of making the Paschal moon (*i.e.*, the moon whose fourteenth day falls at the earliest on the equinox) agree for a series of years as closely as possible with the sun's course, the Churches were forced to change their

---

[1] Mansi, *Concilia*, II, col. 471.
[2] Cf. L. Duchesne, *La question de la Pâque au concile de Nicée* (*Revue des questions historiques*, XXVIII, 1880, pp. 5–42).

computus several times.[1]   At Rome up to the end of the third
century the 16-year cycle of St Hippolytus was followed, and
the festival of the Resurrection was arranged to fall between
the sixteenth and the twenty-second of the lunar month.
After a lapse of time, for this cycle was substituted that of
84 years (the cycle of Augustalis), according to which the
limits for the date of Easter were fixed, for the moon between
the fourteenth and the twentieth day, and for the sun between
March 25th and April 21st.   The cycle of 84 years, which was
considerably modified in 343 and 447, remained in force at
Rome and in the West until 457.   About that time appeared
the cycle of Victorius of Aquitaine, based on a period
of 532 years obtained by multiplying together the solar cycle
of 28 years and the Alexandrian lunar cycle of 19 years,
the extreme limits of Easter being the sixteenth and the
twenty-second of the lunar month.   This system remained in
use in Gaul till the end of the eighth century.   In A.D. 525
a new Easter cycle was drawn up by Dionysius Exiguus,
which was based on the Alexandrian cycle of 19 years.   In
it the equinox was fixed on March 21 and the celebration
of Easter on the Sunday which fell, on the one hand, between
the fifteenth and the twenty-first of the lunar month, and, on
the other, between March 22 and April 25.   Although
Dionysius composed his cycle in 525, there is no trace of its
having been immediately adopted by any Church, and, contrary to an accredited opinion,[2] it was not the computation
accepted by Rome under Pope Gregory the Great.   In his time
the Roman Church still adhered to the cycle of Victorius, and
this was the computus which was introduced into England in
597 by St Augustine, the envoy of Gregory the Great, and
his companions, and which the Roman missionaries, or rather
their successors, had such trouble in inducing the Celtic
Churches to adopt.[3]

It is generally received as certain that these Churches in the

---

[1] Cf. A. Giry, *Traité de diplomatique* (Paris, 1894), pp. 141–45.
[2] B. Krusch, *Die Einführung des griechischen Paschalritus im Abendlande* (*NA*,
IX, 1884, p. 114).
[3] By Reginald L. Poole the conclusion of B. Krusch is regarded as
unproved. See *The earliest Use of the Easter Cycle of Dionysius* (*EHR*, XXXIII,
1918, pp. 57–62).

sixth century followed the 84-year cycle in the form in which
Rome had observed it before 343.[1] Alfred Anscombe, however, demurs to this belief.[2] In any case, it is beyond doubt
that the insular Celts made their Easter oscillate between, on
the one hand, the fourteenth and twentieth days of the moon
inclusive [3]—an arrangement which caused the Resurrection
festival to coincide with the Jewish Passover whenever the
fourteenth day of the moon fell on a Sunday—and, on the
other, between March 25 and April 21, the spring equinox
being fixed by them on March 25.[4] Hence their Easter was
doubly faulty in nature.

The 84-year cycle had probably found its way into Great
Britain in the fourth century,[5] and had thence been introduced into Ireland before the coming of St Patrick.   It had
taken so firm a hold in the two islands that, when they learnt,
in the sixth century, of the changes which had meantime taken
place in Rome and on the Continent, it was very hard to
dislodge it ; nor could that result be attained until the
question had been repeatedly debated throughout one, two
or even three centuries, according to the locality.   We will
now proceed to relate the chief phases of this long controversy.

Pope St Gregory had placed the British bishops under the
jurisdiction of St Augustine of Canterbury.[6] Wishing to
enter into relations with them, Augustine invited them to an
interview at a place south of the Severn, since known as

---

[1] B. Krusch, *art. cit.*, pp. 143–44, 167 ; *s.a.*, *Studien*, pp. 71–72.—The use
of the cycle of 84 years is attested for the Britons by Bede, *HE*, II, 2, III, 25 ;
in Ireland, *ib.*, III, 25 ; Cummian, *DCP*, col. 975 ; for the Picts, by Bede,
HE, III, 25, V, 21.
[2] A. Anscombe, *The Paschal Canon attributed to Anatolius* (*EHR*, X, 1895,
pp. 531–33) ; *s.a. The Obit of St Columba* (London, 1893), p. 27.—According to A. A., the insular Celts used the Alexandrine computus of 19 years.
According to E. Schwartz (*Christliche und jüdische Ostertafeln* in *Abhandlungen
der k. Gesellschaft der Wissenschaften zu Göttingen*, Philol.-hist. Kl. N.F.,
VIII, 1905, p. 103), it is impossible to know which system was followed by
the islanders.
[3] Bede, *HE*, II, 2, 4, III, 25.
[4] Cf. Bede, *HE*, V, 22.   Cf. Anscombe, *art. cit.*, 1895, p. 518.
[5] G. B. de Rossi's view, according to which this cycle was introduced
into Britain by the British bishops who attended the Council of Arles of
314 (*Inscr. Christ. Urbis Romae*, I, 1857–61, p. LXXXVI), is deemed unaccept-
able by B. Krusch (*NA*, IX, p. 167).
[6] Bede, *HE*, I, 29.

Augustine's Oak (602 or 603).[1] At this gathering the archbishop of Canterbury called upon the British clergy to join
his missionaries in the work of evangelizing the Saxons and
asked them to renounce their erroneous Paschal cycle as well as
the other faulty practices which they held. A long discussion
followed ; neither Augustine's exhortations nor entreaties
availed to bend the stubborn Britons. They refused point-
blank to collaborate with the Roman missionaries in the conversion of their deadly enemies. In spite of a miraculous cure
wrought under their very eyes, so Bede tells us, by the Roman
prelate, they declared they could not renounce their ancient
customs without consulting their brethren. Accordingly, it
was decided that the parties should meet again soon after.

Before agreeing to this second conference with Augustine,
seven British bishops, accompanied by learned men belonging
for the most part to the celebrated monastery of Bangor-is-
Coed, went to get the advice of a holy anchorite on the decision to be adopted. When subsequently the Britons presented
themselves before the archbishop, the latter, who was seated,
did not rise from his seat. The susceptible Celts were deeply
wounded. Guided by the oracle given them by the anchorite,
they saw in his behaviour a mark of arrogance ; they were
moved to wrath and refused more emphatically than ever to
come to an agreement. This second meeting took place before
the year 605.[2]

On the death of St Augustine on May 12, 605, Laurentius,
his successor in the see of Canterbury, in concert with Mellitus,
bishop of London, and Justus, bishop of Rochester, made
new overtures by means of a letter to the British clergy. But
this attempt was as vain as the previous ones. In the year
731, the time when the Venerable Bede (to whom we owe our
knowledge of these facts) was writing, the Britons still remained
obdurate.[3]

Another letter from Laurentius and the same two bishops,

[1] Bede, *HE*, II, 2.—The identification of the spot with the modern Aust
(Gloucester) put forward by Lloyd, *HW*, I, pp. 174–75 does not seem
conclusive to E. MacClure, *British Place-Names in their historical Setting*
(London, 1910), pp. 163–67.
[2] Bede, *HE*, II, 2.
[3] Bede, *HE*, II, 4.

written between 605 and 617 to the bishops and abbots of Ireland, shows that the clergy of that island clung to the same peculiarities of ritual as the Britons and were as little anxious to enter into relations with the Anglo-Saxon Church. " Before reaching Britain," said this letter, " we held in equal reverence Britons and Scots. But we have since learnt, from bishop Dagan, on his passage through Britain, and from the abbot Columban who is a sojourner in Gaul, that in respect of discipline the Scots differ in nothing from the Britons. On his arrival here this bishop Dagan disdained not only to eat at our table, but even under the same roof with us." [1]

In Gaul Columban had found the canon of Victorius of Aquitaine in full sway. [2] He was determined to abide by the custom he had followed at Bangor. The Burgundian bishops were shocked at seeing Luxeuil celebrate Easter at a date different from their own, especially when the fourteenth day of the Paschal moon fell on a Sunday and the Irish unblushingly celebrated the Resurrection of the Saviour on that very day. In their eyes Columban was neither more nor less than a Quartodeciman. [3] To defend himself the abbot of Luxeuil resolved to write to Pope St Gregory the Great (c. 595/600). In his letter he asserted that he took his stand on the authority of Anatolius of Laodicea, whose work on Easter had, he said, been quoted by Eusebius of Caesarea and praised by St Jerome, the oracle of the West. [4] Anatolius, bishop of Laodicea, in the third century, had, as a matter of fact, treated of the Paschal computus, but with conclusions as remote as possible from the views held by the Scots. The work to which Columban had appealed was an apocryphal treatise issued under the name of Anatolius, a forgery executed in the British Isles less than fifty years previously in order to support the insular theory about Easter. [5] The computation of the

---

[1] Bede, ib. For the date of the letter see Kenney, Sources, I, p. 219.
[2] Columban, Ep. 1 (MG. Epist., III, pp. 156–60). Cf. Giry, op. cit., p. 114 ; J. Schmid, Die Osterfestberechnung auf den britischen Inseln (Regensburg, 1904), pp. 24–31 ; L. Duchesne, L' Église au sixième siècle (Paris, 1925), p. 544.
[3] Columban, op. cit., pp. 157–58.
[4] Columban, op. cit., pp. 156–57.
[5] L. Duchesne, l. cit.—The Pseudo-Anatolian Paschal treatise has been edited by B. Krusch, Studien, pp. 311–25. On that forgery see B. Mac-

Pseudo-Anatolius does indeed bear superficially the stamp of the 19-year cycle, but is really based on that of 84 years ; it recognizes the same lunar terms for Easter as the Celts and, like them, fixes the equinox on March 25.[1] As for the canon of Victorius, which makes Easter fall between the sixteenth and the twenty-second days of the moon and authorizes the celebration of the festival as early as March 23 or 24, it was, according to Columban, a faulty and reprehensible amalgamation. For how, he asks, can the triumph of Christ over death, a work of the Light, be commemorated after the twentieth day of the lunar period, when the moon no longer rises till the second half of the night and consequently darkness prevails over light ? For this reason he calls the Easter of his opponents an " Easter of darkness." On the other hand, since the equinox falls on March 25, to celebrate Easter on the 23rd or 24th is to celebrate the Resurrection before the Passion, for it is an established fact that Jesus died after the vernal equinox.[2] This is the reason, adds the abbot of Luxeuil, why the canon of Victorius has never been accepted by our Irish doctors, philosophers, mathematicians and learned scholars, who have condemned it, believing it to be absurd.[3]

However, if the Victorian computus had not found favour in Celtic lands before St Columban left Ireland, it was not slow in gaining acceptance there in certain quarters. The *Catalogue of the Saints* tells us that among the different systems of calculation in vogue between 598 and 665, that which fixed the first lunar term on the sixteenth (namely, the cycle of Victorius) had its adherents [4] ; and this testimony is confirmed by Cummian about 632.[5] The Briton who in the eighth century compiled the *Historia Brittonum* also used the cycle of Victorius in fixing his dates.[6]

Carthy, *AU*, IV, pp. cxviii–cxxvii ; Mario Esposito, *PADM*, p. 200 ; *s.a.* *Latin Learning*, I, pp. 233–34. On this and other forgeries in relation to the Paschal controversy see Kenney, *Sources*, I, p. 217.

[1] Krusch, *Studien*, p. 315 ; Schmid, *Die Osterfestberechnung*, p. 9.

[2] Columban, *l. cit.*—Malnory (*Quid Luxov.*, p. 8) points out the existence of an old festival of the Passion fixed on March 25.

[3] On the passage see Esposito, *Latin Learning*, I, pp. 234–35.

[4] " Alii enim Resurrectionem xiv. luna vel xvi. cum duris intentionibus celebrabant " (*Catalogus*, p. 293). Cf. Krusch, *NA*, IX, p. 152.

[5] Cummian, *DCP*, col. 969.

[6] Nennius, *HB*, 31, 46 (pp. 172, 209). Cf. Schmid, *op. cit.*, p. 31.

If the arguments employed by Columban were not all of the highest value, the tone of his letter was that of a man warmly convinced of the truth of the cause he was defending. He laid it, so to speak, as a duty on the Pope to decide in its favour. To his letter he added a memorandum ; but neither letter nor memorandum ever reached the person to whom they were addressed. The Irish monk wrote two other letters on the Paschal question, one to the Gaulish bishops assembled in council at Chalon-sur-Saône in 603 to discuss his case, the other to a pope whom he does not name, probably Sabinian (604–606). His tone in both these letters is less vehement ; the controversialist finally contents himself with asking that he may be suffered to live in peace in his desert, holding by the traditions of his forerunners in respect of Easter observances.[1] We know neither the decrees of the Council of Chalon nor the answer of the pope.

If St Patrick had become accustomed to the cycle in use on the Continent at the time of his wanderings there, he does not seem to have introduced it into Ireland, or at any rate to have succeeded in establishing it there. Already in his time Ireland was in possession of the " old style " cycle of 84 years, such as it had been before the changes made in 343.[2] It remained dominant throughout the entire island till about the year 632. At that time the south of Ireland, first of all Celtic territories, went over to the orthodox Easter under circumstances which we will proceed to relate.

Certain individuals (or communities) began by adopting the cycle of 532 years.[3] Why that cycle (the Victorian one) instead of the cycle of Dionysius ? Apparently because the latter had not yet been adopted by Rome, for, as we have seen, the Victorian system remained in use there until about the middle of the seventh century.[4] It is at the synod of Whitby in 664 that we first find the Dionysian reckoning

---

[1] Columban, *Epp.* 2, 3 (pp. 160–65).

[2] Cummian writes : " Primum illum [cyclum] quem sanctus Patricius papa noster tulit et f[e]cit, in quo luna a XIV. usque in XXI. regulariter et aequinoctium a XII. kl. Apr. observatur " (*DCP*, col. 975). On this passage and other errors in Cummian's treatise see Esposito, *Latin Learning*, I, pp. 240–45, and Kenney, *Sources*, I, pp. 220–21.

[3] Cummian, *DCP*, col. 969.

[4] See Poole, *art. cit.*, pp. 58–59 ; Kenney, *Sources*, I, p. 215.

formally brought forward as the orthodox Roman computation by Wilfrid.[1]

Cummian, our chief authority in the matter, tells us, in his treatise *De controversia paschali*, that he, for his part, before accepting this innovation, determined to devote a year to the study of the question. During that period he searched the Scriptures, studied the computus, consulted with his elders, the men who had succeeded Saints Ailbe of Emly, Ciarán of Clonmacnois, Brendan of Birr, Nessan of Mungret and Lugaid (or Molua) of Clonfertmulloe, and finally persuaded his fellow-clergy to assemble in synod on the plain of Lene (or Mag Léna), probably not far from Birr.[2] There it was agreed that in the following year Easter should be celebrated simultaneously with the universal Church. But shortly after the synod an adversary arose, " a whitewashed wall " (*paries dealbatus*), as Cummian charitably styles him, who, under pretext of respect for tradition, renewed the dissensions and frustrated the decision which had been made. Then, to put an end to the conflict, some discreet and humble-minded persons were sent as deputies to Rome.[3] They did not return for three years and announced that in the Eternal City they had witnessed a spectacle of unity which had deeply impressed them. In St. Peter's they had seen, gathered together in the celebration of a common Easter, a Greek, a Hebrew, a Scythian and an Egyptian, and these people, whose testimony had been confirmed by miracles wrought under their eyes, had declared to them that the whole world commemorated the Resurrection on the same date as Rome. As it happened, the Irish that year were celebrating the festival at an entire month's interval.

Cummian, who has furnished us with all these details, does not tell us the year in which this remarkable divergence occurred ; but we may perhaps determine it. The *De*

---

[1] Bede, *HE*, III, 25 ; Stephen, *Vita Wilfridi*, 10 (p. 203). Cf. Poole, *art. cit.*, p. 60.

[2] Cf. B. MacCarthy, *AU*, IV, p. cxxxviii.—" A plain in Offaley, around Durrow " (Kenney, *Sources*, I, p. 220).

[3] In accordance with the synodal decree, that major causes should be referred to the chief of cities. Cf. *Hibernensis*, xx, 5 *b* (p. 61) and *Liber Angeli* (*LA*, p. 42).

controversia paschali is a letter addressed jointly to Segéne, abbot of Iona, and Beccán the solitary, with the purpose of bringing them round to the canonical celebration. Segéne was abbot from 623 to 652. During that period [1] there was only one year in which Easter was celebrated in Rome and in Ireland at a month's interval, the year 631. As the journey of the Irish mission was prolonged till the third year after it had set out, we may fix the synod of Mag Léna in 628 or 629 and assign the approximate date of 632 to Cummian's letter. [2]

The southern Irish seem to have been led to entertain doubts as to the correctness of their Easter by the letter of Laurentius of Canterbury, written about 615, and still more by a letter of Pope Honorius I (625–638). The Pope exhorted the little Scottic Church, situated on the confines of the inhabited world, not to consider themselves wiser in their calculations than the Churches of Christ, both ancient and modern, established throughout the universe. [3] We meet with the same reflection from the pen of Cummian. " Rome," he says ironically, " is mistaken ; Jerusalem is mistaken ; Antioch is mistaken ; the whole world is mistaken ; the Britons and the Scots alone hold the truth." [4] It happened that in 628 by a harmonious coincidence Easter fell at Rome on the same day as in the British Isles, March 27. The Pope perhaps took advantage of this fortunate circumstance to inculcate permanent uniformity in the future. [5] In any case, it is certain that the south of Ireland had completely submitted by the second quarter of the seventh century, for Bede, speaking of Aidan of Lindisfarne (bishop from 635 to 651), who never gave up the cycle of 84 years, takes care to tell us that the Scots of southern Ireland had since then learnt

---

[1] And even a few years earlier, in the event of these facts happening before Segéne's abbotship. At all events, Cummian seems to have penned his letter immediately after the return of the Irish delegation. Cf. B. Mac-Carthy, p. CXL.

[2] Here is the tentative chronology given by Kenney, *Sources*, I, p. 221 : Epistle of Pope Honorius written, 628 ; arrival in Ireland, 628-629 ; synod of Mag Léna, 629-630 ; delegates set out, 630 ; in Rome, 631 ; returned, 632 ; letter of Cummian, 632-633.

[3] Bede, *HE*, II, 19.

[4] Cummian, *DCP*, col. 974. Cf. col. 972.

[5] For the date of this letter see C. Plummer's note, Bede, *HE*, Vol. II, p. 125.

to celebrate according to the canonical practice, thanks to the exhortations of the Holy See : *ad admonitionem apostolicae sedis antistitis Pascha canonico ritu observare didicerunt*.[1]

About the same time as the synod of Mag Léna another conference was held at Magh Ailbe, *in campo albo* (on the borders of the present counties of Carlow and Kildare). There a discussion took place between Laisrén (or Molaisse), abbot of Leighlin (or Lethglenn, Co. Carlow) and Fintan (or Munnu), abbot of Taghmon (Co. Wexford), the former holding by the new system " lately brought from Rome," the latter by the old one.   The result of this conference cannot be clearly ascertained.   The hagiographer says : *Postea consentientes populi cum sanctis ad sua reversi sunt*.[2]   That is to say, finally the two saints and all present at the meeting professed themselves of the same opinion.   But was it the opinion of Laisrén or that of Munnu which triumphed ?   We cannot tell.

The clergy of the north of Ireland had addressed a letter to the Holy See explaining the reasons why they did not deem it fit to imitate the southerners.   This letter reached Rome in 640.   Pope Severinus had just died and the answer was dispatched by the archpresbyter Hilary, before the consecration of John IV, the pontiff elect, and with his approval. In this missive the Easter of the fourteenth lunar day was sternly condemned and the northern Irish were ordered to adopt the Dionysian computus [3]—a command which remained fruitless.

It was during the rule of abbot Segéne that Aidan left Iona to found Lindisfarne.   He introduced among the Angles the Paschal cycle to which his abbot and his brother monks had remained faithful [4] ; and, following his example, his successor, Finan, maintained it firmly.   But during his episcopacy opposition began to spring up in England, thanks to one of his compatriots, a certain Ronan, who was an ardent

---

[1] Bede, *HE*, III, 3.
[2] *Vita Munnu*, 26, 27 (*VSH*, II, p. 236).   Cf. *Sal. ASH*, cols. 409–11, 501–502.
[3] Bede, *HE*, II, 19.   Cf. Poole, *art. cit.*, pp. 59–60 ; Kenney, *Sources*, I, p. 223.
[4] Bede, *HE*, III, 3, 17.

partisan of the orthodox Easter. Ronan had studied in Gaul and at Rome and had abjured the error of the Scots. In Northumbria he succeeded in converting to his views a large number of dissentients ; he even engaged in a somewhat bitter controversy with Finan, without however succeeding in shaking the bishop's convictions.[1]

In 661 Colmán succeeded to the see of Lindisfarne. The controversy now entered on its acute and decisive stage. The settlement was precipitated by the zeal, enterprise and resolution of the famous Wilfrid. A Northumbrian by birth, Wilfrid had entered Lindisfarne at the age of fourteen.[2] During his youth he knew and practised only the discipline of the Scots. But having heard the orthodoxy of their customs called in question, he wished to come to a clear issue on the subject and set out to study ecclesiastical rules and traditions abroad. He went to Lyons, thence to Rome, stayed a second time for three years at Lyons, and returned in 658 to England. In 661 he received from his friend and patron Aldfrid, son of the king of Northumbria, the monastery of Ripon. The Scottic monks had deserted it, choosing to take refuge in Melrose rather than celebrate the Roman Easter.[3]

Wilfrid had in the course of his travels become convinced that the Scots were in error on the question of Easter as well as of the tonsure, and on his return set to work to eradicate their customs from his country. He felt assured of being upheld in his campaign by numerous adherents ; Romanus, chaplain of the queen of Northumbria, the deacon James, who had been left at York by the Roman bishop Paulinus on his departure in 633, Tuda, a bishop who had come from southern Ireland, Agilbert, former bishop of Dorchester and future bishop of Paris, by whom Wilfrid had himself been ordained, and others had determined to lend him their support. Moreover, the champion of the Roman customs counted on some warm friends at court, notably Aldfrid and Queen Eanfled, who had been instructed in the faith by Paulinus.

---

[1] Bede, *HE*, III, 25.
[2] Stephen, *Vita Wilfridi*, 2 (pp. 194–95).
[3] Bede, *HE*, v, 19 ; *s.a. Vita Cuthberti*, 8 (*PL*, XCIV, 744).

King Oswy, a spiritual disciple of the Scots, was, it is true, in favour of Colmán, bishop of Lindisfarne, but he was eager for uniformity. The inconvenience due to ritual divergence had been recently manifested at court in a very striking manner. On the very day when the king was holding the Easter festival, the queen and her followers were only celebrating Palm Sunday.[1] To make an end of the matter, it was decided to open a conference in which the opinions of both parties should be thoroughly discussed.

At Whitby, in the celebrated monastery of Abbess Hilda, this conference took place in 664. There, with Oswy as president, met together Wilfrid and Colmán with their respective partisans.[2] At the very opening of the discussion, the king put the question concisely : whether the Roman or the Scottic tradition about the observance of Easter was the true one ? Colmán was the first to state his case. He held, he said, his customs from his forerunners, Columba and the successors of Columba, men eminent for their holiness and their miracles. Could they have been victims of an error on the question ? He also claimed on his side Anatolius, a holy man, who had fixed the limits of the festival on the fourteenth and the twentieth days of the moon. Was anything to be found in the divine Law or the holy Gospels opposed to that teaching ? For that matter, the system went back to St John himself, the apostle who rested his head on the Saviour's breast.[3]

Wilfrid spoke next. The Easter which he defended was that of Rome, Italy and Gaul, a fact which he had himself ascertained in the course of his travels. Further, he had learnt that Africa, Asia, Egypt and Greece observed no other. The Irish alone and their abettors the Britons and the Picts, inhabitants of the remotest parts of these islands, had the hardihood to hold out against the rest of the world. Anatolius, Wilfrid admitted, was a very holy, learned, and worthy man ; but what had the Scottic practice in common with his cycle ? The Anatolian cycle was one of 19 years, theirs one of 84.

[1] Bede, *HE*, III, 25.
[2] Bede, *HE*, III, 25, 26 ; Stephen, *Vita Wilfridi*, 10 (pp. 202–204).
[3] Cf. Stephen, *Vita Wilfridi*, 10 (p. 203). Cf. Pseudo-Anatolius, *Liber de ratione paschali*, 7, ed. Krusch, *Studien*, p. 321.

Anatolius did indeed give the fourteenth and twentieth days of the lunar month as the limits within which the festival might fall, but he was speaking after the manner of the Egyptians, to whom these numbers really meant the fifteenth and the twenty-first. The Scots had so little understood this that they actually went so far as to celebrate Easter on the thirteenth day. As for Columba and his successors, they were undoubtedly very holy men, but they were mistaken. They had certainly acted in good faith ; if anyone had been there to deliver them from their error and show them the fallacies in their calculations, they would no doubt have reformed their customs. Colmán had no longer their excuse and he sinned in obstinately resisting the commands of the Holy See. Columba was a saint and wrought miracles, that was beyond dispute ; but was it lawful to set him up against St Peter, to whom the Lord had said : " Thou art Peter and upon this rock (*super hanc petram*) I will build my Church, and the gates of hell shall not prevail against it ; and I will give thee the keys of the kingdom of heaven ? "

On hearing these words of the Gospel text, Oswy was impressed and asked Colmán if he acknowledged that Christ had really uttered them. On the bishop's replying in the affirmative, the king asked him if he could bring forward a text giving equal powers to St Columba. This was an embarrassing challenge. Colmán replied simply that he could not bring forward any such text. Whereupon Oswy closed the debate by saying that St Peter was a custodian of the keys whom he would take good care not to oppose, lest, when he appeared at the gate of Paradise, he should find none to open to him.[1] The king, the majority of the assembly, and Bishop Cedd himself, who had been raised to the episcopacy by the Scots and who on this occasion acted as interpreter to both parties, ranged themselves on Wilfrid's side.

The Irish monks and about thirty Northumbrians of the Lindisfarne community remained faithful to Colmán's teaching. Finding himself defeated, Colmán asked Oswy to

[1] Bede observes that the debate on the form of the tonsure was equally animated at Whitby (*HE*, iii, 26).

nominate his successor, since he was resolved to return to Ireland ; and, at his suggestion, Eata, abbot of Melrose, was appointed. After this he went back to Lindisfarne, where he took some of the bones of St Aidan, and with his band of faithful disciples departed to Iona.[1] From Iona they sailed to Inishboffin, an island situated off the coast of Mayo. There, about 675, Colmán ended his days.[2]

We can readily forgive both Colmán and Columban for cleaving so faithfully to an archaism. No doubt they both believed up to the end that they possessed the true tradition. There is something pathetic in the figure of the Irish monk, vanquished but unyielding, who departs, laden with the venerated relics of a saint of his race, to seek in the land of his forefathers the right of preserving the discipline bequeathed by them, a discipline which for him might be said to form an integral part of the faith.

Like his predecessors Oswald and Oswy, Aldfrid, who ascended the throne of Northumbria in 685, had in his early youth been in exile among the Scots. During that time he had known Adamnán, the ninth abbot of Iona (679–704), and had even been his pupil.[3] On account of their old relations, the abbot was charged with two embassies to the king, in 686 and 688.[4] He was cordially received by Aldfrid, and on the second occasion made a rather long sojourn in his states, during which he visited the celebrated monastery of Jarrow, of which Ceolfrid was abbot. Ceolfrid, a zealous worker in the cause of ritual uniformity, did not fail in the course of their interviews to tackle his Irish colleague on the subjects of Easter and the tonsure ; and with such efficacy as to succeed in converting him. When Adamnán returned to his monastery, he became in his turn the advocate of the canonical practice among his monks, without however inducing them to adopt it. He was more successful in Ireland. He had occasion to go there in 697 to bring his

[1] Bede, *HE*, iii, 26.
[2] Bede, *HE*, iv, 4. See C. Plummer's notes, Vol. II, pp. 210–11.
[3] *V. sup.* ch. v, § 2.
[4] Bede, *HE*, iv, 26 ; v, 15, 21.

campaign against military service for women to a conclusion.[1] He took advantage of his stay, which seems to have been prolonged to the year of his death (704), to preach the adoption of the orthodox Easter. The whole north of Ireland accepted the reform, save only the " family of Columba."

In Iona and its affiliated monasteries the reform was not brought about till 716. Their final conversion was due to Egbert, a holy man who had long studied in Ireland and remained much attached to the Scots.[2] Bede relates that this much revered person lived for thirteen years at Iona, until his death in 729. He died on Easter Day, the eighth of the calends of May (April 24), a day on which before that time the Resurrection of the Saviour had never been commemorated at Iona.[3]

In 710 Naiton, or Nechtan, king of the Picts, suspecting the disciplinary practices introduced by the Scottic missionaries into his country to be faulty, sent to Ceolfrid, abbot of Jarrow, a deputation commissioned, in the first place, to get enlightenment on the questions of Easter and the tonsure, and, in the second, to procure him architects capable of building a stone church *iuxta morem Romanorum*. We do not know whether the abbot of Jarrow was able to get architects for the Pictish king, but it is certain that he willingly bestowed the desired canonical instructions. In a lengthy letter addressed to Naiton he commends him for his religious zeal, indicates the foundations in Scripture and tradition on which the canon of Dionysius Exiguus was based, and concludes by telling how he has led Abbot Adamnán back to the straight path and how Adamnán on his part, despite his reverse at Iona, has laboured successfully to convert his fellow-countrymen of Ireland.[4]

This letter dispelled all Naiton's doubts. He caused it to be

---

[1] The provisions for this reform were laid down in the tract called *Law of Adamnán* (*Cáin Adamnáin*), edited by Kuno Meyer (*Anecdota Oxoniensia*, Med. & Modern Ser., XII, Oxford, 1905).

[2] Bede, *HE*, III, 27.

[3] Bede, *HE*, v, 22.

[4] Bede, *HE*, v, 21.—In an eleventh-century catalogue of the library of the abbey of St. Oyan (Saint-Claude, Dept. Jura, France), Ceolfrid's letter is mentioned, *Item insignis epistola Teolfridi abbatis de pascha* (L. Delisle, *Le Cabinet des manuscrits*, Paris, 1881, III, p. 387).

translated and published, and enjoined his clergy to conform to its regulations. Clerics and monks without more ado adopted the so-called Roman tonsure. The cycle of 84 years was done away with and replaced by that of 19. A further result, which is recorded in the Annals, was the banishment beyond the Grampian Mountains of all monks in communion with Iona who had not yet been won over to the new discipline.[1]

The Britons were the last to hold out stubbornly in the practice of the ancient Celtic customs. Those of Strathclyde separated politically from the Britons of the south since the battle of Chester (c. 615), were bound soon to follow the example of their neighbours, the Northumbrians, Scots and Picts.[2] Those of Cornwall submitted at the beginning of the eighth century. Their conversion was the consequence of a letter which St Aldhelm, abbot of Malmesbury and later bishop of Sherborne, had, at the request of an English synod,[3] addressed to Geraint, king of Dumnonia and the clergy of that region in A.D. 705. " Your priests," wrote Aldhelm, " follow the 19-year cycle of Anatolius or rather the 84-year one of Sulpicius Severus ; they keep the Paschal feast along with the Jews on the fourteenth day of the moon. But the Roman pontiffs recognize neither of these cycles, nor yet that of Victorius of 532 years ; and those who celebrate the Resurrection on the fourteenth are to be condemned on the same grounds as that heretical and excommunicated sect known as the *Tessareskaedecaditae*." [4] In addition, the abbot attacks the Celtic tonsure, calling it the tonsure of Simon Magus and opposing it to the tonsure of St Peter. Finally, he complains

---

[1] *AU*, a.a. 716 ; *AT*, p. 225.

[2] Bede, *HE*, v, 15. Cf. Acts of Council held in Rome, A.D. 721, the signatures of which include the names of " Sedulius episcopus Britanniae de genere Scottorum " and " Fergustus episcopus Scotiae Pictus " (*CED*, II, pp. 6–7). Cf. Kenney, *Sources*, I, p. 223.

[3] Bede, *HE*, v, 18.

[4] " Quod tessereskaedecaditae vocatur id est quartadecimani, eo quod quarta decima luna cum Iudeis Christum blasphemantibus et margaritas evangelii ritu porcorum calcantibus paschae solemnitatem peragunt " (Aldhelm, *Ep.* 4, ed. R. Ehwald, *MG. Auct. ant.*, XV, pp. 483–84). Cf. Isidore, *Orig.*, VIII, 5, 61 ; Cummian, *DCP*, col. 976.—On Geraint see *Two of the Saxon Chronicles parallel*, ed. C. Plummer I, 42, II, 36 ff. ; F. Lot in *Romania*, XXV, 1896, p. 10.

of the conduct of the priests of Demetia (South Wales), the region beyond the Severn, who persisted in their refusal to worship in the same church or sit at the same table with a Saxon.[1] In spite of its grandiloquent style and many inaccuracies of detail, the letter to Geraint succeeded in bringing over numerous Christians of Cornwall to the orthodox tonsure and Easter observance.[2]

The Welsh, on the contrary, did not consent to adopt the reforms till the second half of the eighth century. The northern Welsh were the first to yield, thanks to the endeavours of Elfodd († 809), to whom the *Annales Cambriae* give the title of " chief bishop in the land of Gwynedd." According to the same Annals, the reform took place in the year 768.[3]

§ 2.—THE CELTIC TONSURE

Another cause of hot dispute between the Anglo-Saxon and the Celtic clergy was the particular form of tonsure which the latter insisted on retaining.

It does not appear that any tonsure was adopted by clerics and monks before the fourth century. Up to that time they were only charged not to wear their hair too long.[4] Probably monks were the first to shave their heads, following the example of the Nazarites, and in imitation of them the secular clergy adopted the practice of tonsuring.[5] The primitive tonsure was the so-called tonsure of St Paul, the complete tonsure, which was preserved in the East as late as the seventh century.[6] The tonsure of St Peter, which consisted in leaving only a circle of hair around the shaven

---

[1] Aldhelm, *Ep.* 4 (pp. 482, 484).

[2] Bede, *HE*, v, 18.—On some traces of heterodoxy in Cornwall in the tenth century, *v. inf.*, ch. XI, § 7.

[3] *AC*, pp. 162, 163. Nennius was a disciple of Elfodd (*HB*, p. 143), whom he calls " episcoporum sanctissimus " (p. 207). Elfodd is styled bishop of Bangor by late writers only (*Gwentian Brut*, *a.a.* 755 ; *Iolo* MSS., 117, 127), who could not imagine an " archi episcopus guenedote regione " (*AC*, *l. cit.*) seated in any other place. Cf. Lloyd, *HW*, I, p. 204, note 43.

[4] See notice on Pope Anicetus († *c.* 153) in the *Liber Pontificalis* and L. Duchesne's note thereon (Paris, 1886, I, p. 134).

[5] See Smith's dissertation, *De tonsura clericorum*, an appendix to Bede's edit. of *HE* in Migne (*PL*, XCV, 327–32) and Hauck, art. *Tonsur* in *Realencyclopädie für protestantische Theologie und Kirche* (1907).

[6] Bede, *HE*, IV, 1.

head, is not recorded before the sixth century. St Gregory of Tours († 595) is the first to mention it.[1] It was the tonsure worn by Pope St Gregory the Great [2] and introduced into England by St Augustine and his companions.

These latter were scandalized on beholding the odd fashion in which the Celtic monks cut their hair. With regard to this Celtic tonsure, two opinions have obtained among modern writers. Some hold that the forepart of the head, in front of a line drawn from one ear to the other, was completely shaved, whilst behind this line the hair was left to grow in abundance.[3] According to others, the Celtic clergy did indeed wear their hair long behind, but the forepart of the head was not wholly denuded, for a semicircle of hair ran from ear to ear above the forehead.[4] This latter view appears to me the more likely.

The most explicit statement on the subject is furnished by the letter of Ceolfrid to king Naiton already referred to. Unlike the greater number of the contemporary writers who speak of the Celtic tonsure, Ceolfrid had seen it with his own eyes in his meetings with Adamnán as well, no doubt, as with the envoys of the Pictish king.[5] Having enlightened the abbot of Iona on his erroneous Paschal observance, he had likewise undertaken to make him renounce his incorrect tonsure. With this aim he addressed him in figurative style : " I ask thee, holy brother, thou who aspirest to the ever-lasting crown of life, why dost thou persist in bearing on thy head, in contradiction to thy faith, the semblance of an imperfect crown ? " Then, addressing Naiton, to whom he is relating the conversation, the abbot proceeds to describe this tonsure, which in his opinion is none other than the tonsure

---

[1] *Vitae Patrum*, xvii, 1, ed. Krusch (*MG. Scr. RM*, I, p. 728). Cf. Thomassin, *Ancienne et nouvelle discipline de l' Église* (Paris, 1725), I, cols. 714 ff.

[2] John the Deacon, *Vita Gregorii*, iv, 84 (*PL*, LXXV, 230).

[3] The following adhere to that opinion : Varin, *Mémoire*, p. 161 ; J. H. Todd, *Saint Patrick*, p. 67 ; C. Plummer, Bede, *HE*, Vol. II, p. 354.

[4] This opinion has been supported by Smith, Appendix to Bede's *HE* (*PL*, XCV, cols. 317–27) ; Daniel Rock, *Church of Our Fathers* (London, 1903), I, pp. 144–46 ; Loofs, *Antiquae Britonum Scotorumque Ecclesiae quales fuerint mores*, p. 21 ; William Bright, *The Roman See and the early Church* (London, 1896), p. 414 ; B. Krusch in *MG. Scr. RM*, IV, p. 6.—The matter has been dealt with in a particularly convincing manner by John Dowden in *An Examination of original Documents on the Question of the Form of the Celtic Tonsure* (*PSAS*, 1895–96, pp. 325–37).

[5] *V. sup.* § 1.

of Simon Magus : " In front thou dost indeed see a sort of crown ; but look behind and thou wilt perceive that it is an incomplete one (*decurtatam eam, quam tu videre putabas, invenies coronam*)." [1] Evidently the Celtic tonsure, viewed in front, had the appearance of a crown or circle, but it was only a semicircle.

Other upholders of the Roman customs, Aldhelm of Malmesbury and also the compilers of the Irish Collection of canons (the latter on the authority of a text which they believed to be by Gildas), attribute the origin of the Celtic tonsure to Simon Magus. [2] But, according to a statement attributed by the aforementioned Collection to St Patrick, the first individual to wear it in Ireland was the swineherd of king Loegaire [3]—another statement hardly flattering to the dissentients.

St Columban, as may be readily imagined, did not renounce his tonsure any more than his Easter when he crossed the seas [4] ; but we have no proof that he succeeded in imposing it on his continental followers.

From a portrait of St Mummolinus of Noyon it has been held that that bishop must have adopted the insular fashion of cutting the hair. But the Celtic tonsure, if such as we take it to have been, does not appear in this portrait. [5]

The British emigrants, for their part, retained the insular tonsure in Brittany. It remained in vogue in Landévennec

---

[1] Bede, *HE*, v, 21.

[2] Aldhelm, *Ep.* 4 *ad Geruntium* (*MG. Auct. ant.*, XV, p. 482) ; *Hibernensis*, LII, 6 (pp. 212–13). It is noteworthy that Adamnán, in his discussions with Ceolfrid, does not seem to have questioned the Simonian origin of his tonsure. For the tonsure as well as for the Easter calculation the Irish claimed also the authority of St John (J. O'Donovan, *Three Fragments*, Dublin, 1860, p. 112).—On the tonsure of Simon Magus and his followers, who " caput radebant et ab aure usque ad aurem per medium caput quasi plateam (unde adhuc vulgo *platta* dicitur)," see Honorius Augustodunesis, *Gemma animae*, I, 196 (*PL*, CLXXII, 603).

[3] ". . . priorem autem auctorem huius tonsurae in Hibernia subulcum regis Loigairi filii Neili extitisse Patricii sermo testatur, ex quo Hibernenses pene omnes hanc tonsuram sumpserunt " (*Hibernensis, l. cit.*). On the swineherd Cass Macc Glais resuscitated and baptized by Patrick and reinterred see *Vita Trip.*, 122–23 ; Tirechán, p. 27.

[4] Jonas, *Vita Col.*, II, 9 (p. 126).

[5] A reproduction of this portrait may be seen in *MG. Scr. RM*, V, Pl. 20. See the conclusions of B. Krusch and W. Levison thereupon (*ib.*, pp. 417, 734).

down to the year 818.[1] Those who settled in Galicia
propagated it in that territory, but the fathers of the fourth
Council of Toledo, held in 633, viewed it with disfavour and
demanded its suppression. The terms in which they describe
the tonsure they condemned are not indeed very precise ; the
clerics of Galicia would seem to have worn long hair like the
laity, contenting themselves with shaving a small circle on the
crown of the head.[2] But the Celtic tonsure may easily have
undergone some change when transported to such a distance
and in a foreign Church. The description given by the fathers
of Toledo may be clumsily expressed or even intentionally
exaggerated ; even as it stands, it fits in fairly well with the
very explicit text of Ceolfrid.

What was the origin of the Celtic tonsure ? It was probably
of insular invention. The druids of Ireland wore a tonsure.[3]
According to one manuscript of the *Hibernensis*, they shaved
even the forepart of the head *de aure ad aurem*, except for a tuft
of hair allowed to grow on the forehead.[4] As Simon was the
magician or druid *par excellence* and, moreover, the father of all
heresies, we can well conceive that the orthodox party did not
hesitate to make him responsible for the tonsure they con-
temned.[5] Doubtless, however, the tonsure was not the
exclusive privilege of the druids. It was very likely affected
by certain other classes of ancient Celtic society ; the Breton
warriors of Weroch were shaven.[6] It is probable then that the

---

[1] Morice, *Preuves*, I, col. 228 ; *CED*, II, p. 79. Cf. H. d'Arbois de
Jubainville in Le Men and Ernault, *Cartulaire de Landévennec* (Collection de
documents inédits sur l'histoire de France.—Mélanges historiques, Paris,
1886, p. 539). Note the form of the tonsure still worn by Robert of Arbrissel
(† 1117), " capillis ad frontem circumcisis," according to Marbod (*PL*,
CLXXI, 1483).

[2] Can. 41 (Mansi, *Concilia*, X, 630).

[3] Tirechán, p. 24.—On this important passage see Bury, *Pat.*, pp. 239–42 ;
Hitchcock, *St Patrick and his Gallic Friends*, p. 18 ; Maud Joynt, *Airbacc
giunnae* (*Ériu*, X, 1928, pp. 130–34). " From this passage it seems that the
native name given to the druidic tonsure [*norma magica*] was *airbacc
giunnae* . . . words interpreted as ' frontal curve of the tonsure ' " (M.
Joynt).

[4] " . . . ut a Simone Mago christianos discerneret in cuius capite
cesaries ab aure ad aurem tonsa anteriore parte, cum a ntea Magi in fronte
cirrum habebant " (Cotton MS., Otho E. XIII, fol. 112ᵛ). The beginning of
the sentence is missing, the leaves having been burnt all round the edges
in the fire of 1731.

[5] Varin, *Mémoire*, p. 160.

[6] In order not to be recognized by the enemy, the Saxons of Bayeux

tonsure to which the insular clergy clung with such infatuation rests ultimately on some national tradition.

St Patrick opposed this national tonsure. One of the canons in the series placed under his name and those of the bishops Auxilius and Iserninus (a series which may, we believe, with some important reservations, be held as authentic) [1] actually pronounced excommunication on those Irish clerics who should refuse to shave themselves *more Romano*.[2] In St Patrick's time the Roman tonsure, as has been already said, was not the " corona " but the complete tonsure, and this fact explains the amazement expressed by the Irish druids in their strange pseudo-prophecy : " The adze-head will come with his bent staff." [3] Nevertheless, we must conclude that Patrick's efforts to make the Roman tonsure prevail were powerless, since the *Catalogue of Saints* declares that from the first age (A.D. 432–544) a single tonsure was uniformly adopted which passed only *de aure ad aurem*.[4]

The promoters of the Roman Easter were also the advocates of the " corona," which was generally accepted by the various Celtic Churches at the same time as the orthodox Easter. According to Bede, such was the course of events in Iona.[5] The Annals of Tigernach, on the other hand, assert that the " corona " did not find acceptance there till two years after the Roman Easter.[6]

At the time when Bede was putting the final touches to his *Ecclesiastical History*, the Britons were as far from conform-

who were fighting with the Bretons shaved their heads "iuxta ritum Brittanorum " (Gregory of Tours, *Hist. Franc.*, x, 9, ed. W. Arndt : *MG. Scr. RM*, I, p. 416).—". . . ex quo Hibernenses pene omnes hanc tonsuram susceperunt " (*Hibernensis*, LIII, 6, p. 213). But at the back of the head the hair was left to grow in abundance, for Irish warriors considered it a dishonour to be deprived of that part of their hair. Cf. *Táin Bó Cúailgne*, ed. E. Windisch (Leipzig, 1905), p. 246 ; H. d'Arbois, *L'épopée celtique en Irlande* (Paris, 1892), pp. 369–70 ; Windisch, *Irische Texte*, III, p. 465 ; Kuno Meyer, *Otia Merseiana*, II, p. 90.

[1] Cf. Kenney, *Sources*, I, p. 169.

[2] *CED*, II, p. 328.

[3] " Adueniet asciciput cum suo ligno curui capite, etc." (Muirchu, *LA*, p. 4). " Asciciput," *i.e.*, *asciae caput*, " adze-head," Ir. *táilchenn*. Cf. *Vita Trip.*, pp. 34–35 ; Bury, *Pat.*, p. 299 ; White, *Patrick*, pp. 124–25.

[4] *Catalogus*, p. 292.

[5] Bede, *HE*, v, 22.

[6] *AT*, pp. 225–26 ; *AU* simply say : " Easter is changed in the monastery of Ia " (*a.a.* 715 = A.D. 716).

ing to Roman discipline in respect of the tonsure as of Easter.[1]

§ 3.—THE ADMINISTRATION OF BAPTISM

One of the three conditions laid down by Augustine as essential to a good understanding between the British Church and the Roman mission was, so the Venerable Bede tells us, that the Britons should administer baptism according to the rites of the Holy Roman Apostolic Church.[2] How did the administration of baptism among the Britons differ from the practice of Rome ? It is hard to find out. No writer up to the present has arrived at a satisfactory solution. F. C. Conybeare, the most extreme in his views, has advanced the theory that the British manner of administering baptism was not only irregular but actually invalid.[3] He finds what he considers the strongest argument for this opinion in a letter from Pope Zachary to St Boniface (May 1, 748 ?), in which mention is made of the decree of a synod of Great Britain declaring that whosoever is washed without the invocation of the three Persons of the Holy Trinity is not baptized.[4] To Conybeare the synod in question can be none other than that of Augustine's Oak, where Augustine and the British bishops met together ; consequently, the decree must have been prompted by the British practice of not administering baptism in the name of the Father, the Son and the Holy Spirit.[5] But Conybeare is wrong in his identification of the synod. As a matter of fact, in another letter of the same Boniface to the same Pope Zachary, written in 742, there is an allusion in almost identical terms to the same synod (*synodus et ecclesia in qua natus et nutritus fui*), and, moreover, this time the spot where the synod met is indicated : *Lundunensis synodus*.[6] The reference is therefore to a synod held at London, in the Saxon territory, and not to the synod of the Oak.[7]

---

[1] " Capita sine corona praetendunt " (Bede, *HE*, v, 22).

[2] Bede, *HE*, II, 2.

[3] F. C. Conybeare, *The Character of the Heresy of the early British Church* (*TSC*, 1897–98, pp. 84–117).

[4] *Ep.* 80 (*MG. Epist.*, III, p. 357).

[5] Conybeare, *op. cit.*, pp. 101 ff.

[6] *Ep.* 50 (p. 301).

[7] So Hugh Williams, *Heinrich Zimmer on the History of the Celtic Church* (*ZCP*, IV, 1903, pp. 542–44).

The difference cannot have consisted in the number of immersions,[1] since St Gregory saw no difficulty in allowing either single or triple immersion.[2] Did it lie in omitting to anoint the baptized person with the chrism or with the oil of catechumens ? This feature of the baptismal rite seems to have been neglected in Ireland in the eleventh century,[3] but there is nothing to show that it was the irregularity with which Augustine charged the Britons of the seventh century.[4]

In the twelfth century another custom appears established in Ireland, that of baptizing new-born infants at home without recourse to the priestly ministry. The Council of Cashel (1172) prohibited this abuse, and also, we are assured, another one, serious in a different way, which consisted in baptizing the children of the rich by plunging them thrice in milk.[5] We have no reason to suppose that such practices were already prevalent among the Britons in the time of Augustine. Had the last-mentioned custom been in question, the archbishop would certainly not have failed to declare distinctly that such a baptism was null and void. We must further remark that the prohibition of the triple immersion in milk was attributed to the Council of Cashel only by Benedict of Peterborough († 1193)[6] and that in this passage that writer might very well have referred at second-hand to some profane rite practised at the birth of a child, which perhaps did not exclude a baptism administered in regular form.[7]

In short, we cannot determine what shortcoming the Roman missionaries found in the baptism of the Britons, nor whether their objections related to the matter or the form of the sacrament. We possess, it is true, a canon attributed to Theodore

[1] Such was the opinion of Warren (*Lit.*, pp. 64 ff.) and of Loofs (*Antiquae*, p. 25).
[2] See C. Plummer, Bede, *HE*, Vol. II, p. 75 ; H. A. Wilson, *On some liturgical Points relating to the Mission of St Augustine* in *The Mission of St Augustine to England according to the original Documents, being a Handbook for the Thirteenth Centenary*, edited by A. J. Mason (Cambridge, 1897), p. 249.
[3] Lanfranc, *Ep.* 38 *ad Terdelvacum regem* (*PL*, CL, 536).
[4] H. A. Wilson, *op. cit.*, p. 250.
[5] Mansi, *Concilia*, XXII, 133. Cf. Varin, *Mémoire*, p. 105.
[6] *The Chronicle of the Reigns of Henry II and Richard I known commonly under the Name of Benedict of Peterborough*, ed. W. Stubbs (*RS*), Vol. I, p. 28.
[7] See John Salmon, *The ancient Irish Church as a Witness to Catholic Doctrine* (Dublin, 1897), pp. 64–65. Cf. *Betha Bhrighdi* (*Lismore*, pp. 36, 184, and W. Stokes' note, p. 318).

of Canterbury († 690), which ordains that any persons who, because they had been baptized by dissentient Scots or Britons, had doubts of the validity of their baptism, should be rebaptized.[1] But the reason which caused this fresh baptism to be prescribed was not any defect either of matter or of form. The only ground given for the decision—contrary as it is to the habitual practice of the Roman Church—is that the sacrament had been administered by "non-Catholic" priests, by those Scots and Britons "who are excluded from the Church by their Easter and their tonsure," in a word, by "heretics."

§ 4.—EPISCOPAL CONSECRATION

Besides Easter, the tonsure and the administration of baptism, the Britons and Scots were at variance with the Roman discipline and liturgy on some other points.[2] They did not conform to the canonical rule which required that at least three bishops should take part in an episcopal consecration.[3]

The sixth answer of St Gregory to St Augustine of Canterbury empowered him not to be too exacting in this matter towards the Britons.[4] Augustine therefore brought no charge against them in respect of it. As St Ninian was probably the only bishop among the southern Picts and St Patrick the only one in Ireland at the beginning, they were compelled to officiate alone in consecrating the first priests whom they raised to the episcopacy; it was thus that Fiacc was consecrated.[5] What was at first due to necessity seems to have become a custom in the course of time. The custom was not however universally observed in the Celtic Churches; in 665 we hear of two British bishops joining with Wini, bishop of Winchester,

---

[1] Theodore, *Canones*, II, IX, 3 (p. 324).
[2] "Sed et alia plurima unitati ecclesiasticae contraria faciebant," says Bede speaking of the Britons; and St Augustine speaking to the same: "In multis quidem nostrae consuetudini, immo universalis ecclesiae, contraria geritis" (*HE*, II, 2). And Bede again relating the discussions at the synod of Whitby: "Mota ergo ibi quaestione de pascha, uel tonsura, uel aliis rebus ecclesiasticis, etc." (*HE*, III, 25).
[3] See A. W. H[addan], art. *Bishop* in W. Smith and S. Cheetham, *Dictionary of Christian Antiquities*.
[4] Bede, *HE*, I, 27.
[5] *Vita Niniani* 6, ed. Forbes, p. 148; *Additions to Tirechán's Memoir* (*LA*, p. 35).

to consecrate Chad (Ceadda) ; and to consecrate Cedd, Chad's brother, Finan, bishop of Lindisfarne, called in the aid of two other bishops.[1]

Jocelin of Furness, speaking of the episcopal ordination of St Kentigern, the first bishop of Glasgow (?), by a single bishop, mentions this practice as commonly received among the Britons as well as the Scots.[2] But we must not forget that the biographer wrote more than five centuries after the time his hero lived. It is, nevertheless, certain that from the seventh century on ordinations performed by dissentients were held in suspicion in England, as likewise all sacraments administered by them. To guard himself against being contaminated by Scottic bishops, Wilfrid went for his consecration to Compiègne in the land of the Franks.[3] About the same time Bishop Chad had the validity of his ordination called in question by Archbishop Theodore because of the share which the two British bishops had had in it. On this occasion Chad displayed a praiseworthy humility which reflects honour on his spiritual masters, the disparaged Scots. " If you believe," he said, " that I have not been consecrated canonically, I am quite ready to resign an office of which I have never felt myself worthy and which I accepted only through obedience." [4] Theodore would not deprive a man of such disinterested nature of his episcopal dignity, but he subjected him to reordination *per omnes gradus*.[5] Likewise the Theodorian canons ordered that a second laying on of hands by a " Catholic " bishop should take place in the case of all priests ordained by Scottic or British bishops.[6]

It is rather interesting to note that the same man who showed

---

[1] Bede, *HE*, iii, 28. Cf. iii, 22. See Loofs, *Antiquae*, pp. 26, 76 ; Paul Fournier in *RHE*, VII, 1906, p. 771.

[2] *Vita Kentigerni*, 11, ed. Forbes, p. 182. See editor's important note, pp. 335–40. In this chapter Jocelin points out another British peculiarity in the consecration of bishops.

[3] Stephen, *Vita Wilfridi*, 12 (pp. 206–207) ; Bede, *HE*, iii, 28.

[4] Bede, *HE*, 2.

[5] Stephen, *Vita Wilfridi*, 15 (pp. 209–10).

[6] " Qui ordinati sunt a Scottorum vel Brittonum episcopis qui in pascha vel tonsura catholica non sunt adunati ecclesiae iterum a catholico episcopo manus impositione confirmentur " (Theodore, *Canones*, II, ix, 3 (pp. 323–24). Cf. D recension, 116 (*Ib.*, p. 248) ; *Canones S. Gregorii papae*, 187 (*Ib.*, p. 270).

himself such an unrelaxing corrector of Celtic breaches of the canonical law, did not scruple himself to consecrate in 678 three bishops *inordinate solus*, as Eddius informs us.[1]

It remains an undeniable fact that episcopal consecration by a single bishop had become a current custom in Ireland in the eleventh and twelfth centuries. We have in proof several letters from Lanfranc and St Anselm to princes of that country.[2]

For Brittany let us recall a canon of the Council of Tours of A.D. 567 already quoted, which runs as follows : " Let no pontiff presume to give episcopal consecration in Armorica either to a Briton or a Roman without the sanction of the metropolitan or the bishops of the province ; otherwise he shall hold himself excommunicate." [3]

§ 5.—ROME AND THE CELTIC CHURCHES

In the course of these controversies both parties displayed equal ignorance and equal reliance on illusory authorities. In the conferences, in the treatises and the letters exchanged, the arguments brought forward are nearly always of signal weakness. To hide their weakness the writers make a great parade of mystical reasons and appeal for support to apocryphal works. We have already pointed out the true nature of that treatise of Anatolius, which in the eyes of both parties passed for authentic. Other forged documents, such as the Acts of the Council of Caesarea or synodal Epistle of Theophilus, the treatise ascribed to Athanasius on the Paschal system, a Pseudo-Cyrillus, a Pseudo-Morianus, were used to supply arguments in the controversy.[4] Both sides appeal to fictitious traditions ; the partisans of the Roman observances trace the origin of these to St Peter, the dissentients claim that they hold their Easter from St John ; the former accuse their

---

[1] Stephen, *Vita Wilfridi*, 24 (p. 218).
[2] Lanfranc, *Ep.* 38 *ad Terdelvacum regem* (*PL*, CL, 536) ; Anselm, *Ep.* 147 *ad Muriardachum regem* (*PL*, CLIX, 179).
[3] Can. 9 (Mansi, *Concilia*, IX, 794 ; *MG. Leges : Sect. III, Conc.*, I, p. 124). *V. sup.* ch. IV, § 5
[4] On this group of forgeries relating to the paschal controversy see Krusch, *Studien*, pp. 302–10, 328–36 ; B. MacCarthy, *AU*, IV, pp. cxv–cxiii ; Esposito, *Latin Learning*, I, pp. 233–34 ; *s.a. PADM*, pp. 199–200.

opponents of wearing the tonsure of Simon, and the latter do not even think of protesting against such an assertion.

Those who have cherished traditions to defend are, as a rule, little concerned about criticism or logic. We have seen how attached the insular Celts were to their traditions. There are many reasons to account for this passionate adherence to old customs : their insular position, the invasion of western Europe by Barbarians in the fifth century and the invasion of Great Britain by the Saxons during the same period. The Christians of the isles were cut off by the sea and by the Barbarians from the rest of the world. In the course of the fifth and sixth centuries important changes were effected in the discipline and liturgy of the Roman Church of which they received only belated tidings.[1] Rumours of these innovations did indeed reach them, but they may be excused for doubting their authenticity, inasmuch as they received no direct official notice from the centre of Catholicism before the second quarter of the seventh century. With regard to Easter, the letter of Pope Honorius I (625–638) was the first admonition to reach them from Rome.[2] This letter was not without results ; it was followed in a short time by the conversion of all the south of Ireland. As early as 455 the British Churches, having been informed of an ordinance issued by Pope St Leo the Great touching the date of Easter, hastened to comply with it.[3]

Intermediaries such as St Augustine of Canterbury and the other Italian envoys had sought to open the eyes of the insular Celts ; but the Britons to whom they addressed themselves in the first instance felt an invincible reluctance to submit to disciplinary rules announced to them by the apostles of their enemies.[4] In their eyes the archbishop of Canterbury and his clergy were emissaries of the Anglo-Saxons, just as for the Britons of Armorica the archbishop of Tours was the tool of the Frankish monarch. As a result of political exasperation, religious traditions and old national customs were confounded

---

[1] Bede, *HE*, III, 4, 17, 25.
[2] On the date of this letter *v. sup.*, § 1.
[3] " Pascha commutatur super diem dominicum cum papa leone episcopo rome " (*AC, a.a.* 453, pp. 152–53).
[4] Bede, *HE*, v, 23.

and finally amalgamated, together forming the invisible heritage of the past.

Fundamentally the controversy turned solely on matters of pure discipline or liturgy. It is hard for us at the present date to account for such protracted conflict over some of the questions in dispute. The difference in the date of the Easter festival, it is true, led to a regrettable divergence in the arrangements of the whole ecclesiastical year ; but why should the shape of the tonsure arouse such violent animosity and give food for such long disputes ? Nowadays the Irish Catholic clergy no longer wear any kind of tonsure. Disciplinary laws are open to change. But that idea never occurred to the minds of the early ages, fast bound in the cult of local traditions. Nor did they find it any easier to fix the boundary between questions of pure discipline and dogmatic beliefs.[1] Throughout the entire duration of the controversies over Easter and the tonsure each side excommunicated its opponents and hurled at their heads such epithets as " schismatic " and " heretic " in spirited fashion.[2] Archbishop Theodore (or the canons placed under his name) went so far as to command the reordination of clerics ordained by Scottic or British bishops, *qui in Pascha et tonsura catholicae non sunt adunati ecclesiae*.[3]

However, except for the short-lived irruption of the Pelagian tenets in one part of the Celtic world, it does not seem that the integrity of the faith was ever in danger. In the fourth and fifth centuries the British bishops were manifestly in communion with those of Western Europe.[4] In 431 the Pope

[1] Aldhelm, *Ep.* 4 *ad Geruntium*, p. 485.

[2] Cummian, *DCP*, col. 977 ; Bede, *Vita Cuthberti*, 39 (*PL*, XCIV, 780) ; Stephen, *Vita Wilfridi*, 12 (p. 206) ; Aldhelm, *l. cit.*—" Silete et nolite nos haereticos vocare " (Cummian, *DCP*, col. 975).—" De provinciis et personis devitandis ad judicandum. Institutio Romana : Cavendum, ne ad alias provincias aut ecclesias referantur causae, quae alio more et alia religione utuntur ; sive ad Judeos, qui umbrae magis quam veritati deserviunt, aut ad Britones, qui omnibus contrarii sunt et a Romano more et ab unitate ecclesiae se abscindunt, aut hereticos, quamvis in ecclesiasticis docti et studiosi fuerint " (*Hibernensis*, XX, 6, pp. 61–62).—" Il y a lieu de se demander si l'on donnait au mot *hérétique* toute sa signification quand on l'appliquait aux Bretons " (Louis Saltet, *Les réordinations*, Paris, 1907, p. 99).

[3] Theodore, *Canones*, pp. 270, 323–24.

[4] They attended the Councils of Arles (314) and Rimini (359) ; they called to Britain St Victricius of Rouen and St Germanus of Auxerre. *V. sup.*, ch. II, §§ 1, 2.

sent to Ireland her first bishop. At the beginning of the seventh century Augustine demanded the co-operation of the British clergy in his missionary enterprise ; plainly therefore he had no suspicion of their doctrinal purity. In the seventh and eighth centuries we have Jonas of Bobbio and the Venerable Bede to attest the orthodoxy of the Scots in matters of dogma.[1]

And yet, if we are to believe certain writers, the Celtic Church was distinctly separatist and independent and resolutely withdrew from the jurisdiction of the Pope.[2] It is indeed abundantly clear that for long, in the bosom of the great Catholic unity that Church stood a little aloof and in the shade and preserved a physiognomy all its own ; but to assert that it showed feelings of hostility or even of distrust towards the Mother Church of Christianity is to flout openly our best sources of information.[3]

One of St Patrick's *dicta*,[4] Cummian's treatise on Easter, the *Liber angeli*, the *Collectio canonum Hibernensis*, furnish unquestionable proofs that the Church of Ireland recognized the papal supremacy. But as all these texts, except the first, are of later date than the conversion of South Ireland to Roman discipline, their testimony is sometimes set aside as being the echo of the triumphant Romanizing party.[5] However, from Cummian's little work we may draw a conclusion of far-reaching import, to wit, that even before any part of Ireland had returned to the common Paschal observance, no one in the country felt any objection, when doubt arose on some canonical matter, to sending a deputation to Rome, the centre of Christianity, *velut natos ad matrem*, in order to procure light on the subject.[6] This, it will be remembered, was the decision made in 628 or 629.[7]

---

[1] Jonas, *Vita Col.*, I, 2 (p. 67) ; Bede, *HE*, III, 25.
[2] Rice Rees, *An Essay on the Welsh Saints* (London, 1836), pp. 289, 292 ; W. S. Kerr, *The Independence of the Celtic Church in Ireland* (London, 1931). See a refutation of Archdeacon Kerr's main arguments in *RHE*, XXVIII, 1932, pp. 174–75.
[3] Varin, *Mémoire*, p. 452.
[4] *LA*, p. 17.
[5] Thomas Olden, *Church of Ireland* (London, 1895), p. 153.
[6] Cummian, *DCP*, col. 977.
[7] Cf. Canon of St Patrick in *LA*, p. 42 ; " Patricius : Si quae questiones in hac insula oriantur, ad sedem apostolicam referantur " (*Hibernensis*, xx, 5, p. 61). About A.D. 746 the Scot Virgilius of Salzburg

The attitude of the Scots towards Rome before they had rallied to her call in the field of discipline is further made known to us by the Venerable Bede, who tells us that king Oswy, although educated by Scottic monks, none the less professed quite orthodox opinions on the Catholic and Apostolic character of the Roman Church.[1]

Finally, the attachment of the Irish to the Roman See and the respect which they professed for its doctrinal authority and its supreme jurisdiction are clearly shown in the correspondence of St Columban. We must not be misled by the liberties of speech into which the writer's ardour sometimes led him ; we could find parallels for these in the writings of men whose attachment to the Chair of Peter cannot be disputed, St Irenaeus or St Boniface. Columban salutes the bishop of Rome as " the Head of the Churches of Europe," " the Pastor of pastors." He regards him as the depository of the orthodox Faith, and in his infatuation for his own error he bids him call to order the Gaulish " quasi-schismatics " who surround him.[2] What plainer proof can be found of recognition of the Roman supremacy ? In the letter written by St Columban to Pope Boniface IV in 612 or 613 on the celebrated question of the Three Chapters, some critics have seen an expression of opinion from which it would be legitimate to regard Columban as the precursor of that mediaeval school which admitted that on a charge of heresy the Pope might be deferred to the judgment of the Church. But this is going too far. A dispassionate perusal of the text must lead to the conviction that the Irish abbot was simply inviting the Pope to defend himself from charge or suspicion of heresy before a council summoned by himself. Nothing in the letter goes to prove that Columban did not unreservedly accept the maxim : *Prima sedes non iudicatur a quoquam.*[3]

wrote to Pope Zachary requesting a decision concerning the question of rebaptization (Zachary, *Ep. ad Bonifatium* : *MG. Epist.*, III, p. 336).

[1] Bede, *HE*, III, 29. " Si creditis unitatem aeclessiae ? " is one of the questions put by Patrick to the daughters of King Loegaire before baptism (Tirechán, p.23).

[2] Columban, *Ep.* 1 *Gregorio I. Papae*, p. 151. Cf. Funk, *Zur Geschichte der altbritischen Kirche (Kirchengeschichtliche Abhandlungen und Untersuchungen*, Paderborn, 1887), I, p. 430.

[3] Columban, *Ep.* 5 *Bonifatio IV*, pp. 173-74. Cf. Jean Rivière, *Saint*

Such were the feelings professed towards Rome by one of the most illustrious representatives of the Scottic Church.[1] What were those of the Britons of the same period in the course of their quarrel with Augustine ? Here we have a very decided pronouncement : an answer addressed by an individual of whom we have some knowledge, Dinoot, abbot of Bangor-is-Coed, to St Augustine of Canterbury himself, printed by Migne in the same volume as the correspondence of St Columban. " I am willing," says Dinoot, " to show the Pope of Rome the affection and charity which I ought to feel for every Christian ; more I do not owe to him whom you call the Pope and who wrongfully claims to be the father of fathers. We know no other head than the bishop of Caerleon ; he it is whom God has charged to watch over us." [2] No more explicit text has ever been adduced in favour of the independence of the early Celtic Church. It has only one drawback, but that one of no small consequence : it was composed, not by Dinoot in the seventh century, but by a Welsh Protestant of the sixteenth, who placed his own sentiments on the Papacy in the mouth of the abbot of Bangor. The original text was written in Welsh,[3] and it was translated into Latin by Spelman. No one at the present day entertains any doubt about the " fabrication " of this document.[4]

Widely different from the views held by some Welsh writers of the last century, like Rice Rees or J. W. Willis Bund, are those adopted by present-day historians on the relation of ancient Celtic Christianity to the See of Peter, as the following

Colomban et le jugement du pape hérétique (Revue des sciences religieuses, III, 1923, pp. 277–82) ; M. V. Hay, A Chain of Error in Scottish History (London, 1927), pp. 108, 210–31 ; s.a. Columban and Rome (R. Cel., XXXVIII, 1920–21, pp. 315–18) ; J. C. McNaught, The Celtic Church and the See of Peter (Oxford, 1927), pp. 47–56.

[1] Daniel Rock, Did the Early Church in Ireland Acknowledge the Pope's supremacy ? (London, 1844) ; J. C. McNaught, op. cit.

[2] Dinothi responsio ad Augustinum monachum (PL, LXXX, 21–24).

[3] Printed in CED, I, p. 122.

[4] In 1902, however, Joseph Turmel still believed this document to be genuine. Cf. An. Br., XVII, pp. 315-16. That it is clearly spurious has been shown anew by J. Loth, La prétendue lettre de Dinoot (An. Br., XVIII, pp. 139–40). Cf. R. Rees, Essay, p. 290 ; Walter, Das alte Wales, pp. 229–30 ; John Pryce, The Ancient British Church (London, 1878), p. 171 ; C. Plummer's note in Bede, HE, Vol. II, p. 75.

lines from the pen of a prominent scholar of our day will show. " There was no insurmountable barrier, it would seem, between Augustine and the British bishops," writes Professor John Edward Lloyd, of the University of Wales. " No theological differences parted the Roman from the Celtic Church, for the notion that the latter was the home of a kind of primitive Protestantism, of apostolic purity and simplicity, is without any historical foundation." [1]   And in a still more recent work the same scholar concludes in this way : " The British Church was orthodox and differed from Rome only in minor matters, of which the date of the celebration of Easter was the chief.   Ecclesiastical arrogance on the one hand and national pride on the other were the forces which brought about the schism, which, nevertheless, persisted for over a hundred and fifty years.   It was not until 768 that Bishop Elfodd induced his countrymen to abandon the hopeless attitude of isolation and, by accepting the Roman Easter, to enter into communion with the Churches of the West. Henceforth, the loyalty of the Welsh to the See of St Peter is not in question ; their Churches had many peculiarities, the result of their previous history, but these were not challenged by the papal power, which found its commands as readily obeyed in Wales as in other Western regions." [2]

[1] Lloyd, *HW*, I, p. 173.
[2] J. E. Lloyd, *A History of Wales* (Benn's Sixpenny Library), London [1930], pp. 15–16. Cf. Walter, *op. cit.*, pp. 228 ff. ; J. C. McNaught, *op. cit.*

CHAPTER VII

THE CLERGY AND ECCLESIASTICAL INSTITUTIONS

§ 1.—The Episcopate in Great Britain

ROMAN Britain had possessed bishops with fixed sees ; such were those of York, of London and of another see (Lincoln or Colchester) who were present at the Council of Arles in 314.[1]

We have seen that seven British bishops took part in the conference assembled by the efforts of Augustine of Canterbury in 602 or 603 [2]; but the Venerable Bede does not tell us the sees of these prelates. In Celtic Britain there were no definite territories ruled by diocesan bishops.[3] The monastic element was very strong in the country. Zimmer has noticed that the earliest episcopal sees were established in monasteries, at Bangor, St. Asaph, Menevia and Llandaff. He has further asserted that " in the majority of cases " the Welsh diocesan bishops were at the same time abbots.[4] This assertion admits of no certain proof, for we have scarcely any information about the organization of the Welsh Church of the seventh and eighth centuries, except from the Lives of saints of a late period (twelfth and following centuries), whose testimony must be accepted with caution.

However, we possess an early Life of St Samson, written within about sixty years after the saint's death, which occurred about the year 565. According to this work, Samson, being already an abbot, was consecrated bishop without a see before he went to Brittany and became bishop of Dol.[5] And this was very likely not an isolated instance ; Haddan and Stubbs mention several Welsh abbots who received the dignity of the

---

[1] *V. sup.* ch. II, § 1.
[2] *V. sup.* ch. VI, § 1.
[3] Cf. Lloyd, *HW*, I, p. 157.
[4] H. Zimmer, *Keltische Kirche*, p. 222 ; *CC*, p. 59.
[5] *Vita Sam.*, I, 44 (pp. 139–40). *V. sup.* ch. IV, § 4.

episcopate without being furnished with sees ; these prelates they term " honorary bishops." [1] But there is no doubt that there were also monastery-bishoprics in Wales. Menevia was one, for it cannot be doubted that St David was at the same time head of the abbey and bishop.[2] St Teilo also was a bishop, and Llandaff, where he had his seat—termed a " monasterium " and even an " archimonasterium " by the *Book of Llandaff*,[3] was another example of a monastery-bishopric.

The history of the episcopal sees of Cornwall is even more obscure than that of the Welsh ones. William of Malmesbury in the twelfth century affirms that he had no certain knowledge about the early dioceses of Cornwall or the succession of bishops in that district. He locates one episcopal see *apud sanctum Petrocum confessorem, i.e.,* Padstow. Padstow, the city of St. Petroc, situated on the estuary of the River Camel, preceded Bodmin as the most important religious centre of the district.[4] The same author adds that, according to some sources, there was an episcopal see on the south coast, at St. Germans, near the river Lynher. Other texts, too, confirm the belief that at one time there existed a monastery-bishopric at St. Germans.[5] Another monastery-bishopric has been claimed for Dinnurrin, a place which some writers propose to identify with a little village called Gerrans on the south Cornish coast.[6]

---

[1] *CED*, I, pp. 142–43.

[2] " A Davide episcopo . . ." (*Catalogus*, p. 293) ; " Dauid episcopus moni iudeorum " (*AC*, p. 156), *i.e.*, " moniu Desorum " = " the grove of the Desi," as interpreted by J. Loth (Académie des Inscriptions et Belles-Lettres, Comptes rendus, 1929, p. 332). " This place took the name from the Irish *muni*, which means *rubus*, grove " (Wade-Evans, *David*, p. 78). St. David's was still called a " *monasterium* " by Asser towards the end of the ninth century (*De rebus gestis Ælfredi*, 79, Oxford, 1904, pp. 65–66).

[3] *The Text of the Book of Lan Dâv*, ed. J. G. Evans (Oxford, 1893), pp. 73, 74, 115, 129, 144, 214. Cf. Lloyd, *HW*, I, pp. 207–208 ; Chevalier, *Essai*, p. 377.

[4] William of Malmesbury, *De gestis pontificum Angliae*, II, ed. Hamilton (*RS*), I, p. 204. Cf. G. H. Doble, *Saint Petrock, n.d.*, p. 25.

[5] *Missa Germani* (*CED*, I, p. 696). Cf. Duine, *Inventaire*, pp. 39–41 ; L.G., *La question des abbayes-évêchés* (*Revue Mabillon*, XII, 1922, p. 95).

[6] Cf. *CED*, I, p. 674 ; L.G., *art. cit.*, p. 96. " Gerrans is named after Gereint, a Cornish Prince whose capital, called *Dingerein* (*i.e.*, Gereint's Castle), is undoubtedly the same place as the Cornish monastry of *Dinurrin*, in which Kenstec was Bishop in the 9th century " (Charles Henderson,

In Wales the incessant political rivalry between the kings drew the bishops into contests for supremacy. We do not hear of any metropolitan organization from Gildas. But after his time we find the bishops of Caerleon, St. Asaph, Llandaff and Menevia claiming each in turn a kind of supremacy over the other Welsh sees.[1] This state of affairs has led some writers to believe that in the Welsh Church of that age there existed a sort of movable primacy, in which the predominance devolved always on the head of the worthiest and consequently was attached now to one see, now to another. " This chief bishop is at the same time the head of a monastery," observes Arthur de la Borderie, one of those who uphold the theory.[2] But there seems to be nothing in the texts to make us believe that such a state of things ever existed.

During the Roman period Caerleon was the capital of the province. Its religious supremacy in subsequent times is attested only by the letter ascribed to Dinoot, which we have already seen to be a notorious forgery.[3] In support of the early supremacy of Menevia, the see of the popular St David, arguments have been based on the term *archescob* used in the laws of Hywell Dda (tenth century) to designate the titular of that see. But since on the following page of the code several Welsh *archesgyp* are mentioned, it is likely that the term was purely honorific and did not mean *archbishop* in the sense now attached to the word.[4] The *Annales Cambriae*, on the other hand, give the title of *archiepiscopus* to Elfodd, bishop of Bangor, and the Chronicle of the princes of Gwent dignifies the same individual with the title of *archescob*[5] ; but Bangor,

Parochial History of Cornwall, in *The Cornish Church Guide*, Truro, 1928, p. 100).

[1] See Walter, *Das alte Wales*, pp. 233–37 ; W. L. Bevan, *St. David's* (Diocesan Histories), London, 1888, pp. 42–44.

[2] La Borderie, *HB*, I, p. 278. Cf. Rice Rees, *An Essay on the Welsh Saints*, p. 244.

[3] *V. sup.* ch. vi, § 5.

[4] *Ancient Laws and Institutes of Wales*, ed. Aneurin Owen (London, 1841), pp. 164, 165 ; *CED*, I, pp. 212–13, 216–17.

[5] *AC*, p. 163 ; *Brut y Tywysogion* (Gwent), ed. A. Owen (London, 1863), p. 8. Cf. Hugh Williams, *Some Aspects of the Christian Church in Wales during the Fifth and Sixth Centuries* (*TSC*, 1893–94, p. 131).—In the third decade of the twelfth century, Geoffrey of Monmouth created Dubricius († 612 ?) archbishop of Caerleon (*Historia regum Britanniae*, ed. Acton Griscom

so far as I know, never claimed the rank of a metropolitan see. The ultra-patriotic Asser, who wrote about 893, is the earliest author to style the bishop of Menevia " *archiepiscopus* " in Latin.[1]

At the end of the eleventh century Rhygyfarch, the biographer of St David, writes as follows : " Blessed and extolled by the mouth of all, he (David) is, with the consent of all the bishops, kings, princes, nobles and all grades of the whole Britannic race, made archbishop, and his monastery too is declared the metropolis of the whole country, so that whoever ruled it should be accounted archbishop." [2]

In the twelfth century the claims of Menevia to the title of metropolitan see were formally and with zeal maintained by Giraldus Cambrensis. But the Welshman did not secure the victory for his cause, which, his opponents asserted, was based on fictions and inventions as little worthy of belief as the legends of Arthur.[3] Menevia had to acknowledge the metropolitan and primatial jurisdiction of Canterbury. In Wales, as in Brittany, after long disputes and stubborn resistance, British independence had to yield to the demands of Rome for organization and centralization.[4]

§ 2.—The Irish Episcopate.—Principle of Monastic Exemption in Ireland and Abroad

According as it spread in the Roman Empire, Christianity established its hierarchy within the framework of the civil administration. In Ireland, which had escaped the clutches of Rome, ecclesiastical institutions were necessarily modelled on a political and social organization wholly different. Here there were no towns and the country was devoid of unity, parcelled out among a multitude of hostile *tuatha*, all animated

---

(London, 1929), VIII, 12 (p. 413) ; IX, 1 (p. 432) ; IX, 4 (p. 437) ; IX, 12 (p. 453) ; IX, 13 (p. 455) ; IX, 15 (p. 458).

[1] *De rebus gestis Ælfredi, l. cit.*

[2] Ricemarch, *Vita Davidis*, 53, ed. A. W. Wade-Evans (*YC*, XXIV, 1913) ; Wade-Evans, *David*, p. 27.

[3] Giraldus, *De invectionibus*, IV, 2, ed. J. S. Brewer (*RS*), p. 78.—In his *Retractationes* (Works, I, p. 426) Giraldus confesses that in these discussions he followed " magis famam publicam et opinionem quam historiae cuiuspiam certitudinem."

[4] *V. inf.* ch. XI, § 6.

by intense and exclusive devotion to tribal and local interests, and with ill-defined boundaries. To tell the truth, we do not know how St Patrick, who for some time was the only bishop of the country, organized the episcopate which was called on to continue his work. But he is credited with having ordained a very large number of bishops.[1] Very likely he appointed one in every *tuath* which had been converted or was in process of conversion.[2] The *Ríagail Pátraic* (Patrick's Rule), a tract which is not the work of the saint but which, in view of its early date, has some likelihood of representing the actual state of things, contains the following injunctions : " Here for the souls of the men of Ireland is what is written in the Testament of Patrick. Each tribe is to have a *primescop* (chief bishop) to ordain its clergy, to consecrate its churches, for the spiritual guidance of princes and chieftains, and for the sanctification and blessing of their offspring after baptism. For the tribe and the nation which have not bishops to fulfil these duties behold the law of their belief and their faith perish." [3]

The term *primescop* can hardly denote a sort of metropolitan archbishop exercising jurisdiction over suffragans, but doubtless means rather the territorial bishop or bishop of the *tuath* as opposed to other kinds of bishops of whom we shall speak anon.

We have already referred to the vast preponderance of the monastic element in the Church of Ireland from the beginning. The monks, who at the start were missionaries, lost none of their importance nor their influence after the conversion of the country. The monasteries, endowed with rich domains and thronged with monks, remained focuses of piety and missionary enterprise, centres to which all turned for learning both sacred and profane, in short, oases of peace, light and civilization in

---

[1] " Primus ordo catholicorum sanctorum erat in tempore Patricii. Et tunc erant episcopi omnes, clari et sancti et Spiritu sancto pleni, CCCL numero, Ecclesiarum fundatores " (*Catalogus*, p. 292).—" De episcoporum numero quos [Patricius] ordinauit in Hibernia CCCCL " (Tirechán, p. 18). —" Ordinavit episcopos trecentos sexaginta quinque aut eo amplius . . ." (Nennius, *HB*, 54, p. 196).

[2] Cf. Bury, *Pat.*, pp. 180, 375-79 ; C. Plummer, *VSH*, p. cxiii, n. 1 (*introd.*).

[3] *Ríagail Pátraic*, ed. J. G. O'Keeffe (*Ériu*, I, 1904, pp. 216-24).

the midst of the prevailing barbarism.   In the eyes of the
Christian inhabitants their prestige to some extent eclipsed
even that of the episcopate.

The question whether there were episcopal dioceses in
Ireland in the early centuries of the Middle Ages is still under
discussion.[1] The territory within which the bishop's jurisdiction was exercised was certainly not well defined.[2] The
first attempt to fix diocesan boundaries was not made till the
synod of Rathbreasail (to which we shall recur) at the
beginning of the twelfth century.[3] But the cause which above
all must have tended to bring confusion into the episcopal
system and to lessen episcopal authority was the fact that
important districts were placed in dependence on the
monasteries.

The several foundations of the same holy abbot formed
what was called the *familia* (Ir. *muinter*) of the saint.[4] Into
this *familia* were grafted the foundations made in the course
of centuries by the coarbs or successors of the first abbot.[5]
The territories belonging to these monastic *familiae* or those
over which, in virtue of spiritual or material services rendered
to the inhabitants, they exercised a kind of protectorate,
receiving offerings and raising tributes, constituted the
paruchia (Ir. *fairche*) of the saint who was the original founder.[6]
These monastic " parishes " were like abbatial dioceses
embracing rich domains scattered throughout Ireland (sometimes even overseas).[7]

It would not do to accept blindly the exaggerated statements of certain of the Lives of saints as to the extent of

[1] See L.G., *Les chrétientés celtiques*, p. 217, note 1.
[2] Ryan, *Monast.*, p. 85.
[3] *V. inf.* ch. XI, § 4.
[4] On the origin of the word " muinter " see J. Pokorny, *A.I. montar,
muinter* (*ZCP*, X, 1914–15, pp. 202–204) ; H. d'Arbois, *R. Cel.*, XXX,
1909, p. 326 ; J. Vendryes, *R. Cel.*, 1926, pp. 210, 232.
[5] A. W. H[addan], art. *Coarb* in Smith and Cheetham, *Dictionary of
Christian Antiquities ;* Kenney, *Sources*, I, pp. 33, 292, 352–53.
[6] Can. 34 of Patrick (*CED*, II, p. 330) ; Tirechán, p. 31 ; *Vita Carthagi*,
11, 16, 37 (*VSH*, I, pp. 173, 176, 183) ; *Vita Iᵃ Brendani Cl.*, 2 (*VSH*, I,
p. 98, note 11) ; *Vita Brendani Cl.*, 11, ed. Paul Grosjean (*AB*, XLVIII,
1930, p. 109) ; *Vita Ciarani de Cluan*, 17, 18 (*VSH*, I, pp. 206, 211) ; *Vita
Endei*, 27 (*VSH*, II, p. 72) ; *Vita Moling*, 6 (*VSH*, II, p. 192) ; *Vita Moluae*,
25 (*VSH*, II, p. 213) ; *Vita Munnu*, 16 (*VSH*, II, p. 232).
[7] Cf. C. Plummer, *VSH*, p. CXII (*introd.*).

some of these *paruchiae*; for instance, that of St Brigid of Kildare, if we are to believe Cogitosus, which *per totam Hibernensem terram diffusa, a mari usque ad mare extensa est*.[1] Nevertheless, we are justified in believing that the lands in subjection to the monastic *familiae* took a large share of jurisdiction out of the hands of the territorial bishops. The abbots themselves were often bishops,[2] or even if they were not, in order to escape episcopal jurisdiction they had attached to their abbey a cloistral bishop, who exercised his functions first of all within the precincts of the principal monastery, but doubtless also within those of the other monasteries belonging to the *familia* (when these were not themselves provided with a similar official) and perhaps even throughout the entire extent of the *paruchia*.[3]

The truly extraordinary privileges enjoyed by the presbyter-abbot of Iona may be here recalled. In sixth-century Ireland almost all jurisdiction was exercised from the monasteries. "About half the leading abbot-rulers were bishops, about half priests," says Fr. John Ryan, "and the more illustrious names were to be found among the latter. In this way the essential connection between the episcopal order and ecclesiastical government bade fair to be lost to view. As regards the power of order, the Irish bishop differed in nothing at any period from bishops elsewhere in Christendom. In personal dignity he ranked superior to any presbyter-abbot, but the monastic concept of his office was that he should be a saint rather than a ruler. In course of time the temporalities, and with them effective government, tended to fall more and more into the hands of the presbyter-abbots." [4]

On the other hand, as monasteries multiplied, it followed that bishop-abbots and cloistral abbots multiplied in equal proportion, "like flies," to use Bury's words.[5] The somewhat fluctuating and precarious nature of their legal position

[1] Cogitosus, *Vita Brig.*, Prol., p. 135.
[2] Ryan, *Monast.*, p. 176.
[3] Ryan, *Monast.*, pp. 298–302.
[4] Ryan, *Monast.*, pp. 189–90.
[5] Bury, *Pat.*, p. 181.—Hence doubtless this strange gloss in a St. Gall MS. : "In Hibernia episcopi et presbyteri unum sunt" (Ekkehard IV, *Liber Benedictionum*, ed. J. Egli, *Mitteilungen zur vaterländischen Geschichte*, St. Gallen, 1909, XXXI, p. 372).

(especially of the latter class) led in many cases to an unsettled life. Hence the numerous wandering bishops (*episcopi
vagantes*) of whom we have already had occasion to speak,
who swarmed through the country and even went to seek their
fortune overseas.[1] The Scandinavian invasions, by which
the greater number of the monasteries were disorganized and
depopulated, only added to the number of these roving and
officeless bishops.

Up to the seventh century the monks in Africa and Gaul
had made only timid efforts to free themselves from the
jurisdiction of the diocesan bishops.[2] The movement towards emancipation had begun to make itself felt before the
arrival of the Scots on the Continent ; but to St Columban
and his disciples, who propagated the Irish tenets, was
certainly due the remarkable progress made thenceforth by
the principle of the exemption of regulars. It does not appear
that on arriving in the diocese of Besançon Columban
troubled himself to ask leave of the Ordinary to set up his
foundations, although he was bound to do so by the Councils
of Agde (506) and Epaone (517).[3] Later, having need
of a bishop to consecrate an altar at Luxeuil, he had recourse
to an insular bishop named Aed and not to the diocesan.[4]

The saint of Luxeuil has nowhere revealed his opinions on
the relations between the monasteries and the diocesan bishop.
We know that he had to maintain a struggle against the
Gaulish episcopate. The chief cause of the conflict was the
Paschal observance to which he tenaciously clung in face of
all hindrances ; but we may believe too that his free and easy
procedure as abbot contributed in no small measure to
increase the misunderstanding.

It is particularly interesting to note that the men who in
the seventh century exerted themselves to withdraw the
Gaulish monasteries from episcopal jurisdiction were either

---

[1] *V. sup.*, ch. v, § 7. Cf. *CED*, II, pp. 330, 337 ; *Hibernensis*, I, 8 *b* (p. 6),
I, 22 *a* (p. 12).
[2] See Mansi, *Concilia*, VIII, 907–908, VIII, 649–54, 841–42. Cf. A.
Marignan, *Études sur la civilisation française* (Paris, 1899), I, pp. 228–03.
[3] Mansi, *Concilia*, VIII, 320, 560. Cf. E. Martin, *Saint Colomban*, p. 76.
[4] Columban, *Ep.* 4 (*MG. Epist.*, III, p. 167).

disciples of the Irish abbot or men who had come directly under the influence of his disciples.[1]

In the foundation charter of the monastery of Solignac, established by St Eligius while still a layman on lands which he held by a royal bounty, the founder, following a custom which was destined to become popular, placed the new monastery under the joint Rule of the Fathers Benedict and Columban (632). He recommends the monks and those who should come after them to observe the practice of the holy monks of Luxeuil and then goes on to stipulate that neither the local bishop nor any other person save the king (*gloriosissimus princeps*) shall be able to exercise any power or right over the persons or the property of the monastery; but that if the observance should at any time become lax, on the abbot of Luxeuil shall devolve the task of reforming it.[2]

St Faro of Meaux too, another friend of the Irish,[3] in a privilege granted to Rebais in 637 or 638, stipulates that whenever it shall be needful to consecrate altars or chrism or to hold an ordination in that monastery, the abbot shall be at liberty to call in any bishop whatsoever; and that, once his pontifical function is accomplished, the bishop so summoned shall speedily take his departure.[4] The same injunction is found in the charter of St Omer (Audomarus), a former monk of Luxeuil, in favour of the abbey of St. Bertin (Sithiu) (663), a charter subscribed by St Mummolinus of Noyon, himself a scion of Luxeuil,[5] and in other charters of the period,[6] notably that of Numerianus, bishop of Trèves, in favour of the monastery of Galilee founded by St Deodatus (*c.* A.D. 667).[7]

---

[1] Cf. K. F. Weiss, *Die kirchlichen Exemtionen der Klöster von ihren Entstehung bis zur gregorianisch-cluniacensischen Zeit* (Basel, 1893), pp. 16–27; A. Hüfner, *Das Rechtsinstitut der klösterlischen Exemtion in der abendländischen Kirche* (*Archiv für katholisches Kirchenrecht*, LXXXVI, 1906, pp. 301–10).

[2] Charter edited by Bruno Krusch in *MG. Scr. RM*, IV, pp. 746–49. Cf. *ib.*, V, p. 88. *V. sup.*, ch. v, § 3.

[3] *V. sup.*, ch. v, § 3.

[4] Ed. J. M. Pardessus, *Diplomata chartae*, etc. (Lutetiae Parisiorum, 1849), II, pp. 39–41. Cf. Krusch, *MG. Scr. RM*, IV, p. 28; V, p. 171; W. Levison, *ib.*, V, p. 538.

[5] Ed. Pardessus, *Dipl.*, II, p. 124. Cf. W. Levison, *MG. Scr. RM*, V, p. 733, n. 6.

[6] Cf. B. Krusch, *MG. Scr. RM*, V, p. 171; W. Levison, *Die Iren*, pp. 14–15.

[7] Ed. Pardessus, *Dipl.*, II, pp. 147–48.

The Rules of St Benedict and St Columban were both alike followed in the latter monastery, as likewise in the female monastery of St. Mary of Soissons. It is likewise to Irish influence that we must attribute the immunities granted to this house in 667 by Bishop Drausius, which are modelled on those granted about the same time to male monasteries.[1]

The case of Bobbio calls for special notice. Abbot Bertulf in 628 besought its exemption from the Holy See. It was granted him by a privilege of Honorius I, declaring the abbey freed from all episcopal jurisdiction and placing it immediately under that of the Pope. This is the earliest privilege of the kind.[2]

Strange to say, in the foregoing cases it is the Gaulish bishops themselves, imbued with Irish doctrines, who labour on behalf of monastic emancipation. There were, however, some who withstood the impulse emanating from Luxeuil ; among the number St Audoen (or Ouen) of Rouen, who set himself to maintain the old discipline steadfast in his diocese.[3]

As for the Abbey of St. Gall, the bishops of Constance in the eighth century laid a heavy yoke on its liberties. But Abbots Gozbert (816–836) and Grimald (841–872) succeeded in obtaining from Louis the Pious and Louis the German privileges of immunity by which the abbey was withdrawn from the suzerainty of the bishop of Constance.[4]

§ 3.—THE PRIMACY OF ARMAGH

The origin of the primacy of Armagh is very obscure. Without accepting the legendary details with which Muirchu, and other biographers of St Patrick after him, surround the foundation of this ecclesiastical centre, we may believe the apostle of the Irish really did about the year 444 [5] found a double monastic establishment there, one at the foot of the

---

[1] Ed. Pardessus, *Dipl.*, II, p. 138. Cf. W. Levison, *MG. Scr. RM*, V, p. 540 (St Ouen [Audoenus] subscribed this charter).

[2] *PL*, LXXX, 483–84. Cf. Grützmacher, art. *Mönchtum* (*Realencyclopaedie f. prot. Theol. und Kirche*, XIII, p. 231).

[3] Cf. A. Hauck, *Kirchengeschichte Deutschlands* (Leipzig, 1904), I, p. 312 (same page in ed. 1914, 1922).

[4] B. Krusch, *MG. Scr. RM*, IV, p. 231 ; Maud Joynt, *The Life of St Gall*, pp. 13–14.

[5] Muirchu, pp. 290–92 ; *Vita Trip.*, pp. 228–31.

hill of Macha and the other on its summit, on land given to him by Dáire, a powerful chief, possibly even king of Oriel.[1]

According to the tradition, of all the Churches established by him Patrick favoured that of Armagh especially. There he is said to have fixed his episcopal see and spent the last years of his life.[2]

Patrick's successors, as bishops occupying the see of Armagh or perhaps as abbots placed over the monastery there, put forth the claim of exercising over all Ireland a supremacy ostensibly derived from the saint himself. It is hard to say what Patrick's intentions in this matter really were. In the middle of the fifth century the powers of archbishops, metropolitans and primates were still ill-defined and fluctuating in Western Europe.[3] During his sojourn in the south of Gaul the saint had surely heard of the primacy of Arles, at that time a subject of lively debate. But for a primacy like that of Arles, the outcome of a peculiar political situation, there would have been no justification in Ireland. Patrick must evidently have organized his church on some other system.

In the twelfth century the Patrician origin of the primacy of Armagh was accepted without question. In his *Vita Malachiae* St Bernard writes that it was through reverence and honour for Patrick that from the beginning not merely the bishops and priests of Ireland, but even her kings and princes submitted to the metropolitan of the city where Patrick was laid to rest.[4] Let us note in passing that St Bernard is mistaken in fixing Armagh as the burial place of Patrick ; a claim not made even by the *Liber Angeli*, the compilation most openly favourable to the interests of the primatial see. Giraldus Cambrensis on his part affirms that the apostle of Ireland fixed his see at Armagh and made it a quasi-metropolis (*quam etiam quasi metropolim constituit*), the regular seat of the primacy of all Ireland. However, on the next page he makes a statement which it seems difficult to reconcile with the

---

[1] Bury, *Pat.*, pp. 159–60, 308.
[2] Muirchu, p. 296 ; *Liber Angeli* (*LA*, pp. 40–41).
[3] See E. Lesne, *La hiérarchie épiscopale* (Lille and Paris, 1905), Part I, ch. I ; Part III, ch. XI.
[4] Bernard, *Vita Mal.*, 10, col. 1086.

preceding : *Archiepiscopi vero in Hibernia nulli fuerant, sed tantum se episcopi invicem consecrabant donec Johannes Papiro, Romanae sedis legatus, non multis retro annis huc advenit.*[1] The legateship of Cardinal Paparo in Ireland belongs to the years 1151 and 1152.

We must go farther back in order to form a less summary notion as to the role and the powers of Patrick's successor. From the seventh century onward there set in a current of ideas favourable to the establishment or the consolidation of the privileges of Armagh.[2] Tirechán busied himself to that end by hunting up all the Churches throughout Ireland which owed their origin to the national apostle. The entire group of such Churches formed what was called the *paruchia Patricii*,[3] over which the apostle's successors claimed rights which we shall discuss presently. The additional notes to Tirechán in the Book of Armagh show the same eagerness to forward the interests of the *paruchia* and of the " apostolic city." [4] The *Tripartite Life* of St Patrick is inspired by the same motives. But of all the texts in favour of the extension of the rights and privileges of the Church of Armagh, the most important and the most characteristic is assuredly the *Liber Angeli*, composed in the eighth century and inserted in the Book of Armagh.[5] The title *Book of the Angel* is given to it because it calls in the intervention of a celestial messenger who announces to Patrick in the name of God the singular privileges bestowed on him personally and on his see after him. " The Lord hath given all the nations of the Scots *in modum paruchiae* to thee and to thy city which the Scots call in their tongue Ard Macha." To the pontiff of that Church is due special veneration. By privilege and in virtue of the supreme authority of the sovereign pontiff its founder, its superiority holds good over

---

[1] Giraldus, *TH*, III, 16 (pp. 161, 162–63). Cf. L.G., *Les chrétientés celtiques*, p. 223, n. 3.

[2] Writing to the clergy of Northern Ireland in A.D. 640, Pope John IV gives the first place in the address of his letter to Tomianus (Bede, *HE*, II, 19), who is to be identified with Tomméne mac Ronáin, abbot and bishop of Armagh († 660 *AU*).

[3] Tirechán, p. 21. Cf. Bury, *Pat.*, p. 249.

[4] *LA*, p. 32. Cf. Bury, *Pat.*, p. 253.

[5] *LA*, pp. 40–43. On the *Liber Angeli* see Bury, *Pat.*, p. 287 ; J. Gwynn, *LA*, pp. LXXV–LXXVIII.

all the Churches and monasteries of Ireland. This text, moreover, prescribes the manner in which the successor of Patrick should be received in the course of his visitations and the penalties which fall on those who are guilty of offence towards him or his house or his " parish." Any difficult case or one which the judges of Ireland may be unable to decide is to be brought before the tribunal of " the archbishop of the Irish " ; if he, with the aid of his learned scholars, does not feel himself competent to settle it, the matter shall be deferred to the Holy See. Finally, the *Liber Angeli* speaks of a tribute to be collected for the benefit of Armagh throughout the entire *paruchia*.

With the help of these documents, especially the last, we may form an approximate idea of what must have been the nature of the primacy of Armagh previously to the reforms undertaken by Malachy and others. In memory of Patrick the see enjoyed a pre-eminence of dignity and certain honorific privileges, the right of visitation, that of being the ultimate court of judgment in certain cases and perhaps of appeal, and finally the right of levying a tribute.

We must not, however, take too literally certain hyperbolic expressions used in the *Liber Angeli* which might lead us to infer the existence of a centralized organization such as would have been wholly inconceivable in the Ireland of that age. Taken all in all, the authority of the primatial see amounted to very little. There is but faint trace of a metropolitan organization in the Irish canonical collection, which dates from the beginning of the eighth century. We find in it mention of " *comprovinciales* " bishops and of the right possessed by the metropolitan to judge the causes of his " province " [1] ; but these regulations are contained in texts of foreign origin introduced into Ireland by the partisans of juridical and liturgical uniformity, who were active at that time. Beyond doubt there was nothing correspondingly definite in actual practice. The native canonical texts are quite silent on the matter. In 816 the Council of Celchyth rigorously excludes from sacred functions Scottic priests staying in England, and that for various reasons, one of which is that in their own

[1] *Hibernensis*, I, 3 ; xx, 3 (pp. 4, 61).

country small account is taken of the rank and dignity of metropolitans.[1]

In our final chapter we shall have to tell how in the twelfth century the institution of metropolitan sees was definitely regulated in Ireland and of the new basis on which Rome placed the primacy of Armagh.

§ 4.—The Lower Hierarchy

The lower degrees of the ecclesiastical hierarchy seem to have been constituted in Celtic countries just as in other Churches. The order of acolyte, however, is not so well attested as the other grades. The only trace we can find of it is in two Irish glosses of Würzburg (eighth century), in which the Latin word *acolytus* is glossed by the Irish *caindlóir* (from the Latin *candelarius*).[2]

A piece in the Leabhar Breac sets forth the duties of the rural priest : " Of him is required baptism and communion, that is Sacrifice, and singing intercession for the living and the dead, and Mass every Sunday and every chief solemnity and every chief festival ; celebration of every canonical hour ; the three fifties (the psalter) to be sung every day unless teaching or spiritual direction prevent him." [3]

We have little information touching the garb of clerics. The sixth canon of the first series attributed to St Patrick orders churchmen to wear a *tunica*.[4]

Up to the beginning of the ninth century the clergy of Armagh appear to have been subject to compulsory military service. We are told that they gained exemption from it under the following circumstances. King Aedh Ordnidhe having in the year 803 called upon the bishop of Armagh and his clergy to join his troops in a campaign against Leinster, the bishop pointed out to the king how utterly at variance warlike expeditions were with the obligations of the priest-hood and begged to be exempted from them. The king left

[1] Can. 5 (*CED*, III, p. 581).
[2] Stokes and Strachan, *TP*, I, pp. 654, 703.
[3] In Stokes, *Trip. Life*, p. clxxxiii. Cf. *On the Duties of a Priest* (*The Rule of St Carthage*, ed. Mac Eclaise, *Irish Ecclesiastical Record*, 4th Ser., XXVII, 1910, pp. 502–503).
[4] Can. 6 (*CED*, II, p. 328).

it to his counsellor Fothad to consider the petition. After mature deliberation Fothad gave his verdict in verse ; it was favourable to the wishes of the clergy. Henceforth clerics were exempted from military service.[1]

We have already shown how the parochial system arose in Brittany [2] ; we have no reliable data about its rise in the other Celtic countries.[3]

§ 5.—ECCLESIASTICAL CELIBACY

That the Celtic clergy from the fifth century onward observed celibacy is a fact clearly evident from texts ; but since many writers have endeavoured to make these texts say something quite different from their real meaning, it becomes our duty to pass them carefully under review in our turn and try to give the interpretation which we hold to be in accord with truth.

As we have already stated, monks took a vow of chastity.

Certain historians lay great stress on the genealogy of Patrick, which that saint prefixes to his *Confessio*, and from which it appears that he was the son of the deacon Calpurnius and grandson of the priest Potitus. There is nothing, however, to tell us that the children of Potitus and Calpurnius were born after their ordination ; and, further, if it were proved that such was the case, there would be nothing extraordinary in the fact. The date of Patrick's birth must be placed in the last quarter of the fourth century. Now, Pope Siricius, writing in 385 to Himerius, bishop of Tarragona, in order to recall the Spanish priests and deacons to the practice of celibacy ordained by the Council of Elvira (*c.* 300), assumes that these priests and deacons may have transgressed through ignorance of the canons.[4] Such ignorance is *a fortiori* to be assumed within the confines of the island of Britain where Patrick's parents lived. That region might very well not yet

---

[1] See Kenney, *Sources*, I, p. 473.

[2] *V. sup.* ch. IV, § 4.

[3] "I doubt very much whether any true 'parochial system' had developed itself by this time [in Britain], outside some of the greater towns" (F. C. Burkitt, *St Samson of Dol* in *JTS*, XXVII, 1926, p. 51).

[4] Siricius, *Ep. ad Himerium* (*PL*, LVI, 558-59). See also notification of the same injunction to African bishops (col. 728).

have been affected by the injunctions from Rome. In his
De officiis, written after 386, St Ambrose does in fact say that
there were priests in the remoter countries who continued to
live in the married state.[1]

The references to sons or wives of priests or bishops which
we meet in subsequent insular texts cannot furnish any
argument against the law of ecclesiastical celibacy. Ussher
instances the son of a priest named Benlanus and the priest's
wife Laeta in Great Britain towards the end of the seventh
century.[2] It is known that Gildas requires of a bishop that
he shall be *vir unius uxoris*. A sound proof, according to
William Reeves, that clerical marriage existed in the Church
founded by Patrick, is the demand which the apostle of Ireland makes of the future bishop of Leinster, that he should be
" a man of one wife unto whom hath been borne only one
child." [3] Finally, a passage is adduced in the *Senchus Mór*
which deals with the penalties to be inflicted on guilty bishops
and in which a distinction is made between the bishop who is
a virgin and one who has had a wife.[4]

What conclusion are we to draw from all this ? Simply the
twofold certainty, first, that in a period when men were pro-
moted to the diaconate, the priesthood and the episcopate at
a much maturer age than in the present day, candidates for
orders were very often married [5]; and, second, that in
accordance with the instructions laid down by St Paul for
the bishop's office, those who had married twice were
excluded from holy orders.[6] But from none of the texts
adduced have we any right to conclude that after their
ordination priests and deacons lived in conjugal relations

---

[1] *De officiis*, I, 50 (*PL*, XVI 105).
[2] Ussher, *A Discourse of the Religion anciently professed by the Irish and British* (*Works*, IV, p. 295).
[3] W. Reeves in Adam., *Vita Col.*, p. 344. The reference is to Fiacc's election. See *Additions to Tirechán's Memoir* (*LA*, p. 35).
[4] *Senchus Mór*, I, 57. Cf. T. Olden, *Church of Ireland*, pp. 121 ff. ; H. C. Lea, *History of Sacerdotal Celibacy in the Christian Church*, 3rd ed., London, 1907, I, p. 360.
[5] See *Hibernensis*, I, 11 (p. 8).
[6] On the exclusion of " bigami " in the fifth century see Innocent I, *Ep.* 37 *ad ep. Nucer.*, 2 (*PL*, XX, 604) ; Leo I, *Ep.* 12 (*PL*, LIV, 652). Cf. E. Valton, art. *Bigamie*, II, in *Dictionnaire de théologie catholique*, edited by Vacant and Mangenot.

with their wives. The treatise *De duodecim abusionibus saeculi*, the composition of which, sometimes wrongly ascribed to St Patrick, is now by general consent placed in Ireland before the year 700, traces almost word for word after St Paul the portrait of the perfect bishop, which is contrasted with that of the *episcopus negligens ;* but instead of reproducing simply and unchanged the words of the Apostle, "*unius uxoris virum,*" it says " *ante episcopatum non plures habens uxores quam unam* " [1]— a significant substitution. Wherever mention is made of the son or wife of a priest or bishop, we are justified in supposing a marriage contracted before entry into orders and in which connubial intercourse is broken off by ordination.

Against this conclusion, however, another text is brought forward, one which the objectors deem to be irrefragable ; it is taken from the first series of the canons of St Patrick.[2] We have already had occasion to refer to it in other connections, but this time it may be well to quote it verbatim in its curious tenor : *Quicumque clericus ab hostiario usque ad sacerdotem sine tunica visus fuerit atque turpitudinem ventris et nuditatem non tegat et si non more romano capilli eius tonsi sint, et uxor eius si non velato capite ambulaverit, pariter a laicis contempnentur et ab Ecclesia separentur.*[3] Here we have a command relating not only to the attire of the cleric, from porter to priest, but also to that of his wife ; the latter is not to go out save with veiled head. The text in fact says " *uxor eius* " *;* it admits of no evasion ; it is certainly the cleric's wife that is meant. But it would be idle to attempt to construe the text as implying that the said cleric and his wife did not live together in continence as brother and sister. It actually implies the contrary. That a wife under the conditions was required to wear a veil proves, in fact, that she was no longer to be regarded by the world as an ordinary married woman, but as a sort of widow.[4]

---

[1] *PL*, IV, 879 ; ed. S. Hellmann in *Texte und Untersuchungen*, edited by Harnack and Schmidt, XXXIV, 1 (Leipzig, 1909), p. 56.

[2] Whitley Stokes (*Tr. Life*, p. CLXIX) and H. C. Lea (*op. cit.*, I, p. 78) have particularly laid stress upon this text.

[3] Can. 6 (*CED*, II, p. 328).

[4] On the " *palliatae* " or " *velatae* " see *Hibernensis*, XLV, 10, 12, 13 (pp. 182–83). " Velato capite ambulare," is, I think, wrongly translated " to take the veil " in the sense of entering a convent by J. Salmon (*The ancient Irish Church*, p. 131).

If this interpretation be accepted, it follows that in Ireland in the fifth century even the inferior grades of the clergy were bound to continence. And the inference raises no difficulty. There is nothing surprising in it in an age of ardent asceticism, and similar conditions are to be met elsewhere in ecclesiastical antiquity.[1] However, the wives of the clergy, becoming their sisters after ordination, were not obliged to quit their husband's homes. It will be remembered that the Irish saints of the first order did not shun the society of women, *quia super petram Christi fundati ventum tentationis non timebant.*[2] St Leo, who wrote just at the time when our Irish canon was drawn up, even advises ministers of the altar not to repudiate their wives, but only to convert the former union of the flesh into a spiritual bond. Sidonius Apollinaris, likewise a contemporary, when made bishop of Clermont, did not banish his wife from the bishop's house, nor did St Paulinus of Nola.[3]

Before we proceed to set forth in detail the positive proofs which exist of the observation of ecclesiastical celibacy in the Celtic Churches, there remains one last objection to dispose of. Robert King, in his work on the origin of the primacy of Armagh, draws up, with the aid of the *Annals of the Four Masters*, a list of the abbots of Lusk from the end of the eighth century to the year 927, and shows that the office of abbot was held in succession by direct line throughout that entire lapse of time. For instance, Conall († 784) succeeds his father, Crunnmael. After Conall the place of abbot falls to his brother Colga († 787). Conall's son, Cormac, becomes in 796 his fourth successor. Moenach († 805), son of Colga, succeeds him ; and so on. From which King draws the decided conclusion that the abbots of Lusk, though monks, were married.[4] Monks they probably were not, in any sense. We have here simply to deal with secular abbots. It was the Irish custom that the coarb or successor of the founder of an abbey should always be

---

[1] Thomassin, *Ancienne et nouvelle discipline*, Part I, Bk. II, chs. LXI, LXV (Paris, 1735), I, pp. 907, 922–23.

[2] *Catalogus*, p. 292.

[3] Leo I, *Epist. ad Rusticum*, 3 (*PL*, LIV, 1201). Cf. Paul Allard, *Saint Sidoine Apollinaire* (Paris, 1910), pp. 127–28 ; A. Baudrillart, *Saint Paulin de Nole* (Paris, 1905), pp. 58, 67, 164.

[4] Robert King, *A Memoir introductory to the early History of the Primacy of Armagh* (Armagh, 1854), p. 20.

chosen in the kindred of the founder.[1] Since the abbots were bound to celibacy, the successor was chosen from the collateral branches. But if in the collateral branches no monk was forthcoming fitted to become abbot, the *ecclesiastica progenies* thus failing, the *plebilis progenies*, that is to say, the secular members of the family of the coarb, often laid hands on the government of the abbey and thus there came to be established a succession in direct line of lay abbots.[2]

This is not pure conjecture. St Bernard expressly states that such was the plight of the monastery of Bangor. Such was likewise the plight of several other monasteries in Ireland and Wales, according to Giraldus Cambrensis.[3] If the Annals made no mention of the lay character of the coarbs, it was because the family holding the succession was powerful and would have resented it had the annalist noticed any breach on its part of the discipline of the Church.[4]

There was also a bishop at Lusk. The Annals mention six bishops of Lusk between 731 and 927, but in their case there is no trace of succession in direct line.[5] The bishopric of Armagh, on the contrary, fell into the hands of laymen in the eleventh century. It came to pass, as St Bernard says with mournful irony, that the family which usurped this see " was sometimes lacking in clerics, but never in bishops." Eight pseudo-bishops governed in succession the church of Armagh before Cellach, the predecessor of St Malachy. All these individuals were married, but none of them had taken orders.[6] It would not be difficult to adduce many parallel cases on the Continent in the same period, either of lay abbots who were placed or placed themselves at the head of monasteries, or of pseudo-bishops appointed by feudal lords to certain sees, who, not having received holy orders, were ecclesiastics only in name.[7]

---

[1] *Ancient Laws and Institutes of Ireland*, III, pp. 73, 75. Cf. Kenney, *Sources*, I, pp. 353, 747.
[2] W. Reeves, *On the early System of Abbatial Succession in the Irish Monasteries* (*PRIA*, VI, 1857, p. 447). Cf. Skene, *CS*, II, pp. 67–69.
[3] Giraldus, *IK*, II, 4 (pp. 120–21).
[4] King, *op. cit.*, p. 23.
[5] King, *op. cit.*, p. 20.
[6] Bernard, *Vita Mal.*, 10 (col. 1086).
[7] See H. Lévy-Brühl, *Les élections abbatiales en France* (Paris, 1913), I,

According to Reeves, such monastic and episcopal usurpations occurred from the end of the eighth century onwards. They coincide therefore with the era of the Norse invasions, and were very likely one of its most disastrous consequences.[1] Once the monastery had been pillaged and the monks scattered or driven into exile by the foreigners, the family by whose members it had been governed (though hitherto not till they had regularly embraced the monastic life) considered themselves at liberty to dispose of the monastic property, abandoned or laid waste, as of their patrimony, and to retain it even after the restoration of order. Thus may be explained the succession of so-called abbots who were married in Lusk and other monasteries which had suffered a similar fate.

The prohibition of connubial intercourse after ordination is explicitly formulated in the penitentials. The penitential of St Columban has the following words on the subject : *Si quis autem clericus aut diaconus vel alicuius gradus, qui laicus fuit in saeculo cum filiis et filiabus, post conversionem suam iterum suam cognoverit clientelam* [2] *et filium iterum de ea genuerit, sciat se adulterium perpetrasse et non minus peccasse quam si ab iuventute sua clericus fuisset et cum puella aliena peccasset, quia post votum suum peccavit, postquam se Domino consecravit, et votum suum irritum fecit.*[3] From this text we learn that the clerics in question were bound by vow to chastity on the same footing as monks, and that the cleric who had a child born of his wife after ordination was considered not less guilty than a man who had entered the clerical profession in early youth unmarried and had subsequently an intrigue with some woman. Columban even likens the transgression of the married cleric to the sin of adultery. It is idle to say that this penitential,

---

pp. 191–92 ; Karl Voigt, *Die karolingische Klosterpolitik und der Niedergang des westfränkischen Königtums, Laienäbte und Klosterinhaber (Kirchenrechtliche Abhandlungen*, edited by U. Stutz, XC–XCI, Stuttgart, 1917) ; W. Levison in Gebhardt's *Handbuch der Deutschen Geschichte* (Stuttgart, 1926), p. 263 ; Thomas Allison, *English Religious Life in the Eighth Century* (London, 1929), pp. 55–56, 58–59.

[1] Reeves in Adam., *Vita Col.*, p. 325, note *c*.   Cf. King, *op. cit.*, p. 22.

[2] See Du Cange, *Glossar. s.v.* " *Clientela* " ; M. Esposito, *Latin Learning*, I, pp. 238, 240.

[3] *Poenitentiale*, ed. Seebass (*ZK*, XIV, p. 744) ; ed. Migne (*PL*, LXXX, 226).

being written on the Continent, gives only an imperfect reflection of insular discipline ; for when Columban in his letter to St Gregory has occasion to speak of married Gaulish deacons who are guilty of having taken back their wives, he states that the serious nature of that transgression and its close affinity to adultery are among the principles of morality held by the Irish divines.[1] We are able, moreover, to trace the sources of Columban's penitential, namely, the penitential of Finnian, which he reproduces almost verbatim and from which Cummian's text, too, differs but little.[2]

Such, then, was the ecclesiastical law in Ireland in the sixth and seventh centuries, and such it subsequently remained. The intense ascetic spirit which prevailed during the period of expansion of Christianity renders it highly probable that infractions of the law of celibacy were very rare. We know the sad degeneracy which crept into the morals of the clergy in the tenth and eleventh centuries. But it does not appear that in the darkest ages the Celtic Churches were invaded by such lamentable excesses.

We do indeed read in the Chronicle of the Princes of Gwent under the year 961 that when the priests of Llandaff were ordered not to marry without the Pope's permission, there resulted such a commotion in the diocese of Teilo that it was thought better to allow priests to marry.[3] Who gave this permission ? On this point we have absolutely no information from the text, which has a pronounced anti-papistical tendency and whose authenticity is perhaps as doubtful as that of the famous letter of Dinoot to Augustine.[4] But in all likelihood it was not by the ecclesiastical authority that the authorization was given. As for the civil authority, it looked with strong disfavour on married priests. Take, for example, the estimate given of them in the laws of king Hywell the Good († 949 or 950). They place the married priest among the thirteen things which corrupt the world. His testimony

---

[1] Columban, *Ep.* 1 (*MG. Epist.*, III, pp. 158–59).
[2] *Poenitentiale Vinniai*, 27 (*Buss.*, p. 114) ; *Poenitentiale Cummeani*, 3.
[3] *Brut y Tywysogion, The Gwent Chronicle*, ed. A. Owen, pp. 28–29.
[4] There is nothing on the matter in the *Brut y Tywysogion* edited by William ab Ithel in *RS.*—On the unreliable character of the *Chronicle of Gwent* see A. G. Little, *Mediaeval Wales* (London, 1902), pp. 37–38.

is not to be accepted in courts of justice " because he has disobeyed his law." Three classes of sons are deprived of their paternal inheritance, chief among them the son of a priest born after his father has entered holy orders.[1]

Whatever may have been the shortcomings of individuals, in face of such texts and of the protests of Giraldus Cambrensis,[2] it is surely absurd to speak, as Willis Bund does, of the marriage of priests as recognized by public feeling and to say that " there can be no doubt that such marriages were regarded as perfectly lawful by the Welsh Church until after the Norman conquest." [3]

Jeuan tells us in his *Carmen de vita et familia Sulgeni* that Sulien, bishop of St. David's († 1091), had four sons : " *quattuor ac proprio nutrivit sanguine natos.*" [4] But he does not say that these sons were born after their father had been raised to the episcopate or even after his entry into holy orders.

We admit that in the eleventh and twelfth centuries there set in a sad lowering of the standard of clerical morality in Brittany, Wales and Scotland ; but the canonical law remained none the less intact and obligatory in all these countries.[5]

The evil of concubinage does not appear to have invaded Ireland to the same extent during that period. Giraldus does indeed record certain scandals which arose in the district of Wexford, but declares that they were occasioned by Welsh clerics, his own countrymen, who had crossed the sea in the train of the English invaders.[6] Considering Gerald's wholly unsympathetic attitude towards Ireland, we may be certain that if he had seen the least signs of laxity among the Irish clergy he would have mentioned it in his books. Far from doing so, he declares that among the virtues of the clergy of Ireland continence was pre-eminent.[7]

[1] *Welsh Laws*, ed. A. Owen, pp. 493, 556, 564, 595.
[2] Giraldus, *DK*, II, 6 (p. 214) ; *s.a. De jure et statu Menevensis Ecclesiae*, I (*Works*, III (*RS*), pp. 129 ff.).
[3] W. Bund, *The Celtic Church of Wales*, p. 292.
[4] Jeuan, *Carmen de vita Sulgeni (CED*, I, 666).
[5] *CED*, II, p. 179. Cf. Lloyd, *HW*, I, pp. 215–16 ; H. Thurston, *Clerical Celibacy in the Anglo-Saxon Church (Month*, No. 542, 1909, pp. 180–94). V. *inf*., ch. XI, § 8.
[6] Giraldus, *De rebus a se gestis*, II, 13 (*Works*, I, p. 66).
[7] Giraldus, *TH*, III, 27 (p. 172).—If we are to trust Friar Malachy, a

Once again, it was owing to the outburst of asceticism in the previous ages, which continued to act, though weakened, in the midst of the disorders produced by the Scandinavian invasions, that the Church of Ireland preserved its purity in a time of almost universal licence. This immunity is all the more striking in a Church so imperfectly organized. We have given a summary view of the almost incredible disorder which prevailed. Dioceses with ill-defined borders ; an episcopate motley though numerous, with its authority lessened by that of powerful abbots ; the functions of abbot, too, often usurped by members of the same kindred ; few or no synods ; no metropolitan organization and a primatial see whose influence in matters of discipline amounted in practice to very little : such is the state of the Church of Ireland presented to us, and also, as far as can be observed, the state of several other Churches of the Celtic world, before the epoch of the Roman reforms. It was our original intention to entitle this chapter " Ecclesiastical organization." But we quickly came to see that of " organization " there was no trace. In all ages the Celts have been slenderly gifted with the genius for organization. We must wait for the twelfth century to find a really " organized " Church in Ireland.

most zealous rebuker of vices who inveighs in violent terms against the degradation and corruption of the people of Ireland in the thirteenth century, morality seems to have sunk to its lowest ebb at this epoch, especially among the ecclesiastics " quorum luxuria multo excedit incontinentiam laicorum," says the friar in his *De Veneno* (fol. 23ᵇ), quoted by Mario Esposito, *Friar Malachy of Ireland* (*EHR*, XXXIII, 1918, p. 361).

CHAPTER VIII

INTELLECTUAL CULTURE AND THEOLOGICAL DOCTRINES

§ 1.—FUNDAMENTAL STUDIES

SINCE Britain had been subject to the sway of Rome, it is not surprising to find the monks of that country in the sixth century (Gildas, for instance) possessing a certain amount of classical culture. But how did Ireland, a land which had never been incorporated in the Empire, acquire the knowledge of letters? We may first begin by inquiring what is known about the introduction of writing among the Irish Celts. They possessed a writing of some sort before the conversion of the country to Christianity in the fifth century. The oldest monuments which attest the fact are stones bearing Ogham inscriptions, which are especially numerous in the south and south-east of Ireland and the south of Wales.[1]

The dating of the extant Ogham inscriptions is a matter of great difficulty. "No evidence has been found that enables us to date any of the known inscriptions earlier than the middle of the fifth century," according to Eoin MacNeill. "A small proportion of them can be dated in the seventh century. The sixth century may be regarded as the period during which the cult was most in vogue." [2] It is possible that Ogham may have been inscribed on wood before being

---

[1] Ogham inscriptions in Ireland : R. A. Stewart Macalister, *Studies in Irish Epigraphy*, 3 vols., London, 1897–1907 ; *s.a.*, *AI*, ch. IV ; *s.a.*, *The Ecclesiology of Ogham Inscriptions* (*Transactions of the St. Paul's Ecclesiological Society*, IV, 1900, pp. 53–64) ; Eoin MacNeill, *Notes on the Distribution, History and Import of the Irish Ogham Inscriptions* (*PRIA*, XXVII, Sect. C, 1909). In Wales : Westwood, *Lapidarium Walliae* (Oxford, 1876-1879). Cf. Lloyd, *HW*, I, p. 113. In Scotland and the Isle of Man : R. A. S. Macalister, *Studies in Irish Epigraphy* (Vol. II) ; Joseph Anderson in Allen, *ECMS*, pp. XIX–XXIII.

[2] Eoin MacNeill, *Archaism in the Ogham Inscriptions* (*PRIA*, XXXIV, Sect. C, 1931, p. 33). Cf. *s.a.*, *Phases*, pp. 173–74 ; Macalister, *The ancient Inscriptions of Wales* (A. Cam., 7th Ser., VIII, 1928, p. 331).

incised on stone.[1]   Indeed, in the ancient epic, the *Táin Bó Cúalnge*, we read of a message being cut on a branch of a tree, and the old tales contain several allusions to the " staves " used by *filid* to keep their records.[2]

There can be no doubt that the Ogham script originated in Ireland. The Ogham characters were based on the Roman alphabet [3] ; but the earliest extant inscriptions in the Latin language and in Roman letters found in Britain and Ireland are posterior to the Ogham inscriptions.

The great majority of sepulchral inscriptions in Wales are in the Gaelic tongue and in Ogham characters. They are memorials of Irish settlements in that country.[4] Some of these Welsh stones with Oghams bear also inscriptions in the Latin language and in debased Latin capitals.[5] A large number of Christian epitaphs in the Gaelic language and in Irish script carved in the early Middle Ages have survived.[6] But of inscriptions in the Brythonic language we possess only two ancient examples.[7]

St Patrick's biographers tell us that the apostle was accustomed to distribute to his neophytes abecedaries (*abgitoria, elementa*),[8] a word which may be taken either in a literal or a

---

[1] Macalister, *AI*, pp. 213, 222. Cf. *s.a.*, *The " Druuides " Inscription at Killeen Cormac, Co. Kildare* (*PRIA*, XXXII, Sect. C., 1914, pp. 234–35).

[2] *Táin Bó Cúalnge*, ed. Windisch, p. 89. Cf. p. 148 ; J. Vendryes, *R. Cel.*, XXXIII, 1912, pp. 383–84.

[3] The Ogham alphabet contains the letter *ng* (called *agma* in Lat., *ngedal* in Ir.), which was originally one of the Latin alphabet also. Cf. H. d'Arbois, *R. Cel.*, XXX, 1909, p. 115.

[4] R. A. S. Macalister, *The ancient Inscriptions of Wales*, p. 287.

[5] For instance, memorial of Voteporius (*A. Cam.*, 6th Ser., VII, 1907, p. 242), St Dogmael's stone (*A. Cam.*, 6th Ser., V, 1905, p. 166, 2 plates), Lewannic stone in Cornwall (A. G. Langdon and J. Romilly Allen, *Catalogue of the early Christian Inscribed Monuments in Cornwall* (*A. Cam.*, 5th Ser., XII, 1895, p. 53, fig. 1). On the bilingual inscription at Killeen Cormac (Co. Kildare) see R. A. S. Macalister, *art. cit.*, *PRIA*, 1914 ; H. Gaidoz, *Notice sur les inscriptions latines de l'Irlande* (*Mélanges publiés par les sections historique et philologique de l'École des Hautes Études*, Paris, 1878, p. 127) ; John Rhys, *Studies in early Irish History* (*PBA*, 1903–1904, p. 25 ff.) ; Bury, *Pat.*, p. 298, 305.

[6] George Petrie, *Christian Inscriptions in the Irish Language from the earliest known to the end of the Twelfth Century*, edited by Margaret Stokes (Dublin, 1870–1878) ; R. A. S. Macalister, *Mem. slabs*.

[7] Pillar at Towyn (Merionethshire) and one fragment on Bardsey Island (Macalister, *The ancient Inscriptions of Wales*, p. 285).

[8] Bury, *Pat.*, p. 311.

figurative sense—in the latter as signifying a compendium of Christian doctrine.[1]

But to return to the question with which we started : how did Ireland make acquaintance with classical letters? Through the students of Gaul who, driven from their country by the victorious arms of the Barbarians, Burgundians, Visigoths and Franks, carried their teaching to the island of the Gaels—so answer H. d'Arbois de Jubainville, Zimmer and Kuno Meyer.[2] The two latter writers have drawn with much ingenuity upon a rather vague passage in a Glossary at Leyden, which tells incidentally of such an exodus of Gaulish scholars to transmarine parts ; they have even discovered in these learned Gauls the *rhetorici* who raised difficulties for St Patrick and thwarted his apostolic mission. That such a flight of Gaulish scholars before the barbarian hordes took place, is by no means unlikely ; but the passage in the Leyden text, relied upon as the chief proof of the fact, seems to us as well as to other critics to be too indefinite in its details to permit of its being used as a decisive argument.[3]

According to other writers, literary culture was brought to Ireland by monks hailing from Alexandria or Byzantium [4]— a conjecture still less solidly grounded than the preceding.

Others, finally, are inclined to believe that the great development of Latin learning in Ireland is to be attributed to the activity of British monks who, while initiating the Irish cenobites in monastic discipline, trained them at the same time in the classical culture. " The great stimulus to monastic development and to the concurrent development of Latin literary culture came from South Wales," says E. MacNeill, " especially from St Cadoc and St David, and from their monasteries of Llancarvan and Menevia." [5]

---

[1] MacNeill, *Phases*, p. 174 ; Bury, *l. cit.*

[2] H. d'Arbois, *Introduction à l'étude de la littérature celtique* (Paris, 1883), p. 367 ; Kuno Meyer, *Learning in Ireland in the Fifth Century and the Transmission of Letters* (Dublin, 1913). Cf. Kenney, *Sources*, I, pp. 142–43.

[3] Roger, *Enseignement*, pp. 203–207 ; Esposito, *Latin Learning*, I, pp. 231–32 ; E. MacNeill, *Beginnings of Latin Culture in Ireland* (*Studies*, XX, 1931, pp. 39–48).

[4] Roger, *Enseignement*, pp. 203–204.

[5] MacNeill, *Beginnings*, p. 48. Cf. *s.a.*, art. *Ireland* (*Economic and cultural Development*) in *Encyclopaedia Britannica*, 14th edit., 1929, Vol. XII, p. 601 ;

The British Church had been established and had developed in a country subject to the domination of Rome. From what we know of the close relations between the two countries, it does indeed seem likely that the British Church, having imbibed a certain amount of Latin culture, should have served as the agent of transmission in this respect as in many others.

The pioneer missionaries, British or continental, who brought the faith to Ireland in the fifth century, had no doubt little leisure to engage in study and to work for the diffusion of secular knowledge. St Patrick's whole energy was claimed by the evangelization of the land. That great missionary, moreover, was not a man of learning ; he speaks of himself as " *indoctus*." [1] But he was steeped in the Bible, and his writings abound in reminiscences and quotations from it. [2]

But before long the study of the liberal arts became incumbent on the native clergy. In order to celebrate divine service, to read the Scriptures, to investigate the truths of religion and expound them to the faithful, it was in that age absolutely necessary to learn the Latin tongue. Along with biblical texts and the writings of the Fathers, the works of the ancient authors were imported by degrees from the neighbouring island and the Continent. The large number of monasteries contributed to the rapid progress of intellectual culture. [3] For all those great abbeys which we have seen springing up in the sixth century, besides being centres of religion, were before very long much-frequented centres of study to which flocked all those eager for instruction, even from foreign parts. Among the most celebrated, the schools of Aranmore in Galway Bay, of Clonard, Bangor, Moville, Armagh, Clonmacnois and Ros Ailithir must be named [4] ; and we might mention other famous schools in Ireland of the early Middle Ages without falling into the exaggerations of Archbishop Healy, the ever popular author of the *Insula Sanctorum*

Ryan, *Monast.*, p. 380 ; Evan J. Jones, *History of Education in Wales* (Wrexham, 1931), I, pp. 286–88.

[1] " Ego primus rusticus profuga indoctus " (*Confessio*, 12, p. 9).

[2] Bury, *Pat.*, p. 206.

[3] Roger, *Enseignement*, pp. 227–32 ; Robin Flower, *Ireland and Medieval Europe* (*PBA*, XIII, 1929, p. 8).

[4] *V. sup.*, ch. III, § 4. " Ciuitas in qua semper manet magnum studium scholarium quae dicitur Ross Ailithry " (*Vita Mochoemog*, 4 : *VSH*, II, p. 165).

et Doctorum, of whom a critic has observed that " the smallest huts in which anchorites prayed became in his eyes important centres of learning." [1]

Moreover, in order to train their recruits, the Irish monks settled abroad, in Britain or on the Continent, opened schools there also. The Venerable Bede tells us that the schools of Lindisfarne and Northumbria were largely frequented by the sons of the Angles and that the instruction given in them was carried to an advanced stage *(maiora studia)*. [2]

If we would form some idea of the way in which studies were organized in the Irish monastic schools, we must glean what we can in many texts ; by so doing we gain some meagre information about the scholastic buildings, the methods of instruction, the curriculum of studies and other matters of the kind.

We have found only a single text dealing with the scholastic buildings. In a passage in the Life of a certain St Daig, who studied at Devenish under St Molaisse, there is mention of a little monastery *(monasteriolum)* which adjoined the main one and which served as a *schola*. [3] In it Daig learned his letters and the art of writing, and, in addition, a handicraft, that either of smith or carpenter *(fabrilem artem)*. [4]

As a general rule, a child was taught to read before being handed over to the monks. More than once the age of seven is mentioned as the time for beginning elementary studies. [5] The child learned to read in the Latin Psalter, a custom which was in vogue in all countries in the Middle Ages and persisted for centuries. [6] Thus he fixed in his memory simultaneously the text of the psalms and the hymns and canticles of the

---

[1] Roger, *Enseignement,* p. 257. Cf. Hugh Graham, *The early Irish monastic Schools* (Dublin, 1923) ; W. G. Hanson, *The early monastic Schools of Ireland* (Cambridge, 1927).

[2] " Imbuebantur praeceptoribus Scottis paruuli Anglorum una cum maioribus studiis et observatione disciplinae regularis " (Bede, *HE,* III, 3).

[3] *Acta Dagaei,* 1, 5 (*Sal. ASH,* col. 891, 893–94).

[4] More likely " smith." Cf. *Vita Comgalli,* 36 (*VSH,* II, p. 15).

[5] *Betha Finnchua Bri Gobunn* (Lismore, pp. 85, 232). Cf. C. Plummer, *BNE,* II, pp. 326, 362 ; *VSH,* I, p. cxv (*introd.*).

[6] *Vita Ciarani de Cluain,* 4, 16 (*VSH,* I, pp. 201, 205) ; *Vita Maedoc,* 39 (*VSH,* II, p. 157) (cf. *VSH,* I, p. cxv (*introd.*) ; *Acta Finniani de Cluain Eraird,* 2 (*Sal. ASH,* col. 190) ; *Acta Darercae,* 2 (*Sal. ASH,* 166) ; Conchubran, *Vita Mon.,* 3 (p. 209). Cf. Ursmer Berlière, *L'ascèse bénédictine des origines à la fin du XIIe siècle* (Paris, 1927), p. 181.

psalter and was enabled by degrees to follow the celebration
of the liturgical office intelligently and even take part in it.[1]
As soon as he had acquired these rudiments from a teacher,
he was sent to pursue his studies in a monastery. In the *Acta*
of St Columba of Terryglass there is an apposite passage on
the subject. From it we learn that the child was first entrusted to a holy man of the name of Colmán Cule, founder
of the place called Cluain Cuin. Colmán took entire charge
of the boy, body and soul, and taught him to read the psalms
and hymns ; then, when Columba was well grown and had
become a young man (*iuvenis*), he went to the famous Finnian,
abbot-bishop of Clonard, to study under him as a pupil,
in his school.[2] The great number of eminent disciples
trained at Clonard won for Finnian the title of " Tutor of
the saints of Ireland " or " Master of all the chief saints of
Ireland."

In order to save parchment, the scholars were given waxed
tablets, which were in general use for dictation and literary
exercises.[3] It was on such tablets that Adamnán, the abbot of
Iona, wrote down at the dictation of the pilgrim Arculf the
description of the Holy Places which Arculf had visited.[4]

Where text-books are few, the scholar is obliged to make
use of his memory. The teaching in the monastic schools was
mainly oral, and the memory of the pupils, through much
exercise, acquired a retentive power far greater than is to be
found in our days. In the schools of the *filid*, where an official
class of scholars and men of letters were trained, memorizing
and oral exercises likewise played a preponderant part.[5]

In Latin texts dealing with the monastic schools of Ireland,
the masters are called *magistri, praeceptores, didascali, sapientes,
lectores.*[6] To the term *lector* used for a teacher corresponded

---

[1] *Acta Columbae de Tyre Da Glass*, 4 (*Sal. ASH*, 446) ; *Acta Finniani de
Cluain Eraird*, 2 (*ib.*, 190).

[2] *Acta Columbae de Tyre Da Glass, l. cit.*

[3] Cf. C. Plummer, *VSH*, I, p. cxv (*introd.*) ; L. J. Paetow, *A Guide to
the Study of Medieval History* (New York, 1931), p. 529.

[4] Adamnán, *De locis sanctis*, Prol. ; I, I, ed. P. Geyer, *Itinera Hierosolymitana* (*Corp. SEL*, XXXIX, pp. 221, 227).

[5] Kenney, *Sources*, I, pp. 2–3.

[6] Bede, *HE*, III, 3, 13, 27 ; Alcuin, *Vita Willibrordi*, 4 (ed. A. Poncelet,
Boll., *AS*, Nov. III, 439 ; ed. W. Levison, *MG. Scr. RM*, VII, pp. 118–19) ;
s.a. Versus de sanctis Euboricensis Ecclesiae, V, 462 (*MG. Poet. Lat.*, I, p. 180) ;

the Irish *fer léiginn* (*i.e.*, " man of reading," lecturer, master of studies).

The remuneration of the teacher in the Irish educational system offers some singular features. The cost of instruction was paid in kind ; a cow, a heifer or a pig, furnished by the family of the pupil, in such consisted the fee of the *didascalus*. On this head there is a curious passage in the Rule of the Céli Dé which is worth quoting. " Any one, moreover," so runs the text, " with whom the boys study who are thus offered to God and to Patrick, has a claim to reward and fee at the proper seasons, namely, a milch-cow as remuneration for [teaching] the Psalms with their hymns, canticles and lections, and the rites of baptism and communion and intercession, together with the knowledge of the ritual generally, till the student be capable of receiving Orders. A heifer and a pig and three sacks of malt and a sack of corn are his fee every year, besides tendance and a compassionate allowance of raiment and food in return for his blessing. But the milch-cow is made over immediately after the student has publicly proved his knowledge of the Psalms and hymns, and after the public proof of his knowledge of the ritual the fee and habit are due. Moreover, the doctor or bishop before whom proof in the Psalms has been made is entitled to a collation of beer and food for five persons the same night." [1]

We can imagine the youthful student wending his way to the monastery to read the Scriptures there and driving before him the milch-cow which represented his master's fee. What could be more picturesque than the story of the good cow which accompanied Ciarán, the future abbot of Clonmacnois, to Clonard ? [2]

In 1169 Rory O'Connor, king of Ireland, wishing to make Armagh a national centre of learning, determined to give " ten cows each year from himself and from every king after him till Doomsday to the *fer léiginn* of Armagh, in honour of

---

Vita Cadoci, 7 (*CBS*, p. 15). Cf. C. Plummer, Bede, *HE*, Vol. II, p. 161 ; Ricemarch, *PM* (Lawlor's *introd.*, I, p. ix).

[1] *Rule of the Céli Dé* (*Tallaght*, 1927, p. 83).

[2] *Vita Ciarani de Cluain*, 15 (*VSH*, I, p. 205) ; *The Latin and Irish Lives of Ciaran*, by R. A. S. Macalister (London, 1912), pp. 23, 45–46. See a similar instance in *Vita Tathei* (*CBS*, p. 258).

Patrick, to give lectures to students of Ireland and Scotland." [1]

What are we to understand by the *maiora studia* of which Bede speaks in connection with the Irish schools of Northumbria ? Other passages of that author's *Ecclesiastical History* throw light on the subject, besides furnishing other important details. Indeed, our knowledge of the Irish schools would be greatly lessened if we had not the information afforded by this invaluable book. In speaking of the great plague of 664, Bede mentions the presence of numerous Anglo-Saxons in Ireland. " Many of the nobles of the English nation and lesser men also had set out thither," he writes, " forsaking their native island either for the sake of sacred learning or a more ascetic life (*vel divinae lectionis vel continentioris vitae gratia*). And some of them, indeed, soon dedicated themselves faithfully to the monastic life, others rejoiced rather to give themselves to learning, going about from one master's cell to another (*circumeundo per cellas magistrorum*). All these the Irish willingly received and took care to supply them with food day by day without cost, and books for their studies, and teaching free of charge." [2] Irish hospitality has often been lauded,[3] but of all testimonies this one, coming from a writer so well qualified to speak with authority, is perhaps the worthiest of remembrance.

Grammar (*i.e.*, Latin grammar) formed the basis of all instruction.[4] Aldhelm of Sherborne tells us that besides grammar, geometry, natural philosophy and the allegorical interpretation of Scripture were also taught in the Irish schools.[5]

The Irish monks have often been credited with being distinguished Hellenists. It is true that, even before the time of Sedulius Scottus and Johannes Eriugena, monks may have been found who studied Greek, but, it seems, only on their own individual behalf. The arguments adduced to prove that

[1] *AU, a.a.* 1169.
[2] Bede, *HE*, III, 27.
[3] " Cultores vero Hybernie probati sunt in fide catholica, et in dogmatibus ecclesiasticis ; et plus omnibus nacionibus hospitalitatem sectantur " (*Vita Abbani*, 1 : *VSH*, I, 3).
[4] Alcuin, *Ep.* 280 (*MG. Epist.* IV, pp. 437–38).
[5] Aldhelm, *Ep. ad Ehfridum*, ed. Ehwald (*MG. Auct. ant.*, XV, pp. 490–91).

Greek was taught in the Irish schools are weak and do not go very far.[1] It was otherwise in the neighbouring island. We have proof that the Greek language was seriously studied by the pupils of Theodore of Tarsus and the abbot Hadrian, who arrived in Canterbury, the former in 669, the latter in the following year. " They gathered a crowd of disciples," says Bede, " and rivers of wholesome knowledge daily flowed from them to water the hearts of their hearers ; and, together with the books of Holy Scripture, they also taught them the metrical art, astronomy and ecclesiastical arithmetic. A testimony whereof is, that there are still living at this day some of their scholars, who are as well versed in the Greek and Latin tongues as in their own, in which they were born." [2] There is no such testimony extant as regards the study of Greek in Ireland. It has been asserted that the Greek teaching imparted at Canterbury by Theodore and Hadrian extended its effects to the isle of the Scots also, but this is a gratuitous assumption unsupported by any proof.[3]

The students in the monastic schools were nearly all either monks or aspirants to the monastic life. Some exceptions, however, can be pointed out. The Northumbrian princes Oswald, Oswy and Aldfrid were educated " in the isles of the Scots," where they even learned Irish [4] ; for the national language and literature seem to have been held in honour at that time, as they have come to be once more in the Irish schools of our day. Some poems in the Gaelic tongue have been preserved which are believed to be the composition of Aldfrid.[5] Let us recall another royal exile who also made a stay in Ireland, the young Austrasian prince destined to rule later under the name of Dagobert II. He passed about twenty years among the *Scotti*, probably as inmate of a monastery.[6]

[1] Mario Esposito, *The Knowledge of Greek in Ireland during the Middle Ages* (*Studies*, I, 1912, pp. 665–83).

[2] Bede, *HE*, IV, 2. Cf. *ib.*, V, 20, 23.

[3] Save Aldhelm's rigmarole in his letter to Eahfrid (ed. Ehwald, *MG. Auct. ant.*, XV, p. 493), no support can be found, so far as I am aware, for that view.

[4] *V. sup.*, ch. v, § 2.

[5] *V. sup.*, ch. v, § 2.

[6] *V. sup.*, ch. v, § 5.

We possess but scanty information touching the education of girls. It was in the natural course of things that those who looked forward to embracing the religious life should also learn the Psalter ; as did St Moninne who, while yet a child, was entrusted to a holy priest for that end.[1] It is more surprising to find at Clonard a daughter of the king of Tara, also destined to consecrate her virginity to God. She was brought to St Finnian to study Holy Writ under his direction. Ciarán was at the time among Finnian's pupils, and the master thought it no harm for the young monk and the handmaiden of Christ to read the Scriptures together till such time as a cell of virgins should be built for her. She was wont to take her meals and to sleep with a certain holy widow, so we are told by Ciarán's biographer, who further records the strict discretion observed by Ciarán in his relations with the young princess.[2]

Under the year 1053 the chronicler Marianus Scottus tells of a singular person called Aed the bearded clerk, a man, he says, of admirable piety and enjoying high repute. Aed, however, had his oddities. He conducted a school, a mixed one, it would appear, and he took it into his head to shave all his pupils, girls as well as boys, leaving them only a circular fringe of hair on the crown, *more clericorum*. The eccentricities of this pedagogue led to his banishment from Ireland.[3]

We may form some notion of the methods used by the master in his grammar lessons if we turn to the commentary on Virgil based on Philargyrius, compiled by a certain Adananus, whom it has been attempted to identify with the famous Adamnán, abbot of Iona, though the fact has not been strictly proved. In his explanations the master avails himself of current Latin, of Irish and occasionally of Greek. His commentary comprises remarks on grammar, definitions, and details of history, biography, mythology and archaeology ; it is at once grammatical, allegorical and encyclopaedic.[4]

---

[1] Conchubran, *Vita Mon.*, 3 (p. 209).
[2] *Vita Ciarani de Cluain*, 16 (*VSH*, I, pp. 205–206) ; Macalister, *The Latin and Irish Lives of Ciaran*, p. 25.
[3] Marianus, *Chronicon* (*PL*, CXLVII, 785–86).
[4] Roger, *Enseignement*, pp. 262, 266 ; Kenney, *Sources*, I, pp. 286–87 ; James, *Learning*, p. 507.

Donatus and Priscian, grammarians in vogue throughout the whole western world, were naturally so in Ireland also. We have commentaries on them composed by Scottic masters, probably not until the writers had crossed to the Continent.[1] The same may be said of all the treatises on grammar and prosody, the glossaries and commentaries on classical authors, due to the Irishmen Malsachanus,[2] Dicuil,[3] Clemens Scottus,[4] Cruindmelus,[5] Sedulius Scottus,[6] and Johannes Eriugena.[7]   All these masters (to whom we shall return when speaking of the part taken by the *Scotti* in the Carolingian renaissance) were able to fill up the gaps in their knowledge and to widen the circle of their intellectual interests on the Continent.   In the continental schools they turned their talents to account, and the manuscripts of their didactic works (preserved in more than one case in the form of notes taken down by their pupils) are all to be found in continental libraries.

The Latin of the insular scholars presents some peculiar features which are partly to be explained by the phonetic laws and grammatical constructions of the writer's native tongue.   Those belonging to the Brythonic branch and to the

---

[1] Kenney, *Sources*, I, pp. 552, 553, 560, 564, 572, 648, 674–77, 679 ; Manitius, *Geschichte*, I, pp. 11, 319.

[2] *Ars Malsachani.   Traité du verbe publié d'après le* MS. *Lat.* 13026 *de la Bibl. Nat.* (Paris, 1905), by M. Roger. Cf. Kenney, *Sources*, I, pp. 551–52 ; Manitius, *Geschichte*, I, pp. 521–23, II, p. 809.

[3] Dicuil, *De arte grammatica*, ed. Dümmler (*MG. Poet. Lat.*, II, pp. 667–68).   Cf. Kenney, I, pp. 545–46 ; M. Esposito, *An Irish Teacher at the Carolingian Court : Dicuil* (*Studies*, III, 1914, pp. 653–54).

[4] Clemens Scottus, *Ars grammatica*, ed. J. Tolkiehn (*Philologus*, Supplementband, XX, 3, Leipzig, 1928). Cf. Kenney, *Sources*, I, pp. 537–38 ; M. Esposito, *Bibliography*, pp. 503–504 ; Manitius, *Geschichte*, I, 456–58. On Tolkiehn's edition, see K. Barwick in *Gnomon*, VI, 1930, pp. 385–95.

[5] Cf. Kenney, *Sources*, I, pp. 552–53 ; Manitius, *Geschichte*, I, pp. 523–25.

[6] Cf. Kenney, *Sources*, I, pp. 563–64 ; M. Roger, *Le commentariolum in artem Eutycii de Sedulius Scottus* (*Revue de philologie*, XXX, 1906, pp. 122–23) ; Manitius, *Geschichte*, I, p. 318 ; Esposito, *Bibliography*, pp. 563–64.

[7] Commentary on Martianus Capella, ed. Manitius, *Didaskaleion*, I, 1912, pp. 157–72, II, 1913, pp. 43–61. Cf. Kenney, *Sources*, I, pp. 574–75 ; Manitius, *Geschichte*, I, pp. 335–37 ; Esposito, *Bibliography*, p. 506 ; *s.a. Irish Commentaries on Martianus Capella* (*ZCP*, IX, 1913, pp. 159–63) ; *s.a. A Ninth-century Commentary on Donatus* (*Classical Quarterly*, XI, 1917, pp. 94–97) ; M. L. W. Laistner, *Martianus Capella and his Ninth-century Commentators* (*Bulletin of the John Rylands Library*, IX, 1925, pp. 130–38).

Gaelic have alike their own idioms.[1] In the Latinity of Irishmen of the early Middle Ages singularities have been pointed out in vocabulary (Latin words formed from Gaelic ones),[2] spelling (very numerous these),[3] and syntax (a marked tendency to use the nominative absolute instead of the ablative absolute, and, conversely, to use the ablative where the construction with nominative would be more natural).[4]

But all this is nothing beside the faults of taste and the intentional obscurity of those writers who adopted the stylistic methods exhibited in the *Latinitas Hisperica*. In the British and Irish monasteries from the sixth century, there came into fashion—and the fashion held its own through several centuries—a fantastic, inflated, enigmatical, and indeed for the most part absolutely unintelligible Latin style, of which our chief specimen is the *Hisperica Famina*.[5] The vocabulary is highly eccentric. Either words are coined from other Latin words and perverted from their real meaning, or they are formed from Greek or even Hebrew. Often instead of the proper word we meet with a baffling periphrasis. The style is formless and spasmodic, and the connection of the words is nearly always lacking.[6] The treatises of the grammarian Virgilius Maro, which found their way into Ireland,

---

[1] Duine, *Memento, passim* ; W. H. Stevenson, *Asser's Life of King Alfred*, pp. xci–xcii (*introd.*) ; J. Vendryes, *R. Cel.*, XLIII, 1926, pp. 252–53 ; F. C. Burkitt, *St Samson of Dol*, *JTS*, XXVII, 1926, p. 57.

[2] Holger Pedersen, *Vergleichende Grammatik der keltischen Sprachen* (Göttingen, 1909), I, pp. 189–242 ; C. Plummer, *VSH*, II (*Glossary*) ; J. Vendryes, *R. Cel.*, XL, 1923, p. 190.

[3] Manitius, *Geschichte*, I, p. 11, n. 3 ; Paul Lehmann, *Aufgaben und Anregungen der lateinischen Philologie des Mittelalters* (*Sitzungsberichte der Bayerischen Akad. der Wissenschaften*. Philos.-philol.-und historische Klasse, 1918, pp. 38–39) ; Lawlor, *Cathach*, pp. 253–56 ; L. Traube, *MG. Poet. Lat.*, III, p. 795 ; *s.a. Vorlesungen*, II, pp. 61–62 ; P. von Winterfeld, *MG. Poet. Lat.*, IV, p. 178, n. 4 ; S. Hellmann, *Sedulius Scottus* (München, 1906), pp. 118–20 ; M. Roger, *Enseignement*, pp. 265–66 ; *s.a. Ars Malsachani*, p. xviii ff. ; G. F. Warner, *Stowe*, II, pp. xvii–xx (*introd.*) ; F. E. Warren, *An. Ban.*, I, pp. xxiv–xxv (*introd.*) ; Bernard and Atkinson, *LH*, II, pp. 104 ; M. Esposito, *The so-called Psalter of St Columba* (*Notes and Queries*, 11th Ser., XI, 1915, pp. 467–68 ; XII, pp. 253–54).

[4] C. Plummer, *VSH*, I, pp. xciv–xcv (*introd.*).

[5] Ed. F. J. H. Jenkinson, *The Hisperica Famina* (Cambridge, 1908).

[6] On the origin, spread and latinity of the Hisperic writings, see Kenney, *Sources*, I, pp. 255–58 ; Roger, *Enseignement*, pp. 238–56 ; Evan J. Jones, *History of Education in Wales*, I, pp. 175–88 ; E. K. Rand, *The Irish Flavor of Hisperica Famina* (*Studien zur lateinischen Dichtung des Mittelalters, Ehrengabe für Karl Strecker*), Dresden, 1931, pp. 134–42.

could not but favour this fashion,[1] among whose most prominent votaries were the authors of the hymn *Altus Prosator*, attributed to St Columba of Iona,[2] and of the *Lorica* ascribed to Gildas.[3]

St Columban's style is often grandiloquent and obscure. Muirchu, Cellanus, Cummian and Adamnán, though they do not write elegant Latin, are, on the whole, free from the faults of Hisperic Latinity. All these authors had read the secular literature of Rome, especially Virgil's works. Columban had studied prosody ; we have three metrical epistles written by him, two in hexameters, one in Adonic verses followed by six hexameters,[4] and other poems, some of doubtful authenticity.[5] The study of the classical writers does not seem to have been regarded with suspicion and laid under an interdict in the monasteries of Ireland as it was in the majority of continental cloisters in the Middle Ages.

The pedantic Latinity of which we have just spoken was only one indication of the decided bent of Celtic clerics and monks who had some smattering of letters for all that was uncommon, difficult and esoteric. They were singularly attracted by unusual combinations of ideas and of words, enigmas, acrostics, cryptology and cryptography.[6] This craze is clearly shown in some lines appended to the cryptogram of Bamberg, which run as follows : " This is the inscription which was offered as an ordeal by Dubthach to the learned Irishmen at the castle of Mermin, King of the Britons. For he so far thought himself the best of all the Irish and the Britons as to believe that no Irish scholar, much

---

[1] Kenney, *Sources*, I, pp. 143–45, 256 ; Manitius, *Geschichte*, I, pp. 119–27 ; Roger, *Enseignement*, pp. 110–26, 226, 231, 259, 260, 262 ; H. Zimmer in *Sitzungsberichte d. k. Preuss. Akad. d. Wissenschaften*, 1910, LI, 1031–98 ; K. Meyer, *Learning in Ireland* (Dublin, 1913), p. 22 ; D. Tardi, *Sur le vocabulaire de Virgile le Grammairien* (*Bulletin Du Cange*, 1927) ; *s. a. Les Epitomatae de Virgile de Toulouse* (Paris, 1928).

[2] Ed. *LH*, I, pp. 62–83.

[3] Ed. *LH*, I, pp. 206–10.

[4] Ed. W. Gundlach, *MG. Epist.*, III, pp. 182–88. Cf. Kenney, *Sources*, I, pp. 193–94 ; Manitius, *Geschichte*, I, pp. 181–87, II, p. 798 ; P. Lugano, *San Colombano monaco e scrittore* (*Rivista storica Benedettina*, XI, 1916, pp. 5–46).

[5] Kenney, *Sources*, I, pp. 194–96.

[6] See L.G., *Les chrétientés celtiques*, p. 244, n. 2.

less British, would be able to interpret that writing before King Mermin. But to us, Caunchobrach, Fergus, Dominnach and Suadbar, by the help of God, it did not remain insoluble." (Then follows the interpretation of the cryptogram—" Mermin rex Conchen salutem "—and the explanation of the method by which it was composed, that of substituting, in accordance with a fixed table, Greek letters for Latin). " Please understand, wise and estimable Colgu, our very learned teacher, that we are not transmitting this exposition to you as to one needing such enlightenment ; but we humbly ask that in your kindness you would give this information to such of our simple and unsophisticated Irish brethren as may think of sailing across the British sea, lest perchance otherwise they might be made to blush in the presence of Mermin, the glorious king of the Britons, not being able to understand that inscription." [1] I have thought it well to quote this text, which is typical in its naïve boastfulness. It affords us a glimpse of certain sides of the mentality of these scholars of a remote past, inquisitive and prying minds, ardent collectors and devourers of books, engaging with equal willingness in the solution of a futile puzzle or a theological problem, yet withal so childish in their eagerness to parade their often ill-digested learning, for instance their smattering of Greek, and so headstrong in their convictions, often derived from doubtful sources.

A manuscript preserved in the monastery of St Paul in Carinthia, consisting of some leaves, the remains of what has been called " the commonplace-book of an Irish student monk of the ninth century," contains a little poem in Irish which may fitly be reproduced here, for it admits us to the privacy of the cell of a solitary whom we find engaged in studious research ; he diverts himself by comparing his own occupation with the activity of his companion in solitude, a cat called Pangur Bán.

---

[1] Ed. Whitley Stokes, *On a Mediaeval Cryptogram* (*The Academy*, XLII, 1892, pp. 71–72). Cf. Kenney, *Sources*, I, 556 ; J. Loth, *Étude sur le cryptogramme de Bamberg* (*R. Cel.*, XIV, 1893, p. 91) ; s.a. *An. Br.*, VIII, 1892, pp. 289–93 ; Slover, *Channels*, pp. 110–11. Mermin has been identified with Merfyn Frych, king of Gwynedd, who died 844, according to *AC* (p. 165). Cf. Lloyd, *HW*, I, pp. 323–24.

I and Pangur Bán, my cat,
'Tis a like task we are at ;
Hunting mice is his delight,
Hunting words I sit all night.

Better far than praise of men
'Tis to sit with book and pen ;
Pangur bears me no ill will,
He too plies his simple skill.

'Tis a merry thing to see
At our tasks how glad are we,
When at home we sit and find
Entertainment to our mind.

Oftentimes a mouse will stray
In the hero Pangur's way ;
Oftentimes my keen thought set
Takes a meaning in its net.

'Gainst the wall he sets his eye
Full and fierce and sharp and sly ;
'Gainst the wall of knowledge I
All my little wisdom try.

When a mouse darts from its den,
O how glad is Pangur then !
O what gladness do I prove
When I solve the doubts I love !

So in peace our task we ply,
Pangur Bán, my cat, and I ;
In our arts we find our bliss,
I have mine and he has his.

Practice every day has made
Pangur perfect in his trade ;
I get wisdom day and night,
Turning darkness into light.[1]

---

[1] Edited with Engl. transl., Stokes and Strachan, *TP*, II, pp. 293–94.
The translation here given (with kind permission of its author) is by Robin
Flower (from Eleanor Hull's *The Poem Book of the Gael*, London, 1912,
pp. 132–33). Cf. Kenney, *Sources*, I, pp. 677–78.

The controversies on the Paschal question obliged the Irish to engage in the study of astronomy, chronology and the ecclesiastical computus. We have spoken elsewhere of the forgeries of the computists.[1] According to a Latin note dating probably from the ninth century and written in a Gospel of St Matthew in the library of the University of Würzburg, Mosinu maccu Min, also called Sillan, a scribe and abbot of Bangor, who died in 610 and who in the *Antiphonarium Benchorense* is entitled *famosus mundi magister*, was the first in Ireland to learn a computus taught him by a Greek sage ; he retained it in memory until his disciple Mocuaroc maccu Neth Semon of Cranny Island committed it to writing.[2]

Speaking of scientific subjects, we must mention the dissertation written by Dungal, a recluse of St. Denis, at Charlemagne's command, on the two solar eclipses which occurred in the year 810 ; in it Macrobius is largely quoted.[3] Dicuil is the author of a treatise on astronomy and the computus (814–816), which he dedicated to Louis the Pious,[4] as well as of a compendium of geography, the *Liber de mensura orbis terrae*, a very curious work, composed, like the preceding one, on the Continent and finished in 825.[5] We possess another medieval treatise on geography in verse, which is attributed to a certain Mac Coisse, *fer légind* of Ros Ailithir, who lived in Ireland in the second half of the tenth century.[6]

The spherical shape of the earth was admitted by more than one among the ancients, notably by the Pythagoreans,

---

[1] *V. sup.*, ch. VI, § 1.

[2] Ed. Georg Schepss, *Die ältesten Evangelienhandschriften der Würzburger Universitätsbibliothek* (Würzburg, 1887), p. 27. Cf. W. Sanday, *Byzantine Influence in Ireland* (*The Academy*, Sept. 1, 1888, pp. 137–38) ; Roger, *Enseignement*, p. 206 ; Kenney, *Sources*, I, p. 218.

[3] Ed. Dümmler, *MG. Epist.*, II, p. 552. Cf. Manitius, *Geschichte*, I, p. 461 ; Kenney, *Sources*, I, p. 539.

[4] Ed. M. Esposito, *An unpublished astronomical Treatise by the Irish Monk Dicuil* (*PRIA*, XXVI, sect. C, 1907, pp. 378–446). Cf. *Modern Philology*, 1920, pp. 177–88. The poems have been edited by K. Strecker, *MG. Poet. Lat.*, IV, pp. 659–60. Cf. Kenney, *Sources*, I, p. 546.

[5] Ed. G. Parthey, *Dicuili Liber de mensura orbis terrae* (Berolini, 1870). Cf. Kenney, *Sources*, I, 546–48.

[6] Ed. T. Olden, *On the Geography of Ros Ailithir* (*PRIA*, II. Ser., II, 1884, pp. 219–52). Cf. Kenney, *Sources*, I, 682–83. Ros Ailithir (now Rosscarbery, Co. Cork) was founded by St Fachtna (see Ryan, *Monast.*, p. 131).

and the question of the antipodes was debated by a goodly number of Fathers of the Church, St Augustine, Lactantius, Isidore of Seville, Bede and others.[1] Is it true, as has been asserted, that in the eighth century an Irishman, Virgil of Salzburg, put forward a novel theory on this subject, more in conformity with modern cosmography ? The matter has been much discussed, but, in spite of all that has been written about it,[2] it is very hard to determine exactly wherein consisted these cosmological speculations of Virgil, which gave St Boniface such alarm and were by Pope Zachary, in a letter written to the apostle of the Germans, stigmatized as " a perverse and unrighteous doctrine, an offence alike to God and to his own soul." [3] In fact, we have only a single text bearing on the matter, the reply sent by the Pope to the charges made by St Boniface. The letter (dated May 1, 748 ?) was written only about three years after Virgil's arrival in Salzburg. The doctrine objected to is " that there are under the earth another world and other men or sun and moon (*quod alius mundus et alii homines sub terra sint seu sol et luna*)." [4] These are the words which have been construed as proof of the belief in the antipodes, which is surely extracting a great deal of meaning from them ! We think it wiser to accept the conclusion of an expert critic : " It will be seen that the words of Zacharias contain nothing to support (and nothing to bar) this explanation." [5]

§ 2.—HOLY SCRIPTURE

It has been justly observed that " the religious instruction and the literary education of Ireland were two concurrent and

[1] Ph. Gilbert, *Le pape Zacharie et les antipodes* (*Revue des questions scientifiques*, XII, 1882, pp. 478–503) ; H. Krabbo, *Bischof Virgil von Salzburg und seine kosmologischen Ideen* (*MIÖG*, XXIV, 1903, pp. 1–28). Cf. H. d'Arbois, *R. Cel.*, XXIV, 1903, p. 221.

[2] John Ryan, *Early Irish Missionaries on the Continent and St Vergil of Salzburg* (Dublin, 1924), pp. 18–20 ; Francis S. Betten, *St Boniface and St Virgil* (Washington. 1927); Hamard, art. *Sphéricité de la terre* in A. d'Alès, *Dictionnaire apologétique* (cols. 1476–77) ; H. Van der Linden, *Virgile de Salzbourg et les théories cosmographiques au VIIIᵉ siècle* (*Bulletin de l'Académie royale de Belgique.* Classe des lettres, 1914, pp. 163–87). Cf. Kenney, *Sources*, I, p. 523.

[3] Ed. E. Dümmler, *MG. Epist.*, III, p. 360.

[4] *Ib.*

[5] James, *Learning*, p. 513.

simultaneous facts." [1] The great founders of schools were, in fact, saints, and their disciples monks. The word *sage* (Ir. *suí*), so often used in the religious literature of the Scots, is frequently applied to a scholar versed alike in sacred and profane science.[2] In truth, there was only one science, that of the Scriptures. Other studies were regarded only as servants or auxiliaries of religious education. The liberal arts, the study of the ancient languages, all secular culture had, in theory, for sole end to render the mind fit for the *lectio divina*, that is to say, the study of the divine thought embodied in the words of the Bible and in tradition.[3] In the same way, calligraphy and illumination (arts held in high honour in the isles) were employed almost wholly, as we shall see, in multiplying and adorning religious books, liturgical or biblical texts. Such is indeed the theory of education laid down by Aldhelm of Malmesbury, who had received instruction from an Irish master, and also by Alcuin in a letter addressed to the students of the schools of Ireland.[4]

It has been already said that from the seventh century on crowds of foreigners thronged to the Irish schools as well as to those which the Scots opened outside their native isle. Among the Anglo-Saxons who crossed the Irish Sea, many were destined later to attain great fame or were perhaps already well known. We may name Cynefrid, ex-abbot of Gilling (Yorkshire) [5] ; the ascetic Egbert who, having reached Ireland at the age of twenty-three, spent the rest of his life there and exercised considerable influence " in the islands of the Scots " [6] ; Willibrord, the future apostle of the Frisians [7] ; Egbert's companion Edilhun, who was carried

[1] H. Pirenne, *Sedulius de Liége* (Mémoires couronnés et autres mémoires publiés par l' Académie royale de Belgique, XXXIII, 1882), p. 9.

[2] Lawlor in Ricemarch, *PM*, I, p. IX (*introd.*).

[3] Roger, *Enseignement*, p. 237 ; Ryan, *Monast.*, p. 379.

[4] Aldhelm, *Ep. ad Aethilwaldum*, ed. Ehwald, *MG. Auct. ant.*, XV, pp. 499–500 ; Alcuin, *Ep.* 280 (*MG. Epist.*, IV, pp. 436–39).

[5] *Historia Abbatum auct. anonymo*, 2, ed. C. Plummer, *Bedae opera historica*, I, p. 388.

[6] Bede, *HE*, III, 27, IV, 3, V, 22 ; Alcuin, *Versus de sanctis Euboricensis Ecclesiae*, v. 1012-20 (*MG. Poet. Lat.*, I, p. 192).

[7] Bede, *HE*, III, 13 ; Alcuin, *Vita Willibrordi*, I, 4, ed. A. Poncelet (Boll., AS, Nov. III, p. 439) ; ed. W. Levison (*MG. Scr. RM*, VII, pp. 118–19).

off by the plague during his stay in Ireland [1] ; his brother
Ediluini,[2] and Chad,[3] these last two destined to become
bishops, the former of Lindsey, the latter of Lichfield. Agilbert, a Frank by birth, was already a bishop when he repaired
to the Scots.[4] In his letter, already quoted, to Eahfrid, who
had studied for six years in Ireland, St Aldhelm speaks of
students who at the time (about 686–690) were crossing the
water in troops and in flotillas (*Hibernia, quo catervatim istinc
lectitantes classibus advecti confluunt*), "when," he avers, "they
could get just as good instruction from the masters of Canterbury." [5]   The biographers of many British saints, Cadoc,
Carantoc, Cybi, Petroc and Samson, represent them as having
likewise studied in Ireland.[6] The Scotchman Cadroe and a
Pictish bishop, whose name we do not know, are also said to
have visited Irish schools.[7] Likewise a certain Marcus, of
whom we have spoken already, also a bishop, and a Briton
by birth, whom we find living as an anchorite at Soissons
in the second half of the ninth century,[8] as well as a
host of other students whose names are for ever lost.[9]

Bede says that Egbert and Chad were young men when
they crossed the Channel ; we know in fact that Egbert was
twenty-three. Willibrord was twenty when he arrived and he
spent twelve years in Ireland. Agilbert made a stay of some
length (*non parvo tempore*) ; and in the eleventh century the
Welshman Sulgen (Sulien) spent thirteen years there.[10]

What all these foreigners, Anglo-Saxons, Britons, Scotchmen, Picts or Franks, came to seek from the Scottic masters
was above all else the science of the Scriptures. " *Ad scrip-
turam sanctam addiscendam* "—" *discendarum studio scripturarum* "

---

[1] Bede, *HE*, iii, 27.

[2] *Ib.*

[3] Bede, *HE*, iv, 3.

[4] Bede, *HE*, iii, 7.

[5] Aldhelm, *Ep. ad Ehfridum*, MG. Auct. ant., XV, pp. 489–92.

[6] *CBS*, pp. 35–36, 59, 17–98, 184–86. Cf. C. Plummer, *VSH*, I,
p. cxxiv (*introd.*).

[7] *Vita Cadroe*, i, 10 (Boll., *AS*, Mart., I, p. 475) ; *Vita Findani*, 6 (*MG.
Scr.*, XV, i, p. 504).

[8] Heiric, *Miracula S. Germani*, i, 8 (*PL*, CXXIV, 1245).

[9] Cf. K. Meyer, *Ags. Berechtuine in Alt-Irland* (*Archiv für das Studium der
neueren Sprachen und Literaturen*, CXXX. 1913, pp. 155–56).

[10] Jeuan, *Carmen de vita Sulgeni* (*CED*, I, pp. 665–66).

—" *legendarum gratia scripturarum* "—such are the common expressions.[1] Of these students so eager to study the Scriptures most were already monks and had the further wish to perfect themselves in the ascetic discipline.[2] The Irish monasteries, containing as they did so many holy monks and distinguished scholars, offered them all the means they could desire for advancing towards their double goal. Moreover, the Irish libraries were abundantly furnished with manuscripts, especially biblical texts,[3] and books were supplied gratis to the students along with board and lodging.[4]

All the great churchmen of Celtic Christianity, Patrick, Gildas, Columban, Cummian, Aidan, Adamnán and Sedulius, were steeped in Holy Writ. Speaking of Aidan, Bede says that all who followed him, whether tonsured or laymen (*sive adtonsi, seu laici*), had to practise meditation, to wit, the reading of the Scriptures and the study of the Psalms.[5] Of Adamnán, Bede declares that he was " a good and wise man and versed in the knowledge of the Scriptures in a remarkable degree." [6]

The abbot of Iona had the good fortune to welcome on the shores of his island a pilgrim from the Holy Land. Driven by contrary winds to that distant coast, the Frank Arculf dictated to Adamnán some notes which enabled the latter, who had himself never visited those sacred spots, to indite a treatise *De locis sanctis*.[7] He presented this book to his friend king Aldfrid of Northumbria.[8] It was the chief source of the work of Bede's which bears the same title.[9]

---

[1] See texts already referred to above and in addition : *Vita Ruadani*, 1 (*VSH*, II, 240) ; *Vita Moluae*, 27 (*ib.*, 214).

[2] Bede, *HE*, III, 27, IV, 3 ; *Historia Abbatum, l. cit.* ; Alcuin, *Vita Willibrordi, l. cit.*

[3] " Hibernian properavit et in ea aliquandiu commoratus est eorum volumina volvens " (Aethicus Ister, *Cosmographia*, ed. Wuttke, p. 14) ; " The host of the books of Erin " (*Fél. Oeng.*, p. 270). Cf. Kuno Meyer, *Learning in Ireland*, p. 11 ; Kenney, *Sources*, I, p. 624 ; Ryan, *Monast.*, p. 380.

[4] Bede, *HE*, III, 27.

[5] Bede, *HE*, III, 5.

[6] Bede, *HE*, v, 15 ; *s.a. De locis sanctis*, 20 (*PL*, XCIV, 1190).

[7] Ed. P. Geyer, *Itinéra Hierosolymitana* (*Corp. SEL*, XXXVIIII, pp. 219-97).

[8] Bede, *HE*, v, 15.

[9] Cf. Kenney, *Sources*, I, p. 286.

The Latin biblical texts in use in the Celtic Churches up to the sixth century were versions anterior to St Jerome's Vulgate.[1] St Patrick quotes the Bible according to an Old Latin version of the type known as European.[2] The *Codex Usserianus I* (sixth–seventh century)[3] contains a " European " text of the Gospels in a recension which is believed to be peculiar to Ireland.[4] Some other early Gospels which have an Old Latin text have been adduced as belonging to the Irish family, but their origin and their Irish relationship remain doubtful.[5]

Some hagiographical narratives speak of a text of the Gospels brought from Rome by an Irish saint—in one place St Finnian of Magh Bile (Moville) († 579) is the hero of the incident,[6] in another St Fridian or Frediano of Lucca (*c.* 560–588)[7] ; the exploits of these two saints have very often been confounded. Elsewhere the deed is attributed to St Laisrén or Molaisse of Leighlin († 639).[8] None of these narratives make it clear that a new translation of the Gospels was brought. However, as the saints named above all lived either in the sixth or at the beginning of the seventh century, the period when the Vulgate text was beginning to become known in Ireland, it has been inferred that the hagiographical works in question may allude to the introduction of St Jerome's translation.[9] But here we tread on unstable ground ; it is quite possible that no historical information can be drawn from any of these narratives.[10]

[1] See especially N. J. D. White, *Libri S. Patricii : the Latin Writings of St Patrick* (*PRIA*, XXV, sect. C, 1905, pp. 230–33, 300, 316) ; H. J. Lawlor, *Chapters on the Book of Mulling* (Edinburgh, 1897) ; John Gwynn in *LA*, pp. cxxxv–cclviii (*introd.*) ; Samuel Berger, *Histoire de la Vulgate pendant les premiers siècles du moyen âge* (Paris, 1893), chs. iii & iv. Cf. Kenney, *Sources*, I, pp. 623–27.

[2] N. J. D. White, *op. cit.*

[3] ms. Trinity College, Dublin, 55 (A. 4. 15).

[4] J. Gwynn, *LA*, p. cxli.

[5] Kenney, *Sources*, I, pp. 627–28 (Nos. 450–52).

[6] *Fél. Oeng.*, Sept. 10th (p. 193). Cf. pp. 204–205 ; Kenney, *Sources*, I, p. 391.

[7] *Vita II^a Fridiani*, 3 (Colgan, *ASH*, p. 638). Cf. Kenney, *Sources*, I, pp. 184–85.

[8] *Acta Lasriani*, 7 (*Sal. ASH*, col. 794) ; *Vita Lasriani*, 22 (*VSH*, II, p. 136).

[9] Lawlor, *Cathach*, pp. 315–16.

[10] M. Esposito, *The Cathach of St Columba* (*Louth Archaeological Journal*, IV, 1917, p. 82).

The Vulgate is clearly the source of many of Gildas' quotations. It gained further ground with Columban, Cummian, Adamnán and the Irish canonical collection, a compilation Roman in its inspiration.[1] It is an ascertained fact that the diffusion of the Vulgate becomes more marked in Celtic territories in proportion as Roman customs take root in them.[2]

The earliest Hieronymian texts of indisputably Irish origin which we possess are the Cathach of Columcille (sixth–seventh century),[3] a fragmentary Psalter which presents Jerome's second version (the " Gallican " Psalter) with a small admixture of pre-Hieronymian readings, and the Book of Durrow (seventh–eighth century), containing the four Gospels in a remarkably pure type of Vulgate.[4]

However, the introduction of the Vulgate into Ireland did not entail the suppression of the older texts. " The new translation of the Scriptures was welcomed, no doubt, by scholars ; but it is unlikely that it was used for the purpose of edification by preachers, or in the ordinary services of the Church." [5]

Apart from the two codices just mentioned, the Irish manuscripts of the same period and those of following centuries offer a mixed text and might be classed under two heads, those based on the Old Latin with occasional Vulgate readings, and those based on the Vulgate but retaining important traces of the Old Latin.

Every Gospel Book of the mixed type copied by an Irish scribe has its textual peculiarities, as regards the proportions in which the two elements, Old Latin and Vulgate, are mixed, their distribution (sometimes very erratic) through the text, doublets and conflate readings. These Gospels are the following : 1. The Book of Mulling (seventh–eighth cen-

---

[1] See biblical quotations collected in *CED*, I, Append. G (pp. 170–98).
[2] S. Berger, *op. cit.*
[3] MS. deposited in RIA library, Dublin. Cf. Lawlor, *Cathach ;* M. Esposito, *The Cathach ;* Kenney, *Sources*, I, pp. 620–30.
[4] MS. *TCD*, 57 (A. 4. 5). Cf. Lawlor, *Cathach*, p. 320 ; Kenney, *Sources*, I, pp. 630–31.
[5] H. J. Lawlor, *The Biblical Text in Tundal's Vision* (*PRIA*, XXXVI, Sect. C, 1924, p. 351).

tury).[1] 2. Book of Dimma (seventh–eighth century).[2]
3. Cambridge Irish Gospels (eighth century ?).[3] 4. The
Domnach Airgid Manuscript (eighth–ninth century).[4]
5. The Gospels of St Chad (eighth–ninth century).[5] 6.
Book of Kells (eighth–ninth century).[6] 7. The Gospel of
MacRegol (eighth–ninth century).[7] 8. The Stowe Gospel
of St John (eighth–ninth century).[8] 9. The St. Gall Gospel
of St John, Stiftsbibl. 60 (eighth–ninth century).[9] 10. Book
of Armagh (A.D. 807).[10] 11. The Garland of Howth : Codex
Usserianus II (ninth–tenth century).[11] 12. The Gospels of
MacDurnan (ninth–tenth century).[12] 13. The Oxford
Corpus Christi College Gospels (eleventh–twelfth century).[13]
14. The Gospels of Mael Brigte (A.D. 1138).[14] 15. Codex
Harleianus 1023 (twelfth century ?).[15]

In addition to the Psalter of St Columba already mentioned,
the psalters copied by Irish scribes are as follows : 1. Codex
Palatino-Vaticanus 68 (eighth century), an incomplete copy
accompanied by a Latin commentary.[16] 2. The Southampton Psalter (ninth–tenth century), complete.[17] 3. Vitellius
F. XI (tenth century ?), incomplete.[18] 4. Psalter of St
Caimin (eleventh–twelfth century), a fragment of manuscript containing only a part of Ps. cxviii (*Beati immaculati*).[19]

---

[1] MS. *TCD*, 60. Cf. Lawlor, *Chapters* (1897) ; Kenney, *Sources*, I,
pp. 632–33.
[2] MS. *TCD*, 59 (A. 4. 23). Cf. Kenney, *Sources*, I, p. 633.
[3] MS. Cambridge Univ. Libr., Kk. 1. 24. Cf. Kenney, *Sources*, I, p. 636.
[4] MS. *RIA* (Dublin), 24. Q. 23. Cf. Kenney, *Sources*, I, pp. 638–39.
[5] MS. Lichfield Cathedral Lib. Cf. Kenney, *Sources*, I, p. 639.
[6] MS. *TCD*, 58 (A. 1. 6). Cf. Kenney, I, 640–41.
[7] Or Rushworth Gospels, MS. Bodl. Auct. D. II, 19. Cf. Kenney, I,
pp. 641–42.
[8] MS. *RIA*, D. II, 3. ff. 1–11. Cf. Kenney, I, pp. 637–38.
[9] Cf. Kenney, I, p. 640.
[10] MS. *TCD*. Ed. J. Gwynn, *LA*. Cf. Kenney, I, pp. 642–44.
[11] MS. *TCD*, 56 (A. 4. 6). Cf. Kenney, I, 646.
[12] MS. Lambeth Palace, London. Cf. Kenney, I, 644–45.
[13] MS. *CCC*. 122, Oxford. Cf. Kenney, I, 647–48.
[14] MS. *BM*, Harl. 1802. Cf. Kenney, I, 648.
[15] MS. *BM*. Cf. Kenney, I, 648.
[16] Kenney, I, p. 465.
[17] *Ib.*, p. 476.
[18] *Ib.*, p. 478.
[19] *Ib.*, p. 479 ; M. Esposito, *On the so-called Psalter of Saint Caimin*
(*PRIA*, XXXII, Sect. C, 1913, pp. 78–88. with 1 plate.

5. Codex Palatino-Vaticanus 65 (twelfth–thirteenth century), complete.[1]

These psalters are divided into three fifties, each fifty being followed by the biblical canticles and, in some cases, collects. The text of the Psalms is that of the " Gallican " redaction.[2]

Outside the Psalms, very little of the Old Testament has been preserved to us.[3]

Of the New Testament, besides the Gospels we possess three copies of St Paul's Epistles : 1. Codex Wirceburgensis (Würzburg Universitätsbibl. M.th. 12, eighth century), complete except for the closing part of Hebrews, lost with the last folio.[4] 2. Book of Armagh (A.D. 807). " The Book of Armagh," says Dr. John Gwynn, " stands forth to the student of Biblical literature without a rival in the whole range of Irish antiquity, as the only entire New Testament as read in the early Irish Church, and copied by Irish scribes, that is now extant." [5] This codex contains even the apocryphal Epistle to the Laodiceans, with the warning that it is rejected by St Jerome.[6] 3. Codex Vindobonensis 1247 (A.D. 1079). Here also the authentic Epistles of St Paul (Vulgate), copied by the hand of Marianus Scottus of Ratisbon, are accompanied by the Epistle to the Laodiceans.[7]

The Epistles of Würzburg, as well as the copy made by Marianus, contain marginal comments and interlinear glosses. Among the commentators drawn upon is Pelagius ; 1,311 glosses of Pelagian origin have been counted in the Würzburg codex [8] ; while the Book of Armagh contains the *Prologus Pilagii in omnes epistolas*.[9]

Setting aside the Book of Armagh, which contains the entire

---

[1] H. M. Bannister, *Pagine scelte (Codices e Vaticanis selecti*. Ser. minor, II (1910) ; *s.a. JTS*, XII, 1911, pp. 280–84 ; *ZCP*, VIII, 1911, pp. 246–59 ; Ehrle and Liebaert, *Specimina codicum*, 1912, Tab. 24, p. XXI.

[2] On Irish psalters see H. M. Bannister, *Irish Psalters (JTS*, XII, 1911, pp. 280–84).

[3] Cf. Kenney, I, p. 650 (n. 488).

[4] Kenney, I, pp. 635–36.

[5] *LA*, pp. XV–XVI.

[6] *LA*, p. 271, " Incipit aepistola ad laudicenses sed hirunimus eam negat esse pauli " (fol. 139ʳ).

[7] Kenney, I, pp. 618–19.

[8] *Ib.*, p. 636.

[9] *LA*, pp. 206–207. Cf. Kenney, I, p. 643, note 66.

New Testament, we know of no other books of the New Testament besides the Pauline Epistles, save a fragment of the second Epistle of St Peter ; it is preserved on the last page (a palimpsest) of a codex of Turin coming originally from Bobbio (Bibl. Nazion., F. IV. 24, 1, eighth–ninth century), and is accompanied by glosses in Old Irish.[1]

Thus our only material for a comparative study of Old Testament texts outside the Psalter, and of New Testament ones outside the Epistles of St Paul and the books contained in the Book of Armagh, are the quotations made from those parts of the Bible by insular ecclesiastical writers, and there is nothing to guarantee that the scribes who copied their works in the course of the ages had any scruple in replacing the early readings by those of the Vulgate, with which they were perhaps more familiar. However, a study of this kind, even though it be based on a single text (provided the exact date of that text be known) such as those made by Mario Esposito on the treatise *De Mirabilibus sanctae Scripturae* and by H. J. Lawlor on the Vision of Tundal, may lead to results worthy of record. M. Esposito concludes his examination of the biblical quotations in the *De Mirabilibus*, which was written in Ireland in 655, with the following words : " From the above examples we see that while a considerable number of our author's biblical citations come directly from the Vulgate, a somewhat larger portion does not, and can be traced to the Old Latin Version. Several other readings do not, as far as we are aware, occur elsewhere." [2]

The Vision of Tundal was written at Ratisbon in the year 1149 by an Irishman named Marcus. It has been shown that this Irishman, writing in the middle of the twelfth century, still quotes the Old Latin text of the Gospels and Apocalypse as well as of James and 1 Peter. The Pauline Epistles he quotes from a text fundamentally Old Latin but not without Vulgate mixture. On the other hand, his Psalter seems to have been Vulgate with Old Latin mixture.[3]

The biblical manuscripts carried off to their own countries

[1] Kenney, I, p. 639.
[2] Esposito, *PADM*, p. 205.
[3] H. J. Lawlor, *The Biblical Text in Tundal's Vision* (*PRIA*, XXXVI, Sect. C, 1924, pp. 351–75).

by foreigners who had come to study in Ireland, those taken to Great Britain and the Continent by the Irish *peregrini* themselves, finally those which they copied abroad, have not all perished. In the libraries of England and the Continent there is to be found at the present day a considerable number of Irish texts of the Vulgate, in some of which it has been kept pure, in others more or less contaminated. The greater part of these manuscripts come from monasteries where the influence of the *Scotti* was felt, Deer in Scotland,[1] Lindisfarne,[2] some Welsh centres,[3] Echternach,[4] Landévennec,[5] Tours,[6] St. Gall,[7] Reichenau,[8] Pfäffers,[9] Würzburg,[10] Bobbio,[11] and other places.[12]

The earliest monuments of the Old Irish language are biblical glosses, the oldest of which go back to the eighth century. Their number is comparatively large. They have been published with an English translation in the first volume of the *Thesaurus Palaeohibernicus* by Whitley Stokes and John Strachan (1901). No medieval biblical gloss in any other Gaelic dialect or in the languages of the Brythonic branch has reached us.[13]

---

[1] Book of Deer (Cambridge Univ. Libr., I. 1. 6. 32) *s.* ix/x (Kenney, I, p. 656).

[2] Gospels of Lindisfarne (*BM*, Cotton, Nero D. iv, *s.* viii? (Kenney, I, pp. 651–52).

[3] St. Chad Gospels (Kenney, No. 468) ; Psalter of Ricemarch (Kenney, No. 508).

[4] Maihingen Gospels : Oettingen-Wallersteinische Bibl., Maihingen (Bavaria), *s.* vii/viii : Kenney, I, pp. 633–34. Gospels of Willibrord, MS. B.N. Lat. 9389 (*s.* viii ?) : Kenney, I, p. 634.

[5] Gospel-book written at Landévennec of the latter part of the ninth century, now in New York Public Library : C. R. Morey, E. K. Rand, C. H. Kraeling, *The Gospel-book of Landevennec* in *Art Studies*, VIII, Part II, 1931, pp. 225–86 (with 40 plates). Berne Gospels (MS. 85), also from Landévennec (?) : cf. C. R. Morey, *art. cit.*, p. 260. Troyes Gospels, MS. 960 (A.D. 909) : cf. A. Wilmart, *Notes sur les Évangiles datés de Troyes N.* 960 (*R. Bib.*, XXXIII, 1924, p. 393). Note subscription, fol. 17ʳ. This MS. also may come from Landévennec.

[6] Kenney, I, p. 653 (No. 494), p. 654 (No. 496, 497).

[7] Kenney, I, p. 649 (No. 486), p. 650 (No. 488).

[8] *Ib.*, p. 655 (Nos. 500, 501).

[9] *Ib.*, p. 654 (No. 498).

[10] *Ib.*, p. 636 (No. 462).

[11] *Ib.*, p. 639 (No. 469), p. 649 (Nos. 484, 485).

[12] *Ib.*, Nos. 473, 487, 489, 491. Cf. Hans Glunz, *Britannien und Bibeltext. Der Vulgatatext der Evangelien in seinem Verhältnis zur irisch-angelsächsischen Kultur des Frühmittelalters* (Kölner Anglistische Arbeiten, XII. Leipzig, 1930).

[13] See J. Bellamy's articles *Bretonnes—Gaéliques—Galloises (Versions) des*

The importance of the Glosses is mainly linguistic ; from the commentaries properly so called on the books of the Bible, composed or copied by Celts, we can gain some information about their method of interpreting Holy Scripture.

Among the writings falsely ascribed to St Augustine of Hippo, there is one which is certainly the work of an Irishman bearing the same name, the treatise *De Mirabilibus sanctae Scripturae*, written in the year 655.[1] In his preface the author of this little book says that he has undertaken it at the request of one Manchianus, whom he calls his " venerable brother," and that, despite his incapacity, he has been able to accomplish the task thanks to the enlightenment he has received from that master and from another named Bathanus. These Latinized names represent the common Irish names Baetán or Baedán and Manchén or Manchán. Among the author's contemporaries we find a Manchén, abbot of Mendroichet (now Mundrehid, near Borris-in-Ossory, Co. Leix), who died in 652, and an abbot of Clonmacnois, Baetán moccu Cormaic, who fell a victim to the great plague of 664.[2]

Augustine passes in review the chief marvellous events of the Old and New Testaments and, without attempting to explain their allegorical and figurative meaning, endeavours to show in each case that in all occurrences which fall outside the ordinary course of things and natural laws, God does not create a new nature, but contents Himself with directing the one He has created. The author's nationality is further betrayed by the way in which he speaks of Ireland (the only part of the western world which he mentions, and that twice)[3] and discusses the cycles, the fauna of islands, and the problem of tides.[4] To the neaptide and springtide he gives the respective names *ledo* and *malina*, which are found in Bede's *De Natura rerum* (ch. xxviii). The *De Mirabilibus* thus affords us some interesting glimpses of the theories current in Ireland

---

Saintes Écritures in Vigouroux's *Dictionnaire de la Bible* (I, col. 1921–27, III, 34–43, 99–102).

[1] *PL*, XXXV, 2149–2200.

[2] *AU*, a.a. 663. Cf. W. Reeves, *On Augustine, an Irish Writer of the Seventh Century* (*PRIA*, VII, 1861, p. 515) ; M. Esposito, *PADM* ; Kenney, *Sources*, I, pp. 275–77.

[3] *De Mirabilibus*, I. 7, II, 4.

[4] *Ib.*, I, 7, 20, II, 4.

in the seventh century in natural philosophy, theology and exegesis. He excludes the deuterocanonical books of the Maccabees from the canon of Scripture and regards as apocryphal the story of Bel and the dragon, as well as the miraculous transportation of Habacuc.[1]

A Latin commentary on Job (Oxford, Bodl. MS. Laud 460, eleventh–twelfth century), written by an Irish hand, contains some Gaelic glosses.[2]

Lathcen or Laidcen († 661), a monk of Clonfertmulloe, made an abridgment of the *Moralia in Job* of St Gregory the Great, of which only the beginning has been published.[3] In it we find a quotation from the *De ortu et obitu Patrum* of St Isidore of Seville.[4] Some manuscripts ascribe also to the monk Laidcen the *Lorica* elsewhere attributed to Gildas.[5]

The Psalter, the basis alike of liturgical and private prayer, was made the object of especially thorough study. The monks used to learn it by heart. It is not uncommon for the biographer of an Irish saint to mention as worthy of remembrance the person from whom the saint while yet a child learned his psalms.[6] We possess several psalters glossed in the vernacular and also some commentaries on the psalms.[7]

Of St Columban his biographer Jonas tells us that he had laid up so great a store of Holy Scripture in his heart that he composed in his early manhood a commentary on the Psalms in polished style.[8] Perhaps this is the commentary mentioned under the title *Expositio Sancti Columbani super omnes Psalmos* in a ninth-century catalogue of the library of St. Gall

[1] *Ib.*, II, 34.
[2] Ed. Whitley Stokes in Kuhn's *Zeitschrift*, VIII, pp. 254–55.
[3] Alfred Holder, *Die Reichenauer Handschriften*, Leipzig, I (1900), pp. 328–29; II (1914), pp. 668–69; L.G., *Le témoignage des manuscrits sur l'œuvre littéraire du moine Lathcen* (*R. Cel.*, XXX, 1909, pp. 39–43); M. Esposito, *Miscellaneous Notes on Medieval Latin Literature* (*Hermathena*, XVII, 1912, pp. 104–106); Kenney, *Sources*, I, pp. 278–79.
[4] Isidore, *De ortu et obitu Patrum* (PL, LXXXIII, 136). Cf. Esposito, *art. cit.*, p. 106; Manitius, *Geschichte*, I, p. 100, II, p. 796.
[5] L.G., *art. cit.*, pp. 43–46; M. Esposito, *Bachiarius, Arator, Lathcen* (*JTS*, XXX, 1929, pp. 289–91).
[6] *V. sup.*, § 1.
[7] Southampton Psalter; Palat. Vatic. 65; St Caimin's Psalter (*v. sup.*).
[8] Jonas, *Vita Col.*, I, 3 (p. 69).

and another of Bobbio of the tenth century.[1]   Has this work
been lost ? Some critics identify it with a Latin commentary
on the Psalter transcribed in the eighth century by an Irishman called Diarmait, which came originally from Bobbio and
is now preserved in the Ambrosian Library in Milan.[2]
This work is accompanied by glosses in Old Irish. It has
been recognized as a compilation based on a commentary
on the Psalms by Theodore of Mopsuestia or more directly
on a Latin adaptation of that commentary made by the
Pelagian bishop Julian of Eclanum, a friend of the bishop of
Mopsuestia.[3] It has been further observed that the
character of the Psalter used by the final compiler is such that
the most likely habitat which could be assigned to him would
be " a Celtic *milieu* anterior to the spread of the Vulgate." [4]
Consequently, more than one critic—notably Dom Germain
Morin—is inclined to attribute the commentary hailing from
Bobbio to St Columban.

Another fragmentary commentary on the Psalter, written
in an Irish cursive of the eighth century and coming likewise
from Bobbio, has been preserved in a codex of Turin (Bibl.
Nazionale F. IV. I, fasc. 5, 6).[5]

We possess two treatises on the Psalms in Old Irish, one
the original composition of which may go back to the year
850 and whose author mentions Hilary, Ambrose, Jerome,
Augustine, Cassiodorus, Gregory the Great and Isidore [6] ;

---

[1] G. Becker, *Catalogi bibliothecarum antiqui*, 32, nos. 216–217. Cf. M.
Esposito, *An ancient Bobbio Catalogue* (*JTS*, XXXII, 1931, p. 341).

[2] Milan ms. Bibl. Ambros. C. 301 inf. Cf. Kenney, *Sources*, I, pp.
200–202 ; Stokes and Strachan, *TP*, I, p. xv ; C. Plummer, *Notes on some
Passages in the Thesaurus Palaeohibernicus* (*R. Cel.*, XLII, 1925, pp. 376–78).

[3] R. L. Ramsay, *Theodore of Mopsuestia and St Columban on the Psalms*
(*ZCP*, VIII, 1912, pp. 421–51) ; *s.a. Theodore of Mopsuestia in England and
Ireland* (*Ib.*, pp. 452–97) ; A. Vaccari, *Nuova opera di Giuliano Eclanese :
Commento ai psalmi* (*Civiltà cattolica*, 1916, pp. 578–93) ; *s.a. Il salterio ascoliano
e Giuliano Eclanese* (*Biblica*, IV, 1923, pp. 337–55) ; D. Germain Morin, *Le
Liber S. Columbani in psalmos et le MS. ambros. C. 301 inf.* (*RB*, XXXVIII,
1926, pp. 164–77) ; R. Devreesse, *Le commentaire de Théodore de Mopsueste
sur les psaumes* (*R. Bib.*, XXXVII, 1928, pp. 340–66 ; XXXVIII, 1929,
pp. 35–62) ; *s.a. Par quelles voies nous sont parvenus les commentaires de Théodore
de Mopsueste ?* (*Ib.*, XXXIX, 1930, pp. 362–77).

[4] G. Morin, *art. cit.*, p. 177.

[5] Kenney, I, p. 665 (No. 515).

[6] Ed. Kuno Meyer, *Hibernica minora* (*Anecdota Oxoniensia, Mediaeval and
Modern Series*, Pt. VIII, Oxford, 1894). Cf. Kenney, I, p. 665 (No. 516).

the other, an epitome of the former, in mnemonic verses, written in 982 by Airbertach macCoisse of Ros Ailithir.[1]

The commentary on the Psalter found in the Codex Palatinus 68 of the Vatican, written in the eighth century by an Irishman, contains Gaelic and Northumbrian glosses.[2]

The only book of the Old Testament outside the Psalter on which, so far as we know, a commentary of Irish origin exists, is the book of Isaias, commentated by Joseph the Scot. This commentary, taken from St Jerome, is unedited; only the dedication has been published.[3]

As regards the Gospels and the Epistles of St Paul, we are better off. Aileran the Wise, *lector* of Clonard, who died of the plague in 665, has left a Latin poem on the canons of Eusebius [4] and (of greater importance) a mystical and moral explanation of the names of Christ's ancestors, *Interpretatio mystica progenitorum Christi*.[5] The edition reproduced in Migne is that of Fleming and is incomplete ; the lacking part was published in 1861 by Charles MacDonnell from a manuscript of the former Imperial Library of Vienna.[6] Aileran's treatise, slightly abridged, is found inserted in some MSS. of an unedited work by Sedulius Scottus, the *Collectaneum in Mattheum*.[7]

In the field of exegetical work, Sedulius has left us *Explanationes in praefationes sancti Hieronymi ad Evangelia* and *Explanatiuncula de breviariorum et capitulorum canonumque differentia*, some *Explanatiuncula* of the arguments of St Matthew, St Mark and St Luke, a commentary on the ten canons of Eusebius, and, above all a *Collectaneum in epistolas Pauli*, a compilation in which is to be found a good deal that is borrowed from the commentary of Pelagius.[8]

[1] Ed. B. MacCarthy, *Codex Palatino-Vaticanus* 830 (Royal Irish Academy. Todd Lectures Series, III, 1892). Cf. Kenney, I, p. 682 (No. 545) ; R. L. Ramsay, *art. cit.*, pp. 474–76.

[2] Stokes and Strachan, *TP*, I, p. 3.

[3] Dedication to his master Alcuin printed in *MG. Epist.*, IV, 483–84 ; *PL*, XCIX, 821–22. Cf. Manitius, *Geschichte*, I, p. 548.

[4] *PL*, CI, 729. Cf. Kenney, pp. 280–81 ; D. De Bruyne, *Une poésie inconnue d'Aileran le Sage* (*RB*, XXIX, 1912, pp. 339–40).

[5] *PL*, LXXX, 327–42.

[6] *PRIA*, VII, 1857–1861, p. 369–71. Cf. Kenney, pp. 279–80.

[7] Cf. Kenney, pp. 565–66.

[8] *PL*, CIII, 9–270 ; 271–72 ; 331–48 ; 348–52. Commentary on the

Let us further mention a fragment of a commentary on Mark in a manuscript of Turin, already referred to, hailing from Bobbio (Bibl. Nazion, F. IV. 1, No. 7), and in another manuscript of the same collection (F. VI. 2, No. 4), a fragment of a commentary on Matthew, both works in Irish minuscule and copiously glossed in Latin and Irish.[1]

A homily on the first chapter of St John, fragments of a commentary on the same Gospel, and possibly some glosses on the Old Testament, are all that remain of the exegetical work of Johannes Eriugena.[2]

Judging by some of the authorities (Pelagius, Breccán, Bercán mac Aido, Manchian " *doctor noster*," Lodcen, Lath and Bannbán) mentioned by the compiler of a commentary on the Catholic Epistles, of which we possess a manuscript of the ninth century coming from Reichenau, we are justified in concluding that we have to do with an Irish work, perhaps from the pen of Augustine, the author of the *De Mirabilibus*.[3]

We shall later have occasion to speak at greater length of the Commentary of Pelagius on the Epistles of St Paul, to which several references have already been made.[4]

In a pseudo-Hieronymian treatise on the four Gospels, sometimes ascribed to Fortunatianus of Aquileia, Dom Germain Morin is inclined to see " a product, probably Irish, of the beginning of the Carolingian era."[5]

---

ten canons of Eusebius, ed. M. Esposito (*PRIA*, XXVIII, Sect. C, 1910, pp. 83–91) ; *Explanatiuncula* (*ib.*, pp. 91–95). Cf. A. Souter, *The Sources of Sedulius Scottus' Collectaneum on the Epistles of St Paul* (*JTS*, XVIII, 1917, pp. 184–228) ; Kenney, I, pp. 565–66 ; Manitius, *Geschichte*, I, p. 317 ; II, p. 802.

[1] Kenney, I, pp. 660–61 (Nos. 510, 511).

[2] *PL*, CXXII, 283–96 ; 297–348 ; 1241–44 ; Stokes and Strachan, *TP*, I, pp. 1–2. Cf. Kenney, I, pp. 585–87 (Nos. 394–96).

[3] Kalrsruhe, Codex Aug. CCXXXIII. Cf. A. Holder, *Die Reichenauer Handschriften*, I, pp. 531–32 ; *s.a. Altirische Namen im Reichenauer Codex* ccxxxiii (*Archiv für celtische Lexicographie*, III, 1907, pp. 266–67) ; M. Esposito, *A Seventh-century Commentary on the Catholic Epistles* (*JTS*, XXI, 1920, pp. 316–18). Cf. Kenney, I, pp. 277–78 (No. 105).

[4] *V. inf.*, § 5.

[5] *PL*, CXIV, 861–916. Cf. D. Germain Morin, *RB*, XXIX, 1912, p. 495 ; Bardenhewer, *Geschichte der altkirchlichen Literatur* (Freiburg i. Br., 1912), III, p. 486 ; A. Wilmart, *Deux expositions d'un évêque Fortunat sur l'Évangile* (*RB*, XXXII, 1920, pp. 160–74).

§ 3.—THE APOCRYPHAL LITERATURE

The thought of the early Irish Christians was impregnated with the Bible, and their religious literature affords striking testimony of the fact. When hagiographers lacked traditional data concerning their heroes, or when their imagination was exhausted, they had recourse to the Bible and drew from it such parallels, transpositions and episodical details as were needed to touch up their narratives. A single verse of a psalm has sometimes suggested an entire scene to the narrator.[1]

Tirechán expressly notes the points of resemblance between St Patrick and Moses,[2] points which henceforth all biographers of the saint endeavour to bring into relief.[3] Like Moses, he was a law-giver ; he aided in the codification of the *Senchus Mór*. Like Moses, he lived one hundred and twenty years. It was in the midst of a burning bush that the angel Victor spoke to him. Patrick's dealings with the druids are singularly reminiscent of those of Moses and Aaron with Pharaoh's magicians. On the day of his death the sun stood still, as it did in the Book of Josue.

The saints of the New Testament are compared individually with those of the Old.[4] In the Life of Patrick in the Book of Lismore, Patrick is compared in turn with the most famous personages of both Testaments.[5] Under the rubric: *Hic incipiunt sancti qui erant bini unius moris*, the Book of Leinster gives a list including the patriarch Job, the Apostles and Evangelists, the Holy Virgin, the great hermits, monks, popes and doctors of the Church, and opposite each name is that of the Irish saint who deserves to be associated with it on account of some resemblance.[6] Needless to say, the resemblance is often arbitrary. In this holy list, Brigid is coupled with the Virgin Mary. By a flight of imagination outsoaring all bounds, the abbess of Kildare was not only compared to our

---

[1] Cf. C. Plummer, *VSH*, I, pp. CXXXIII–CXXXIX, n. 2, CXLVII, CLXVII–CLXVIII, n. 6, 7.

[2] Tirechán, p. 30.

[3] Cf. H. d'Arbois, *R. Cel.*, IX, 1888, pp. 113–14.

[4] H. J. Lawlor, *Chapters on the Book of Mulling*, p. 170.

[5] *Lismore*, pp. 165–66.

[6] *Book of Leinster, Facs.* (1880), p. 370. Cf. *Lismore*, pp. 298–99.

Lady, but was commonly identified in a way with her. She was called " Mary of the Gaels." In a hymn in her honour, Broccán calls her " mother of my High King " (*Brigit máthair mo ruirech*).[1] And in Ultan's hymn, *Brigit bé bithmaith*, we read the following stanza :

> " May she extirpate in us
>   the vices of our flesh,
>   she, the branch with blossoms,
>   the mother of Jesus ! " [2]

The exceptional fate of Elias and Enoch made a deep impression on the imagination of the Celts. There are frequent allusions to them in prayers, eschatological writings and other works.[3] According to a theory enounced several times, these two persons lead a life of innocence on a desert isle of the ocean, awaiting the end of the world, when they will taste of death by martyrdom.

There was a lively belief in the continuance of the gift of prophecy. The Irish Christian literature includes a host of prophecies attributed to national saints or made concerning them, sometimes even by pagans.[4]

As might be expected, biblical texts figure largely in the liturgy ; but what is more remarkable, the influence of the Bible appears in a marked degree, as we shall see presently, in the canonical collections, one of which bears the title *Liber ex lege Moysi*.

Knowing the bent of the Celtic temperament, we might infer *a priori* that our insular writers, not content with finding their mental nutriment in the canonical books of the Bible, would probably be strongly attracted also by the extra-biblical apocryphal literature. And, indeed, we need not go

---

[1] *LH*, I, 112, II, 40.

[2] *LH*, I, 110, II, 39. Cf. note Vol. II, p. 107.

[3] Augustine, *De mirabilibus script.*, I, 3 ; *Litany of Jesus*, 1 (*Ir. Lit.*, pp. 32–33. Cf. Editor's note, p. 111) ; *BC*, p. 103 ; Cod. Harl. 7653 (ed. Warren, *An. Ban.*, II, p. 95) ; *The Voyage of Snedgus and Mac Riagla*, ed. W. Stokes (*R. Cel.*, IX, 1888, p. 23) ; *Les deux chagrins du royaume du ciel*, ed. G. Dottin (*R. Cel.*, XXI, 1900, pp. 386–87). Cf. Kenney, *Sources*, I, p. 738 (No. 614).

[4] See Best, *Bibl.*, pp. 171, 234. Cf. P. Grosjean, *AB*, XLVIII, 1930, p. 399.

very far in the study of their literature to discover that they drew abundantly from that source. It is much to be desired that this point of literary and religious history should be thoroughly investigated, but the contents of the Irish manuscripts are as yet too imperfectly known for anyone to attempt such a study. Here we give a few general hints on the subject.

A good part of the early Gaelic literature is composed of amplifications of the Bible narrative. The following are some of the titles of pieces of religious fiction on biblical or eschatological themes : *Of the Wonders of the Birth of Christ.—The Testament of the Virgin.—The evernew Tongue.—Tidings of Doomsday. —Tidings of the Resurrection.—The two Sorrows of the Kingdom of Heaven.*[1] Most of these productions have, however, counterparts in Latin, in other ancient literatures, and in the European literatures of the Middle Ages. Plainly their origin is to be sought in the apocryphal books, which were early disseminated in the East. We have explicit proofs that a goodly number of these writings were also in circulation later in the British Isles.

The mutilated fragments of an Irish sacramentary of the tenth or eleventh century contain a Mass of the Circumcision, in which the gospel is taken, not from the canonical Gospels, but from an apocryphal Gospel, hitherto unknown, of James the son of Alphaeus.[2]

In the pieces entitled *The fifteen Tokens of Doomsday (Airdena Brátha)* and *Tidings of Doomsday (Scéla Laí Brátha)*, the mortals summoned to appear before their sovereign Judge are divided into four classes, the *mali valde*, the *mali non valde*, the *boni non valde* and the *boni valde*,[3] a division also found (though couched in different words) in the *Vision of Adamnán*, " the finest of all medieval visions that existed prior to Dante,"[4] a composition dating from the tenth or eleventh century. According to this text, the not quite perfect remain in Para-

---

[1] On the apocryphal literature in Old and Middle Irish see Best, *Bibl.*, pp. 115-17, 231-34, 241-43 ; Kenney, *Sources*, I, pp. 736-42.

[2] See H. M. Bannister, *Liturgical Fragments (JTS,* IX, 1908, pp. 417-18).

[3] Ed. Wh. Stokes, *R. Cel.*, IV, 1880, p. 250 ; XXVIII, 1907, p. 317. Cf. Best, *Bibl.*, p. 232.

[4] St John D. Seymour, *The Vision of Adamnan (PRIA,* XXXVII, Sect. C, 1927, p. 304).

dise, the perfect are in Heaven, the not very bad wander in waste places until Doom, and the utterly bad are cast into Hell.[1]

The expressions *mali non valde* and *boni non valde* recur in the *Vision of Tundal*, written in the year 1149, but besides these two classes the author recognizes five other divisions of the Other World.[2]

The influence of the Irish religious temperament is clearly discernible in the Book of Cerne, a collection of Latin prayers compiled in England in the ninth century. As far as the foundation of the book goes, many of the prayers are drawn wholly or in part from the *Acta Johannis*, the *Passio Petri et Pauli*, and the *Passio Andreae*.[3]

The letter of Christ to Abgar was inserted in the Irish *Liber Hymnorum*,[4] and used to be read in a religious office, an outline of which is given in a psalter of Basel (coming from Ireland?).[5] The Law of Sunday (*Cáin Domnaig*), which played an important part in Ireland and contributed much to establish Sunday observance, was based on a letter of Jesus said to have fallen from Heaven.[6]

A collection of one hundred and fifty poems was called a "psalter." The *Saltair na Rann* (Psalter of the Staves or Quatrains) is a "psalter" of this kind, which recounts in a hundred and fifty poems the sacred history from the creation of the world to the death of Christ.[7] Its composition goes back to 987. The poets who wrote it made use, besides the canonical texts, of at least three apocryphal documents, namely, the *Vita Adae et Evae*, the *Apocalypse of Thomas* and

---

[1] *Ib.*, pp. 305–306.
[2] Ed. Albrecht Wagner, *Visio Tnugdali* (Erlangen, 1882), p. 40, 41. Cf. St John D. Seymour, *Studies in the Vision of Tundal* (PRIA, XXXVII, Sect. C, 1926, pp. 98–99) ; *s.a. Irish Visions of the Other World* (London, 1930), pp. 133–34.
[3] *BC*, p. 233.
[4] *LH*, I, pp. 93–95, II, p. 30.
[5] H. J. Lawlor, *Chapters on the Book of Mulling*, p. 165.
[6] Ed. J. G. O'Keeffe, *Ériu*, II, 1905, pp. 189–214 ; *Anecdota from Irish Manuscripts*, III, 1910, pp. 21–27. Cf. Kenney, *Sources*, I, pp. 476–77, 782 ; Donald Maclean, *The Law of the Lord's Day in the Celtic Church* (Edinburgh, 1926).
[7] Ed. Wh. Stokes, *Saltair na ʼRann* (Anecdota Oxoniensia, Mediaeval and Modern Series, I, III, Oxford, 1883).

the *Apocalypse of Moses*, of which they possessed Latin versions.[1]

The *Saltair* names the biblical angels Gabriel, Michael and Raphael and, in addition, many others mentioned in none of the inspired books—Sarmichiel, Sarachel, Sariel, Darachel, Arachel, Babichel, Hermichel, Lonachel, etc. In the West, the apocryphal writings were the chief factors in spreading these fantastic names of angels, of which popular superstition laid hold with enthusiasm, alike in the islands and on the Continent.[2] The councils condemned, but to no effect, the forms of incantation, adjurations or prayers whose efficacy was supposed to depend on some of these magic names.[3] Enamoured of strange and mysterious prayers, as well as of magical formulas, the Celts eagerly welcomed this extra-canonical angelology.[4] The names of the following angels, Ariel, Axal, Azael, Panahiael, Panchel, Panithibh, Phanuihel, Rumihel, Sairiel, Uriel, are found in Latin prayers going back to the early Middle Ages (Book of Cerne[5]; B. M. MS. Harl. 7653[6]; *Lorica* of Leyden[7]) and in Irish texts (Amra of St Columba[8]; *Evernew Tongue*[9]; *Prayer to the seven Archangels for the days of the week*[10]). In the *Vision of Adamnán*, Ariel keeps guard over the second gate of Heaven and Abersetus over the torrent of fire which flows in front of that gate.[11] Even in our own days, in the recesses of

---

[1] Cf. St John D. Seymour, *The Book of Adam and Eve in Ireland* (*PRIA*, XXXVI, Sect. C, 1922, pp. 121–33); *s.a. Notes on Apocrypha in Ireland* (*PRIA*, XXXVII, Sect. C, 1925, pp. 107–17). Cf. Kenney, I, pp. 736–37.

[2] G. A. Barton, *The Origin of the Names of Angels and Demons in the Extra-canonical Apocalyptic Literature to* 100 A.D. (*Journal of Biblical Literature*, XXXI, 1912, pp. 156–67).

[3] See a charm against various ailments transcribed in the Missal of Bobbio (ed. E. A. Lowe, *HBS*, 1920, p. 153); Council of Laodicea, 35 (Mansi, *Concilia*, II, 659–70); Gelasian decree (*ib.*, VIII, p. 152); Council of Rome, A.D. 745, ed. A. Werminghoff, *MG. Leges : Sect. III, Conc.*, I, 1, p. 43.

[4] M. R. James, *Names of Angels in Anglo-Saxon and other Documents* (*JTS*, XI, 1910, pp. 569–71).

[5] *BC*, p. 153.

[6] *An. Ban.*, II, pp. 85, 92.

[7] Ed. Williams, *Cymmrodor Record*, No. 3, p. 294.

[8] *LH*, II, p. 66.

[9] *Une rédaction moderne du Teanga bithnua*, ed. G. Dottin (*R. Cel.*, XXVIII, 1907, pp. 298–99).

[10] Ed. T. P. O'Nolan, *Ériu*, II, 1905, pp. 92–94.

[11] Ed. J. Vendryes, *R. Cel.*, XXX, 1909, p. 367.

Scotland and the adjacent isles, Ariel, Uriel and Muriel are invoked.[1] In time we may perhaps discover the ultimate source of all these angelic names. Several of those mentioned are to be found in the *Book of Enoch*, the fourth book of Esdras, the Sibylline books and the apocalypses of Moses, Baruch, Sophonias and Elias.[2]

The *Celestial Hierarchy* of Pseudo-Dionysius contributed especially to make Christians familiar with the division into three hierarchies, each of three orders, together forming the nine angelic choirs ; a division of which the individual elements were furnished by Holy Writ.[3] It was adopted by St Gregory the Great in the West,[4] but it was already known to St Ambrose about the year 385.[5] Nevertheless it is found only in vague outline in the Celtic Churches in the time of the *Altus prosator* attributed to St Columba and that of the *Loricae* of Pseudo-Gildas and of Leyden.[6] On the contrary, " the nine orders of the Church in Heaven " are fully detailed in the *Litany of Jesus* or *Besom of Devotion*, attributed to Colgu, *lector* of Clonmacnois.[7]

§ 4.—CANON LAW

The decisions of the councils of the British Church are wholly penitentiary ; we will therefore deal with them a little later when speaking of penal discipline and penitential books. In the Church of Ireland the amount of literature emanating from councils is not considerable. Two series of canons have been preserved, said to belong to the age of St Patrick. The first series is attributed to a synod of bishops in which Patrick and his helpers Auxilius and Iserninus took

[1] A. Carmichael, *Carmina Gadelica* (Edinburgh, 1900), pp. 10, 94, 232, 244, 294, 314 (2nd edit., London, 1928).

[2] *Book of Enoch*, 9, 10, 20, 21, ed. R. H. Charles (*The Apocrypha and Pseudepigrapha of the Old Testament*, II, Oxford, 1913, pp. 192, 193, 201). Cf. L. Hackspill, *L'angélologie juive à l'époque néotestamentaire* (*R. Bib.*, XI, 1902, pp. 535–36).

[3] *Gen.*, III, 24 ; *Ex.*, XXV, 18 ff. ; *Is.*, VI, 2 ff. ; *Ephes.*, I, 21 ; *Coloss.*, I, 15 ff.

[4] *Homil. in Evang.*, XXXIV, 7. Cf. *Moralia*, XXXII, 8.

[5] Ambrose, *Apologia prophetae David*, v, 20 (*Corp. SEL*, XXXII, p. 311 ; *PL*, XIV, 900).

[6] *LH*, I, pp. 66–67, 207 ; *Cymmrodor Record*, No. 3, *l. cit.*

[7] *Ir. Lit.*, pp. 30–31.

part. The second is ascribed to the sole authority of St Patrick.[1] We may further mention a canon contained in the Book of Armagh and attributed to the bishops Auxilius, Patricius, Secundinus and Benignus.[2] We have more than once already laid these canonical texts under contribution. With J. B. Bury we regard the first series as possibly going back to the time of Patrick. However, these canons could hardly have emanated from a synodal assembly ; probably they simply served the purpose of a circular letter addressed to the Irish clergy.[3] Of this primitive legislation J. F. Kenney has given a good summary in the following words : " It is intended for a Church not yet fully organised, among a people still in part pagan. . . . The following points may be noted : a married clergy is recognised ; the Roman tonsure is enjoined ; clerics are assumed to be inmates of religious houses ; the bishop has some administrative importance, though, on strict interpretation, it may not be great ; rules are laid down to govern the collection of money for the ransom of captives ; alms must not be accepted from pagans ; Christians must not consult witches and soothsayers or believe that there is a witch in a mirror [? crystal] ; the penitential sentences to be imposed are comparatively light. An interesting regulation provides that no cleric who has come ' from the Britons ' without bringing proper credentials shall be permitted to perform the priestly duties." [4]

As for the second series, its Patrician origin is much more open to dispute. One of the canons is in flagrant contradiction with a passage of the Saint's *Confession*.[5] With much ingenuity and great probability, Bury has concluded that these latter canons were elaborated in the course of one or more Irish synods of the seventh century, in which the partisans of Roman reforms exercised a preponderant influence.[6]

Independently of these texts of more or less synodal origin, we have at our disposal for a study of insular canon law

[1] *CED*, II, pp. 328-30, 333-38.
[2] *LA*, p. 42 ; *CED*, II, p. 332.
[3] Bury, *Pat.*, pp. 233-45.
[4] Kenney, *Sources*, 1, p. 170.
[5] Compare Can. 27 (p. 337) with Patrick, *Confessio*, 42 (p. 20).
[6] *L. cit.*

several collections which, though non-official in origin, came before long to be held in high favour. The Irish canonical collection generally styled in brief the *Hibernensis* is the most celebrated of all. It is a compilation of aphorisms and enactments, arranged without any apparent order in sixty-seven books, each subdivided into a certain number of chapters, and dealing with all that pertains to Christian discipline, the religious life and the government of souls. The aphorisms and laws are drawn chiefly from Holy Scripture, the decisions of foreign and local councils and finally the works of the Fathers.

The compilers of the *Hibernensis* do not legislate in virtue of any ecclesiastical authority ; they speak in their own name. Although their work bears an undeniably Irish stamp, it is quickly seen that in collecting the various materials of this singular *florilegium* they have not remained wholly neutral in the great controversies which divided the Irish Church in the seventh century. Their leanings are distinctly " Romanist." It is their aim that the Roman customs lately introduced into their country shall take firm root. They condemn the tonsure of Simon Magus ; they are advocates for the tonsure of St Peter and the appeal to Rome ; they have little sympathy for the Britons " *toto mundo contrarii, moribus Romanis inimici* " ; they are agreed that it is necessary for the prelate who conse-crates a new bishop to call in the aid of at least two other bishops.[1] " The law peculiar to the Church of Ireland is here brought nearer to the law of the universal Church." [2]

As we have already hinted, the influence of the Bible on the *Hibernensis* is very striking. A large number of biblical precepts and examples have found place in it. Still more, this compilation tried to acclimatize in the extreme West many institutions of a distinctly Mosaic character, such as the privileges of the cities of refuge, the year of Jubilee, the obliga-tion of paying tithes, the *quaestiones mulierum*, and the distinction between clean and unclean foods.[3] These injunctions, along

---

[1] *Hibernensis*, xx, 5, 6 ; LII, 6 ; I, 15.
[2] P. Fournier, *De l'influence de la collection canonique irlandaise sur la formation des collections canoniques* (*Nouvelle revue historique de droit français et étranger*, XXIII, 1899, p. 28).
[3] *Hibernensis*, Lib. xxviii, xlv, lii, liii. Cf. Paul Fournier, *R. Cel.*, XXX, 1909, p. 233, note 1.

with others relating to certain cases of legal or ritual impurity, are to be found also in other canonical texts and in writings of Celtic origin of a different nature, and some of them found their way into the ecclesiastical law of the Anglo-Saxons.[1] It might be said that the maxim of St Paul : " To the pure all things are pure," had not yet been wholly accepted in these Western regions. Here we must quote the opinion of a canonist who has brought the subtlety of his criticism to bear on the study of these texts and has grasped their character and scope better than anyone else. " Thus," writes Paul Fournier, " fragmentary extracts from the Bible occupy an important place in the collections composed under Irish influence, where they appear side by side with a certain number of strictly canonical texts and copious quotations from the Fathers of the Church. It is otherwise with the collections which the Latin Church commonly used in the Merovingian period, particularly the *Dionysiana* and the *Hispana*. One need only place these texts beside the *Hibernensis* to perceive the contrast. The *Dionysiana*, the *Hispana* and analogous collections are made up of texts emanating from an official and always active ecclesiastical authority, that namely of the councils and the Popes. For the Western Church is provided with organs corresponding to the degrees of a regular hierarchy, to the functioning of which the faithful are accustomed ; hence they obey the direction of an authority qualified to command and conscious of its mission. In the Irish Church, on the contrary, such an organization, based on the territorial episcopate, has not yet reached full maturity ; in it the councils occupy only a secondary place, as also the bishops, whose authority is strangely subordinate ; the legislative machine works badly. Just as in the civil order the Celt, equipped only with rudimentary institutions, likes to have the authority of some powerful personage or famous jurist to support the decisions which constitute the law, even

[1] J. D. Michaelis, *Mosaisches Recht* (Biehl, 1777) ; Karl Böckenhoff, *Die römische Kirche und die Speisesatzungen der Bussbücher* (*Theologische Quartalschrift*, XXVIII, 1906, pp. 186–220) ; *s.a. Speisesatzungen mosaischer Art in mittelalterlichen Kirchenrechtsquellen des Morgen-und Abendlandes* (Münster, 1907) ; Paul Fournier, *De quelques infiltrations byzantines dans le droit canonique de l'époque carolingienne* (*Mélanges offerts à Gustave Schlumberger*, Paris, 1924, I pp. 67–78).

so in the canonical collections which are peculiarly his own, he quotes incessantly not only the Fathers of the Church and the saints of his race, but also Moses, the prophets and the apostles."[1]

We have spoken of the " compilers " of the *Hibernensis*. Thanks to a colophon in one of the Paris manuscripts which contain this collection, it has been discovered that it is the work of two Irish canonists. This colophon belongs to the original manuscript, and the Breton scribe who copied it has given it incorrectly as follows : " *Hucusq* ; *nuben &* *cucuiminiae & du rinis.*" [2] In these distorted words we have the names of the two compilers. The former is Rubin of Dairinis, a monastery situated on an island in the Blackwater not far from Youghal ; he was called " Rubin mac Connadh, scribe of Munster," and died in 725. The other compiler is Cúchuimne of Iona, entitled "the Wise," who died in 747.[3] To him is attributed a Latin hymn in honour of the holy Virgin in the *Liber Hymnorum*.[4] Accordingly the *Hibernensis* must have been composed in the first quarter of the eighth century, and there is no intrinsic reason to contradict this date.

Up to 1874 the *Hibernensis* was known only by the extracts given by Luc d'Achery and Martène.[5] In that year Wasserschleben published a first edition of the collection [6]; it is, however, to be regretted that the editor, as well as Henry Bradshaw,[7] took the latest redaction to be the oldest and moreover neglected to take into consideration other manuscripts containing related texts.[8]

---

[1] P. Fournier, *Le Liber ex lege Moysi et les tendances bibliques du droit canonique irlandais* (*R. Cel.*, XXX, 1909, pp. 228–29).

[2] Paris, B.N. Lat. 12021, s. xi, fol. 127.

[3] Five scholars have their share in the solution of the puzzle : 1. H. Bradshaw, *Letter to Wasserschleben* in *Hibernensis* (1885), introd., p. LXXII ; 2. Wh. Stokes (*Academy*, July 14, December 1, 1888) ; 3. B. MacCarthy (*Academy*, November 3, 1888) ; 4. E. W. Nicholson (*ZCP*, III, 1901, pp. 99–103 ; VI, p. 556) ; 5. R. Thurneysen (*ZCP*, VI, 1908, pp. 1–5). Cf. Kenney, *Sources*, I, pp. 248–49.

[4] *LH*, I, pp. 32–34.

[5] L. d'Achery, *Spicilegium* (Parisiis, 1723), I, pp. 492–506 ; Martène and Durand, *Thesaurus*, IV, cols. 1–22, reprinted by Migne, *PL*, XCVI, 1281–1308, 1311–14.

[6] The first edition having been almost entirely destroyed by fire, a second edition was issued with H. Bradshaw's letter (pp. LXIII–LXXV) in 1885.

[7] See letter mentioned and, by the same author, *The early Collection of Canons known as the Hibernensis : Two unfinished Papers* (Cambridge, 1893).

[8] S. Hellmann, *Sedulius Scottus* (München, 1906), pp. 136–44 ; P. Fournier, *R. Cel.*, XXX, pp. 225–26 ; Kenney, I, pp. 247–48.

This collection is the most developed and most important of the canonical collections of Celtic origin so far known. Paul Fournier has brought to light a *Liber ex lege Moysi*, a brief series of texts taken from the Pentateuch, extracted and compiled in Ireland in the eighth century and already in circulation on the Continent at the end of that century or at any rate in the following one.[1] From the islands come also the *Canones Adomnani* which contain, in various redactions, prohibitions relating to diet [2] ; their ascription to Adamnán, the famous abbot of Iona, has not been proved ; further, a small collection dealing with tithes, *De decimis et primogenetis et primitivis in lege*, likewise Hebraic in its inspiration.[3] On this subject, as on many others, there is probably much new matter in the manuscripts in reserve for future investigators.

The Irish and British canonical texts crossed the seas from the second half of the eighth century.[4] Received with favour by Anglo-Saxons and Franks, they contributed signally to the formation of the ecclesiastical law of both those peoples. A manuscript of Angers has preserved for us the thirty-one canons ascribed to the second synod of St Patrick. The same collection has borrowed from the *Hibernensis*, especially in passages dealing with monks. The influence of the *Hibernensis* is also to be discerned in the Frankish collection known as that of the 400 chapters (eighth century), in that of Cologne (eighth–ninth century), in the canons of the Council of Tribur (895), in the *De synodalibus causis et disciplinis ecclesiasticis* of Regino of Prüm (about 910) and in other works. The author of the prologue to the Anglo-Saxon laws of Alfred the Great in the ninth century was largely inspired by the *Liber ex lege Moysi*.[5]

It has, moreover, been noticed that five manuscripts

---

[1] *Le Liber ex lege Moysi* (*R. Cel.*, XXX, 1909, pp. 221–34). Cf. *Bulletin de l'Académie des Inscriptions et Belles-lettres*, May 14, 1909 ; Kenney, I, p. 250.

[2] Ed. Wasserschleben, *Buss.*, pp. 120–23 ; *PL*, LXXXVIII, 815 ; XCVI, 1319, 1324–25. Cf. Kenney, I, pp. 245–46.

[3] Ed. Martène and Durand, *Thesaurus*, IV, cols. 11–13 ; *PL*, XCVI, 1314–20 ; *Buss.*, pp. 143–44. Cf. Paul Fournier, *R. Cel.*, XXX, pp. 227–28, 232–33.

[4] ms. Cambrai 619 was transcribed, between A.D. 763 and 790, for Albericus, bishop of Cambrai, from an Irish original (end incomplete).

[5] P. Fournier, *De l'influence de la collection canonique irlandaise*, pp. 20, 36,

transcribed between the ninth and eleventh centuries, bearing a striking family resemblance and all containing the *Hibernensis* and the *Canones Adomnani* and many another Irish or Welsh canonical text, contain names of Breton scribes and glosses in Breton, a fact which attests a Breton origin for them or their prototypes.[1] On the ground of this ascertained fact, P. Fournier is inclined to infer that in the eighth century there must have been direct intercourse between Ireland and Brittany. This is possible, but not certain. There is nothing to assure us that the Irish texts transcribed in these manuscripts did not first make a stay in Great Britain before passing thence to Brittany ; does not the presence of British canons in at least two of them point to that conclusion ?

In any case, by whatever ways Irish texts found access to the Continent, it is quite certain that they exercised an important influence in the legislation of the Frankish Church. Their opportuneness in the first place secured them this fortune. In the *Hibernensis* the reformers of the eighth century found a series of principles after their own heart : the exemption of bishops from the jurisdiction of princes, the intervention of the Holy See in cases hard to decide, severe condemnation of simony, the indissolubility of marriage. They made use of it to propagate these doctrines. In the next place, the continental clergy were still in want of a canonical collection easy to use. The *Dionysiana*, the *Hispana* and the other contemporary collections gave the canons arranged according to their sources in chronological order. A classification according to subject, like that offered by the Irish collection, was far more convenient. Besides, the latter was much more comprehensive and more attractive in its nature. The mind of the reader was agreeably entertained by abundant citations from Holy Writ and the Fathers and by eclecticism of a wholly novel kind, whilst devout and earnest hearts were won by the fragrance of asceticism and

39–41 ; *s.a. R. Cel.*, XXX, p. 230 ; Wasserschleben, *Hibernensis*, p. xxix (*introd.*).

[1] Names of the Breton scribes as follows : Arbedoc (Paris, B.N. Lat. 12021), Maeloc (Paris, B.N. Lat. 3182, previously at Fécamp), Junobrus (Orleans, MS. 193, formerly at Fleury-sur-Loire). Cf. Bradshaw's letter (*Hibernensis* ; p. LXIX) ; *s.a. Collected Papers* (Cambridge, 1889), pp. 210–20, 452–88 ; P. Fournier, *R. Cel.*, XXX, p. 224.

piety which exhaled from texts on monasticism, fasting, relics and prayer.[1]

So far we have spoken only of disciplinary canons. But we cannot study them apart from the penitential canons which were elaborated in the same centres as the former, are often found in juxtaposition with them in general collections and were disseminated at the same time outside the country of their common origin.[2]

When Theodore of Tarsus arrived in England to take over the archiepiscopal see of Canterbury, he ascertained that public penance and the solemn reconciliation of penitents with the Church were practices unknown in the country.[3] It is very likely that they were equally unknown in the Celtic Churches. The penitential system in vogue in all these regions, at any rate from the sixth century on, was based on a kind of scale, a special penitence being imposed on the transgressor by the minister of the sacrament, without any rite whatever, according to the scales of works of satisfaction contained in the little books called " penitentials." [4] These works of satisfaction in the penitentials are of severity and duration proportionate to the offence. For the gravest crimes, such as incest, parricide, perjury, etc., they prescribe according to circumstances either banishment or confinement in a monastery for lifetime or for a term of ten, seven or three years.[5] Thus the satisfaction demanded for serious offences carried with it a certain publicity. In the *Liber Angeli* con-

---

[1] P. Fournier, *De l'influence*, pp. 71–73 ; *R. Cel.*, XXX, p. 231.

[2] On the spread of the penitentials in England and on the Continent see Canons of Aelfric, s. x–xi (Wilkins, *Concilia*, I, 252, can. 21) ; Ratherius of Verona († 974), *Synodica ad presbyteros*, 10 (*PL*, CXXXVI, 562) ; Oscar D. Watkins, *A History of Penance* (London, 1920), Vol. II [cf. H. Thurston, *An Anglican History of Confession* (*Month*, No. 137, 1921, pp. 44–55)] ; Hans von Schubert, *Geschichte der christlichen Kirche im Frühmittelalter* (Tübingen, 1921), pp. 684–87 ; T. P. Oakley, *English penitential Discipline and Anglo-Saxon Law in their joint Influence* (Studies in History, Economics and Public Law, CVII, II, New York, Columbia University, 1923) [Cf. P. Fournier, *RHE*, XXI, 1925, pp. 300–303] ; J. T. MacNeill, *The Celtic Penitentials and their Influence on Continental Christianity* (*R. Cel.*, XXXIX, 1922, pp. 257–300, XL, pp. 51–103, 320–41) and Paris, 1923 ; P. W. Finsterwalder in Theodore, *Canones*, pp. 217–25.

[3] Theodore, *Canones*, U text, I, 13 (p. 306).

[4] Cf. A. Boudinhon, *Sur l'histoire de la pénitence* (*Revue d'histoire et de littérature religieuses*, II, 1897, pp. 496 ff.).

[5] Adam., *Vita Col.*, I, 22, 30, II, 39 ; *Vita Coemgeni*, 38 (*VSH*, I, p. 253) ;

tained in the Book of Armagh mention is made of a class of *poenitentes* besides one of *virgines* and a third one comprising persons *in matrimonio legitimo*.[1] For offences of not so heinous a nature, the satisfaction consists in fasts more or less prolonged, or repeated during periods of forty days or of years, or else in prayers, flagellations, almsgiving, etc.

The theory propounded by H. J. Schmitz, that all the Western penitentials were derived from a Roman one,[2] has not succeeded in finding general acceptance.[3]   It is now commonly admitted that penitentials had their birth and development in the Celtic Churches, whence they passed, just like the disciplinary canons, to the Anglo-Saxons and the Continent in the seventh, eighth and ninth centuries.[4]

We will now proceed to enumerate the monuments which have been preserved of the Celtic penitential discipline, both British and Irish.

It seems impossible to reconstruct with any certainty in their original tenor texts like these, which were copied and recopied in the course of many centuries and subjected more than any others to contamination, mutilation and numerous additions, according to the fluctuations of social habits and ecclesiastical discipline.

The oldest texts seem to have come from Celtic Britain ; they are the *Excerpta quaedam de libro Davidis*, the *Synodus Aquilonalis Britanniae*, the *Altera Synodus Luci Victoriae*, the *Praefatio de Poenitentia* attributed to Gildas,[5] and the *Canones Wallici* [6] ; these range from the sixth to the eighth century.

Columban, *Poenitentiale*, B text, ed. Seebass, pp. 443, 445) ; *Rule of the Céli Dé*, 38 (*Tallaght*, 1927), pp. 74–75 ; " Moechator matris suae annos III cum peregrinatione perenni peniteat " (*Poenit. Cummeani*, II, 7, ed. Zettinger, p. 509).

[1] *LA*, p. 41.

[2] H. J. Schmitz, *Die Bussbücher und die Bussdisciplin der Kirche* (Mainz, 1883), s.a. *Die Bussbücher und die kanonische Bussverfahren* (Düsseldorf, 1898) ; s.a. *Archiv für katholisches Kirchenrecht*, LI, 1884, pp. 25 ff.

[3] P. Fournier, *Étude sur les pénitentiels* (*Revue d'histoire et de littérature religieuse*, Vols. VI–IX) ; P. Fournier and G. Le Bras, *Histoire des collections canoniques en Occident* (Paris, 1931), I, p. 85.

[4] P. Fournier, *Étude*, IX, p. 102.

[5] Accepted as authentic by O. Seebass, *ZK*, XIV, p. 430 ; J. T. MacNeill, *R. Cel.*, XXXIX, 1922, p. 265.

[6] All these texts first printed by Martène and Durand, *Thesaurus*, IV, and in *PL*, XCVI, 1315–24 ; *Buss.*, pp. 103–106, 124–36 ; *CED*, I, pp. 113–20, 127–37.

The oldest Irish penitential is a compilation of the sixth century made by a certain Vinnianus or Vinniaus, " overflowing with words from the fount of the Scriptures, for the blotting out of all men's transgressions." [1] An attempt has been made to identify the author of this penitential with one or other of the two Finnians, him of Clonard or him of Magh Bile (Moville). The reference made by St Columban to a *Vennianus auctor*, who questioned Gildas on a point of monastic discipline,[2] as well as the chronology of the epoch, has led Mario Esposito to conclude with Seebass that the author was the abbot of Moville, who died in 589.[3] Columban's Penitential, drawn up for one of his continental foundations,[4] and also that which bears the name of Cumianus Longus (*Longius* in the MSS.), in Irish St Cuimine Fota († 662),[5] are largely derived from that of Finnian.

Four other penitential *libelli* must be mentioned : 1. The *Poenitentiale Bigotianum* (seventh–eighth century), derived from the Penitential of Cuimine Fota, and probably of Irish origin [6] ; 2. A penitential composed in Old Irish, which dates from about the year 800 and is related to the *Bigotianum* as well as to Cuimine and Theodore [7] ; 3. A treatise, likewise in Old Irish, on the commutation of penances (*De arreis*), which may date from the eighth century [8] ; 4. A penitential of a still more composite nature than the preceding ones, which long passed for being the authentic text of Cumianus

---

[1] " Finit istud opusculum, quod coaptavit Vinniaus suis visceribus filiis dilectionis et religionis obtentu, de scripturarum venis redundans, ut ab omnibus omnia deleantur hominibus facinora " (p. 119). Ed. Wasserschleben, *Buss.*, pp. 108–19.

[2] Columban, *Ep.* 1 (*MG. Epist.*, III, p. 159).

[3] Esposito, *Latin Learning*, I, pp. 236–40. Cf. O. Seebass, *ZK*, XIV, 1894, pp. 435–37. Cf. Kenney, *Sources*, I, pp. 240–41.

[4] Ed. O. Seebass, *ZK*, XIV, 1894, pp. 430–48 ; Wasserschleben, *Buss.*, pp. 353–60.—This penitential, if authentic (the Columbanian authorship is hardly beyond dispute), may contain considerable interpolations. Cf. Kenney, *Sources*, I, p. 200.—The *Regula coenobialis* of Columban (ed. Seebass, *ZK*, XVII, 1897, pp. 215–34 ; *PL*, LXXX, 216–24), a monastic penitential, is our chief source of information for penal discipline in Columbanian monasteries.

[5] Ed. J. Zettinger, *Das Poenitentiale Cummeani* (*Archiv für katholisches Kirchenrecht*, LXXXII, 1902, pp. 501–40). Cf. Esposito, *Latin Learning*, I pp. 245–50.

[6] Ed. Wasserschleben, *Buss.*, pp. 441–60. Cf. Kenney, I, pp. 241–42.

[7] Ed. E. J. Gwynn, *Ir. Pen.* (1914). Cf. Kenney, *ib.*, p. 242.

[8] Ed. Kuno Meyer, *De arreis* (1894).

and which seems to have been compiled on the Continent in the ninth century.[1]

At a fairly early period, under the constraint of various necessities, the system of equivalents and commutations of works of satisfaction was grafted on that of penance regulated according to a fixed scale.[2] Thus several days of fasting, either at intervals or more often consecutively (*biduanae, triduanae, superpositiones*), accompanied by the recitation of the Psalter or other prayers, by vigils, genuflexions, prostrations or other acts of mortification, some of them strange enough, might take the place of a less severe but more prolonged penance originally imposed, which for sundry reasons had become difficult or impossible to carry out. Such commutations or reductions of penance were called *arrea*, from the Old Irish *arra*, meaning " equivalent, substitute." [3]

It is not impossible that such practices paved the way for the introduction of indulgences properly so called.[4] Many penitentials contain lists of *arrea* ; but the most important document in this matter is the Old Irish compilation dealing with commutations of which we have just spoken. In it the *arrea*, like certain of the indulgences of later date, are actually given as being available for the souls of the departed. The booklet begins by speaking of an *arreum* " which saves a soul from hell," consisting of 365 paternosters and an equal number of genuflexions and of lashes each day till the end of the year, and in addition a monthly fast.[5] The influence of the Bible may well have contributed towards the success of the principle of commuting penances.[6]

According to Loening and his supporters, private penance was originally only a claustral practice, introduced into the lay world in the seventh and eighth centuries through the

---

[1] Ed. Wasserschleben, *Buss.*, pp. 460–93. Cf. Kenney, *ib.*, p. 243.
[2] Boudinhon, *art. cit.*, pp. 503–506.
[3] Cf. K. Meyer, *De arreis*, p. 486 ; *Fél. Oeng.*, Epil. 177–88 (pp. 272–73). Cf. Oakley, *English Penitential Discipline*, pp. 69–72 ; Du Cange, *Glossarium*. The French *arrhes* is no doubt of kindred origin. See W. Meyer-Lübke, *Romanisches etymologisches Wörterbuch* (Heidelberg, 1911), *s.v. arra*.
[4] A. Boudinhon, *Sur l'histoire des indulgences (Revue d'hist. et de lit. eligieuses*, III, 1898, pp. 442–43).
[5] *De arreis*, 1 (pp. 487, 492). Cf. St John D. Seymour, *Irish Visions*, p. 23.
[6] See *De arreis*, ch. 27. Cf. P. Fournier, *R. Cel.*, XXX, p. 233.

influence of St Columban and the Irish and Anglo-Saxon missionaries, and gradually transformed into a universal ecclesiastical institution.[1] This theory cannot be admitted.[2] It is, however, true that Columban and his disciples worked zealously to attract the peoples *ad medicamenta poenitentiae*—to use the words of Jonas of Bobbio—and strove to make confession more frequent, chiefly in cloisters, but also among pious laymen.[3] The *Regula coenobialis* and the Penitential of St Columban, the *Regula cuiusdam patris ad virgines*, the Rule of St Donatus of Besançon for the nuns of that city (*Jussanense parthenon*), the customs of Faremoutiers, all of them impregnated with the spirit of Luxueil, prescribe frequent confession for the religious of both sexes.[4] We grant that in many passages of these Rules it is not sacramental confession that is spoken of, but a mere practice of claustral discipline. Nevertheless, there is every reason for believing that sacramental confession itself must have developed concurrently in these cloisters and among those of the faithful who were under the spiritual guidance of the Scots. In Ireland confession was much practised, even among the laity.[5] The name given to the confessor deserves to be noted ; from the Old Irish period he was called *anmchara*, " soul-friend." According to a scholiast of the *Félire Oengusso*, Comgall of Bangor once uttered the following significant words : " My soul-friend has died, and I am headless, and ye, too, are headless, for a man without a soul-friend is a body without a head." [6]

[1] E. Loening, *Geschichte des deutschen Kirchenrechts* (Strassburg, 1878), II, pp. 468 ff. Followed by Malnory, *Quid Luxov.*, pp. 62 ff.

[2] See L. Duchesne, *Bulletin critique*, IV, 1883, p. 366 ; H. Thurston, *An Anglican History of Confession* (*Month*, No. 137, 1921, pp. 51–55) ; E. Carpentier, *De confessione peccatorum venialium ab antiquissimis temporibus* (Boll., *AS*, Oct., IX, 722–24).

[3] Jonas, *Vita Col.*, I, 5, II, 8 (pp. 71, 123). Cf. L.G., *Les chrétientés celtiques*, p. 278, n. 1.

[4] *Regula coenobialis*, ed. Seebass, pp. 218, 220 ; *Poenit. Columbani*, ed. Seebass, p. 448 ; *Regula cuiusdam Patris ad virgines* (*PL*, LXXXVIII, 1059) ; Donatus, *Regula ad virgines* (*PL*, LXXXVII, 281, 282) ; Jonas, *Vita Col.*, II, 19 (p. 139). Cf. O. Seebass, *Fragment einer Nonnenregel des 7 Jahrhunderts* (*ZK*, XVI, 1896, pp. 465–70) ; Ryan, *Monast.*, p. 223.

[5] *Acta Ciarani*, 15 (*Sal. ASH*, col. 815) ; Bede, *HE*, IV, 25 ; *The Battle of Carn Conaill* (*ZCP*, III, 1900, p. 217). Cf. C. Plummer, *VSH*, I, p. cxvi (*introd.*).

[6] *Fél. Oeng.*, pp. 180–83. Cf. H. d'Arbois de Jubainville, *R. Cel.*, XXIV, 1903, p. 107 ; C. Plummer, *l. cit.* ; Ryan, *Monast.*, p. 223.

§ 5.—Theological Doctrines

The Scots who attracted notice in the Carolingian period seem to have been men of encyclopaedic intellect, well equipped for erudite labours, inquisitive and never tired of rummaging in books. Their knowledge was undoubtedly extensive for the age, but it was ill digested and undisciplined. Proud of their intellectual superiority, they were fond of showing it off. Were they equally well endowed with the faculties of speculation ? Had they the philosophic mind ? It is true that the title of philosopher is often bestowed on them, and they sometimes assume it themselves. But we know that philosophy in that period had as yet no domain of its own in which it reigned supreme ; it embraced the entire field of learning, sacred and profane, in its evidential as well as its speculative departments.[1] With their gift of glib reasoning and their wordy erudition, our Scots might well pass for complete philosophers in the eyes of their contemporaries. Besides, it cannot be denied that they applied themselves largely to dialectic ; they made use of the syllogism in season and out of season. St Benedict of Aniane, who had doubtless had the opportunity of meeting some insular masters in the monastic schools, is careful to warn one of his disciples against the *syllogismus delusionis* in favour among the *scholastici* of his time and especially, he avers, among the Scots.[2] Some years later, Prudentius of Troyes, Florus of Lyons, and the Council of Valence in 855 reproved Johannes Scottus for his excessive use of purely ratiocinative methods in theological discussions. For him there was no distinction between philosophy and theology : a consequence of his Neo-Platonic training. Whereas his contemporaries, in order to elucidate points of faith, relied chiefly on arguments based on authority, drawing from the Scriptures, the Fathers and the decisions of the councils, he for his part claimed the right of solving the thorniest problems almost solely by means of dialectic, undertaking to decide all theolo-

[1] Maurice De Wulf, *Histoire de la philosophie médiévale* (Paris, 1924), I, pp. 1–56 ; G. Brunhes, *La foi chrétienne et la philosophie au temps de la Renaissance carolingienne* (Paris, 1903), pp. 51, 63.
[2] Benedict, *Ep. ad Gisarnarium* (*PL*, CIII, 1413).

gical questions by the four logical processes of division, definition, demonstration and analysis.

Hincmar, archbishop of Reims (845–882), and Pardulus, bishop of Laon (847–857), made a great mistake in engaging an intellect so doctrinaire and so daring in the controversy on predestination which Gottschalk had just revived with no little stir.[1] The Saxon monk had been condemned for having admitted a predestination of two kinds, both alike imposing necessity on the predestined. The Scot asserted that prescience and predestination are in God one and the same thing, and he rejected the notion that the wicked are predestined to punishment, recognizing only the predestination of the elect to life. Moreover, his *De Praedestinatione* (851)[2] contained grave errors concerning the fire of hell and the eternity of punishment, as well as several propositions of pantheistic or Pelagian tendency.

A band of theologians, Prudentius, bishop of Troyes, Florus, deacon of the Church of Lyons, and Remigius, archbishop of that city, immediately rose in arms against him.[3] The Councils of Valence (855) and Langres (859) opposed the methods of Eriugena, terming his syllogisms " inventions of the Devil," " inept reasonings," and " old wives' tales," and finally reviving St Jerome's witticism on Pelagius, " Irish porridge " (*Scottorum pultes*).[4]

The other great theological work of John the Scot is the *De divisione naturae* (*c.* 867), which sets forth, in the form of a dialogue between a master and his disciple, a kind of philosophico-theological synthesis on the constitution of the Universe, or Nature, viewed under four aspects : Nature creating but not created ; Nature creating and created ; Nature created but not creating ; and Nature neither created nor creating.[5] " The Neo-Platonic mysticism which Johannes imbibed from Pseudo-Dionysius, Maximus Con-

[1] On Gottschalk, see Kenney, *Sources*, I, p. 576.
[2] *PL*, CXXII, 347–440.
[3] Cf. Kenney, *Sources*, I, pp. 575–77.—A. Wilmart, *Un passage sauté dans l'ouvrage de Florus contre Jean Scot* (*RB*, XLII, 1930, pp. 372–73).
[4] Council of Valence, 4, 6 (Mansi, *Concilia*, XV, 5, 6) ; Council of Langres, 4 (*ib.*, 538).
[5] *PL*, CXXII, 439–1022.

fessor, Chalcidius and others, permeates the whole, and has been developed into a quite thoroughgoing pantheism." [1]

About the same time Ratramnus, a monk of Corbie, wrote a treatise *De qualitate animae*, which has never been published, all we have being the introductory letter addressed to Odo, abbot of Corbie and later (861–881) bishop of Beauvais, to refute a system of monopsychism devised by another Scot, a certain Macarius, who taught that each man's mind was only part of a single universal mind. [2]

All the Irish theologians settled in France in the Carolingian period did not fall into heresy. On the contrary, in 827 Dungal constituted himself the champion of orthodoxy against Claudius, bishop of Turin, who rejected the cult of images, relics and the cross of the Saviour, as well as the practice of pilgrimages and the invocation of saints. The *Liber adversus Claudium* is dedicated to the emperors Louis and Lothair and displays a certain amount of patristic learning. [3]

We have not to speak here of the *Instructiones variae* of St Columban, of which only four out of seventeen have been admitted as authentic and which, moreover, belong rather to the paraenetic or hortatory class of literature [4]; nor yet of the *De Fide*, sometimes attributed to St Mochta of Louth, but really the work of the mysterious Bachiarius, who was neither an Irishman nor a Briton. [5]

---

[1] Kenney, I, p. 584.

[2] Ed. Dümmler, *MG. Epist.*, VI, 153–54. Cf. Kenney, *ib.*, pp. 549–50 ; Manitius, *Geschichte*, I, pp. 412–17.

[3] *PL*, CV, 457–530. Cf. E. J. Martin, *A History of the Iconoclastic Controversy* (London, 1930), pp. 266–67.

[4] Ed. O. Seebass, *ZK*, XIV, 1894, pp. 76–97. Cf. *s.a. Ueber die sogennanten Instructiones Columbani* (*ZK*, XIII, 1892, pp. 513–34) ; *s.a. Ueber die Handschriften der Sermonen und Briefe Columbas von Luxeuil* (*NA*, XVII, 1892, pp. 245–59) ; *s.a. Ueber die beiden Columba Handschriften der Nationalbibliothek in Turin* (*NA*, XXI, 1896, pp. 739–46) ; G. Morin, *Deux pièces inédites du disciple de Fauste de Riez auteur des soi-disant "Instructiones Columbani"* (*Revue Charlemagne*, I, 1911, pp. 161–70) ; Kenney, I, pp. 196–97.

[5] Bachiarius, *De fide* (*PL*, XX, 1019–36). This work has been attributed to Mochta by Moran, *Essays on the Origin, Doctrine and Discipline of the early Irish Church* (Dublin, 1864), p. 94 ; by Salmon, *The ancient Irish Church* (Dublin, 1897), pp. 176–77.—See M. H. MacInerny, *St Mochta and Bachiarius* (Dublin, 1923, reprinted from the *Irish Eccles. Record*) ; O. F. Fritzsche, *ZK*, XVII, 1896–97, pp. 211–15 ; A. Lambert, art. *Bachiarius*, in the *Dictionnaire d'histoire et de géographie ecclésiastiques* edited by A. Baudrillart, De Meyer and Van Cauwenbergh ; Kenney, *Sources*, I, p. 351, n. 181.

On the other hand, the short work which bears the title *De duodecim abusivis saeculi*, attributed in turn to St Cyprian of Carthage, St Augustine of Hippo and St Patrick, had certainly an Irishman for its author.[1] It is a treatise on morality. The twelve abuses which are reproved are of the following classes : " *sapiens sine operibus—senex sine religione—adolescens sine obedientia—dives sine elemosyna—femina sine pudicitia—dominus sine virtute—christianus contentiosus—pauper superbus—rex iniquus—episcopus neglegens—plebs sine disciplina—populus sine lege.*" [2] The author quotes the Vulgate, the Rule of St Benedict, and St Isidore of Seville, or some source drawn on by him in his *Etymologiae.*[3] A long extract from the treatise *De duodecim abusivis* has been inserted in the *Hibernensis*, where it appears under the name of St Patrick,[4] to whom it is also ascribed in the letter addressed to Charlemagne by a certain Cathuulfus or Kathvulf.[5] The treatise is considered to have been composed between 630 and 650.[6]

This work belongs in virtue of a goodly part of its contents to gnomic literature, a class of composition cultivated in Ireland from a very early period. The *Senchus Mór* offers examples of it [7] ; and an old collection of maxims made use of in the *Hibernensis* and known to Sedulius Scottus must also have been placed under contribution by the author of the *De duodecim abusivis.*[8]

We possess another moral treatise in the *De tribus habitaculis ;* it has been printed among the *spuria* of St Augustine, to whose authorship it has sometimes been attributed.[9] A

[1] Ed. S. Hellmann, *Pseudo-Cyprianus De* XII *abusivis saeculi* (Harnack and Schmidt, *Texte und Untersuchungen*, XXXIV, 1, Leipzig, 1909) ; *PL*, XL, cols. 1079–88.
[2] Ed. Hellmann, p. 32.
[3] Cf. Kenney, *Sources*, I, p. 282.
[4] Ed. Hellmann, pp. 51–52 ; *Hibernensis*, xxv, 3–4 (pp. 77–78).
[5] *Epistolae variorum*, VII (*MG. Epist.*, IV, 502–505).
[6] On that work see J. Sajdak, *Stromata in honorem Casimiri Morawski* (Cracoviae, 1908), pp. 1–11 ; Esposito, *PADM*, p. 200 ; P. Fournier, *Les collections canoniques romaines de l'époque de Grégoire VII (Mémoires de l'Institut : Académie des Inscriptions et Belles-lettres*, XLI, 1920, p. 340) ; Manitius, *Geschichte*, I, pp. 107–108, II, p. 796.
[7] Cf. S. Hellmann, *op. cit.*, p. 15.
[8] Cf. S. Hellmann, *ib.*, pp. 96, 137 ff. ; Carl Mrrstrander, *Bídh Crínna* (*Ériu*, V, 1911, pp. 126–41).
[9] *PL*, XL, 991–98.

certain number of manuscripts, however, assign this work to St Patrick, and this is the only reason for connecting it with Ireland. " Internal evidence shows that the work can have been written neither by St Augustine nor by St Patrick." [1] The three habitations referred to in the title are Heaven, the abode of God, of the angels and of the elect ; Hell, that of the damned and of devils, whose pains are eternal (*mors aeterna, poena sine fine*) ; and the terrestrial world. It is hard to say at what date this opuscule was written. It displays a good Latinity, simple in style but not wanting in vigour. The author makes use of ingenious comparisons, such as that he employs in speaking of the threefold vision of the blessed in Heaven. " Before a glass mirror," he says, " a threefold vision is presented to us : we see ourselves in the mirror, we see the mirror, and we see all that is present around us ; even so, in the mirror of the Divine radiance we shall see God as He is, as far as is possible for a creature ; we shall see ourselves, and we shall be able to know others with a true and certain knowledge." [2]

From the *Hibernensis*, the Book of Armagh, the glosses or continuous commentaries on the Epistles of St Paul preserved in manuscripts of Würzburg, Reichenau (Karlsruhe) and St Gall, as well as from the *Collectaneum in omnes beati Pauli epistolas* of Sedulius Scottus and other products of Irish Pauline exegesis or deriving from it, we are aware that the commentary of Pelagius on St Paul's Epistles was read and used in Ireland in the eighth and ninth centuries. Marianus Scottus of Ratisbon still makes use of it in 1079 to annotate the Epistles copied " for his brethren in peregrination." [3] Does this imply that the Pelagian heresy had supporters in Ireland throughout the entire early Middle Ages ? This is not evident. St Columban believes in the necessity of Divine Grace [4] and (except for John the Scot who, while avowing his belief in it, manifests nevertheless a tendency to diminish its sphere of action) we do not observe any deviation from the

---

[1] M. Esposito, *PADM*, p. 200, n. 7.
[2] *De tribus habitaculis*, 6 (*PL*, XL, 996).
[3] Cf. Kenney, I, pp. 661–64.
[4] Columban, *Ep.* 4 (*MG. Epist.*, III, p. 168).

orthodox doctrine on this point in the teachers from the western isles. A concise commentary on the entire series of the Pauline Epistles was, as will be readily understood, highly appreciated in those days. Now the choice of commentaries of this kind was very limited. Outside that of Pelagius, the only ones to be had in Latin were the Ambrosiaster (by the Irish held to be the work of St Hilary), Pseudo-Jerome and Pseudo-Primasius, the two latter being themselves merely revisions of the commentary of Pelagius.[1]

It is true that in a letter addressed in 640 to the clergy of North Ireland to admonish them to adopt the orthodox Easter, Pope John IV, so Bede tells us, enjoined the Scots in addition to reject the Pelagian heresy, which, according to sundry reports, had been revived among them.[2] The Scots who clung to their old Paschal style were in little favour at Rome.[3] It is quite possible that the mere fact of their having used the commentary of the heresiarch in their study of St Paul gave rise to the rumours which reached the Pope's ears. The use of the commentary may have led to the inference that its readers endorsed all the errors of Pelagius. However, I repeat, it is absolutely false to represent Pelagianism as the traditional and endemic heresy of the Celts, whether Irish or Britons.

If space permitted, we should have something to say here about sacramental theology, a subject which has been touched upon elsewhere.[4]

The reader who desires to form fuller acquaintance with the dogmas professed by the Celtic Church should further have recourse to the formulas of faith which have been handed down both by writers and in liturgical books.[5]

---

[1] Cf. Kenney, I, p. 662 ; A. Souter, *A Study of Ambrosiaster* (*Texts and Studies*, VII, ιv, Cambridge, 1905), pp. 162–63.—Victorius Afer (A.D. 355–365) commented on four epistles only ; Jerome on four, and Augustine on two. See A. Souter, *The earliest Latin Commentaries on the Epistles of St Paul* (Oxford, 1927).

[2] Bede, *HE*, ιι, 19. No support can be found in the late *Passio Kiliani* (*MG. Scr. RM*, V, p. 723, n. 6). On alleged Pelagianism in Ireland see further H. Williams, *ZCP*, IV, 1903, pp. 536–38.

[3] See *Laterculus imperatorum Romanorum Malalianus* (*MG. Auct. ant.*, XIII, pp. 426–27).

[4] See L.G., art. *Celtiques* (*Liturgies*), cols. 3019–24.

[5] A. Hahn, *Bibliothek der Symbole* (Breslau, 1897), §§ 76 ff., pp. 209, 226.

There is, however, one particularly ticklish question which cannot be passed over in silence : the fate in store for the souls of the departed. The doctrine of Heaven and Hell set forth by the author of the *De tribus habitaculis* is very definite. "*In regno autem Dei,*" he says, "*nulli mali sunt, sed omnes boni; at in inferno nulli boni, sed omnes mali.*" [1] There is no mention in this treatise of the *mali non valde* nor of the *boni non valde* spoken of (as we have seen) in some visions of the hereafter [2] ; neither is there the least trace of a place of expiation reserved for these *mali non valde* and *boni non valde*. Consequently, some Protestant writers, such as Ussher and W. D. Killen, not finding any mention of Purgatory in the *De tribus habitaculis*, have drawn the conclusion that the theology of the early Irish ignored the existence of that place of purification. [3] It may be answered that the author's only object, as indicated by the title of the opuscule, was to speak of these three abodes of souls, Hell, Heaven and the terrestrial world. Nevertheless it must be admitted that the absence of any incidental allusion to Purgatory in this work, brief as it is (containing only six short chapters), is a little surprising.

Let us recognize the fact that in the Irish writings previous to the tenth century which have reached us, whether theological treatises, narratives of visions of the state after death, or works of any other description, we come across nothing to attest the belief in a Purgatory distinct from Hell [4] ; the word (*purgatorium*, or, in Irish, *purgatóir*)—as well as the idea —does not appear till later in religious literature. However, we must beware of drawing any sweeping conclusions from this negative argument. If the pains of Hell were eternal for the damned properly so called, the *mali* of our author, we see that other souls—those of the *mali non valde* and the *boni non valde*, to use the terms we have already met with—might be delivered from "Hell" by the prayers, the good works and the acts of penance put forth to that end by their friends still

---

[1] *De tribus habitaculis*, i (*PL*, XL, 991).
[2] *V. sup.*, § 3.
[3] Ussher, *Works*, III, pp. 193–200 ; IV, p. 271 ; W. D. Killen, *The Ecclesiastical History of Ireland* (London, 1875), I, p. 87.
[4] St John D. Seymour, *Irish Visions*, ch. II.

living.[1] There is abundant testimony to prove it in the religious literature and liturgy of the Irish before the tenth century.[2] Be it observed, moreover, that none of these early writings in which traces of a Purgatory have been sought in vain, purports to be a didactic work ; they are all products of pure imagination or else works written with the sole aim of edification. We cannot therefore expect to find in them the definiteness of doctrine which we should look for in a scholastic theologian dealing *ex professo De novissimis*.[3] Let it be finally remembered that even at the present day the word *purgatorium* does not once appear in the liturgy for the departed of the Roman Church, and that even in the offertory of the Mass of Requiem we meet with these words : " *Libera animas omnium fidelium defunctorum de poenis inferni*," which are equivalent to the expressions used in the Celtic Churches of the early Middle Ages.

Quite apart from the systems elaborated by daring thinkers like Pelagius and John the Scot, and from the doctrines expounded by theologians or implicit in the liturgy, if we would penetrate into the inmost recesses of the religious sentiment of the Scots, we should have to explore the prolific domain of popular beliefs bordering on superstition, of traditions or customs based on a perversion of the religious instinct ; we should have to trace in all their vagaries those freaks of the Celtic imagination which are to be found especially in eschatological literature and in revelations of the other world.

In all times the Celt has delighted in speculating on the hereafter ; the place occupied by the thought of death among the Bretons even at the present day is well known.[4]

---

[1] *De arreis* (*v. sup.*, § 4) ; J. Pokorny, *Eine altirische Legende aus dem Buch von Leinster* (*Miscellany presented to Kuno Meyer*, Halle, 1912), pp. 210–13 ; *s.a.* in *Irish Texts*, I, 1931, p. 44. Cf. Seymour, *op. cit.*, pp. 39–45.

[2] *Hibernensis*, Lib. XV, *De cura pro mortuis* (pp. 43–45) ; " Missa pro mortuis pluribus " (*Stowe*, p. 23). Cf. J. Salmon, *The ancient Irish Church*, pp. 144–52 ; L.G., art. *Celtiques* (*Liturgies*), § VIII, 8.

[3] " Purgatorius videlicet ignis qui corpore statim egressos et minus per lamenta poenitentiae purgatos ad plenitudinem recipit purgandos " (*De statu Ecclesiae*, PL, CLIX, 1001, a work written by Gilbert, bishop of Limerick, *c.* A.D. 1109).

[4] See Anatole Le Braz, *La légende de la mort chez les Bretons armoricains* (Paris, 1902, new edit., 1923).

According to the Irish visionaries, souls after death sometimes assume the form of birds.[1] The damned suffer alternately from excess of heat and intolerable cold.[2] The
author of the *De tribus habitaculis* himself upholds this doctrine :
" *Frigus intolerabile et calor ignis inextinguibilis,*" these are the
two chief tortures of Hell,[3] and he appeals to the words of
Job : " *De aquis nivium transibunt ad calorem nimium.*" [4] This
alternation of heat and cold is, however, to be met with in
other medieval writings besides those of Ireland.

The Vision of Adamnán depicts " vast multitudes, dwelling
in utter darkness on the shore of eternal pain.   Every other
hour the pain (tide) ebbs away from them, and the next hour
it returns and submerges them.   These are they in whom the
good and evil were equal, and at the judgment their good
shall quench their evil, and they shall be brought to the har-
bour of life." [5] Along with fratricides (or parricides) and
spoilers of churches, the erenaghs (Ir. *airchennech*) or managers
of churchlands who have alienated the money entrusted to
them instead of bestowing it on the poor and needy, are
plunged into a sea of fire up to their chins.   Others stand
immersed in black mire up to their waists, wearing short
cowls of ice and girdles which incessantly torture them with
alternate heat and cold.[6]

In the Vision of Tundal, the monk Marcus again describes
in his own way the tortures inflicted on divers classes of sinners,
among them gluttons and fornicators, both lay and monastic,
and those of the religious orders who lived unchastely.[7]

The belief in a periodical respite granted to the damned

[1] *Les deux chagrins du royaume du ciel*, ed. G. Dottin (*R. Cel.*, XXI,
1900, p. 377). ·Cf. C. S. Boswell, *An Irish Precursor of Dante* (London, 1908),
pp. 46, 160, 162–63, 174 ; L.G., *La croyance au répit périodique des damnés*
(*Mélanges bretons et celtiques offerts à J. Loth*, Rennes, 1927), p. 67.

[2] *Vita II^a Brendani*, 44, 45, 46, ed. C. Plummer, *VSH*, II, pp. 287–88 ;
Vita Brendani, 25, ed. P. Grosjean (*AB*, XLVIII, 1930, p. 118) ; *Vision of
Adamnán*, ed. Boswell, *An Irish Precursor*, p. 40 ; ed. J. Vendryes, p. 373 ;
La langue toujours nouvelle, ed. G. Dottin (*An. Br.*, XXXIV, 1920, p. 296) ;
A Poem on the Day of Judgment, 14, ed. J. G. O'Keeffe (*Ériu*, III, 1907,
pp. 29–33). Cf. C. Plummer, *BNE*, II, pp. 337–38 ; J. Vendryes,
L'enfer glacé (*R. Cel.*, XLVI, 1929, pp. 134–42).

[3] *De tribus habitaculis*, 2 (*PL*, XL, 993)·

[4] " Ad nimium calorem transeat ab aquis nivium " (*Job*, XXIV, 19).

[5] Seymour, *Irish Visions*, pp. 25–26 (sect. 24).

[6] Sect. 25, 26, 27 (Seymour, *Irish Visions*, p. 26) ; Boswell, *op. cit.*, p. 43·

[7] Seymour, *Irish Visions*, pp. 128–30.

is also certainly to be found in the Irish narratives, in which the Sunday *refrigerium* of Judas Iscariot occupies an important place [1]; this belief, too, is found in continental eschatology.

As for the customs and traditions especially dear to Irish piety or superstition, what a long list might be drawn up ! We should have to mention those prayers the repetition of which was deemed to be particularly efficacious, such as the *Biait* (*Beati immaculati*, Ps. cxviii.),[2] the *loricae* and certain celebrated hymns. Persons pressed for time might earn the copious indulgences attached to these formulas by reciting only a part, for instance, the last three stanzas of St Sechnall's famous hymn in praise of St Patrick.[3] We should have also to speak of the certainty of salvation acquired by burial in some cemetery where saints of bygone ages had found a resting-place. " This superstition," observes C. Plummer, " is probably responsible for the crowded condition of many Irish cemeteries to-day." [4]

A very old belief, one still deeply rooted in the minds of many Irishmen, is that they will enjoy the privilege of appearing before Patrick, presiding side by side with Christ, on the Day of Judgment.[5]

According to the Vision of Laisrén, the Irish people were to enjoy another mark of favour in the world to come. Laisrén perceived some of his compatriots set apart in a valley which formed an antechamber to Hell. They were those who had died in sin. In that place they felt no other torment save deep despair.[6]

[1] Cf. Arturo Graf, *Miti, leggende e superstizioni del medio evo* (Torino, 1892), I, pp. 241–70 ; Paul Lehmann, *Judas Ischarioth in der lateinischen Legendenüberlieferung des Mittelalters* (*Studi Medievali*, New Ser., II, 1929, pp.308–309, 326 ff.) ; Seymour, *Irish Visions*, pp. 87 ff. ; L.G., *La croyance au répit périodique des damnés, l. cit.*

[2] *Eine altirische Legende*, ed. J. Pokorny, *l. cit.* ; *L'aventure de Maelsuthain*, ed. J. Vendryes (*R. Cel.*, XXXV, 1914, pp. 203–11) ; *Story of two young Clerical Students* (*Lismore*, pp. x–xii).

[3] *LH*, II, 98. Cf. C. Plummer, *VSH*, I, p. xciii (*introd.*) ; Kenney, *Sources*, I, p. 743.

[4] C. Plummer, *l. cit.*

[5] *Liber Angeli* (*LA*, p. 42) ; Hymn of Fiacc (*LH*, I, p. 102, II, p. 34). Cf. *An. Ban.*, II, p. 51 ; H. Thurston, *St Patrick's Petitions* (*Month*, Nov., 1905, pp. 539–43) ; Paul Grosjean, *A Tale of Doomsday Colum Cille should have left untold* (*SGS*, III, 1929, pp. 80–81) ; L.G., *Gaelic Pioneers*, p. 103.

[6] *Vision of Laisrén*, ed. K. Meyer (*Otia Merseiana*, I, 1899, p. 119) ; Seymour, *Irish Visions*, pp. 20–23.

§ 6.—The Scots and the Carolingian Renaissance

Perhaps throughout the Middle Ages in the western part of continental Europe there was no more barbarous period than that which elapsed between the beginning of the seventh and middle of the eighth century. Classical and ecclesiastical studies had fallen into complete decay. The best educated among the laity, with but few exceptions, were hardly able to read and write. The clerics, with an indifferent knowledge of Latin, despised the popular tongue (*lingua laica*), as yet not fully formed, and were wholly ignorant of Greek. Charlemagne saw the necessity of improving this state of things. To attain that end he summoned to France masters from abroad ; the Italians Peter of Pisa and Paulinus, who later became patriarch of Aquileia, the Lombard Paul the Deacon, the Visigoth Theodulf, whom the emperor made bishop of Orleans, the Anglo-Saxon Alcuin and others. This academic group was completed by the addition of two Irishmen ; one was named Clement (he must not be confounded with the heretic of that name) ; the other, whom it is harder to identify, was either Dungal or Joseph the Scot.[1] The passage of the *Gesta Caroli Magni* in which Notker relates the arrival of the two strangers is well known. The narrative is probably in large part fictitious, but it seems likely that we may take it as based on fact. We will content ourselves with the essential features, which are picturesque and highly characteristic of the time and the people with whom we are dealing. The two Scots land in the company of British traders. Their learning, both sacred and profane, is soon discovered ; they represent themselves as being also traders ; they sell knowledge to him who desires to possess it. Hearing of their intentions, Charlemagne hastens to summon them to the palace and asks the conditions on which they are willing to place their knowledge at the disposal of the youth of his Empire. As is natural in men who in want of the necessaries of life, they are not exorbitant in their demands ; board and lodging and, in addition, teachable pupils will suffice them.[2] And so Clement

---

[1] Dungal, according to B. Simson, *Jahrbücher des fränkischen Reichs unter Ludwig dem Frommen* (Leipzig, 1876), p. 257.

[2] *Gesta Karoli Magni*, i, 1 (*MG. Scr.*, II, p. 731).

remained as a teacher in the palace school. On Charlemagne's death, Louis the Pious kept him in his office and entrusted to him the education of his eldest son Lothair, to whom Clement dedicated his *Ars grammatica*.

He seems to have been still at the imperial court in 826 ; probably he was the " Scotellus " on whom Theodulf vented his sarcasms. Notwithstanding which, the lessons of the Scottic grammarian were so highly appreciated that pupils were sent to him from places so far distant as Fulda,[1] probably also from Reichenau.[2] Clement retired at last to Würzburg near the tomb of St Kilian, where it is likely that he died.[3]

Let us recall the names of the principal Irish scholars who took part in the work of literary revival carried out by the Carolingians, and also the centres of study whence their influence chiefly emanated.

The Joseph who has just been mentioned as being possibly the companion of Clement on his arrival, may doubtless be identified with the " Joseph abbas Scottus genere " who was Alcuin's friend and disciple.[4] We have still remaining poems addressed by him to Alcuin and to Charlemagne.[5] He also composed a commentary on Isaias, as has been already stated.[6]

The name Dungal is often met with in the history of the intellectual and educational movement of the period. We have already come across a letter addressed to Charlemagne in 811, treating of the double solar eclipse of the preceding year, written by a Dungal[7] ; and we know a refutation of the heretical tenets of Claudius of Turin published in 827, likewise the work of a Dungal.[8] Further, we possess letters and poems written by a Dungal[9] ; a Dungal is mentioned

---

[1] *Catalogus abbatum Fuldensium* (*MG. Scr.*, XIII, pp. 272–74).
[2] Walahfrid, *Visio Wettini*, v. 123–24 (*MG. Poet. Lat.*, II, p. 308).
[3] Dümmler, *Forschungen zur Deutschen Geschichte*, VI (Göttingen, 1866), pp. 115–19 ; B. Simson, *op. cit.*, pp. 258–59.
[4] Alcuin, *Epistolae* (*MG. Epist.*, IV, pp. 32, 33, 40, 119, 483).
[5] *MG. Poet. Lat.*, I, p. 149.
[6] *V. sup.*, § 2.
[7] *V. sup.*, § 1.
[8] *V. sup.*, § 5.
[9] Ed. Dümmler, *MG. Epist.*, IV, pp. 578–83 ; *Poet. Lat.*, I, pp. 411–12, II, pp. 664–65.—In a *titulus* written by " Dungalus Magister," Hilduin of

in other compositions both in prose and verse [1] ; in a capitulary of Lothair of the year 825, a Dungal is named as teacher at the school of Pavia.[2] Various descriptions are associated with the name of Dungal in our texts : *reclusus, peregrinus, magister, episcopus, abbas*.[3] Moreover, there has come down to us a series of poems ascribed to a certain " *Hibernicus exul*," the author of which has been identified with Dungal, a recluse of St. Denis.[4] Finally, a catalogue of books belonging to Bobbio gives a list of codices which had been presented to the library of the monastery by Dungalus, " *praecipuus Scottorum*." [5]

Can all these works have been written by a single author, and that one described in such a variety of terms ? After arriving in France at the very beginning of the ninth century, can this Dungal have been still alive at the time when the donation of books was made to the library of Bobbio ? Traube and others have refused to believe that there was only one Dungal, and have distinguished as many as four persons of the name [6] ; they place the donation made to Bobbio in the eleventh century.[7] Another critic, however, who has recently investigated the subject afresh, has reached the conclusion that the catalogue in question must have been drawn up between 862 and 896, and in his opinion the Dungalus, " *praecipuus Scottorum*," was none other than the teacher of Pavia and the recluse of St. Denis, to whom also may be

St. Denis († 840), " egregius abbas," is mentioned (*Carm.*, XVII ; *Poet. Lat.*, III, pp. 664–65).

[1] *Carmen*, XVII (*Poet. Lat.*, I, pp. 406–407) ; *Versus Scottorum*, III (*Poet. Lat.*, IV, pp. 1124–27) ; Alcuin, *Ep.* 280 (*MG. Epist.*, IV, pp. 436–38).

[2] Ed. Boretius, *MG. Leges : Sect. II. Cap.*, I, 327.

[3] (*a*) *Reclusus* (A.D. 811 = *MG. Epist.*, IV, p. 570).—(*b*) *Peregrinus* (*MG. Poet. Lat.*, I, p. 411).—(*c*) *Magister* (*Poet. Lat.*, II, p. 664).—(*d*) *Episcopus* (Alcuin, *Ep.* 280 : *MG. Epist.*, IV, p. 437).—(*e*) *Abbas* (*Versus Scottorum*, III, ed. K. Strecker, *MG. Poet. Lat.*, IV, III, p. 1124). The superposing of these different vocations is not to be wondered at on the part of an Irish churchman of that time.

[4] Ed. Dümmler, *MG. Poet. Lat.*, I, 395–99. Cf. Kenney, I, p. 541.

[5] Becker, *Catalogi bibliothecarum antiqui* (Bonnae, 1885), pp. 64–73. Cf. Kenney, I, p. 516 (No. 322).

[6] L. Traube, *O Roma nobilis* (*Abhandlungen der k. Bayer. Akad. der Wissenschaften*, I. Cl., XIX, Bd. II, pp. 332–37) ; Manitius, *Geschichte*, I, pp. 370–74 ; K. Strecker, *Ein neuer Dungal ?* (*Zeitschrift für romanische Philologie*, XLI, 1921, pp. 566–73).

[7] So believed Gottlieb, *Centralblatt für Bibliothekswesen*, IV, 1887, p. 443 ; Manitius, *Geschichte*, I, p. 374 ; Traube, *O Roma nobilis*, p. 336.

assigned the authorship of all the writings above mentioned ;
on the other hand, the " *Hibernicus exul* " ought to be identified
not with this one Dungal, but with Dicuil.   Such are the latest
views on this difficult question which we owe to the penetra-
tion of Mario Esposito.[1]

Among those with whom Dungal had literary relations
appears Hildoard, bishop of Cambrai (790–816), in whose
honour he composed a short poem.[2]   Cambrai seems to
have been one of the favourite centres of the *Scotti* at the end
of the eighth and beginning of the following century.   The
bishops of Cambrai took advantage of their presence to have
various works transcribed which time has preserved to us.
Thus for Hildoard's predecessor Albericus (763–790) were
transcribed the oldest manuscript we possess of the *Collectio
canonum Hibernensis* (Cambrai MS. 619 [679]),[3] which manuscript also contains a very interesting fragment of a homily in
Old Irish, the earliest piece of continuous Irish prose extant.[4]

During the episcopate of Hildoard and for his church were
also written two sacramentaries (Cambrai MS. 162–163 [158]
and 164 [159]), which suggest " at once the usual character
of the more ordinary Irish codices." [5]   Finally, the penitential composed by Hildoard's successor Halitgar (817–831)
betrays a Celtic influence very likely to be attributed to the
presence of Irishmen in the city.[6]

Not only Cambrai but also Reims, Soissons, Laon and
Liége had colonies of Scots at this period.   The grammarian
bishop Dunchad taught *belles lettres* in the monastery of St.
Remigius of Reims, where in all likelihood he had Remigius of
Auxerre and Gottschalk for pupils.[7]   Dunchad has left some
notes on the computus,[8] but the commentary on Martianus

---

[1] M. Esposito, *Dungalus 'Praecipuus Scottorum'* (*JTS*, XXXIII, 1932,
pp. 119–31.
[2] *MG. Poet. Lat.*, I, p. 411.—A letter in which Dungal " ab episcopo
quodam subsidium petit " (*c.* 800–814) (*MG. Epist.*, IV, p. 578) may also
have been addressed to Bishop Hildoard.
[3] Cf. *Hibernensis*, p. xxx ; A. Molinier, *Catalogue général des bibliothèques
de France. Départements*, XVII, pp. 257 ff.
[4] Stokes and Strachan, *TP*, II, pp. xxvi, 244–47.
[5] E. Bishop, *JTS* ,IV, 1903, pp. 414–15 ; *s.a. LH*, p. 65.
[6] P. Fournier, *Étude sur les pénitentiels* (*Rev. d'hist. et de lit. relig.*, VIII,
1903, pp. 528 ff.).
[7] Traube, *NA.*, XVIII, p. 104.
[8] Ed. M. Esposito, *ZCP*, IX, 1913, pp. 161–62.

Capella which has been edited under his name, is not his work.[1]

Traube has further drawn attention to a Latin poetic style of a special kind in fashion in the ecclesiastical province of Reims in the ninth century and in his opinion due to the imitation of Irish models.[2] He has also edited the *ludicra* of a certain Scot dwelling in Soissons in this period.[3] It was in Soissons that Heiric of Auxerre met a bishop named Marcus, a native of Britain but educated in Ireland, who, after a long and saintly episcopate, had resolved upon exile (*ultroneam sibi peregrinationem indixit*) and was then living as a recluse in the monastery of SS. Medard and Sebastian. From the lips of this aged man Heiric gathered the details about the doings of St Germanus of Auxerre in Great Britain which he afterwards set down in his *Miracula Germani*.[4]

But no town of that district had greater attractions for studious Irishmen than Laon. The most famous among the emigrants of the age, Johannes Eriugena, " towering in gigantic proportions over all his contemporaries," [5] made a stay there under the patronage of Charles the Bald, who had appointed him master of the palace school ; there he enjoyed the friendship of Hincmar the younger, the bishop of the place (858–876), and established his ascendancy over those of his compatriots who had settled in the town—Aldelmus, sometimes given as his brother, perhaps Dunchad, and some others. He seems to have entered the palace school in 845, or even earlier, and to have remained there at least till 870.[6]

No foreigner, if we except Alcuin, exercised a more decisive intellectual influence among the Carolingian Franks. Among his chief disciples were said to be Wicbald, who became bishop of Auxerre, and many of his own compatriots, among them

---

[1] M. Esposito, *Sur le prétendu commentaire de Dunchad sur Marcien Capella* (*Didaskaleion*, III, 1914, pp. 173–82). Cf. Kenney, I, pp. 573–74 ; A. Van de Vyver, *Les étapes du développement philosophique du haut moyen âge* (*Revue belge de philologie et d'histoire*, VIII, 1929, p. 435).

[2] See note *MG. Poet. Lat.*, III, pp. 710–11.

[3] *Ib.*, p. 690.

[4] Heiric, *Miracula Germani*, I, 8 (*PL*, CXXIV, 1245). Cf. L. Traube, *MG. Poet. Lat.*, III, p. 422.

[5] Turner, *Irish Teachers*, pp. 35–36.

[6] L. Traube, *NA*, XVIII, p. 104 ; *s.a. O Roma nobilis*, pp. 362–63 ; *s.a. M.G. Poet. Lat.*, III, pp. 422, 519–20, 523 ; Kenney, I, pp. 571–73.

Helias, who was one of the teachers of Heiric of Auxerre and became bishop of Angoulême, and Martinus Hibernensis († 875), a very learned man who also became a teacher.[1] A codex (Laon MS. 444) written partly by Martinus allows us to form some notion of the extent of his knowledge. This manuscript contains Latin and Greek poems of his composition as well as various pieces transcribed by him, notably a Graeco-Latin glossary ; works which show that he, like his master, was acquainted with the Greek language, though he was not able to write it with perfect correctness.[2]

Johannes Scottus himself has left us verses, both Greek and Latin [3] ; but it is mainly due to his translation of the works of Pseudo-Dionysius the Areopagite and to his own writings in prose, especially the *De divisione naturae*, his chief work (*c.* 867), that his name has lived.[4]

The works of Dionysius, written in Greek and studied eagerly in the East, had hitherto been known only sporadically and in detached fragments in the West. Copies had been sent, first about 758 by Pope Paul I to Pippin the Short, then in 827 by the Byzantine emperor Michael II to Louis the Pious, emperor of the Franks.[5] At the request of Louis, who had asked him for a Latin translation and a Life of Dionysius, Hilduin, abbot of St. Denis, had attempted such a version with the aid of some collaborators [6] ; and in his Life of St Dionysius (835) he had amalgamated the convert of St Paul with the martyr of Paris, in whose honour the great abbey near that city had been founded, and with the author of the theo-

---

[1] Kenney, I, pp. 589–92.

[2] *Ib.*

[3] Ed. L. Traube, *MG. Poet. Lat.*, III, pp. 518–56.

[4] *V. sup.*, § 5.

[5] G. Théry, *L'entrée du Pseudo-Denys en Occident* (*Mélanges Mandonnet*, Paris, 1930), II, pp. 23–30.

[6] M. Grabmann, *Pseudo-Dionysius Areopagita in lateinischer Uebersetzung des Mittelalters* (*Beiträge zur Geschichte des christlhichen Altertums und der byzantinischen Literatur.* Festgabe Ehrhard (Bonn, 1922), pp. 180–99) ; P. Lehmann, *Zur Kenntniss der Schriften des Dionysius Areopagita im Mittelalter* (*RB*, XXXV, 1923, pp. 81–97) ; G. Théry, *Hilduin et la première traduction des écrits du Pseudo-Denis* (*Revue d'histoire de l'Église de France*, IX, 1923, pp. 23–40) ; *s.a. Le texte intégral de la traduction du Pseudo-Denis par Hilduin* (*RHE*, XXI, 1925, pp. 33–50, 197–214). Cf. A.-M. Jacquin, *Revue des Sciences philosophiques et théologiques*, XIX, 1930, pp. 585–86 ; Kenney, I, pp. 579–81 ; M. L. W. Laistner, *Thought and Letters in Western Europe* (London, 1931), pp. 197–201.

logical treatises. For centuries this identification passed unchallenged.[1]

St Denis had been adopted by the Franks as their patron. About 858 Charles the Bald wished to have a new translation of the works of the Areopagite and he asked it from the Irishman John, renowned for his knowledge of the Greek language. Although too literal and retaining too many Greek constructions, the version executed by John the Scot was, on the whole, correct.[2] Amended by Anastasius, the librarian of Pope Nicholas I, it was widely diffused in the Middle Ages and had considerable influence on the pre-scholastic theologians of the eleventh and twelfth centuries, Gerbert, Berengarius, Anselm of Laon, Honorius Augustodunensis, Hugh of St. Victor, Abelard, and even on the schoolmen of the thirteenth century.[3]

Under the influence of the *Scotti* of Laon, dilettanti in Greek scholarship, bishop Hincmar, who was ignorant of the vulgar tongue, set himself, so it appears, to Hellenize, and also acquired a smattering of Gaelic which enabled him to interlard his conversation with Irish words. "You who not only cannot speak, but cannot even understand without the help of an interpreter the language in which you were born," writes to him his uncle, Hincmar of Reims, "have made use of mongrel and corrupt terms, Greek and sometimes Irish, and other barbarisms, as the whim seized you, where Latin words would have amply sufficed."[4]

About the year 848 there arrived on the Continent Sedulius Scottus, accompanied by some of his fellow-countrymen.[5] Hartgar, the bishop of Liége (840–854), detained him in that

---

[1] Kenney, I, p. 580.

[2] Ed. *PL*, CXXII, 1023–1194 ; ed. E. Dümmler, *MG. Epist.*, VI, 1, 158–61 (dedicatory epistle).

[3] J. Dräseke, *Johannes Scottus Erigena und dessen Gewährsmänner* (Leipzig, 1902) ; Grabmann, *Geschichte der scholastischen Methode*, I (1901), pp. 202–10 ; Maurice De Wulf, *Histoire de la philosophie médiévale* (Louvain, 1924), I, pp. 122–23, 129–30.

[4] Hincmar, *Opusculum* LV *capitulorum* (J. Sirmond, *Hincmari opera*, II, 547).

[5] It has been conjectured that Sedulius arrived in France with the embassy sent to Charles the Bald in A.D. 848 by the Irish king Máel Sechlainn (see Prudentius of Troyes, *Annales Bertiniani*, ed. G. Waitz, 1883, p. 36. Cf. Traube, *O Roma nobilis*, pp. 342–43). But this is pure supposition (Kenney, I, p. 555).

city. Fortune was not very kind to him, but his lessons procured him a livelihood. He was besides able by his facile,
copious and agreeable verses to interest in his fate the persons
of most consequence at the time, the bishops Hartgar and
Franco, Charles the Bald, Lothair I, his wife Irmingard, Louis
the German, and others.[1] Sedulius seems to have been
endowed with a happy temperament ; we may judge of it by
the confidences which he has left us :

> " I read or write, I teach or wonder what is truth,
> I call upon my God by night and day.
> I eat and freely drink, I make my rhymes,
>   And snoring sleep, or vigil keep and pray.
> And very ware of all my shames I am ;
>   O Mary, Christ, have mercy on your man ! "[2]

Sedulius knew Greek, but not well enough to be able to
compose verses in it like John the Scot.[3] Like his eminent
compatriot, he possessed encyclopaedic knowledge. Besides
what has been already told of his literary output, he commentated the grammarians Eutyches, Donatus and Priscian,[4] and
composed for Louis II (emperor after 855) a *Liber de rectoribus
Christianis*, a kind of mirror for kings, partly in prose and partly
in verse.[5]

But to appreciate his poetic powers we must read his other
poems. In these he often attains a high level ; he sings the
beauties of springtide with Virgilian grace :

> " The year is at its fairest ; corn shows green,
>   Vines burgeon fast, and with a verdant sheen
>   The fields are gay.
>   The songs of birds re-echo in the air,
>   Earth, sea, and sky a smiling visage wear
>   On this glad day." [6]

[1] Ed. L. Traube, *MG. Poet. Lat.*, III, pp. 166–237.
[2] *Carmina*, II, LXXIV, p. 225. Transl. Helen Waddell, *Mediaeval Latin Lyrics* (London, 1929), p. 123.
[3] See Mario Esposito, *The Knowledge of Greek in Ireland during the Middle Ages* (*Studies*, I, 1912, pp. 677–78).
[4] Kenney, I, pp. 563–64 (No. 371).
[5] Ed. S. Hellmann, *Sedulius Scottus*, pp. 1–91 ; L. Traube, *MG. Poet. Lat.*, III, pp. 154–66 (poems only).
[6] *Carmina*, II, XLIX. Transl. F. A. Wright and T. A. Sinclair, *The History of later Latin Literature* (London, 1931), p. 163.

" Considering the poetry of Sedulius as a whole," says F. J. E. Raby, " we are bound to place him with Theodulf and Walafrid in the front rank of the poets of the Carolingian age. While he shared with them the inevitable defects both of taste and of execution, like them he sought his subjects in experience and in life, and conveyed into his verses the impression of a lively personality. It is for reasons of this kind that modern readers are able to find pleasure in the occasional verses of Fortunatus or Sedulius, while the Middle Ages, true to their peculiar standard, delighted most in poems of extravagant moral and theological allegory, which modern readers can hardly approach without an effort." [1]

In his poems Sedulius names a certain number of his compatriots and comrades, Dermoth, Fergus, Blandus, Marcus and Beuchell. [2] Many of these names, along with those of other Irishmen, notably Dubthach, appear in the margins of manuscripts still extant which were either written by them or circulated in the coterie of Sedulius. [3] Another *peregrinus*, who signs himself Electus Scottigena, writes to Franco, bishop of Liége, to complain that he has been robbed on his way back from Rome. [4] Not all these Irishmen were scholars ; another pilgrim who likewise describes his distress in full, confesses that he is neither a grammarian nor a skilled Latinist : " *Non sum grammaticus neque sermone Latino peritus.*" [5] But all of them seem to have been in straits, and those who had skill and learning had only one desire, to turn them to the best possible account in order to fill their own shrunken purses.

> " Nos tumidus Boreas vastat—miserabile visu—
>   Doctos grammaticos presbiterosque pios :
> Namque volans Aquilo non ulli parcit honori
>   Crudeli rostro nos laniando suo.
> Fessis ergo favens, Hartgari floride praesul,
>   Sophos Scottigenas suscipe corde pio." [6]

---

[1] F. J. E. Raby, *A History of Christian-Latin Poetry from the Beginnings to the Close of the Middle Ages* (Oxford, 1927), p. 196.
[2] Sedulius, *Carmina*, II, xxvii, p. 193. Cf. Kenney, I, pp. 555 ff.
[3] Kenney, *l. cit.*
[4] *Epistolae variorum*, 31, 4 (*MG. Epist.*, VI, pp. 196–97).
[5] *Epist. var.*, 31, 2 (*ib.*, p. 196).
[6] Sedulius, *Carmina*, II, iii, p. 168.

The education of the Irish monks, firmly grounded on religion, such as we have endeavoured to describe it, made them thoroughly fit agents for carrying out the intellectual reform undertaken under the auspices of Charlemagne. It was, in truth, by no means the emperor's aim to produce humanists, animated by a disinterested and purely secular passion for ancient literature; he simply desired to train priests and monks capable of understanding and copying Latin, and to provide them with books for study and church books well and correctly written. During the reigns of the great emperor and his successors, the Irish taught the Franks orthography and grammar; they commentated the Scriptures; they brought from their island biblical and liturgical manuscripts, collections of canons and penitentials [1]; above all, they copied many books on the Continent. The libraries of continental Europe preserve to the present day a large number of such books which they scattered along their route—and whither did they not make their way? Especially great was the wealth of codices of Irish origin possessed by the libraries of Bobbio, St. Gall and Reichenau.

St Columban himself no doubt bequeathed a goodly collection of manuscripts to his foundation beyond the Alps. The library of that cloister was further enriched by an important acquisition from the manuscripts brought together at Vivarium by Cassiodorus in the sixth century [2]; and Dungal, "*praecipuus Scottorum*," bequeathed to it, as we have seen, another batch of twenty-nine works. The books of the Irish bishop Marcus, the uncle of Moengal or Marcellus († 871), remained at St. Gall.[3] As for Reichenau, the library of St. Gall was transferred thither for the sake of safety during an inroad of

---

[1] *Additamentum Nivialense de Fuilano*, ed. B. Krusch (*MG. Scr. RM*, IV, p. 449).—Kuno Meyer has suggested that the Laon MS. 55 [see Kenney, I, p. 680, No. 540] might have been written at Armagh (*Sitz. d. k. Preuss. Akad. d. Wiss.*, 1914, pp. 480–81).

[2] Rudolf Beer, *Bemerkungen über den ältesten Handschriftenbestand des Klosters Bobbio* (*Anzeiger der philos.-hist. Kl. der k. Akad. der Wissenschaften in Wien*, 1911, XLVIII, pp. 78–104); Paul Lejay, *Bobbio et la bibliothèque de Cassiodore* (*BALAC*, III, 1913, pp. 265–69); James, *Learning*, p. 486; A. Van de Vyver, *Cassiodore et son œuvre* (*Speculum*, VI, 1931, p. 283). Cf. D. A. Wilmart, art. *Bobbio* (MSS. *de*) in *DACL*.

[3] Ekkehard, IV, *Casus S. Galli*, II, pp. 78 ff. Cf. Clark, *The Abbey of St. Gall*, pp. 32 ff.; Kenney, I, pp. 599–600.

the Magyars in the year 925. When the danger was past, an
equal number of codices was restored by the monks of
Reichenau to those of St. Gall, but not all the identical
volumes.[1]   Reichenau had other opportunities besides of
enriching its library with Irish books.[2]

Not only the palace school and the schools of the episcopal
cities, but also those of some monasteries benefited by the
instruction of the Irish teachers. Dunchad taught at St. Remi
(Remigius) in Reims, Moengal and Faillan at St. Gall.[3]

Under Charles the Bald, a prince of some learning, the
scheme of studies was enlarged.   Dialectic and philosophy (the
latter a province open only to readers of Greek), both
hitherto insufficiently studied, made great progress with John
the Scot and the scholars associated with him. A wider
acquaintance was formed with Greek literature, both the
works of the Fathers and of classical writers. How far did this
acquaintance go ? On this question researchers are of divided
opinion.

We have seen that it cannot be admitted that Greek was
studied, save in exceptional cases, in Ireland before the
departure of John the Scot, Sedulius and their companions in
the ninth century.[4] In the second half of that century a
limited number of Irish emigrants on the Continent gave
proof of some acquaintance with the language. They were
capable of copying biblical Greek manuscripts, some of which
we still have [5] ; they made use of, or annotated, Greek works
of which no Latin translations are known.[6] Among them all
Johannes Eriugena distinguished himself by his translation of
the works of the Areopagite. This translation, as has been
said, was certainly not free from defects, obscurities and mistakes, but all the same it is unquestionably a fine achievement
when we remember that among contemporary continental
scholars scarcely three or four can be mentioned who possessed

[1] Kenney, I, p. 10.
[2] Cf. Kenney, I, pp. 518 ff., 550, 668 ff.
[3] *Ib.*, pp. 573–74 (No. 377) ; Clark, *op. cit.*, p. 44. *V. sup.*, ch. v, § 3.
[4] *V. sup.*, § 1. Cf. M. Esposito, *The Knowledge of Greek*, pp. 665–83.
[5] Cf. *Epistolae variorum*, 33 (*MG. Epist.*, VI, pp. 201–205) ; M. Esposito,
The Knowledge of Greek, p. 678.
[6] James, *Learning*, pp. 502–506.

any knowledge of Greek.[1] Such is pretty much the judgment passed on it by the papal librarian Anastasius, who, after examining the translation and making some criticisms, was yet able to write the following words of praise to Charles the Bald : " It is a wonderful thing how that barbarian, living at the ends of the earth, who might be supposed to be as far removed from the knowledge of this other language as he is from the familiar use of it, has been able to comprehend such ideas and translate them into another tongue. I refer to John Scotigena, whom I have learned by report to be in all things a holy man." [2]

On the other hand, the Irish emigrants of that generation themselves profited very largely from the intellectual point of view by their sojourn on the Continent. Men like Dungal, Dicuil, John the Scot and many others perfected their knowledge abroad. It has been proved that Johannes Eriugena, at the time when he wrote the *De Praedestinatione* (851), that is to say, in the early years of his stay in France, had as yet only a slight smattering of Greek and was almost wholly ignorant of Greek patristic literature.[3] The Neo-Platonic ideas which he parades at this period are borrowed, at least in their main principles, from Latin writers.[4] It has been shown also that the field of study of Sedulius, especially with regard to classical authors, was widened by frequenting the Frankish libraries.[5] Nevertheless, when we collect the testimonies borne by contemporaries to the scholars who came from Ireland, it becomes evident that they were conscious of owing to these latter much

[1] Walahfrid Strabo, Heiric of Auxerre, Christian of Stavelot (Manitius, *Geschichte*, II, p. 802). Cf. M. L. W. Laistner, *The Survival of Greek in Western Europe in the Carolingian Age* (*History*, N.S., IX, 1924, pp. 177–87), s.a. *A Ninth Century Commentator on the Gospel according to Matthew* (*Harvard Theological Review*, XX, 1927, pp. 141–43) ; s.a. *Thought and Letters in Western Europe* (London, 1931), ch. x.

[2] *Ep.* 13, *Carolo imp.*, ed. E. Perels and G. Laehr (*MG. Epist.*, VII, p. 431).

[3] A.-M. Jacquin, *Le néo-platonisme de Jean Scot* (*Revue des sciences philosophiques et théologiques*, I, 1907, pp. 674–85). Cf. E. M. Deutsch, art. *Scotus* (*Johannes*) in *Realencycl. f. prot. Theol. u. Kirche*, p. 90.

[4] A.-M. Jacquin, *art. cit.*—On the Neo-Platonic system of John see M. De Wulf, *Histoire de la philosophie médiévale* (Louvain, 1924), I, pp. 123–24 ; Hermann Dörries, *Zur Geschichte der Mystik Erigena und des Neuplatonismus* (Tübingen, 1925) ; Marguerite Techert, *Le plotinisme dans le système de Jean Scot* (*Revue néo-scolastique de philosophie*, XXIX, 1927, pp. 28–68).

[5] S. Hellmann, *op. cit.*, pp. 99 ff. Cf. Kenney, I, p. 555.

of their own progress in their studies. The Irish learning was in their eyes out of the common and worthy of the most grandiloquent encomiums.

The Venerable Bede had highly appreciated the value of the principles of learning and piety instilled into the children of the Angles by the monks of Lindisfarne, and equally the unexampled generosity with which the Irish in the seventh and eighth centuries welcomed strangers eager for instruction.[1] Other writers can find only superlatives wherewith to express their admiration for the learned *Scotti*. The Welsh biographer of St Cadoc represents his hero leaving home to follow the courses of those excellent teachers from whose lips he gathers " the sum of Western knowledge." [2] Alcuin recalls the services rendered to Christendom by " the very learned Irish masters, who enabled the Churches of Christ in Britain, Gaul and Italy to make so great progress." [3] Notker depicts Clement and his companion as men " incomparably well versed in letters secular and sacred." [4] Another representative of German learning in the ninth century, Ermenrich of Ellwangen († 874), in his letter to Abbot Grimwald extols the island " whence such brilliant luminaries have come to us . . . for, imparting philosophy alike to small and great, it has filled the Church with its knowledge and its doctrine." [5]

Charlemagne and his successors certainly made it their aim to make the utmost use of the zeal and learning of the Irish teachers in order to raise the intellectual level of the clergy in their states, and bestowed on them constant proofs of their interest. If an anecdote handed down by William of Malmesbury may be taken as authentic, we may even believe that the most familiar relations existed between Charles the Bald and John the Scot.[6]

The most influential churchmen and the great abbeys likewise showed themselves ready to welcome the learned *Scotti*,

---

[1] *V. sup.* §§ 1, 2.
[2] Lifris, *Vita Cadoci*, 7 (*CBS*, p. 36).
[3] Alcuin, *Ep.* 280 (*MG. Epist.*, IV, p. 437).
[4] *MG. Scr.*, II, p. 731.
[5] *Epistola ad Grimaldum abbatem* (*MG. Epist.*, V, p. 575).
[6] William of Malmesbury, *Gesta pontificum Anglorum*, v, 240, ed. Hamilton (*RS*), p. 392. Cf. Kenney, I, p. 589.

aiding and encouraging them and knowing how to turn their talents to account. We know how Alcuin, Hilduin, Hincmar of Reims and many bishops behaved towards them. The most celebrated men of the time, Hrabanus Maurus, abbot of Fulda and afterwards archbishop of Mainz (847–856),[1] Walahfrid Strabo, abbot of Reichenau (838–849),[2] Servatus Lupus, abbot of Ferrières († c. 862), entered into literary relations, sometimes even ties of friendship, with the Irish.[3] A learned Scottic priest named Probus, who lived at Mainz and died in 859, was the intimate friend of Walahfrid and Lupus,[4] and Rudolf, abbot of Fulda, devoted to him a highly eulogistic obituary notice in the Annals of that monastery.[5] One Thomas Scottus, " praeceptor palatii," exchanged verses with Walahfrid, with Prudentius, later bishop of Troyes, and with Florus of Lyons.[6]

In the ninth century unhappy Ireland fell a prey to the Vikings ; her monasteries were pillaged, her monks scattered, her great schools deserted. No longer able to live by their learning amid the turmoils of their native isle, the Irish teachers were driven to leave home. The exodus of scholars had already begun before the Scandinavian invasions set in, but was greatly stimulated by these misfortunes, as well as by the warm welcome accorded to them by the Carolingian princes. " Why should I mention Ireland," writes Heiric of Auxerre about the year 866, " of which almost the whole people, despising the dangers of the sea, migrate with their crowd of philosophers to our shores ? The more learned a man is, the more likely is he to sentence himself to exile that he may serve the wishes of our most wise Solomon." [7] This new Solomon was Charles the Bald.

---

[1] Kenney, I, p. 550.

[2] *Ib.*, pp. 550–51 (No. 358).

[3] Lupus, *Ep.* 34 (*PL*, CXIX, 502) ; ed. and transl. L. Levillain (Paris, 1927), I, pp. 70–71.

[4] Walahfrid, *Carm.*, XLV (*MG. Poet. Lat.*, II, pp. 393–94). Cf. Kenney, I, p. 551.

[5] Rudolf, *Annales*, a.a. 859 (*MG. Scr.*, I, p. 373).

[6] Cf. Kenney, *Sources*, I, p. 549 ; Manitius, *Geschichte*, I, p. 457, n. 1, II, p. 806.

[7] Heiric, *Vita Germani*, Epist. dedicat. (*PL*, CXXIV, 1133). Cf. *Vita Burchardi Herbipol.* (*MG. Scr.*, XV, 1, p. 52).

Enough has now been said for the reader (while making due allowance for the exaggerations of Heiric and his contemporaries) to realize the high esteem in which Irish learning, in its happiest hour, was held by the most enlightened men in the Frankish empire.

CHAPTER IX

LITURGY AND PRIVATE DEVOTION

§ 1.—Sources

THROUGHOUT the period with which we are dealing the several Celtic Churches did not possess a uniform liturgy. In their ritual observances there were differences greater or less ; and indeed it would be surprising had it been otherwise.

It was not till the nineteenth century, and only towards its close, that anyone began to speak of a " Celtic liturgy." Mabillon mentions only an " Irish liturgy " (*liturgia Hibernica*[1]) ; and, as a matter of fact, the Irish ritual practice is the one about which our information is least meagre. However, since the publication of F. E. Warren's work, *The Liturgy and Ritual of the Celtic Church* (Oxford, 1881), which is now indeed out of date but marks an important stage in the series of historical investigations into the Western liturgies, it has been recognized that Mabillon's term is too narrow and the wider expression " Celtic liturgy " or " liturgies " has been generally adopted.[2]

Among the early monuments of the Irish liturgy are two books of outstanding importance, the Antiphonary of Bangor and the Stowe Missal, both of monastic origin.

The Antiphonary of Bangor is a collection of canticles, hymns, antiphons and versicles, intended for the use of an abbot of the celebrated monastery of Bangor founded by St Comgall, in which St Columban received his religious training. The composition of the book must be placed between the years 680 and 691. In the last hymn of the Antiphonary, [*In*] *memoriam abbatum nostrorum,* fifteen abbots of Bangor are named,

---

[1] Mabillon, *De liturgia gallicana,* I, II, 3 c (*PL*, LXXII, 114, 119).
[2] In 1908 Henry Jenner entitled " *Celtic Rite* " his important article for the *Catholic Encyclopedia.*

of whom the second last, Camanus, who died in 680, is said to be " singing hymns with Christ," whereas of his successor Cronanus, who died in 691, it is said : " *Conservet eum Dominus*." [1] We may therefore conclude that the book dates from the abbotship of Cronanus. It was carried from Ireland to Bobbio at an unknown date and remained in the library of the monastery there till about 1606, when it was transferred to the Ambrosian Library at Milan. [2]

The Stowe Missal was probably composed for the abbey of Tallaght in the first decade of the ninth century. [3] Several scribes collaborated in writing it. Warner has distinguished at least five different hands in the original text, as well as that of a corrector called Moelcaích, who signed his name in the Missal. [4] St Máel Rúain of Tallaght, who died in 792, figures in a long list of saints written by one of the original scribes, and none of the others mentioned is of later date. [5]

The original hands, which resemble one another closely, are in an Irish minuscule of a peculiar angular type ; Moelcaích's writing on the contrary is very different, being " a smaller, rounder and more facile minuscule." [6] " On palaeographical grounds," says Warner, " no less than for the other reasons before stated, there seems to be sufficient warrant for dating the original text in the early part, or even within the first decade, of the ninth century." [7]

The manuscript was not found on the Continent, as was formerly believed ; in all likelihood it never left the British Isles. [8] After having been for some years in the possession of the Duke of Buckingham and Chandos, the owner of Stowe House in Buckinghamshire, then in that of the Earl of Ash-

---

[1] *An. Ban.*, II, p. 33.

[2] *An. Ban.* or some Irish book of a similar type may have circulated in the abbeys of Faremoutiers and Sithiu, both influenced by Luxeuil, as may be gathered from : (*a*) Jonas, *Vita Col.*, II, 16 (p. 135) ; (*b*) *Vita Audomari*, ed. W. Levison (*MG. Scr. RM*, V, p. 753). Cf. Levison, *Die Iren*, p. 5.

[3] Cf. G. F. Warner, *Stowe*, II, pp. xxxiv, xxxvi.

[4] Fol. 37 (*Stowe*, II, p. 18). Cf. pp. xii, xx–xxii.

[5] Fol. 33 (*Stowe*, II, p. 16). Cf. Warner, p. xxxii.

[6] Warner, p. xxi.

[7] Warner, II, p. xxxvi.

[8] See T. F. O'Rahilly, *The History of the Stowe Missal* (*Ériu*, X, 1926, pp. 95–109)

burnham, it has belonged since 1883 to the Library of the Royal Irish Academy of Dublin, its press mark being D. II, 3.

The full contents of the Stowe MS. comprise the following items, all of which, except the last two, are in Latin : 1. Extracts from the Gospel of St John ; 2. The ordinary and canon of the Mass, followed by a few special Masses ; 3. The Order of Baptism, with the communion of the newly baptized ; 4. The Order of the visitation of the sick, with the administration of Extreme Unction and Communion ; 5. A short treatise in Irish on the Mass ; 6. Three short spells in Irish.

Other missal fragments of Irish origin are found in the Book of Armagh (ninth century),[1] in the St. Gall MSS. Nos. 1394 and 1395 (eighth or ninth century),[2] in the Reichenau fragments now preserved at Karlsruhe (App. Aug. clxvii, eighth or ninth century),[3] and those of Piacenza (ninth or tenth century ?),[4] etc.

Besides the ritual parts of the Stowe MS. already mentioned, we have prayers for the visitation of the sick or the administration of the last sacraments in the Irish books of Mulling and of Dimma (both of the eighth or ninth centuries) [5] and in some pages written in the ninth century in a Scotch MS. known as the Book of Deer.[6]

Another fragmentary MS. coming from Bobbio and now in the Biblioteca Nazionale at Turin (F. IV, 1) may be placed beside the Antiphonary of Bangor, and is said to be of even earlier date than the latter. It contains canticles, psalms, collects and the *Te Deum*.[7] All these items are in the Antiphonary of Bangor, except four collects, of which one is in the Southampton Psalter, a MS. written in Irish minuscule (ninth or tenth century) now at Cambridge, St. John's College 59.[8]

---

[1] Fol. 19ʳ (*LA*, p. 37).
[2] Ed. Warren, *Lit.*, pp. 174–79, 179–84.
[3] Ed. H. M. Bannister, *Some recently discovered Fragments of Irish Sacramentaries* (*JTS*, V, 1903, pp. 49–75).
[4] Ed. H. M. Bannister, *art. cit.*, pp. 66–70.
[5] Ed. Warren, *Lit.*, pp. 167–71, 171–73.
[6] Ed. Warren, *Lit.*, pp. 164–65.
[7] Ed. Wilhelm Meyer, *Das turiner Bruchstück der ältesten irischen Liturgie* (*Nachrichten von der kön. Gesellschaft der Wissenschaften zu Göttingen*. Philol.-hist. Kl., 1903, pp. 163–214).
[8] On the Southampton Psalter, *v. sup.*, ch. VIII, § 2.

The Leabhar Breac, a codex of the early fifteenth century, contains several treatises dealing with liturgical subjects, one of them on the consecration of a church, which, according to Whitley Stokes, may on linguistic grounds be dated as far back as the eleventh century.[1]

Hymns, Latin or perhaps even some Irish ones, held an important place in the liturgy. The Antiphonary of Bangor has preserved several Latin hymns composed in Ireland. Adamnán speaks of a *hymnorum liber septimaniorum* written by St Columba of Iona with his own hand.[2] The early hymnology of the Irish monasteries is known to us chiefly from two collections which have been published under the title of the *Irish Liber Hymnorum*.[3] In these collections, which, strictly speaking, are rather antiquarian than liturgical compilations, the various items are often preceded by prefaces in which a commentator gives, if not the history, at any rate the legend of the origin of the hymn, sometimes also information as to the uses (generally superstitious) to which it was put. The commentator further provides the texts with glosses, either Latin or Irish.

The *Liber Hymnorum* and other collections have preserved also a fairly large number of old prayers destined not for liturgical but private use, the recitation of which has been faithfully handed down through the ages. They bear as a rule the stamp of a piety *sui generis* and give us a far deeper insight into the intimate devotion of the ancient Celts than do the liturgical texts. Those which have the title of *lorica* or " corslet " are especially illuminating in this respect.[4]

No early British liturgical book has been preserved. The

---

[1] Whitley Stokes, *The Lebar Brecc Tractate on the Consecration of a Church* (*Miscellanea linguistica in onore di Graziadio Ascoli*, Torino, 1901, pp. 363–87).—On other liturgical treatises in the L.B. see Best, *Bibl.*, p. 225.

[2] Adam., *Vita Col.*, II, 9.

[3] Ed. J. H. Bernard and Robert Atkinson, 2 vols. (*HBS*), 1898.

[4] On " loricae " and cognate prayers see Best, *Bibl.*, pp. 227–28 ; Wilhelm Meyer, *Gildae oratio rythmica* (*Nachrichten von der kön. Gesellschaft der Wissenschaften zu Göttingen.* Philol.-hist. Kl., 1912, pp. 48–108) ; *s.a. Poetische Nachlese aus dem sogenannten Book of Cerne in Cambridge und aus dem Londoner Codex Regius 2 A. xx* (*Nachrichten*, 1917, pp. 597–625) ; Mario Esposito, *The " Lorica " of Lathcen* (*JTS*, xxx, 1929, pp. 289–91) ; L.G., *Étude sur les " loricae " celtiques et sur les prières qui s'en rapprochent* (*BALAC*, I, 1911, pp. 265–81, II, 1912, pp. 33–41, 101–27).

earliest Breton missal is that of Saint-Vougay, dating from the end of the eleventh or beginning of the twelfth century.[1] A considerable number of Celtic saints, especially Breton ones, are mentioned in the litany of Holy Saturday [2] ; therein lies its chief interest for us. It contains some neumes.

§ 2.—ORIGINS

When tracing the origin of the insular Churches, we gave a rapid sketch of the influence exercised on each of them by the great apostles and missionaries who came from the Continent or crossed from one island to the other, Ninian, Germanus of Auxerre and his companions, Palladius and Patrick. And, side by side with these leading figures, there worked no doubt many others from the outset in founding, consolidating and developing the Christian life in the islands, men of whom we have no longer any trace, whose very names are unknown to us. What influence may such workers have had in moulding the liturgical institutions of the insular Churches ? It is, of course, impossible to tell with any precision or certainty. Nevertheless, there are some texts which enable us to give a partial answer to the question.

The first of these texts is an anonymous treatise entitled *Ratio de cursus (sic) qui fuerunt ex auctores (sic)*, which claims to give an account of the fortunes of the six great *cursus*, one of which is the *cursus Scottorum*.[3] This treatise was probably written on the Continent by an Irishman acquainted with the traditions of Luxeuil and Bobbio, after the publication of the Lives of St Columban and his disciples, the abbots Eustasius and Attala, a work finished about 642.[4] According to this anonymous author, the *cursus Scottorum* owed its formation to St Mark, said to have evangelized not only Egypt but Italy. It was adopted by Gregory of Nazianzus and the Eastern

---

[1] Facs. in *Paléographie musicale* edited by the Solesmes monks (II, Pl. 80). See F. Duine, *Bréviaires et missels des églises et abbayes bretonnes de France antérieurs au XVIIᵉ siècle* (Rennes, 1906), pp. 169–70 ; *s.a. Inventaire*, p. 57.

[2] J. Loth, *Les anciennes litanies de Bretagne* (R. Cel., XI, 1890, pp. 135–51).

[3] Ed. *CED*, I, pp. 138–40 ; Ed. J. Wickham Legg, *Cursus* (1910), pp. 149–67.

[4] " The place of writing apparently is in Gaul in the eighth century " (J. Wickham Legg, *Cursus*, p. 151).

monks, Basil, Antony, Paul, Macarius, John and Malchus. Through Cassian it found its way into Gaul and took root at Lérins, where it was followed by Honoratus, Caesarius of Arles, Lupus and Germanus. The last two instructed the blessed Patrick in Holy Scripture and bequeathed to him the *cursus*, which he carried to Britain and Ireland. The *cursus* of St Mark, now become the *cursus Scottorum*, was reintroduced on the Continent at the end of the sixth century by Columban of Luxeuil and his companion Wandilochus (? Waldolenus). Such, in brief, is the history of the *cursus* of the Scots according to the anonymous writer of the seventh or eighth century.

It is certain that many of the statements in this work are confused and that many of the authorities alleged are fabrications.[1] Nevertheless, it is not to be summarily rejected. All that is recorded as to the transmission of the *cursus* from the time of Cassian to St Patrick and St Columban is fundamentally in agreement with what we know of the connection of the insular religious world with Gaul in the fifth and sixth centuries. We have spoken of the relations which St Patrick seems to have kept up with Lérins and St Germanus of Auxerre. As for Caesarius of Arles, he is believed likewise to have had a real influence on the ecclesiastical ideas of the Irish.[2] Taken as a whole, then, this account of the genesis of the *cursus Scottorum* is not wholly devoid of probability.[3]

The *Catalogus sanctorum Hiberniae secundum diversa tempora*, also dating from the eighth century, furnishes incidental information as to the origin not alone of the canonical hours, but also of the Eucharistic liturgy. To appreciate the significance of this text properly, we must, as B. MacCarthy has shown,[4] follow the readings adopted by Ussher and reproduced by Haddan and Stubbs, leaving aside the less correct text of the Salamanca codex and Fleming's edition. According to the Catalogue, the saints of the first order, comprising St Patrick's helpers and first successors down to the year 544,

---

[1] See Levison, *Bischof Germanus von Auxerre* (*NA*, XXIX, 1903, p. 150).

[2] Cf. Paul Lejay, *Revue d'histoire et de littérature religieuses*, X, 1905, pp. 468 ff. ; *Revue critique*, N.S., LXII, 1906, p. 369.

[3] Cf. Warren, *An. Ban.*, II, p. xxiv ; L.G., *Les chrétientés celtiques*, p. 300.

[4] B. MacCarthy, *On the Stowe Missal* (*TRIA*, XXVII, Lit. and Antiq., VII, 1877–86, pp. 161–62).

*unum ducem Patricium habebant ; unamque missam, unam celebra-
tionem, unam tonsuram,* etc. The saints of the second order (from
544 to 598) *diversas missas celebrabant et diversas regulas. . . . A
Davide episcopo et Gilla et a Doco Britonibus missam acceperunt.*
The saints of the third order (from 598 to 665) *diversas regulas
et missas habebant et diversam tonsuram . . . et diversam solemnitatem paschalem.*[1]

By the uniform *celebratio* of the first period and no doubt also
by the *diversas regulas* of the two following is meant the divine
office. As for the *unam missam* of the first age, we must doubtless understand by it the Mass introduced into Ireland by the
undisputed leader (*dux*) of the time, St Patrick. Tirechán
mentions a *missa Patricii* as having been adopted by the community of Achad Fobuir during St Patrick's lifetime.[2] Unfortunately, we have no information whatsoever as to its
nature.[3]

As for the reputed introduction of a new Mass into Ireland
by the three British saints David, Gildas and Docus (or Cadoc),
of which the Catalogue speaks, given the close relations which
then existed between the two countries, it seems quite possible.

A fragment ascribed to Gildas, but rightly printed by
Mommsen under the rubric " *Fragmenta dubia,*" is almost the
only text which tells us anything about the liturgy of the
Britons. From it we learn that Roman customs, especially
with regard to the Mass, were not in favour among them :
*Brittones toto mundo contrarii, moribus Romanis inimici, non solum
in missa, sed etiam in tonsura.*[4] The *responsiones* of St Gregory
the Great to St Augustine of Canterbury, which seem now to
be definitely regarded as authentic, show that the British
liturgical customs already differed widely from the Roman
ones in the sixth century, that is to say, in the time of Gildas,
Cadoc and David.[5]

It was probably from the seventh century on, the period

---

[1] *CED*, II, pp. 292–93.
[2] Tirechán, p. 26.
[3] *V. sup.*, ch. II, § 10.
[4] *Epistularum Gildae deperditarum fragmenta*, ed. Mommsen (*MG. Auct.
ant.*, XIII, p. 88). Cf. *ib.*, p. 12.
[5] Bede, *HE*, I, 27. Cf. A. Gasquet, *St Gregory's Responsiones ad interro-
gationes B. Augustini* (*Miscellanea Amelli*, Montecassino, 1920, pp. 1–16).

when southern Ireland adopted the Roman Easter, that the Irish liturgy began to assimilate Roman elements. Judging these problems of liturgical origins with the aid of the few historical texts at our disposal, it seems on the whole that Gaul exercised the first and chief influence on the formation of the insular liturgies, and that the British Church in its turn had a considerable share in the development of the Irish rites. The internal evidence afforded by the liturgical texts does not conflict with this conclusion.

§ 3.—THE LITURGICAL YEAR

As will be readily understood, it is hopeless to think of reconstructing the entire arrangement of the liturgical year in the early Celtic Churches ; all that can be done is to make out some of its features. Besides, every church had its own calendar, which was added to as time went on.

The following terms, inserted as variants in the *Communicantes* of the Mass in the Stowe Missal, acquaint us with the principal festivals of the *Temporale* observed at the time and in the church (Tallaght) in which this missal was in use : *In natale domini.—Kalendis* (Circumcision).—*Stellae* (Epiphany). —*Pasca.—In clausula pasca* (*Dominica in albis*, Low Sunday). —*Ascensio.—Pentecosten.*[1]

As in other Latin Churches, the return from Egypt, the presentation of Jesus in the Temple and his victory over the Devil were the subject of liturgical celebrations in Ireland in the ninth century, for instance at Tallaght.[2] The observances of this monastery contain the following words : " *Eductio Christi ex egipto* and the presentation in the Temple and the defeat of the Devil : on these days Sunday's office is to be said : we never saw dinner in the daytime on those feasts." [3]

In the passage referred to of the Stowe Missal there is also mention of the *dies sacratissima natalis calicis domini nostri iesu*

---

[1] *Stowe*, pp. 11–12.

[2] *Tallaght* (1911), 55, p. 148. Cf. L.G., *Sur trois anciennes fêtes de Notre-Seigneur* (*BALAC*, IV, 1914, pp. 208–10).

[3] *Tallaght* (1927), 96, pp. 56–57. Cf. *Martyrology of Tallaght*, ed. Best and Lawlor (*HBS*) (1931), p. 7.

christi,[1] a name bestowed on the *Cena Domini* (Maundy Thursday) which recurs elsewhere in the Christian Church of the early Middle Ages.[2] Maundy Thursday was in Irish called *cennlá* (supper day),[3] *dia dardaín cennlá*,[4] *lá senaid an Tigerna* (" the day of the Lord's synod," *Cena Domini*),[5] or *caplait* (from Low Latin *capillatio*, Welsh *dydd iau cablyd*).[6] This day was specially devoted to the care of the person. The monks washed their heads, had their hair cut and pared their nails[7] ; nuns cleansed their hair.[8] Why on this day above others ? Perhaps on account of the words of St Peter which were read in the Gospel for Holy Thursday : " *Domine, non tantum pedes meos, sed et manus et caput* " (John xiii, 9).

The *Rule of the Céli Dé* (ninth century) informs us, moreover, that the ceremony of the *mandatum* (whence the English term Maundy Thursday) was also observed among these religious, as it is still observed in the Catholic Church at the present day : " At the washing of feet the *Beati* is recited as long as the washing lasts. After that comes the sermon on the Washing." [9]

In other places a regular bath was taken on this day,[10] a

---

[1] *Stowe*, p. 11.

[2] Eligius, *Homilia* 10 (*PL*, LXXXVII, 628). Cf. Du Cange, s.v. *Natalis calicis*.

[3] Treatise on the Mass in *Stowe*, 16 (*Stowe*, pp. 38, 41) ; *Tallaght* (1927), 19, p. 68. Cf. *Lismore*, p. LXXXIII.

[4] *Betha Bhrighdi*, l. 1437 (*Lismore*, pp. 43, 191). See Glossary, p. 387.

[5] *Betha Brenainn*, 63, 77 (*BNE*, I, pp. 56, 60). See Glossary, I, p. 343.

[6] " Dardáin caplaite " (*Fél. Oeng.*, p. 244. Cf. p. 307). Cf. Bury, *Pat.*, p. 241 ; *Lismore*, p. LXXXIII.

[7] *Fél. Oeng.*, pp. 244–45.

[8] " pectinamque eius ligneam, qua capud pectinabat semel, ut refertur, in anno, id est in coena Domini, vel quando necessitas infirmitatis cogebat, honorifice conservantes secum habent, merito magis pretiosam quam si de auro fuisse facta " (Conchubran, *Vita Mon.*, III, 1, p. 228).

[9] *Rule of the Céli Dé*, 19, 20 ; *Tallaght* (1927), pp. 68–69. Cf. *Teaching of Máel Rúain*, 25 ; *ib.*, pp. 16–17.—On the Lat. word " obsequium " (Ir. *ósaic*), also used in the technical sense of foot-washing, see C. Plummer, *VSH*, I, p. CXIV and Glossary (p. 383), *BNE*, notes to Br. 1, 38, 65 (pp. 329, 331), Maed., II, 16 (p. 350), Bede, *HE*, Vol. II, p. 238.

[10] *Vita Iᵃ Brendani*, 38 (*VSH*, I, p. 121) ; *Betha Brenainn*, 81 (*BNE*, I, p. 60, II, p. 59).—In the tenth century English Benedictine monks used to take a bath and shave on Good Friday or Holy Saturday. See *Regularis concordia* (*PL*, CXXXVII, 494).—Some Irish ascetics refrained from ever taking any hot baths by reason of mortification. So Fintan of Rheinau (*Vita*, 12 : *MG. Scr.*, XV, 1, p. 506), Kevin of Glendalough (*Vita*, 30 : *VSH*, I, p. 250).

survival of an ancient custom which was observed by catechumens in the primitive Churches and of which St Augustine
of Hippo has given a clear explanation.[1]

A canon attributed to St Patrick mentions three baptismal
festivals : *Octavo die chatechumeni sunt ; postea solemnitatibus
Domini baptizantur, id est, Pascha et Pentecoste et Epiphania.*[2]

The rite of the new fire on Holy Saturday, unknown to the
ancient Greek, Roman and Gallican books,[3] was perhaps
practised in Ireland from the time of Patrick, at any rate from
the seventh century. We have as proof the passage in the
notes on St Patrick written about 690 by Muirchu : " *Sanctus
ergo Patricius sanctum pasca celebrans incendit diuinum ignem ualde
lucidum et benedictum, qui in nocte refulgens a cunctis pene per plani-
tiem campi habitantibus uisus est.*" [4]

The faithful used to discharge their Paschal duty on Easter
night, *in qua qui non communicat fidelis non est.*[5]

In the *Comes* of the Gospel-Book of Landévennec the rubric
In pascha annotina occurs after the words *Dominica octavum
Paschae.*[6] " This ' Pascha annotinum,' kept on or near Low
Sunday, denoted the solemn and public renewal of their
baptismal vows on the part of those who had been baptized at
Easter-tide in the preceding year." [7]

At Iona a season of forty days was observed in preparation
for the Easter festival.[8] A remark of Tirechán's seems to
imply that a meatless Lent was the rule.[9] Several texts

---

[1] Augustine, *Ep.* LIV, 9–10, ed. A. Goldbacher (*Corp. SEL*, XXXIV,
p. 168). Cf. J. Zellinger, *Bad und Bäder in der altchristlichen Kirche* (München,
1928), p. 30.

[2] *CED*, II, II, p. 336.

[3] L. Duchesne, *Les origines du culte chrétien* (Paris, 1920), p. 264 ; J. G.
Carleton, art. *Festivals and Feasts (Christian)* in *ERE*, V, 1912, p. 846.

[4] Muirchu, p. 279. Cf. Tirechán, p. 19 : " Kannanus episcopus quem
ordinauit patricius in primo pasca *hiferti* uirorum *feicc*, qui portauit secum
ignem primum benedictum, etc." See *Vita Trip.*, pp. 40–43.—" Et sanctus
senex Kiaranus [de Saigir] nolebat ignem alium in suo monasterio, nisi
conservatum ignem a pascha usque ad pascha sine extinccione " (*Vita
Ciarani de Cluain*, 30 : *VSH*, I, p. 212).

[5] Can. 22 (*CED*, II, II, p. 336).

[6] C. R. Morey, E. K. Rand, C. H. Kraeling, *The Gospel-Book of Landevennec* (*Art Studies*, VIII, II, 1931, p. 267).

[7] F. E. Warren, *The Leofric Missal* (Oxford, 1883), p. LXIII. See further
information in Du Cange, *s.v. Pasca annotinum.*

[8] Adam., *Vita Col.*, II, 39 (p. 109).

[9] Tirechán, p. 31.

mention two other Lents besides that preceding the Easter festival.[1]

In the Celtic Churches Saturday bore something of a festive character, which was expressed by greater length and solemnity in the liturgy and also in monasteries by a less rigorous diet.[2]

The observance of Sunday (sometimes in Pharisaic fashion) is enjoined by various Irish texts, the most celebrated being the *Cáin Domnaig*, which seems to have had a great influence on the religious mentality of the country.[3] Muirchu and other Irish writers of tales endeavoured to inculcate respect for Sunday observance by striking examples[4] ; so did some continental hagiographers.[5]

It seems that from an early time the *Sanctorale* of the Celtic Churches included the celebration of the feast-days of the great saints of Christendom and of the national ones.[6]

§ 4.—THE MASS

The Irish word for Mass is *oifrenn* (from Lat. *offerendum*), in Welsh *offeren*.

Gildas reproaches the British priests with celebrating the holy sacrifice too seldom.[7] It seems that in Iona in St Columba's time it was celebrated only on Sundays and feast-days and when tidings came of the death of some friend of the

---

[1] *Tallaght* (1911), 24 (p. 136). Cf. n. 136, 11 (p. 168) ; *Fél. Oeng.*, p. 42 ; C. Plummer, *VSH*, I, p. cxx, n. 1 ; Ryan, *Monast.*, pp. 392, 393.

[2] *Rule of the Céli Dé*, 27 (*Tallaght*, 1927, pp. 70–71) ; *Teaching of Máel Rúain*, 1, 82, 83 (*Ib.*, pp. 2–3, 48–49) ; *Tallaght* (1911), 69 (p. 156) ; *Vita Winwaloei*, ed. Latouche, p. 107. Cf. Ryan, *Monast.*, pp. 341, 344.

[3] *V. sup.*, ch. VIII, § 3 ; Ryan, *Monast.*, p. 349.

[4] Muirchu, p. 289 ; *Vita Aedi*, 30 (*VSH*, I, 43), ed. P. Grosjean, 41 (Boll., AS, Nov., IV, p. 514-15) ; *The Voyage of the Húi Corra*, ed. Wh. Stokes, 61 (*R. Cel.*, XIV, 1893, pp. 50–51) ; *The Wooing of Becfola*, ed. Standish Hayes O'Grady, *Silva Gadelica*, II, p. 92.

[5] Bili, *Vita Machutis*, 1, 53, ed. F. Lot, *Mélanges*, p. 385 ; Rembertus, *Vita Anskarii*, 37, ed. G. Waitz (Hannover, 1884), pp. 71–72. Cf. R. Flower, *Catalogue of Irish Manuscripts in the British Museum* (London, 1926), II, pp. 307–10.

[6] *Tallaght* (1911), 22 (p. 135). Cf. Ryan, *Monast.*, p. 341. *V. sup.*, ch. II, § 10, ch. III, Conclusion. On the dedications of the ancient Welsh ministers see an instructive note of A. W. Wade-Evans in his paper, *Bonedd Y Saint, E.* (*A. Cam.*, 1931, pp. 170-72).

[7] Gildas, *De exc.*, 66 (p. 162).

monastery.[1] In Brittany, Riwenno and Condeluc, the disciples of St Conwoïon of Redon († 868), used to celebrate it
daily.[2]

As a general rule, Mass was said in the morning.[3] Adamnán
however tells of a case of Mass being said in the afternoon ;
on the occasion to which he refers, the celebration was preceded by the washing of hands and feet.[4] Was this an acci-
dental circumstance due to the needs of the moment, or was
it a ritual ablution ? If the latter, we should no doubt be
right in regarding the practice as a reminiscence of a command given in Exodus (xxx, 18–20). Besides, Warren believes
that in a Gaelic composition [5] he has come across the Oriental
custom of taking off the sandals on entering the sanctuary, a
custom for the origin of which we have also to look to Exodus
(iii, 5).[6]

We cannot enter here upon a detailed analysis of the rites
and prayers of the Mass. That has been done elsewhere.[7]
We will content ourselves with mentioning the most salient
features of the liturgy of the Holy Mysteries, taking as our
chief guide the Stowe Missal.

In the preparatory part of the Mass there is found in this
book the text of a litany of saints containing, besides the
names of apostles, martyrs and confessors honoured throughout
the universal Church, those of twenty-six Irish saints, men and
women.[8]

After the *Gloria in excelsis*, which is followed by various
collects, and after the Epistle, followed likewise by collects,
there comes the Gradual and next the *Alleluia* with a versicle
taken from Psalm cxvii.[9]

Next we find another collect (*Sacrificiis presentibus . . .*)
which in the modern Roman missal serves as the Secret for

---

[1] Adam., *Vita Col.*, ii, 12, 23, 45.
[2] Ed. Mabillon, *Acta Sanct. O.S.B.*, IV, ii, p. 205.
[3] Warren, *Lit.*, p. 142.
[4] Adam., *Vita Col.*, ii, 45.
[5] Ed. Wh. Stokes, *Lismore*, p. 313.
[6] Warren, *The Liturgy and Ritual of the Ante-Nicene Church* (London, 1897),
p. 225.
[7] See H. Jenner, art. *Celtic Rite* in *Catholic Encyclopedia*, and L.G., art.
Celtiques (Liturgies) in *DACL*.
[8] *Stowe*, pp. 3, 14.
[9] *Stowe*, pp. 4–6.

the fourth Sunday in Advent. Here, under the rubric *Depre-catio sancti Martini pro populo incipit. Amen. Deo gratias*, there follows a prayer in the form of a litany which is not found else-where in this place. Let us note in passing the following formula of this bidding-prayer, one hardly to be expected in an Irish book : *Oramus . . . pro pi[i]ssimis imperatoribus et omni romano exercitu.*[1] " By comparing this litany with those found in the Oriental liturgies, from that of the Apostolic Constitutions onwards," writes L. Duchesne, " we shall see that they are all absolutely of the same type. We may go even further and say that the examples given are nothing more than translations from a Greek text." [2] The bidding-prayer is followed by two collects.

Some of the rubrics of the missal are drawn up in Irish. The words : *Lethdirech sund* (half-uncovering here), which occur before the Gospel, are followed by a Latin rubric : " *Dirigatur domine* " *usque* " *vespertinum* " *ter canitur . . . hic eliuatur lintiamen de calice*, which seems to mean that the rite began by partly uncovering the chalice and the *oblatae* by removing a first veil, the complete uncovering not taking place till the Offertory.

The verses indicated of the psalm *Dirigatur* were sung thrice, then after the partial uncovering the following formula was sung, also thrice : *Ueni, domine, sanctificator omnipotens, et benedic hoc sacrificium preparatum tibi. Amen.*[3]

With regard to this rite, the treatise on the symbolism of the ceremonies of the Mass appended to the Stowe Missal must here be quoted. In it we read : " The uncovering, so far as half, of the Host and of the Chalice, and what is chanted thereat, both Gospel and Alleluia as far as *oblata*, it is a com-memoration of the law of the Prophets, wherein Christ was manifestly foretold, save that it was not seen until He was born." [4]

The " half-uncovering " referred to by the rubric of the Stowe Missal quoted above is also spoken of in the treatise on the Mass in the same manuscript and in another version of it

---

[1] *Stowe*, p. 6.
[2] L. Duchesne, *Christian Worship* (London, 1919), p. 200.
[3] *Stowe*, p. 7.
[4] *Treatise on the Mass*, 6 (*Stowe*, pp. 37, 40).

preserved in the Leabhar Breac [1] ; it very likely signifies the removal of a first veil, and the " full uncovering " that of a second one.

After the Gospel and the Credo have been chanted, comes the Offertory, which comprises the following rites and formulas : (1) the full uncovering of the chalice (*lándírech sund*) ; (2) *Ostende nobis domine missericor[diam] et salutare tuum dabis* (= *da nobis*), with the rubric : *Ter canitur ;* (3) *Oblata domine munera sanctifica nosque a peccatorum nostro[rum] maculis emunda, per dominum.* [2]

At this point an elevation of the chalice took place, as we learn from the treatise on the Mass symbolism already quoted, in which it is said ; " The elevation of the Chalice, after the full uncovering thereof, *quando canitur oblata*, that is a commemoration of Christ's birth and of His glory through signs and miracles." [3]

Next comes the prayer *Hostias quesumus*, then the prayer *Has oblationes . . . immolamus tibi domine iesu christe . . . pro animamus* (= *animabus*) *carorum nostrorum .n. et cararum nostrarum quorum nomina recitamus et quorumcumque non recitamus sed a te recitantur in libro uitae aeternae propter missericordiam tuam eripe qui regnas*, etc.,[4] which shows that, in conformity with the Spanish and Gallican practice, the reading of the diptychs of the dead took place at this conjuncture, whereas the *Memento* of the living followed the prayer *Te igitur* of the canon as at the present day.

Next in the Stowe Missal come the preface and the *Sanctus*. The *Te igitur* is preceded by the words *Canon dominicus pape gilasi.*[5]   The canon of the Mass presents only very slight variations ; but the Irish treatises already quoted add some interesting details on the rites of consecration : " *Quando canitur : accepit Jesus panem*, the priest bows himself down thrice to repent of his sins. He offers it (the Chalice) to God [and

---

[1] The Leabhar Breac Tract has been edited by Wh. Stokes in the *Zeitschrift für vergl. Sprachforschung*, XXVI, 1883, pp. 497–519, and by B. MacCarthy, *On the Stowe Missal*, pp. 245–65.

[2] *Stowe*, p. 9.

[3] *Treatise*, 7 (pp. 37, 40).

[4] *Stowe*, p. 9.

[5] *Stowe*, pp. 9–10.

chants *Miserere mei Deus*], and the people kneel, and here no voice cometh lest it disturb the priest, for this is the right of it, that his mind separate not from God while he chants this lesson. Hence its *nomen* is *periculosa oratio.*" [1]

Cuimine's penitential inflicts a penance of fifty stripes on any priest guilty of having once stumbled in pronouncing the *periculosa oratio.* [2] The penitential attributed to Gildas leads us to believe that the word *periculum* was sometimes written on the margin of missals opposite the words of the consecration, in order to put the celebrant on his guard. [3]

The Stowe treatise continues : " The three steps which the ordained man steppeth backwards and which he again steps forward, this is the triad in which everyone sins, to wit, in word, in thought, in deed ; and this is the triad of things by which he is renovated *iterum* and by which he is moved to Christ's Body." [4]

At the point where at present the *Memento* of the dead is recited, we find in the Stowe Missal a list containing the names of more than a hundred of the righteous, both of the Old Law and the New, and of a number of Irish and other non-biblical saints. Among these last are the names of SS. Martin, Gregory and Gildas and of St Augustine's first three successors in the see of Canterbury, Laurentius, Mellitus and Justus. [5]

St Patrick, already named in the opening litany, figures here again. His name recurs in the *Nobis quoque peccatoribus*, after those of the Apostles Peter and Paul, and finally in the *Libera nos, Domine* after the same Apostles.

After the *Per quem haec omnia* an elevation of the Great Host took place, and half of the Host was immersed in the chalice. [6]

At Iona a curious rite of confraction was practised. If the

---

[1] *Treatise*, 8 (pp. 37, 40).

[2] *Poenitentiale Cummeani*, XI, 29, ed. J. Zettinger (*Archiv für kath. Kirchenrecht*, LXXXII, 1902, p. 523).

[3] Gildas, *De poenitentia*, 20 (*CED*, I, p. 115 ; ed. Mommsen, p. 90).

[4] *Treatise* 9 (pp. 37–38, 40).—The Leabhar Breac Tract prescribes the recitation of the psalm *Miserere* by the priests at the moment of the Consecration (ed. Wh. Stokes, p. 512).

[5] *Stowe*, pp. 15–16.

[6] *Stowe*, pp. 16–17.

celebrant was a simple priest, another priest joined him in order to break the Body of the Lord with him. If the celebrant was a bishop, he broke the Host alone.[1] A similar rite prevailed also in Brittany, at any rate from the seventh century.[2]

The treatise of the Stowe Missal contains the following words : " The particle that is cut off from the bottom of the half which is on the [priest's] left hand is the figure of the wounding with the lance in the armpit of the right side ; for westwards was Christ's face on the Cross, to wit, *contra civitatem*, and eastwards was the face of Longinus ; what to him was the left to Christ was the right." [3] The same text proceeds to enumerate diverse complicated modes of fraction of the Host according to festivals and tells how the particles should be arranged on the altar at Easter and Christmas.[4]

The custom of giving the Pax at Mass is attested by different texts of Celtic origin.[5] A rather curious detail is that at Bangor the kiss of peace seems to have been observed during the canonical office itself,[6] outside the Mass. It should be noticed that in all the Celtic languages the word used to denote the ordinary kiss is derived from the Latin *pacem*, the name of the liturgical kiss.[7]

It is well known that the *Agnus Dei* was introduced into the Roman Mass by Pope Sergius (687–701). It finds a place in the Stowe Missal.[8]

In conclusion, we may mention some of the peculiar features which F. Duine considers worth noting in the Mass as it was celebrated in Brittany in the seventh century,

---

[1] Adam., *Vita Col.*, I, 44 (pp. 56–57). Cf. L.G., *Les rites de la consécration et de la fraction dans la liturgie celtique de la messe* (*Nineteenth Eucharistic Congress Report*, London, 1908, pp. 348–61).

[2] *Vita Sam.*, I, 44 (p. 140) ; *Vita Iᵃ Tuduali*, 4 ; *Vita tertia*, 13 (ed. A. de La Borderie, *Les trois Vies anciennes de S. Tudual*, 1887, p. 13). Cf. F. Duine, *Inventaire*, p. 236.

[3] *Treatise*, 15 (pp. 38, 41).

[4] *Ib.*, 16–18 (pp. 38–39, 41–42).

[5] *Stowe*, p. 17 ; Liturgical fragments in MS. 1394 (Warren, *Lit.*, p. 177) ; Liturg. fragm. in B. of Dimma (*ib.*, p. 170) ; *Vita Cainnici*, 20 (*VSH*, I, p. 159).

[6] *An. Ban.*, II, p. 21. Cf. D. Germain Morin, *Destination de la formule* " *Ad pacem celebrandam* " *dans l'Antiphonaire de Bangor* (*RB*, XII, 1895, p. 202).

[7] Cf. L.G., *Celtiques* (*Liturgies*), cols. 3012–13.

[8] *Stowe*, p. 18.

according to the oldest Life of St Samson of Dol.[1] The officiating bishop was assisted by a deacon, who chanted the Gospel and offered the chalice [2] ; further, the reading of the diptychs in which were inscribed the names of the departed who were entitled to share in the eucharistic sacrifice [3] ; the rite of fraction or, more probably, the Celtic rite of confraction of the Host already referred to ; and the distribution of the unconsecrated bread (*eulogium*) after the solemn Mass.[4] Also, in the ninth century, according to the *Vita secunda Samsonis* : the presence of the *Agnus Dei* [5] ; and a final collect at the end of the mass, the expression *ultimam collectam complere* being used.[6]

As for Scotland, Turgot, the biographer of Queen Margaret († 1093), relates that in some places in that country Mass was celebrated in an irregular manner *contra totius Ecclesiae consuetudinem*.[7] But he does not tell us in what these irregularities, which he terms *ritus barbarus*, exactly consisted.[8]

§ 5.—THE DIVINE OFFICE

The celebration of the divine office was the chief occupation of the monks. The office comprised the canonical hours of day and night, varying in number in different monasteries and at different periods. An Irish gloss of the eighth century, written in the Codex Palatinus 68 of the Vatican, enumerates seven canonical hours : *Septies in die laudem dixi tibi, .i. antert, tert, sest, noon, fescer, midnoct, maten, quod convenit, quia septies in*

---

[1] Duine, *Inventaire*, pp. 236–37.

[2] *Vita Sam.*, I, 13 (pp. 111–13).

[3] *Vita Sam.*, I, 1 (pp. 99–100). According to F. C. Burkitt (*JTS*, XXVII, p. 49), these passages apply to Llantwit, Illtud's monastery in Wales, not to Dol. For Ireland see Lawlor and Best, *The Ancient List of the Coarbs of Patrick* (*PRIA*, XXXV, Sect. C, 1919, pp. 333–36). Cf. Duine, *Inventaire*, p. 236.

[4] *Vita Sam.*, I, 45 (p. 140). Cf. J. Leverdier, *Le pain bénit* (*La vie et les arts liturgiques*, XII, 1926, pp. 393–401).

[5] *Vita IIa Samsonis*, II, 9, ed. Plaine (*AB*, VI, 1887, p. 130) ; Bili, *Vita Machutis*, 22, ed. F. Lot, *Mélanges*, p. 367.

[6] *Vita IIa Samsonis*, *l. cit.*

[7] Turgot, *Vita Margaritae* (*CED*, II, p. 158).

[8] M. V. Hay, *A Chain of Error in Scottish History* (London, 1927), pp. 231–34 ; *s.a.* " *Nescio quo ritu barbaro* " (*SGS*, II, 1927, pp. 30–33).

die cadit iustus.[1] But another gloss written in the *Liber Hymnorum,* after the hymn *In te Christe* attributed to St Columba, runs as follows : " Colum Cille was wont to celebrate ten canonical hours, *ut ferunt,* and he got this number from the history of John Cassian." [2] There is nothing in Cassian to support this statement.

No monastic Rule gives us such full information about the arrangement of the office as that of St Columban, which may rightfully be placed beside the Antiphonary of Bangor, since it was at Bangor that the great Irish monk received his ascetic and liturgical training. Once on the Continent, he was not likely to make innovations in aught pertaining to the constitution of the divine office, and, indeed, we know that he remained to the end a stickler for tradition.[3] In his chapter on the *cursus psalmorum* he appeals twice to the traditions of the early Irish.[4]

The canonical hours of night mentioned in the Antiphonary of Bangor are also found in Columban's Rule ; as for the other hours, they are called in the Rule *horae diurnae,* but nothing is said of their number or their several names. At Bangor the *horae diurnae* were five in number : *secunda* (corresponding to prime), *tertia, sexta, nona* and *vespertina* [5] ; the nocturnal *vigiliae* comprised three offices, that of the *initium noctis,* the *nocturna* (midnight office, mentioned also in Adamnán's *Vita Columbae* [6]) and the *matutina* or *ad matutinum* (Columban's term), celebrated in the early morn.[7] The monks went to bed after the office of *initium noctis* and again after the midnight one.[8]

The longest office in the *cursus* of St Columban was the last of the nocturnal vigils, that styled *ad matutinum.* In speaking of this office, Columban makes a distinction between the nights which usher in Saturday and Sunday and the five others. From November 1 to March 25 each of the last

[1] Stokes and Strachan, *TP,* I, 3. Cf. Kenney, *Sources,* I, p. 637.
[2] *LH,* I, p. 33. Cf. II, p. 124.
[3] Columban, *Ep.* 2 (*MG. Epist.,* III, p. 160).
[4] Columban, *RM,* 7 (p. 379).
[5] *An. Ban.,* pp. 10–21.
[6] Adam., *Vita Col.,* III, 23 (p. 159).
[7] *An. Ban.,* pp. 11, 13, 21, 23, etc.
[8] *An. Ban.,* No. 58 (p. 24), No. 120 (p. 32).

two nights of the week admitted seventy-five psalms and twenty-five antiphons *ad matutinum*, one antiphon to each set of three psalms, forming a *chora*.[1] From March 25 to June 24 an antiphon and three psalms were cut off each week, so that by June 24 there were only twelve antiphons and thirty-six psalms, the minimum for the lauds of the last nights. Conversely, when the nights began to lengthen after June 24, an antiphon and three psalms were added weekly, until on November 1 the full number of twenty-five antiphons and seventy-five psalms prescribed for winter was attained.[2]

For the remaining five nights of the week Columban allots *ad matutinum* twenty-four psalms for the summer and thirty-six for the winter, without saying whether any graduation was made between the minimum and maximum according to season.

As for the diurnal hours, according to the traditions of the elders, they ought to consist of three psalms and terminate in a series of six petitions in versicle form : (1) *pro peccatis nostris*, (2) *pro omni populo christiano*, (3) *pro sacerdotibus*, etc., (4) *pro eleemosynas facientibus*, (5) *pro pace regum* and (6) *pro inimicis*.[3]

The office of vespers, as well as those *ad initium noctis* and *ad medium noctis*, had twelve psalms.

Some Irish psalters, the Turin fragments and the Antiphonary of Bangor furnish proof that canticles taken from Holy Scripture were also recited at office ; unfortunately, we cannot determine how they were distributed.

According to the Bangor rubrics, the *Te Deum* was sung on Sundays and the *Gloria in excelsis* at vespers and matins.[4] Other hymns are assigned to the office of night, the festivals of martyrs, the matins of Saturday and those of Sunday.

Every psalm recited in church was followed by an act of humiliation.[5] The so-called Rule of St Ailbe of Emly prescribes a hundred genuflexions at matins for a certain

---

[1] Columban, *RM*, 7 (p. 379). Cf. D. Germain Morin, *Explication d'un passage de la Règle de S. Colomban relatif à l'office des moines celtiques* (*RB*, XII, 1895, p. 203).
[2] Columban, *RM*, 7 (pp. 379–80).
[3] *Ib.*, p. 379.
[4] *An. Ban.*, pp. 10, 31.
[5] *L. cit.*

period of the year and at all times the recitation of the verse *Deus in adjutorium, etc.*, at the end of each psalm.[1] St Columban's Rule enjoins on penitents only the triple recitation of this verse *sub silentio*.

According to Cassian, in the monasteries of Egypt the recital of the psalm was followed by a mental prayer offered kneeling, then by a prostration, and finally a collect.[2] The office of lauds at Bangor was likewise interspersed with collects. In the Antiphonary we come across eight collects *post canticum*, seven *post Benedicite*, one *post tres psalmos* and six *super Laudate dominum de caelis*.

The Celtic monks were great reciters of psalms, whether in the routine of the *cursus* or of their own accord. St Columban ordered the entire Psalter to be recited in two offices. The " three fifties " had to be recited daily at Menevia in the time of St David, as well as by the monks who followed the rules of St Ailbe, St Comgall and Máel Rúain.[3]

We have given the Irish names of the seven canonical hours as preserved by a gloss of the eighth century : *antert, tert, sest, noon, fescer, midnoct* and *maten*.

Antert or *anteirt* (*ante tertiam*)[4] was the Irish word for the hour of prime, also called *prím*.[5]

Medón laí (midday) was another name for sext.[6]

For vespers the term *esparta* (later sometimes *espartain*, from Lat. *vespertina* [*hora*]) is also found.[7]

The eighth century gloss has nothing corresponding to the office called at Bangor and by Columban *ad initium noctis*. Probably this hour fell into disuse after the seventh century ; it was replaced by compline (Ir. *compléit*).[8]

[1] Ed. J. O'Neill, 17, 20 (*Ériu*, III, 1907).

[2] *De institutis coenobiorum*, II, 7, ed. M. Petschenig (*Corp. SEL*, XVII, p. 23).

[3] *V. sup.*, ch. III, § 12.

[4] *Antert. Rule of Ailbe* (*Ériu*, III, 1907, p. 100) ; *Teaching of Máel Rúain*, 90 (*Tallaght*, 1927, pp. 52–53) ; *The Lebar Brecc Tractate on the Canonical Hours*, ed. R. I. Best (*Miscellany presented to Kuno Meyer*, Halle a. S., 1912, pp. 165–66).

[5] *L. Br. Tractate*, 8 (pp. 146–47), v. 145–53 (pp. 158–59). Cf. p. 165 ; *Tallaght* (1927), p. xxv.

[6] *Medón lai.* Cf. *L. Br. Tractate*, 2 (pp. 144–46), 21–39 (pp. 148–51) ; *Tallaght* (1927), p. xxv.

[7] *Esparta.* Cf. *Tallaght* (1927), *l. cit.*

[8] *Compléit. L. Br. Tractate*, 5 (pp. 146–47), 94 (pp. 154–55). Cf. *ib.*, p. 161 ; *Tallaght* (1927), *l. cit.*

The midnight office was called *midnocht* or *iarmérge*, a word which means " after rising." [1]

The last hour of the night was named *maiten*,[2] or *tiugnáir* (a word derived from *tiug* " final " and **ndir* " night " ?),[3] or *gairm an choilig* " cockcrow." [4] But in some texts the word *iarmérge* is also applied to the last office of the night. The confusion between *iarmérge* and *maiten* among Irish writers of the late Middle Ages is evidently to be accounted for by the fact that in their time lauds were celebrated immediately after matins, and thus the office of dawn and that of midnight fell together, so to speak.

The hour of compline, as has been said, did not exist in the primitive *cursus*.[5] Such allusions to it as are found in certain Lives of saints (*Vita Brioci*,[6] *Vita prima Brendani* [7]) are probably to be attributed to the imagination of hagiographers who introduced the customs of their own day into the biographies of saints belonging to a remote age.

The divine office was called *cursus, synaxis, horae, celebratio*. To the last two terms correspond the Irish words *trátha* and *celebrad*.[8]

Each of the canonical hours had its mystical meaning (sometimes indeed several), as is set forth in various texts dealing with the matter.[9]

---

[1] *Iarmérge*. Cf. *The Voyage of Mael Duin*, ed. Wh. Stokes (*R. Cel.*, IX, 1888, p. 453) ; Best, *L. Br. Tractate*, pp. 162–63 ; Gwynn, *Tallaght* (1927), *l. cit.*

[2] *Maiten*. Cf. Gwynn, *l. cit.*

[3] *Tiugnáir*. Cf. *L. Br. Tractate*, 7 (pp. 146–7), v. 113–117 (pp. 156–57) and pp. 162–64.

[4] *Gairm an choilig*. Cf. Best, *L. Br. Tractate*, pp. 162–63. " Gallorum, Christe, cantibus " (*Collectio ad matutinam*, 25, *An. Ban.*, p. 20). In some liturgical texts " Gallorum cantus " also denotes the midnight office (cf. Warren, *An. Ban.*, II, p. 60), but in *An. Ban.* it is used for the daybreak office, *ad matutinam* (*v. sup.*), as is the case in the *Regula Magistri*, c. 33 : " Pullorum cantus declinantis est terminus noctis, qui mox diem parit " (*PL*, LXXXVIII, 1002).

[5] " Its introduction seems to date at the earliest from the ninth century " (Ryan, *Monast.*, p. 336, n. 1).

[6] *Vita Brioci*, 49, ed. F. Plaine (*AB*, II, 1883, pp. 183–84. Cf. p. 161).

[7] *Vita I^a Brendani* 13, 32 (*VSH*, I, pp. 105, 118).

[8] On " celebrare " and " celebrad " see B. MacCarthy, *op. cit.*, pp. 162, 182–83.

[9] On the mystical significance of each canonical hour see : 1. *An. Ban.*, Nos. 10, 19, 20, 23, 25, 28, 29, 37, 57, 121 and notes, II, pp. 59–60 ; 2. R. I. Best, *The Canonical Hours* (*Ériu*, III, 1907, p. 116) ; 3. *s.a. The*

The monk was bound to demean himself correctly during the divine office. St Columban ordains appropriate punishments for the monk who coughs *in exordio psalmi* or allows himself to smile or spits in unseemly wise.[1] Likewise the Welshman Rhygyfarch, who composed a Life of St David of Menevia in the last quarter of the eleventh century, relates that yawning and sneezing, as well as spitting, were absolutely forbidden in the oratory of David's monastery.[2]

We have the testimony of St Bernard that the *laus perennis* was practised in the monastery of Bangor in Ireland at an early period—when exactly, he does not say.[3]

In the time of Bishop Gilbert (1106–1145 ?) and St Malachy, the divine office, it appears, was greatly neglected in Ireland or celebrated with slight regard to liturgical rules.[4] The liturgy was one of the points in which these reformers endeavoured to gain sway for the Roman customs.[5] Their efforts were not vain ; St Bernard affirms that the Irish people had come to celebrate the canonical hours and to sing the psalms *juxta morem universae terrae*.[6]

In winter, when the glacial north wind was blowing, it was no petty mortification for a monk to leave his couch and repair to the night offices. We have a witness to the fact in the following avowal preserved to us in the Rule of the Grey Monks (*Ríagul na manach líath*) : "To go to *iarmérge*, great labour ; the wind stings my two ears ; were it not dread of the blessed Lord, though sweet the bell, I would not go to it." [7]

§ 6.—CHARACTERISTICS AND INFLUENCE

What is there, in fine, that is fundamentally and specifically Celtic in the insular liturgies ? It is not easy to say. Edmund

Lebar Brecc Tractate on the Canonical Hours, pp. 160–66 ; 4. Ryan, *Monast.*, p. 336.

[1] Columban, *Reg. coenobialis*, ed. O. Seebass (*ZK*, XVII, 1897, pp. 215–34).

[2] *Vita Davidis*, 25, ed. A. W. Wade-Evans (*YC*, 1913, p. 14). Cf. L.G., *Anciennes coutumes claustrales* (Ligugé, 1930), pp. 41–48.

[3] Bernard, *Vita Mal.*, 6 (*PL*, CLXXXII, col. 1082).

[4] Gilbert, *SE*, col. 994–95.

[5] Bernard, *Vita Mal.*, 3, col. 1079.

[6] *L. cit.*

[7] Ed. J. Strachan, *Ériu*, II, p. 229. Cf. R. I. Best, *L. Br. Tractate*, p. 165.

Bishop used the expression " tinkering method " to characterize the *modus operandi* of Irish liturgical compilers.[1] They were, above all, eclectics. In the liturgical texts of Celtic composition which have reached us we find a mixture of elements drawn from Roman, Gallican and other sources.

If we would seek the distinctive traits of the religious temperament and piety of the early Celtic Christians, we must turn not so much to liturgical texts as to the more spontaneous effusions of private devotion. Read their *loricae*, their petitions in form of litany, the prayer of Colcu úa Duinechda of Clonmacnois,[2] that of St Brendan,[3] the Confession placed under the name of St Patrick [4] and his *lorica* (still popular),[5] and a host of other prayers of the same kind,[6] and you will be struck by their original style, the outcome of a somewhat roving imagination, by the reiterated entreaties, the copiousness of language, the outpourings of trust and self-abandonment, finally by the rhetoric which give the tone to these compositions.[7]

That the reader may form some notion of their character, here are a few passages from one of the most famous among early Irish prayers, the *Scúap Chrábaid* or " Besom of Devotion " of Colcu úa Duinechda († 796). It begins as follows :

" I entreat Thee, O holy Jesus, by Thy four evangelists who wrote Thy divine gospels, to wit, Matthew, Mark, Luke and John ; I entreat Thee by Thy four chief prophets who foretold Thy Incarnation, Daniel and Jeremiah and Isaiah and Ezekiel." There follow fifteen adjurations beginning with the same words " I entreat Thee," in which every category of saint is mentioned, those of the Old Testament, the Virgin

---

[1] E. Bishop, *JTS*, VIII, 1907, p. 279 ; *s.a. LH*, p. 166.

[2] See below.

[3] Ed. P. Moran, *Acta S. Brendani* (Dublin, 1872), pp. 27–44. Cf. L.G., *Étude sur les " loricae " celtiques et sur les prières qui s'en rapprochent* (*BALAC*, I, 1911, pp. 266–67) ; A. Wilmart, *The Prayers of the Bury Psalter* (*Downside Review*, XLVIII, 1930, pp. 212–14).

[4] Ed. *BC*, pp. 95–99. Not to be confounded with the saint's authentic *Confessio*.

[5] Ed. *LH*, I, pp. 133–35 ; II, 49–51 ; Stokes and Strachan, *TP*, II, pp. 354–58.

[6] See *Ir. Lit. ;* L.G., *Étude sur les " loricae."*

[7] " The ejaculatory, litanic, asyndetic type of prayer is peculiarly suited to the Irish genius " (E. Bishop, *LH*, p. 148).

Mary, the Holy Innocents, angels, apostles, martyrs and confessors. The first part of the prayer ends with the following words :

" That Thou wilt take me under Thy protection and defence and care, to preserve and protect me from demons and all their promptings, against all the elements of the world, against lusts, against transgressions, against sins, against the crimes of the world, against the dangers of this life and the torments of the next, from the hands of enemies and every terror, against the fire of hell and doom, against shame before the face of God, against attacks (literally " seizures ") of demons, that they may have no power over us at the entry of the other world ; against every man that God knows to have ill will towards us under the ten stars of the world ;

" May God keep far from us their rage, their violence, their anger, their cruelty, their craft ;

" May God kindle gentleness and love and affection and mercy and forgiveness in their hearts and in their thoughts and in their minds and in their bowels."

All this is only the first part of the prayer. The author goes on : " O holy Jesus ; O gentle friend ; O Morning Star ; O mid-day Sun adorned." Twelve other invocations of the same kind follow. After them come sixteen fresh adjurations, of which the first runs :

" For the sake of Thy kindliness, [Thy affection, Thy love and Thy mercy], hear the entreaty of this man and wretched [poorling and] weakling for the acceptance of this sacrifice on behalf of all Christian churches, and on mine own behalf."

Finally, the long *lorica* concludes as follows :

" Give and grant and impart [to me] Thy holy grace and Thy Holy Spirit, to protect me and preserve me from all my sins present and future, and to kindle in me all righteousness, and to establish me in that righteousness to my life's end ; and that He may receive me after my life's end into heaven, in the unity of apostles and disciples, in the unity of angels and archangels, in the unity which excels every unity, that is, in the unity of the holy and exalted Trinity, Father, Son and Holy Ghost ; for I have nothing unless I have it according to the word of the Apostle Paul : *Quis me liberabit*, etc. Amen." [1]

To the recitation of these prayers were attached promises, often extravagant, of their efficacious action both in spiritual and temporal matters, as also to that of certain liturgical hymns (or sometimes only their closing stanzas). For instance, the indulgences attached to the celebrated hymn of Secundinus in honour of St Patrick could be gained by all who recited the last three stanzas only on getting up and on lying down. [2]

These prayers enjoyed great popularity in the Middle Ages and some of them have retained their vogue down to our own days. [3] Very often they were invested with a superstitious regard as if they were magical incantations, to which they are not without resemblance. From the fact that they were introduced into a number of collections of *preces* in use in England or on the Continent, and from the imitations of them to be found in such collections, we may gather that they were in high favour in those countries from about the eighth to the twelfth century. [4]

Prolixity, repetition of the same formulas, and verbosity are certainly patent marks of the productions due to private devotion among the insular Celts as well as of their liturgical compositions. Their contemporaries did not fail to remark the note of eccentricity and extravagance both in their formulas and their rites. At the Council of Mâcon in 627 a charge was preferred by one Agrestius against the disciples of Columban, who were blamed for making the sign of the

[1] Ed. C. Plummer, *Ir. Lit.*, pp. 30-45.   Cf. Kenney, *Sources*, I, No. 580.
[2] See *LH*, I, p. 6, II, p. 6 ; P. Grosjean, *A Tale of Doomsday Colum Cille should have left untold* (*SGS*, III, 1929, p. 83) ; Kenney, *Sources*, I, p. 259 (No. 310).
[3] L.G., *Étude sur les " loricae*," pp. 122–27.
[4] *Harleian Prayer-Book* (Kenney, *Sources*, I, No. 575) ; *Royal Library Prayer-Book* (*ib.*, No. 576) ; *Book of Nunnaminster* (*ib.*, No. 577) ; *Book of Cerne* (*ib.*, No. 578) ; *De psalmorum usu liber cum variis formulis*, attributed to Alcuin (*PL*, CI, 461–508) ; *Officia per ferias*, attributed to the same (*ib.*, 509–612) ; *Libellus precum ex* MS. *Floriacensi* (*ib.*, 1383–1416) ; Prayers of the Bury Psalter : Vat. Reg. 12 (fols. 165-81), ed. A. Wilmart (*v. sup.*) ; *A Prayer Book from St. Emmeran, Ratisbon* [Munich, S.B., Clm. 14248], ed. M. Frost (*JTS*, XXX, 1929, pp. 32–45).   Cf. E. Bishop, *About an old Prayer Book* [Galba, A. xiv] (*LH*, pp. 384–91).

cross too frequently on things of daily use and for uttering too many benedictions on entering and quitting different places, even *intra coenubium*.[1]   In speaking of the Mass in the Stowe Missal we have already noticed its multiplicity of collects. This was also one of the special points laid to the charge of the Columbanians by Agrestius, " *et multa alia superflua.*"   In the ninth century we find Walahfrid Strabo noting the Scottic habit of multiplying genuflections.[2]

Such then are some of the undeniable traits of the Celtic genius as manifested in liturgical worship and in private devotion, traits widely different from the Roman sobriety. We have moreover seen that the Irish showed themselves rabid compilers and deft manipulators of liturgical texts, eclectics both by temperament and of necessity.

Did they then introduce nothing new ? The Church of Gaul was endowed by Mamertus, bishop of Vienne (*c.* 470), with the custom of Rogations, which was subsequently adopted by the Roman Church.   Many other Churches in like manner brought their stones to lay on the perennial edifice of the Christian liturgy.   Can it be that Celtic Britain, that Ireland, whose population of monks sent forth such large swarms beyond the seas, remained wholly without a share in this kind of ecclesiastical co-operation ?   That it was not so, one fact at least seems to indicate, a fact which has been already touched on ; namely, the solemn benediction of the new fire on Holy Saturday.   This, according to all appearance, was the special contribution of the Irish.   To them, perhaps to their apostle St Patrick himself, a contemporary of Mamertus, is due the introduction into the Paschal liturgy of this picturesque rite, beautiful in its symbolism.   It may be surmised that the *Scotti* scattered throughout England and the continental countries first made it known to the Anglo-Saxon missionaries with whom they had such close relations, and that the latter, practising it themselves on their own behalf, helped to diffuse it abroad.[3]

---

[1] Jonas, *Vita Col.*, II, 9 (p. 125). Cf. Ryan, *Monast.*, p. 234 ; Bernard Capelle, " *Collecta* " (*RB*, XLII, 1930, pp. 197–204).

[2] *V. sup.*, ch. III, § 12.

[3] *V. sup.*, § 3.

CHAPTER X

CHRISTIAN ARTS

THERE remain a sufficient number of monuments to enable us to form some idea of the way in which the Celts adapted architecture and the other plastic arts, including the transcribing and adornment of manuscripts, to the needs of contemporary Christian life. We propose here to give a summary of their artistic achievement, endeavouring to trace the influences to which it may have been subjected and to show in what respects it contributed to the general progress of the arts.

§ 1.—ARCHITECTURE

In the early Middle Ages architecture, civic or religious, was at a low stage in the British Isles.[1] Churches were originally built of wood; either in wattle-work (*ex virgis*)[2] or rough-hewn timber (*de robore secto*)[3] or smooth planks (*de lignis levigatis*[4]; *tabulis dedolatis*).[5] Indeed, that style of construction was regarded as a peculiarity of Irish or British architecture,

---

[1] For the monuments discussed in this section the reader is principally referred to the following works : 1. George Petrie, *The Ecclesiastical Architecture of Ireland anterior to the Anglo-Norman Invasion* (*TRIA*, XX, 1845) ; 2. Lord Dunraven, *Notes on Irish Architecture*, 2 vols. (London, 1875–77) ; 3. Margaret Stokes, *Early Christian Architecture in Ireland* (London, 1878) ; 4 *s.a. Early Christian Art in Ireland* (London, 1887), re-edited by G. N. Count Plunkett (Dublin, 1911) ; 5. G. Baldwin Brown, *The Arts in early England*, I, II (London, 1903) ; 2nd edit., I (1926), II (1925) ; 6. A. C. Champneys, *Irish Ecclesiastical Architecture* (London, 1910).

[2] *Vita Coemgeni*, 19 (*VSH*, I, pp. 243–44) ; *Betha Brighdi* (*Lismore*, l. 1573). —At Dublin Henry II had a palace built for his use outside the walls, near the church of St. Andrew ; it was a structure of wattle-work, " *de virgis ad morem patriae illius* " (*The Chronicle of the Reigns of Henry II and Richard I known commonly under the Name of Benedict of Peterborough*, ed. W. Stubbs (*RS*), Vol. I, pp. 28–29).

[3] Bede, *HE*, III, 25.

[4] *Vita Kentigerni*, 24 (ed. Forbes, p. 203 ; ed. Pinkerton, p. 248) ; *Vita Samthannae*, 6, 15 (*VSH*, II, pp. 254–55, 257) ; *Vita Moling*, 10, 11 (*VSH*, II, pp. 194–95).

[5] Conchubran, *Vita Mon.*, III, 12 (p. 237).

as is shown by the expressions used of it in contemporary texts : " *iuxta morem Scotticarum gentium,*" " *iuxta morem Hibernicae nationis,*" " *opus Scotticum,*" " *more Scottorum,*" " *more Brittonum.*" [1] The use of stone in building churches was considered Roman or Gaulish. [2] When St Malachy, the ex-archbishop of Armagh, determined to build a large stone oratory at Bangor, the inhabitants did not disguise their astonishment and uneasiness on seeing the foundations, and one of the malcontents voiced their feelings, saying to the man of God : " Why have you thought good to introduce this novelty into our regions ? We are Scots, not Gauls. What is this frivolity ? What need was there for a work so super-fluous, so proud ? " [3]

However, St Ninian, the apostle of the southern Picts, built his church of *Candida Casa* in Galloway in the fourth century in masonry [4] ; and, as we shall presently see, in Ireland also there existed ecclesiastical structures (oratories or small churches) of stone long before St Malachy's time.

Where wood and stone were not forthcoming, clay was used. St Patrick is said to have built two earthen churches, one at Clebach, the other near Killala. [5] According to his biographer Tirechán, the latter was square. [6] A curious druidic oracle concerning Patrick applies to that apostle's churches the epithets " *angustae et quadratae.*" [7] The little oratories built of unhewn stone, generally put together without mortar, of which numerous specimens are still to be found in Ireland and Scotland, generally took the shape of the keel of an upturned boat or of a truncated pyramid or a round beehive. Though circular or oval in external form,

---

[1] Conchubran, *l. cit.* ; Adam., *Vita Col.*, II, 45 ; Bede, *l. cit.* ; *Vita Kentigerni, l. cit.* ; Bernard, *Vita Mal.*, VI, 14, col. 1083. Cf. C. Plummer, edit. of Bede, Vol. II, pp. 101–102 ; *s.a. VSH*, I, p. xcix (*introd.*) ; Macalister, *AI*, p. 239 ; Josef Strzygowski, *Early Church Art in Northern Europe* (London, 1928), ch. III, pp. 77–115 (Half-timber churches in Western Europe).

[2] Bede, *HE*, v, 21 ; *s.a. Historia abbatum*, 5 (ed. C. Plummer, p. 368).

[3] Bernard, *Vita Mal.*, XXVIII, 61 (col. 1109).

[4] " qui locus . . . uulgo uocatur Ad Candidam Casam, eo quod ibi ecclesiam de lapide, insolito Brettonibus more fecerit " (Bede, *HE*, III, 4).

[5] Tirechán, pp. 24, 28.

[6] " aecclesiam terrenam de humo quadratam, quia non prope erat silua."

[7] Muirchu, p. 274.

they were quadrangular inside. The principle of construction employed was that of the primitive monastic cell of beehive type known as *clochán*. Instead of perpendicular walls supporting a dome, these cells and oratories were built with walls gradually inclined towards the centre by means of overlapping courses, till they met overhead in a cap which formed the roof of the little structure.

The pre-Norman Cornish oratories of Perranzabulo (St Perran's) and of Gwithian are without ornament and of the rudest description. After having lain for centuries in the sand they were excavated in the last century ; the former is now cased in a shell of protective concrete, but the latter has become buried again.[1]

Among the Irish oratories of the oldest type which remain at the present day, intact or partly ruined, may be mentioned those of Gallerus on the Dingle peninsula (Co. Kerry), of Valencia, off Kerry, and those of Skellig Michael. In some of these buildings the stone which formed the primitive altar is still to be seen at the east end.

The Great Skellig, a precipitous rock situate 7½ miles from the nearest coast (south-west of Valencia), its highest point being 704 feet high, is dedicated to the archangel Michael, like the similar rock-islets off Normandy and Cornwall, but is much more difficult of access than these latter. The Skellig contains a platform measuring 300 feet by 100, on which in the early Christian ages daring ascetics built their cells and erected oratories of the type just described. Many of these diminutive structures are still intact, after weathering the fierce squalls of the Atlantic for over twelve centuries.

On various points of the Scottish or Irish coast are still to be seen similar groups of beehive-shaped cells standing apart from each other and of oratories, enclosed within a cashel, the former habitations of small cenobitic communities or the *dínearts* of hermits, though they are not generally so well

---

[1] *Ancient Oratories of Cornwall* (*AJ*, II, 1846, pp. 228–39, with plans) ; Charles Henderson, *Parochial History of Cornwall* in *The Cornish Church Guide* (Truro, 1928), pp. 107, 179–80, Pl. 4) ; Clifton Kelway, *The Church in Cornwall* (Truro, 1928), Plate, p. 9 ; G. H. Doble, *St Perran, St Keverne and St Kerrian* (1931), Frontispiece fig., and pp. 38–48 (by C. Henderson).

preserved as those on the Skellig Michael.[1] They occur chiefly on the following small islands off the west coast of Ireland : Inishmurray, 4½ miles off Streedagh Point (Co. Sligo) ; Inishglora, off the Mullet peninsula (Co. Mayo) ; Ardoilén (High Island), south of Inishboffin, off Connemara ; and Oilén Senaig (St. Senach's Island), one of the Magharee islands at the entrance of Tralee Bay (Co. Kerry).

The oratories of these early ascetic colonies were of modest dimensions ; they measured only about 15 feet in length by 9 feet in width and 12 in height.

The churches properly so called were also on a small scale. They were generally roofed with stone [2] ; the use of lead in roofing is not recorded in Ireland before the year 1008.[3] According to tradition the church of St Ciannán at Duleek (Co. Meath) was the first stone church built in Ireland ; hence the name of the village, Daim-liac, " house of stone." [4]

An important religious building of which we have a detailed description was the monastery church of Kildare, described by Cogitosus († c. 680) in his *Vita Brigidae*. It was spacious and lofty and adorned with mural paintings. The bodies of " archbishop " Conlaed and of St Brigid were deposited in it in monuments of gold and silver studded with gems on either side of the altar ; above these tombs were suspended crowns of gold and silver. The church contained three oratories (chapels ?). A transverse wall, decorated with paintings and hangings and pierced by two doorways, separated the east part from the rest of the building ; the various celebrants in the service entered by the door on the right, the abbess and her nuns repaired " to the banquet of the Body and Blood of

[1] On beehive-shaped cells see chiefly R. A. S. Macalister, *Ireland in Pre-Celtic Times* (Dublin, 1921), pp. 259–60 ; *s.a. AI*, p. 242, Pl. v–vii ; *Royal Commission on Ancient and Historical Monuments and Constructions of Scotland. Ninth Report with Inventory of Monuments and Constructions in the Outer Hebrides, Skye and the small Isles* (Edinburgh, 1928), p. xli, Figs. 7–10. Views of the Skellig cells in A. Kingsley Porter, *The Crosses and Culture of Ireland* (New Haven, Yale University Press, 1931), Figs. 42, 43.

[2] The church of Lindisfarne was at first covered with a rush thatch, but Eadberct, who succeeded St Cuthbert, " *ablata harundine, plumbi lamminis eam totam, hoc est, et tectum, et ipsos quoque parietes eius, cooperire curauit* " (Bede, *HE*, 25). Cf. Bede, *Vita Cuthberti*, 46 (*PL*, XCIV, 787–88).

[3] *AU*, a.a. 1008. The oratory of Ard Macha was roofed with lead in this year. Cf. *Lismore*, p. civ.

[4] *Vita Mochua*, 8 (*VSH*, II, p. 187). Cf. *VSH*, I, p. xcix.

Christ " by that on the left. A partition at right angles to this wall divided the body of the church into two parts, reserved respectively for men on the right and women on the left.[1] This *basilica maxima,* as Cogitosus calls it, could accommodate a large congregation. Light entered freely through numerous windows ; these were not glazed, for the use of glass panes was unknown in that period in Ireland as well as in Great Britain.[2] The altar in this church was placed at the east, in conformity with the traditional rule alluded to in the prophecy of the druids about St Patrick : " His table in the east of his house." [3]

The small church with perpendicular side-walls and gables, generally very pointed, at the east and west ends, bearing a stone roof marks a new phase of Irish religious architecture (oratories of St. Brendan in Inishglora, of MacDara on the island of Cruach MacDara off Connemara, etc.). The entrance door in the west end is surmounted by a horizontal lintel and has sloping sides or jambs ; this inclination is still found in a large number of buildings even of the Romanesque period. The lintel of the door of the church at Maghera (Co. Londonderry) is surmounted by a piece of rude sculpture representing the Crucifixion.

The churches of this early period have small square windows, the top being either pointed (formed by two inclined stones propped against each other) or round (with an arch cut out of a single stone slab).

The primitive oratories consisted of only a single chamber. Those of later construction have two, nave and chancel, both quadrangular in plan. Finally, at a period which it is hard to determine (eighth cent. ?), appears the semicircular arch, both at the west door of the building and in the partition between nave and chancel.[4] The door of an old church in the neighbourhood of the village of Banagher (Co. Londonderry) has a horizontal lintel in the outer door and in the interior a semicircular arch above the lintel. Examples of the oldest

[1] Cogitosus, *Vita Brig.,* 8 (p. 141).
[2] Cf. L.G., *Les chrétientés celtiques,* p. 318, n. 1.
[3] *Vita Trip.,* pp. 34–35.
[4] See F. Henry, *SI,* pp. 178–79.

chancel-arches and semicircular doorways, decorated with chevrons, pellets, human heads and other sculptures, may be seen at Trinity Church, Glendalough (Co. Wicklow), Rahen (Co. Offaly), Teampull Mac Duach (Aranmore), Temple na Neave (Teampull na Naomh) at Inchagoill (Loch Corrib), Kilmalkedar (Co. Kerry), Killeshin (Co. Leix), Roscrea (Co. Tipperary), and elsewhere.

The two finest monuments of Irish Romanesque style are the Cathedral of Clonfert (Co. Galway) and Cormac's Chapel built on the Rock of Cashel (Co. Tipperary). The decoration of the west portal of Clonfert is both rich and highly original, the capitals and archivolts being elaborately wrought. It is surmounted by a pediment on which are to be seen ten human heads, carefully carved and enclosed in triangles.[1] The human head is frequently used in the decoration of churches of this period, appearing on capitals, key-stones and other parts of the building (Kilmalkedar, Inchagoill, Killeshin, Cormac's Chapel, etc.).

Cormac's Chapel marks the zenith of the Hiberno-Romanesque style. It was consecrated in the year 1134. Like all the Irish churches of that age, it is small (only 44 feet long), but it offers a large number of interesting features to the archaeologist.[2] The north portal is surmounted by a tympanum on which is sculptured a centaur with bow and arrows taking aim at a lion. The chancel arch is very effective. The chapel is vaulted and there are chambers between the barrel vault and the outer stone roof, an arrangement found in other churches also, for instance, St. Flannan's oratory at Killaloe, St. Columba's House at Kells, and St. Kevin's at Glendalough.[3] Two other features are, first, the two square towers which rise at the end of the nave

---

[1] H. S. Crawford, *The Romanesque Doorway at Clonfert* (*JRSAI*, XLII, 1912, pp. 1–7).

[2] Françoise Henry, *La chapelle de Cormac à Cashel. Note sur les influences étrangères en Irlande au début du XIIᵉ siècle* (Institut d'art et d'archéologie. —Travaux des étudiants du groupe d'histoire de l'art de la Faculté des lettres de Paris. Année 1927–28, Paris, 1928, pp. 109–117).

[3] *Ancient and National Monuments, Ireland : Glendalough.—Extract from the Eighth Annual Report of the Commissioners of Public Works in Ireland*, 1911–12. Revised 1925, p. 71, Figs. 23, 27, 28, 29 ; F. Henry, *SI*, p. 183 ; Kingsley Porter, *Crosses and Culture*, Fig. 71.

at its junction with the chancel, and, second, the decoration of the walls by means of blank semicircular arcades. It has been noticed that these peculiarities recur in several Romanesque churches on the banks of the Rhine, notably St. Gereon's and St. Kunibert's at Cologne, and the inference has been drawn that in these points the architect of the chapel may have been an imitator.[1]

But if, on the other hand, we examine the symbolic sculptures and decoration of the celebrated north portal of the Jakobskirche, the church of the Irish monks of Ratisbon, which dates from about the year 1180, we are struck by the discovery of traces of Irish inspiration and technique in the choice of decorative motifs and in the representation of human forms. Inside the church is carved the figure of a monk, bearing a bolt intended to close the door and a key, with the accompanying name Rydan ; and it has been suggested that this Rydan was one of the artists who wrought at this " *Rätselarbeit* "—for such indeed is this piece of work, laden with symbolism the interpretation of which is still a matter of dispute.[2]

The earliest record extant of a round tower dates from the year 965,[3] but it is possible that these structures may have begun to be built close to churches and monasteries long before that date. They were not intended to serve as belfries, for the only bells in use in Celtic lands at that period of the Middle Ages were small portable handbells. Some writers, however, are still inclined to regard them as imitations of the Italian campaniles.[4] It seems likely that the round towers of Ireland are to be explained as places of refuge where in case of danger the monks could secure themselves with their articles of value. The lowest entry could only be approached by means of a ladder. Only two examples of a tower joined

---

[1] Charles MacNeill, *The Affinities of Irish Romanesque Architecture* (*JRSAI*, XLII, 1912, pp. 140–47).

[2] *V. sup.*, ch. v, § 12.—Cf. Wilhelm Hausenstein, *Das Bild. Atlanten zur Kunst*, V–VI (München, 1922), pp. 14–18 ; M. Leonia Lorenz, *Das Schottenportal zu Regensburg* (Waldsassen, 1929), Fig. 1 ; Richard Wiebel, *Das Schottentor* (Augsburg, Köln, Wien, n.d.), Fig. 28 ; F. Henry, *La chapelle de Cormac*, p. 116 (see *Addenda*).

[3] *Chronicon Scottorum*, ed. W. M. Hennessy (*RS*), pp. 216–17.

[4] Macalister, *AI*, p. 257 ; J. Vendryes, *MHMA*, p. 762.

to a church are extant, one is MacCarthy's tower at Clonmacnois joined to Teampull Finghin, the other the little church of St. Kevin at Glendalough, for which its peculiar appearance has earned the name of " St. Kevin's kitchen." [1]

As for the religious architecture of Brittany, there are but rare vestiges left of buildings going back to the times with which we are dealing here. Almost the only ones to be mentioned are the crypt of St. Mélar of Lanmeur (in the arrondissement of Morlaix), two or three pillars and arcades in the nave of Plougasnou (canton of Lanmeur),[2] and probably also the nave of the church of Locquénolé near Morlaix and the "Temple" of Lanleff (arrondissement of St. Brieuc).[3] Two or three crosses at crossways go back perhaps to the ninth and tenth centuries.[4] The monumental calvaries of granite which excite admiration in many spots in Brittany, and the ossuaries, structures peculiar to the country, date for the greater part only from the sixteenth and seventeenth centuries.[5]

§ 2.—SCULPTURE

Before the tenth century sculpture is rarely employed in the decoration of religious buildings. However, the sculptor did not wait till that century to exercise his art, as is proved by a host of monumental crosses erected in all parts of the Celtic insular world. No other countries of Christendom can

---

[1] *Ancient and National Monuments, Ireland : Glendalough* (1925), pp. 15–18 ; A. C. Champneys, *Irish Ecclesiastical Architecture*, pp. 208–11 ; L.G., art. *Clonmacnois* (*DACL*, col. 2017). In some cases a later church has been unmistakably attached to an earlier round tower (see Champneys, *op. cit.*, pp. 60–61).

[2] J.-M. Abgrall, *Crypte de Saint-Mélar à Lanmeur* (*BSAF*, XXXV, 1908, pp. 301–10). Cf. G. H. Doble, *Saint Melor* (Long Compton, 1927, pp. 26–27).

[3] A. Martin, *Le temple de Lanleff* (*RA*, 4th Ser., XV, 1910, pp. 212–16) ; André Rhein, *Le temple de Lanleff* (Congrès archéologique de France, LXXXIe session [Brest and Vannes, 1914], Paris and Caen, 1919, pp. 542–53).

[4] J.-M. Abgrall, *Les croix et calvaires du Finistère* (*Bulletin monumental*, LXVI, 1902, pp. 177–78)

[5] J.-M. Abgrall, *Les ossuaires bretons* (Congrès, LXXXIe session, pp. 529–41); s.a. *Les grandes époques de l'architecture religieuse en Basse-Bretagne* (Compte rendu du IVe Congrès scientifique international des catholiques tenu à Fribourg, 1897 [Xe section], Fribourg, 1898, pp. 11–18).

boast of having preserved or even of having produced such a number and such a variety of monuments of the kind.

In the tenth and following centuries, especially in Ireland, burial crosses and other memorial crosses of the well-known type styled " Celtic " attained a high degree of beauty and wealth of ornament. But before reaching such perfection they underwent several transformations ; and archaeologists have succeeded in determining the chief phases of their evolution.[1]

The custom of erecting memorial stones was inherited by the first Christian Celts from their ancestors. Tirechán speaks of the burial stone of a druid of St Patrick's time which was still to be seen in his own day.[2]

Christian burial stones in the form of lechs or rude pillar stones scarcely touched by the stone-cutter's tool, which go back to the seventh and sixth centuries, possibly even to the end of the fifth, have been preserved in Galloway. Five of them bear Latin Christian inscriptions in Roman capital letters, and four of these (three at Kirkmadrine and one at Withorn) have the monogram of Christ in a peculiar form engraved within a circle above the inscription.[3] The Chi-Rho figures also on a stone at Penmachno (Carnarvonshire) [4] and on numerous crosses in Cornwall.[5]

Opinions are divided as to the signification originally attached by insular converts to this combination of circle and cross. Some see in it a transformation of the sacred monogram enclosed in a circumference in imitation of the garland which surrounded it on the *Labarum* ; a device which is reproduced on a large number of sarcophagi of the post-Constantinian period.[6] Others find in it a blending of the

---

[1] Allen, *CA*, pp. 180–94 ; G. Baldwin Brown, art. *Art (Celtic)* in *ERE*, II (1909), p. 840.

[2] Tirechán, p. 19.

[3] G. Baldwin Brown, *The Arts in Early England*, Vol. V (London, 1921), pp. 42–50, 55–56, with fig. ; Joseph Anderson, *Inscribed Monuments of Scotland* in Allen, *ECMS*, pp. xiii–xvii ; *ib.*, Figs. 532, 533, 534, 537, 538, 539 ; W. G. Collingwood, *Northumbrian Crosses in Pre-Norman Age* (London, 1927), Figs. 1–5.

[4] G. Baldwin Brown, *The Arts*, V, p. 43, Pl. iv, Fig. 1.

[5] A. G. Langdon, *Old Cornish Crosses* (Truro, 1896), p. 5 ; C. G. Henderson, *The Celtic Crosses in Cornwall* in *The Cornish Church Guide* (Truro, 1928), p. 243.

[6] Allen, *CA*, pp. 162–64 ; *s.a. Early Christian Symbolism in Great Britain and Ireland before the Thirteenth Century* (London, 1887), Lect. ii. See H.

circular sun-symbol known to the pagan Celts with the Christian cross.[1]

The Chi-Rho monogram has never been found on the early monuments of Ireland.[2] It is possible that the circle around the cross is merely an artistic ornament, a halo surrounding the sacred symbol.[3]

Originally the representation of the cross within a circle occupied only part of the surface of the stone. The cross carved in relief on an upright fixed stone is chiefly found in Scotland (crosses of St. Madoes, Perthshire, and Aberlemno, Forfarshire)[4]; the cross incised on erect or recumbent tombstones is seen in Ireland. The best known slabs of this kind are those of Clonmacnois and Inis Cealtra.[5] The surface of these slab-stones presents the three following elements, either singly or in combination : (1) the cross, varying in design, (2) some simple decoration, (3) an inscription in the Gaelic language and characters. The inscription is very brief, generally consisting of the words OROIT (usually abbreviated OR) DO " a prayer for," followed by the name of the person whose grave is marked by the stone. Some of these slabs go back to the eighth and ninth centuries, as can be ascertained by the names which occur in the inscriptions.[6]

Not all the early stone crosses are burial monuments ; a large number of sculptured crosses mark the scene of some event the memory of which it was desired to perpetuate.[7]

Leclercq, art *Labarum* (*DACL*) ; Max Sulzberger, *Le symbole de la croix et les monogrammes de Jésus chez les premiers chrétiens* (*Byzantion*, II, 1925, pp. 393, 428).

[1] Coffey, *Guide*, pp. 85–86.

[2] R. A. S. Macalister, *Muiredach, abbot of Monasterboice* (890–923), *his Life and Surroundings* (Dublin, 1914), p. 67. Cf. G. Baldwin Brown, *The Arts*, V, p. 54.

[3] Macalister, *Muiredach*, *l. c.*

[4] Allen, *CA*, pp. 183, 185, with fig. ; *s.a. ECMS*, Figs. 227A, 227B, 309A, 309B.

[5] Macalister, *Mem. Slabs* ; *s.a. Inis Cealtra.*

[6] Macalister, *Mem. Slabs;* L.G., art. *Clonmacnois* (*DACL*, cols. 2019–23).

[7] Tirechán, pp. 25, 27, 28 ; *Vita Trip.*, pp. 106–107, 124–27, 138–39, 234–35, 236–37, 238–39 ; *Lismore*, l. 3970 ; Jocelin, *Vita Kentigerni*, 41 (pp. 232–34) ; *Vita Abbani*, 27 (*VSH*, I, p. 17) ; *Vita Barri*, 14 (p. 73) ; *Vita Cainnici*, 19, 31 (p. 159, 163) ; *Vita Carthagi*, 57, 79 (pp. 192–93, 199) ; *Vita Ciarani de Cluain*, 4 (p. 201) ; *Vita Comgalli*, 4 (*VSH*, II, p. 4) ; *Vita Declani*, 35 (p. 56) ; *Vita Endei*, 9, 27 (pp. 63, 72) ; *Vita Maedoc*, 13,

From the erect stone bearing a cross carved on its face was evolved by degrees the free-standing cross. First the stone is rounded at the top so as to follow the curve of the circle containing the cross, till in time both outlines meet in one. Then its surface contracts likewise at the base, forming beneath the rounded top what will in time become the shaft of the developed cross (wheel crosses of Grutne, of Conbelin, at Margam, Glamorganshire).[1] Simultaneously, by an inverse tendency, the summit and arms of the cross gradually emerge from the confining circle, whilst the shaft is lengthened below (Penmon Cross, Anglesey).[2] Finally, the stone, now reduced to the periphery of the cross, is pierced between the arms and the connecting ring from which they project. The evolution is now complete ; we have the free-standing cross, pierced with four holes around the meeting-point of its arms, of which there are numerous and varied specimens.

In Wales the cross properly so called is of small dimensions and often assumes the form of a Maltese cross within a circle, as at Nevern and Carew (Pembrokeshire) [3] ; it is mounted on a slender stele adorned on all faces with interlaced and geometric patterns, hardly ever with human or animal forms. This type is also found in Cornwall [4] ; but the one most commonly seen there is the wheel cross, bearing a Maltese cross on an unpierced disc and decorated either not at all or very rudely.[5]

The crosses of the Isle of Man display runes, animals and dragons.[6]

(p. 145) ; *Vita Munnu*, 13 (p. 231). Cf. G. Baldwin Brown, *The Arts in Early England*, V, p. 155.

[1] J. O. Westwood, *Lapidarium Walliae* (Oxford, 1876–79), Pl. xiv (2), xv ; Allen, *CA*, p. 187, Fig.

[2] Allen, *CA*, p. 185, Fig.

[3] Allen, *CA*, p. 191, Fig. ; *An Inventory of the Ancient Monuments of Wales and Monmouthshire*, VII, *County of Pembroke* (London, 1925), Figs. 85, 86, 211. Cf. Macalister, *AI*, p. 313.

[4] See Langdon, *op. cit.* ; Henderson, *op. cit.*

[5] " The majority of the Cornish crosses are of great antiquity, perhaps of the 8th and 9th centuries " (Henderson, p. 244). " It is true that the execution and ornament are inferior [to the Irish crosses], but Cornish *Moorstone*, or surface granite, has never been a suitable material for delicate carving " (p. 245).

[6] H. Bradley, *The Runic Crosses in the Isle of Man* (*The Academy*, 1886, pp. 126, 194, 213, 248) ; P. M. C. Kermode, *Manx Crosses* (London, 1907) ;

In Scotland few free-standing crosses are found with a circular ring like the great Irish crosses ; the rare examples of this type occur on the islands of the western coast (Iona, Islay) and do not appear to be of great age.[1] The upright cross-slabs of Scotland, either rectangular or tapering upwards, deserve special mention. The cross, carved in relief, is filled with ornamental designs (interlaced, spiral, fret patterns, etc.), and around it various other designs and figures are also sculptured in relief (animals, horsemen, biblical scenes, symbols). The symbols of Scottish sculpture are particularly numerous, curious and enigmatic. Very common are the double disc and Z-shaped rod ; the crescent and V-shaped rod ; arch or horseshoe ; mirror and comb ; serpent and Z-shaped rod ; various beasts, etc. The meaning of these is a problem so far unsolved.[2]

The beautiful " High Crosses " of Ireland, erected from the seventh or eighth to the twelfth century in cemeteries, near round towers or beside roadways, are the most artistic of all.[3] They are mounted on a socle. The shaft, generally square, the arms and the shrine-shaped top are divided into compartments, sometimes filled in with carvings of biblical scenes, the Fall of Man, the Sacrifice of Isaac, the Children in the Furnace, the Flight into Egypt, the Crucifixion, the Last Judgment, etc. : *pictura laicorum litteratura*.[4] " In a world where books were few and dear," writes Professor R. A. S. Macalister, " the unlettered were taught by symbols and by pictures, and it was for the instruction of such simple folk that this great art treasure was added to the riches of Ireland." [5]

Haakon Shetelig in *Opuscula archaeologica Oscari Montelio dicata* (Holmiae, 1913), pp. 391–403.
    [1] Allen and Anderson, *ECMS*, pp. LXVI–LXVII, 381–84, 387, 391–93.
    [2] Allen, *ECMS*, pp. 57–128, Figs. 180, 213, 263–65.
    [3] See F. Henry, *Origines*, p. 102.
    [4] Lists of biblical scenes : Romilly Allen, *On some Points of Resemblance between the Art of the early Sculptured Stones of Scotland and Ireland* (*PSAS*, XXXI, 1896–97, p. 323) ; Crawford, *Handbook*, ch. x. See Kingsley Porter, *Crosses and Culture*, Figs. 107–275.—No biblical scene is carved on the time-worn cross of Tuathgall at Bealin (Co. Westmeath), but it exhibits zoomorphic designs and a hunting scene, and also bears a Gaelic inscription in relief of considerable interest which has enabled Mlle. Françoise Henry to date it from *c.* A.D. 800. See F. Henry, *L'inscription de Bealin* (*RA*, 5th Ser., XXXII, 1930, pp. 110–15, Pl. IV and V).
    [5] Macalister, *Muiredach*, p. 66.

The finest specimens of these crosses are at Ahenny (Co. Tipperary), Kells (Co. Meath), Monasterboice (Co. Louth), Clonmacnois, Durrow (Co. Offaly), Castledermot, Moone (Co. Kildare), Drumcliff (Co. Sligo). The cross of Muiredach at Monasterboice, the most beautiful of all, is 17 feet 8 inches in height and dates from the tenth century, as do also those of Durrow and the " Cross of the Scriptures " at Clonmacnois.[1]

The only crosses in Great Britain which can be set beside these marvels of Irish art are the celebrated ones of Bewcastle (Cumberland) and Ruthwell (Dumfries), the former mutilated. Both these crosses are richly decorated like the Irish ones but loftier in height ; they are not, however, the work of Celtic sculptors and evidently belong to a different technique.[2]

§ 3.—WOOD, LEATHER AND METAL WORK

We have now to pass in hasty review the following objects : processional crosses, pastoral staffs, chalices and patens, portable bells and shrines.

The two early processional crosses which call for mention are those of Cong, now preserved in the National Museum of Dublin, in which a relic of the true cross was formerly enshrined,[3] and that of Clogher, preserved in the museum of the diocesan seminary of Monaghan. Both are of oak covered with laminae of copper or bronze remarkable for the designs, the enamels and filigree work with which they are enriched.[4] Both crosses date only from the twelfth century.

The pastoral staff in use in the insular countries in early

---

[1] " Cross na screaptra " (L.G., art. *Clonmacnois*, col. 2016).—H. C. Crawford, *A descriptive List of the early Irish Crosses* (*JRSAI*, XXXVII, 1907, pp. 187–239) ; *s.a. Handbook ;* Margaret Stokes, *The High Crosses of Durrow and Castledermot* (Dublin and London, 1898) ; *s.a. Notes on the High Crosses of Moone, Drumcliff, Termonfechin and Killamery* (*TRIA*, XXXI, 1896–1901, pp. 541–578) ; F. Henry, *Origines.*

[2] G. Baldwin Brown, *The Arts in Early England*, V (1921) ; Allen, *ECMS*, pp. 442–48 ; W. G. Collingwood, *Northumbrian Crosses of Pre-Norman Age* (London, 1927), pp. 82–98, 117–19, Figs. 101, 102, 135 ; A. W. Clapham, *English Romanesque Architecture before the Conquest* (Oxford, 1930), Pl. 11 ; F. Henry, *SI*, p. 164.

[3] M. Stokes, *ECAI*, Fig. 44 ; Allen, *CA*, p. 213.

[4] J. E. Mackenna, *The Clogher Relics* (*UJA*, VII, 1901).

times was of wood and of small size [1] ; it has even been asserted that it did not differ from a walking-stick.[2]   Not only bishops but abbots were equipped with it.   The earliest mention of an abbot's staff known is, I believe, that of St Columban's *cambutta*, which was sent after his death to his disciple St Gall [3] ; two fragments of it, encased in silver croziers, are still preserved in Bavaria, at Kempten on the Iller and at Füssen.[4]

Representations of the pastoral staff used in Ireland in early times may be seen on the socle of the north cross of Ahenny (ninth century), as well as on some other Irish or Scottish sculptured stones [5] ; in two miniatures in the Gospel-book of MacDurnan (tenth century) [6] ; and on the *cumdach* of the Stowe Missal.[7]

The manufacture of these staffs and their appurtenances (mountings, cases) seems to have formed a regular branch of Irish monastic art.   Among famous craftsmen are mentioned Tassach, who made a case for the *Bachall Ísa*, (St Patrick's staff),[8] and Daig MacCairill, who made divers articles pertaining to religious service, " *quaedam horum nuda, quaedam vero alia auro atque argento gemmisque pretiosis circumtexta.*" [9]   A note in the *Félire Oengusso* ranks Daig, who was the craftsman of Ciarán of Saigir, among the " three chief artisans of Ireland " —all three of them bishops, the two others being Tassach, St Patrick's craftsman, and Conlaed, St Brigit's craftsman. The same note credits him with having made 300 bells, 300 *bachalls* and 300 gospel-books.[10]

[1] See Coffey, *Guide*, Fig. 55 ; Crawford, *Handbook*, Figs. 147, 148.

[2] Lord Talbot de Malahide, *The Quigrich, or Crozier of St Fillan* (*AJ*, XVI, 1859, pp. 46–47) ; M. Stokes, *ECAI*, Pt. I, pp. 96–97.

[3] *V. sup.*, ch. v, § 3.—On the word " cambuta " see Du Cange, *Gloss.*, s.v. ; M. H. Longhurst, *English Ivories* (London, 1926), p. 36 ; J. J. Savage, *An Old Irish Gloss in Codex Laur.* xlv, 14 (*ZCP*, XVII, 1928, pp. 371–72).

[4] Margaret Stokes, *Six Months in the Apennines* (London, 1892), p. 14 ; Maud Joynt, *The Life of St Gall* (London, 1927), p. 101.

[5] Coffey, *Guide*, Fig. 55 ; Crawford, *Handbook*, Figs. 148, 149, 150 ; Allen, *ECMS*, Figs. 4, 4A (p. 7), Fig. 6 (p. 11), Fig. 370 (p. 357), Fig. 255B (p. 240).

[6] L.G., *L'art celtique chrétien* (*Revue de l'art chrétien*, 1911, Figs. 9, 10) ; s.a. art. *Crosse* (*Chrétientés celtiques*) in *DACL*, Fig. 3433.

[7] Warner, *Stowe*, II, Pl. vi.

[8] *LH*, I, p. 102 ; II, p. 185.

[9] Colgan, *ASH*, p. 133.

[10] *Fél. Oeng.*, pp. 186–87.

In the *Mabinogi* of Peredur the term *balawc* (cf. the Breton *baelec*) is used for a priest, a word derived from *baculus* : a proof that to the imagination of the Welsh and the Breton the priest appeared in the guise of an itinerant churchman.[1]

The *baculus* of a famous saint was preserved as a treasure. In Wales, Scotland and Ireland oaths were sworn on it as on a relic.[2] Troops marching to battle hoisted it aloft like a palladium.[3] Many staffs were credited with healing powers.[4]

To guard against injury and the risk of loss, it was confided to the guard of a family, generally the *plebilis progenies* of the saint, who were bound to hand down the precious deposit in hereditary succession to their descendants. This accounts for the fact that so many ancient pastoral staffs have been preserved to our own days in the British Isles.[5] Some of the primitive wooden staffs, when worn or damaged by use, were embellished, plated with gold and silver, encased in bronze croziers, sometimes even adorned with jewels, according to the taste of following ages. But such croziers still recall by their shape the primitive walking-stick; the crook, instead of forming a circular or spiral curve, has a flattened end which falls vertically. The collar and head of the crozier were divided into little rectangular or lozenge-shaped compartments filled as a rule with filigree work.[6]

We possess two beautiful specimens of these richly adorned croziers, that of Clonmacnois, measuring 3 feet 2¼ inches in height, now preserved in the National Museum of Dublin,[7] and that of Lismore, the property of the Duke of Devonshire, measuring 3 feet 4 inches in height, preserved at Lismore Castle (Co. Waterford).[8] From an inscription engraved

---

[1] *Le roman de Pérédur*, ed. J. Le Roux (Bibliothèque bretonne armoricaine publiée par la Faculté des lettres de Rennes, V, Rennes, 1923, 87, p. 139). See E. Ernault, *Glossaire moyen-breton* (Paris, 1895), II, p. 50 ; Chevalier, *Essai*, p. 364. Cf. " baculatus " : *Vita Cainnici*, 38 (*VSH*, I, 166. Cf. II, p. 381, Glossary) ; " baglar " in the *Islendigabók* (Knut Gjerst, *History of Iceland*, London, 1924, p. 22).

[2] Giraldus, *IK*, I, 1 (pp. 17–18) ; *Breviarium Aberdonense*, Vol. II, in festo S. Servani, fol. xvi ; C. Plummer, *VSH*, I, pp. cv, n. 9, clxxvi (*introd.*).

[3] M. Stokes, *ECAI*, Pt. I, p. 100.

[4] C. Plummer, *VSH*, I, pp. clxxvi–clxxvii (*introd.*).

[5] See L.G., art. *Crosse (Chrétientés celtiques)* (*DACL*).

[6] Allen, *CA*, pp. 205 ff.

[7] Coffey, *Guide*, Pl. xv.

[8] Allen, *CA*, Pl. facing p. 206.

on the latter crozier by its maker Nechtán we learn that it was made for Niall Mac Aeducáin, who was bishop of Lismore from 1090 to 1113.[1]

No staff was more highly venerated in Ireland than that of St Patrick, the *Bachall Ísa*, so called from a legend that the saint had received it from the hands of Our Lord himself.[2] It was burnt in the time of the Reformation (1538) as being an object of superstition.[3]

In the Museum of Scottish antiquities at Edinburgh, the British Museum, the National Museum of Dublin and some private collections, a fair number of early Celtic staffs are still preserved.[4]

A note in the Book of Armagh states that Patrick " *portauit per Sininn* [5] *secum .l. clocos, .l. patinos .l. calices, altaria, libros legis, aeuangelii libros, et reliquit illos in locis nouis.*" [6] Patrick's disciple Assicus,[7] a craftsman-bishop like those already mentioned, was a skilful worker in bronze (*faber aereus*). He fashioned various liturgical articles, including altars, cases for books (*bibliothicas*) and patens, among the last three square ones which Tirechán affirms he had seen.[8]

The two-handled chalice of Ardagh in the National Museum of Dublin, thoroughly Celtic in its decoration, may possibly go back to the eighth century.[9] Gold, silver, bronze, lead, enamel, glass, amber and mica are the materials of which it is composed.[10] The chalice of Kremsmünster (Upper Austria), of nielloed bronze inlaid with silver, is by several archaeologists considered akin to Irish goldsmith's work.[11]

---

[1] M. Stokes, *ECAI*, Pt. I, p. 84.

[2] *Vita Trip.*, pp. 30–31 ; Giraldus, *TH*, III, 34 (p. 180). Cf. Bury, *Pat.*, p. 320 ; Lawlor, *BLM*, p. 54, n. 1.

[3] Todd, *Book of Obits and Martyrology of the Cathedral Church of the Holy Trinity* (Dublin, 1844), pp. VIII–XX.

[4] *See* L.G., art. *Crosse*.

[5] The Shannon.

[6] *LA*, p. 16.

[7] Another name for Tassach.

[8] Tirechán, p. 22. Cf. *Vita Trip.*, pp. 96–97.

[9] M. Stokes, *Inquiry as to the Date of the Tara Brooch and Chalice found near Ardagh* (*PRIA*, 2nd Ser., II, 1879–88, pp. 451–55) ; G. Baldwin Brown, art. *Art (Celtic)* in *ERE* ; Allen, *CA*, Fig. facing p. 216 ; M. Stokes, *ECAI*, Fig. 31 ; Coffey, *Guide*, Pl. V, VI.

[10] Allen, *CA*, p. 216.

[11] H. Leclercq, art. *Calice* (*DACL*, cols. 1630–32).—A silver chalice (not

We have just seen that, according to the Book of Armagh, Patrick brought fifty bells with him across the Shannon. The text alludes to the small portable bells, 4 to 11 inches in height, the only kind known in the early Celtic communities. Nearly all the districts evangelized or visited by British or Irish saints preserve some specimens of these little bells, to which the lasting veneration of the devout still clings. In Ireland we hear of a bishop receiving a pastoral staff and a bell among other insignia at his consecration.[1] These small bells were used to summon the monks and the faithful to church. They were also employed, when occasion required, as instruments of malediction ; the saint who had been offended by some chieftain cursed him, at the same time striking his bell with the butt of his staff. The bell of St Carthach of Rahen and Lismore is styled by one of his biographers " *clog rabhaydh Blaithmecc, id est, cymbalum extinguens Blaithmecc, eo quod per pulsacionem eius rex Blaithmecc cum semine suo extinctus est uelocius.*" [2]

In the Book of Armagh, as we have just seen, bells are denoted by the Latin plural *clocos*. Adamnân, abbot of Iona, uses the singular form *clocca*.[3] According to linguists, this latter term is the original Celtic word itself, from which are derived the O.Ir. *cloc* and the Welsh and Breton *cloch*, and which later passed into the Teutonic languages (German *Glocke*, English *clock*, etc.).[4]

The oldest specimens of these portable bells are of extremely simple make and wholly devoid of artistic elaboration. Two

necessarily of Celtic origin) found near St. Austell (Cornwall) is preserved in the British Museum.

[1] Additions to Tirechán's Memoir (*LA*, p. 35). A bell is carved on the cross of Old Kilcullen (Co. Kildare) : Coffey, *Guide*, Fig. 65 ; Crawford, *Handbook*, Fig. 149 and p. 73.

[2] *Vita Carthagi*, 58 (*VSH*, I, p. 193). " The writer takes the name as a sentence : ' clocc ro baid Blaithmacc,' *i.e.*, the bell which destroyed B. ; more probably it is : ' clocc robaid Blaithmeicc,' *i.e.*, the bell of the proclamation (*i.e.*, excommunication) of Blathmac " (Plummer's note). Cf. *The Bodleian Amra Coluimb Cille*, ed. Wh. Stokes (*R. Cel.*, XX, 1899, p. 427-28) : *The death of Muirchertach mac Erca*, ed. Wh. Stokes (*R. Cel.*, XXIII, 1902, p. 403) ; C. Plummer, *VSH*, I, p. clxxvii (*introd.*).

[3] Adam., *Vita Col.*, I, 8 ; III, 23 (pp. 24, 159).

[4] G. Dottin, *Le celtique "clocca"* (*Revue des études anciennes*, XXII, 1920, pp. 39–40). Cf. J. Vendryes, *R. Cel.*, XXXIX, 1922, pp. 403–404 ; R. Bauerreiss, *Irische Frühmissionäre in Südbayern* (*Wissenschaftliche Festgabe zum zwölfhundertjährigen Jubiläum des hl. Korbinian*, München, 1924, pp. 48–49).

plates of sheet-iron, riveted together, bent into a quadrangular shape and finished off with a handle at the top and an
iron clapper inside, the whole being then plunged into a
bronze bath, such are the materials and method of construction.[1] St Patrick's bell, now preserved in Dublin, is said to
be the oldest iron relic of the Christian period.[2]

From the ninth century at latest small bronze bells began
to be cast, which still preserved the quadrangular shape of the
earlier iron ones. Those of St Fillan (Edinburgh Museum),[3]
of Clogher and Armagh (Dublin),[4] of St Goulven (at Goulien,
near Pont-Croix), of Saint-Pol-de-Léon (Finistère), and of
St Mériadec (at Stival, Morbihan) are of this description.[5]
Some of them bear inscriptions.

Artistic elaboration found its scope in the making of metal
caskets, adorned with plates of silver, tallow-topped gems and
gold filigree work, which were intended to serve as cases or
shrines for the most highly prized bells. The oldest of these
shrines, those of St Patrick's bell (in the Dublin Museum)[6]
and of St Culan's bell (in the British Museum),[7] date from
the end of the eleventh or the twelfth centuries. The former
is a work of truly artistic stamp, which would be an ornament
in the window of any jeweller's shop at the present day.

The shrines intended to contain relics are of rectangular
form with a roof-shaped top. They are of wood, generally
yew, covered with plates of metal, bronze, copper or silver,
decorated with the designs familiar to Celtic craftsmen, interlaced patterns, spirals, cruciform ornaments, etc.[8] In the
National Museum of Dublin is preserved a shrine found in
1891 in the waters of Lough Erne, which it is believed may

---

[1] L.G., art. *Clochettes (Celtiques)* (*DACL*).
[2] Allen, *CA*, pp. 193 ff. ; Coffey, *Guide*, pp. 47–49, Pt. 1, Fig. 51 ; M.
Stokes, *ECAI*, p. 58.
[3] *Catalogue of the National Museum of Antiquities of Scotland* (Edinburgh,
1892), pp. 282–83.
[4] Coffey, *Guide*, pp. 65–67 ; Figs. 64, 65.
[5] Allen, *CA*, pp. 199 ff. ; Rosenzweig, *Répertoire archéologique du Morbihan*,
1863, col. 120 ; Abgrall, *Notice sur quatre vieilles cloches* (*BSAF*, XXII, 1895,
pp. 17–23).
[6] Coffey, *Guide*, pp. 47–49 ; Pl. IX, X ; Allen, *CA*, Pl. facing p. 204.
[7] M. Stokes, *ECAI*, Figs. 19, 20.
[8] On the cult of relics in early Irish Christianity see C. Plummer,
VSH, I, pp. CXXVII-CXXIX (*introd.*) ; Ryan, *Monast.*, pp. 358–59.

perhaps date from the ninth century.[1] The Monymusk shrine, preserved from time immemorial at Monymusk House in Aberdeenshire, is a box hollowed out of a piece of wood, covered with plates of bronze and silver, decorated with zoomorphic designs and trumpet-patterns and set off with enamels.[2] The shrine of the Museum of Copenhagen bears runes similar to those observed on the monumental crosses of the Isle of Man.[3] The shrine discovered in 1906 at Melhus in Norway, to which country it had been taken as plunder by the Vikings, like the Copenhagen one, displays trumpet patterns, but has no trace of interlaced work or zoomorphic elements. It is believed to be the oldest of all and to go back to the seventh century.[4] None of the shrines mentioned is adorned with human figures. But the bronze shrine of St Maedóc (Dublin), made probably in the eleventh century, originally possessed a large number of human forms, of which now only eleven remain on the front panel and one (David playing the harp) on one side ; they are treated with great uniformity, especially as regards costume.[5]

In order to carry shrines and liturgical books for a distance, leather bags furnished with a strap were used. The National Museum of Dublin preserves the satchel of the so-called shrine of St Maedóc ; it is decorated on all four sides with interlaced and other patterns.[6] Besides it only two others remain, that of the missal of Corpus Christi College in Oxford and that of the Book of Armagh in Trinity College, Dublin.[7] A bag or satchel specially intended to carry books was called in Irish

[1] Allen, *CA*, Fig. facing p. 210 ; Coffey, *Guide*, Fig. 50.

[2] J. Anderson, *Scotland in early Christian Times* (Edinburgh, 1881, first ser.), frontispiece and p. 249 ; *s.a. Architecturally-shaped Shrines and other Reliquaries of the early Celtic Church in Scotland and Ireland* (*PSAS*, XLIV, 1909–10, Fig. 2, p. 261).

[3] J. Anderson, *op. cit.* (1881), p. 248 ; *s.a. PSAS*, XLIV, Fig. 7, p. 270.

[4] J. Anderson, *PSAS*, XLIV, p. 272 ; Figs. 8, 9 ; Th. Petersen, *A Celtic Reliquary found in a Norwegian Burialmound* (Trondhjem, 1907) ; A. W. Brögger, *Funde aus Norwegen* (*Praehistorische Zeitschrift*, I, 1909, Fig. 4).

[5] M. Stokes, *Observations on the Breac Moedog* (*Archaeologia*, XLIII, 1871, pp. 131–50) ; Coffey, *Guide*, pp. 50–51 ; Fig. 52 ; Pl. xi.

[6] Coffey, *Guide*, p. 53 ; Fig. 53 ; J. J. Buckley, *Some early ornamented Leatherwork* (*JRSAI*, XLV, 1915, pp. 300–309).

[7] *The Book of Trinity College*, 1591–1891 (Belfast, 1892), pp. 164–65 ; J. J. Buckley, *art. cit.*

a *tiag lebair* (book wallet or satchel).[1] The word *tiag* (gen. sing. *téige*, dat. *téig*) is an early derivative from the Latin *theca* (Gk. θήκη) and is used in Middle Irish literature of a bag or wallet of various description, often of a bag intended to carry provisions on a journey, but also of one carried by a labourer, presumably for his tools and gear.[2] In one of the earliest instances of the word, in the *Saltair na Rann*, it is applied to the wallet into which David put the stones with which he meant to kill Goliath and corresponds to the *peram pastoralem* of the Vulgate (1 Reg. xvii, 40).[3] The *tiag lebair* seems to have been used by monks and churchmen, especially on journeys, to carry their gospels and liturgical books, sometimes relics and also provender for the way, and to have formed a regular part of their equipment. It was probably made of leather, and, from different texts in which it is spoken of, we gather that it was furnished with a strap and was carried on the shoulders like a knapsack or suspended from the neck,[4] and could be hung on a peg or rack when not in use. It formed, in fact, a portable bookcase, sufficing the needs of an age when books were few and possessed by few. The term *tiag lebair* may have been suggested by the Latin *bibliotheca*, which in a few religious texts is used of a receptacle or case for books, *e.g.*, in the Book of Armagh, where we read that Assicus made *bibliothicas quadratas* (these however may possibly have been of metal)[5] ; but the Latin word *theca* occurs alone in the same sense,[6] also *cetha*[7] and more frequently *scetha*,[8] both of which may be corruptions of *theca*. The

---

[1] *Fél. Oeng.*, pp. 198, 204 ; *Lismore*, l. 968.

[2] *Betha Colmáin*, ed. K. Meyer, 60, 3 ; *Lebar Laigen* (*Book of Leinster*), Facs., 126ᵇ, 22 ; 303ᵃ, 48 ; 304ᵇ, 33 ; *Betha Mochuda*, xxi (32) (*BNE*, I, p. 297) ; *AU*, *s.a.* 1012.

[3] *Saltair na Rann*, ed. Wh. Stokes (1883), l. 5868.

[4] A satchel suspended from the neck may be seen in Scottish sculptures : Bressay stone (now Edinburgh Museum), Allen, *ECMS*, Figs. 4, 4A (p. 7) ; Papil stone (now Edinburgh Museum), *ib.*, Fig. 6 (p. 11).—" . . . pendentem collo capsellam " (Walahfrid Strabo, *Vita Galli*, I, 11, p. 293).

[5] " . . . suus liber . . . in sua bibliotheca " (*Vita Moling*, 4 : *VSH*, II, p. 192).

[6] " sed et thecas, in quibus multa inerant librorum volumina, et reliquiarum capsas abstulit " (Willibald, *Vita Bonifatii*, 8, ed. W. Levison, 1905, p. 50).

[7] " sarcina cethe, que erat de pelle facta, in qua euangelium positum erat " (*Vita Ciarani de Cluain*, 27 : *VSH*, I, p. 211).

[8] " duas scethas libris plenas suis humeris imposuit " (*Vita Carthagi*,

terms *capsella* [1] and *capella* [2] are also found in early Latin hagiographical literature for a wallet or case for carrying books and relics.

Another article which seems to have formed part of a travelling ecclesiastical outfit is denoted by the Irish word *pólaire*, which is by philologists derived from the Latin *pugillaris* and by Whitley Stokes translated " writing-tablets," [3] though this meaning does not appear satisfactory in all cases. The earliest instance we have of the word is in the Book of Armagh, where we are told that Fiacc, on being consecrated bishop, received from St Patrick a *poolire* along with a bell, a staff and a *menstir* or service-set, the whole contained in a *cumtach* (or *cumdach*).[4] In the *Tripartite Life* we read (in two different versions) of St Patrick journeying on foot with nine companions, the youngest of whom, Benén or Benignus, brought up the rear carrying his *pólaire* [5] (or, according to one of the versions, Patrick's *pólaire*) [6] on the back of his shoulders. In a gloss on one of these passages, the word is explained as equivalent to *tiag lebair*,[7] but in a passage in the Lismore Lives of the Saints the *pólaire* and the *tiag lebair* appear as separate items in an ecclesiastical equipment.[8]

In Ireland the most treasured books were preserved in rectangular caskets known by the name of *cumdach*. The *cumdachs* of the Books of Durrow, Armagh and Kells, executed

18 ; *VSH*, I, p. 177) ; " aperiens iam Fyachra sanctus scetham suam ad ducendum inde librum baptismi " (*Vita Comgalli*, 58 : *VSH*, II, p. 21).

[1] *Vita vetustissima Galli*, 7.—*Capsella* containing relics of the Blessed Virgin (Walahfrid, *Vita Galli*, I, 11, p. 293).—*Capsella* in which St Gall used to place his hairshirt and chains (*Ib.*, I, 32, p. 309).

[2] " Capellam (*i.e.*, capsam) qua itinerans [Landolaus ep. Trevisanus] utebatur, cum reliquiis et libris et omnibus utensilibus sacris " (Ekkehard IV, *Casus S. Galli*, A.D. 895 : *MG. Scr.*, II, p. 82).—On the text " libros in pelliceo reconditos sacculo " (Adam., *Vita Col.*, II, 8), see W. Reeves's note, pp. 116–17.

[3] Cf. *Vita Trip.*, II, p. 655 (index of Irish words).

[4] Additions to Tirechán's Memoir (*LA*, p. 35). Cf. *Vita Trip.*, p. 190.

[5] *Vita Trip.*, p. 46.

[6] Leabhar Breac Homily on St Patrick, ed. Wh. Stokes, *Vita Trip.*, II, p. 458.

[7] ms. H. 3, 18, p. 523 (*Vita Trip.*, p. LI).

[8] *Betha Coluim Chille* (Lismore, l. 969).—" Pugillarius " = writing-tablet in *Hibernensis* (XXXVII, 3, p. 132) ; and Clark (*St Gall*, p. 27) writes : " Von Arx (*Berichtigungen u. Zusätze*, p. 29) conjectured that it was they [the Irish] who introduced writing-tablets into Germany, because in Codex 242, p. 28, they are called *pugilares Scottorum*."

between the ninth and eleventh centuries, are lost ; but we still possess those of the Gospel-book of St Molaisse (dating from 1001–1025),[1] of the Stowe Missal (1023–1052 in its oldest parts),[2] of the Cathach or Psalter of St Columba (1084),[3] of the Book of Dimma (1150),[4] and, finally, the one known as the *Domnach Airgid* (*dominica argenti*, " house of silver ").[5] This last includes three small cases fitting one into another, the smallest being of yew, the second of copper plated with silver, the third of silver plated with gold. An inscription proves that this last case was executed as late as the fourteenth century ; the others are older. It was long believed that this *cumdach* was intended to hold the so-called St Patrick's Gospel-book, a manuscript of the eighth century which now belongs to the Royal Irish Academy and is itself known by the name of the receptacle ascribed to it as the *Domnach Airgid*.

No medieval book-shrine is now known to exist in Scotland.[6]

The *flabellum* (Ir. *culebad*, O.Ir. *culebath*) or eucharistic fan was in use in Ireland in the early Middle Ages. It is mentioned in various texts of this epoch,[7] and the thing itself is represented in ancient Irish illuminations, notably in the Book of Kells.[8] But no specimen has come down to us, nor have we any of those small vessels called *chrismals* employed by monks for carrying the Blessed Sacrament with them when going to work in the fields or on voyages, of which frequent mention is made in medieval Irish and British texts.[9]

[1] Coffey, *Guide*, Pl. viii ; M. Stokes, *ECAI*, Figs. 34, 36.

[2] Allen, *CA*, Fig. facing p. 170 ; *Stowe*, II, pp. xliv–lviii, Pl. i–vi.

[3] Lawlor, *Cathach*, pp. 390–96 ; Pl. xxxv–xxxviii.

[4] M. Stokes, *ECAI*, Fig. 38 ; H. S. Monck Mason, *Description* (*TRIA*, XIII) ; Petrie, *Christian Inscriptions in the Irish Language* (ed. M. Stokes), II, pp. 100–102.

[5] J. H. Bernard, *On the Domnach Airgid MS.* (*TRIA*, XXX, 1893, pp. 304, 305) ; E. C. R. Armstrong and H. J. Lawlor, *The Domnach Airgid* (*PRIA*. XXXIV, Sect. C, 1918). Cf. G. H. Orpen, *EHR*, XXXIII, 1918, p. 533– Cf. Kenney, *Sources*, I, pp. 638–39.

[6] J. Anderson, *Scotland in early Christian Times*, I, p. 145.

[7] Gloss in the Karlsruhe Cod. Augiensis cxcv (Stokes and Strachan, *TP*, II, p. 8) ; *AU*, *s.a.* 1034, 1128. Cf. T. Olden, *PRIA*, II, Ser., II, 1886, pp. 355–58 ; K. Meyer, *Contributions to Irish Lexicography*, I, 1906, p. 558.

[8] Westwood, *MO*, Pl. liii, Fig. 7. Cf. Warren, *Lit.*, p. 144.

[9] *Poenitentiale Cummeani*, xi, 3, ed. Zettinger, p. 521 ; Giraldus, *TH*, ii, 19 (p. 102). Cf. Ryan, *Monast.*, p. 352 ; M. Cahen and M. Olsen, *L'inscrip-*

§ 4.—Manuscripts and Illumination

Once Christianity was introduced, it became necessary to provide for the new needs, intellectual, liturgical and spiritual, of the believers ; and the scribes set resolutely to work to copy manuscripts in large number, both profane and sacred, grammatical tracts, works of the ancients, books of the Bible, liturgical books, treatises of the Fathers, etc. We shall here have to confine ourselves almost entirely to the palaeographical achievements of the Irish, for the manuscripts coming from the other Celtic countries are far less numerous and ancient, as well as less interesting from an aesthetic point of view. The Irish of the Middle Ages nowhere displayed more manual dexterity, ingenuity, resourcefulness and invention than in the art of copying and adorning religious manuscripts, and many of their works deserve to be classed among the fairest specimens of calligraphy and illumination now extant.

The scribes were held in high respect in monasteries, as were likewise secular scribes in following ages. The Annals of Ulster record the death in 821 (= 822) of Macriaghoil úa Magléni, scribe and bishop, and abbot of Birr ; he has been identified with Mac Regol (more correctly Mac Réguil), the scribe who wrote a celebrated gospel-book now preserved in the Bodleian Library.[1] The Annals and other texts furnish numerous examples in the eighth, ninth and tenth centuries of scribes who were similarly honoured with episcopal rank. The oldest Irish ecclesiastical law places the scribe on the same footing as the bishop, the anchorite and the *excelsus princeps* in regard to the penalty inflicted for violence perpetrated against their persons.[2]

Under the authority of the chief scribe, there worked in the monastery scriptorium (if indeed we may venture to use that term, for it is not known whether the early Celtic monasteries were provided with an apartment specially set aside

---

tion runique du coffret de Mortain (Collection linguistique publiée par la Société de linguistique de Paris, XXXII, Paris, 1930, pp. 44–54) ; L. G., *Jahrbuch für Liturgiewissenschaft* (1930), X, 1931, pp. 322–23.

[1] ms. Auct. D. ii. 19.

[2] *Hibernensis*, i, 29 ; iii, 1 ; iv, 6 (pp. 138, 140, 142). See *AU*, index (s.v. *scribes*).

for the scribes) a whole band of subaltern copyists, to whom their task seemed sometimes irksome and monotonous. They readily took into their confidence the parchment on which they toiled. The *marginalia* and colophons of manuscripts give us intimate details concerning the life of these workers with pen and brush.[1]

Besides the trite marginal comments which often recur in manuscripts of the Middle Ages, such as : *Tres digiti scribunt sed totum corpus laborat.—Sicut naviganti dulcis est portus, ita scriptori novissimus versus.—Vinum scriptori detur de meliori*, etc., in Irish manuscripts we come across many original remarks, some pious, others plaintive, others naïve, others facetious. Some are written in Latin, others in Irish. A few examples may be given. Complaints concerning bad materials : " The vellum is defective and the writing " ; " New vellum and bad ink to say nothing else " (St. Gall Stiftsbibl. 904 ; *Thes. Palaeohib.*, II, pp. xxi–xxii).—Cold : " A blessing on the soul of Fergus. Amen. I am very cold " (*ibid*). In a letter written in 764 Cuthbert, abbot of Wearmouth and Jarrow, complains of the delay caused in the work of the scribes by the cold and inclemency of a severe winter.[2]—Fatigue : " Let no reader blame that script, for my arm is cramped through excess of labour " (Annals of Loch Cé, II, 328) ; " Oh ! my hand " (St. Gall Stiftsbibl. 904).—Rapid work : " That column was written very slowly " (St. Gall Stiftsbibl. 904) ; " Three pen-dips did that last column " (Book of Armagh, ed. Gwynn, p. 151) ; " Dubtach copied these verses in a brief space of time ; pardon, reader, the errors you may notice " (Leyden Universiteitsbibl. F. 67, fo. 7^v) ; " This page has not been written very slowly " (St. Gall Stiftsbibl. 904).—Invocations and requests for prayer : " May Mary and Patrick help my hand " (Rawl. B. 487, fo. 35^v) ; " A prayer for Maelbrigte, *qui scripsit hunc librum;* the slaying of Cormac MacCarthy by Turlough O'Brien " (Harl. 1802, fo. 60); " *Horum ergo lectorem ammoneo experimentorum, ut pro me misello peccatore*

---

[1] See C. Plummer, *On the Colophons and Marginalia of Irish Scribes* (*PBA*, 1926). There is a reference to the division of labour between the scribe and the illuminator in Ricemarch's verses (Ricemarch, *PM*, I, p. 29).

[2] *MG. Epist.*, III, p. 405.

eorundem craxatore [1] *Christum iudicem saeculorum exorare non neglegat* " (Colophon of Adamnán's *De locis sanctis*).—Various remarks : " *Sudet qui legat, difficilis est ista pagina* " ; " *Tertia hora* " ; " *Tempus est prandii* " ; "Nightfall and time for supper " (St. Gall Stiftsbibl. 904) ; " Alas O hand, how much white vellum hast thou written ! Thou wilt make famous the vellum, while thou thyself wilt be the bare top of a faggot of bones " (Trin. Coll. H. 3, 18, p. 478) ; " It is pleasant for us to-day, O incluse Moelbrigte, in the incluse's cell in Mainz, on the Thursday before the feast of Peter, in the first year of my sentence, that is, in the year of the killing of Diarmait, king of Leinster ; and this is the first year I came from Scotland (Albain) *in peregrinitate mea. Et scripsi hunc librum pro caritate tibi et Scotis omnibus, id est Hibernensibus, quia sum ipse Hibernensis* " (Cod. Palatino-Vaticanus 830, fo. 33 ; reflections of a companion of the chronicler Marianus Scottus).

Some writers are inclined to regard these *marginalia* as tags of " written conversations " carried on between the copyists, who were compelled by the monastic rule to keep silence.[2] It is possible that this may be the explanation of some. But many are mere *probationes pennae* ; a large number are the effusions of sad or weary hearts ; finally, many—those, for instance, requesting prayer—are obviously addressed to future readers.

At the end of the codex the scribe or illuminator seldom failed to implore the prayers of the reader in a humble and urgent colophon. At the end of his Gospel-book MacRegol writes the following words : " *Macregol depincxit hoc euangelium : quicumque legerit et intelligerit istam narrationem orat pro macreguil scriptori.*" Although often several scribes collaborated in copying the same manuscript, it might happen that the one who finished it, or perhaps the chief of the band, did not scruple to draw up the colophon as if he alone had written the whole.[3]

---

[1] Instead of " scribere " the Irish often used the verb " caraxare," also written " charaxare ; craxare ; crassare ; xraxare " (see Fowler in Adam., *Vita Col.*, p. 2).

[2] W. M. Lindsay, *Early Irish minuscule Script* (St. Andrew's University Publications, VI), Oxford, 1910, p. 42 ; R. A. S. Macalister, *Muiredach*, p. 64–66.

[3] W. M. Lindsay, *op. cit.*, pp. 5, 6, 36.

Minute examination of some of these colophons has led to interesting discoveries. R. I. Best has succeeded in proving that in those (four in number) of the so-called Book of Dimma the name Dimma was substituted for that of the real scribe of the Gospels.[1] The forger who made this substitution at the end of the tenth or beginning of the eleventh century no doubt wished to have it believed that the Gospel-book was the very one written miraculously in forty days by one Dimma, who is mentioned in a Life of St Cronán, the founder of Roscrea.[2]

The colophon of the Book of Durrow (written on what is now folio 12^v) has also given rise to discussion. It is drawn up as follows :

" *Rogo beatitudinem tuam sc̄e praesbiter patrici ut quicumque hunc libellum manu tenuerit meminerit columbae scriptoris. qui hoc scripsi [mi]himet euangelium. per xii dierum spatium. gatia dni nri s.s.*"

Can the author of these lines have been Columba, abbot of Iona ? That is one of the questions raised. However, it is the concluding part of the colophon which is most likely to arouse the reader's curiosity. If this manuscript containing the four gospels was, as is asserted in the colophon, actually written in the space of twelve days, it must be admitted that the feat is one which well nigh passes belief. The Book of Durrow contains 245 leaves ; of these the four gospels alone occupy folios 14^r to 234^r. This would give a daily task of more than eighteen leaves. It is true that an even more extraordinary performance has been placed to the credit of Ferdomnach, the scribe of the Book of Armagh, for he is said to have written the whole gospel of St Matthew in a single day, September 21, the festival of the Evangelist. Such, at least, was the interpretation at first given by Professor Lindsay to Ferdomnach's statement written at the end of St. Matthew's gospel (fo. 53^v) : *explicit . . . scriptum. atque finitum in feria Mattei.*[3] But Professor Lindsay has since recognized his error ; he had overlooked the full stop after " *scriptum.*" Ferdomnach was indicating the day on which his task of

---

[1] R. I. Best, *On the " subscriptiones " of the Book of Dimma* (Hermathena, XX, 1926, pp. 84–100).

[2] *Vita Cronani*, 9 (*VSH*, II, p. 24).

[3] W. M. Lindsay, *Notes on Two Manuscripts from Irish Scriptoriums* (Hermathena, XVIII, 1914, pp. 44–45).

copying was ended, not that on which it was begun.[1] With regard to the Book of Durrow, Professor Lindsay believes that " *Columba scriptor* " was really St Columba of Iona, but is of opinion that the colophon was copied from the original manuscript into the Book of Durrow by a devotee of the saint ; so that it would have been the original manuscript which was written by St Columba in the space of twelve days.

St Columba left behind him the reputation of an indefatigable scribe. The closing scenes of his life recall in some measure the death of the Venerable Bede ; but, whereas the latter showed himself a commentator and teacher to the very end, Adamnán recounts that, on the very eve of his death, the abbot of Iona still wished to transcribe a few verses of the Psalter.[2]

Another Irishman, Marianus Scottus of Ratisbon († 1184/1185), also furnishes a fine example of *Schreiblust*. " Such great talent for writing did Divine Providence confer on Blessed Marianus," his biographer tells us, " that with his speedy pen he completed many extensive volumes. To tell the truth without any dissimulation, among all the achievements which the Divine Mercy deigned to work through the instrumentality of that man, I deem worthy of most praise and admiration, and I myself admire most, the fact that, with scanty food and clothing, assisted by his brothers both of the Upper and the Lower Monastery, who prepared the parchment, he, for the sake of an eternal reward, wrote through with his own hand, not once or twice, but innumerable times, the books of the Old and New Testament with their prefaces. Moreover, during the same time he had written many little books and many manual psalters for poor widows and clerks of the same city (Ratisbon), for the benefit of his soul, without any hope of earthly reward. Moreover, many monastic communities which, recruited from Ireland through faith and charity and the desire to imitate Blessed Marianus, inhabit Bavaria and Franconia as *peregrini*, are supplied for the most part with the writings from his hand." [3]

[1] W. M. Lindsay, *The Colophon of the Durrow Book* appended to Lawlor, *Cathach*, pp. 403–407. Cf. Lawlor, *Cathach*, p. 317 ; Kenney, *Sources*, I, p. 631.
[2] Adam., *Vita Col.*, III, 23 (p. 157).
[3] *Vita Mariani Ratisp.*, II, 9 (Boll., *AS.*, Febr., II, p. 367).

We have seen that scribes frequently had occasion to complain of the roughness of their parchment. The parchment used by the Irish during the early Middle Ages was in fact much thicker and coarser than that in use on the Continent in the same period. Nevertheless, the parchment of the Book of Kells is very fine and in places even transparent. The skin of sheep, calves and goats was used. As regards quality, the writers were not very exacting ; there are occasionally holes in the leaves ; sometimes sorry clippings of insufficient size take the place of a leaf. The instrument employed for writing was the quill of a swan, goose or raven.[1]

To save time and parchment the scribes made use of numerous abbreviations. The Irish had their own special system of abbreviation, well known to palaeographers.[2]

During the earlier centuries of the Middle Ages, they used chiefly two kinds of script, both derived from the Latin script : a semi-uncial of a peculiar type, preserving however the rounded forms of the Roman semi-uncial, and a minuscule with fine and more or less pointed letters, the angularity of which became more pronounced as time went on.

The same letter appears in different forms sometimes on the same page. Two forms of *d* are found in the semi-uncial ; the minuscule has likewise two forms of *d*, as well as of *a*, *e* and *r* ; the letters *g* and *t* have nearly the same shape in semi-uncial and minuscule. The cross-bar of *f* is placed lower in the semi-uncial than in the minuscule, sometimes almost at the end of the down-stroke. The treatment of the minuscule *s* and that of *g* both in semi-uncial and minuscule, while not exclusively Irish, are particularly consistent in Scottic script.

The Irish semi-uncial probably took shape about the sixth century.[3] " To Ireland," says E. A. Lowe, " belongs the

[1] W. Wattenbach, *Das Schriftwesen im Mittelalter*, 3rd ed., Leipzig, 1896 ; W. Reeves, *Early Irish Calligraphy* (*UJA*, VIII, 1860, pp. 221, 222, 293).

[2] W. M. Lindsay, *Notae Latinae* (Cambridge, 1915), pp. 498–500 ; L. Schiaparelli, *Note*, pp. 172 ff., 191–228 ; *s.a. Avviamento allo studio delle abbreviature latine nel medioevo* (Firenze, 1926) ; R. I. Best, *Palaeographical notes* (*Ériu*, VII, pp. 117–20) ; R. I. Best and O. Bergin, *Lebor na Huidre* (Dublin, 1929), pp. xxiv–xxvii ; R. Thurneysen, *Lat./. = ir. Edón* (*ZCP*, XVIII, 1929–30, pp. 427–28) ; F. E. Warren, in *An. Ban.*, I, pp. xxiii–xxv ; G. F. Warner in *Stowe*, II, pp. xli–xlii.

[3] E. M. Thompson, *An Introduction to Greek and Latin Palaeography* (Oxford, 1912), p. 372 ; Schiaparelli, *Note*, pp. 134, 147–54.

credit of having been the first to develop a minuscule in the true sense of the word." The minuscule was already in use in the country from the first half of the seventh century.[1] The Antiphonary of Bangor (A.D. 680–691) is the oldest book extant containing this script.

The following manuscripts are written in semi-uncial : the Cathach of Colum Cille (sixth–seventh century), the Book of Durrow (seventh–eighth century), the Book of Kells (eighth–ninth century), the *Domnach Airgid* (eighth–ninth century), the Gospel-book of MacRegol (eighth–ninth century), and Codex Usserianus II (ninth–tenth century).

The chief examples of manuscripts written in minuscule, besides the Antiphonary of Bangor already mentioned, are the following : the Book of Mulling (seventh–eighth century), the so-called Book of Dimma (eighth century ; Irish cursive for the first three gospels, minuscule for John), Book of Armagh (A.D. 807), Gospel-book of MacDurnan (ninth–tenth century), and the Southampton Psalter (ninth–tenth century).

Irish script underwent very little change in the course of the Middle Ages ; consequently, as all palaeographers agree, it is an extremely difficult task to date Irish MSS. solely on the ground of the writing.[2]

Just as the so-called " Roman " type of the printed books of our day is derived from the humanistic minuscule, itself derived from the Carolingian minuscule,[3] even so the printed characters known as " Irish " go back to the insular minuscule of the early Middle Ages.[4]

The library catalogues of the Middle Ages give evidence of a considerable number of *libri scottice scripti*.[5] The libraries of Bobbio and St. Gall possessed a particularly rich store of Irish manuscripts. Among the modern libraries which pre-serve important ones may be named, besides those of the

[1] E. A. Lowe, *Handwriting*, in *The Legacy of the Middle Ages*, edited by C. G. Crump and E. F. Jacob (Oxford, 1926), pp. 203, 212 ; Schiaparelli, *Note*, pp. 134, 154–68.

[2] E. M. Thompson, *op. cit.*, p. 371.

[3] Louis Havet, *Que doivent à Charlemagne les classiques latins* (*Revue bleue*, 5th Ser., V, 1906, p. 133) ; Lowe, *Handwriting*, pp. 200–201.

[4] On Irish characters in the past see P. W. Lynam, *The Irish Character in Print* (*The Library*, IV, 1924, pp. 286–325).

[5] See list in Kenney, *Sources*, I, p. 620.

British Isles, those of St. Gall, Turin, Milan, Berne, Karlsruhe and Vienna, the Vatican Library and the Bibliothèque
Nationale of Paris ; a complete list would include many other
names.

Many of these manuscripts were doubtless brought overseas
to the Continent by travelling *Scotti*.[1] But the greater
number were written by them either in England or on the
Continent, where their talent as copyists was highly appreciated and often laid under contribution.[2] Thus the
scriptura Scottica came to be well known among Continentals in
the eighth and ninth centuries. It did not, however, find
many imitators, and after the year 1000 people had forgotten
how to read it. Speaking of certain charters of Fulda drawn
up in Irish script, Eberhard, a monk of that monastery, wrote
between 1152 and 1155 : " *Nec poterat quaeque scedula leviter
legi prae nimia vetustate et inexperientia Scoticae scripturae et apicum
vilitate.*" [3] And thus many a Scottic manuscript, deemed
useless, was taken to pieces and its leaves were used to bind
other manuscripts ; in consequence, fragments of Irish liturgical books have sometimes been discovered in examining
early bindings.[4]

The Anglo-Saxon script proceeds directly from the Irish,
so much so that it is often hard to distinguish one from the
other. And it is evident from the psalter and the martyrology
of Ricemarch, written by a Welshman (Ithael) and decorated
by a Welsh illuminator (Johannes),[5] that Irish script as well
as Irish decorative art were also prevalent in Wales at the end
of the eleventh century.[6] On the contrary, the Scottic
manuscripts had scarcely any influence on the Carolingian
script ; though the skill displayed by the Irish in illustrative

---

[1] *Additamentum Nivialense de Fuilano*, ed. B. Krusch (*MG. Scr. RM*, IV,
p. 449).
[2] Ethelwulf, *Carmen*, ed. Dümmler (*MG. Poet. Lat.*, I, p. 589 [Ultan]).
[3] Quoted by Traube, *Perrona Scottorum* (*Vorlesungen*, III, p. 115).
[4] See Kenney, *Sources*, I, p. 701. On bookbinding in Irish monasteries
see Ryan, *Monast.*, p. 291, n. 10 ; L.G., *Les chrétientés celtiques*, p. 335.
[5] By whom also was transcribed and ornamented MS. 199 C. C. C.
Cambridge (Augustinus, *De Trinitate*). See M. R. James, *A Descriptive
Catalogue of the* MSS. *in the Library of C.C.C.C.* (Cambridge, 1912), I,
pp. 481–83.
[6] Ricemarch, *PM, l. cit.*

decoration found admirers and imitators on the Continent as well as in Great Britain.

On leaving Luxeuil, where he spent but a few years, St Columban led his countrymen across the Alps and probably carried all his manuscripts with him as well, for no Irish manuscript has reached us by way of Luxeuil ; the oldest ones extant which come from that quarter bear no trace of insular influence.[1] Although, on the contrary, a considerable number of Scottic manuscripts were stored in the libraries of Bobbio, St. Gall and Reichenau, they do not seem to have exercised great or lasting influence on the writing in those *scriptoria*.[2] At Tours, which in the Carolingian period was a highly important centre in the production of manuscripts, E. K. Rand has discerned only a slight current of Irish influence which " was only of passing significance " during what he calls the second period of the history of that *scriptorium*, namely, some time before the middle of the eighth century.[3]

Moreover, we must not lose sight of the fact that some Irish emigrants, Moengal at St. Gall, Martinus Hibernensis at Laon, Marianus Scottus at Ratisbon and others, occasionally adopted the continental way of writing, as may be proved by manuscripts still extant written by them.[4]

On the other hand, it is, as we have already said, in illustrative decoration that the influence of Irish manuscripts is clearly manifest, and also in the choice of abbreviations, the continental scribes having borrowed several symbols from the Irish system.[5]

---

[1] Cf. Lowe, *Handwriting*, p. 212 ; Laistner, *Thought and Letters in Western Europe*, p. 181 ; Kingsley Porter, *Crosses and Culture*, p. 68. See facsimiles of Luxeuil mss. in E. H. Zimmermann, *VM*, I, Pl. 44–74.

[2] Lowe, *Handwriting*, pp. 213, 215–16 ; K. Löffler, *Die Sankt Galler Schreibschule in der 2. Hälfte des VIII. Jahrhunderts (Palaeographia Latina*, edited by W. M. Lindsay, VI, 1929, pp. 1–66) ; Schiaparelli, *Note*, pp. 228–38 ; s.a. *Influenze straniere nella scrittura italiana dei secoli* VIII *e* IX (*Studi e Testi*, XLVII, 1927, pp. 15–23) ; Achille Ratti, *Reliquie di antico codice Bobbiese ritrovate* (*Miscellanea Ceriani*, Milano, 1910, pp. 791–810) ; W. M. Lindsay, *The Bobbio Scriptorium* (*Zentralblatt für Bibliothekswesen*, XXVI, 1909, pp. 293–306).

[3] E. K. Rand, *Studies in the Script of Tours*, I, A Survey of the Manuscripts of Tours (Cambridge, Mass., 1929, pp. 25, 34–35).

[4] See Kenney, *Sources*, I, pp. 590, 597, 618, 649.

[5] Levison, *Die Iren*, pp. 19–20.

The close resemblance between the script of the Anglo-Saxons and that of the *Scotti* led to these two national scripts being confounded in the seventeenth century under the common denomination of *scriptura Saxonica*, canonized by Mabillon. It was only at the beginning of the nineteenth century that, thanks to the patriotic researches of Charles O'Conor (1764–1828), librarian of the Duke of Buckingham, the distinction between the two insular scripts was established once more and the right of priority due to the *scriptura Scottica* was recognized.[1]

The decoration of Irish manuscripts claims attention even more than the peculiarities of their script. The most highly decorated codices are psalters and gospel-books, especially the latter. The oldest Irish gospel-book is apparently that of Durrow, which dates from the seventh or eighth century. The most beautiful is indisputably the Book of Kells, which is of slightly later date. The oldest illuminated Scottish gospel-book is the Book of Deer (ninth–tenth century), much inferior to the two preceding in every respect.

In the gospel-books the decoration assumes various forms. First of all, we meet with the Eusebian canons, drawn up at the beginning of many Gospel-books, in columns under highly ornate arches.[2] Next comes the representation of the symbols of the four evangelists, generally united on the same page, which is divided by a cross into four compartments, each containing a symbol; the whole being surrounded by a framework of interlaced, geometric or zoomorphic patterns.[3] Sometimes the page is divided into four triangular sections by a St. Andrew's cross.[4] The same gospel-book often contains several repetitions of the symbols thus grouped. There are

---

[1] On the *Scriptura Scottica* and the *Scriptura tunsa* (name given by the Irish scribes to their own handwriting) see Append. I and II to Traube's *Perrona Scottorum* (*Vorlesungen*, III, pp. 114–19). Cf. Schiaparelli, *Note*, pp. 135, 138–39.

[2] B. of Kells: Zimmermann, *VM*, III, Pl. 166, 167. Cf. L.G. *Répertoire des facsimilés des manuscrits irlandais*, I (*R. Cel.*, XXXIV, 1913, p. 19). —On the Eusebian canons see Vigouroux, *Dictionnaire de la Bible*, s.v. *Eusèbe*, and Kenney, *Sources*, I, pp. 280–81.

[3] B. of Kells: Zimmermann, *VM*, III, Pl. 174, 175.—B. of Armagh: Zimmermann, *VM*, III, Pl. 206; L.G., *Répertoire*, I, p. 30.—MacDurnan Gospels: L.G., *Répertoire*, II (*R. Cel.*, XXXV, 1914, p. 420).

[4] B. of Kells: Zimmermann, *VM*, III, Pl. 176.

others in which the symbols appear separately, each occupying a page to itself.[1]

A third element of decoration to be noticed is the portrait of the Evangelist, in most cases very rudely drawn, which is placed in front of each gospel.[2] Sometimes the symbol of the Evangelist appears again above his head.[3] Besides these portraits we find in some manuscripts biblical subjects depicted, the drawing of these also being generally barbaric ; for instance, the Virgin and the child Jesus, Jesus tempted on the pinnacle of the Temple, Jesus seized by the Jews (Book of Kells),[4] Christ on the Cross,[5] the Last Judgment (Gospels of the eighth–ninth century, St. Gall Stiftsbibl. 51).[6] In the psalters, we see David playing the harp (Brit. Mus. Vitellius F. xi, tenth century ?),[7] David and Goliath (*ibid.* and Southampton Psalter).[8]

A further opportunity for copious decoration offers itself in psalters at the beginning of each fifty of the psalms,[9] and in gospel-books at the head of each gospel,[10] or else at the verse "*Christi autem generatio*" of St Matthew (i, 18),[11] or some

---

[1] B. of Durrow : Zimmermann, *VM*, III, Pl. 161, 162 ; L.G., *Répertoire*, I, p. 21.—B. of Dimma : Zimmermann, *VM*, III, Pl. 195d.—Gospels of Maelbrigte (London, B.M. Harl., 1802) ; L.G., *Répertoire*, II, p. 426.

[2] B. of Mulling : Zimmermann, III, Pl. 194 a, b, c.—B. of Dimma : Zimmermann, III, Pl. 195.—B. of Kells : *ib.*, III, Pl. 171, 172, 173.—St Gall, 51 : *ib.*, III, Pl. 190a, 191a, 198a, 198b.—St Gall, 1395 : *ib.*, III, Pl. 191b.—MacDurnan Gospels : *ib.*, III, Pl. 205a.

[3] St Gall, 51 : *ib.*, III, Pl. 189.—St Gall, 60 : *ib.*, III, Pl. 193a.—Gospels of MacRegol : *ib.*, III, Pl. 199, 201a, 202a.

[4] Zimmermann, *VM*, III, Pl. 168, 169, 170 ; Kingsley Porter, *Crosses and Culture*, Fig. 70 (according to the latter the picture represents Moses, Aaron and Hur).

[5] St Gall, 51 ; Southampton Psalter : Zimmermann, *VM*, III, Pl. 188b, 213a. Cf. L.G., *The earliest Irish Representations of the Crucifixion* (*JRSAI*, VI, Ser., X, 1921, pp. 128–39).

[6] St Gall, 51 : Zimmermann, *VM*, III, Pl. 188a.

[7] London, B.M., Vitellius, F. xi : L.G., *Répertoire*, II, p. 424.

[8] Vitellius, F. xi : L.G., *Répertoire*, II, p. 424.—Southampton Psalter : Zimmermann, *VM*, III, Pl. 213b.

[9] Psalter of Ricemarch, ed. Lawlor, II, Pl. lix, lxi, lxviii : Zimmermann, *VM*, III, Pl. 314 a, b, c.—Vatican Pal. 65 : L.G., *Répertoire*, III (*R. Cel.*, XXXVIII, 1920, p. 9).

[10] St Matthew : Zimmermann, *VM*, III, Pl. 203a.—St Mark : *ib.*, Pl. 160, 181, 186a, 202b, 210a, 218a.—St Luke : *ib.*, Pl. 185b, 200, 217b. —St John : *ib.*, Pl. 183, 186b, 193b, 201b, 218b.

[11] B. of Kells : *ib.*, Pl. 178.—B. of Armagh : L.G., *Répertoire*, I, p. 29. —St Gall, 51 : Zimmermann, *VM*, Pl. 187.—Gospels of MacDurnan : *ib.*, Pl. 205b.

other passage of major importance.[1] The entire page is
occupied with the seven or eight opening words of such
passages, written in highly ornate capitals. The letters of the
first word (in the case of the above-mentioned verse of St
Matthew, the abridged form XPI = Christi) are larger than
the rest. The initial letter itself is of great size ; its down-
stroke reaches nearly to the foot of the page, of which it takes
up the entire left side, the lower part and the right-hand side
being marked off by two pieces of framework composed of
geometric and interlaced patterns, animals with elongated
bodies, serpents, birds, etc.

The designs of these pages, as well as those of the less ornate
initials and the other decorations of the manuscript, are done
with pen and filled in with colour with amazing sureness of
touch.[2] With regard to the colours used, we have a well-
qualified guide in Professor A. P. Laurie. This investigator,
at once a historian of art and a chemist, has engaged in a
minute study at first hand of the pigments and mediums
employed by the insular illuminators, Irish and Anglo-
Saxon, based chiefly on the Book of Lindisfarne.[3] His
researches have led to the following discoveries.[4]

Unlike the Byzantines, the insular illuminators of the early
Middle Ages did not employ vermilion, but red lead, of which
they used a large quantity, especially in the myriads of red
dots with which they made a rule of surrounding their initial
letters (sometimes even some of the letters following the
initial), their framework and other designs. These innumerable red dots have in general kept their brilliancy well.

The palette of the miniaturists further included the colours
yellow, blue, green and purple. The yellow pigment was
made of orpiment, a sulphide of arsenic ; the orpiment used
in Ireland is not very bright " and has a scaly appearance,

[1] B. of Kells : ib., Pl. 179, 180.
[2] See reproductions (many of them in colour) of small initials and other
ornaments in Stanford F. N. Robinson, *Celtic Illuminative Art in the Gospel
Books of Durrow, Lindisfarne and Kells* (Dublin, 1908).
[3] This MS. should be regarded as an Irish work, according to R. A. S.
Macalister, *The Colophon of the Lindisfarne Gospels (Essays and Studies presented
to William Ridgeway*, Cambridge, 1913, pp. 299–305).
[4] *The Pigments and Mediums of the old Masters* (London, 1914),
pp. 70–77.

almost resembling litharge, and is in some cases fibrous in structure. It is not nearly so bright as the highly crystalline orpiment to be found on Italian manuscripts."

The blue resembles that of Byzantine manuscripts ; " it is badly washed ultramarine, and must therefore have been obtained by a similar process from lapis lazuli." [1] Green was furnished by a copper carbonate called malachite. The purple, which has the appearance 'of Tyrian purple, was probably prepared by the Celtic monks themselves, who extracted it from a shellfish (murex) of the family of the buccinoids, which they found on the coasts of Ireland and Great Britain and the properties of which are mentioned by Bede. [2]

The colours of the Irish miniaturists, combined with exquisite taste, produce the happiest effect, and in many manuscripts still preserve an astonishing freshness after the lapse of nine, ten or eleven centuries. This is to be attributed partly to the quality of the gum used as a medium and partly to the nature of the parchment. The medium in question was particularly well adapted to fix the colour firmly, for although the pages of these manuscripts have been turned times innumerable, the colours show no sign of flaking off ; and this is all the more remarkable, inasmuch as they were generally applied in thick coats, even to the point of standing out in relief from the surface of the page. As for the nature of the parchment, according to A. P. Laurie, it offered the following advantages to the illuminator. " It is notorious," he says, " that the pigments flake off Byzantine manuscripts. This is at once explained on examining the surface of the vellum. Either the Byzantine method of preparation was different, or some different skin was used, because the surface under the microscope has a smooth polish, while even the finest of Western vellums under the microscope is simply a mass of fibres with a rough surface." [3] On such a vellum the colours remained more firmly encrusted.

[1] On ultramarine ash and the recipe for obtaining a pure blue from lapis lazuli see A. P. Laurie, *Persian Miniatures*, a letter printed in *The Times*, February 6, 1931.
[2] Bede, *HE*, I, 1.
[3] Laurie, *The Pigments and Mediums*, p. 64. Cf. G. Baldwin Brown, *The Arts in early England* (London, 1921), V, pp. 370–76.

Gold never appears in the decoration of Celtic manuscripts, and this is surprising, for we know that in early times gold abounded in Ireland and was skilfully wrought by Irish goldsmiths.[1]

Where and how did the Celtic monks procure the various ingredients necessary in preparing their colours ? That is by no means the least of the problems which beset the investigator. The purple, we have seen, was supplied by a shellfish of their own coast ; but what of the other colouring matters ? The orange tint of the red lead leads experts to believe that it was obtained by roasting white lead. But we cannot tell whether the red lead was manufactured in the monasteries or procured from some centre where lead was treated chemically.

The malachite came from a district producing copper. The orpiment was also a foreign product. A. P. Laurie declares that " the orpiment in Irish manuscripts is so characteristic throughout the centuries that one must suppose that it was all obtained from one source, though there is no indication where this source of supply can have been." [2] Finally, the monks must have imported their lapis lazuli from distant Asia, whether they purchased the stone itself or the pigment already manufactured.

It now remains to examine the various motifs contained in the grammar of ornament of Celtic Christians and determine how far they were original : motifs which are found on stone and metal as well as on vellum, but some of which have been developed by the miniaturists with unequalled felicity.

§ 5.—Decorative Motifs

The weak point in Celtic art, as we have already implied, is the representation of living beings, especially of the human form. All sense of proportion, relief, perspective and expression is wanting. The Evangelists have a stiff and forbidding aspect. It is occasionally hard to decide whether the minia-

---

[1] See George Coffey, *The Distribution of Gold Lunulae in Ireland and North-Western Europe* (*PRIA*, xxvii, Sect. C, 1909) ; R. A. S. Macalister, *Ireland in Pre-Celtic Times* (Dublin and London, 1921), pp. 118–20, 140–43.
[2] Laurie, *The Pigments and Mediums*, p. 72.

turist meant to represent them standing or seated, so crude
and formless is the drawing. There is not the least verisimi-
litude in the arrangement of the costumes ; the figures in the
pictures have nearly always the appearance of being swathed
in a cloth or in bandages. On the shrine of St Maedóc, where
the drapery is somewhat better indicated, there is great
monotony, each series of three persons being clad in identically
the same fashion.[1] Subordinate details are arranged with a
symmetry wholly fantastic. The hair is long and ringleted ;
the nostrils are invariably formed by two spirals, as if they
were seen from below. The limbs appear to be anchylosed ;
the hands have no joints. In these appalling caricatures of
the human form, some students have discerned Oriental
influence of some kind or other, chiefly Egyptian.[2] We may
frankly declare with Auguste Molinier : " These figures are
of wood, and many a painting reproduced by Westwood is
an ugly reminder of the worst grotesques of the Far East." [3]

There are even designs so diagrammatic in character as to
exceed imagination. In the Book of Deer, for instance, the
human body is represented by a rectangle or trapezium surmounted by a circle, without any sign of arms.[4] The
crucified Christ of the bronze plaque found at Athlone and
preserved in the National Museum of Dublin has the same
form with the addition of arms—but such arms !—, and the
head takes up a third of the entire length of the body.[5]
There are even cases in which one might suppose that a
caricature was intended. In the Southampton Psalter David
has a head of utterly grotesque type, the nose and chin being
outrageously pointed, while the equipment of the figure is odd

---

[1] Coffey, *Guide*, Pl. xi.

[2] F. Keller, *Bilder und Schriftzüge in den irischen Manuscripten der Schweiz-
erischen Bibliotheken* (*Mittheilungen der antiquarischen Gesellschaft in Zürich*,
VII, 1851, pp. 61–97), an essay translated into English under the supervision
of William Reeves and published in *UJA* with the title *Early Irish Calligraphy*
(VIII, 1860). See pp. 229–30 ; André Michel, *Histoire de l'art* (Paris, 1905),
I, p. 315.

[3] A. Molinier, *Les manuscrits et la miniature* (Paris, 1892), p. 97.

[4] John Stuart, *The Book of Deer* (Spalding Club, Edinburgh, 1869), Pl. i,
vi, vii, xv, xx.

[5] Coffey, *Guide*, Pl. xvi. See Crucifixion on a Manx Cross (Kermode,
Manx Crosses, F ⁺.16, Pl. xvi).

in the extreme.[1] The crucified Christ of the Gospels of St. Gall (Stiftsbibl. 51, p. 266) has the body oddly swathed in a cloth, from which there emerge arms coloured red and legs painted blue.[2] The picture of the Crucifixion in the Southampton Psalter (fo. 38ᵇ) displays incredible grotesqueness in its details and general effect ; Longinus has a bird's head, while the bodies of the angels placed above the cross are represented by triangles surmounted by a head and have hands without any arms.[3] But, destitute as it may be of artistic value, the Crucifixion scene, whether treated on vellum, stone or metal, offers none the less details possessing a certain archaeological interest.[4]

The fauna introduced into decoration reveals, as a general rule, an almost equal ignorance of anatomy and scientific drawing. However, the four dogs carved on each side of the upright cross-slab of St. Madoes (Perthshire) are fairly successful ; the lower dogs are biting the upper ones ; they have tails of inordinate length coiled in spirals.[5] The animals most commonly employed are those with long, slim, elastic forms of the type called *lacertine*, greyhounds, serpents, lizards, and birds with long necks and claws. The " artist " still further elongates and attenuates their bodies and develops their limbs, ears, tongues, tails and crests to an extraordinary degree, coiling, interlacing and knotting them at pleasure in the strangest fashion. When an animal has to be drawn after nature or by itself, the result is a complete failure.[6] Among the symbols of the Evangelists in the Book of Durrow are an eagle without claws, a bovine animal of triangular shape and a two-legged lion.[7]

But once he no longer has to copy living beings and objects as they are in nature, once he is forced, on the contrary, to

---

[1] Zimmermann, *VM*, III, Pl. 212a, 213b ; Kurt Pfister, *Irische Buchmalerei* (Potsdam, 1927), Pl. 29.

[2] Westwood, *MO*, Pl. 28.

[3] L.G., *The earliest Irish Representations of the Crucifixion* (*JRSAI*, VI, Ser., X, 1921, Pl. vii, Fig. 2).

[4] L.G., *art. cit.*

[5] Allen, *CA*, Pl. facing p. 182 ; *s.a. ECMS*, Fig. 227.

[6] Westwood, *MO*, Gospels of St Chad (Fig. 1) ; Gospels of MacDurnan (Fig. 1) ; Irish mss. (Fig. 1) ; Irish Bibl. mss (p. 6) ; Coffey, *Guide*, Pl. viii. Cf. Bernard Salin, *Die altgermanische Thierornamentik* (Stockholm, 1904), ch. v.

[7] Zimmermann, *VM*, III, Pl. 165b.

draw upon his own fancy and imagination for complex and varied combinations of lines, the craftsman, whether his task be that of a sculptor in stone, a decorator in metal or a miniaturist, is forthwith in his element. Then his marvellous powers of fertile invention, ingenuity, patience and precision reveal themselves ; then he rises to true art. He excels in infinitely varied treatment of those geometric ornaments which have been classed by archaeologists under the heads of spiral, star- and fret-patterns and have been minutely analyzed by two of them, Romilly Allen and Henry S. Crawford.[1] In this field the Irish artists were thorough innovators. If they were not the first to introduce spiral and interlaced designs into decoration,[2] they applied them with so felicitous a fancy, such width of scope and such freedom of treatment, that the definitive adoption of these motifs in the artistic repertory of the West is due to Irish decorative art and the imitation of it by the Anglo-Saxon and Franco-Saxon schools. In this sense it is not rash to say that, but for the graphic and pictorial impulse which found its full expression in the Book of Kells, the Book of Lindisfarne would never have attained the kind and the degree of beauty which call forth our admiration, nor the most highly prized French paintings on vellum in the ninth and tenth centuries either.

Interlacement is certainly the most characteristic motif of Celtic decoration. Irish artists have drawn wonderful value from it. We are filled with amazement as we gaze at these labyrinths of ribbons and straps endlessly unrolled, crossing and recrossing one another in an extremely complicated and varied entanglement of lines without ever offending our eyes by a suggestion of disorder or confusion. So innate was the taste for interlacement in the artistic genius of the Irish that

[1] Allen, *CA*, ch. vIII ; *s.a. ECMS*, pp. 140–403 ; Crawford, *Handbook*, pp. 12–56 ; Pl. xv–xxxII.
[2] See E. Müntz, *La miniature irlandaise et anglo-saxonne au IX⁰ siècle* in *Études iconographiques et archéologiques sur le moyen âge* (Paris, 1887) ; *s.a. Recherches sur l'origine des ornements connus sous le nom d'entrelacs (R. Cel.*, III, pp. 243–45) ; Hyvernat, *Album de paléographie copte* (Paris and Rome, 1888), Pl. xxII, xxxI, xxxIV, xxxV, xxxVII, xxxVIII ; A. Michel, *op. cit.*, pp. 306 ff. ; O. M. Dalton, *Byzantine Art and Archaeology* (Oxford, 1911), pp. 89–99 ; Allen, *CA*, ch. vII ; Coffey, *Guide*, pp. 1–19 ; Macalister, *AI*, pp. 275 ff. ; W. R. Hovey, *Sources of the Irish illuminative Art (Art Studies*, VI, 1928, pp. 105–20) ; F. Henry, *Origines* (pp. 89–109) ; *s.a. S.I.*, pp. 30–47.

they even used it in combinations of the forms of living beings ; arms, legs, hair and beards are found interlaced and plaited together.[1] On the recumbent monument of Meigle (Perth-shire), four naked men are arranged in the form of a swastika, each holding the leg of the man behind him, while the legs intersect one another at right angles.[2] In the Gospel-book of MacRegol two nude individuals have their legs and fingers enormously elongated and crossing each other diagon-ally.[3] Irish sculpture also offers instances of naked men or monsters arranged in various attitudes with their limbs curiously intertwined.[4] Interlacements of birds, swans, peacocks, storks and cormorants, or of serpents often produce a pretty decorative effect.[5] It is important, above all, to note that genuine Celtic art has borrowed nothing worth speaking of from the vegetable kingdom, which, on the con-trary, was laid under contribution by the Anglo-Saxon and Franco-Saxon schools.[6]

In conclusion, we will here reproduce two appreciations of the works of Irish pen and brush, made at an interval of seven centuries. The first is from Giraldus Cambrensis, who in the course of his Irish travels had the opportunity of examining an illuminated Irish manuscript at Kildare. " This book," he says, " which contains the four gospels, offers almost as many different figures, variously coloured, as it has pages. In it are seen the countenance of the Divine Majesty divinely represented, and the mystical symbols of the Evangelists with six, four or two wings ; here are the eagle, the ox, the face of a man and the head of a lion, besides other figures in almost infinite number. Looking at these paintings with a super-

---

[1] See plates reproducing illuminations from the Books of Durrow and Kells in Zimmermann, *VM*, Vol. III.

[2] Allen, *CA*, Pl. facing p. 288 ; *s.a. ECMS*, Fig. 319 (p. 304).

[3] Plate facing p. 291 in *AJ*, Vol. X (1853).

[4] Crawford, *Handbook*, Pl. xxxiii ; F. Henry, *SI*, pp. 82–87.

[5] B. Salin, *op. cit.*, Figs. 727, 729 ; Zimmermann, *VM*, III, Pl. 163, 167, 177, 187a, 197.

[6] F. Henry, *SI*, pp. 109–14 ; J. O. Westwood, *On the Peculiarities exhibited by the Miniatures and Ornamentation of ancient Irish illuminated* MSS. (*AJ*, VII, 1840, pp. 17–25) ; *s.a. On the distinctive Character of the various Styles of Ornamentation employed by the early British, Anglo-Saxon and Irish Artists* (*AJ*, X, 1853, p. 280) ; F. M. Unger, *La miniature irlandaise, son origine et son développement* (*R. Cel.*, I, 1870, p. 15).

ficial and casual glance, you are more struck by their defects than by their beauty and do not notice the subtlety in this art, which nevertheless is subtle throughout. But if, on the contrary, you fix your attention on the pages and set yourself to examine their secrets minutely, you will see interlacements so delicate and subtle, so finely traced and close together, so intercrossed and intermingled and so vivid in colouring, that their beauty seems rather to be attributed to the industry of angels than to human hand. The more often and more attentively I contemplated these wonders, the greater was my amazement and the stronger my desire to admire them again and again." [1]

Now for the estimate of a palaeographer who had spent a good part of his life in studying Irish and Anglo-Saxon manuscripts, John Obadiah Westwood :

" I have examined, with a magnifying glass, the pages of the Gospels of Lindisfarne and Book of Kells, for hours together, without ever detecting a false line or an irregular interlacement ; and, when it is considered that many of these details consist of spiral lines, and are so minute as to be impossible to have been executed with a pair of compasses, it really seems a problem not only with what eyes, but also with what instruments they could have been executed. One instance of the minuteness of these details will suffice to give an idea of this peculiarity. I have counted in a small space, measuring scarcely three-quarters of an inch by less than half an inch in width, in the Book of Armagh, not fewer than one hundred and fifty-eight interlacements of a slender ribbon-pattern, formed of white lines edged by black ones upon a black ground. No wonder that an artist in Dublin, lately applied to by Mr. Chambers to copy one of the pages of the Book of Kells, excused himself from the labour on the ground that it was a tradition that the lines had been traced by angels." [2]

§ 6.—MUSIC

The Celts had a reputation for their musical talents in the Middle Ages. Giraldus Cambrensis informs us that the Irish

---

[1] Giraldus, *TH*, II, 38 (pp. 123–24).
[2] Westwood, *On the distinctive Character*, pp. 278–79.

music had a singular charm ; the melodies of that country, he says, were not slow and harsh like those of Wales, but, on the contrary, quick and lively, and withal sweet and blithe in tone. He names two musical instruments in use in Ireland, the *cithara* (harp) and the *tympanum*, while the Scotch, in addition to these two, also played the *chorus* and the Welsh exercised their musical talents on the *cithara*, the *tibiae* (flute) and the *chorus*.[1] It will be seen that the harp was cultivated in all the insular Celtic territories.

The harpers of the Arthurian romances were Bretons or Welshmen. In the *Lai de l'Épine*, however, there is mention of an Irish (*Ireis*) *jongleur* who sweetly sings the lay of Aelis while accompanying himself on the " rote," [2] and other texts go to show that the fame of the Irish harpers was not confined to their native island.[3]

In the north of Great Britain (and probably in other parts of the island as well), the harp bore the name of *rotta* or *rottae*.[4] An instrument of the same nature is said by Venantius Fortunatus to have been used by the Britons ; he calls it *chrotta*, a word evidently akin to the Irish *cruit* and the Welsh *crwth*, names for the harp.[5]

The *cruit* (or *crot*, as the word is occasionally written) is frequently mentioned in early Irish literature. We have a reference to it in the *Amra Coluim Cille* or elegy on St Columba written by Dallán Forgaill at the end of the sixth century.[6]

As far as can be judged by the representations on sculptured monuments, some of which have suffered the ravages of time, the Irish of the early Middle Ages were acquainted with several kinds of harp differing in respect of size, shape and

---

[1] Giraldus, *TH*, pp. 153–54.—On those various musical instruments see H. Leclercq, art. *Instruments de musique* (*DACL*). On the " timpan " see W. H. Grattan Flood, *The Story of the Harp* (London, 1905), p. 13. According to a Welsh triad, " the race has three jewels, the Book, the Harp, and the Sword " (*Myvyrian Archaiology of Wales*, Denbigh, 1870, p. 922 [54]).

[2] Ed. R. Zenker, *Der Lai de l'épine*, v. 175–78 (*Zeitschrift für romanische Philologie*, XVII, 1893, p. 246).

[3] See G. Lyman Kittredge, *Sir Orfeo* (*American Journal of Philology*, VII, 1886, pp. 187, 199) ; T. P. Cross, *The Celtic Origin of the Lay of Yonec* (*R. Cel.*, XXXI, 1910, p. 426).

[4] Cuthbert, *Lullo episc.* (*MG. Epist.*, III, p. 406).

[5] Venantius, *Carmina*, VII, 8

[6] *LH*, I, p. 170 ; II, p. 63.

the number of strings.[1] On the south cross of Castledermot (Co. Kildare) a harper appears seated, " illustrating an early form of harp and the method of playing it. The material of the carving is a rough granite, and the details are not well preserved, but the harp is clearly square with an arched top and six strings. It forms a strong contrast to the triangular harp seen elsewhere, for instance, on the shrine of St. Maedóc. A harper is carved on the cross at Ullard, in Kilkenny, but is almost worn away." [2]

The seated figure playing on a harp on St. Maedóc's shrine represents David. The instrument, as has just been said, is of triangular form. " It is one for which both hands are re-quired—the left for treble, and the right for bass—and so accurate is the representation that the manner of playing, by pulling the strings with the nails, is clearly shown." [3]

David, too, is most likely represented by the figure on the *cumdach* of the Stowe Missal, plucking a three-stringed harp.[4]

Larger and of altogether different shape is the twelve-stringed harp played by the psalmist in a miniature of the psalter Vitellius F. xi in the British Museum.[5] But perhaps no value as testimony can be attached to the whimsical fancy of the dauber who decorated this manuscript.

The only question with which we are concerned in these pages is that of the cultivation of the art of music in monas-teries and the use made of it in the ritual of worship. Here again it is Giraldus Cambrensis who informs us that the bishops, abbots and saints of Ireland were wont to carry their harps with them on their journeys and that the sounds they drew from them were a source of pious delight. He adds that in his day St Kevin's harp was still exhibited and was

---

[1] See the representation of a twelve-stringed harp from a ninth-century St Blasian MS. with the inscription " *cythara anglica* " in H. Leclercq, *art. cit.*, Fig. 5910. On Celtic harps see R. B. Armstrong, *The Irish and the Highland Harps* (Edinburgh, 1904), and Maurice Duhamel, *Les harpes celtiques* (*Mélanges bretons et celtiques offerts à Joseph Loth*, Rennes and Paris, 1927, pp. 178–85).

[2] Crawford, *Handbook*, Fig. 158, p. 75.

[3] Coffey, *Guide*, Fig. 52.

[4] *Stowe*, p. LIII, Pl. VI.

[5] Fol. 2ʳ. J. O. Westwood, *On the Peculiarities exhibited by the Miniatures and Ornamentation of ancient Irish illuminated MSS. (AJ, VII, 1840, pp. 24–25).*

held by the natives in singular veneration as a valued relic.[1]

Not all Irish saints, however, seem to have been so favourably disposed towards music. If we are to believe two anecdotes, one relating to Brendan of Clonfert,[2] the other to Máel Rúain of Tallaght, these two saints closed their ears to all earthly music, piously reserving them for the harmonies of heaven ; so a cleric who played the harp was told by Brendan, and the anchorite Cornan of Glen Essa, a player on the pipes, by Máel Rúain.[3]

Gildas speaks briefly of the " tuneful voices of Christ's servants, sweetly modulated, singing the praises of God," and of " the strains of ecclesiastical melody," [4] but we do not know to what melodies the Celtic monks chanted their long psalmodies. Neither do we know whether the liturgical chant was accompanied by any instrument. The organ was known to St Aldhelm of Malmesbury († 709),[5] but perhaps not as an instrument of accompaniment. In Brittany, the earliest allusion to the use of that instrument in accompanying sacred hymns is found in the Life of St Paul Aurelian written by Wrmonoc in the ninth century.[6]

As for all that has been written about the part said to have been taken by Irish monks in the development of the Gregorian chant,[7] we had better say nothing ; for there is no evidence forthcoming in texts to justify these theories. Speaking of Moengal, who settled at St. Gall, Ekkehard says that he was " *in divinis aeque potens et humanis ; septem liberales eos* (*i.e.*, his disciples) *duxit ad artes*," and he adds " *maxime autem ad musicam*." [8] In these last four words, as well as in

---

[1] Giraldus, *TH*, III, 12 (p. 155).

[2] *Lismore*, pp. XIII–XV.

[3] *Teaching of Máel Rúain* (*Tallaght*, 1927, pp. 30–31). Cf. *Tallaght* (1911), pp. 130–31.

[4] Gildas, *De exc.*, 34 (p. 46).

[5] Aldhelm, *De virginitate*, v. 71–73 (*MG. Auct. ant.*, XV, p. 356).

[6] Wrmonoc, *Vita Pauli Aurel.*, 20 (*AB*, I, 1882, p. 252). Cf. Duine, *Memento*, p. 60.

[7] Chiefly by the late W. H. Grattan Flood. See his paper on *Intimate Connection between Gregorian Chant and Irish Music* (*Rassegna Gregoriana*, III, 1904, cols. 253–56) and his book, *Instruction Sketch of Irish musical History* (London, 1922), pp. 1–9.

[8] Ekkehard IV, *Casus Sancti Galli* (*MG. Script.*, II, p. 94).

the assertion (wholly unjustified) that Tuotilo, another musician of St. Gall and a composer of tropes, was an Irishman,[1] and other conjectures equally devoid of foundation, some writers gifted with a fertile imagination have found sufficient basis for daring hypotheses, quickly accepted as facts, and have made of the abbey of St. Gall an important centre for diffusing the musical art and the melodies of Ireland. In history we must resign ourselves to remain ignorant of many things.

CONCLUSION

Whence is Irish art derived ? What foreign civilizations— Anglo-Saxon, Scandinavian, Continental or Oriental—may have in one way or another influenced any of its iconographic themes ? And which of these themes may, on the other hand, be regarded as the native product of the Irish genius ? These are questions which various investigators have attempted to answer, but no one has as yet got beyond the stage of hypothesis.[2]

There is a further question of an interest no less engrossing, that of the influence exercised by Irish art on the conceptions and the technique of foreign schools of art : can we hope to gain more light on this ? In the course of the preceding pages we have pointed out all that may in the light of sound criticism be affirmed on the subject.

We have seen that the Scottic monks left their mark in the sculptures of the celebrated church of Ratisbon (Jakobskirche) which belonged to them for centuries. Moreover, the rich ornamentation of the Irish manuscripts was much copied overseas, though nowhere, save in Northumbria (Book of Lindisfarne), did the imitators approach the artists of Ireland, where this branch of art, especially in the treatment of interlaced designs, was carried to a marvellous degree of perfection.

---

[1] According to Grattan Flood, his real name would have been Tuathal (*Instruction Sketch*, p. 4). Like Notker, Tuotilo was probably a Swabian. See J. M. Clark, *The Abbey of St. Gall as a centre of Literature and Art* (Cambridge, 1926), p. 111.

[2] See W. R. Hovey, *Sources of Irish illuminative Art* (*Art Studies*, VI, 1928, pp. 105–20) ; A. Kingsley Porter, *Notes on Irish Crosses* (*Amici amico :* Johnny Roosval Festschrift, Stockholm, 1929, pp. 84–94) ; J.-G., Lemoine, *Les origines de la miniature irlandaise* (*L'art vivant*, V, 1929, pp. 274–79). Cf. F. Henry, *Origines ; s.a. S.I.*, Conclusion.

With regard to music, we have already stated our opinion that it has not yet been clearly established that the Irish played any conspicuous part in the development of musical compositions at St. Gall. In plastic art, however, we have the authority of an explicit text which tells us that, in the time of Bernward, bishop of Hildesheim († 1022), richly wrought " Scottic vessels " (*ex Scotticis vasis, quae regali maiestati singulari dono deferebantur*) were much admired in Germany, and that artists endeavoured to imitate their elegant form.[1]

Finally, after years of zealous research, historians of art are convinced that they have found fairly numerous traces of Irish art on the Continent in the mural paintings discovered in 1923–24 in an old country church at Naturns (Naturno), now in the Italian province of Alto Adige (formerly South Tyrol),[2] and in divers forms of pre-Romanesque or Romanesque ecclesiastical plastic art (Scandinavian art [3] ; metal work of Godefroy de Claire, of the twelfth century ; sculptures in San Michele of Pavia, in the churches of Moissac, Souillac, Saint-Martin d'Ainay at Lyons, Vézelay,[4] in the cathedral of Bayeux,[5] and elsewhere). Those who have devoted themselves to these researches have discovered, in continental works of art, curious analogies to the decoration and iconographic

[1] *Vita Bernwardi*, 6 (*MG. Scr.*, IV, p. 760 ; *PL*, CXL, 397). Cf. V. C. Habicht, *Des heiligen Berward von Hildesheim Kunstwerke* (*Niedersächsische Kunst in Einzeldarstellungen*, Bd. 3–4, Bremen, 1922).

[2] G. Gerola, *Gli affreschi di Naturno* (*Dedalo*, VI, 1925) ; J. Garber, *Die romanischen Wandgemälde Tirols* (Wien, 1928), pp. 37 ff. ; Federico Halbherr, *St Paul as in a Swing : early Irish Frescoes found in the Alps* (*Illustrated London News*, May 23, 1925, pp. 998–99) ; Kurt Pfister, *Irische Buchmalerei*, p. 7 ; Cornelius Kniel, *Die vorkarolingischen Wandergemälde von Naturns* (*Benediktinische Monatschrift*, XIII., 1931, pp. 192–98) ; Kingsley Porter, *Crosses and Culture*, p. 77.

[3] F. Henry, *S.I.*, pp. 73–75.

[4] A. Kingsley Porter, *The Chronology of Carolingian Ornament in Italy* (*Burlington Magazine*, XXX, 1917, pp. 98 ff.) ; *s.a. The Tomb of Hincmar and Carolingian Sculpture in France* (*Ib.*, L, 1927, pp. 75–91) ; *s.a. Notes on Irish Crosses* (Johnny Roosval Festschrift, Stockholm, 1929) ; *s.a. An Egyptian Legend in Ireland* (*Marburger Jahrbuch für Kunstwissenschaft*, 1930). Two lectures on Irish art, its origin and influence, given by M. Henri Focillon at University College, Dublin (May 26, 27, 1931) must also be mentioned.

[5] Jean Vallery-Radot, *La sculpture française au XIIᵉ siècle et l'influence irlandaise* (*Revue de l'art ancien et moderne*, XLV, 1924, pp. 335–44) ; *s.a. La Cathédrale de Bayeux* (Paris, 1915), pp. 42–45.

themes found in the illuminated manuscripts and High Crosses of Ireland. But is there more than analogy? Has it been shown with any degree of probability that in such cases there was actual borrowing or imitation? Hardly, we think.[1] In all the various hypotheses set forward, it must be admitted that the link between the Irish model and the continental work of art is, in general, very slight. Nevertheless, investigation of this kind is to be encouraged. Studies of comparative archaeology have been so fruitful in other fields of research within the last forty or fifty years that in this domain also, we may hope, research pursued in a critical spirit and without losing sight of historical data will lead in the future to results more solid and positive than those hitherto attained.[2]

[1] See Mlle. F. Henry's pertinent remarks in *Origines* (pp. 107–109).
[2] On what remains to be done in this rich field of research, see R. A. S. Macalister, *The Present and Future of Archaeology in Ireland* (Dublin, 1925).

CHAPTER XI

THE GRADUAL DECLINE OF CELTIC PARTICULARISM

§ 1.—RETROSPECTIVE SURVEY

BEFORE passing on, it may not be amiss to set before the reader a rapid summary of the history of the Churches of the Celts from the beginning down to the era of the Scandinavian invasions.

The earliest positive fact which attests the existence of a British Church is the presence of three of its bishops as delegates at the Council of Arles in 314. In the first quarter of the fifth century Christianity was carried by St Ninian to the regions of the north, the Britons of Strathclyde and the southern Picts.

At that time the monk Pelagius was propagating his erroneous doctrines far and wide ; and they soon spread in Britain to such a degree that the British bishops, unable of themselves to check their diffusion, appealed to the Church of Gaul for aid. In consequence, St Germanus of Auxerre crossed the Channel twice ; on the first occasion (429–431) he was accompanied by St Lupus of Troyes, on the second (446–447) by Severus, bishop of Trèves. Germanus had a considerable influence on the formation of the insular Churches. Not only did he gain a brilliant triumph over Pelagianism, but he also contributed towards consolidating religion, developing monasticism, and probably also towards establishing the insular liturgies. At the end of the twelfth century Giraldus Cambrensis mentions several religious practices still in use in his day which he traces back to Germanus.[1]

The year 428 witnessed the first settlement of Anglo-Saxons in Great Britain. The era of the Saxon conquests was a period of ruin and desolation for religion as well as for social

---

[1] Giraldus, *DK*, i, 18 (pp. 202–203).

institutions. Teutonic paganism took possession of the island down to the coming of Augustine in 597, thrusting back to the north and west what still survived of the Christian faith.

On the other hand, the neighbouring island, called " barbarous " by Prosper of Aquitaine because it had never borne the Roman yoke, had already before the year 432 been visited by missionaries, notably by Palladius, who made but a fleeting stay; and in the course of the fifth century it was won for the Gospel by St Patrick. That apostle, by dint of superhuman labours and aided by zealous helpers, succeeded in rescuing the land from idolatry, and ere long it became a nursery of saints. In the sixth and seventh centuries monasteries increased in number and in population in an extraordinary degree, while the Christian life, asceticism and zeal for winning converts had a marvellous development. Thither from the neighbouring countries flocked all who desired to be trained in the perfect life and instructed in secular and sacred learning ; for to that island, lying on the verge of the inhabited world, knowledge, assailed on every side by barbarism, had fled for refuge.

Meantime, an important section of the insular Celtic world had broken away from Great Britain and taken possession of the Gallo-Roman Armorica. The Celtic Church established in that peninsula for long preserved its own peculiar features, and for centuries refused to acknowledge the rights of the Frankish metropolis under whose jurisdiction it was placed by canon law.

The insular Churches, no less, displayed a spirit of pertinacious particularism and inveterate confidence in their own traditions. Hence arose the long and acrimonious controversies on the Easter question and the form of the tonsure. But at last, in the course of the seventh or beginning of the following century, their resistance was overcome and contact became more frequent between the representatives of Celtic Christianity and the English and continental Churches.

In that age monks, solitaries, clerics, bishops and scholars quitted Ireland in numbers to spread the Christian faith, religious life and knowledge abroad. The latest of these emigrants laboured in the revival of learning under the Carolingian monarchs. We have already indicated the various causes which impelled these Scots to cross the sea. A contemporary writer, beholding them engage in wandering in such numbers and with such zest, is fain to see in this predilection for a roving life an instinct of their nature : *Quibus consuetudo peregrinandi iam pene in naturam conversa est.*[1] But, whatever natural inclination they may have had for voyages across seas, at the time when Walahfrid Strabo wrote these words expatriation was becoming a painful necessity for them. Their island had already been visited several times by the Vikings, who covered its face with ruins and installed themselves as masters. We must here proceed to tell what injuries resulted to religion from the Scandinavian invasions of the Celtic territories, and how those invasions in turn, by the dispensation of Providence, opened the way to the ecclesiastical reforms of the twelfth century.

§ 2.—The Norsemen in Brittany

The first aggression of the Norsemen in Brittany was that which led to the sack of Nantes in 843.[2] This city was subsequently attacked and pillaged several times by the sea-rovers, notably in 853 and 886. From the year 870 on, the valleys of the Loire and the Vilaine were constantly visited by the enemy. The northern coast of the peninsula was not spared ; Hasting took possession of the island of Batz and between 878 and 882 sacked Tréguier and Dol. Alain I at last succeeded in winning an important victory over the invaders in 888 ; but after his death in 907 there was no longer any check to their daring and their conquests.

In 913 or 914 the abbey of Landévennec was destroyed. The monks took flight, bearing the body of their founder St Guénolé (Winwalloc), and settled at Montreuil on the Canche.[3] " In the year 919," writes Flodoard, a contemporary, " the

---

[1] Walahfrid, *Vita Galli*, II, 46 (p. 336).
[2] On the invasions of the Norsemen see La Borderie, *HB*, II, pp. 73 ff.
[3] J. Loth, *Le date de la destruction de Landevennec par les Normands* (*An. Br.*, VIII, 1893, pp. 492–93 ; Régis de L'Estourbeillon, *Itinéraire des moines de Landévennec fuyant les invasions normandes* (Saint-Brieuc, 1889) ; R. Rodière, *Les corps saints de Montreuil* (Paris and Montreuil, 1901) ; A. Oheix, *Les reliques bretonnes de Montreuil-sur-Mer* (*Mémoires de l'Association bretonne*, 1905).

Norsemen lay waste the whole of Brittany lying within the horn of Gaul, on the sea-coast ; they overwhelm and destroy it, selling, carrying off or driving away all the inhabitants." [1] In fact, during the second quarter of the tenth century, there took place more than one important emigration of Bretons from their country, alike of nobles and of monks, as well as deportation of the relics of their saints. Only those whom the Chronicle of Nantes terms the *pauperes Britanni* remained attached to the soil under the Scandinavian dominion. [2]

Many Bretons crossed to England. The relations between Bretons and Anglo-Saxons appear to have been frequent and friendly from the ninth to the eleventh century. Alfred the Great (871–901) sent gifts to the monasteries of the peninsula and received Bretons at his court. [3] At that of his grandson Athelstan (924–940), Matuedoi, count of Poher, took refuge with his young son Alain, the future liberator of Brittany, and also *cum ingenti multitudine Britonum,* as the Chronicle of Nantes adds (931). [4] Even after the period of the Norse invasions in Brittany, the Bretons still continued to be received with special favour in England, as is attested by an interesting passage in the laws with which Edward the Confessor (1043–1064) is credited : " *Britones vero Armorici, cum venerint in regno isto, suscipi debent et in regno protegi sicut probi cives. De corpore regni huius exierunt quondam, de sanguine Britonum regni huius.*" [5] The Breton names in the inscriptions of the church of Wareham (Dorset) lead us to believe that just in the tenth century that place had a colony of Breton refugees. [6] It may be assumed that some of those legendary traditions native to Brittany which found a place in the so-called Arthurian romances and

---

[1] Flodoard, *Annales,* ed. Ph. Lauer (*Collection de textes pour servir à l'étude et à l'enseignment de l'histoire*), Paris, 1905, p. 1.

[2] *Chr. Nam.,* 34 (p. 83).

[3] Asser, *De rebus gestis Aelfredi,* ed. W. H. Stevenson (Oxford, 1904), pp. 60, 89.

[4] *Chr. Nam.,* p. 82.

[5] *Leges Edwardi Conf.,* 23 c, ed. F. Liebermann, *Die Gesetze der Angelsachsen,* I, p. 658. The *Leges Edwardi Conf.* were actually compiled, in all probability, about 1135–36, but the prologue represents the text to be a statement of the law as declared to king William I in an assembly held in or about 1070. See Liebermann, *Gesetze,* III, 341 ; J. E. Edwards, *Hywel Dda and the Welsh Lawbooks* (Bangor, 1929), p. 10.

[6] On these inscriptions see E. MacClure, *British Place-names in their historical Setting* (London, 1910), pp. 161–62.

together with the Welsh traditions constituted the " *matière de Bretagne* " were transmitted at the time of these emigrations.

Moreover, in the matter of religion, the numerous names of Breton saints which occur in several Anglo-Saxon litanies and calendars were no doubt imported at this time also.[1] It is to such centres of Breton refugees in England that, according to F. Duine, we must assign the origin of two litanies in which names of Anglo-Saxon saints are found along with those of Celtic ones, many of the latter Bretons.[2]

However, the great mass of the Breton monks did not cross the Channel, but sought refuge in France with the relics of their saints.[3] That was the course taken by the monks of Redon, whose abbey was pillaged during their absence, and also by those of Ruis, Léhon, Dol and other places.

From 921 to 936 the Norsemen remained absolute masters of the whole of Brittany. But in 936 Alain Barbetorte, who had grown to manhood in exile, crossed the Channel and after three years of struggle succeeded, with the aid of the counts of Rennes and the Maine, in ridding his country completely of the invaders.

§ 3.—THE SCANDINAVIANS IN THE CELTIC TERRITORIES OF THE BRITISH ISLES

The Norsemen easily gained a foothold in the northern and western archipelagoes of Scotland, the Shetland and Orkney Islands and the Hebrides. After they had become masters of the Hebrides, where their dominion lasted for 450 years and whence they made frequent descents on Scotland and Ireland,[4] those islands received the name of Innsegall, " the isles of the foreigners," among the Celtic peoples of the mainland. The Norsemen for their part called them *Sudreyar*

---

[1] Cf. A. Gasquet and Ed. Bishop, *The Bosworth Psalter* (London, 1908), pp. 53–56.

[2] Duine, *Inventaire*, pp. 41–48. Cf. L.G., *Mentions anglaises de saints bretons et de leurs reliques (An. Br.,* XXXIV, 1920, pp. 273–77) ; *s.a. Notes sur le culte des saints bretons en Angleterre (An. Br.,* XXXV, 1923, pp. 601–609).

[3] La Borderie, *HB,* II, pp. 507 ff. ; F. Plaine, *Les invasions des Normands en Armorique et la translation générale des saints bretons* (Paris, 1899) ; F. Lot, *Date de l'exode des corps saints hors de Bretagne (An. Br.,* XV, 1899, pp. 60–76).

[4] Cf. *Grette's Saga (c.* 874), 4, in Anderson, *Early Sources,* I, p. 326.

(islands of the south) in opposition to the Orkney and Shetland groups, which they called *Nordreyar* (islands of the north). Hence the English names of Sudreys and Nordreys and the title (still in use) of the Bishop of Sodor and Man, the inhabitants of the Sudreys being in ecclesiastical Latin termed *Sodorenses*.

The monastery of Lindisfarne was one of the first points of the English coast bordering the North Sea to be attacked by the pirates. Its church was pillaged and destroyed in 793.[1] In 795 the Scandinavians made their first appearance off the coasts of Ireland.[2] A few years later, in 798, they established themselves in the Isle of Man,[3] which remained in their power for several centuries. Naturally, they directed their first attacks to small and thinly-peopled islands. The monastery of Iona was burnt for the first time in 802 by these sea-robbers, who are frequently called " Gentiles " in Irish texts ; and the island was subsequently ravaged on very many occasions.

The brevity with which the Annals record these repeated ravages is in itself eloquent. " Devastation of the islands of Britain by the gentiles " (A.U. 793 = 794).—" The burning of Rathlin by the gentiles ; and Skye was pillaged and devastated " (A.U. 794 = 795).—" Patrick's Island was burned by the gentiles ; and they took away tribute from the provinces, and Dochonna's shrine was broken by them, and other great incursions [were made] by them, both in Ireland and in Scotland " (A.U. 797 = 798).—" Iona of Columcille was burned by the gentiles " (A.U. 801 = 802).

During this period St Columba's relics were carried either to Scotland or Ireland on several occasions by their custodians, anxious to save them from the greed and impiety of the

---

[1] *Anglo-Saxon Chronicle* (RS), I, p. 101 ; II, p. 48.

[2] A. Sommerfelt, *Recherches sur l'histoire du vieux-norrois en Irlande* (R. Cel., XXXIX, 1922, p. 175). Cf. Lawlor in Ricemarch, *PM*, I, p. x (*introd.*) ; Todd in *Cogadh Gaedhel*, pp. xxxi–xxxvi (*introd.*).

[3] See Todd, *Cogadh Gaedhel*, p. xxxv (*introd.*) ; Lloyd, *HW*, I, p. 322. "Norse was still spoken in the Isle of Man at least in the twelfth century, and it survived even longer in the Hebrides and the Shetlands" (Eilert Ekwall, *How long did the Scandinavian language survive in England?* in *A grammatical Miscellany offered to Otto Jespersen*, London and Copenhagen, 1930, p. 18).

Vikings.[1] The relics of St Cuthbert underwent many similar transportations.

Wales does not appear to have suffered any serious incursion of the Norsemen before the second half of the ninth century. In 853 Anglesey was laid waste by the " black gentiles " [2] ; thenceforth the attacks became fairly frequent. The monasteries of Llanbadarn, Menevia, Llanilltud, Llancarvan and Llandydoch were sacked in 987 and in the course of the following years. Menevia had a special attraction for the pirates ; Bishop Morgeneu fell at their hands in 999.[3]

They conquered the territory of the Picts, Northumbria, the north-west of England and Strathclyde.[4] It would be impossible to record the havoc of all kinds wrought by these northerners, and their ever-increasing conquests. The Annals of the various regions we have spoken of are filled with the enumeration of their raids, their devastations and their permanent settlements.

Not one of the great Irish monasteries, still flourishing in the eighth century, escaped their clutches. Once masters of the coastland, they made their way up the rivers to the heart of the country. Their fleets were anchored in the lakes of the interior, whence on a favourable opportunity they descended upon churches and monasteries, slaughtering the monks or putting them to flight, seizing on all articles of value, rifling reliquaries and casting the contents, in their eyes useless, into the waters, and plundering the libraries.

In 832 Armagh was pillaged thrice in a month by the Gentiles. In 845 Forannán, its abbot, was taken prisoner by them with his reliquaries and his community and carried off by the ships to Limerick.[5] A great number of monasteries, Clonmacnois, Brendan's foundation of Clonfert, Lorrha, Terryglass and Inis Cealtra, were ravaged by the hordes of Turgeis (Turgesius). His wife Ota profaned the sanctuary of Clonmacnois, giving audience mounted on the altar of its

---

[1] J. Dowden, *The Celtic Church in Scotland* (London, 1894), I, pp. 195–96.
[2] " Mon uastata a gentibus nigris " (*AC, a.a.* 853, p. 165).
[3] *AC;* Giraldus, *IK*, II, I (p. 104). Cf. Lloyd, *HW*, I, p. 352.
[4] A. Mawer, *The Vikings* (*CMH*, III, 1922, pp. 303–39). Cf. MacNeill, *Phases*, p. 255 ; Henry Bradley, *EHR*, XXXIV, 1919, p. 425.
[5] *AU, a.a.* 831, 844.

church. Being taken prisoner by Máel Seachlainn, then king of Meath, Turgesius met his end, being drowned in Loch Uair (Owel) in 845.[1]

The monastery of Kells (Meath), where the monks driven from Iona found refuge, did not escape the ravages of other bands ; it was pillaged on several occasions and some of its monks were killed or carried off captives.[2]

In the ninth and tenth centuries the Vikings made fortified settlements on various points of the Irish coast, especially near the mouth of the Liffey, where they founded Dublin, anciently known (and still known in modern Irish) as Ath Cliath, " the ford of the hurdles," from the ford which crossed the river in that locality [3] ; at the estuary of the Shannon, where they founded Limerick ; and also at Waterford and Wexford. Under their dominion these towns became busy commercial ports.[4]

The conquest of the country by the foreigners was facilitated by the divisions between the native kings and tribes, who did not cease waging war on one another instead of uniting their forces against the invader. Some Irish rulers even went so far as to make alliance with the foreigners. At last, however, a brave champion arose. Made king of Ireland in 1002, Brian Bóramha undertook to free his country from the yoke of the *Genti* (Gentiles). While passing through Armagh he had himself styled *Imperator Scotorum* in an inscription written in his presence by the royal historiographer in the Book of

---

[1] *Cogadh Gaedhel*, pp. 12–15.

[2] *AU*, 806 = 807 ; 919 or 920 = 920 ; 950 = 951 ; 969 or 970 = 970 ; *AT*, 1018 = 1019 (p. 357).

[3] Cf. D. A. Chart, *The Story of Dublin* (London, 1907) ; C. Haliday, *The Scandinavian Kingdom of Dublin* (2nd ed., Dublin, 1884), p. 23 and Appendix I.—The following passage from the *Vita Coemgeni*, 29, must obviously be treated as an anachronism : "[Garban] prope ciuitatem Ath Cliath habitabat, que est in aquilonali Laginensium plaga, super fretum maris posita. Et illud scotice dicitur [Duibh Linn], quod sonat latine nigra terma ; et ipsa ciuitas potens et belligera est, in qua semper habitant uiri asperrimi in preliis et peritissimi in classibus " (*VSH*, I, p. 249). " No trace has been found in Irish records or tradition of anything approaching in character to a city on the site occupied by Dublin until the Norsemen fortified themselves here in 841 " (MacNeill, *Phases*, pp. 137–38).

[4] Giraldus, *TH*, III, 43 (p. 186). Cf. A. Walsh, *Scandinavian Relations with Ireland during the Viking Period* (Dublin, 1922), pp. 21–28, 29–34 ; MacNeill, *Phases*, pp. 265, 273 ; A. S. Green, *History of the Irish State to* 1014 (London, 1925), pp. 352–54.

Armagh.[1] A great battle was fought at Clontarf on the outskirts of Dublin on Good Friday, April 23, 1014. The Irish army was commanded by Brian's son Murchadh, the Norse forces by Sigurd and Brodir. The Norsemen were routed and Sigurd was killed. But Murchadh and Brian Bóramha himself also perished, the king being slain by Brodir, who, in his turn, fell in the combat. The victory of Clontarf, dearly bought, arrested the progress of the invaders, though the Norse kingdom of Dublin survived until the conquest of Ireland by the Anglo-Normans.[2]

These wars and the concomitant political and social revolutions were the source of the greatest evils to the Church in Ireland.

In the first place, learning decayed for want of teachers and books. The fugitive monks had carried their most precious manuscripts with them to the Continent. Those left in the libraries were dispersed or destroyed ruthlessly by the Vikings. When Brian Bóramha sought to revive learning, he was obliged, so a chronicler tells us, to send scholars to purchase books beyond seas.[3] However, it must not be concluded that all intellectual life was extinguished in the tenth and eleventh centuries, for the national literature and plastic arts continued to be cultivated.[4] Cormac's Glossary—if it was really composed by the bishop-king of Cashel, Cormac mac Cuilennáin, who met his death in the battle of Belach Mughna (Ballaghmoon) in 908—shows that the sources of knowledge were not altogether dried up.   John or Jeuan, son of Sulgen (Sulien), relates that his father († 1091), before he was made bishop of St. David's, " stirred by the example of the fathers," went to Ireland to prosecute his studies and remained there for thirteen years.[5]

As for monasticism, it had certainly lapsed from its early glory. It would indeed be going too far to believe with St Bernard that, prior to the reforms of St Malachy and the

---

[1] Fol. 32b.
[2] *Cogadh Gaedhel*, pp. 190–203.
[3] *Cogadh Gaedhel*, pp. 138–39.
[4] *V sup.*, ch. x, §§ 1, 2, 3 ; Lawlor in Ricemarch, *PM*, I, p. xii (*introd.*).
[5] *Carmen de vita Sulgeni* (*CED*, I, pp. 665–66). Cf. *Vita Cadroae* (Boll., *AS*, Mart., I, 481).

introduction of the Cistercians in Ireland, monks were known in the island only by the memory of institutions of the past.[1] But in the midst of such political and social upheaval, can we wonder that there ensued a deep lowering of the standard both of faith and morals ? As a consequence of the capture of Armagh by Turgesius, the worship of Thor was established in the holy city. The entire country was plunged anew into a barbarism hardly less profound than that before the arrival of Patrick. The word " barbarous " recurs constantly to the pen of St Bernard as an epithet for the people whose morals it was St Malachy's task to reform, a people more like beasts than men, Christians in name, but in fact pagans.[2]

Fifty years later, Giraldus Cambrensis lavishes the darkest hues in depicting the degradation of the Irish : *gens spurcissima, gens vitiis involutissima, gens omnium gentium in fidei rudimentis incultissima.*[3] We know that impartiality towards Ireland was not the dominant characteristic of the Welsh writer. Nevertheless, even if his political animus and his rhetorical tendencies led him to deepen his colours, some of his allegations must be accepted as well grounded, since they are corroborated by other testimonies of weight. The letters written by Lanfranc (1070–1093) and St Anselm (1093–1109), for instance, deserve our attention in this matter ; they likewise attest a remarkable depression of faith and morals in Ireland.

Sacraments had fallen into disuse or were profaned. In some remote districts penance, confirmation, even baptism were no longer practised. Irregular unions had become common ; married men exchanged or sold or repudiated their wives at pleasure ; marriages took place within the degrees forbidden by the canons. The dead were no longer interred with Christian rites. The people refused to pay tithes.[4]

As for the ecclesiastical hierarchy, we know how frail its

---

[1] Bernard, *Vita Mal.*, 16, col. 1095.
[2] *Ib.*, 8, col. 1084.
[3] Giraldus, *TH*, III, 19 (p. 164).
[4] Lanfranc, *Ep.* 37 (*PL*, CL, 535) ; *Ep.* 38 (col. 536) ; Anselm, *Ep.* 142 (*PL*, CLIX, 174) ; Giraldus, *TH*, III, 26 (p. 170) ; *s.a. De rebus a se gestis*, 14 (*Opera*, I, p. 68) ; Bernard, *Vita Mal.*, 3, col. 1079 ; 8, col. 1084.

constitution was in Ireland. After as well as before the
Scandinavian invasions, bishops continued to grow in number
without cause and without sees to fill. On the other hand,
there was a dearth of priests. Episcopal consecration was
still performed by a single bishop.[1] The lack of diocesan and
metropolitan organization, which in earlier times had not
entailed any very deplorable consequences owing to the zeal
and faith which animated the clergy, had now, in the midst
of general disorder and demoralization, resulted in complete
anarchy. Even where the liturgy was not once and for all
given up, a spirit of independence and arbitrary caprice laid
down the law.[2]

The Irish Annals throw very little light on the religion of
the Scandinavians. The conversion of several of their chiefs
to Christianity, notably that of Olaf Cuaran, king of Dublin
and Northumbria (934–981), about the year 943, set an
example which led a good number of their subjects to embrace
the Christian faith.[3] Mixed marriages between Gaels and
Scandinavians, which appear to have been common in Ireland,
may have contributed to hasten the diffusion of the Christian
religion among the worshippers of Thor, though, on the other
hand, such unions were in many cases harmful to the beliefs
of the Christian partners.[4]

About the year 1040, the Scandinavian colony of Dublin
possessed a sufficient number of converts to have a bishop of
its own. Dunan was the first to occupy the see. Under his
episcopate the cathedral of Holy Trinity (now Christ Church)
was founded. The first bishops of the Scandinavian colonies
in Ireland were all Irishmen by birth, but several of them,
before their elevation to episcopal rank, had practised the
monastic life in England. In the see of Dublin Dunan was
succeeded by Gilla Pádraig (1074). His successor was

---

[1] Lanfranc, *Ep.* 38 (*PL*, CL, 536) ; Anselm, *Ep.* 147 (*PL*, CLIX, 179) ;
Bernard, *Vita Mal.*, 10, col. 1086.

[2] Bernard, *Vita Mal.*, 3, col. 1079 ; Gilbert, *SE*, cols. 995–96.

[3] *Anglo-Saxon Chronicle*, a.a. 942, 943. Cf. Haliday, *The Scandinavian
Kingdom of Dublin*, pp. 124–26 ; A. Walsh, *Scandinavian Relations*, pp. 48,
53. After the battle of Tara (980) Olaf laid down his kingship and retired
into religious life at Iona, where he died (*Annals of the Four Masters*, a.a. 979).
Cf. MacNeill, *Phases*, p. 212 ; Mawer, *The Vikings*, pp. 329–30.

[4] A. S. Green, *op. cit.*, pp. 354–57 ; Sommerfelt, *art. cit.*, p. 176.

Donough O'Hanley, a monk of Canterbury, who was followed by his nephew Samuel O'Hanley, a monk of St. Albans. These bishops, except perhaps Dunan, made a profession of canonical obedience to the Primate of England.

We lack information touching the earliest ecclesiastical history of Wexford.

The first bishop of Waterford, Malchus (Máel Ísa úa hAinmire), who had been a monk of Winchester, was consecrated at Canterbury in 1096 and made profession of obedience to St Anselm as one of his suffragans.[1]

Gilbert (Gilla Easpuig) became bishop of Limerick about 1105. He did not receive his consecration from the English Primate, although he kept up friendly relations with Anselm. As Papal Legate in Ireland he exercised a great influence on the fortunes of the Irish Church.

These four sees were the first to be occupied by a bishop who was not head of an abbey, the first centres of an episcopal diocese with clearly defined territory—of limited extent, it is true, in Dublin, Wexford and Waterford—, but vast in Limerick. This was a great innovation in Ireland. "Large or small, each of these dioceses presented to the eyes of the Irish a model of Church government similar to that in vogue on the Continent, and utterly different from that to which they were accustomed."[2]

In truth, the work of unification had already made great strides since the seventh and eighth centuries, when the Celts had first been brought to conform with the customs of the Church of Rome in several matters of discipline. Rome, as we have seen, had never ceased to be regarded as the Mother Church, the capital of the Christian world ; her Pontiff was looked upon as the supreme Head. But the direct influence of Rome rarely made itself felt within the confines of the local

---

[1] Eadmer, *Historia novorum in Anglia*, II, ed. M. Rule (*RS*), pp. 76–77.—A letter of Walkelin, bishop of Winchester, to St Anselm (*Ep.* 10) and another from Malchus to the same (*Ep.* 13) have recently been published by Dom André Wilmart, *La tradition des lettres de Saint Anselme : Lettres inédites de S. Anselme et de ses correspondants* (*RB*, XLIII, 1931, pp. 51, 52). Cf. F. S. Schmitt, *Zur Ueberlieferung der Korrespondenz Anselms von Canterbury. Neue Briefe* (*RB*, XLIII, 1931, p. 227).

[2] Lawlor, *BLM*, p. XIX. Cf. Lawlor, *The Reformation of the Irish Church in the Twelfth Century* (*Irish Church Quarterly*, IV, 1911, pp. 216–28).

hierarchy, which remained vague and ill-defined. Compared with the Anglo-Saxon Church, bound to the Holy See by ties so close and filial and so completely moulded by it, the Church of Ireland might well seem almost independent and auto-nomous. The Scandinavian invasions had made its relations with the Papacy still less frequent, as the Saxon invasions had formerly done for the British Churches. Again, the entire character of insular religious society, the outcome rather of impulse than of deliberate organization, was out of harmony with the Roman spirit, disciplined, practical and fond of order and unity. How many inconsistencies and abuses, how much easy-going slackness needed to be suppressed alike in the liturgy, in the religious life and in morals ! All this called for serious reform. It remains for us to tell how this work of organization and unification was accomplished not only in Ireland but in the Churches of Wales, Scotland and Brittany, where conditions were much the same, with the result that the Churches of the Celtic world were finally deprived of their last traits of originality.

§ 4.—The Ecclesiastical Reformation in Ireland
(c. 1110–1172)

The work of reform was carried on in the Irish Church throughout the entire twelfth century. The impulse came from Canterbury. The archbishops of Canterbury, holding, on the one hand, that Gregory the Great, when giving St Augustine primatial authority over the " Britons," had included the Irish under that designation, and, on the other hand, taking account of the ill-defined and insecure nature of the supremacy of Armagh, did not hesitate to claim spiritual rights over Ireland and Scotland and all adjacent islands.[1] We have seen that Lanfranc brought the newly formed Scandinavian dioceses under the dependence of Canterbury. Eadmer, St Anselm's biographer, explicitly attaches the diocese of Waterford, whose bishop Malchus had been consecrated by Anselm, to the " province " of Canterbury

---

[1] Eadmer, *Historia novorum*, I, p. 26. For Limerick, *ib.*, p. 236 ; A. J. Macdonald, *Lanfranc* (Oxford, 1926), pp. 84–85, 193); Lawlor, *BLM*, p. xxiii.

(1096).[1] We possess the text of the professions of obedience made to the archbishops of Canterbury by the bishops Gilla Pádraic, Donough, Samuel and Gregory of Dublin, as well as by Malchus of Waterford and Patrick of Limerick, the latter Gilbert's successor and consecrated by archbishop Theobald, probably in 1140.[2] St Anselm as well as his predecessor wrote to the bishops of Ireland as suffragans, not alone to those of the Norse kingdoms, but to the others as well, pointing out to them the abuses which required correction and the reforms they ought to promote in their dioceses.[3]

Gilbert, bishop of Limerick, was the initiator of the reform movement in Ireland. About the year 1109 he wrote a treatise entitled *De statu Ecclesiae*, a kind of summary of Christian doctrine and ecclesiastical law, which he dedicated to all the bishops and priests of Ireland, many of whom, he states, had eagerly desired such a work. In the circular letter placed at the head of this composition, Gilbert begins by calling the attention of the clergy to the disorders and the liturgical irregularities which presented such a sorry spectacle throughout nearly all Ireland and which he does not hesitate to term " schismatic." [4] He urges uniformity with the rest of the Christian Church in these respects, as also in all relating to ecclesiastical organization. He proceeds to draw a succinct plan of the edifice of the Church and enumerates and defines all the hierarchical degrees, noting the functions attached to each, from the rank of *ostiarius* up to the supreme Pontificate. Among the points on which the Irish clergy require most enlightenment, he mentions specially the necessity for a bishop to hold two synods yearly, one in summer and the other in autumn. He then speaks of the functions of a metropolitan ; to him it belongs to consecrate bishops, assisted by the bishops of his province. Above the archbishops is placed the primate, a dignitary who occupies the same place in the West as the patriarch in the East. Archbishops and primates receive the pallium from the sovereign Pontiff and are bound to go to

---

[1] Eadmer, *op. cit.*, p. 76.
[2] Kenney, *Sources*, I, p. 762 (No. 649). Cf. Lawlor, *BLM*, p. 73.
[3] Kenney, *Sources*, I, pp. 757-58, 761 (Nos. 640, 642, 643, 646).
[4] " Diversi et schismatici illi ordines, quibus Hibernia pene tota delusa est, uni catholico et Romano cedant officio " (Gilbert, *SE*, col. 995).

Rome to seek it in person ; only weighty causes, such as infirmities or war, can exempt them from this step.[1]

A few other points of Gilbert's treatise deserve mention. Priests are to administer baptism by means of triple immersion and, except in cases of urgent necessity, in the church. They are to give communion to the baptized immediately after baptism. All the faithful are bound to communicate thrice yearly, at Easter, Whitsuntide and Christmas. Finally, monks are not entitled to baptize, administer the Sacrament or exercise any other sacerdotal ministry among the laity, except in case of urgent need or by command of the bishop.[2]

Gilbert's zeal drew on him the notice of Rome. He was appointed legate of the Holy See in Ireland, an office which none before him had ever held in the country.[3] It was in his capacity as legate that he was called on to preside at the important synod which met at Rathbreasail in 1110 or 1111.

From the year 1106 on, the see of Armagh was occupied by a coarb of Patrick, who was a bishop—a contingency which had not arisen since the year 957.[4] This prelate, named Cellach (Celsus), behaved from the very outset as a metropolitan archbishop. Having embraced Gilbert's views on the reorganization of the Irish Church, he had decided that the south of Ireland ought to have an archbishopric also, and with the aid of Murtough O'Brien, *ardrí* of Ireland and a zealous promoter of the reform, Cashel was chosen as the archiepiscopal see of Munster, and Malchus, bishop of Waterford, was called to occupy it. For these two archbishoprics it was necessary to supply suffragans, and this was the chief task which was in contemplation in convoking the synod of Rathbreasail.

Under the presidency of the legate Gilbert, the two archbishops, the king Murtough O'Brien and some fifty bishops assembled. Fifty bishops were indeed far too many for the number of episcopal dioceses which it was proposed to establish. It was decided that ecclesiastical Ireland should be divided into twenty-four bishoprics : twelve, including

[1] *Ib.*, cols. 1002–1004.
[2] *Ib.*, cols. 998, 1000, 1001.
[3] Bernard, *Vita Mal.*, 10, col. 1087.
[4] Lawlor, *BLM*, pp. xxxiv–xxxv.

Cashel, for the southern province (Leath Mogha), and twelve, including Armagh, for the northern one (Leath Cuinn). The members of the synod pledged themselves to fix the limits of each diocese, leaving many points (and those not the least important) to be settled after the close of the assembly.

Armagh retained its supremacy of honour over the rest of Ireland, and Dublin remained attached to the province of Canterbury.[1]

The decrees of Rathbreasail were very imperfectly carried out. The new delimitations of the dioceses remained drawn up on paper, but in many cases had no further effect. These changes, which amounted to a regular revolution, were hindered by divers causes. The repeated alterations made in the dioceses of Meath, Oriel, Ulaidh (Ulster), Cloyne, Kilmore and elsewhere, show that the execution of the synod's arrangements was hampered in many places by local rivalries, wars, political changes and probably above all by the resistance of the great abbeys, which for centuries had been centres of religious life and of learning, and whose prestige and interests were seriously infringed by the new order of things.[2]

Gilbert had spoken of the pallium in his *De statu Ecclesiae*, although in his day and for a considerable time after that badge of honour was unknown in Ireland. It was St Malachy who in 1139 took the first step to secure its being granted to the insular metropolitans. Thanks to St Bernard, his friend and later his biographer, no other Irish personality of that age is better known to us than St Malachy.

He was born at Armagh in 1095 of a distinguished family, his Irish name being Mael-Maedóc úa Morgair. A recluse named Imar living in that city trained him in piety and turned his thoughts towards the ecclesiastical calling, and at the age of twenty-five he was ordained priest by the archbishop Cellach. After being made coarb of Comgall at Bangor, he was called when about thirty years old to the episcopal see of Connor (1124), in spite of his strenuous resistance. The barbarism, ignorance and degradation of his

---

[1] Keating, *Foras Feasa ar Éirinn*, II, 28 (Irish Texts Society, London, 1908), ed. P. S. Dineen, p. 299. Cf. Lawlor, *BLM*, pp. xlvi ff.

[2] See H. J. Lawlor, *A fresh Authority for the Synod of Kells*, 1152 (*PRIA*, XXXVI, Sect. C, 1922, pp. 18, 21–22).

       D D

flock were great. He had already, before being raised to the episcopate, set to work to reform morals and to restore the liturgy, religious chant and ecclesiastical discipline in the churches entrusted to his ministry. " He made regulations full of righteousness, full of moderation and integrity," we read in his Life. " Moreover in all churches he ordained the apostolic sanctions and the decrees of the holy fathers, and especially the customs of the holy Roman Church." Thus, as we see, he had thrown himself fully into the plan outlined about 1109 by Gilbert of Limerick. " Hence it is," continues the saint's biographer, " that to this day there is chanting and psalmody in these churches at the canonical hours after the fashion of the whole world. For there was no such thing before, not even in the city (Armagh). He, however, had learnt singing in his youth, and soon he introduced song into his monastery, while as yet none in the city, nor in the whole bishopric, could or would sing. Then Malachy instituted anew the most wholesome usage of confession, the sacrament of confirmation, the marriage contract—of all of which they were either ignorant or negligent. And let these serve as an example of the rest, for [here] and through the whole course of the history we omit much for the sake of brevity." [1]

But when Conor O'Loughlin, king of northern Ireland, ravaged his diocese, Malachy was forced to forsake his church and fly southwards (1127). He sought refuge first at Lismore (where he had previously made a stay with the aged bishop Malchus, who had resigned the archbishopric of Cashel in order to end his days in his old diocese) and then at Iveragh in Kerry where he founded a monastery. [2]

In the meantime archbishop Cellach died (1129), and the see of Armagh fell into the hands of usurpers. A deliverer was called for, and all eyes turned towards Malachy, whom, moreover, Cellach on his death had named as his successor. To gain possession of the see was a formidable enterprise and one involving risk of life ; and several years of struggle were needed to oust the unlawful holders. After finally becoming

---

[1] Bernard, *Vita Mal.*, III, 7, col. 1079 (Lawlor's transl., *BLM*, pp. 17–18). See ch. VIII, cols. 1084–85 and Lawlor's note on St Bernard's description of the state of the Irish Church (*BLM*, pp. 161–63).
[2] Bernard, *Vita Mal.*, IX, col. 1085.

master of the situation and restoring order in the metropolitan city, Malachy resigned his archbishopric in 1137, having occupied that exalted position for only three years. He retired to his former diocese of Connor, which he divided into two districts, leaving the more important one to the titulary of the new see and reserving for himself the lesser one (Down), along with his monastery of Bangor for residence.

He consecrated Gelasius (Gilla mac Liag) († 1174), the new archbishop of Armagh. It was this Gelasius who occupied the primatial see at the date of the Anglo-Norman invasion. Giraldus Cambrensis relates that when the old primate of Ireland went to Dublin to do homage to the king of England, he brought with him his white cow to provide him with milk, the only nourishment the old man required.[1]

Far from remaining idle in his retreat, Malachy now took in hand more resolutely than ever the general interests of the Church of Ireland. Two points specially claimed his attention. The first was to have the elevation of the see of Cashel to the rank of a metropolitan see confirmed by the Holy See ; the second to obtain the pallium both for his successor, the archbishop of Armagh, and for the new archbishop of the south, in case the Holy See consented to recognize the latter. In order to plead his two-fold request Malachy made a journey to Rome in 1139.

On his way he made a stay at Clairvaux. The lively faith, the benevolence, the disinterestedness and the simplicity of the holy pastor at once won the heart of St Bernard, who later in his Life of Malachy wrote with warm feeling : " To me also it was granted to see the man on that journey, and by the sight of him and by his word I was refreshed, and I rejoiced as in all riches ; and I, in turn, though a sinner, found grace in his sight then, and from that time up to his death, as I said in the Preface. He also, deigning to turn aside to Clairvaux, when he saw the brothers was deeply moved ; and they were not a little edified by his presence and his speech. So accepting the place and us, and gathering us into his inmost heart, he bade us farewell and departed." [2]

---

[1] Giraldus, *EH*, I, 35 (p. 283).
[2] Bernard, *Vita Mal.*, xvi, col. 1094 (Lawlor's transl., *BLM*, pp. 70–71).

Malachy was likewise received with great cordiality by Pope Innocent II. " He spent a whole month in the city, visiting the holy places and resorting to them for prayer. During that time the chief Pontiff made frequent and careful inquiry of him and those who were with him co ncerning the affairs of their country, the morals of the people, the state of the churches, and the great things that God wrought by him in the land." [1]

The confirmation of the new metropolis of Cashel was granted without gainsay. As for the question of the palliums, the Pope required that the matter should first of all be carefully investigated in a national council ; if all the Irish clergy were agreed in soliciting the favour, it would be granted. To bestow on Malachy a manifest pledge of his goodwill, Innocent, before dismissing him, conferred on him the legateship of Ireland, an office which the aged Gilbert felt himself henceforth unable to discharge with profit.

It is not clear what cause hindered the council required by the Pope from being at once held. Seven years elapsed before it was convened. At last, in 1148, it was held at Inishpatrick, a small island off Skerries.[2] Fifty bishops and two hundred priests met there, and it was decided that the legate should once more repair to Rome in order to remind Eugene III of the promises made by Innocent II regarding the palliums.

In virtue of his office as legate, Malachy immediately set out again. As on the former occasion, he wished to pass through Clairvaux, where he arrived on October 13 or 14, 1148. It was his intention to rest there for a few days only before continuing his journey, but on the 18th he fell ill, and on November 2 expired in the arms of St Bernard.[3]

A friend of monks and once an abbot himself, the Irish prelate had been so edified by the life of the monks of Cîteaux and the holiness of Bernard, that he would fain have ended his career among them, had his ecclesiastical duties allowed it. But at least he had, after his first stay, sent some Irish novices thither to be trained in monastic discipline with a view to

---

[1] *Ib.*, col. 1095 (Lawlor's transl., p. 73).
[2] Co. Dublin.—Bernard, *Vita Mal.*, xxx, 67, cols. 1112–13. Cf. *Annals of Four Masters, a.a.* 1148 ; Lawlor, *BLM*, p. 118, note 2.
[3] Bernard, *Vita Mal.*, xxxi, cols. 1114–18.

founding Cistercian monasteries in Ireland. St Bernard was able in 1142 to send back a first batch, who settled at Mellifont, in the diocese of Armagh. This first foundation was prolific ; by 1151 five daughter establishments had already gone forth from it, Bective (1147), Baltinglass (1147–1148), Boyle (1148), Shrule (1150) and Monasternenagh (1151).[1]

Before the arrival of the Cistercians, it is likely that the monks of Ireland adhered to the practice of their own Rules. On this point of monastic history Mabillon had once occasion to declare himself, when certain of his brethren took him to task for having excluded from his *Acta sanctorum ordinis sancti Benedicti* as not being Benedictines many holy monks (and especially several saints belonging to early Celtic monasticism), who in their opinion really lived under the Rule of St Benedict. In a memoir written to justify himself, the renowned Maurist gave it as his opinion that the Celtic monks had embraced the Benedictine Rule in so far as they conformed to the practices of the Roman Church.[2] This, however, we hold to be a generalization which it is not easy to accept. It is true of the Northumbrian monasteries of Irish foundation and also perhaps of Landévennec, where the Rule of St Benedict was introduced, in the former at the same time as the Roman Easter and tonsure as a result of the Council of Whitby (664),[3] in the latter at the moment when Louis the Pious enjoined on the abbot Matmonoch to renounce the tonsure of the Scots.[4] But we have no proof that any similar change took place in the monasteries of Ireland in 690 or at Iona in 716, as Mabillon would have it believed. Assuredly the Rule of St Benedict was known through literature in Ireland in the seventh and

---

[1] *Ib.*, XVI, col. 1095. Cf. Janauschek, *Origines Cistercienses* (Vindobonae, 1877), pp. 70, 92, 113, 114, 123. Cf. J. Vendryes, *Mellifont, fille de Clairvaux (Medieval Studies in Memory of Gertrude Schoepperle Loomis*, Paris and New York, 1927).—The monastery of Inislounaght (Co. Tipperary) also existed before A.D. 1148 ; it is mentioned as " Suriense monasterium " (the monastery on the River Suir) in *Vita Mal.*, XXIX, 64 (col. 1111). Cf. Lawlor, *BLM*, p. 76, note 1, p. 114, note 5.

[2] Paul Denis, *Dom Mabillon et sa méthode historique. Mémoire justificatif sur son édition des Acta Sanctorum O.S.B.* (Paris, 1910), p. 37.

[3] Stephen, *Vita Wilfridi*, 14, p. 209 ; Bede, *Vita Cuthberti*, 16 (*PL*, XCIV, 754. Cf. 732).

[4] *V. sup.*, ch. IV, § 4.

eighth centuries,[1] but no written record allows us to affirm that it had established itself as law in any Irish monastery before the arrival of the Cistercians.

Before the English conquest, very few of the continental religious orders had succeeded in gaining foothold in Ireland. Apart from the Cistercians, we can name only the Congregation of Savigny (St. Mary's Abbey, Dublin)[2] and several houses of Augustinian Canons.[3] After the conquest, the continental orders took root under more favourable auspices. The Premonstratensians and, still more, the Friars Minor and Dominicans developed rapidly and soon became popular.[4] On the other hand, the Black Monks never flourished in Ireland, and the Carthusians made only a single settlement there, which had but a short existence from 1280 to 1321.[5]

Let us now see how the work of ecclesiastical reform progressed after Malachy.

We may well suppose that immediately after the death of his friend, St Bernard set himself to make sure that the desires of the Irish Church reached Rome, especially as the reigning Pope, Eugene III, had been a disciple of his. At any rate, in 1151 Cardinal John Paparo arrived in Ireland in the capacity of legate *a latere* to settle the ecclesiastical questions at issue. In March, 1152, a synod was convened at Kells, presided over conjointly by Paparo in his capacity of *Legatus a latere* and by Christian, the first abbot of Mellifont and now bishop of Lismore, who had lately succeeded Malachy as *legatus natus*. The synod effected deep-reaching alterations in the constitution of the Irish Church. Many petty dioceses were suppressed, an archpresbyter taking henceforth the place of the bishop. But an innovation even more radical and more unexpected was the decision, taken by Rome and

---

[1] S. Hellmann, *Pseudo-Cyprianus de XII abusivis saeculi* (Leipzig, 1909), pp. 5 ff. ; Warren in *An. Ban.*, II, pp. 90, 98.

[2] The date of its foundation is unknown. Cf. Léon Guilloreau, *Les fondations anglaises de l'abbaye de Savigny* (*Revue Mabillon*, V, 1909, pp. 322–24).

[3] Bernard, *Vita Mal.*, xiv, 32 (col. 1092). Cf. Lawlor, *BLM*, p. 63 and note, *AU*, 1170. Cf. Lawlor, *ib.*, p. 113, note 3.

[4] R. Flower, *Ireland and Medieval Europe* (*PBA*, XIII, 1929, pp. 10 ff.).

[5] Carthusian house " de Domo Dei " at Kinaleghin (Dioc. of Clonfert). See Margaret Thompson, *The Carthusian Order in England* (London, 1930), pp. 156–57 ; J. MacErlean, *Studies* (xx, 1931, p. 339).

announced by the legate Paparo, of dividing Ireland into four
metropolitan provinces, two new archbishops being created,
one at Dublin and the other at Tuam.   The metropolitan of
Armagh, designated as " *Primas totius Hiberniae*," retained
only eight suffragans ; the metropolitan of Cashel had twelve
(perhaps fourteen).   To Dublin were assigned as suffragans
Glendalough, Ferns, Kilkenny, Leighlin and Kildare, and to
Tuam, Mayo, Killala, Roscommon, Clonfert, Achonry and
Kilmacduagh.[1]

The bishops of Dublin had long since ceased to be docile
suffragans of Canterbury.[2] Already in a letter addressed to
Lanfranc (1074 ?) the Norse Church of Dublin entitled itself
" the metropolis of the island of Ireland," [3] and bishop
Samuel O'Hanley had been called to order by Anselm (about
1100) for presuming to have a cross borne before him in
processions, that being a prerogative of archbishops who wore
the pallium.[4] Henceforth the pontiff of Dublin, exalted to
the rank of metropolitan archbishop, would be able to exercise
this prerogative lawfully.   The legate, in fact, brought from
Rome not two palliums only, one for Armagh and one for
Cashel, as the council of Inishpatrick had desired in 1148,
but four, one for each of the Irish metropolitans.

Up to 1152 the Church of Ireland had presented in respect
of organization a spectacle of chaos probably without a
parallel in any other part of Christendom.   Henceforth it was
provided with regular organs and a sound framework.   Its
physiognomy was wholly altered.   " There was at last,"
observes Dean Lawlor, " one Church in Ireland, which
embraced within it not only the Celtic parts of the island, but
all the Danish dioceses as well.   And the whole Church was
ruled by the bishops.   The reformation may not have been
complete in every detail—there was indeed much left for the
Anglo-Normans to do—but the synod of Kells had set the crown
on the work of the Irish reformers.   And this consummation

---

[1] H. J. Lawlor, *A fresh Authority for the Synod of Kells*, pp. 16–22.   Cf.
Kenney, *Sources*, I, pp. 768–69.
[2] Lawlor, *BLM*, p. LXIV.
[3] *PL*, CL, 536–37.
[4] *PL*, CLIX, 109–10.

was mainly due to the wisdom and the untiring zeal of St Malachy of Armagh." [1]

We might at this point break off the history of the Celtic Church of Ireland ; but just then there occurred the most memorable event in the history of the country, one the consequences of which last to the present moment, namely, the conquest of the island by Henry Plantagenet, second monarch of the name, between 1169 and 1171 ; and we cannot but say something of those consequences.

Much discussion has been waged as to the authenticity of the famous Papal Bull *Laudabiliter*, by which the English Pope Adrian IV authorized King Henry, from the year 1155, to undertake that conquest " in order to extend the boundaries of the Church, to bear the knowledge of the truth to ignorant and uncivilized peoples and to root out the weeds of wickedness from the field of the Lord." [2] The arguments put forward by those who uphold its authenticity are, in our opinion, the strongest. Although the Bull is not drawn up in strict conformity with the rules followed at the time by the papal Chancery, it can nevertheless be proved that in substance it is in accord with other contemporary and uncontested witnesses. [3]

It still remained to improve discipline, the liturgy and the observance of sacraments in certain points, in conformity with the wishes of Lanfranc and St Anselm. The synod of Cashel, convened in 1172 by command of Henry II, under the presidency of Christian, bishop of Lismore and apostolic legate,

[1] Lawlor, *BLM*, p. LXIV.

[2] See text of the Bull in Giraldus, *EH*, II, 5 (pp. 317–18).

[3] Among the many studies on Pope Adrian's Bull we may refer the reader to the following outstanding ones : 1. Paul Scheffer-Boichorst, *Zwei Untersuchungen zur päpstlichen Territorial-und Finanzpolitik* (*MIOG*, Ergänzungsbd., IV, 1892) ; 2. Kate Norgate, *The Bull " Laudabiliter "* (*EHR*, VIII, 1893, pp. 18–52) [gives extensive bibliography] ; 3. O. J. Thatcher, *Studies concerning Adrian IV* (University of Chicago.—The Decennial Publications. I. Ser., 1903, pp. 153–238) ; 4. H. Thurston, *The English Pope and his Irish Bull* (*The Month*, April and May, 1906) ; 5. G. H. Orpen, *Ireland under the Normans*, 1169–1216 (Oxford, 1911), pp. 274–78 ; 6. H. P. Russell, *The Popes and the Norman Invasions of Britain and Ireland* (*American Catholic Quarterly Review*, XXXIX, 1914, pp. 527–39) ; 7. Anna Eggers, *Die Urkunde Papst Hadrian IV. für K. Heinrich II. von England über die Besetzung Irlands* (*Historische Studien*, CLI, Berlin, 1922) ; 8. R. I. Best, *Pope Adrian's Bull* (*Times Literary Supplement*, November 30, 1922, p. 783) ; 9. C. Bémont, *La bulle Laudabiliter* (*MHMA*, pp. 41–53).

undertook the task of settling these matters.   Gelasius, the archbishop of Armagh, was prevented by his infirmities from taking part in the synod, but the three other archbishops, one of whom was Lorcan (St Lawrence O'Toole), the new arch-bishop of Dublin, their suffragans, abbots and many other prelates, were present in the assembly.   The canons relating to prohibited degrees in marriage were re-enacted.   Children were to be catechized at the church doors and baptized at the font of the baptisteries.   The faithful were bound to pay tithes to the parochial church.   Glebe lands and ecclesiastical property were exempted from the levies of the native kings, nobles and potentates.   Clerics were not obliged to com-pound for a homicide perpetrated by a layman of their kindred.   When dangerously ill, the faithful were to make their will solemnly and in presence of their confessor and neighbours, taking care to provide for the payment of their debts.   All good Christians should have a proper funeral, and Masses and vigils should be offered for the repose of their souls. Finally, the liturgy was to be celebrated in conformance with the rules followed in the universal Church, the English Church being taken as a model.[1]

With the synod of Cashel the reformation was accomplished in its essentials.   We shall here end our account of Ireland and pass to Scotland.

§ 5.—ECCLESIASTICAL REFORMS IN SCOTLAND
(TENTH TO TWELFTH CENTURIES)

In 825, in the course of a sudden descent made by the Danes, the monk Blathmac was put to death by the pirates while celebrating the sacred mysteries in the church of Iona. The news of his martyrdom before long reached Reichenau, where Walahfrid Strabo composed a poem in his honour.[2] The isle of Iona was ravaged by the Vikings several other times in the ninth and tenth centuries.[3]   On the night of

---

[1] Giraldus, *EH*, I, 34, 35 (pp. 280–83) ; Mansi, *Concilia*, XXII, 133–36. Cf. J. Lanigan, *An Ecclesiastical History of Ireland* (2nd edit., Dublin, 1829). IV, pp. 206–16.

[2] *AU*, a.a. 824 = 825 ; Walahfrid Strabo, *Versus de B. Blaithmaic vita et fine*, ed. Dümmler, *MG. Poet. Lat.*, II, 297–301.

[3] *CED*, II, I, pp. 143, 148–49.

Christmas 986 the abbey was pillaged and the abbot killed, with fifteen of his elders.[1]

In 848–849 some of the relics of Colum cille had been carried to Dunkeld (Strathtay) through the exertions of king Kenneth Mac Alpin († 858), the same monarch who effected the fusion of the two different national elements in North Britain, the Picts of Alba and the Scots of Irish descent.[2] He caused the monastery of Dunkeld to be built, thenceforth the most important religious centre in Scotland. The deaths of the abbots of Dunkeld are recorded in the Annals of Ulster : Tuathal in 865, Flaithbertach in 873, Dubscuile in 964 and Donnchad in the same or the following year. Tuathal, the son of Artgus, is entitled " chief bishop of Fortrenn and abbot of Dunkeld." However, Dunkeld did not escape the destructive raids of the Scandinavians.

In the reign of Constantine, son of Aed (900–943), a council was held (906) on the hill of Credulity, near the royal city of Scone (Perthshire), at which the king and the bishop Cellach were present. There an engagement was entered into to observe, " in conformity with the customs of the Scots (*pariter cum Scottis*), the laws and discipline of the faith and the rights of churches and the Gospels." [3]

At what date did the dignity of chief ecclesiastical city pass to St. Andrews ? It is hard to say, so dense is the obscurity which enfolds the history of Scotland in this period. Among the earliest bishops of that see may be named Maelduin (before 1055), Tuathal (about 1055–1059), and Fothad († 1093), called by the Annals of Ulster " *ardepscop Alban* " (chief bishop of Scotland). Fothad was succeeded by Turgot, a Saxon by birth and prior of Durham, who was elected on June 20, 1107, and consecrated at York on August 1, 1109.

Neither can it be said with certainty at what time the relics of the Apostle who gave to St. Andrews its name were brought thither from Constantinople.[4]

---

[1] *AU*, a.a. 985 or 986 = 986.

[2] *Chronicle of the Kings of Scotland*, Version A, ed. Skene, *Picts and Scots*, p. 8. Cf. Anderson, *Early Sources*, I, note, p. 279.

[3] *Chronicle of the Kings of Scotland*, p. 9 ; *CED*, II, i, p. 144. Cf. Anderson, *Early Sources*, I, pp. 224, 445.

[4] See Anderson, *Early Sources*, I, pp. 266–68 ; A. S. Cook, *The Old English " Andreas " and Bishop Acca of Hexham (Transactions of the Connecticut*

No one in Scotland laboured in the interests of uniformity in ritual and discipline with such zeal as the pious queen Margaret, wife of king Malcolm III (1054–1093), and grand-niece of Edward the Confessor. Up to her time it had been the custom in Scotland not to begin the Lenten fast until Monday in the first week of Lent. Margaret caused it to begin on Ash Wednesday, as was usual in the Roman Church by that time. The queen, moreover, exerted herself to banish from the office of the Mass " certain barbarous rites," concerning whose nature we have no other information. Finally, she insisted that Sunday should be kept as a holy day and that the canon law forbidding marriage within certain degrees of kinship should be observed. Her biographer Turgot tells us that she reformed many other abuses, but has not judged it expedient to give us any details about them.[1]

In accordance with an agreement made at the Council of Windsor (1072) between Lanfranc and Thomas I, archbishop of York, the Church of Scotland was placed in the dependence of the northern English metropolis, an arrangement subsequently sanctioned by the Holy See.[2] But in 1119 Ralph d'Escures, who succeeded St Anselm, claimed that Scotland should be attached to his own see, taking his stand on the theory on which we have already seen his predecessors base their claims with regard to Ireland, to wit, that St Gregory the Great had subjected the entire Britannic group of islands to the jurisdiction of Augustine.[3] There ensued prolonged confusion and hot disputes, until at last Pope Clement III, by a Bull of March 13, 1188, established the independence of the Church of Scotland in respect of both English sees and placed it under the immediate jurisdiction of the Apostolic See.[4]

The assimilation of the Church of Scotland was thus in a fair way to being realized. At that time it numbered nine bishoprics, St. Andrews, Glasgow, Dunkeld, Dunblane,

---

Academy of Arts and Sciences, XXVI, 1924, pp. 245–332) ; W. C. Mackenzie, *Scottish Place-names* (London, 1931), p. 251.

[1] Turgot, *Vita Margaritae*, 8 (*CED*, II, 1, pp. 156–59).

[2] *CED*, II, 1, pp. 159, 167, 191, etc.

[3] *CED*, II, 1, pp. 193–95.

[4] *CED*, II, 1, pp. 273–74. Cf. J. Dowden, *The Medieval Church in Scotland* (Glasgow, 1910), pp. 11–12.

Brechin, Aberdeen, Moray, Ross and Caithness. Galloway remained under the jurisdiction of York.

The first bishops of the Orkneys were sent to the islands by Adam of Bremen († *c.* 1076). Their successors in the eleventh and twelfth centuries, Ralph, Roger and Ralph Nowell, were consecrated by the archbishop of York. William the Old († 1168) was bishop of the Orkneys at the time when the see of Trondhjem was raised to the rank of an archbishopric (1152), Norway, the Orkneys, the Hebrides, Iceland and Greenland being included within its sphere of authority. The bishops of the Orkneys remained suffragans of Trondhjem down to the year 1472, when they passed into the dependence of St. Andrews.[1]

It would be extremely difficult to give an accurate account of the Scottish monasteries in the ninth century and the two or three following ones. During that time we find Culdees (Keledei), monks whom we have already met with in Ireland, established in several places, Dunkeld, Lochleven, St. Andrews, Brechin and elsewhere.[2]   On the other hand, the great religious orders of continental origin, Benedictines, Cistercians and Canons Regular of St Augustine, installed themselves in the monasteries from the twelfth century onward. The first Cistercian settlement was made at Melrose in 1136.[3]

" And thus," says Skene, " the old Celtic Church came to an end, leaving no vestiges behind it, save here and there the roofless walls of what had been a church, and the numerous old burying-grounds to the use of which the people still cling with tenacity, and where occasionally an ancient Celtic cross tells of its former state. All else has disappeared ; and the only records we have of their history are the names of the saints by whom they were founded preserved in old calendars, the fountains near the old churches bearing their name, the village fairs of immemorial antiquity held on their day, and here and there a few lay families holding a small portion of

---

[1] A. W. Brøgger, *Ancient Emigrants : a History of the Norse Settlements of Scotland* (Oxford, 1929), pp. 164–65. Cf. Anderson, *Early Sources*, II, pp. 7–9, 228–30, 266.
[2] See map showing the Culdee stations in Scotland in W. Douglas Simpson, *The Origin of Christianity in Aberdeenshire* (Aberdeen, 1925), p. 46.
[3] *CED*, II, 1, pp. 181–82.

land, as hereditary custodiers of the pastoral staff or other relic of the reputed founder of the church, with some small remains of its jurisdiction." [1]

§ 6.—ECCLESIASTICAL REFORMS IN WALES
(c. 900–1207)

The supremacy of one Welsh see over the rest was, as we have seen, always a subject of debate and uncertainty. It is possible that Cyfeiliawg of Llandaff († 927) and several other Welsh bishops of the ninth or tenth century were consecrated by the archbishop of Canterbury.[2] But it was after the conquest of the country by the Normans that the influence of the English primate gained ground in the Principality. A Norman, Bernard, was elected bishop of St. David's in 1115 ; consecrated at Canterbury, he made profession of canonical obedience to the primate of England.[3]

At the end of the twelfth century Giraldus Cambrensis, archdeacon of Breckon, one of the most cultured men of the time, but of an ambitious, restless and intriguing spirit, engaged in a series of attempts to detach the bishopric of St. David's (Menevia) from the jurisdiction of Canterbury.

To this end he collected a host of documents of all kinds and from all quarters, wrote his *De invectionibus* and his *De iure et statu Menevensis Ecclesiae*,[4] and thrice made a journey to Rome to set forth his case. But his arguments were finally judged insufficient by the Holy See, and the Welsh bishops, including the bishop of Menevia, were called on by Innocent III in 1207 to submit to the jurisdiction of Canterbury.[5]

The order of Cîteaux found in Wales as in Ireland a thoroughly congenial soil for its plantations. The oldest Cistercian abbeys were those of Tintern in Monmouth (1131),

---

[1] Skene, *CS*, II, p. 418.
[2] *CED*, I, pp. 208, 287–88. Cf. Lloyd, *HW*, I, p. 347 ; II, p.4 86 (note on the alleged archbishopric of St. David's). Hervé, a Breton, one of the favourite chaplains of Rufus, having been appointed to the bishopric of Bangor, was consecrated in 1092 by Thomas, archbishop of York, *vacante sede Cantuar.* (*CED*, I, p. 299).
[3] Eadmer, *Historia novorum*, v, pp. 235–36 ; *CED*, I, pp. 306–307.
[4] *Opera* (*RS*), Vol. III.
[5] *CED*, I, pp. 452–53. Cf. H. Owen, *Gerald the Welshman* (2nd ed., London, 1904).

Whitland in Carmarthen (1140), Cwmhir in Radnor (1143) and Margam in Glamorgan (1147).[1] In 1147 there were handed over also to the Cistercian order the two abbeys of Neath (Glamorgan) and Basingwerk (Flint), which had hitherto belonged to the Congregation of Savigny ; Neath had been founded in 1130 and Basingwerk in 1133.[2]

The Benedictines, on the contrary, were represented only by priories of little importance and dependent on English or continental abbeys, such as Monmouth, founded about 1095 by the Breton Wihenoc and belonging to Saint-Florent-le-Vieil, Abergavenny, a dependent of Saint-Vincent in Le Mans, Goldcliff at the mouth of the Usk, a cell of Bec, and others.[3]

§ 7.—CORNWALL (NINTH TO ELEVENTH CENTURY)

The profession of canonical obedience made to Ceolnoth, archbishop of Canterbury (833–870), by a bishop of Cornwall named Kenstec has been preserved to us. This Kenstec, stated to have been elected " *in monasterio quod lingua Brettonum appellatur Dinnurrin,*" a place otherwise unknown, may well have had his see at Gerrans. This is the earliest profession of obedience made by a Celtic bishop to the archbishop of Canterbury that we possess.[4]

In the twelfth century William of Malmesbury declared that he had no certain knowledge touching the ancient bishoprics of Cornwall and the succession of its bishops. He mentions the see of St. Petroc and says that, according to some, a bishopric had also existed at St. Germans.[5] We may be sure that in the monasteries of Cornwall, as in the other Churches of the Celtic world, there were bishops attached to these monasteries, but not provided with dioceses.[6] In the eighth

[1] Janauschek, *Origines Cistercienses*, pp. 19, 61, 74, 107 ; Alice M. Cooke, *The Settlement of the Cistercians in England* (*EHR*, VIII, 1893, pp. 637 ff.), with a map of the Cistercian abbeys in England and Wales.

[2] Janauschek, *op. cit.*, pp. 98, 99. Cf. L. Guilloreau, *Les fondations anglaises de l'abbaye de Savigny* (*Revue Mabillon*, V, 1909, pp. 319–21, 323).

[3] A. G. Little, *Mediaeval Wales* (London, 1902), p. 105 ; E. J. Newell, *A History of the Welsh Church* (London, 1895), pp. 290–93.

[4] *CED*, I, p. 674.

[5] William of Malmesbury, *Gesta pontificum Anglorum* (*RS*), II, 95, p. 204. See Charter of Edward the Confessor, A.D. 1050 (*CED*, I, p. 694).

[6] *V. sup.*, ch. VII, § 1.

century the jurisdiction of the bishop of Sherborne extended over Cornwall. The diocese of Crediton (Devon) was founded in 909, and over it was placed the Saxon Eadwulf, who was bound to visit the Cornish people yearly and endeavour to root out their errors, " for," so we read in a text preserved to us in Leofric's Missal, " they had hitherto resisted with all their might the truth and the apostolic decrees, refusing to obey them." [1]

With the sanction of Pope Leo IX and king Edward the Confessor, Leofric, bishop of Crediton, transferred his see to Exeter in 1050 and established his cathedral in St. Peter's monastery,[2] in which he installed canons, who lived, says William of Malmesbury, " *ad formam Lotharingorum*," in other words, followed the Rule of St Chrodegang of Metz.[3]

A letter written at the end of December, 1049, by the Pope to king Edward on this matter, contains a passage of particular interest. " It has come to the knowledge of our Holiness," writes Leo, " that the bishop Leofric occupies a pontifical see without a city (*sine civitate sedem pontificalem tenet*). We are much surprised not only by this particular case, but by that of the other bishops who accept a like condition. As we have sent you our legate to speak to you of other matters, we command you at this time and beseech you in the name of the Lord and for love of us to aid our brother Leofric that he may be able to transfer his episcopal see from the *villula* of Crediton to the *civitas* of Exeter." [4] Evidently at Rome it was not considered fitting that an episcopal see could be established elsewhere than in a city of the ancient Roman empire. In the month of May of the following year we shall find the same Pope in another letter expressing his amazement at the claims made by the bishop of Dol in Brittany to the title of archbishop, " seeing that one who has neither a see in a city nor the pallium cannot be considered an archbishop." [5]

[1] *Missale vetus Leofrici*, ed. F. E. Warren (Oxford, 1883), pp. 1–2 ; *CED*, I, p. 676.
[2] *Ep. Leonis ad Edw. regem.*, *PL*, CXLIII, 639 ; *CED*, I, pp. 691–92.
[3] William of Malmesbury, *Gesta pontificum Anglorum* (*RS*), II, 94, p. 201.
[4] Letter quoted above.
[5] Letter to Eudo of Penthièvre, regent of Brittany (*PL*, CXLIII, 648–49). Dol is not mentioned in the *Notitia Galliarum ;* see Mommsen's edition, *MG. Auct. ant.*, IX, pp. 586–87.

§ 8.—Reforms in Brittany (936–1199)

The Breton Church suffered acutely in the eleventh century from the evils which infected well nigh the universal Catholic hierarchy in that gloomy period, namely, concubinage and simony. In the episcopal sees of Rennes and Quimper a scandalous succession from father to son is known to have prevailed in the tenth and eleventh centuries.[1] Budic, bishop of Nantes, who had obtained the episcopal dignity by simony, was deposed at the Council of Reims in 1049.[2] Juthaël, bishop of Dol, a simoniac and openly married, who in a letter addressed to his protector William the Conqueror by Gregory VII is called a " Nicolaitan," provided his daughters with dowries out of the lands and rents of his church.[3] Placed under an anathema by the sovereign Pontiff, Juthaël attempted resistance, but the clergy and people of Dol, revolted by his exactions and infamies, expelled from his see the reprobate who called himself an archbishop, but was in truth an arch-wolf (*non tam archiepiscopum quam archilupum*) (1076).[4] A large number of the lower clergy were corrupted by the scandalous example of the episcopate.

The popes, as may well be imagined, did not remain impassive in the face of such relaxation of clerical morals and discipline. After the deposition of Budic, Leo IX appointed to the see of Nantes an abbot of St. Paul's in Rome named Airard, who set to work to prevent the laity from usurping ecclesiastical benefices and to reform the morals of the clergy. But the imperious bearing of this prelate and his followers irritated the Bretons, who drove them out in 1054.[5]

The secular clergy, ignorant and corrupt as they were and at the mercy of the lay aristocracy, were very indifferent tools for the work of reform which it was the earnest desire of Rome to carry out. It was needful to resort to the monks. Brittany

[1] La Borderie, *HB*, III, pp. 168–71. Cf. B. A. Pocquet du Haut-Jussé, *Les papes et les ducs de Bretagne* (*Bibliothèque des Écoles françaises d'Athènes et de Rome*, CXXXIII, Paris, 1928), I, pp. 1–43.
[2] Mansi, *Concilia*, XIX, 741.
[3] *PL*, CXLVIII, col. 674 ; Morice, *Preuves*, I, pp. 442–43.
[4] *Vita Gilduini* in Du Paz, *Histoire généalogique de plusieurs maisons illustres de Bretagne* (Paris, 1619), p. 502.
[5] La Borderie, *HB*, III, pp. 179–81.

possessed already a large number of monasteries ; and in addition, the dukes of Brittany, the bishops and the barons who were zealous in the good cause appealed to the French abbeys of Marmoutiers, St. Florent, St. Aubin and St. Serge in Angers, and Mont-Saint-Michel, in order to secure as great a number as possible of religious to whom the moral and spiritual uplifting of the parishes might be entrusted.[1] Thanks to the efforts and example of these monks, not only were the churches governed according to the canons, religious worship sedulously maintained and the tone of morals raised in all classes of society, but, while thus cultivating the souls of the people, they set to work also on the barren Breton soil and cleared considerable tracts of it, giving a strong impetus to agriculture throughout the extent of the duchy.[2]

Dol nevertheless still persisted in its claims to independence from the metropolis of Tours. But the importance of Dol had been much diminished. Vannes and Quimper had already united themselves to Tours.[3] The worthless Juthaël was succeeded by the virtuous Even, to whom Gregory VII granted the pallium, reserving however the settlement of the metropolitan question (1076).[4] Both Even's successors John and Rolland obtained the same badge of honour. But in 1094 Urban II commanded the bishops of Brittany to submit to their lawful metropolis, declaring that after Rolland his successors should no longer receive the pallium.[5] Rolland outlived Urban, and the following pope, Paschal II, in spite of the declaration of 1094, granted the pallium to Rolland's successor Baudry, the learned abbot of Bourgueil (1107–1130), who went to Rome to claim it in 1109.

Dol was losing ground in another direction also. Of the four Breton bishoprics which remained faithful to it, St. Pol-de-Léon, St. Brieuc, Tréguier and Alet, the one last named broke away in 1120 ; and St. Pol did the same after the death of bishop Galon († 1128 or 1129).[6]

---

[1] Duine, *Métropole*, p. 12.
[2] La Borderie, *HB*, III, pp. 185–88.
[3] Cf. L.G., *Les chrétientés celtiques*, p. 374, note 2.
[4] *PL*, CXLVIII, 459 ; Morice, *Preuves*, I, 446.
[5] Martène and Durand, *Thesaurus*, III, 878–81.
[6] La Borderie, *HB*, III, p. 199 ; Duine, *Métropole*, pp. 118, 119.

Hildebert of Lavardin, elected archbishop of Tours in 1125, presided about two years later over a provincial council at Nantes, in which various abuses were amended—at any rate on paper. Especially it was decreed that the sons of priests could not be ordained unless they had previously been professed in a monastery of canons regular or of monks.[1] The acts of this council do not state whether the metropolitan question was brought forward at it. But, be that as it may, soon afterwards Hildebert wrote to Pope Honorius II begging him not to grant the pallium in future to the bishop of Dol, who was his suffragan, inasmuch as the right to wear it had been accorded to Baudry only in consideration of his personal merits and not in virtue of his see (1130).[2] This proceeding of the metropolitan remained however without effect, for Geoffroy Le Roux, Baudry's successor, received the pallium from the hands of Innocent II.

The Breton metropolis still kept two faithful suffragans, St Brieuc and Tréguier. But in 1144 Pope Lucius II enjoined on the bishops of both these sees to submit to the metropolitan of Tours.[3]

During the pontificate of Eugene III (1145–1153), St Bernard of Clairvaux put forward a proposal for an arrangement between Dol and Tours, which however fell through.[4]

At last Innocent III put an end to the long strife by a bull dated June 1, 1199. He decreed that the archbishopric together with the title of archbishop of Dol should be henceforth suppressed and that the bishop of that see should no longer have the pallium, but should be subject to the metropolitan of Tours on the same terms as the other Breton bishops.[5] The Papal decision met with no resistance in Brittany, except at Dol; for at the moment when it was made St. Brieuc and Tréguier, the last two suffragans of the pseudo-metropolis, had already forsaken it. John VI, who

---

[1] Hildebert, *Ep.* II, 30 (*PL*, CLXXI, 253–54).
[2] Hildebert, *Ep.* II, 35 (cols. 258–59).
[3] Martène and Durand, *Thesaurus*, III, 890. Cf. Duine, *Métropole*, p. 124.
[4] Morice, *Preuves*, I, 761 ; Martène and Durand, *Thesaurus*, III, 855, 897, 898.
[5] Morice, *Preuves*, I, 759–67 ; *PL*, CCXIV, 625.

had for several years been bishop elect of Dol, was consecrated at Tours, probably towards the end of September, 1201.[1]

In addition to this age-long quarrel, the state of Christian society in the tenth, eleventh and twelfth centuries offers a spectacle far from edifying. Among clergy and laity alike little was to be seen but violence, a barbarous state of morals and disorders of all sorts. We may recall the words of Peter Abelard touching his monks of St. Gildas of Ruis : " *O quoties veneno me perdere tentaverunt !* " [2] " *Duram provinciam nactus sum,*" wrote Jean de la Grille, bishop of St. Malo (Alet), to St Bernard.[3]

About the middle of the eleventh century a visionary of the name of Éon de l'Étoile, a fanatic and anarchist, roamed through Brittany preaching war on the clergy and their property and winning many adepts. He was condemned by the Council of Reims in 1148.[4]

Gloomy as the picture may be, it must, however, be admitted that all these irregularities of belief, discipline and morals, had their counterpart or something very near it in the rest of the Christian world in that age of violent contrasts, in which the most extravagant disorders were to be found side by side with marvellous examples of holiness. Heresies were rife in Brittany about the year 1147, if we are to believe Hugh of Amiens, archbishop of Rouen, who wrote at that date a work in three books *Contra haereticos sui temporis*, in which he gives battle to a large number of heterodox ideas.[5] But were all these heresies peculiar to the Brittany of his day ? It is hardly likely. After alluding in the dedication of his work to a certain heresy prevalent in the country, which, however, he does not describe (can it have been that of the Eounites or initiates of Éon de l'Étoile ?), for the remainder of his three books he discourses only of generalities without adducing a single concrete instance and without further mention of Brittany or any Breton whatever—a singular

---

[1] Cf. Duine, *Métropole*, pp. 135–40.
[2] Abelard, *Ep.* I, *seu Historia calamitatum* (*PL*, CLXXVIII, 179).
[3] John of Alet to St Bernard (*PL*, CLXXXII, 681).
[4] See F. Vernet, art. *Éon de l'Étoile* in the *Dictionnaire de théologie*, edited by Vacant and Mangenot.
[5] Hugh of Amiens, *Contra haereticos* (*PL*, CXCII).

method of prosecuting a charge, and one on which it were better not to place too much reliance. Old Brittany had its troubles, like the rest of Christendom, but, again be it said, let us not deepen the shades in a picture which is already dark enough.

CONCLUSION

With the era of the Scandinavian invasions the Christian Churches in Celtic lands enter on the path of decline. The Scandinavians were followed by other conquerors. The yoke of foreigners pressed more and more heavily on these unhappy peoples. Powerless to reform their discipline and to complete their hierarchical organization, imperfectly developed as it was, the Celtic Churches yielded without resistance, but also without any great enthusiasm, to the reforming influence exercised on them at the instigation of Rome by the great neighbouring ecclesiastical centres—Canterbury and York in the case of the islands, Tours in that of Brittany. On the old and half-withered stock it was sought to graft new branches in the hope that their young sap would kindle life anew. By the end of the twelfth century the work of reform, unification and centralization was being everywhere carried on, if not fully accomplished.

To appreciate the part played by these Churches in the religious evolution of western Europe we certainly must not take our standpoint in this last period of their history ; we must go back some centuries in the course of time. Their period of expansion falls between the beginning of the sixth and the middle of the ninth century. During that time they appear to us at the height of their beneficent activity and their glory, full of youth, ardour and originality, and inspired by a remarkable zeal in winning converts. Surely it was a privileged region of the Christian world which, in the space of a few generations, produced Patrick, Gildas, David, Columba, Brendan, Columban, Aidan, John the Scot, besides those pioneers of the Gospel who implanted Christian life in the soil of Brittany and the swarms of ascetics and missionaries who spread over the whole of Europe. These were, in truth, men of memorable breed !

What country ever better deserved the name of " Isle of Saints " than Ireland, a land covered with monasteries and hermitages, churches and schools, in which legions of holy and learned men embraced renunciation, poverty and chastity, and gave themselves up to a life of lofty asceticism and to the cultivation of religious learning ? These men were wonderful in their power alike of stimulating intellectual life and of winning souls. An undefinable mixture of fervour with austerity, of independence with respect of tradition, of naïve simplicity with keen sensibility, along with an eager imagination, enamoured of singularity and often carried away to fantastic extremes—all these contrasting traits which united to form the religious temperament of the early Celts exercised far and wide an irresistible charm. Foreigners of the highest type, attracted by their ardent piety and superior knowledge, were seen flocking to the masters of the isles, from whose influence they could not henceforth loose themselves.

In the later centuries of the Middle Ages, when their religious life had ceased to put forth such fair blossoms, the Celts still kept their hold on the imagination of Europe by other means. From their race, small in numbers, restricted in territory, even subject, all the other nations vied with one another in borrowing their literary romances. Arthur, Lancelot, Perceval, Merlin, Tristram and Isolt were known in all countries and were the delight of numberless generations. " In the dreamy, melancholy and passionate imagination of this [Celtic] race, the fairest fictions of the Middle Ages were elaborated, if not originally formed " [1]—for many of them go back to a far remoter past.

The obstinacy with which the Celts clung to their own opinions in the course of those controversies in matter of discipline, which they made the leading concern of their religious history, was certainly injurious to their reputation for orthodoxy, even after they had made a final submission. By dint of calling them " schismatics " and even " heretics " in season and out of season, their adversaries came at last to believe, and to persuade the world at large to believe, that they were really such. Besides, were not Pelagius and John the Scot of their kin ? Fewer reasons would have sufficed for those hasty and ill-

[1] Gaston Paris, *Légendes du moyen âge* (Paris, 1904), p. 117. Cf. E. Renan, *La poésie des races celtiques* (*Essais de morale et de critique*, p. 376).

matured generalizations by which the current of public opinion was determined. Thus, even after they had finally yielded the field in the domain of discipline, Scots and Britons found themselves invested, down to the ninth century and even later, with a vague suspicion, if not of actual heresy, at any rate of being rash and too free and easy in their opinions and methods, a suspicion which the freedom of their manners and their frankness of speech appear to have helped to establish.

Their neighbours, the Anglo-Saxons, were the chief to cast discredit on them, instigated by principle, by difference of temperament, and very likely also by jealousy. Theodore of Tarsus, on his arrival in England in 669, took his stand as a determined adversary of the Celtic spirit. In his eyes the Scots of Northumbria, as well as those of Ireland, were indeed pious men, animated by great zeal and able to inspire lively enthusiasm, but they were bad administrators, unacquainted with canon law and the latest decisions of Rome, men of undisciplined and quarrelsome behaviour, whose influence must at all costs be checked in England. The canonical texts ascribed to the archbishop of Canterbury preserve unequivocal traces of this attitude.

We find the same feelings entertained by Wilfrid towards the Irish. Their impulsive nature and proneness to extremes were an offence to the sober Anglo-Saxons, imbued with the Roman spirit and ever on the look-out for the minutest direction emanating from the Roman Curia. If (as there is room for believing) the Holy See laid in its stock of information concerning the life of the Celtic Churches from that furnished by the English churchmen who were incessantly plying to and fro between their country and the Eternal City,[1] it is easy to account for the prejudices to which more than one Roman document testifies.

That the ascendancy held by the Scottic teachers in the Catholic world at large awakened at last a certain jealousy in their English neighbours, is superabundantly proved by a letter of Aldhelm of Sherborne which has been quoted in another connection.

[1] " Angli, qui maxime familiariores apostolicae sedis semper existunt " (*Gesta abbatum Fontanellensium*, ed. S. Loewenfeld (Hannoverae, 1886, p. 42).

And yet the Celtic influence made its way in spite of all obstacles. From the Irish books of devotion the Anglo-Saxons themselves in the eighth and ninth centuries borrowed a goodly proportion of their formulas of prayer. Nor was it otherwise on the Continent. St Columban's inflexible character set the bishops against him ; notwithstanding, the cloisters opened by him or his disciples were filled, his practices spread, and his Rule, in association with that of St Benedict, continued during the seventh century to be the guide of numerous monasteries.

In the following century Celtic canons and penitentials were received everywhere with favour. But that favour was not destined to endure for long. The Frankish councils of the ninth century are by no means flattering to the Scots. Those of the beginning of the century direct their censures chiefly against the *episcopi vagantes* and other peripatetics. The later ones condemn the theological extravagances of John the Scot and his followers. These condemnations of the councils created a current of opinion little favourable to the spread of the insular canonical collections, and that just at a moment when, on the other hand, the reputation of the Scots for learning was at its height. However, these canons were intended rather, as it has been said, " to lay down principles than to give hard and fast rules for the action of the various organs of ecclesiastical society." Besides, other independent canonical tendencies were beginning to make themselves felt. A collection of the end of the eighth or beginning of the ninth century, drawn up in a reforming spirit and one of the most widely spread of the age, has borrowed nothing from the *Hibernensis* or the insular penitentials. Nevertheless, the Irish canons continued to be transcribed in the tenth century and in the eleventh enjoyed a brief renaissance in Italy.[1]

One admires the Celtic societies for their utter contempt of aught savouring of opportunism. Yet one might wish they had shown in the course of their medieval history greater political insight, and better realized what principle of strength and duration union is. Whenever an enemy has

[1] P. Fournier, *De l'influence de la collection canonique irlandaise* (*Nouvelle revue d'histoire de droit français et étranger*, XXIII, 1899, pp. 74–78).

appeared among them he has always found their kings at utter variance, rending one another in intestine conflict instead of forming a united body against foreign arms. The same inability for cohesion, organization and prolonged common effort hastened the decline of the religious institutions of the Celts. What Paul Fournier has said of their canonical work may well be applied to their ecclesiastical institutions as a whole : " Here, as elsewhere, the Celtic genius, when it was no longer a question of stimulating individual action, but of organizing and governing, was unable to construct anything destined to endure ; here, as elsewhere, the victory remained with the Latin genius." [1] " The Irish race has always been fertile of individualities, but insusceptible of organization," it has been said also [2] ; and again it has been observed that " The Celt [was] better suited to win converts than to train and manage them when won." [3] But many pages of this book will result in showing that this latter opinion at least admits of more than one reservation.

We have followed for nearly a thousand years the historical development of the Churches of the Celtic world. It is our earnest hope that we may not have given an altogether unfaithful picture. We have confined ourselves to main outlines and outstanding figures, being too diffident of the use of imagination in historical research to venture more deeply into details in order to reproduce the animation and picturesque vividness of life. To endeavour to resuscitate the past is a delicate task, and he who attempts it too often succeeds only in presenting a caricature. For, as it has been said with perfect justness, " of all truths, the most variable and the most uncertain is historic truth." [4] The historian must never weary of searching the past ; but let him beware of believing that he can explain all its mysteries.

[1] P. Fournier, *art. cit.*, p. 78. Cf. *R. Cel.*, XXX, p. 234.

[2] E. J. Gwynn, *Some Saints of Ireland* (*Church Quarterly Review*, LXXIV, 1912, p. 67).—" Man gewinnt den Eindruck, dass der irische Einfluss auf dem Festland genau wie der Columbas von Iona oder der Aidans in Nordhumbrien viel mehr von der Persönlichkeit der Beteiligten als von der zwingenden Macht ihrer Lehre oder ihres Systems ausging " (Hans Glunz, *Britannien und Bibeltext* (Kölner Anglistische Arbeiten, XII, Leipzig, 1930), p. 72).

[3] H. W. Hoare, *Our English Bible* (London, 1911), p. 31.

[4] A pronouncement of Ferdinand Brunetière.

ADDENDA

xlv.—*Sources : Ireland ; Bibliography of Sources.*—National Library of Ireland, Dublin.—A list of the MSS. in the Irish language acquired in 1931 by the Library from the collection of the late Sir Thomas Phillips, compiled by the Librarian, Dr. R. I. Best, is printed in the Appendix of the *Report of the Council of Trustees for* 1930–1931 (Dublin, 1932, pp. 15–27).

Ib.—Franciscan Library, Merchant's Quay, Dublin : Sir John T. Gilbert, *The Manuscripts of the former College of Irish Franciscans, Louvain,* in *Fourth Report of the Royal Commission on Historical Manuscript.* Pt. 1. Report and Appendix C. 857 (London, 1874), pp. 599–613.

xlvi.—*Sources : Ireland ; Hagiography.*—On the works of St Patrick, see Martin Schanz, *Geschichte der römischen Literatur,* IV, II (Müller's *Handbuch*), München, 1920, pp. 530–33.

9.—On the age and character of the Welsh Laws and their codification, see J. Loth, *L'étude et l'enseignement du droit dans le Pays de Galles du Xe au XIIIe siècle (R. Cel.,* XLVIII, 1931, pp. 293–311).

10.—On the *cenedl,* legal compensation in Wales and Ireland, etc., see J. Loth, *Un genre particulier de compensation pour crimes et offenses chez les Celtes insulaires (R. Cel.,* XLVIII, 1931, pp. 332–51).

21.—On St Alban of Verulam and St Aaron and St Julius of Caerleon, see P. Hippolyte Delehaye, ' *In Britannia* ' *dans le Martyrologe Hiéronymien (PBA,* XVII, 1932, pp. 13–15 of reprint).

31–47.—In his paper, *Der hl. Patrick (Nachrichten von der Gesellschaft der Wissenschaften zu Göttingen ; Philol.-hist. Kl.,* LXXXII, 1931, pp. 62–116), K. Müller treats of St Patrick's mission and writings with special reference to the views held by Zimmer and J. B. Bury.

48, note 4.—The passage referred to has just been reproduced in facsimile in *Senchas Már. Facsimile of the oldest Fragments, with descriptive Introduction* by R. I. Best and Rudolf Thurneysen (Dublin, 1931), P. 48-49.

49, note 6.—See also H. Delehaye, *Commentarius perpetuus in Martyrologium Hieronymianum ad recensionem H. Quentin* (Boll., *AS*, Nov., II, ɪɪ, Bruxellis, 1931, p. 148).

113, note 4.—" Dolo monasterio." Cf. H. Delehaye, *Op. cit.*, pp. 399, 401.

133, l. 2.—" . . . . sometimes even by way of ordeal." Cf. Mary E. Byrne, *On the Punishment of sending adrift* (*Ériu*, XI, 1930, pp. 97–102).

144, l. 10.—On the epitaph of " dominus Cumianus episcopus," who died at Bobbio in 736, see M. Esposito, *The Poems of Colmanus " Nepos Cracavist" and Dungalus " praecipuus Scottorum"* (*JTS*, XXXIII, 1932, p. 131).

168-69.—Pilgrimage to Rome. See Latin poem on St. Brigid by Colmanus styled " nepos Cracavist," stated in one MS. to have been written in Rome, edited by M. Esposito, *art. cit.*, pp. 116–18.

On the verses against Rome " *Nobilibus quondam* " (p. 169, n. 4), see M. Esposito, *art. cit.*, p. 118, n. 7, and Paul Kletler, *Johannes Eriugena. Eine Untersuchung über die Entstehung der mittelalterlichen Geistigkeit* (Beiträge zur Kulturgeschichte des Mittelalters und der Renaissance herausg. von Walter Goetz, Bd. 49, Leipzig and Berlin, 1931), p. 54.

173-77.—Texts and remarks on travelling methods, together with a map of N.W. Europe between 600 and 900 in Paul Kletler, *Nordwesteuropas Verkehr, Handel und Gewerbe in frühen Mittelalter* (Wien, 1924).

175, note 2.—For the exact situation of Quentavic (Quentovic, Quantovic), see L. Levillain, *Études sur l'abbaye de Saint-Denis à l'époque mérovingienne* (*Bibliothèque de l'École des Chartes*, XCI, 1930, pp. 25–28, 58).

180.—M. Esposito (*art. cit.*, p. 129) refers to possible relations of Donatus, bishop of Fiesole, with Dungal.

PAGE

254.—Dr. Robin Flower's translation of Pangur Bán has been re-issued in his *Poems and Translations* (London, 1931), pp. 129–30.

304.—On the personality of Johannes Eriugena, his knowledge of Greek, his translations and poems, see the above-mentioned book of Paul Kletler, *Johannes Eriugena*, pp. 43–52.

335.—On a conjectural influence of Syrian devotion and piety on Western Europe and notably on Ireland during the 6th, 7th and 8th centuries, see E. Bishop, *LH*, pp. 161–63, and F. J. Badcock, *A portion of an early Anatolian Prayer-Book* (*JTS*, XXXIII, 1932, pp. 167–80).

345.—On a fresh examination of the sculptures of the Jakobskirche at Ratisbon, Mlle. Henry is not so much inclined (she writes to me) to recognize Irish inspiration in the choice of decorative motifs and in the representations of human or animal forms as she was when she wrote on the matter in 1928.

347.—On the earliest Christian monuments in Scotland, see also John A. Duke, *The Columban Church* (Oxford, 1932), pp. 139–42.

364–65.—See examples of fast writing scribes noted by C. H. Jones, Jr., in *A quickly written Manuscript* (*Speculum*, VII, 1932, pp. 94–95).

376.—In his work, *Christus am Kreuz in der Bildkunst der Karolingerzeit* (Studien über christliche Denkmäler, N.F. 21, Leipzig, 1930), Johannes Reil devotes only a few lines (pp. 32–33) to the Crucifixion in Irish art.

413.—On Gerald's writings, see Manitius, *Geschichte*, III (1931), pp. 622–37.

419.—Another little-flattering appreciation by Baudry de Bourgueil, " *Dolensium metropolitanus* " of the people of Brittany, " *in qua cum scorpionibus habito* " (*Vita Roberti de Arbrisello*, Prol. 2 : *PL*, CLXII, 1045), may be added.

IRELAND

Rathlin I

Derry · Banagher
Maghera
Connor
Bangor

Donegal
L. Derg
Moville
(Magh Bile)
Manes I
(Nendrum)
Strangford L.
(Loch Cuan)
L. Erne
Clogher
Devenish
(Daminis)
Armagh
Downpatrick
Saul (Sabal
Patraic)

Inishmurray
Drumcliff
Monaghan

Inishglora
Killala
Achonry
MAGH
SLECHT
Louth · Ardpatrick

Boyle ·
Kilmore ·
Duleek ·
Mellifont · Monasterboice
Kells

Achagower
(Achadfobuir)
Mayo
Roscommon
Ardagh
Bective · Tara
St Patrick's I
(Inis Patraic)

Inishbofin
Croagh Patrick
Cong
Tuam
L. Owel
Clonard ·

High Island
(Ardoilén)
Inchagoill
Shrule
Dublin · Howth
Clontarf

St Macdara's I
L. Corrib
Clonmacnois
Durrow
Clondalkin
Tallaght

Galway
Clonfert
Rahen
Kildare
Naas
Killashee

Inishmore
Killeany
Lorrha
Burr
Saigir
Glendalough

Aran Is
Kilmacduagh
Terryglass
(Ter dá Glass)
Roscrea ·
Clonfertmulloe
Mundrehid
(Men Droichet)
Moone
Wicklow

Inis Cealtra
Aghaboe
Timahoe
Sletty
(Slébte)
Killeshin
Baltinglass
Castledermot

Lough
Derg
Kilkenny
Leighlin

Scattery
Limerick
Mungret
Cashel
Ferns

Monasternenagh
Emly
St Mullins
(Techmoling)

Magharee
Is
Ardfert
Killeedy
Inislounaght
Ahenny
R. Suir
Taghmon · Wexford

Kilmalkedar
Gallarus
Innisfallen
L. Loane
Lismore
Waterford

Valencia
Is
Cork ·
Youghal · Dairinis
Clayne

Skellig
R
Roscarberry
(Ros Ailithir)

MONASTERIES
AND OTHER PLACES OF CONTINENTAL EUROPE
KNOWN TO HAVE BEEN FREQUENTED BY
IRISH MONKS AND SCHOLARS.

Verden

Paderborn

St Odilienberg

Ghent
BELGIUM
Nivelles

Cologne

GERMANY

Erfurt

Liege

Lahnheim
Rodheim
Lich
Wieseck
Horloff
Schotten
Bauernheim
Sternbach

Fulda

Aubigny
Gerthe
Méxerolles
Cambrai
Péronne
Quierzy
Noyon
Soissons

Lobbes
Fosses
Waulsort
Hastières
THIÉRACHE
St
Michel
Oise R
Aisne R
Laon

Mainz

Bamberg
Würzburg

Disibodenberg

Nuremberg

Meaux
Lagny
Rebais
St Denis

Reims
Verdun
Metz
St Mihiel
Toul

Hohenburg

Strasbourg
Honau

Eichstätt
Ratisbon
Kelheim

Danube R
Göttweig
Melk
Stockerau
Vienna

Clairvaux

Auxerre

Fontaine
Luxeuil
Annegray
Sackingen
Moutiers-
Grandval

Murbach
Rheinau
Arbon
St Gall
Viktorsberg

Memmingen
L. of Constance
L. Chiemsee
Salzburg

CARINTHIA

FRANCE

Mazerolles

Angoulême

Verona

Pavia
Piacenza

Bobbio

I
T
A
L
Y

Cahors

Lucca

Lérins Is

Fiesole

Rome

H. Goodwin 1932

SCOTLAND, ENGLAND, WALES,
CORNWALL

ORKNEY Iˢ

CAITHNESS

HEBRIDES

Moray Firth

Elgin

Isle of Skye

Grampian Mts

R. Dee

Aberdeen

Eigg

Brechin

Tiree

Dunkeld

Meigle

I. of Mull

Scone

St Andrews

Iona
Ross of Mull

ARGYLL

Dunblane

Culross

Firth of Forth

DAL RIADA

Dumbarton
Glasgow

R. Clyde

Islay

Melrose

Lindisfarne I.

R. Tweed

Bamborough

STRATHCLYDE

GALLOWAY

Ruthwell

Bewcastle

Jarrow
Wearmouth

Candida
Casa

NORTHUMBRIA

CUMBRIA

Gilling

Whitby

Lastingham

I. of Man

Ripon

York

Hatfield

LINDSEY

Anglesey

Penmon

St
Bangor Asaph

Basingwerk
Chester

GWYNEDD

Wrexham

Bangor-is-Coed

R. Dee

Bardsey I.

Wroxeter

Lichfield

Cnobheresburgh
(Burgh Castle)

Cmwhir

R. Severn

Nevern

St David's
(Menevia)

DYFED

Whitland

R. Usk

R. Wye

Carew

Neath

Tintern

Caldey
I.

GWENT

Caerleon

Abingdon

St Albans

Margam

Llandaff

Caerwent

Malmesbury

London

Llantwit
Llangarvan

Silchester

Glastonbury

DUMNONIA

Sherborne

Bosham

R. Camel

Crediton

Exeter

Padstow

R. Lynher

Bodmin

Perranzubuloe
Gwithian

St Germans

Gerrans

SHETLAND Iˢ

ENGLAND, WALES,
BRITTANY

INDEX

Aar, 142
Aaron, high priest, 271
—— of Caerlon, St., 21, 426
Abbán of Abingdon, St., 140
—— of Magh Arnaide, St., 93, 98, 247, 348
Abbott, T. K., xxix, xxxii, xxxix
Abel, archb. of Reims, 153–54
Abelard, 304, 419
Aberdeen, 136, 353, 357, 412
Abergavenny, 414
Aberlemno, 348
Abersetus, 275
Abgar, 274
Abgrall, J.-M., xxi, 346, 356
Abingdon, 140
Abraham, patriarch, 130
Abraham, L., 182
Acca of Hexham, 410
Achadfobuir (Aghagower), 50, 319
Achelis, Hans, 87, 88
Achery, Lucas D', xviii & passim.
Achonry, 407
Actard, 109, 125
Adalbero I, 155, 177
—— II, 155, 177
Adam of Bremen, 173, 412
Adamnán of Coldingham, 98
—— of Iona, xxxi, xxxv, xl, 11–12, 55, 198–99, 202, 259, 324, 363 & passim.
——, author of Vision, 296
Adananus, 249
Adomnanus, 281, 282
Adraste, 17
Adrian IV, 408
Adso of Montier-en-Der, 146
Aed mac Bricc, St., 85, 103, 333
Aed, bp. of Slébte, 48
——, bp. in Gaul, 224
—— the Bearded Clerk, 249
Aedan, St. See Maedóc of Ferns.
Aedh Ordnidhe, 230
Aedhán mac Gabhráin, 136
Aelfric, 283
Aethicus Ister, 259
Africa, 224

Agaune, 74
Agde, 224
Aghaboe, 151
Agilbert, 174, 258
Agilus (Ayeul), St., 142, 167
Agrestius, 337–38
Agricola, Gnaeus Julius, 5, 12
——, heretic, 25
Ahade (Ath-Fithot), 45
Ahenny, 351
Aidan, St. See Maedóc of Ferns.
—— of Lindisfarne, 76, 85, 98, 102, 103, 137–38, 175, 193, 194, 259
Ailbe of Emly, St., 27, 79, 90, 93, 98, 170, 192, 331–32
Ail Clúade, 32, 43
Ailech, 7
Aileran the Wise, 269
Ailred of Rievaulx, 26
Ainmire, 70, 71
Airard, 416
Airbertach mac Coisse, 255, 269
Airgialla. See Oriel.
Aisne, 177
Alain I, 388
Alain Barbetorte, 390
Alban of Verulam, St., 21, 426
Albericus, 301
Albion, 3, 134
Alcadus, 157
Alcuin, 99, 130, 139, 151, 166, 245, 247, 257, 259, 269, 298–300, 310, 311, 337
Aldegisus, St., 159
Aldelmus, 302
Aldfrid, 195, 198, 248, 259
Aldhelm, St., 88, 95, 107, 139, 148, 200–201, 203, 212, 247, 248, 257, 258, 382, 423
Alemannia, 143, 163, 165, 183
Alès, A. d', 128, 256
Alet, 110, 114, 115, 123, 417, 419
Alexandria, 185, 186, 187, 242
Alfred the Great, 281, 389
Algisus, St, 159
Allard, Paul, 234

431

G G